CW01246390

Subsea Manned Engineering

Subsea Manned Engineering

Gerhard F. K. Haux
Director, Haux-Life-Support GmbH, Waldbronn, West Germany

with contributions by

Jörg Haas
General Manager, Bruker Meerestechnik GmbH, Rheinstetten, West Germany

and

Anthony Lovell Smith
Director, Underwater Security Consultants Ltd, London, England

English translation by
Eberhard Kern and Anthony Lovell Smith

Best Publishing Company · Carson, California

A BAILLIÈRE TINDALL book published by
Cassell Ltd.,
35 Red Lion Square, London WC1R 4SG

and at Sydney and Toronto

an affiliate of
Macmillan Publishing Co. Inc.
New York

© 1982 Baillière Tindall
a division of Cassell Ltd

All rights reserved. No part of this publication may be reproduced, stored in a retrieval system or transmitted, in any form or by any means, electronic, mechanical, photocopying or otherwise, without the prior permission of Baillière Tindall, 35 Red Lion Square, London WC1R 4SG

First published 1982

ISBN 0-941332-00-4

Published in the United States of America by
Best Publishing Company,
23005/2 S. Avalon Blvd.,
Carson, California

Designed by Peter Powell MSTD
Typeset by Santype International Ltd., Salisbury, Wilts, UK,
and printed in the United States of America by
Maple Vail Book Manufacturing Group, New York

Contents

	Preface	vii
	Acknowledgements	viii
	Introduction	ix
1 **Hyperbaric Diving Simulators and Test Facilities** *Gerhard F. K. Haux*	Basic design options	4
	Basic diving simulator complexes	9
	Large-scale testing facilities	24
	Worldwide distribution of diving simulators and large pressure testing facilities	27
	Examples of hyperbaric diving simulators	31
2 **Deck Compression Chambers** *Gerhard F. K. Haux*	Stationary compression chambers for divers	66
	Compression chamber modules	76
	Mobile compression chamber	78
	Compression chambers for saturation diving	78
	Compression chamber components	79
3 **Deep Diving Systems** *Gerhard F. K. Haux*	General layout and procedures	109
	Design criteria	116
	Deck compression chamber configurations	118
	Component parts of a diving system	123
	SCC handling and winch systems	145
	Sanitary systems	165
	Diving equipment	167
	Capsule systems	169
4 **Submersible Compression Chambers, Open Diving Bells and Observation Chambers** *Gerhard F. K. Haux*	Submersible compression chambers (diving bells)	172
	Open diving bells	202
	Observation chambers	206
5 **Transportable Recompression Chambers for Divers** *Gerhard F. K. Haux*	Transportable one-man recompression chambers	209
	Transportable two-man recompression chambers	223
	Life-support in transport chambers	226
	Evacuation of divers under pressure	230
6 **Under-water Habitats** *Gerhard F. K. Haux*	Conventional designs	235
	Advanced designs for habitats with integrated pressure hulls	238
	Mobile under-water habitats	240
	Construction of habitats	241
	Logistic support systems	249

		Support of a habitat in an emergency	258
		Safety and rescue	263
		Lowering procedures, ballast and trim systems	269
		Personnel transfer to manned under-water stations	275
		Materials and equipment	276
		Life-support systems	281
		Brief descriptions	292
7	**Submersibles** *Jörg Haas*	Contemporary submersible development	308
		Life-support systems	316
		Deck compression chamber installations	319
		Operational procedures and control	322
		Submersible support requirements	324
		Transfer under pressure to DCCs and under-water capsules	349
		Gas supply systems for different deep diving procedures	360
		Diver monitoring equipment	369
		Diver heating	371
		Manipulators	376
		The diver lock-out: the future	380
8	**Submarines** *Gerhard F. K. Haux*	History	381
		Submarine design	381
		The justification for a commercial submarine	384
		Specific submarine designs	386
		Existing submarines	389
		Proposed submarine designs	390
		Safety	396
9	**One-atmosphere Diving Systems** *Anthony Lovell Smith*	Development of the one-atmosphere suit	397
		Modern one-atmosphere suits	399
10	**Life-support Systems and Commercial Diving Equipment** *Gerhard F. K. Haux*	Primary life-support factors	409
		Secondary life-support factors	414
		Primary life-support: technical solutions	419
		Commercial breathing equipment for divers	438
11	**Under-water Welding, Repair and Construction Habitats** *Gerhard F. K. Haux*	Subsea welding chambers under ambient pressure	481
		Subsea one-atmosphere chambers	483
		Welding chambers with alignment frames	486
		Current welding chamber units	488
12	**Animal Experiment and Equipment Test Chambers** *Gerhard F. K. Haux*	Experimental chamber applications	495
		Construction of testing chambers	496
		Design of animal experiment chambers	497
		Design of equipment and material test chambers	505
	Appendices	Research centres, institutes, government agencies and training schools	512
		Selected diving contractors	517
		Equipment manufacturers	522
		Scientific and technical journals, newsletters and trade magazines	524
		Bibliography	527
		Picture sources	529
		Index	531

Preface

Subsea technology has in the last decade made dramatic advances to meet the requirements of the off-shore oil and gas industries as they have responded with increasing urgency to the world's energy needs. In no other commercial industry have pressures been more demanding and sustained than those imposed on subsea engineering disciplines. In less than twenty years, the emphasis has moved from the less immediate demands of salvage, civil engineering and naval warfare to an almost total commitment to ensure that oil, gas and eventually minerals will continue to be extracted from ever-increasing depths.

This book presents a summary of recent developments and illustrates current techniques for engineers, designers and users. However, all who are involved in the planning and preparation of diving programmes will find the detailed description of equipment and its uses of the greatest value. The text covers a wide scope in order to review in detail recent important advances in the methods by which man, either under pressure or encapsulated, but directly controlling his movements, can undertake work under water.

It is hoped that this comprehensive survey of existing practice will provide the necessary platform of knowledge for future development and technical advance.

Until relatively recently diving was the only means of intervention in the sea and, although there are clearly limitations and some drawbacks in operating divers in deeper and more hostile waters, it is far from certain that they will be removed from the task except in the deepest waters. The diving industry has to keep ahead of the offshore operator's requirements and although there are inherent risks in exposing a man to increasing pressures the advances in subsea engineering and diving medicine will allow an increase in present operational depths with greater safety. Divers will only be removed from working in deeper waters when significant advances are made in the other methods which are described in the book. These cover one-atmosphere systems, submersibles, habitats and autonomous submarines, their design and operating factors. After studying this text readers will be able to arrive at their own conclusions with regard to the future but it seems likely that no one system will be able to carry out all the tasks under water.

Clearly it has not been possible to cover all the varying systems and types of equipment and to give separate recognition to all the manufacturers, service companies and research institutions that make up a varied industry, but those who want to explore deeper in the subject will find useful the appendixes listing the main companies and institutions.

June 1981   GERHARD F. K. HAUX

Acknowledgements

I wish to thank my co-authors, Jörg Haas and Anthony Lovell Smith, for their valuable assistance which has contributed to the solution of problems that face present day under-water working techniques and the use of available equipment. I also have to thank many people, institutes and companies who have contributed to the success of this work by supplying information and photographs.

I am particularly grateful to Eberhard Kern who undertook the laborious task of a first translation from German into English, and to Anthony Lovell Smith who did the final translation and important technical supervision of it, and finally to Herbert Hörter for considerable assistance with the photographs and drawings. My total devotion is due to my dear wife Erna who not only typed the entire manuscript but also provided encouragement when I was prepared to capitulate before the mountain of work.

Introduction

Within the broad scope of ocean technology, diving is a relatively small but highly developed and demanding discipline, which should not be considered separately but in the context of supporting offshore ocean industries. The installations, vessels and systems which are needed in support of offshore exploration and production have increased rapidly in size, scope and application since the 1960s and diving research and development have had to keep pace and develop research techniques into applied technology.

The practical and economic considerations of conventional saturation diving have led to investigation and development of alternative remote-controlled systems in the deeper depths and if these can also be used in the intermediate depths where divers now operate, the question arises whether this would not be more beneficial in terms of cost and practicability. In cost terms this is possibly true, as the cost of diving operations escalates as the depths increase, but when faced with the ultimate reality of having to carry out a complex task at depth, man does possess some clear advantage over remote manipulators and sensors. As long as man, the diver, is equipped with the correct tools for the job and the depths are feasible, he can be more cost-effective than other alternative systems. A well known British diving scientist has summed it up thus: 'Some of the diver's qualities are irreplaceable: his sense of touch, his ability to adapt work methods to changing conditions and to make the right decisions quickly. If this integration of sensory perception, decision-making and action dictate the solution to the problem, then divers are indispensable.'

It is essential that we should consider the use and probable overlap of divers and remote unmanned systems individually in respect of cost effectiveness. In the deeper depths beyond the limit of operational diving, the exciting development of one-atmosphere systems represents a great stride forward, although it still introduces a man in the water. However, current technology is not yet at a stage where a remote-controlled system may be developed which can be totally substituted for man.

In the future, mineral exploration for the extraction of ores at 2000 m or of manganese nodules at 3000–5000 m will need to rely on remote systems, submersibles and submarines. By this time the development of manipulator systems will in all probability have achieved the high performance required.

The varied tasks that can be carried out by divers are numerous ranging from salvage to offshore oil and gas production, to ocean biology and fish farming to mention only a few. Fig. 3.2 (p. 107) summarizes current applications of various diving systems by which man and machine can work in the sea. Whilst diving within the shallow range of 50 m is relatively simple since the diver is more or less in full control of his actions and destiny, the more complex diving techniques in deep waters of 300–400 m, and perhaps deeper, demand a greater involvement and performance from other personnel and equipment. The physiological problems alone compel us to use highly developed equipment and techniques, many of which are based on space technology.

The development of various components of an under-water diving system, such as the vessel, pressure chambers, diving bell habitats, recovery and ancillary systems, needs to be integrated into a reliable balanced system with the comparable research and training facilities ashore. It is all these units which make up the balance that are reviewed in this book.

Hyperbaric Diving Simulators and Test Facilities

1

In spite of the significant advances made in the last decade in manipulator and remote-control technology used by submersibles, remote-controlled vehicles, one-atmosphere and robot systems, the need to operate divers at deep depths has not decreased.

The operation of divers at the depths at which exploration for oil and the subsequent production takes place has demanded the preparation of deep diving breathing tables, equipment and not least the divers themselves. In the initial phase of off-shore exploration, it was necessary to enable divers to make short-duration dives to observe and to carry out quick repairs on drilling systems which were, as far as is possible, designed to operate without the use of divers. It is rare for exploration drilling to be carried out without the back-up of divers as a precaution against failures and difficulties and to provide a very necessary secondary function. The divers carry out their work within relatively short periods and, although exploration drilling will always be leading the search into deeper waters, the actual working time spent on the bottom is short.

The requirements for the off-shore production of oil and gas are different from those of the exploration phase. The construction of off-shore production facilities, followed by a continuous inspection, maintenance and repair programme over the whole operating life of the field, demands long and sometimes continuous periods of work. Whilst, for instance, the mission cycles of divers on survey or remedial work in an exploratory drilling programme might be carried out within 20 minutes, the mission cycle for divers working on production platforms and subsea systems might involve many weeks of continuous work with teams of divers under full saturation conditions. The emphasis is on designing and operating deep diving facilities which can accommodate large numbers of divers over extended periods. In comparison, the exploration phase requires fewer divers, with shorter periods under pressure, advancing into deeper waters as the search for oil and gas extends off-shore. The advance in deep diving techniques has been very fast in the last ten years and developments made within the last decade could not have been foreseen 20 years ago. Diving compression and decompression profiles need to be tested in shore test facilities, first on animals and then on man, before an operational dive at sea. The record dive at sea by Comex to 500 m in 1977 was the result of a careful progression from experiments with monkeys to the important stage of divers testing the equipment and diving tables under simulated conditions to 610 m in a dry pressure chamber, followed by trials. A record depth of 686 m was reached in 1981 at Duke University, extending the previous record of 660 m held by the UK Royal Navy.

Various hyperbaric simulators, from very simple to very large and advanced facilities, are essential to the basic operational research to evaluate and prove the following before any dives in the sea can be made:

1. Theoretically calculated compression and decompression tables.
2. The physical and mental capability of divers to withstand the dives.
3. The breathing, i.e. life-support, equipment required to keep the diver comfortable.
4. The actual working techniques required to complete an essential under-water task at that depth.

The range of tests is extensive and the essential dictate now and for the future is to establish the tasks that need to be carried out under water at various depths and then work towards an overall solution. This should include the evaluation of whether tools and working techniques can be used at those depths. Man's ability to withstand great pressure is not in doubt: the problem lies in man's ability, while under pressure, to undertake useful work with efficient tools and pressure simulators for various tests are therefore essential. Simulators need to conform to the highest safety standards and to be capable of reproducing, as nearly as possible, the environment at depth with regard to pressure, temperature, particle suspension, water motion and salinity.

Diving simulators have been used for many years. One of the oldest is at Lübeck (Fig. 1.1) and was used for experiments with submarine escape apparatus, semi-closed-circuit and scuba breathing equipment using mixed gas and compressed air. Where the need was to carry out straightforward functioning tests on breathing equipment, it was more important to immerse the equipment in shallow water than the deeper pressures needed later. Open-ended water towers have been built, some 30 m high, to train naval crews in submarine escape techniques where a closed pressure chamber cannot be used to simulate this operation.

The need to simulate working depths of 500 m and more demanded the construction of complex pressure chambers in various configurations to simulate the different wet or dry environmental conditions. There are about 70 systems in use or planned worldwide in 1980. Systems are increasing both in number and in sophistication. In the Federal Republic of Germany there are now four in use, two

Fig. 1.1. A veteran diving simulator (Dräger) installed in 1913 in Lübeck in the Federal Republic of Germany, with an operating pressure of 20 bar.

under construction and one planned; in 1971 there was only one. There are even greater proportional increases in the USA. The number of systems in the USSR, as far as is known, is relatively small. A large system is under construction near the Black Sea for the Institute of Oceanology and there will be another in Moscow. Other facilities are planned.

The divers' efficiency is not assessed solely by the absolute water depth and the time that they can spend at that depth, but also by the work that they can undertake and complete at depth. Many smaller tools and items of equipment required for these tasks can be tested in pressure chambers designed primarily for divers. However, subsea engineering also demands unmanned or one-atmosphere systems which, whilst not constrained by the physiological factors of depth, are equally affected by water pressure; this equipment must often be tested in pressure chambers. Furthermore, the tests need to be monitored. Operating pressures can be considerably higher, due to the need to operate in the deeper depths below 500 m, and the size of the chambers is much larger to accommodate the equipment. These chambers may need to accommodate working and research submersibles, unmanned vehicles and other equipment for deep submergence operations.

The cost of designing and building these larger simulators is very considerable and there are few such systems available in the world to cover adequately even the smaller items of equipment. The use of equipment is not related solely to the exploration and production of off-shore oil and gas, but also to the extraction of other materials such as minerals from the seabed, to the obtaining of oceanographic data and geological samples for scientific study and to certain salvage requirements, all in depths in excess of 500 m. The cost of the pressure-testing facilities is well beyond the capabilities of most countries and certainly no single commercial venture could meet the requirements. Some consideration should be given to the joint building of these facilities by various countries for their common use, as is the case in international partnerships for research into energy problems. Such facilities are urgently required for the 1980s.

Basic Design Options

Unlike conventional dry pressure chambers, a diving simulator must always have at least one compartment which can be filled with water. Irrespective of whether there are one or more wet chambers, the increase in water pressure is achieved by increasing the pressure of the gas on the water surface. The gas may be compressed air or mixed, depending on the type of test and whether the diver needs to breath the chamber gas. In a wet chamber there will always be the inherent hydrostatic pressure of the column of water. For example, a wet chamber with water to a depth of 5 m will have a hydrostatic pressure of 0.5 bar at the bottom and this difference from surface pressure must be accounted for, in addition to the increase of chamber gas pressure, to produce a simulated water pressure. Additionally, small differences due to the use of fresh or sea water need to be taken into account, owing to their differing densities. Also, for exactness, the geographical height above sea level needs to be considered.

A different method of achieving a pressurized wet environment, incorporated into the diving complex at Buffalo University, USA, is an important advance in the development of simulators and will be discussed later in this chapter. The financial and material considerations of the design lead, in most cases, to cylindrical pressure chambers for low and medium operating pressures. For high pressures, a spherical design for chambers is usual, with diameters up to 6 m. Variations in the design of pressure systems are not dictated solely by the specific requirements of each system, but also by the available financial resources and the constraints of space for building.

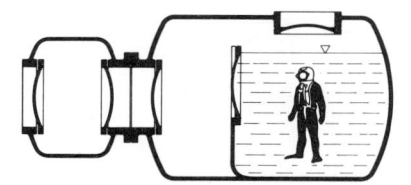

Fig. 1.2. A basic diving simulator. A cylindrical chamber placed horizontally with a small entry lock at the end.

The design in Fig. 1.2 is simple, compact and inexpensive, with construction on one floor level, yet is capable of relatively high pressures using the wet compartment. Modifications can be made to existing dry pressure chambers by incorporating a wet internal chamber. The Swedish Navy procedure for experimental wet dives is to enter the wet compartment from above through a top bulkhead door, after the chamber has been pressurized, and the system is therefore not suitable for extended or saturation diving. The second diver can give only limited assistance to the diver in the water over the top of the intermediate bulkhead. The water is drained away after the wet dive has finished and the intermediate bulkhead is removed, allowing the diver full access to the chamber with the attendant, and decompression can take place in the enlarged area. The arrangement is very economical in space, as fittings such as tables, bunks and stools can be collapsed and stowed away until required for living in an enlarged dry chamber. The overall dimensions of the system are very flexible, although the minimum diameter of the wet compartment should be 2 m. The main advantage of this design is that a large variety of technical and physiological tests can be undertaken using a relatively small volume of gas, but the diver cannot carry out swimming exercises in the wet compartment, except with the limited use of an ergometer. Also, the design does not allow excursion diving in the wet compartment at a depth greater than that of the dry chamber, as the same pressure is maintained throughout the whole chamber. In operational saturation work, it is normal for divers to live at a pressure less than the actual required working pressure at the work site.

The design shown in Fig. 1.3 allows greater flexibility, as the diver can stand up, although he is still unable to swim. Pressures different from that of the diving chamber can be applied to the wet compartment, but the basic disadvantage is that the diver, although under observation from outside, is not in direct contact with a standby diver in the dry chamber. Although this may be just acceptable in the controlled environment of a deep diving facility, and accepting the risks of possible unpleasant psychological pressures imposed on the diver by confinement and isolation, the lack of control through direct contact between the standby personnel and the

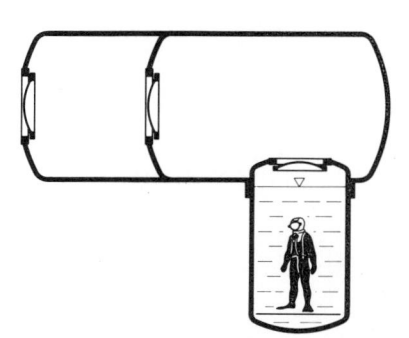

Fig. 1.3. A diving simulator with vertical cylindrical wet chamber installed with separate pressurization.

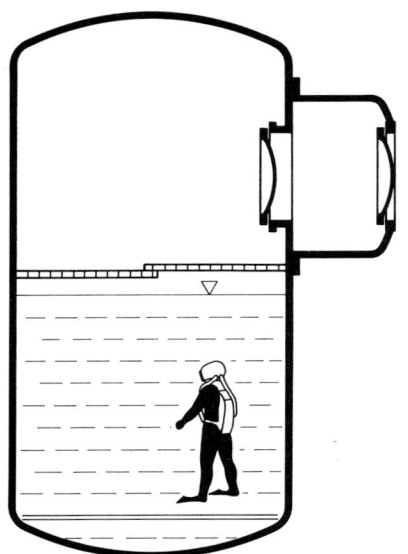

Fig. 1.4. A cylindrical diving simulator installed vertically with a small side entry lock; the wet and dry portions of the main chamber are separated by a grating.

diver is prohibited under generally accepted standard diving safety procedures in open water.

In principle, the design in Fig. 1.4 is much the same as that in Fig. 1.2 and allows for direct control of the diver by the standby diver, which is the procedure in open water. The lower portion of a vertical and cylindrical chamber becomes a wet compartment, separated by a removable grating from the dry upper portion from where the standby diver can tend the diver in the water. There is a small entry lock on the side, but there are obvious constraints on the diving due to the limitations of living space and the problem of humidity control. The design is ideally suited for diver training because instructors are at the same pressure as the divers and, in those facilities where the diameter of the pressure chamber is 2.5–3 m, swimming can be done by one or more divers. For training purposes, large numbers of personnel can be pressurized in a dry chamber with the water removed. Except for large equipment tests, the use of the open cylindrical design for equipment tests requires greater volumes of gas.

The design shown in Fig. 1.5 is the basic design of a complete wet and dry complex, capable of carrying out dives at a medium operating pressure up to 200 m. The wet and dry compartments contained in one vertical pressure cylinder are much the same as in the previous design (shown in Fig. 1.4) and the advantages of the previous three very basic systems are generally incorporated. By installing an intermediate lock in the horizontal plane between the dry compartment and the living chamber, the vertical and horizontal sections can be operated separately, with regard to both pressure and breathing gases. The design has become a standard model and is favoured by navies for trials and diver training. An enlarged entry flange on the top of the vertical pressure chamber can facilitate the use of the wet chamber for equipment trials.

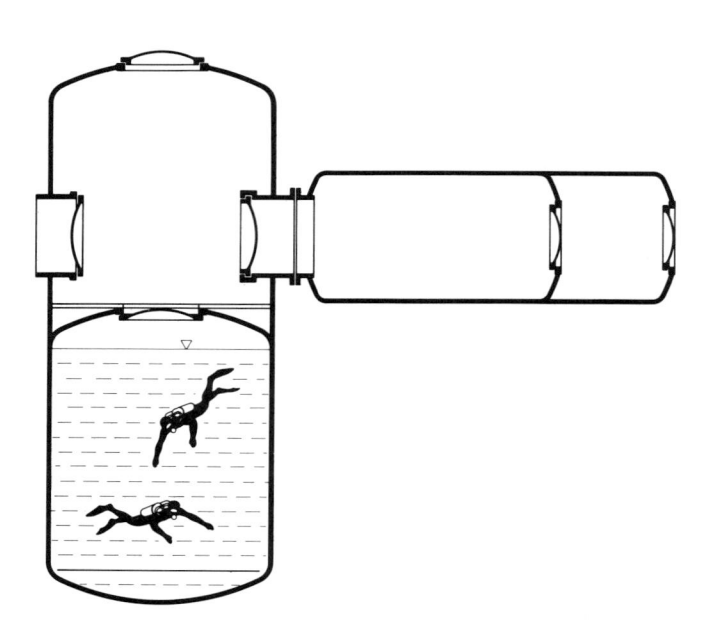

Fig. 1.5. A diving simulator with vertical arrangement of wet and dry chambers and with flanged horizontal living chambers at right angles.

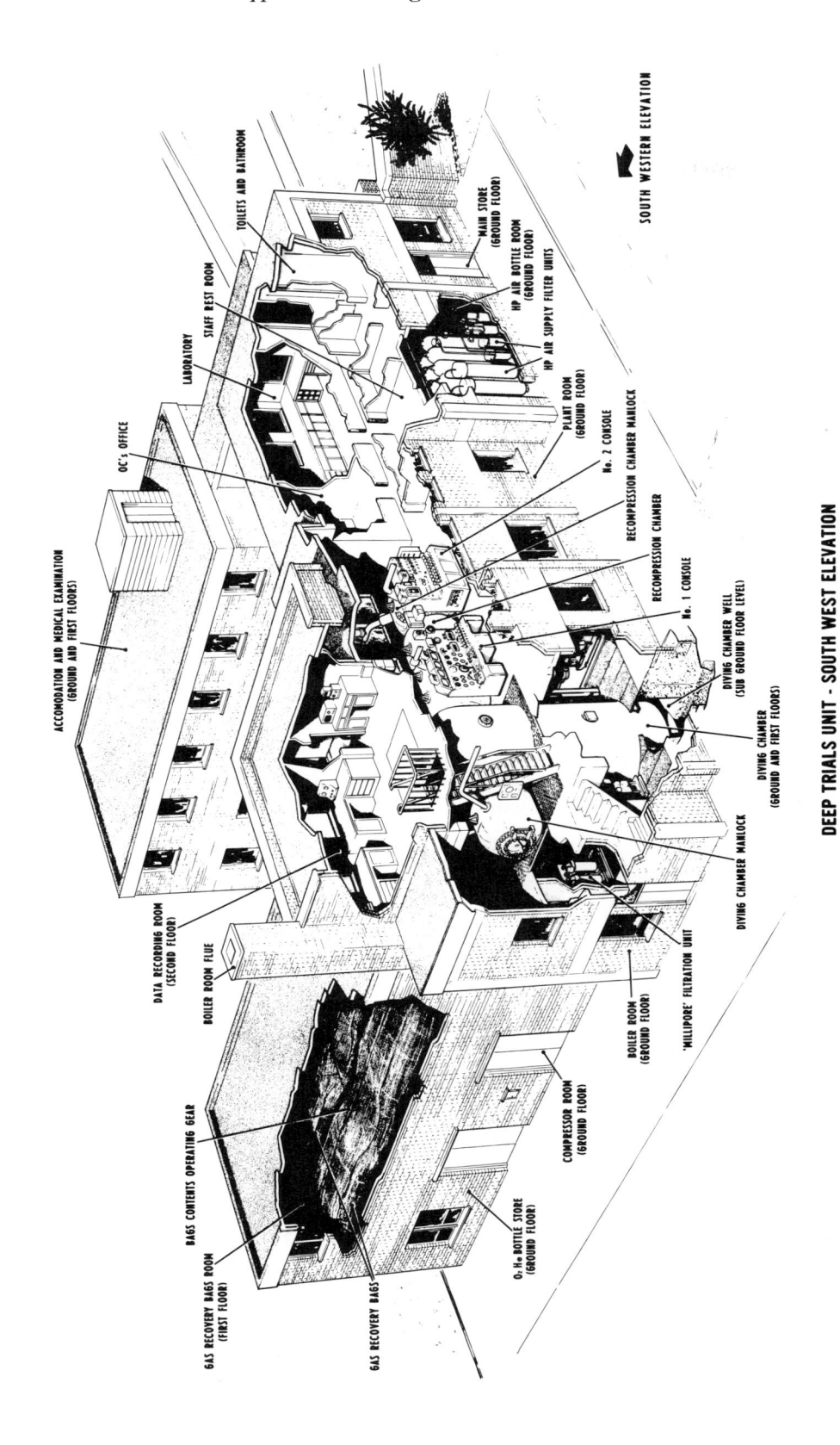

Fig. 1.6. The Royal Navy's deep diving trials unit at Alverstoke, UK, showing the general layout.

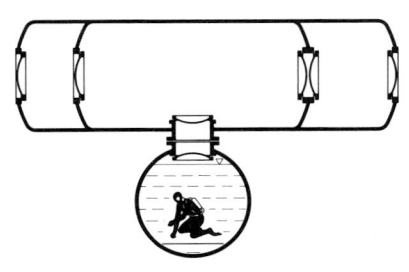

Fig. 1.7. Diving simulator with spherical wet chamber with higher pressure capability and horizontal living compartments at lower pressures.

For operating pressures above 50 bar the use of a pressure cylinder becomes less practicable, owing to design stress considerations, and often the pressure sphere is favoured. Fig.1.7 shows the use of a wet spherical chamber for excursion diving trials into the deeper range with the use of the horizontal living chambers at less pressure. This configuration relates more closely to the operational diving systems used off-shore. The living chambers are comparable in size but the wet chamber, ideally not less than 3 m in diameter, is larger than a diving bell. The design allows the divers in the working wet chamber to be at a greater pressure than the living chamber. A second entry lock can be fitted to the living chamber in a modular design. In place of cylindrical chambers the system can be designed throughout with spherical chambers, as shown in Fig. 1.8. The modular spherical design can be operated at the maximum pressure throughout. This design has been used for the simulator at the Technical University, Aachen. With two-way pressure doors between the spheres, either double doors or a single door with bayonet lock, each compartment can be operated separately.

A significant advance in simulator design was made, after many years of conventional chamber design, with the introduction of the system built at Buffalo University, USA. With one single exception, all the basic systems need to be constructed on two levels. This inevitably leads to special building and, since the control room is usually on the top floor, quick access to the lower layer is impossible. In the two-layer design the attendant inside the wet chamber does not have a clear view of the diver in the water, especially through a disturbed water surface. The Buffalo University design overcame the disadvantages of these previous systems with a one-low-level system where the wet compartment is partitioned off behind a clear acrylic

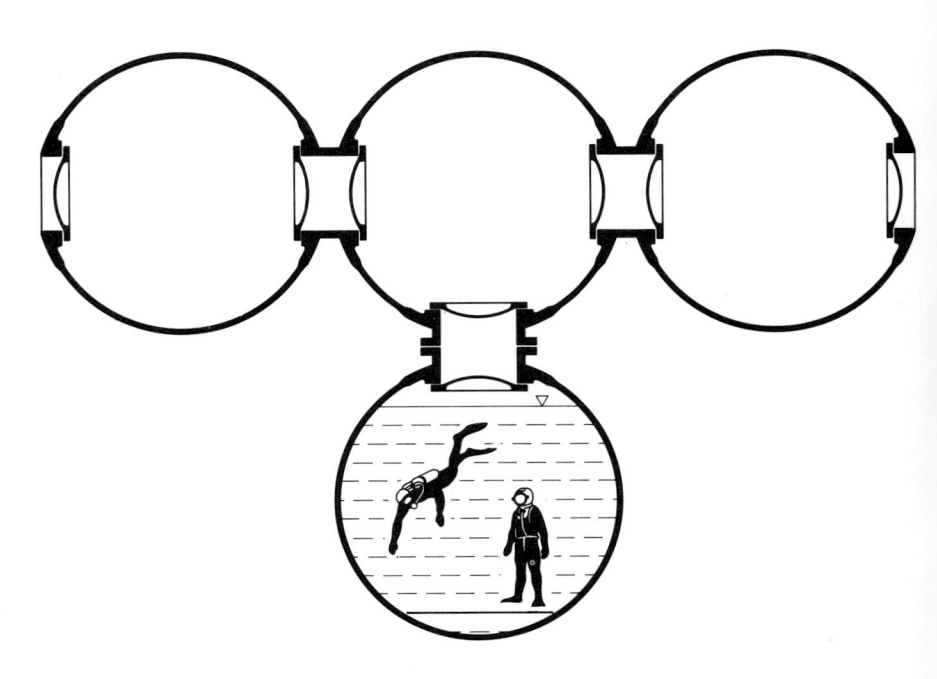

Fig. 1.8. Spherical chamber with equal higher pressure capability integrated into a deep diving simulator—the Aachen system (see Fig. 1.17).

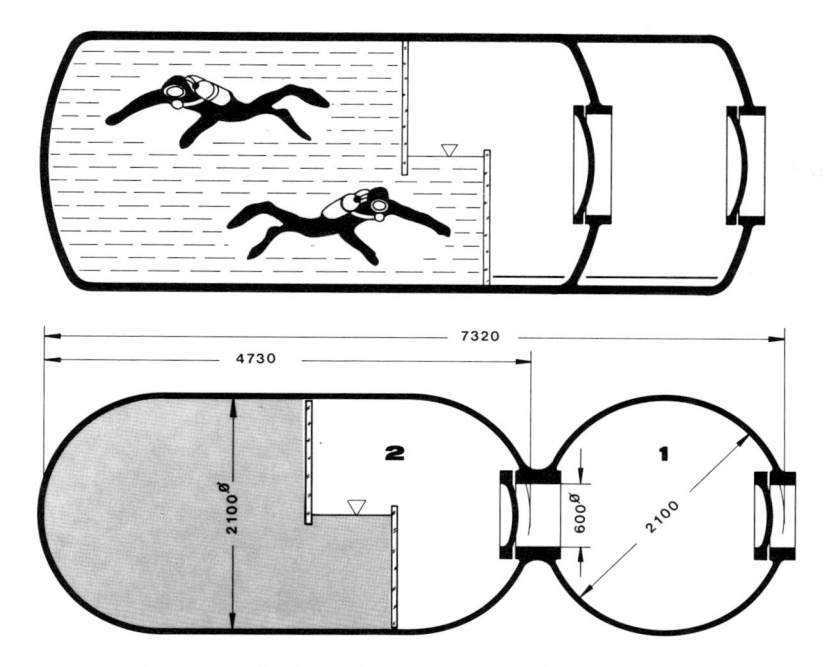

Fig. 1.9. A horizontal diving simulator with an internal clear acrylic partition—the Buffalo system.

screen. Besides reducing the overall height of the simulator, the internal design allows the attendant in the dry compartment to supervise the diver closely and have constant visual contact. A simple design is shown in Fig. 1.9.

Basic Diving Simulator Complexes

From a description of the different design options, we now describe some actual facilities that have been built. The more simple designs, of which there are a greater number, are as important as the larger more sophisticated complexes, which are fewer and more specialized in their use.

Simple Diving Simulator with Small Personnel Lock

A simple diving simulator with small personnel lock (as in Fig. 1.4) built for the Royal Dutch Navy (Fig. 1.11) gives a low-cost simulator for medium operating pressures where there is no necessity for a large living chamber. It is for trials and diver training with relatively short diving exposures. The vertical steel chamber has an internal height of 5 m and the lock a diameter of 1500 mm with a bayonet flange on the outside to allow the connection of one- and two-man portable chambers for therapeutic use. A grating inside the main chamber is fitted above the water level and the water is heated through a heat-exchange coil. The gas supply and life-support system controls are mounted on the same console alongside the chamber, which is of standard design.

Most simulators occupy two levels, with the control console on the upper level (Fig. 1.12) and the wet compartment on the lower level.

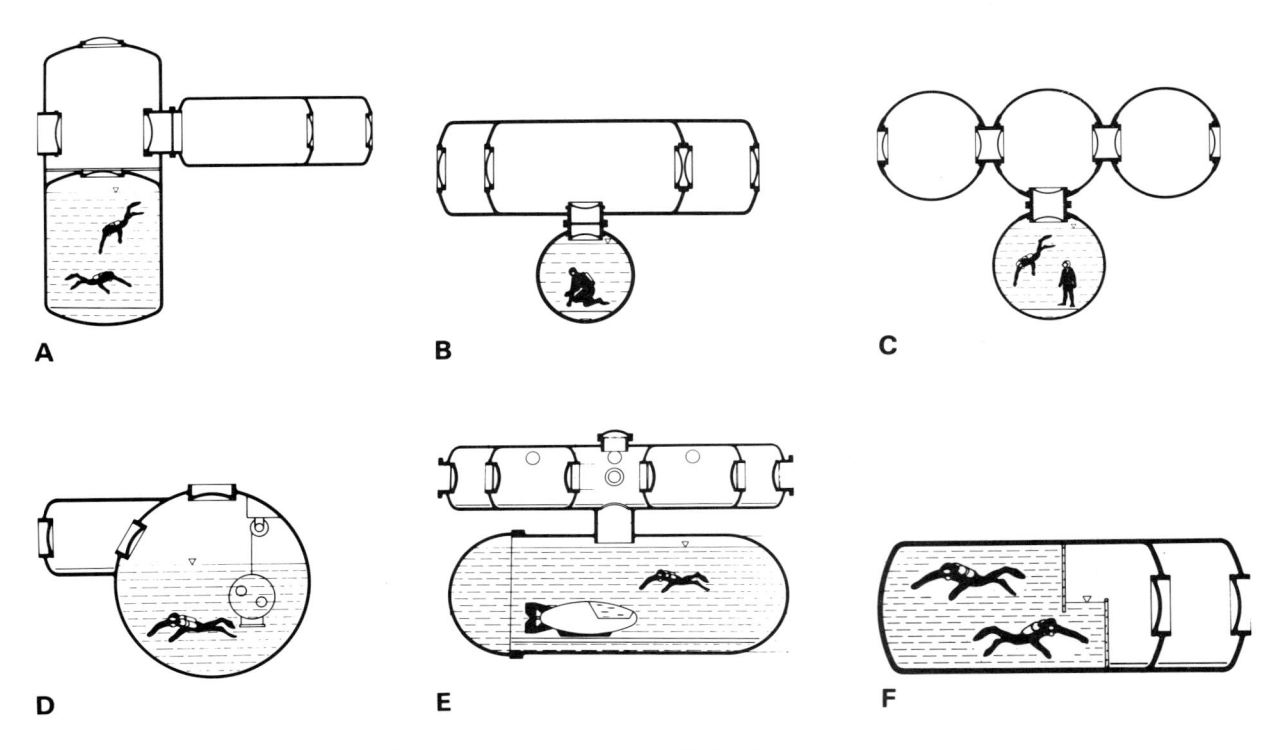

Fig. 1.10. Summary of design configurations for standard deep diving simulators.

- **A** Vertical split-level cylindrical complex. Wet and dry compartments with flanged living chamber at right angles. A standard design for training divers and testing equipment. For low to medium pressures of 10–25 bar
- **B** Vertical split-level complex with spherical wet chamber and horizontal cylindrical living chambers. A small facility for training divers and testing equipment. For maximum operating pressures up to 150 bar
- **C** Vertical split-level complex with spherical wet chamber and horizontal spherical living chamber. A small facility for training divers and testing equipment. For maximum operating pressures up to 150 bar
- **D** A large sphere with a horizontal cylindrical entrance chamber on the upper level. Mainly for diving research and training. For medium pressures up to 30 bar
- **E** A split-level cylindrical complex with a large horizontal wet chamber and a smaller dry chamber above. Primarily for trials of large equipment such as unmanned vehicles and smaller submersibles. For operating pressures up to 70 bar. The need for special steels, other material and fabrication is reflected in the high cost
- **F** The Buffalo system. The wet and dry cylindrical chambers cover a large area. Suitable for diving research and training under close overall supervision. For medium operating pressures up to 30 bar, but can be increased to 172 bar with the use of special steels, other materials and fabrication

This system has rapid wet chamber drainage to evacuate half the water within four minutes from a maximum internal pressure of 10 bar.

Standard Diving Simulator with Vertical Wet Chamber, Transfer Chamber and Horizontal Living and Decompression Chambers

For the training of commercial and military divers in the medium operating pressure range (up to 25 bar), a design built in Bergamo,

Fig. 1.11. Diving simulator of the Royal Dutch Navy before installation.

Fig. 1.12. Diving simulator of the Royal Dutch Navy in Den Helder, Holland.

Fig. 1.13. Diving simulator operated by Sub Sea Oil Services at Bergamo, Italy.

Italy (Fig. 1.13), is sufficient. The vertical chambers are usually subdivided near the middle with two dished bulkheads and two separate chambers. The lower part is filled with water for wet operations and is separated by a door from the transfer chamber above. During a dive the standby attendants are in this transfer chamber and the diver in the water. The transfer chamber can be fitted out as a diving bell in order to train divers in conditions as realistic as possible. In special circumstances the wet chamber can be operated at a different pressure from the transfer chamber by closing the connecting door. In these conditions special safety precautions are needed, as divers in the wet chamber are not in direct contact with the attendants and this is not normally acceptable.

Decompression is carried out in the horizontal living chamber but for saturation diving certain modifications are required. The chambers are usually fitted with a personnel lock for transfer during the dive. The temperature of the water in the wet chamber is controlled and filtered and is separate from the pressure system of the dry chambers.

Fig. 1.14. Deep diving simulator at Cartagena, Spain.

Standard Diving Simulator, Modular Design

In order to carry out the full range of diving experiments, trials, training, operational research with long saturation exposures and equipment trials, a complex such as that shown in Fig. 1.14 is required.

Based on the design in Fig. 1.5, the two main compartments, 1 and 4, are working compartments designed for 50 bar pressure (i.e. water depths of 500 m). The vertical compartments have a diameter of 3 m with a water depth of 3 m. Restricted swimming is therefore possible. Compartments 1 and 4 are connected by a short trunk fitted with a hydraulic door with pressure-tight seals and with an access diameter of 1000 mm allowing equipment to be passed through. Fig. 1.15

Fig. 1.15. Diver entering a wet chamber from a transfer chamber in a diving simulator.

shows a diver entering the wet compartment. The 1000 mm side door with bayonet lock fitting—a two-way pressure door capable of withstanding maximum operating pressures from both sides—can also be seen. The generous capacity of the system allows for an intermediate transfer lock between the wet and dry main compartments and gives a facility for running separate programmes, including saturation diving. The internal dimensions of the living and decompression chambers are approximately 5 m in length and a minimum diameter of 1.8 m in the living chambers to normally 2.2 m.

Although the basic design principles for gas and life-support systems are the same as for the simplest designs, application is considerably more complicated to allow for variable gas mixtures, the continuous monitoring of all life-support systems and some secondary duplication of systems in case the primary functions fail. For example, the following requirements of information and control will need to be displayed and controlled on the console:

1. Gas mixing control.
2. Continuous recording and analysis of breathing mixtures, oxygen and CO_2 content.
3. Humidity and temperature control.
4. Observations and measurement of divers' physiological functions displayed and recorded outside through penetrations in the chamber (i.e. electroencephalogram, electronystagmogram, electrocardiogram and body core temperature).
5. Gas mixture recovery and filtration units to remove CO_2 and moisture and replace oxygen to maintain the necessary partial pressure and depth control.
6. Visual closed-circuit television and sound communication.

Temperature control of the water in the wet chamber is important in order to achieve realistic conditions and this can be varied between $+4°C$ and $+30°C$. The water is treated separately. Throughout the system there are six television cameras and monitors to cover every conceivable operation in the dry chambers and a further under-water television camera in the wet chamber, mounted on a moving base, to cover every part of the compartment. Normal voice communications with all chambers are further backed up with sound-powered telephones in case of power failure or the need to eliminate a potential fire hazard where a high oxygen content has built up inside the chambers. Although television cameras are generally sited outside the chambers, filming through the windows with the use of fibreoptics has yet to be fully developed. Diving schedules for prolonged decompression may be automatically programmed from a computer source with an immediate override facility for manual control.

Diving Simulators for High Operating Pressures

As the requirement for simulated deep water depths has increased, so a number of diving centres have been built to meet the need to achieve water pressures of 100–150 bar (1000–1500 m). Where it is acceptable for pressure to be significantly lower in the dry chambers than in the wet chambers, cylindrical chambers are used, but as the design pressures are increased so the material problem of constructing steel cylinders becomes more expensive and the design of spherical dry chambers can be considered on grounds of cost. Spheres also have special advantages of strength-to-weight ratio. Fig. 1.16 shows the combination of spherical wet chambers and cylindrical dry chambers. There are practical operating disadvantages to the sphere as a dry chamber because of space limitations for the divers and ventilation problems in this configuration.

Fig. 1.16. A diving simulator with a wet sphere, operating to 100 bar, and cylindrical living and decompression chamber operating to 50 bar.

Diving Simulator for Maximum Operating Pressures Using Spheres (the Caterpillar)

To accommodate the commercial need to explore deeper in the sea, particularly in oil exploration, facilities to carry out the required research work in diving to 1000 m have been built. The example shown in Fig. 1.17 at the Technical University, Aachen, shows a perfect symmetry in spherical design. The two large centre spheres have a diameter of 3 m and an operating pressure of 100 bar. The lower of the two spheres can be filled with water. The two side spheres, which also operate as transfer locks, have a diameter of 2 m and are designed with an operating pressure of 50 bar. Also fitted are small supply locks for transfer of food and equipment during dives. Some form of small supply lock is essential in all chamber design. The upper central sphere has a bolted flange for the installation of test equipment and is conveniently sited for the use of an overhead crane.

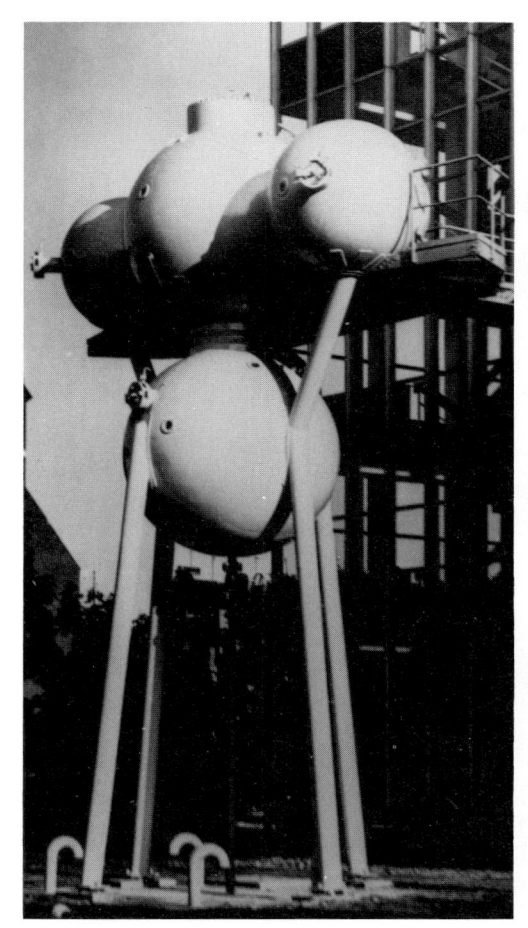

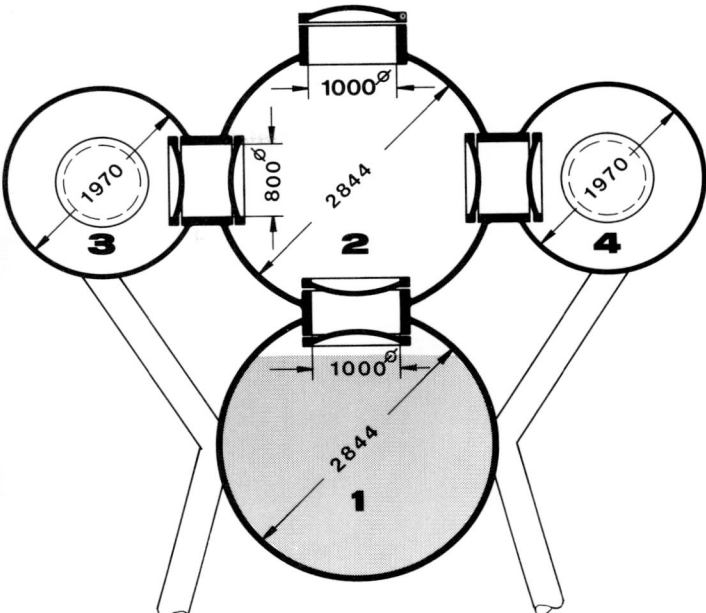

Fig. 1.17. The diving simulator at the Technical University, Aachen, with an operating pressure up to 100 bar. The control room is on the third floor and the weight of the complex is supported on stilts.

Large-volume Spherical Diving Simulator

One of the best known diving simulators, both for its advanced design and for the successful practical research carried out, is the complex at Comex, Marseilles (Fig. 1.18). The main chamber is a large sphere with a diameter of 5 m and an internal volume of approximately 113 m^3, designed for a maximum operating pressure of 30 bar.

The system was operational in the late 1960s but the restriction of depth soon became apparent as commercial pressure relentlessly forced diving companies to go deeper. Nevertheless, the unit is almost a perfect simulation of actual diving in water; with the addition of a diving bell *inside* the sphere, it becomes a near perfect simulation of actual diving bell operations under controlled conditions. Life-support is supplied from a control system which also supplies an adjacent, and separate, chamber complex. This extensive deep diving research complex has the facility to extend even further.

Fig. 1.18. The large wet and dry spherical chamber at Comex, Marseilles, during construction. Because of good weather all the year round the installation needs minimal insulation.

The Buffalo Diving Simulator

Whereas the symmetry of the diving system at Aachen and the sheer size of the unit at the Naval Coastal Systems Laboratory in Panama City, USA, are both magnificent examples of practical simulators, the facility at the University of Buffalo, USA, marks a radical advance in design (Fig. 1.19). The design allows for a horizontal complex including the wet chamber, which in previous designs had to be entered from above and required as much as 5–6 m of overall chamber height to achieve 2–3 m of water depth. Installed on one floor level, the system allows reasonable comfort for the diver in the water and better control and visual contact with the diver by the standby attendant. The partition is made of acrylic, in two semicircular parts, and allows the divers to step in and out of the water. Equal ambient pressure holds the water up to the top of the wet portion of the chamber. The water level is controlled from outside and, if required, the water can be evacuated to allow additional dry chamber space. An additional facility can be installed in the water control system to create water movement through the chamber and a stationary diver can swim realistically against a controlled current of water.

Diving Simulator Facility at the Bundeslehr- und Forschungstätte der Deutschen Lebensrettungsgesellschaft in Berlin

Most, if not all, diving simulators are restricted to water depths not exceeding 3–4 m in the wet chamber. Although large water towers

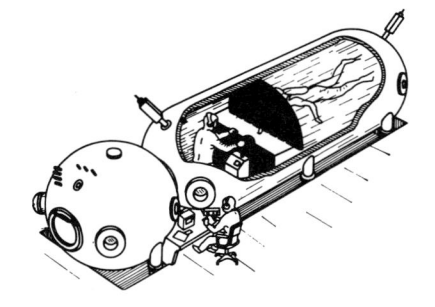

Fig. 1.19. The horizontal diving simulator at Buffalo, USA.

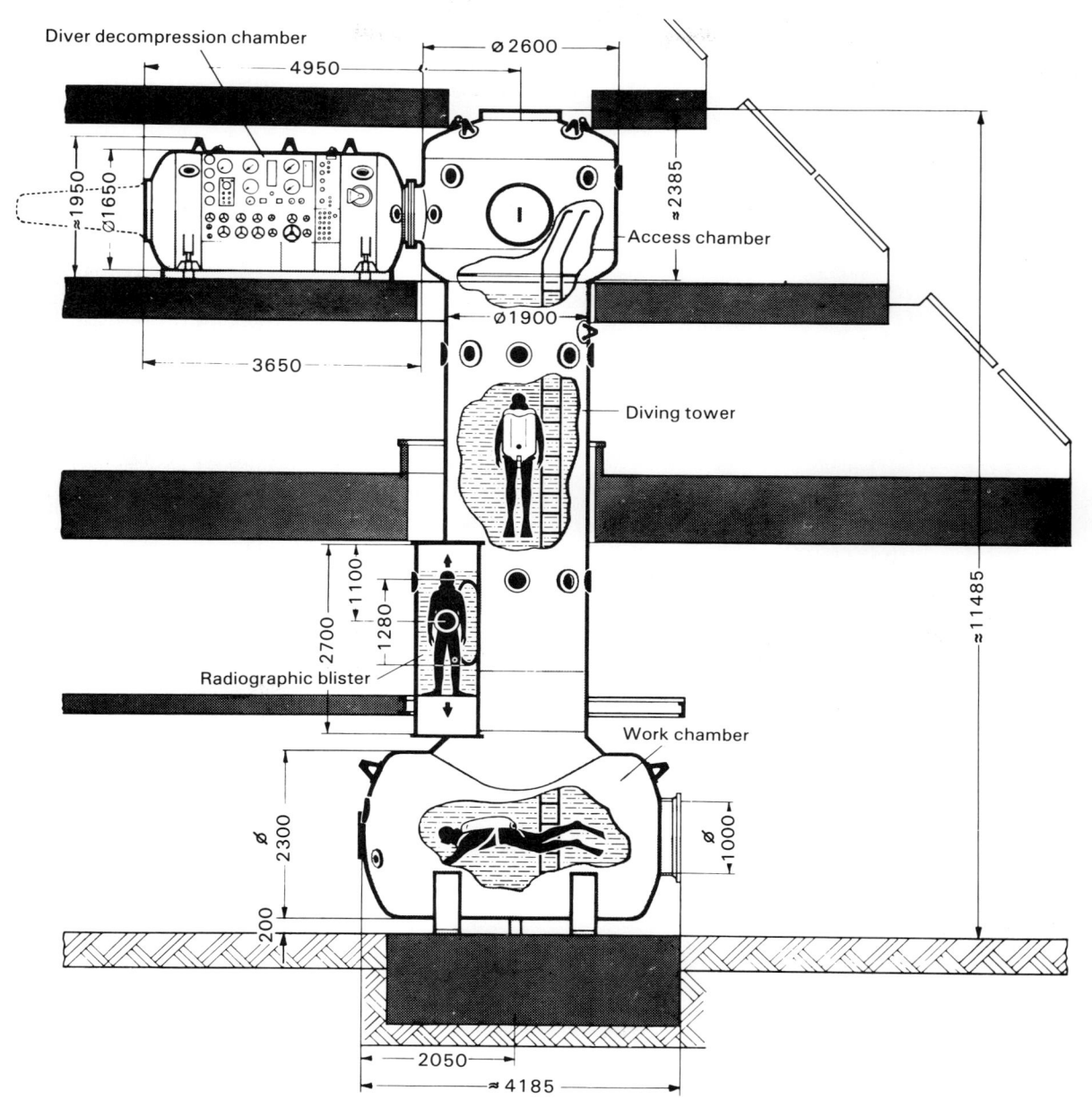

with water depths of 30 m are constructed for training submarine crews in free ascent, these are open-ended at the top. However, one such closed facility has been built and installed in Berlin at the national training and research centre for the German life-guard. A modern building houses the boats, lecture rooms, workshops, accommodation and also a large diving tower chamber, which not only has an operating pressure equivalent to 150 m but also has water of more than 8 m in the tower chamber. Fig. 1.20 shows a cross-section of the installation. The training of divers to appreciate and overcome the extreme psychological pressure of working in confined spaces and

Fig. 1.20. A cross section of the diving simulator installed at the Bundeslehr- und Forschungstätte in Berlin.

Fig. 1.21. Radiographic unit and blister at the diving simulator of the DLRG, Berlin.

with a realistic depth of water above them is very important. For a rescue and salvage diver this training is even more important and the Berlin facility goes as far as possible to provide this special training in a controlled environment. The diver in the lower chamber can operate tools and equipment within the confines of the chamber and this is essential practical training for salvage and rescue work.

The research work of the medical group into certain aspects of recreational diving is specially important and, apart from pulmonary and cardiac laboratory units, there is also a complete radiographic unit installed in the central column of the tower to allow divers under pressure and in the water to be radiographed. For this purpose a blister (Fig. 1.21) is welded to the side of the tower. The height is about 3 m and there are two exposure windows for the radiographic source. The windows are made of specially coated aluminium plates. The radiograph machine is moved towards the blister along a guide rail on the ceiling and, with a direct view of the diver in the water, can radiograph any part of the body. Whilst the X-ray source remains static, the diver is moved upwards or downwards to any desired position opposite the radiograph window by an externally controlled hydraulic platform on which the diver stands. The central diving tower is connected to a standard decompression chamber (Fig. 1.22)

Fig. 1.22. The decompression chamber with central control panel and transfer chamber in the diving simulator at the DLRG, Berlin.

which is designed to be modified for the installation of new research equipment.

Large-volume Diving Simulator Naval Coastal System Laboratory, Panama City, USA

The US Navy built a huge facility which became operational in 1975, after many years of construction, at Panama City, Florida. The large internal volumes increased the scope of the facility and the terms of reference for its usage are as follows:

1. Basic physiological research in respiratory problems.
2. Testing and evaluation of breathing equipment and under-water tools.
3. Pressure testing of unmanned vehicles and submersibles.
4. Under-water measuring instrumentation.

Fig. 1.23 shows the cross-section of the layout of the system and Fig. 1.24 gives an impression of the size of the wet chamber. Fig. 1.25 shows the control room for the system, much like the control room for a space programme. A computer fed with information during a diving or equipment trial will respond if there are any failures in the

Fig. 1.23. The general layout of the US Navy facility at Panama City, Florida.

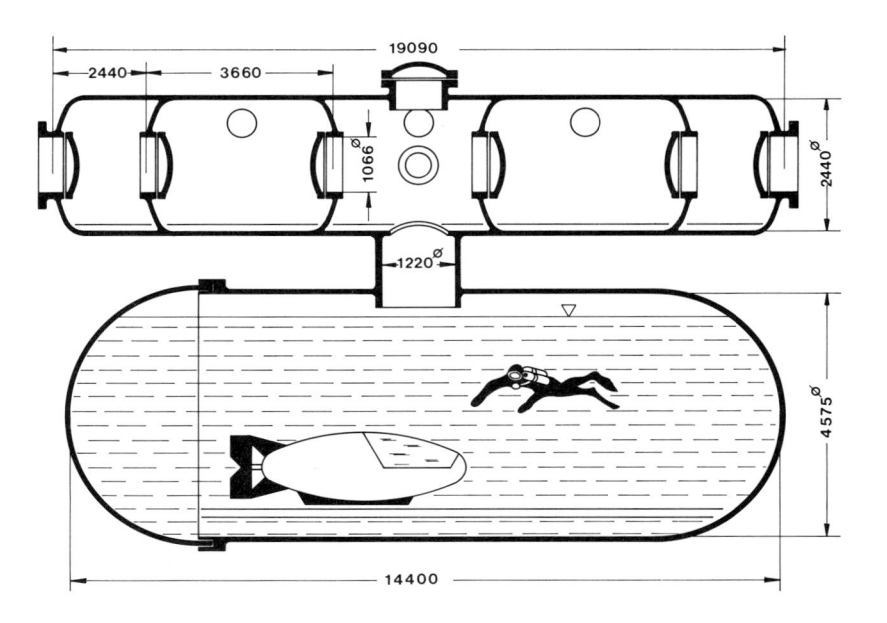

Fig. 1.24. The wet chamber of the US Navy facility at Panama City, Florida. The size of the chamber is indicated by the photograph of Dr George Bond, the American physiologist.

system and can take corrective action. This monitoring and control system can be overridden by manual control. It is questionable whether such a large and expensive facility could be commercially viable, but its use for commercial work would be very important. Joint ventures between governments and commercial interests will be needed to support complexes of this size in the future.

The USSR are considering moving ahead with the design for a large-volume diving system with a capability of 1500 m of simulated water depth.

Diving Simulator of the Kantonhospital, Zürich

The Swiss, despite their geographical position in the centre of Europe, have led some exciting advances in the diving and oceanographic fields. Auguste Piccard, in 1960, with his enclosed one-atmosphere bathysphere, descended into the darkness of the Marianas Trench in the Pacific, the deepest known seabed. In the late fifties and early sixties Hannes Keller, helped by Professor Bühlmann, extended the frontiers of diving in open water with some daring deep dives. Piccard again pressed forward in oceanographic research with the

Fig. 1.25. The control centre of the US Navy facility at Panama City, Florida.

Fig. 1.26. The diving simulator at the research centre of the Kantonhospital, Zürich.

Gulf Stream drift using *PX15*. Professor Bühlmann has continued to be a valued authority on decompression and problems of treating decompression sickness. The research facility at the Kantonshospital in Zürich centres around the diving simulator, fully operational since 1976. The whole system has been carefully considered and constructed with many special refinements.

Fig. 1.26 shows the living chamber, transfer chamber and part of the controls. The spherical wet chamber has an internal diameter of 3.5 m and is large enough to support three to four divers. Above the wet chamber is the transfer chamber and living chamber which is also the decompression chamber. All the chambers are rated for operation at 100 bar. A small transfer lock is connected to the living chamber and there are two-way pressure-tight doors throughout the system, except that there is no door between transfer hatch and wet chamber. The engineering of the steel pressure chamber is designed to accept a very sophisticated life-support system with numerous control and monitoring systems.

Large-scale Testing Facilities

There has always been a need to test equipment and where it is possible this is carried out in diving simulators, inside the wet chamber. Entry, as much as size, restricts the type of equipment and special facilities have been built specifically for testing equipment in water without the need for life-support systems and dry chambers.

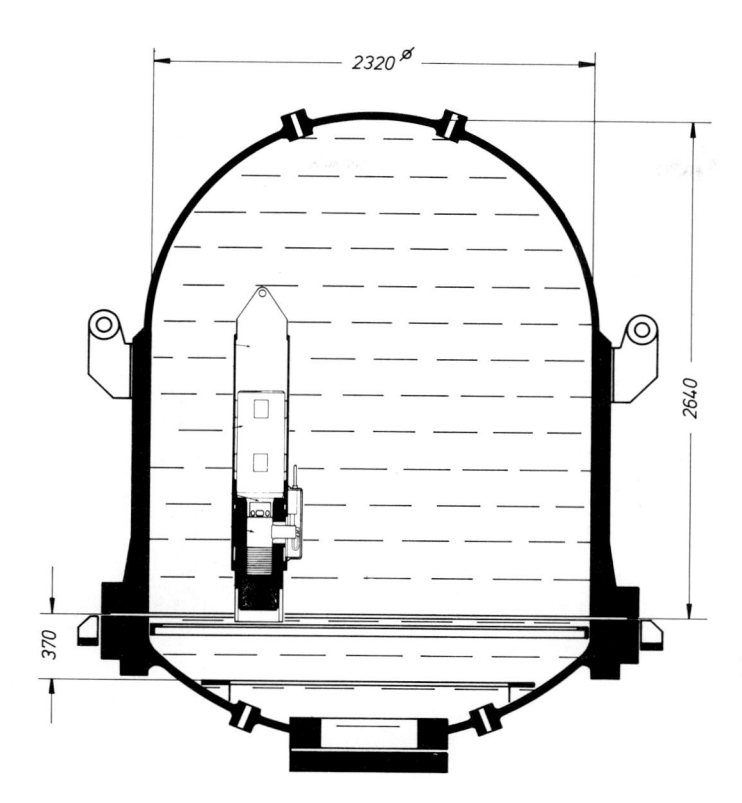

Fig. 1.27. The pressure testing chamber of the Ateliers et Chantiers de Bretagne, France. Operating pressure 50 bar.

The chambers required to test working submersibles, subsea oil production equipment, oceanographic equipment etc. tend to be large and expensive and therefore restricted in number.

Pressure Simulator with Simple Design for Medium-size Equipment

The system installed at the Ateliers et Chantiers de Bretagne is representative of many other installations used in industry where testing of smaller units is needed. The dimensions and the design layout can be seen in Fig. 1.27. The operating pressure is 50 bar to an accuracy of 1%. The upper dome is lifted and the equipment placed on the base plate. The test chamber is filled with either fresh or sea water.

Pressure Simulator for the Testing of Research and Working Submersibles

The use of both manned and unmanned vehicles is accepted in many facets of off-shore work, not solely oil and gas production, but also other commercial uses and oceanographic research. The introduction of the lock-out submersible has enabled divers to operate from such systems and has therefore increased the versatility of the submersible. The present method of testing these units is lowering them into the sea to the depth required. This can be a time-consuming and expensive exercise.

Fig. 1.28. A pressure vessel for external pressure testing of research and working submarines.

Fig. 1.28 shows a pressure chamber with a horizontal chamber 10 m long and 2 m in diameter. The end can be opened to the full extent of the cross-section. Door movements and the four-piece clamping mechanism are operated hydraulically. The test units are moved into the chamber on trolley and rails. The chamber is filled with water and pressure built up by compressed air and a hydraulic system. Ample penetrations allow measurement to be taken and monitored outside and at the same time the test run can be monitored with television and seen through the chamber windows. Dynamic tests can be carried out on the equipment using a hydraulic pumping system adjusted to give pressure and frequency variations. A filtration unit allows the water to be used again.

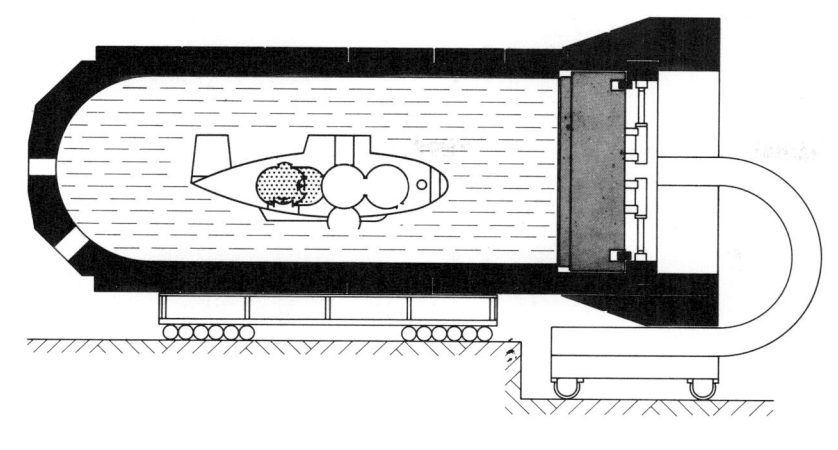

Fig. 1.29. The hydraulic test tank at the Naval Ship Research and Development Center of the US Navy at Annapolis.

Deep Ocean Pressure Facility, Annapolis, USA

Annapolis is the largest pressure vessel facility of its kind (Fig. 1.29) in the world, with a working depth of 843 bar and large enough to test submersibles and large unmanned vehicles. The dimensions are vast, with a clear internal length of 8.2 m and internal diameter of 3.1 m; it is manufactured in HY-100 steel in a multi-layer construction (shrink rings). Either fresh or sea water can be used to fill the interior. The locking system at the end is impressive. It is constructed in the form of a breach shutter, hydraulically operated, which, when open, exposes the full diameter of the cylinder. The door is moved vertically on a trolley and, at full pressure load, 63 500 tonnes is exerted on the door.

An interesting constructional detail is the solution of the door-seal problem. In Fig. 1.30 a cut-away view of the seal section is shown.

Worldwide Distribution of Diving Simulators and Large Pressure Testing Facilities

Tables 1.1 and 1.2 show, as far as can be ascertained, all diving simulators and large pressure testing facilities, their geographical location and their current status.

Classification

It is not easy to classify the range of applications of diving simulators and pressure testing facilities as there is frequently overlap and many of the facilities are used for several purposes. There is always some difficulty in obtaining up-to-date information as most facilities are continuously being modified. In Table 1.2, 43 simulators, some still in the design stage, are evaluated with respect to their main application. It is interesting to see that 19 facilities are used primarily for military research. 16 simulators belong to academic institutions and diving schools and 10 are owned by industrial manufacturers.

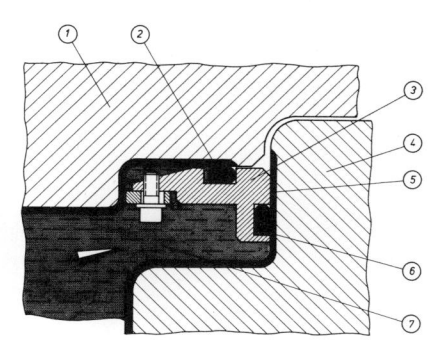

Fig. 1.30. Sealing arrangement for the test tank illustrated in Fig. 1.29.

1 pressure tank
2 O-ring, radial seal
3 supporting ring
4 door plate
5 monel coating
6 O-ring, axial seal
7 water filling, pressure direction

Table 1.1. World-wide hyperbaric simulators with life support (1980)

Country	Operational	Building	Planned	Laid up
Argentina	1	—	—	—
Canada	2	—	—	—
China	2	—	—	—
Czechoslovakia	—	—	1	—
France	4	2	1	1
Germany (Federal Republic)	4	2	1	1
Holland	1	—	—	—
Iraq	1	—	—	—
Italy	4	—	—	—
Japan	1	—	—	—
Norway	3	1	1	—
Spain	1	—	1	—
Sweden	2	—	—	—
Switzerland	1	—	—	—
Taiwan	1	—	—	—
Turkey	1	—	—	—
United Kingdom	5	—	1	—
USA	1	1	—	—
USSR	1	—	4	—
Yugoslavia	1	—	—	—

Purpose	No. of simulators
Basic research	21
Training of divers	25
Testing of diving and underwater equipment	17
Development and trial of new working techniques	6
Testing of materials and structures	6

Applications

Scientific research
    Mental and physical application tests
    Defining medical standards and tolerance tests for divers
    Physiological monitoring
    Evaluation of medical standards
    Development and evaluation of decompression and treatment tables
    Study of the limits of diver performance
    Verification of permissible compression rates
    Study of work in cold water
    Study of drowning accidents

Table 1.2. Geographical location and application of main hyperbaric simulators with life support (1980)

Location	Scientific research	Training and operational evaluation	Testing of diving equipment	Development and testing of new work techniques	Testing of materials and pressure vessels
Mar del Plata		×			
Aachen					×
Berlin	×	×			
Bruchsal		×			
Lübeck			×		
Bonn-Wahn (under constr.)	×				
Geesthacht (under constr.)				×	
Eckenförde (Plg)			×		×
Marseille Hydr.		×		×	
Marseille EMS	×				
Marseille CEMA	×				
Toulon		×			
Aberdeen		×			
Alverstoke	×	×	×	×	
Den Helder	×	×	×		
Bergamo					×
La Spezia		×	×		
Palermo	×				
Zingonia	×	×	×		
Damascus					×
Yokusuka	×	×			
Split		×	×		
Ontario DCIEM I	×	×	×		
Ontario DCIEM II	×	×	×		
Bergen		×	×	×	
Haakonsvern		×	×		
Tromsø (Plg)		×		×	
Stockholm	×	×	×		
Sjödal	×	×	×		
Zürich		×			
Cartagena		×	×		
Prague (Plg)	×				
Istanbul		×			
Annapolis I			×		
Annapolis II				×	×
Belle Chasse		×	×	×	
Bethesda	×				
Panama City		×	×		×
Buffalo		×			
Durham		×			
Groton		×			
Philadelphia		×			
Gelencić		×	×		
Shanghai (2×)		×			

X-ray tests under pressure
Marine biological studies under hyperbaric pressures
Research into treatment of gas gangrene, gas poisoning etc.
Definition of absolute depth limits for safe diving
Experiments with animals
Intensive biological, physiological, psychological and medical studies
Study of bone necrosis and other pressure related problems

Training and operational evaluation
Basic introduction to bounce and saturation diving
Training divers in the use of new equipment and diving procedures
Further training for simulated diving bell operations using the wet chamber
Training and certification of commercial divers
Training in the use of submarine escape gear
Preparation for under-water habitat operations
Oxygen tolerance tests
Training in emergency routines
Training in the use of under-water tools and working procedures

Testing of diving equipment
Testing of diving equipment for use under operational conditions
Trials of one-atmospheric diving suits
Test runs of under-water propulsion units
Tests of diving apparatus and equipment
Testing of compression chamber components
Trials of off-shore equipment
Testing and trials of measuring instruments
Cable testing
Testing under-water TV systems
Testing of probes and ROVs
Testing of under-water satellites
Trials of hot water suits
Trials of submarine escape gear
Trials of special diving suits for radio-active contaminated water

Development and testing of new working techniques
Trials of non-destructive testing methods for off-shore repair
Trials of subsea oil production equipment
Testing of pipeline connectors
Development of under-water cutting and welding procedures
Development of methods and tools for pipeline flanges
Development and trials of spool pieces
Study of the relevance of ergonomics to new working techniques
Pre-operational trials of working procedures
Improvement of the safety and efficiency of diving procedures

Testing of materials and pressure vessels
    Testing of subsea wellheads and production equipment under external pressure
    External pressure tests of diving bells, submersibles, unmanned vehicles and pressure vessels
    Pressure tests of concrete under external pressure of sea water

Examples of Hyperbaric Diving Simulators

Drägerwerk Lübeck

Location:	Lübeck, Federal Republic of Germany (removed in 1960)
Operator:	Drägerwerk, Lübeck
Manufacturer:	Drägerwerk, Lübeck
Completion:	1913

Technical details:

Operating pressure	20 bar
External diameter of wet pot	2000 mm
External length of wet pot	3000 mm
Diameter of lock	1000 mm
Length of lock	1000 mm

Closed by oval man-hole cover
Filled with fresh water to approx. 2 m height
Pressurized with air

Technical equipment:
Simple instrumentation, air inlet and outlet valves
Pressure gauges for internal pressures and gas storage pressures
Slot-shaped windows
Communication by diver telephone

Purpose:
Basic research on diving physiology, for example hyperbaric oxygen tolerance tests (submarine escape gear)
Escape gear trials
Trials of standard diving dresses
Trials of experimental deep diving apparatus

The intensive testing of diving equipment and submarine escape gear, together with the more and more urgent need for basic research in the field of hyperbaric oxygen tolerance, resulted in Dräger at Lübeck constructing this simulator as early as 1913. The facility was at that time unique and influenced later designs. It was the first known recorded simulator. Welding pressure vessels were not feasible and as a rivetted construction capable of 20 bar working pressure, it was no mean technical achievement in those days.

The vertical cylinder with a diameter of 2 m and a height of 3 m was normally filled to about two-thirds with water. Therefore the divers had a chance to reach the air space above them if their equipment failed. The lock with a diameter of approximately 1 m and almost the same height was extremely small and could be used for personnel transfer only with difficulty.

The small observation slots which provided a relatively good view of the interior of the chamber were designed to use the minimum of glass. The equipment and fittings were very basic. A heating coil inside the chamber warmed the water. Air and oxygen storage banks were sited outside the chamber with the minimum number of control valves and pressure gauges. A sound-powered telephone was the only means of communication.

Early reports record that the simulator was extensively used initially for the development of submarine escape gear. In many cases dangerous experiments were carried out to establish the limits of oxygen tolerance as these were of fundamental importance for the development of oxygen rebreathers used as submarine escape gear. Later the testing of standard diving suits and especially autonomous hard hat equipment became more important. In the following years first experiments with autonomous, self-mixing deep diving equipment using oxy-helium were carried out in exhaustive tests. But as the simulator did not include a decompression chamber, further trials were limited. Longer decompression times imposed severe limitations on the divers. Although the water was drained immediately after the test dives it was very uncomfortable to stay in this small, humid and sparsely furnished tank.

In 1960 this historic facility had to be removed to give room for a more modern installation and unfortunately could not be preserved.

Sub Sea Oil Services (Fig. 1.31)

Location: Zingonia, Bergamo, Italy

Operator: Sub Sea Oil Services, Milan

Manufacturer: Drass, Zingonia

Completion: 1970

Technical details:

Operating pressure 60 bar

Dimensions of chamber	1	2	3	4	5
Diameter (mm)	3500	1500	2000	2000	2000
Length (mm)	5000	2300	3500	5000	3500
Hatch diameter (mm)	605	605	605	605	605
Volume (m^3)	36.1	3.1	8.2	11.9	8.2

Filled with water, air or oxy-helium mixtures

Purpose:
Development in the field of deep diving including saturation diving
Verification of theoretically established decompression tables and gas mixtures

Physiological hyperbaric experiments with animals and human beings
Training of deep divers
Human engineering in deep diving
Training and certification of technicians and scientists in the operation of hyperbaric systems (physicians, engineers and managers from diving contractors or the offshore industry)

SSOS is a major European diving company which has done much to advance deep diving technology. Advanced work on decompresison tables has been carried out with the Swiss diving physiologist Dr A. Bühlmann of Zürich University. The simulator was made by Drass with this type of research in mind. The facility has an operating pressure of 50 bar and comprises five chambers, the wet chamber being very large.

The vertical wet chamber has a diameter of 3.5 m and a height of 5 m. This chamber is normally filled with water to about half of its height. Above the wet chamber a smaller chamber simulating a diving bell was installed to give divers realistic training in bell operations. Three horizontal cylindrical decompression and transfer chambers complete the installation. A control panel designed in a semi-circle gives good quality presentation of the operations in the various chambers.

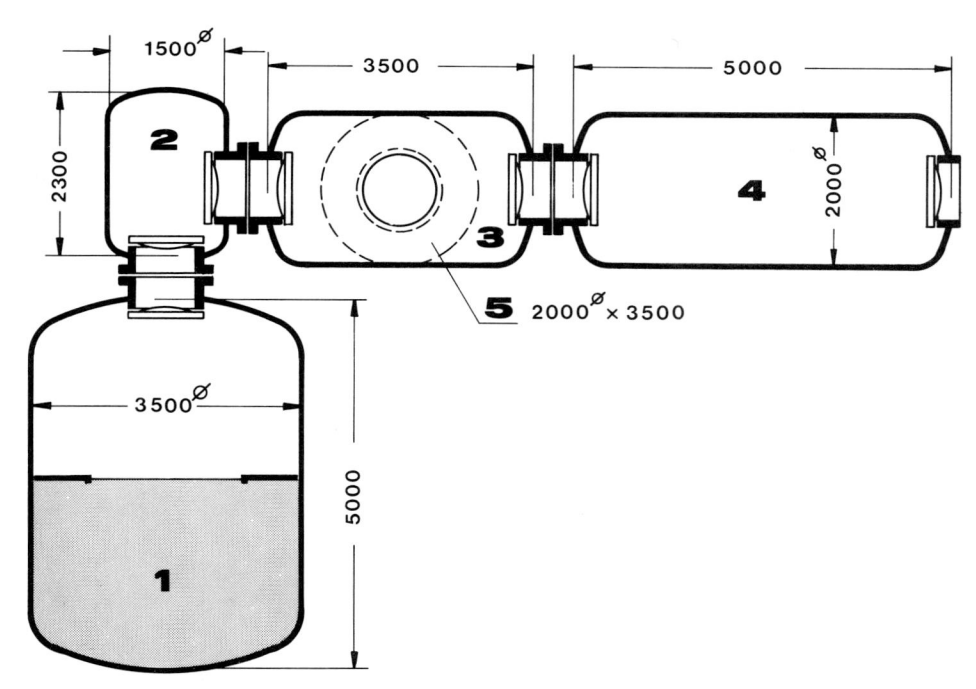

Fig. 1.31. Subsea Oil Services, Zingonia.

Technical University at Aachen

Location:	Aachen, Nordrhein-Westfalien, FRG
Operator:	Technical University, Aachen, Institute of Shipbuilding
Manufacturer:	Drägerwerk, Lübeck, and Neumann, Eschweiler
Completion:	1972

Technical details:
Operating pressure
  Chamber 1 and 2   100 bar
  Chamber 3 and 4   50 bar

Dimensions of chamber	1	2	3	4
Internal diameter (mm)	2844	2844	1970	1970
Hatch diameter (mm)	1000	800/1000	800	800
Volume (m^3)	12	12	4	4

Filled with water, air or helium–oxygen mixtures

Purpose:
Testing of pressure vessels under external pressure
Testing of materials (concrete) under pressure and in water
Development of non-destructive testing methods
Development of under-water working procedures
Evaluation of decompression tables

Largely thanks to the late Professor Ebner, this elegant and sophisticated simulator was installed in 1972. With an operating depth of 1000 m, it will meet most requirements for the future. The T-shaped arrangement is unique, with the chambers elegantly supported on pillars outside a university building so as to allow the control console to be sited on the third floor.

The university facility is used mainly for material testing but under the present direction of Professor Kokkinowrachos may well extend to other aspects of off-shore technology including man-under-pressure and material inspection procedures.

Westinghouse Ocean Research (Fig. 1.32)

Location:	Annapolis, Maryland USA
Company:	Westinghouse Electric Corporation
Manufacturer:	Westinghouse Electric Corporation
Completion:	1965

Technical details:
Depth 457 m (610 m under special conditions)

	Entrance lock	Main chamber	Wet chamber
Diameter (m)	1.2	2.5	2.5
Length (m)	—	3.1	2.9

Volume (m³)	2.9	11.2	dry 1.8
			wet 7.9
			total 9.7
Hatch diameter (m)	0.76	0.76	0.68
No. of view ports	4	5	6
Viewport diameter (m)	0.12	0.12	0.002

Compression capability: wet chamber max. 366 m/min; main chamber 46 m/min

Temperature of wet chamber min. $-1.7°C$ (29°F) at 457 m, min. 12.8°C (55°F) at 610 m; max. 21.7°C (70°F)

Capacity three or four divers, six to eight under special conditions; two in wet chamber

Replenishment lock 0.3×0.5 m

Technical equipment:
Environmental control for temperature and humidity
Diver suit heating two divers at 29°C
Ergometer
Wet chamber water filtration
100% reserve gas supply for endurance of 23 days to date
CCTV and intercom
Gas analysis
Fire suppression system

Westinghouse is well known for the introduction of the Cachalot diving system which was used for the inspection and repair of the Smith Mountain Dam.

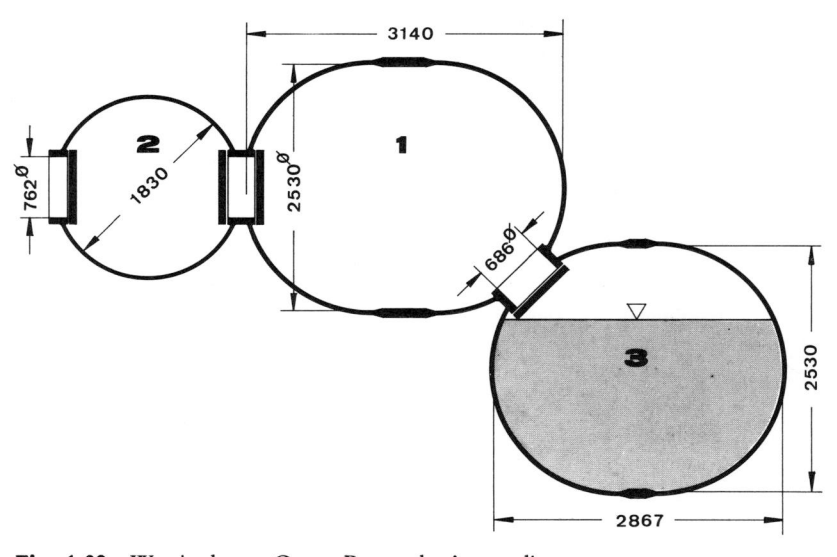

Fig. 1.32. Westinghouse Ocean Research, Annapolis.

Since 1965 when the hyperbaric facility was built a great number of exploratory saturation dives have been carried out. Two divers can be in the wet chamber at any one time and carry out tests on an ergometer frame. Water temperature can be varied between $-1.7°C$ (29°F) and 21.7°C (70°F). An unusual facility is the fast compression rates of 366 m/min in the wet chamber.

New York at Buffalo

Location:	Department of Physiology, State University at Buffalo, New York, USA
Operator:	State University at Buffalo, New York
Manufacturer:	Pressure vessels made by Struthers Nuclear and Process Co., Warren, Pennsylvania, USA
Completion:	1971

Technical details:
Operating pressure: vacuum equivalent to an altitude of 7500 m; hyperbaric pressures up to 170 bar

Dimensions of chamber	1	2
Internal diameter (mm)	2100	2100
Internal length (mm)	—	4730
Hatch diameter (mm)	600	600
Volume (m^3)	4.85	14

Filled with air or helium–oxygen mixtures, partly water

Purpose:
Physiological studies
Research in all fields of deep diving
Testing of deep diving equipment
Research in the vacuum pressure range

This system uses a unique design configuration and other facilities which have based their designs on this system are often known as 'Buffalo systems'. The L or T configuration has always been the standard design form of hyperbaric simulators with the exception of only a few installations. As wet chamber and decompression chambers are never on the same level with these configurations they always required a building with two or more stories.

Disadvantages of this arrangement are not only the higher costs for the building but also the additional cost of installing communication and control systems on separate levels. Therefore the main advantages of the Buffalo system are that the supervisors have a better view of divers in the wet chamber. In the T- or L-shaped configuration the disturbed surface of the water makes observation from the inside very difficult. The Buffalo system allows the divers to be observed through two semi-circular acrylic partitions, allowing the attendants to remain dry whilst the divers operate in the water.

The system, being rated for an operating pressure of 170 bar, will cover most research work in the future. The design feature has been incorporated in the Canadian facility in Ontario, the Norwegian facility in Bergen, the German GUSI in Geesthacht and will undoubtedly be used elsewhere in many future designs.

Norwegian Under-water Institute (NUI) (Fig. 1.33)

Location:	Sotra, Bergen, Norway
Operator:	Norwegian Underwater Institute (Royal Norwegian Council for Scientific Research and Det Norske Veritas)
Manufacturer:	Pressure vessels by Kvaerner Brug, Oslo Instrumentation by Saturation Systems Inc., USA
Completion:	1978

Technical details:
Operating pressure: 50–65 bar

Dimensions of chamber:	1	2	3	4
External diameter (mm)	2200	2200	2200	3000
Chamber length (mm)	3500	4700	3000	8000
Hatch diameter (mm)	800	800	800	3000
Volume (m^3)				50

Filled with air, helium–oxygen mixtures, chamber 4 with water

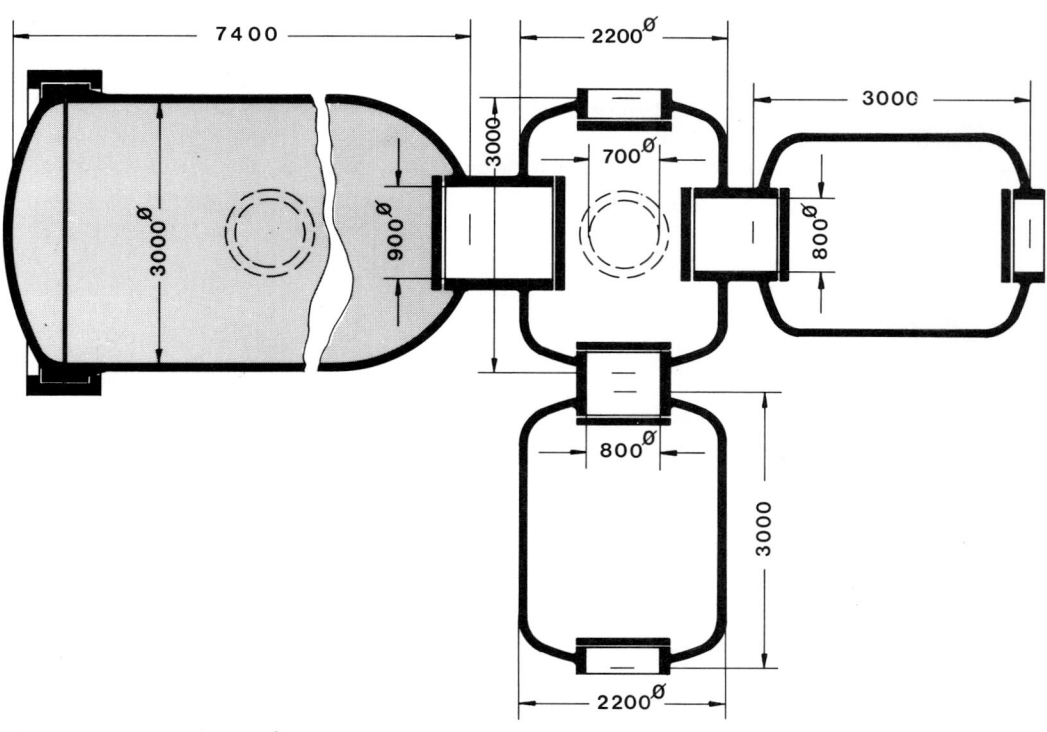

Fig. 1.33. Norwegian Under-water Institute, Bergen.

Purpose:
Medical and physiological research inclusive practical tests to establish a relation between diver performance, diving equipment, depth and temperature conditions
Improvements of the instrumentation to monitor and record physical condition of divers and their equipment during diving operations
Improvements of diver communication equipment for field operations
Tests of diving equipment on breathing machines
Improvements of decompression tables
Measurements of dangerous gas bubble formation
Influence of anaesthetics during pressure treatment
Study of the dangers of electricity under water
Risk analysis of manned submersibles
Treatment of divers after accidents

After several years of intensive planning one of the largest and most modern institutes which deals almost exclusively with research and development in the field of under-water technology was completed in 1978. NUI is run jointly by the Royal Norwegian Council for Scientific and Industrial Research and Det Norske Veritas. It is located at Sotra in the immediate vicinity of Bergen on the Norwegian west coast. Ideal because of adjacent deep waters and the excellent facilities of the institute, it provides the best natural facility for a permanent under-water test range.

The main chamber complex is built to the Buffalo configuration with horizontal chambers and semi-circular internal walls for use as wet compartments. The maximum chamber diameter of 3 m allows large units to be tested with a large exit door. With a maximum operating depth of 650 m in the main chamber it is not likely that this pressure specification will become out-dated since it well exceeds the operating depths in the adjacent Norwegian Trench. The adjacent pressure chamber complex is designed for operating depths of 500 m and includes a central transfer chamber with all the necessary life-support and sanitary arrangements and with two separate decompression chambers, in which independent decompression schedules can be carried out simultaneously.

The transfer chamber and wet chamber have flanges for connection to a diving bell where a complete transfer operation under pressure can be simulated including direct access into the water inside the wet chamber.

A hyperbaric rescue chamber can be connected to the compression chamber complex so that in addition to the facility at Aberdeen a modern hyperbaric medical centre is now available on the other side of the North Sea in Norway.

Duke University, USA (Fig. 1.34)

Location:	Duke University, Durham, North Carolina, USA
Operator:	Duke University Medical School (The F.G. Hall Laboratory for Environmental Research)
Manufacturer:	DIXIE Manufacturing Co. of Baltimore, Maryland

Technical details:

Dimensions of chambers	A	B	C	D	E
Internal diameter (mm)	3200	3200	6100	3200	1981
Chamber length (mm)	4420	2896	Sphere	Sphere	3048
Operating pressure (bar)	6.8	6.8	6.8	31.0	31.0
Volume (m^3)	33.98	21.52	113.28	16.99	7.36
			0.02832		

Dimensions of chambers	F	G	H (lock)
Internal diameter (mm)	3200	2387 sphere / 1981 cyl.	1981
Chamber length (mm)	5639	3048	815
Operating pressure (bar)	31.0	109.0	109.0
Volume (m^3)	36.81	11.04	0.84

Purpose:
Biomedical research
Hyperbaric oxygen treatment of patients
Development of decompression tables
Saturation diving
Cold water studies
Equipment tests

Technical equipment:
Pneumatic automatic and manual controls
Direct manual control
Automatic supervision and regulation of temperature and humidity
Fire supression system with water
Gas storage 8989 m^3

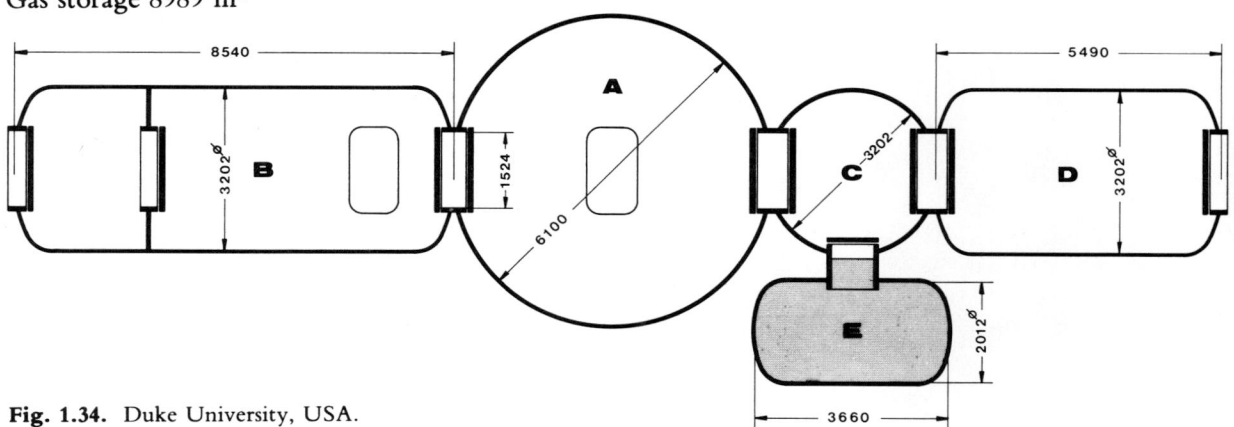

Fig. 1.34. Duke University, USA.

The F. G. Hall Laboratory for Environmental Research is one of the largest hyperbaric complexes of the world and can be used in a number of ways. The enclosed hyperbaric chamber volume amounts to over 255 m³ and is divided into eight chambers. An outstanding feature is a spherical operations room with an internal diameter of 6.1 m. The doors are unusual, being rectangular with an access area of 1524 × 762 mm. Built of flat plates, they have wall thicknesses of 50 mm.

The director of diving research is the well-known physiologist Dr P. Bennett.

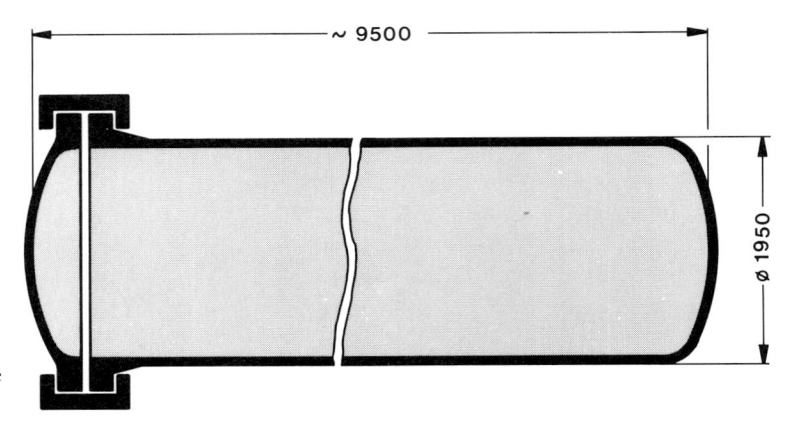

Fig. 1.35. Research Institute of the Armed Forces, Damascus.

Damascus (Fig. 1.35)

Location:	Damascus
Operator:	Research Institute of the Armed Forces of Iraq
Manufacturer:	Drägerwerk, Lübeck
Completion:	1975

Technical details:
Operating pressure: 20 bar
Internal diameter (mm) 1950
Internal length (mm) 9500
Volume (m^3) approx. 35

Capable of carrying out trials on large units, usually of a military nature, the facility can accommodate small submersibles and diver transport vehicles, and can be filled with water.

Technically of interest is the locking technique. One end of the 9.5 m long horizontal cylinder can be opened and makes the full cross-section with a diameter of 1.95 m accessible. Four U-shaped locking segments as well as the whole door are moved hydraulically. The total procedure for opening and closing takes only a fraction of a minute. In order to carry out trials on large units within the overall length of 9.5 m and diameter of 1.95 m the entrance door lock is operated hydraulically moving the door and four-locking segments. To facilitate the entry of heavy objects a pair of rails was installed inside the vessel. The chamber is fitted with observation windows and external lighting.

Argentinian Navy (Fig. 1.36)

Location:	Mar del Plata, Argentina
Operator:	Armada Argentinia
Manufacturer:	Comex Industries, Marseilles, France
Completion:	1977

Technical details:
Operating pressure: 20 bar

Dimensions of chamber	1	2	3
External diameter (mm)	2500	1800	1800
Length overall (mm)	6000	5610	5610
Volume (m^3)		10.7	10.7

Chamber 1 is filled with water, chambers 2 and 3 are operated with air or heliox mixtures
Water temperature: cooling to 5°C

Technical equipment:
Gas storage: 18 storage banks each with 90 m^3 of different mixed gases

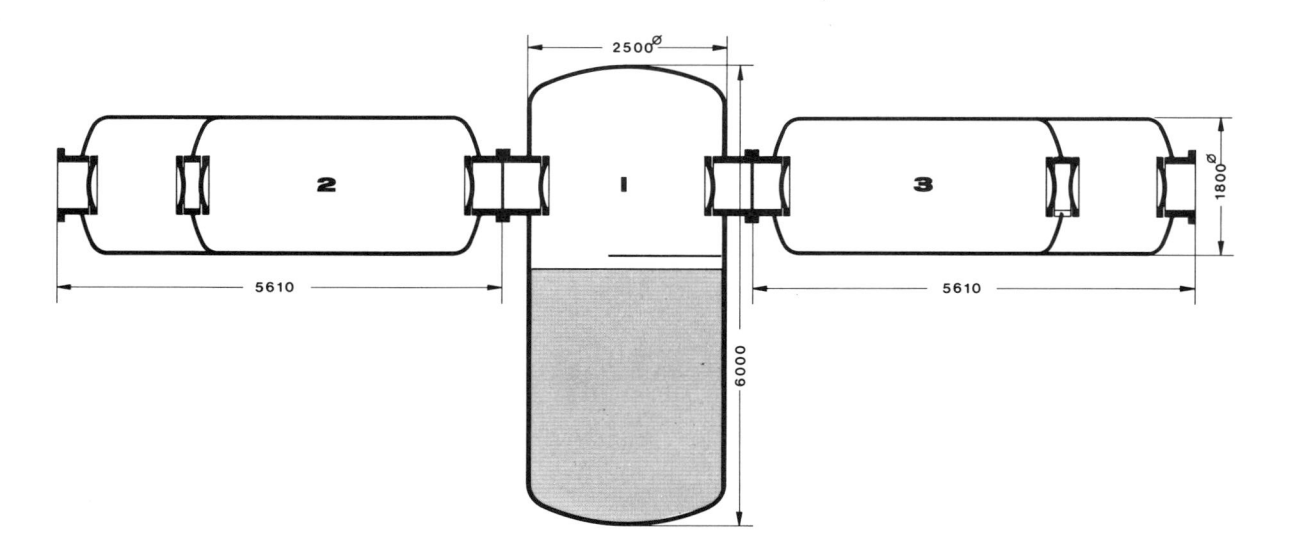

Fig. 1.36. Argentine Navy, Mar del Plata.

Life support: automatic oxygen partial pressure control
Hot water system for chamber heating and hot water diver suits, output 240 000 kcal/hour
Communication system: optical and acoustic emergency communication system

Measuring instruments:
Oxygen monitor
CO_2 monitor
Gas chromatograph
Hygrometer
Electroencephalograph
Electrocardiograph
Connection flange for transportable recompression chambers

Purpose:
Training of divers and personnel
Equipment tests

The hyperbaric simulator of the Argentinian Navy was completed in 1977. The standard design pressure chamber complex was constructed by Comex Industries in Marseilles and installed at Mar del Plata. The configuration is quite similar to comparable facilities of other navies such as the USA, Turkish, Greek or Norwegian Navy. With an operating pressure corresponding to a water depth of 200 m the vertical wet pot allows simulated training of divers and personnel and equipment tests. The water can be cooled to 5°C which allows realistic trials on hot water diving suits and thermal problems. The decompression chamber can be used independently for decompression. On each decompression chamber there is a flange for the connection of a transfer-under-pressure recompression chamber.

Italian Navy (Fig. 1.37)

Location:	La Spezia, Italy
Operator:	Italian Navy
Manufacturer:	Galeazzi, La Spezia, Italy

Technical details:
Operating pressures: wet and dry chamber 30 bar
decompression chambers 20 bar

Dimensions of chamber	1	2	3	4
Diameter (mm)	2200	2200	1920	1920
Length (mm)	—	—	2500	1400
Hatch diameter (mm)	1000	800	800	800
Volume (m^3)	5	4.5	7	3.2

Chamber 1 is water-filled; the other chambers are operated with air or heliox

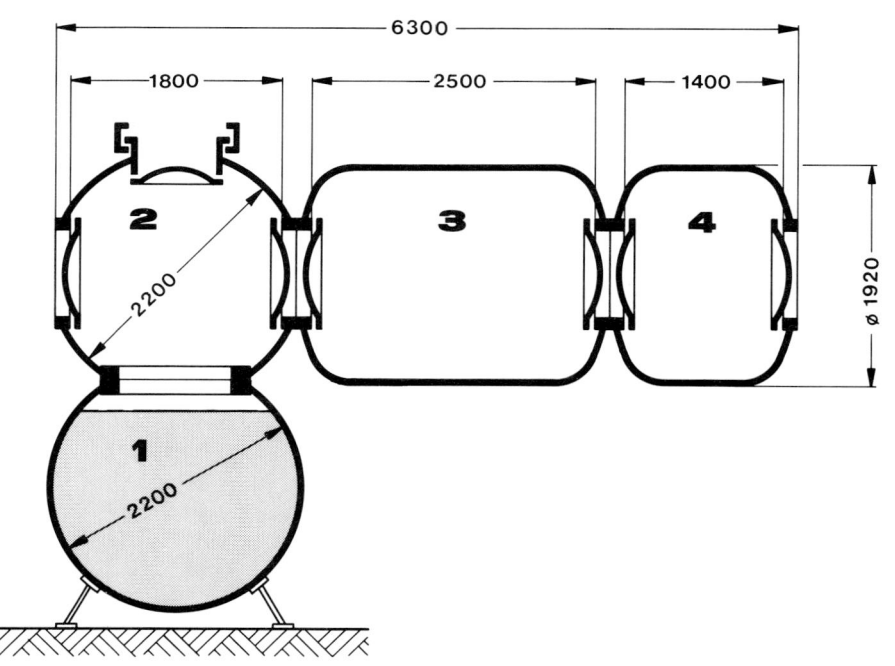

Fig. 1.37. Italian Navy, La Spezia.

Technical equipment:
The facility incorporates all the necessary control and monitoring systems for short-term and long-term diver training and experimental diving.

A diving bell can be mated to the top of the dry chamber and a one-man rescue chamber can be connected to the lock of the decompression complex.

The Italian Navy has always been advanced in under-water techniques, not least the use of under-water vehicles, known as chariots in the Second World War. Very early a hyperbaric complex was built at La Spezia by Galeazzi. The facility has two spherical pressure vessels (wet and dry chamber), one on top of the other, and the adjacent decompression complex with horizontal cylindrical pressure chambers. Whereas the spheres are designed for an operating pressure of 30 bar the cylinders/chambers are restricted to 20 bar.

The installation is utilized for the training of divers but is equally suited for research and development. For the realistic training of divers, a top-transfer diving bell can be connected to the dry chamber. The lock of the decompression complex is furnished with a flange for the connection of a transportable recompression chamber.

Swedish Naval Diving Center (Fig. 1.38)

Location:	Stockholm, Sjödal, Sweden
Operator:	Royal Swedish Navy, Swedish Naval Diving Center
Manufacturer:	Comex, Marseilles, and Kockums Shipyard, Malmö, as joint partners
Completion:	1979

Technical details:

Operating pressure	40 bar		
Dimensions of chamber	1	2	3
Diameter (mm)	2300	2300	2300
Length (mm)	2830	5445	5700
Gas volume (m^3)	12.5	17.3	15.3
Water volume (m^3)	8.0	8.5	

Filled with water, air and heliox
Temperature range:
gas-filled chambers   22–35°C
water-filled chambers   0–35°C

Purpose:
Training of divers
Applied research for rescue of submarine crews
Training of submarine personnel
Development of decompression tables
Tests of diving equipment and accessories
Decompression treatment of injured divers and submarine personnel

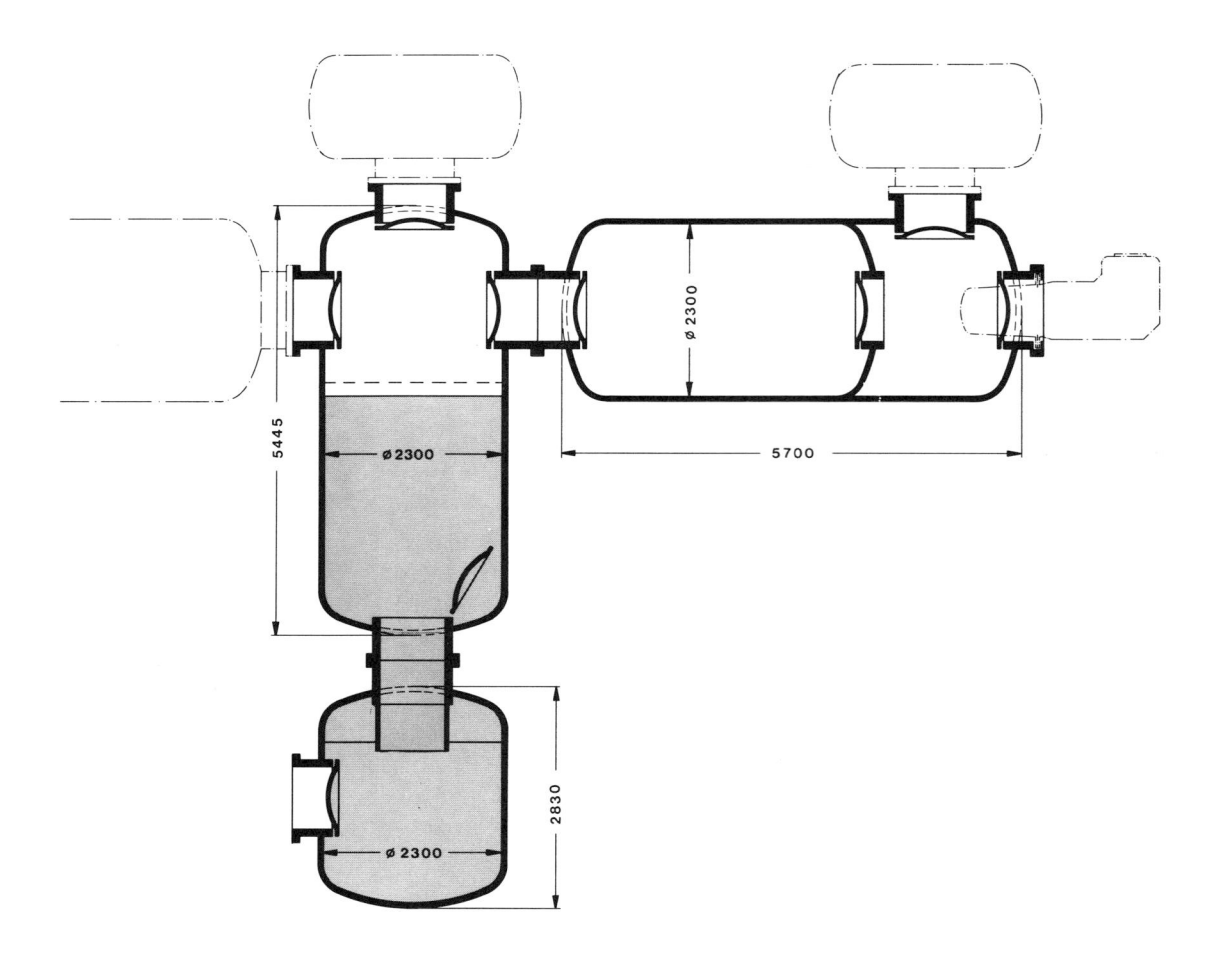

Fig. 1.38. Swedish Naval Diving Centre.

Together with the under-water rescue vehicle (URF), the new hyperbaric simulator of the Swedish Navy, which started operation at Sjödal near Stockholm in 1978, forms part of the Swedish submarine rescue organization. The simulator was built by Comex in cooperation with Kockums and has an operating pressure equivalent to a water depth of 400 m.

This new facility is designed to the standard L configuration of wet pot and decompression chamber common to many naval simulators. Differing from the standard arrangement, a submarine escape chamber is fitted beneath the wet chamber for the training of submarine crew in escape techniques. To transfer crews from the pressurized compartment of the rescue vehicle URF into the decompression complex, there is a transfer chamber which can be connected to the dry chamber of the wet pot or the lock of the decompression chamber.

To simulate realistic cold water conditions, fresh water can be cooled to 6°C and sea water to 0°C. The life-support system consists mainly of a regenerating system (soda-lime and silica gel) and a system for the automatic control of oxygen partial pressure. A hot water heat exchanger is installed to heat the chamber and the life-support and control systems allow for the full range of saturation diving.

Taylor Diving and Salvage (Fig. 1.39)

Location: Belle Chasse, Louisiana, USA

Operator: Taylor Diving and Salvage Co. Inc., Belle Chasse, Louisiana, USA

Manufacturer: Delta Southern County Inc.

Completion: 1967

Technical details:
Operating pressure: 66 bar

Dimensions of chamber	1	2	3	4
Diameter (mm)	3810	3810	2362	2286
Length (mm)	4000	2313	3708	2133
Hatch diameter (mm)	1219	067	762	762
Volume (m^3)	35	28.4	11.4	6

Filled with water, air and heliox
Capacity four to seven divers

Technical equipment:
Complete technical and medical equipment for the performance of simulated saturation dives

Purpose:
Training of divers
Physiological studies
Equipment tests
Development of welding procedures

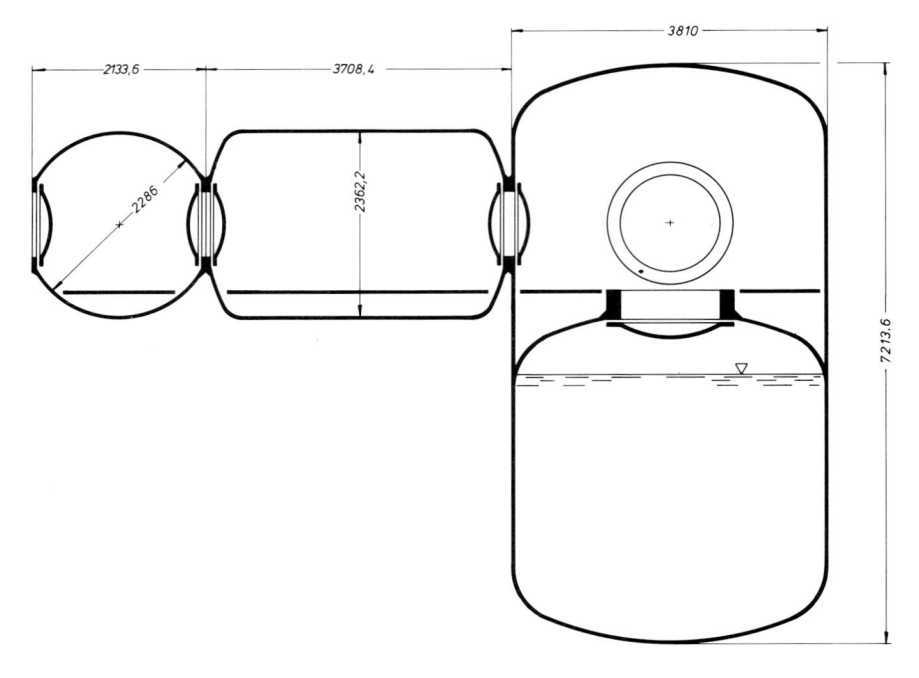

Fig. 1.39. Taylor Diving and Salvage, Belle Chasse.

The company Taylor Diving and Salvage, located at Belle Chasse, Louisiana, is amongst the largest and most successful diving contractors in the world. One of the outstanding features of Taylor's expertise lies in their pipe-welding operations in deep water, a function of pipeline tie-ins and the repair of damaged pipelines using hyperbaric welding habitats. The hyperbaric facility is an important part of the programme where welding certification procedures are carried out. All divers and diver/welders employed by Taylor Diving are trained in this hyperbaric training and research complex located at

Taylor's world headquarters in Belle Chasse, Louisiana. The complex can be pressurized to a simulated depth of 2200 FSW and is equipped with a 'wet pot' where under-water exercises can be performed. Welding procedures are also certified in the complex which is one of the largest units of its type in use by the commercial diving industry. Whilst the deep facility is also used for research, a small separate facility, built in 1962 with a wet and dry chamber, is rated to 11 bar, capable of pressurizing two or three divers and used for training.

Canadian National Diving Research Facility (Fig. 1.40)

Location:	Downsview, Ontario, Canada
Operator:	Defence and Civil Institute of Environmental Medicine (DCIEM)
Manufacturer:	Canadian Vickers Ltd, Montreal (chamber hull)
Completion:	1977/8

Technical details:

Operating pressure: 170 bar

Dimensions of chamber	1	2	3
Diameter (mm)	2440	2740	2440
Length (mm)	7320	—	6400
Hatch diameter (mm)	910	760	760
Volume (m^3)	32	10.8	24

Chamber 1 is gas/water filled; other chambers are pressurized with air or heliox

Technical equipment:
Complete technical and medical equipment for the performance of simulated bounce and saturation dives

Purpose
Thermal studies and protective clothing

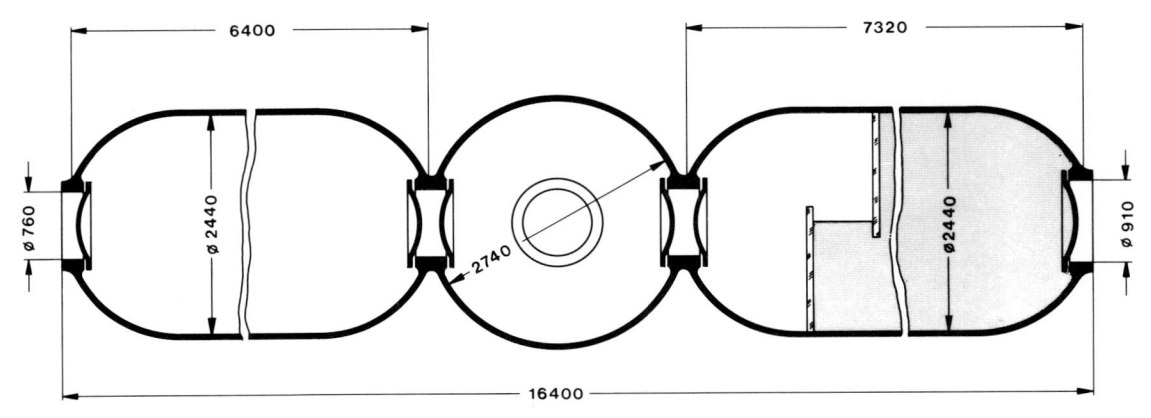

Fig. 1.40. DCIEM, Canada.

Decompression studies related to bounce diving, gas-switching theories, ultrasonic detection techniques, evaluation of excursion tables

HPNS and diver performance

Physiology of sleep during saturation, exposure, cardio-respiratory problems, special studies relating to Arctic conditions

Equipment trials

Canada, with her considerable maritime frontiers and exposure to Arctic conditions, has always been involved in under-water sciences and with the recent inception of the new hyperbaric centre at the Defence and Civil Institute of Environmental Medicine in Toronto, it has a formidable facility. With a minimum of three horizontal chambers the complex is capable of withstanding pressures of 170 bar. The design concept is similar to the Buffalo system with the wet chamber partitioned into a wet and dry area with volumes of 20 and 12 m^3 respectively.

Drass S.p.A. (Fig. 1.41)

Location:	Zingonia (Bergamo), Italy
Operator:	Drass
Manufacturer:	Drass
Completion:	1977

Technical details:

Operating pressure	100 bar
Dimensions of chamber	
Diameter (mm)	3000
Length (mm)	7900
Hatch diameter (mm)	620
Volume (m^3)	52.6
Filled with water	

Technical equipment:
Chamber can be opened to full cross-section
Vessel can be swivelled for vertical and horizontal operation
Viewports and penetrators for measuring connections

Purpose:
Testing of raw and completed pressure vessels under external pressure, such as submersibles and diving bells

Drass at Zingonia (Bergamo) is, together with Galeazzi and Novindustria Acciaio, one of the best known Italian firms engaged in under-water technology. Originally a boiler manufacturer, the move into hyperbaric chamber construction was reached in cooperation with Sub Sea Oil Services (SSOS) in the production of complete systems.

For the testing of pressure vessels under external pressure, a hydrostatic test facility is available in this company which is

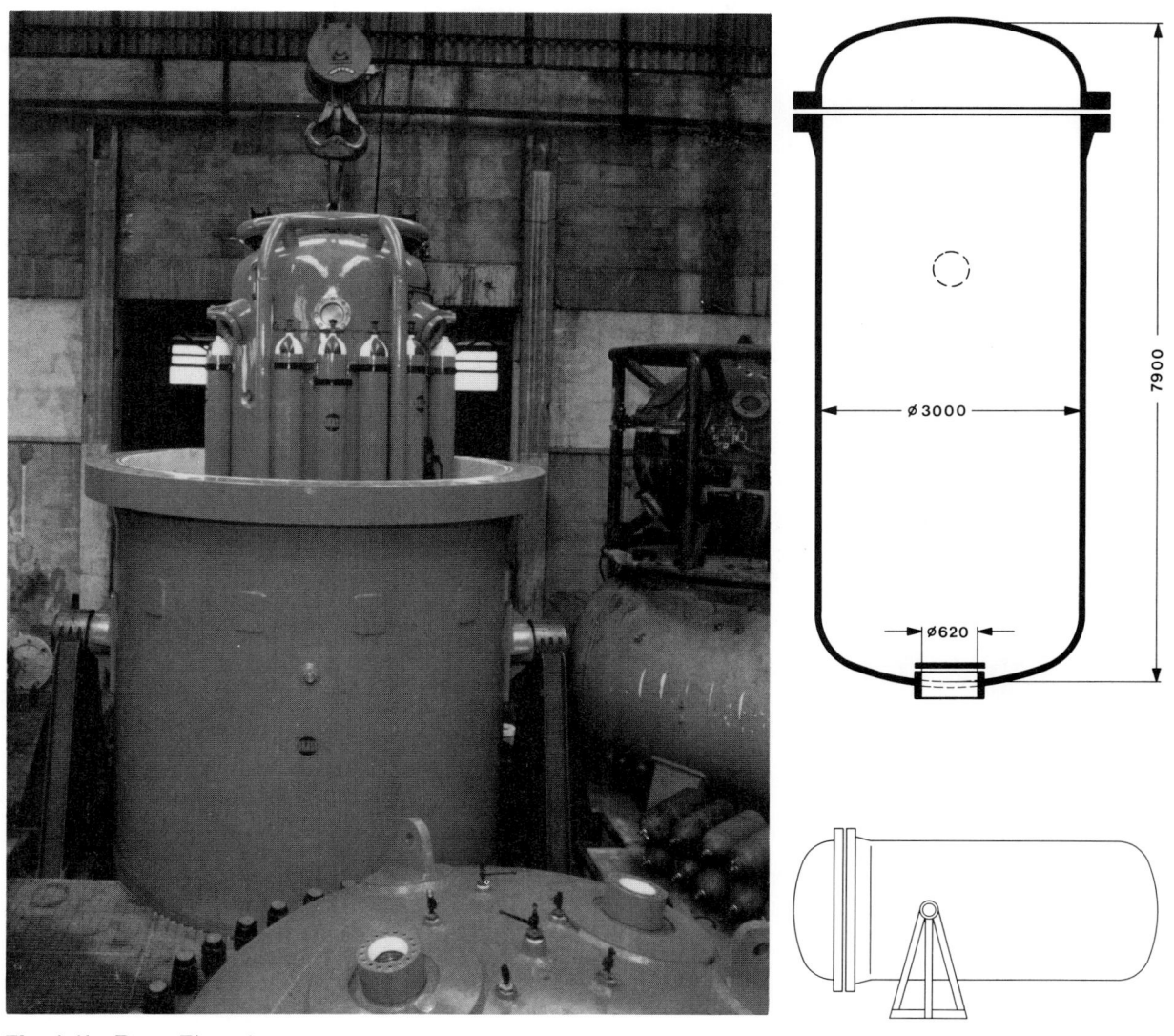

Hyperbaric Diving Simulators and Test Facilities

Fig. 1.41. Drass, Zingonia.

outstanding for both its dimensions and its high pressure rating. The chamber has an entry with 3000 mm diameter and a clear internal length of 7900 mm with a cylindric length of 6450 mm. Especially interesting is that the complete chamber can be rotated about a swivelling axis over 90°. This allows tests to be carried out in either the vertical or horizontal position as required.

A number of viewports are incorporated for the observation of tests. There are 49 penetrations which allow for a wide range of tests. A separate access hatch allows entry to the chamber after the main hatch has been locked and is used, for example, to connect measuring lines to the test object. For hydrostatic tests the chamber can be totally filled with water.

University Hospital, Zürich (Fig. 1.42)

Location:	Zürich, Switzerland
Operator:	University Hospital, Zürich
Manufacturer:	Pressure vessels by Gebrüder Sulzer, Winterthur, Switzerland
Completion:	1975

Technical details:
Operating pressure 0.5–101 bar

Dimensions of chamber	1	2	3	4
Diameter (mm)	2500	2000	2000	3500
Internal length (mm)	—	3200	1600	—
Hatch diameter (mm)	800	800	800	1300
Volume (m³)	8	10	6.5	22

Filled with air, heliox or pure oxygen; chamber 4 only water.

Purpose:
Development of practicable diving procedures for off-shore exploration (field oriented)
Solutions for special problems of deep diving down to 1000 m in form of basic research
Development of decompression and treatment tables
Development of decompression tables for high altitudes (mountain lakes)
Hyperbaric therapy of divers
Hyperbaric oxygen therapy of various deceases or accidents
Investigation of fatal diving accidents

Switzerland, with its deep water lakes and a tradition of highly skilled engineering, has made a great contribution to oceanology starting with Jacques Piccard's bathyscaphe. This bathyscaphe plumbed the depths of the Mariana Trench. In the later 1950s Hannes Keller pioneered the use of oxy-helium gases in the sea. Piccard further designed and had built in 1968 the *PX15* submersible, later known as the *Ben Franklin*, and earlier the *Auguste Piccard* built as *PX8* in 1963 and used for oceanographic studies. Professor Bühlmann at Zürich University has made a notable contribution to diving technology in particular studies related to decompression theory and practice.

More recently the first main hyperbaric simulator was developed under the direction of Benno Schenk at the University Hospital, Zürich. This facility includes the use of the hyperbaric chambers for the treatment of diving accidents and for hyperbaric oxygen therapy. The complex was completed late in 1975.

The basic design of the pressure vessel complex is visible in the cross-sectional drawing whereas different photographs show the cylindric decompression chamber, the spherical working chamber with a connection device for transportable recompression chambers and part of the control and monitoring panels.

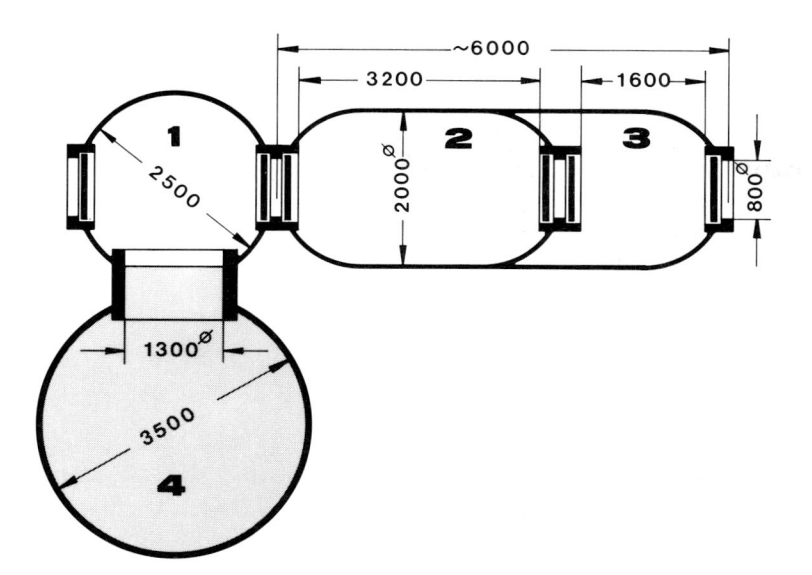

Hyperbaric Diving Simulators and Test Facilities

Fig. 1.42. University Hospital, Zürich.

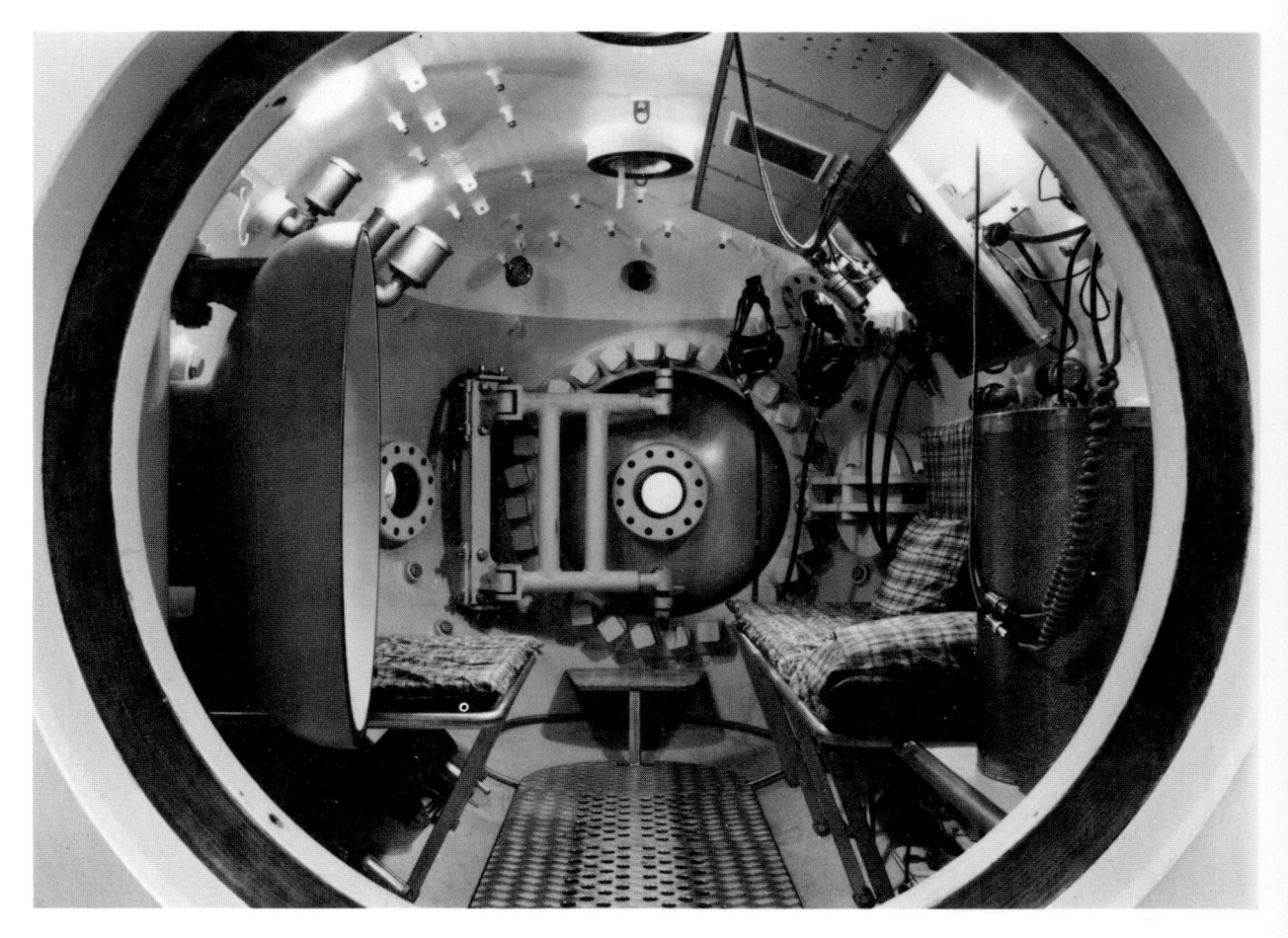

The spherical wet chamber has a clear diameter of 3500 mm and is therefore large enough to allow two or three divers to move freely. Above the wet chamber there is the also spherical work chamber. All chambers are rated to 100 bar.

Horizontally connected to the work chamber is the cylindrical double-lock decompression chamber with one of the two sufficiently large material locks.

All chamber compartments can be separated by adequate pressure-proof doors. An exception is the connection of wet and dry chamber which does not possess a pressure-proof door. In addition to the special method of steel construction, the complete system is very remarkable because a variety of new life-support control and monitoring installations were incorporated.

Royal Navy, UK (Fig. 1.43)

Location:	Alverstoke, Hampshire, United Kingdom
Operator:	Ministry of Defence (Navy)
Manufacturer:	Daniel Adamson & Co., Cheshire
Completion:	1965

Technical details:

Operating pressure	34 bar			
Dimensions of chamber	1	2	3	4
External diameter (mm)	3048	1829	1829	1829
Length overall (mm)	7163	3962.4	1829	1829
Volume (m^3)	52	10	4.6	4.6

Chamber 1 is the wet chamber, Chamber 2 is the diver's living chamber and Chambers 3 and 4 are the two transfer chambers at the extremities.

Technical equipment:

Gas storage in 61 storage bottles, each with 0.26 m^3 up to 272 bar
Life support:
    Automatic oxygen partial pressure control
    2 regeneration systems
    1 helium recovery cyrogenic system
    Hot water system for chamber heating
Communication by standard intercom with helium speech unscrambler
Measuring instrumentation:
    Ergonomic machine in the wet chamber
    Oxygen and CO_2 monitors
    Gas chromatograph
    Hard wire penetrations for electrocardiogram, electronystagmogram and core temperature

Purpose:
The facility completed in 1965 was designed to implement the Royal Navy's commitment to further deep diving to meet operational naval

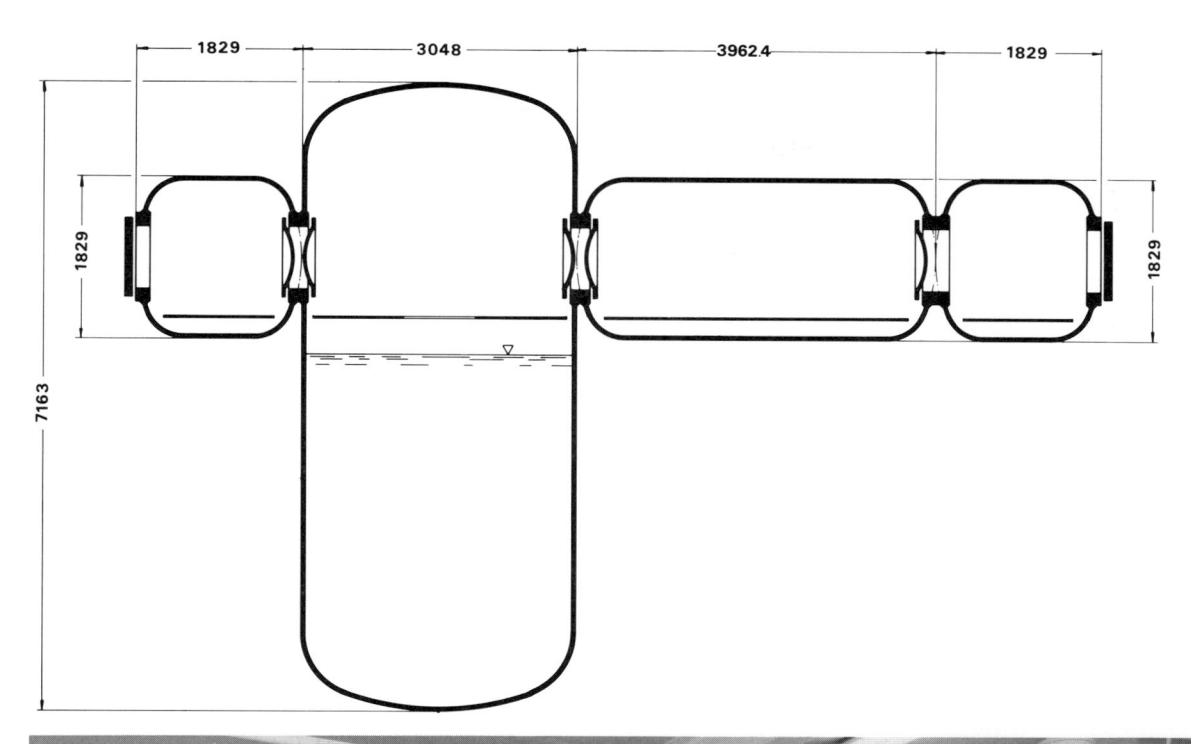

Fig. 1.43. Royal Navy, Alverstoke.

requirements at sea. The RN's deep diving vessel *HMS Reclaim* is to be superseded by the seabed operations vessel *HMS Challenger*. The shore facility carries out research and development work to maintain the vessel's operational capability to 300 m. The facility also meets a training requirement for naval divers and is used for evaluating compression and decompression schedules and procedures for commercial use.

Ocean Simulation Facility, Panama City

Location: Panama City, Florida, USA

Operator: Navy Experimental Diving Unit (NEDU) Ocean Simulation Facility

Manufacturer: Pressure Chamber Complex: Hahn u. Clay, Houston, Texas; Support Systems: Northrop Corporation, Anaheim, Calif.

Completion: 1975

Technical details:
Operating pressure: 68 bar

Dimensions	Wet chamber	Dry main (2)	Chamber locks (2)
Diameter (ID) (mm)	4575	2440	2440
Length (internal) (mm)	13725	3660	2440
Access hatches (mm)	1219	1066	1066
Doors (mm)	4575		
Volume, internal (m^3)	201	17.6	12.5

	Centre lock	Section trunk
Diameter (ID) (mm)	2440	2440
Length (internal) (mm)	3050	1982
Access hatches (mm)	1066	1219
Doors (mm)		
Volume, internal (m^3)	15.3	9.35

Environmental control ranges:

	Wet chamber	Dry chambers	Centre section
Pressure	68 bar	68 bar	68 bar
Temperature	−1.7–32°C	10–42°C	10–42°C
Salinity	as required	—	—
Relative humidity (%)		−50–100	50–100

Purpose:
Tests of marine equipment for under-water use such as diving equipment, propulsion units, submersibles

Performance of saturation dives and respiration–physiological fundamental work

Work mainly associated with US Navy research and operational development

The Ocean Simulation Facility at Panama City is still one of the largest hyperbaric complexes in the world. The hyperbaric chamber complex features the most recent developments in chamber control and computerized diver monitor systems. The wet chamber alone has a volume of 201 m^3 and with five dry chambers is a comprehensive and very large facility. It took many years to complete as there were considerable technical problems to overcome. An interesting technical feature is the large locking system for opening one end of the wet chamber to the full diameter by means of 96 hydraulically operating radial locks.

The facility houses the US Navy Experimental Diving Unit responsible for researching, testing and evaluating diving procedures, equipment and systems.

Comex, France (Figs 1.44, 1.45)

Location: Marseilles, France

Operator: Comex Services

Manufacturer: Comex Services

Completion: 1968

Technical details:
Features of each sphere:
Inner diameter: 2.8 m
Working pressure: 68 bar
Three 800 mm pressure locking access hubs
Eight penetrator plates, each 320 mm diameter
Electrical penetrators
   power supply 100 A standard
   monitoring penetrators for mechanical, electrical and stress measurements
Penetrations for different gases or mixtures
Penetrations for other fluids (water, hydraulic fluid)

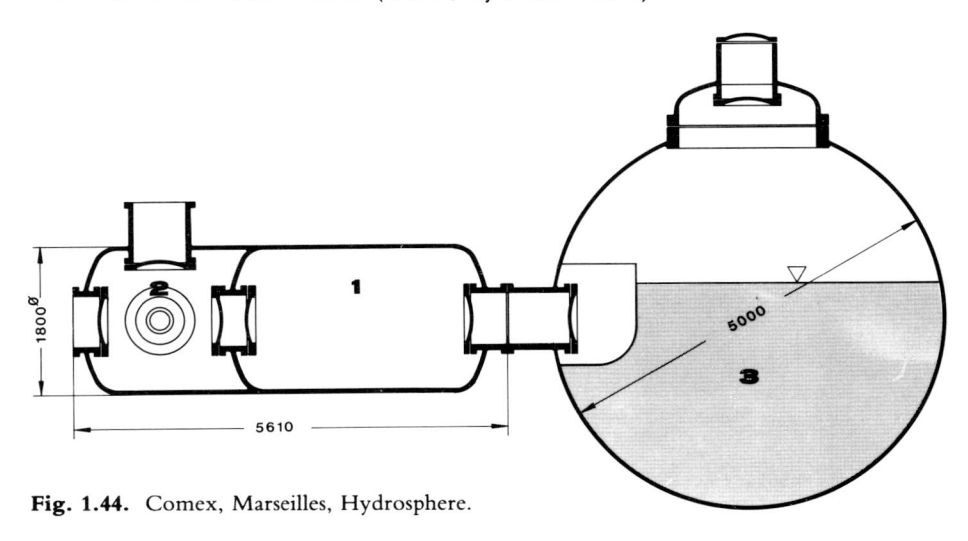

Fig. 1.44. Comex, Marseilles, Hydrosphere.

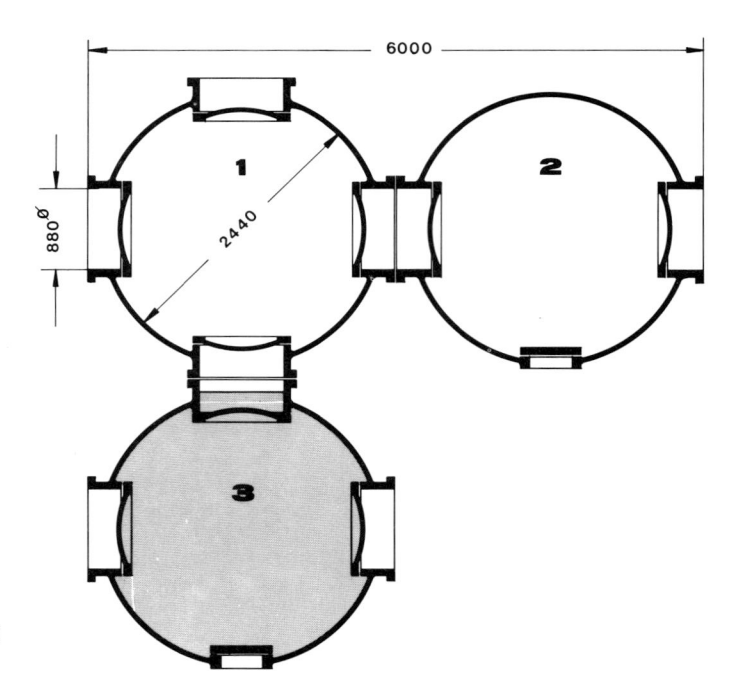

Fig. 1.45. Comex, Marseilles, EMS 600.

The EMS 600 is one of the two simulator complexes at the COMEX installation. The group of three spheres, rated to 68 bar, features full life-support.

One sphere may be used as a wet pot, with controlled water temperatures down to −2°C (28°F). Closed-circuit TV and video recording systems monitor all activities.

The EMS 600 is connected up with all measurement and monitoring equipment in the Hyberbaric Research Center. It also has its own hydraulic, electrical and gas controls.

Purpose:

Since 1965 Comex has been in the forefront of commercial diving research and development. Amongst the projects Physalie was a series of tests in which divers were exposed to record depths for short periods. Project Sagittaire studied the divers' ability to perform useful work during long exposures at depth carried out in the spherical wet chamber. Ultimately these led to the Janus project which simulated operational dives carried out in the hyperbaric chamber prior to dives in the sea. In particular research has been carried out on high pressure nervous syndrome, oxygen tolerances and thermal balance.

Spanish Navy, Cartagena (Fig. 1.46)

Location:	Cartagena
Operator:	Spanish Navy
Manufacturer:	Drägerwerk, Lübeck
Completion:	1968

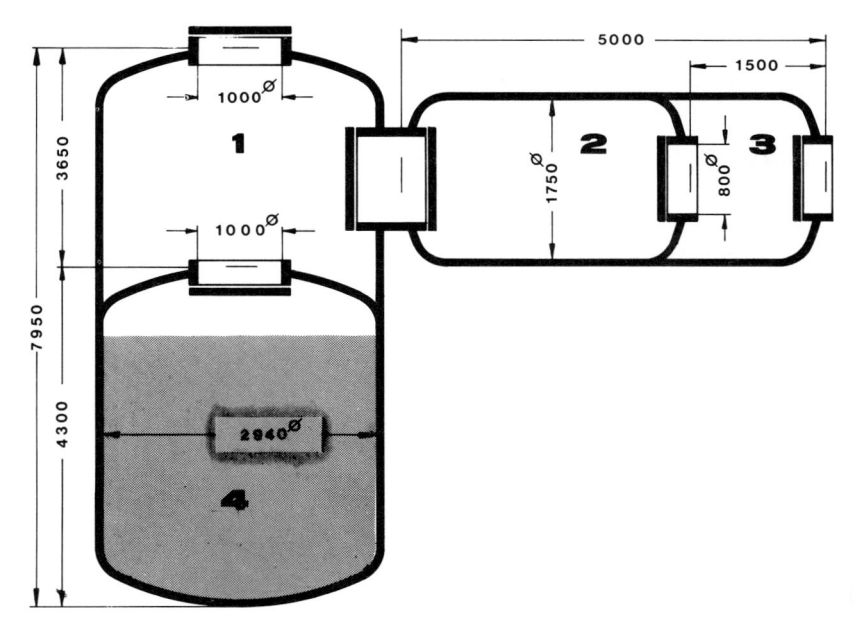

Fig. 1.46. Spanish Navy, Cartagena.

Technical details:

Operating pressure	20 bar			
Dimensions of chambers	1	2	3	4
External diameter (mm)	2940	2940	1750	1750
Length overall (mm)	4300	3550	4500	1500

Chambers 1 and 2 are in one unit, chamber 1, the wet chamber, being separated by a pressure door from the work chamber 2. Chamber 3 is the main living chamber and chamber 4 a transfer lock.

Purpose:
The training of Naval divers, testing equipment in the wet chamber and research into diving physiology.

GUSI, Geesthacht (Fig. 1.47)

Location: Geesthacht, Schleswig-Holstein, FRG

Operator: GKSS Research Center, Institut für Anlagentechnik

Manufacturer: Drägerwerk, Lübeck

Completion: planned for 1982

Technical details:
Wet chamber, horizontal cylinder
Operating pressure: unmanned 100 bar
                         manned 60 bar
Internal diameter: 3500 mm
Internal length 11000 mm
Large opening, clear diameter 3250 mm

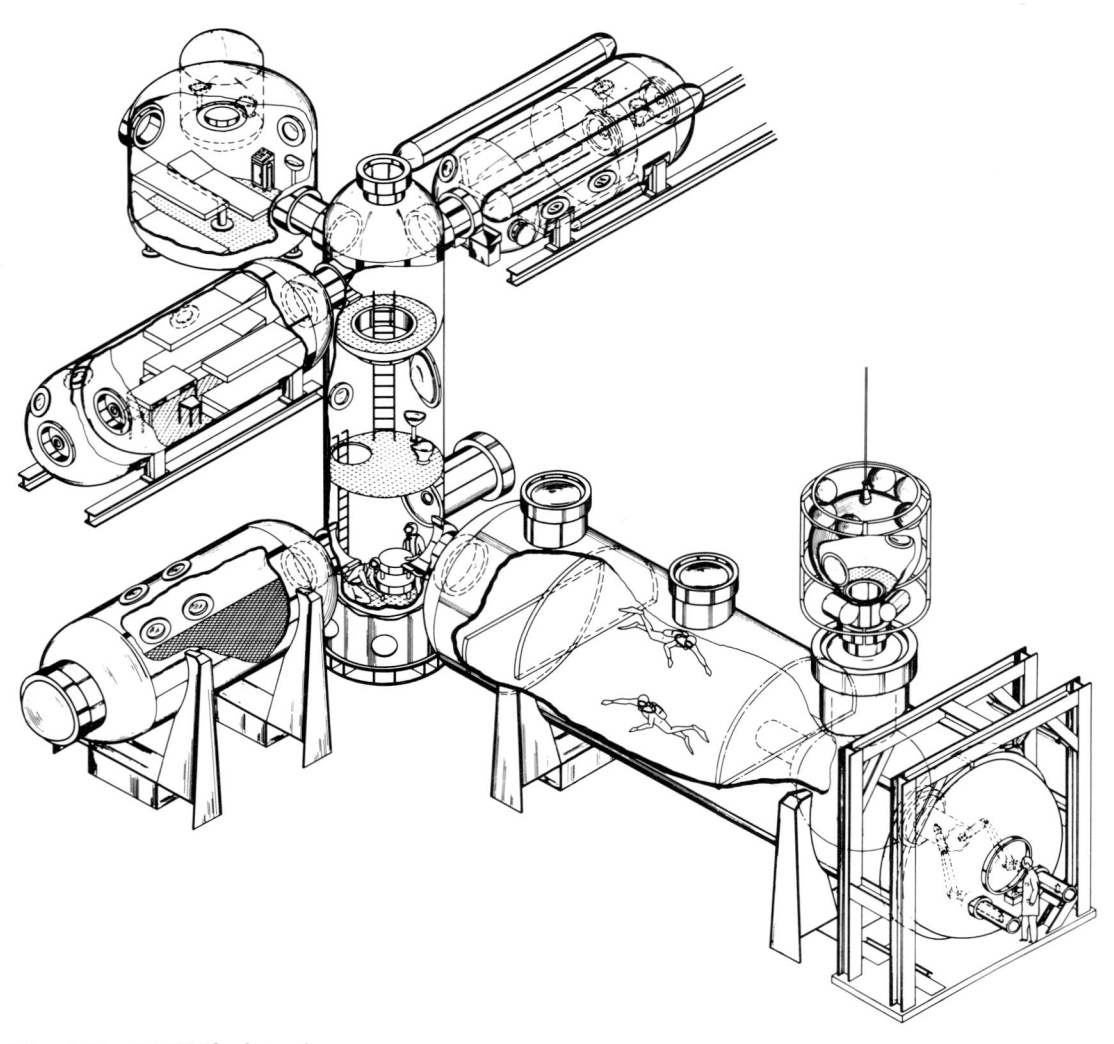

Fig. 1.47. GUSI (final stage).

Connection flange for bell, diameter 1200/700 mm
Hatch diameter: 1000 mm

Dry test chamber, horizontal cylinder
Operating pressure: 60 bar
Internal diameter: 2500 mm
Internal length: 5000 mm
Material hatch diameter: 1200 mm

Central chamber, vertical cylinder:
Operating pressure 60 bar
Internal diameter approx. 2300 mm
Internal height approx. 7300 mm
Connection flange for bell 700 mm diameter
Diameter of hatches 700 mm

Decompression chamber, horizontal cylinder:
Operating pressure 60 bar
Internal diameter 2300 mm
Internal length 5700 mm
Hatch diameter 700 mm

Rescue chamber, horizontal cylinder
Operating pressure 60 bar
Internal diameter approx. 2100 mm
Internal length approx. 4600 mm
Hatch diameter 700 mm

Medical treatment chamber, vertical cylinder
Operating pressure 40 bar
Internal height approx. 3050 mm
Internal diameter approx. 3250 mm
Hatch diameter 700 mm
Fitted with an entrance lock

Diving bell, spherical:
Operating pressure 60 bar, internally
                45 bar, externally
Internal diameter approx. 1900 mm
Lock-out hatch 700 mm clear diameter

Purpose:
Under-water welding technology including welding and cutting procedures, design research and material research and testing
Diving technology including improvement and evaluation of equipment for breathing and communication; power packs; thermal protection studies; improvement and evaluation of working procedures; closed and open diving bell development; working submersibles physiological studies
Equipment development, including handling systems, power packs, power tools, rescue equipment, vehicles and submersibles
Under-water inspection and testing, non-destructive testing methods, equipment evaluation, preparation of certification standards and tests
Under-water work procedures of divers including evaluation of inspection, maintenance and repair; procedures to cover inspection; transport; preparation for repairs; welding procedures; non-destructive testing; application of protective coating
Safety in under-water work including risk and accident analysis; safety at work; rules and regulations
Training of divers, diver/welders, diver/experts, inspectors, paramedics and emergency personnel

The GKSS research centre at Geesthacht, Schleswig-Holstein, is one of the largest research institutions of the Federal Republic of Germany which carries out research and development work that is of national interest. The emphasis is on fundamental research and pre-industrial development.

Programmes are coordinated with the Federal Ministry of Research and Technology, the State Ministries of the coastal federal states and interested industry. There is also a close cooperation with universities and scientific institutions.

In 1970 marine technology was also included in the research and development programme of the GKSS.

By operating the under-water habitat *Helgoland* and the related deep diving equipment the GKSS reached an internationally recognized high technical standard. Whilst diver equipment, operating techniques and non-destructive testing were of a high priority and well covered in the past, the facility when completed will provide additional scope for other areas of research and development. These include short-, medium- and long-term work in the other areas including maintenance, inspection and repair procedures of under-water structures.

The Geesthachter Unterwasser-Simulationsanlage (GUSI) will have a compression chamber complex with a wet chamber of considerable dimensions and a maximum operating pressure of 100 bar, chambers for orientation tests, a diving tower and a test pool as well as all necessary ancillary systems for the safe operation of the facility. In GUSI it will be possible to perform experiments under varied environmental conditions of pressure, temperature, water motion, salinity, visibility and water contamination. Realistic conditions can be simulated to depths of 600–1000 m; in the temperature range 0–32°C and in a dry or wet environment. The complexity of GUSI allows for parallel manned or unmanned experiments.

The capacity of the chambers is sufficient to allow the testing of most actual under-water units. The simulator has a lock-on facility for a diving bell which can be transferred to off-shore. Much of the credit for the simulator must go to G. Schafstall who has developed the concept which should have a great impact on under-water technology.

DFVLR, Bonn-Wahn (Fig. 1.48)

Location:	Bonn-Wahn, Nordrhein-Westfalen, FRG
Operator:	Deutsche Forschungs- und Versuchsanstalt für Luft- und Raumfahrt (DFVLR) Institut für Flugmedizin
Manufacturer:	Drägerwerk, Lübeck
Completion:	planned for 1983

Technical details:
Operating pressure:
Wetpot C   150 bar
Living chamber A   100 bar

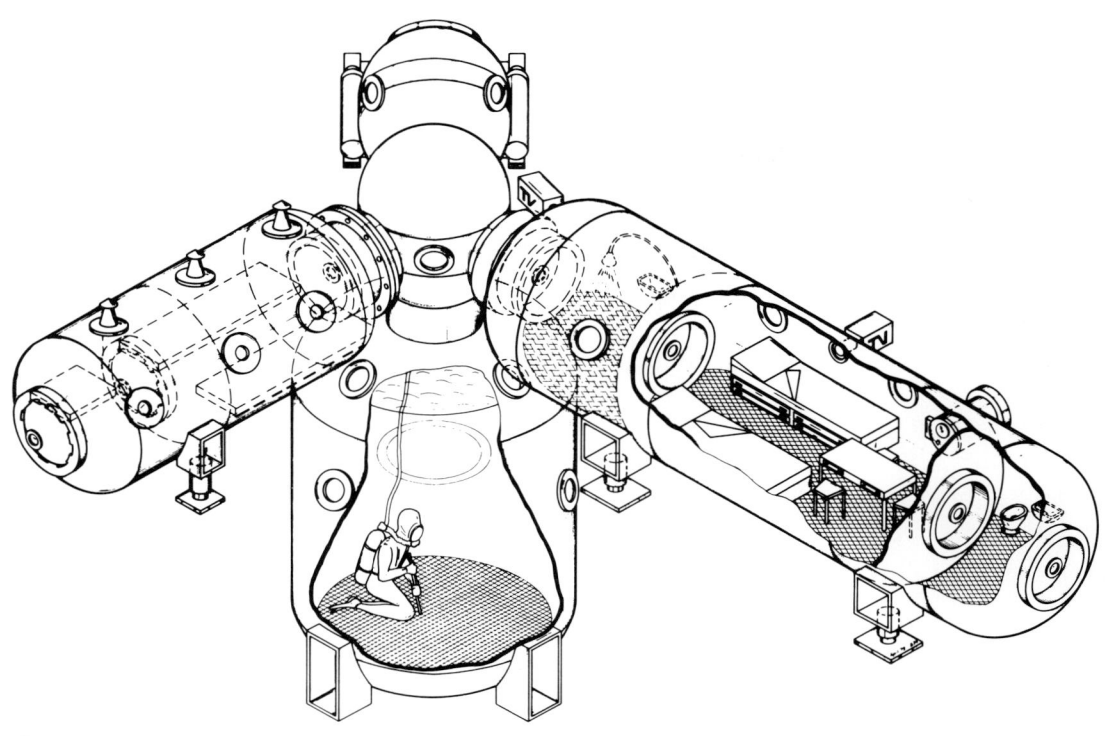

Fig. 1.48. DFVLR (Titan).

Transfer lock B   100 bar
Living chamber C   25 bar

Dimensions of chamber:	A	B	C	D
Internal diameter (mm)	2200	2000	3000	1740
External length (mm)	6400	—	4000	3600
Hatch diameter (mm)	800	800/700	800	800/700
Volume (m^3)	21.5	4.2	19	

Purpose:

Study of physical and chemical principles of gas diffusion in body fluid, body tissue and organs

Studies of physiological adaptation with special consideration of physical and mental work

Development and evaluation of diving and decompression procedures for saturation dives, bounce dives and excursion dives

Determination of objectives, methods and rules for the medical/psychological selection and the training of divers for deep diving operations

In the Federal of Republic of Germany the GKSS at Geesthacht is primarily concerned with the technical aspects of under-water operations, whereas the Institut für Flugmedizin of the DFVLR at Bonn-Wahn has been engaged for more than 15 years in providing the technical/medical prerequisites for human subsea activities. The

Institute pioneered the introduction of mixed gas diving in the Federal Republic and participated in the *Helgoland* habitat operations particularly in respect of the preparation of diving tables in the 50–150 m range.

Since 1964 the institute has operated a hyperbaric facility which is only suitable for dry experiments at pressures of up to 25 bar. The tremendous progress of marine research and technology with divers operating at greater and greater depths has made it necessary to enlarge the existing facilities considerably. A new building available in 1980 will become the location of the modern hyperbaric simulator *Titan* which is planned to start operation in 1982. *Titan* is designed for manned experiments to a maximum diving depth of 1500 m. It provides for hyperbaric studies in gas atmospheres as well as in water.

The complex consists of four chambers which can be pressurized separately or commonly, as far as the pressure rating permits. The internal outfit as well as the technical possibilities are intended for medical research and adequately sophisticated. The central part of the complex is composed of the wet chamber and the spherical transfer lock on top of it. A large three-compartment living chamber and a two-compartment decompression chamber are flanged to the transfer lock at right angles. The wet chamber is located on the ground floor of the building. It is also suited to be used as a separate animal test chamber for experimental studies with larger animals.

Titan will be under the direction of H. D. Fust, who is also well known outside his country for his outstanding work in the field of diving medicine.

Deck Compression Chambers

2

There are throughout the world hundreds of fixed and mobile compression chambers for divers, used for normal decompression in diving operations, for aptitude tests and training and for the therapeutic treatment of divers' illnesses.

These quick-entry treatment chambers, with their integrated life-support systems, may be either fixed installations in shore facilities or installed on board ships. The majority are used operationally at sea as essential equipment for diving operations. These include diving vessels, submarine support vessels, salvage vessels and some oceanographic research vessels.

Smaller mobile compression chambers are used where space is restricted. They may be installed in coastal naval ships or stationed in rescue facilities so as to be quickly mobilized for rescue missions to transport divers under pressure from the scene of an accident. The same basic design factors are relevant to all these chambers irrespective of size. The maximum number of personnel required to be under pressure at any one time will determine the overall volume and, therefore, the diameter and length of the chamber. The minimum requirements should be as follows:

1. At least two chambers, one of which may be smaller to be used for locking in and out personnel, fitted with doors acting as pressure seals and which may be opened from either side.
2. Sufficient space in at least one compartment to enable two divers to lie down inside; if the chamber is to be used for more than 12 hours, the diameter or height of the chamber should also allow the divers to stand upright.
3. Suitable life-support and environmental facilities, taking into consideration the need to minimize noise and the risk of fire, good two-way communications and adequate sanitary facilities.
4. A small lock to allow food and medical supplies to be passed through.

The space requirements therefore determine the diameter and length of the chamber and, together with the design operating pressure, will affect the weight and costs. The final selection of the material will need to take into consideration magnetic properties and corrosion problems.

As a rule, horizontal cylindrical pressure vessel design is the best suited and spheres or vertical cylinders are rarely used for this type of work. The normal arrangement for the transfer of personnel through locks is shown in Fig. 2.1. The chambers arranged horizontally to allow for the transfer of divers undergoing hyperbaric treatment normally have the same size diameter hatches. The overall length of the lock varies from 1000 to 1500 mm and is kept to the minimum size compatible with the transfer of divers, possibly undergoing hyperbaric treatment, so as to minimize the amount of gas needed for pressurization.

Stationary Compression Chambers for Divers

Small One-lock Treatment Chambers

The smallest diameter which is acceptable for a 'crawl-in' chamber is about 1200–1300 mm; therefore only short-duration decompression schedules are possible. The requirement for low cost, low weight and space in the design has to be balanced against the acceptable minimum standards of safety and therefore there is a lower limit in the overall volume beyond which further reductions are unacceptable, except in cases of extreme emergency.

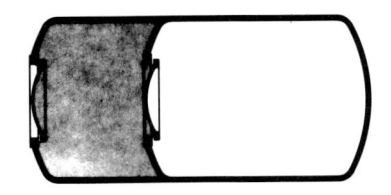

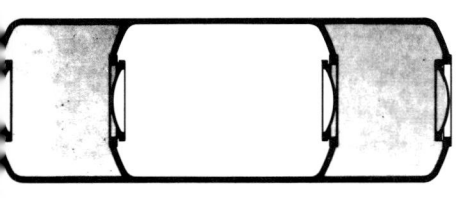

Fig. 2.1. Treatment chambers fitted with one-lock and two-lock personnel chambers.

Fig. 2.2. One-lock compression chamber (1300 mm diameter) with high-pressure air supply.

The identically designed pressure chambers in Figs 2.2 and 2.3 differ in the supply of compressed air. The one-lock chamber (Fig. 2.2) is supplied with air from a high-pressure reservoir whilst the two-lock chamber (Fig. 2.3) is supplied from a low-pressure reservoir. The chambers illustrated are made to a standard 1300 mm diameter design and a length of 3500 mm overall with 2500 mm for the main compartment. With the operating pressure restricted to 5 atmospheres, which covers the maximum requirements for therapeutic treatment within the air range of diving, it is possible to incorporate simple flat panel doors with a diameter of 700 mm and, with pressurization from one side, only one locking bar is required. To cover the basic requirements for the treatment of divers, a single observation window is needed in the main chamber and transfer lock. A simple control panel should have sufficient gauges and valves to control the pressure inside accurately and the additional facility to provide the occupants with pure oxygen breathing, if needed, through oral-nasal masks. Therefore the valves must be designed for. the rapid flushing of the chamber with air, to lower any oxygen content in the chamber to below 25% as a precaution against fire. Also as a precaution against fire, the lighting arrangements should be external; if internal, special light fittings are needed with switches operated from the control panel.

The instrumentation and control panel can therefore be simple and effective and the interior fittings can likewise be functional, with simple retractable bunks and a food lock for the supply of food and small articles. Larger articles can be passed through the main access locks.

The chambers shown in Figs 2.2 and 2.3 differ only in the way in which they are supplied with air. The chamber in Fig. 2.2 is supplied with high-pressure air and therefore the high-pressure cylinders

Fig. 2.3. One-lock compression chamber (1300 mm diameter) with low-pressure air supply.

needed are relatively small in volume and the arrangement is ideally suitable for rapid compression in cases of emergency. The overall size of the chamber and compactness of reservoir cylinders also makes the unit easy to transport and mobilize in an emergency. Skids are fitted for ease of operation.

The chamber shown in Fig. 2.3 has a low-pressure supply with the low-pressure reservoir fitted in place of skids. Two reservoirs with a total volume of 900 litres at a pressure of 25 bar will pressurize the chamber twice to the maximum operating pressure. A compressor capable of delivering 42 m^3/hour would be needed to supply the

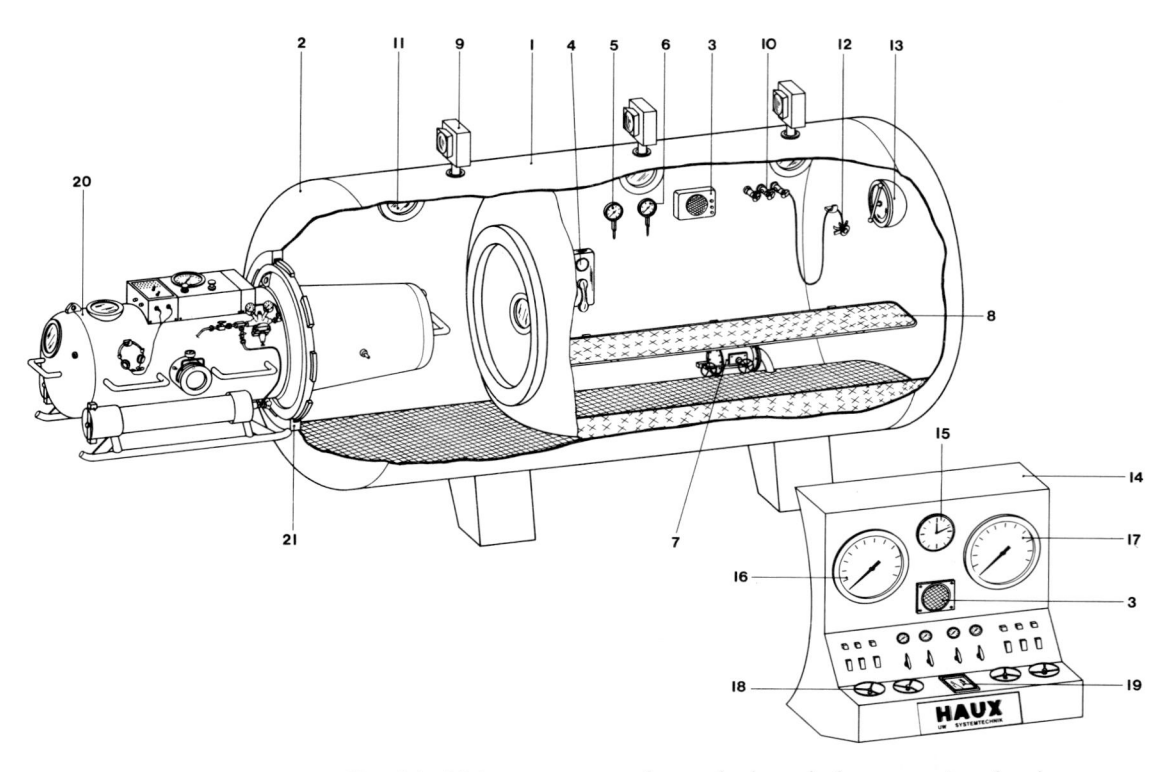

Fig. 2.4. Main components of a standard one-lock compression chamber.

1 main chamber
2 antechamber
3 loud speaker
4 telephone
5 thermometer
6 manometer
7 inner control valves
8 bunk
9 lights
10 oxygen valves
11 viewports

12 oxygen mask
13 supply lock
14 control panel
15 time clock
16 manometer, antechamber
17 manometer, main chamber
18 valves
19 pressure recorder
20 one man chamber
21 bayonet flange

reservoirs. With the ancillary equipment protected in pipe frames in accordance with normal off-shore field practice, the equipment is easy to move around on construction sites and from vessels and off-shore rigs.

Standard Compression Chamber with One Lock, 1500 mm Diameter, Light Alloy Construction

Where the main priority is one of weight, a restriction imposed for reasons of stability in some ships and the deck-loading factor on structures and buildings, lighter materials with a high strength-to-weight ratio are needed. The use of aluminium alloy for the construction of chambers has certain advantages. The non-magnetic quality of the material and its light weight are particularly attractive for use in naval ships, especially for mine counter-measures. The chamber in Fig. 2.4 shows an aluminium alloy construction for a chamber 2250 mm long with an internal lock of 1100 mm and a diameter of 1500 mm. The control panel is neatly faired to reduce the size of external fittings and the operating pressure increased to 10 bar, allowing the system to be operated throughout the full range of air

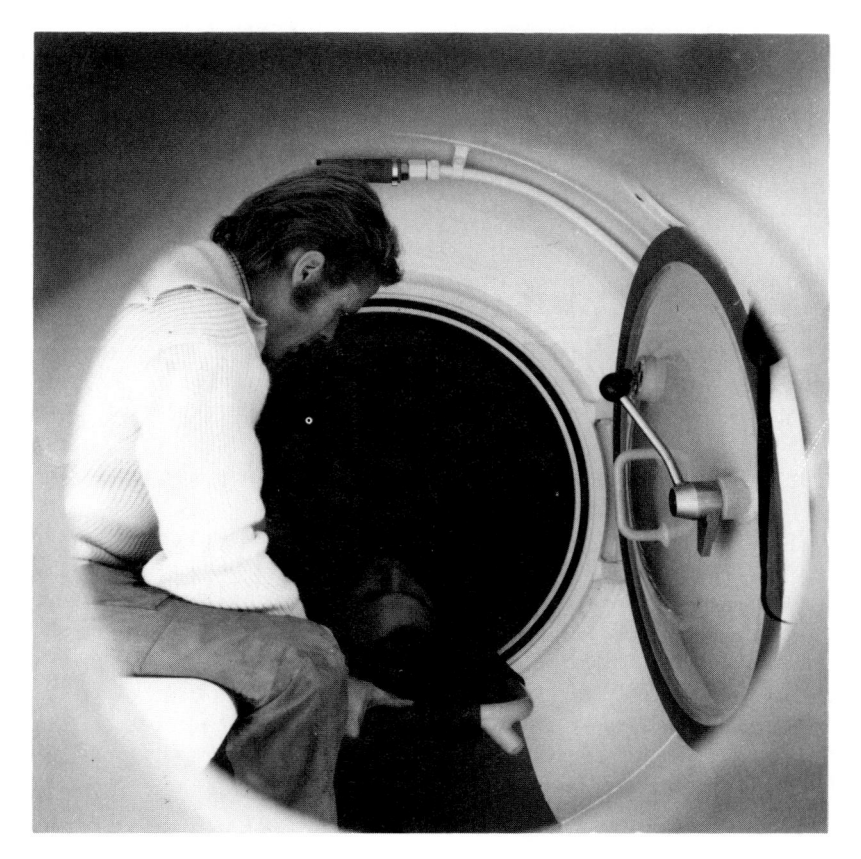

Fig. 2.5. The transfer of injured personnel through the outer transfer compartment to the main chamber.

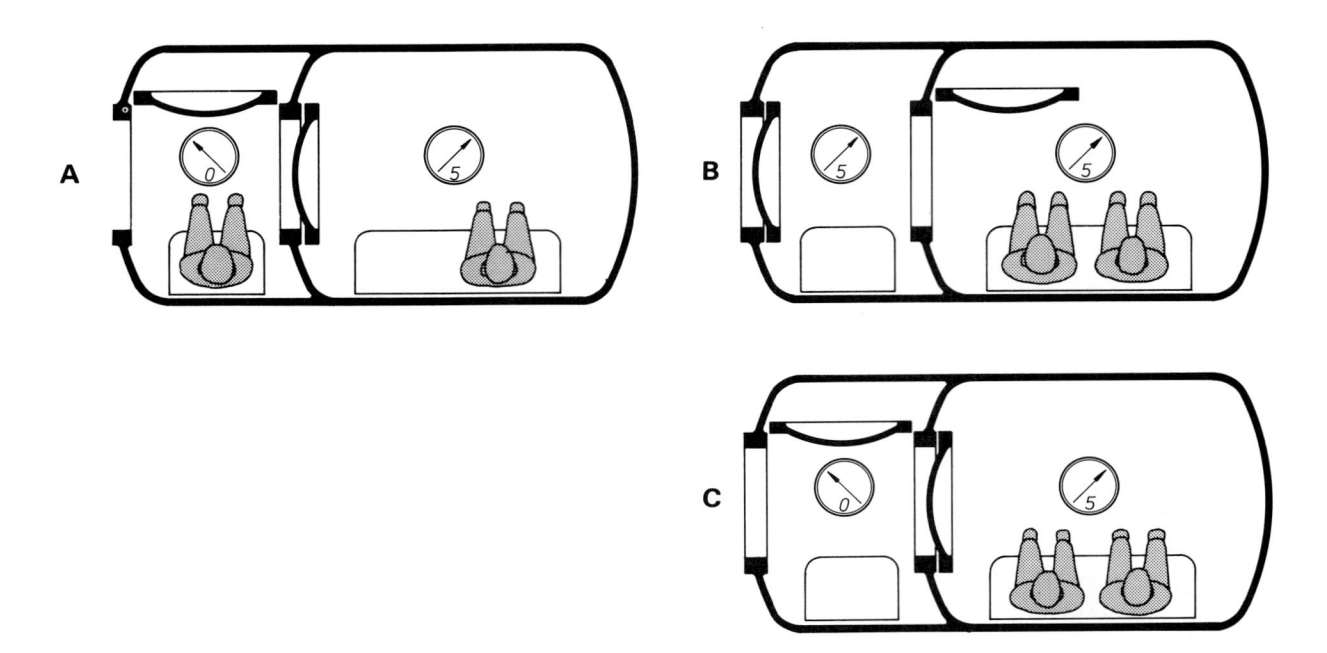

Fig. 2.6. Operation of a standard one-lock compression chamber. A, The diver is in the main compartment awaiting treatment or assistance and the arrival of a doctor or attendant. For example, the diver is pressurized to 5 bar. The doctor or attendant enters the unpressurized transfer lock. The outer transfer door is closed and the chamber pressurized to equal the main chamber exactly, to allow the inner door to free and open, and the attendant to enter (B). The main compartment can now be isolated, the inner door closed and the transfer compartment depressurized (C) to surface pressure for the next transfer if required.

diving. With a total weight of 2000 kg, this chamber is approximately one-third of the weight of a chamber of the same size but built of steel.

The procedure for medical staff and other personnel entering the main chamber at the same pressure as the occupants is shown in Fig. 2.6. The locking-out procedure is the reverse of locking-in. The doors are made to a common diameter of 800 mm and are designed with a flange for the connection of a portable one-man chamber, shown in Fig. 2.6. Although designed to accommodate two with bunks, the chamber can take six on seats and, in an emergency, eight.

There is greater detail in control and instrumentation than in the previous basic designs. With the greater operating pressures, more comfort is needed and provided, such as heating and better communications and breathing systems, all requiring safety controls and some additional secondary back-up supplies.

These standard systems are for maximum operating pressures

between 5 and 10 bar and used for air diving operations. The fittings are generally the same in this range of chambers and are as follows:

Control Panel. Clock; pressure gauges for the lock; pressure gauge for the main chamber; pressure recorder; loudspeaker system; gauge for air supply pressure; gauge for oxygen supply pressure; gauge for oxygen working pressure; thermometer readout; selection valves for the pressure recorder; sound-powered telephone; air inlet valve, main chamber; air inlet valve, transfer; air exhaust valve, main chamber; air exhaust valve, internal, main chamber; oxygen main shut-off valve; air main shut-off valve; oxygen pressure reducer; ventilation valve, exhaust, normal; ventilation valve, exhaust, oxygen; ventilation valve, inlet; power supply switch; switch for lighting; switch for heating; panel illumination.

Transfer compartment. Lighting unit; observation window; oxygen breathing units; silencer for air inlet; silencer for air exhaust; bench; floor boards; internal gauge for local pressure; equalizing valve.

Main compartment. Clock; lights; observation windows; oxygen breathing oronasal mask; silencer for air inlet; silencer for air exhaust; inlet valve; exhaust valve; benches; floor gauge for main compartment pressure; differential pressure gauge; heating; supply lock.

Additional life-support equipment. Temperature recorders; humidity recorders; analysers for the monitoring of oxygen and carbon dioxide; partial pressure of oxygen. Automatic pressure control units may also be installed.

Fig. 2.7 shows schematically the complete compressed-air and oxygen supply system with the instrumentation on the control panel and the chamber. For two-lock chambers the system is appropriately extended. The electrical system is not shown. Chamber pressurization and ventilation are different systems. The chamber compartments are pressurized by a nozzle-injector for temperature control whereas for ventilation purposes the noise level is more important. (This subject is discussed in more detail later when the individual components are described.)

Weight savings with the use of aluminium have to be paid for in higher costs. If stainless steel is used because of its antimagnetic

Table 2.1. Differences in chamber weight and price compared to boiler plate H 1 (BS 1501 Grade 23)

Material	Weight difference (%)	Price difference (%)
Fine-grained structural steel	−20	+ 10
Stainless steel	+40	+200
Al–Mg–Si–Mn	−50	+150

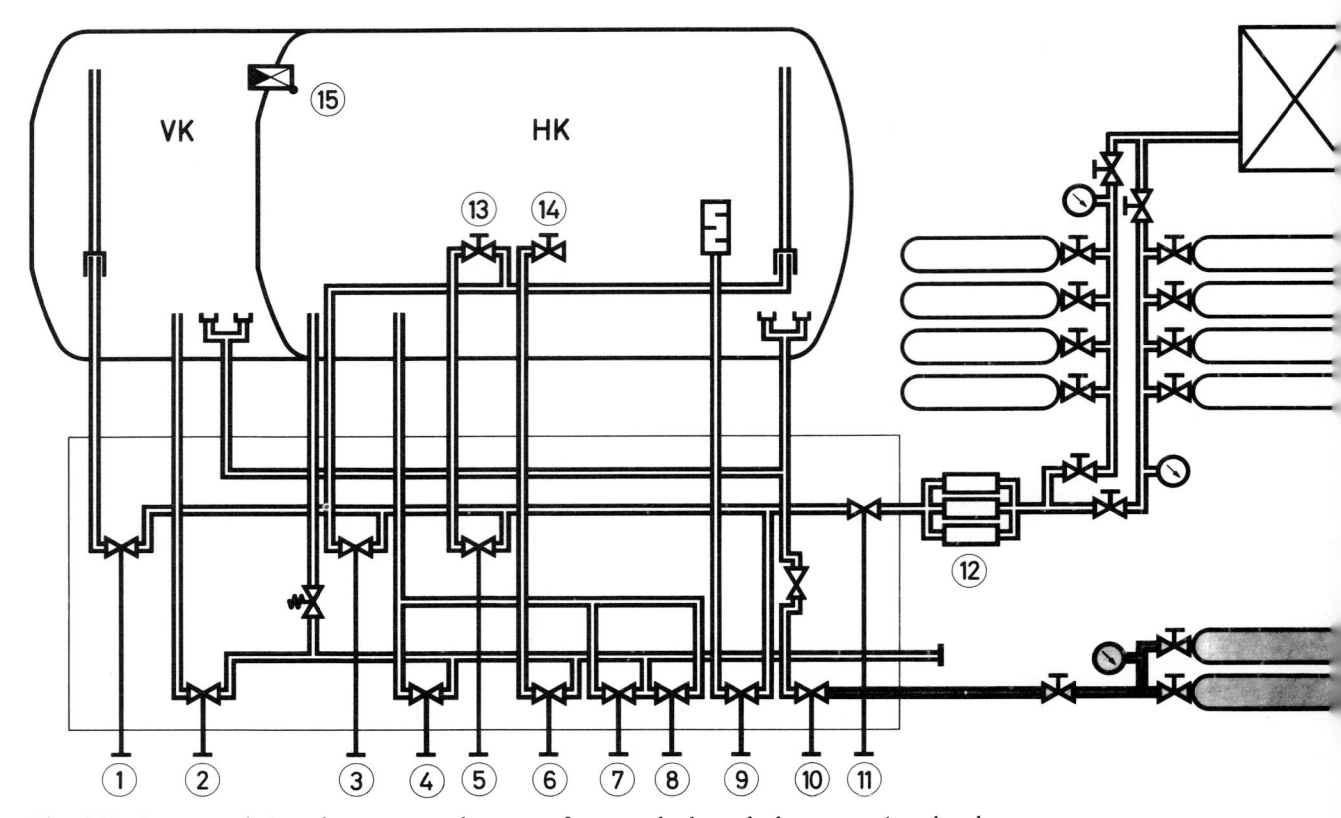

Fig. 2.7. Compressed-air and oxygen supply system for a standard one-lock compression chamber.

1 inlet valve, outer compartment
2 exhaust valve, outer compartment
3 inlet valve, main compartment
4 exhaust valve, main compartment
5 inlet shut-off valve, main compartment, internal control
6 exhaust shut-off valve, main compartment, internal control
7 ventilation exhaust valve, normal
8 ventilation exhaust valve, oxygen breathing
9 ventilation inlet valve
10 main shut-off valve, oxygen
11 main shut-off valve, compressed air
12 air filter
13 inlet valve, main compartment, internal control
14 exhaust valve, main compartment, internal control
15 pressure-equalizing valve

properties and its resistance to sea-water corrosion, the overall weight as well as the cost are increased. Table 2.1 gives approximate figures for the differences in chamber weight (without equipment) and price, as compared to boiler plate H 1 which is normally used for the construction of standard pressure vessels.

Compression Chambers Made of Stainless Steel, Non-magnetic

Some exceptional advantages are obtained with stainless steel chambers. The manufacturing process does require special techniques to avoid the reduction of the low permeability during welding. Equally important is the selection of fittings and quite often special alloys are needed to maintain the non-magnetic qualities. Fig. 2.8 shows a production series of these stainless steel units. There are only minor differences in appearance compared to the aluminium chambers. The door diameter is reduced to 600 mm and requires a special flange to adapt to the 800 mm one-man decompression chamber. Ideally all compression chambers in commercial or naval use should have the same standard connection system to allow a one-man or two-man decompression chamber to be mated. For various reasons, it is impossible to get users' agreement on this and therefore different flanges are required. The steel chambers are not skid-mounted as they are designed for resilient mountings on board minesweepers. Although the cost of the stainless steel chambers is high, the corrosion and magnetic qualities will give the long life and operational efficiency more often required by naval specifications.

One-lock Compression Chambers, 1800 mm Diameter

If space and weight considerations are not of overriding importance, a chamber diameter of at least 1800 mm is preferable in order to allow

Fig. 2.8. Series production of a standard compression chamber (1500 mm diameter) in stainless steel.

Fig. 2.9. A compression chamber (1800 mm diameter) installed as a test facility in the Deutsche Versuchanstalt für Luft- und Raumfahrt in Bonn Bad Godesberg.

the occupant to stand up. It is considered essential for commercial operations off-shore that chambers should be large enough for the occupants to be upright for decompressions longer than 12 hours. The ancillary chamber fittings are identical to the standard 1500 mm series and need no further comment. Fig. 2.9 shows a 1800 mm diameter chamber used for diver training and experimental work. For this purpose the controls are modified for different requirements. High-precision gauges are fitted and recorders maintain a simultaneous record of pressure and chamber temperature and CO_2 and humidity are also recorded separately. The partial pressure of oxygen is recorded and monitored to allow oxygen injection to maintain the correct percentage. Double valves are fitted into the same line with a separate bleed-off valve. The increased height allows more comfort for the divers and therefore longer periods can be sustained under pressure.

Fig. 2.10. Modular components of a compression chamber.

1. chamber A (main chamber)
2. chamber B (antechamber)
3. adaptor flange
4. bench
5. oxygen breathing system
6. lighting
7. medical lock
8. cover
9. one-man chamber

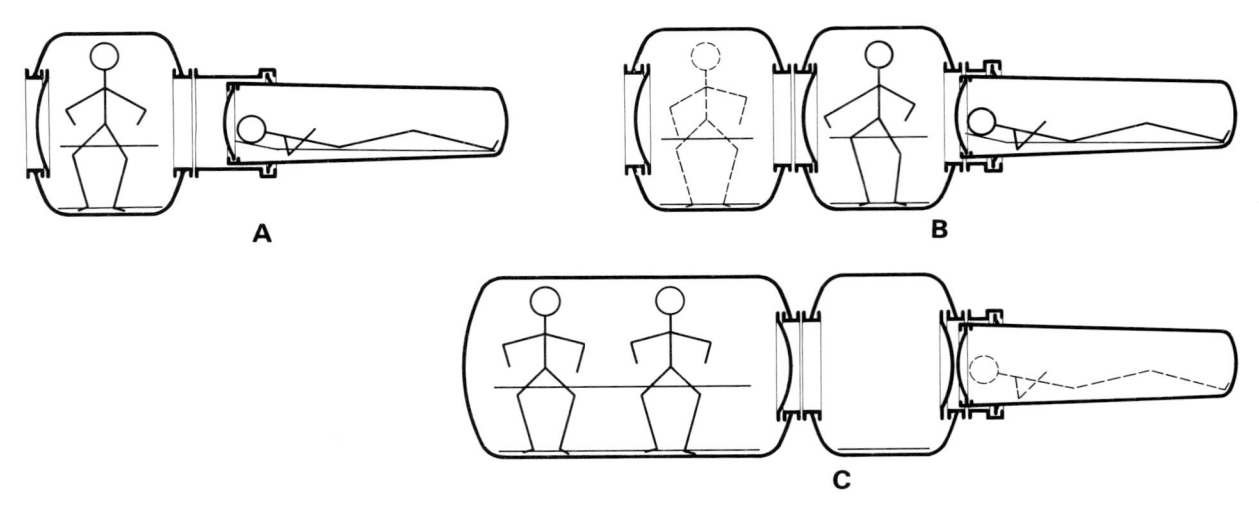

Fig. 2.11. Possible combinations for pressure chamber modules.

- **A** Module B with long adaptor piece for treatment of one-man chamber patients
- **B** Two module B chambers with short adaptor piece for long-term treatment in a one-man chamber lock-out facility for a doctor
- **C** Modules A and B with a short adaptor piece forming a stationary complex lock-out facility connection for a one-man chamber

Two-lock Compression Chambers

The advantage of two transfer locks at each end of the main chamber is for training purposes, allowing divers to enter and evacuate from both ends. This ability to process divers continuously into and out of a main chamber is particularly suited to diver rescue vessels where a submarine accident may require a continuous flow of occupants or to constructional caisson work where labourers need to be decompressed.

Compression Chamber Modules

Diving schools and small diving companies are not always able to provide the full cover of therapeutic compression chambers at the beginning, although conforming to safety regulations. Figs 2.10 and 2.11 show a pre-planned step-by-step programme to equip chambers to a higher standard, without having to dispose of previous equipment. A form of modular development, the mobile one-man chamber, can be a start, but fitted with a standard flange. The system can then be upgraded to a two-man system with chamber B (Fig. 2.11), with a long adaptor flange. This combination can, if necessary, allow a doctor to enter the chamber, which is sufficiently large for the patient to be pulled far enough into the chamber module. With the addition of the large chamber A, a final and reasonably full-size complex can ultimately be achieved. There are clearly a number of variations and combinations. There are even ways to save the costs of instrumentation without reducing safety. A single chamber pressure

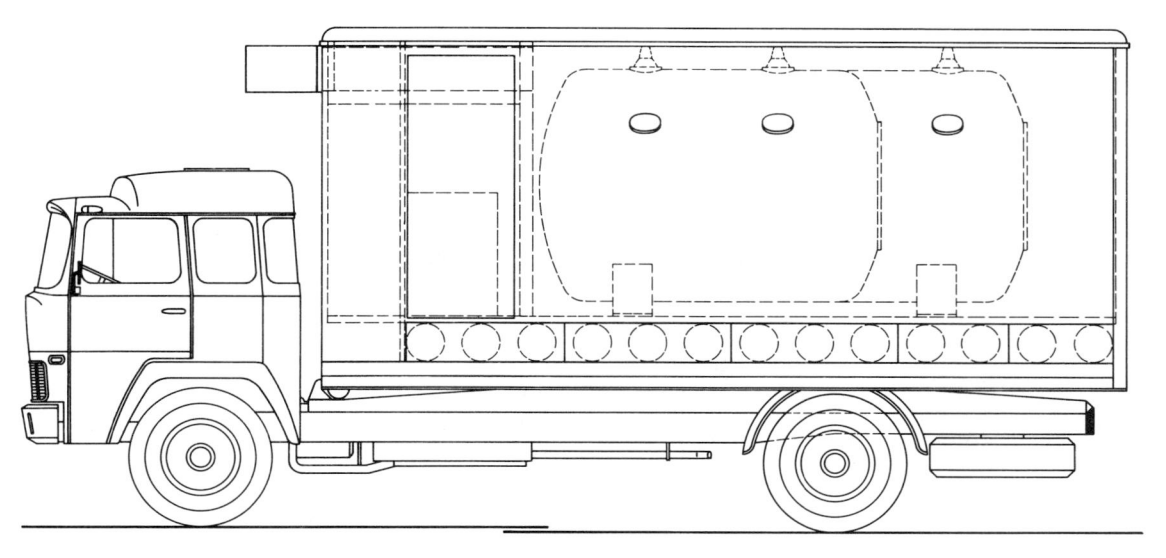

Fig. 2.12. The mobile Galeazzi one-lock transfer compression chamber complete with air compressors, storage banks, pressure chamber and a connector flange for a mobile one-man chamber.

Fig. 2.13. A mobile two-lock compression chamber fi[tted] with air conditioning a[nd] inert-gas fire extinguish[er] (Dräger).

gauge and communication system will suffice. Additional improvements such as internal lighting, oxygen breathing systems and medical supply lock can be incorporated later.

Mobile Compression Chamber

There are certain situations, such as rescue or the provision of diving services in remote inland sites, where a mobile compression chamber has some advantages. A standby rescue facility must naturally be fully autonomous for life-support and power. Smaller one-unit facilities can be designed to fit into a single closed truck, with the compression chamber preferably constructed in aluminium for reduction in weight (Fig. 2.12). Larger units can be transported in containers where there is a need for a larger involvement and the transportable chamber is shown in Fig. 2.13. This chamber, used in temperate climates, does not require protection and can be quickly transported on its trailer. A large chamber nearly 8 m in length and 2.4 m in diameter can accommodate 16 people, with two outer transfer locks of 1500 and 2500 mm in length at either end of the main chamber, which is about 4 m in length. In this chamber there are oxygen breathing units with an overboard dumping device which removes the oxygen exhaled from the divers to the outside of the chamber.

Compression Chambers for Saturation Diving

Operational saturation diving chambers are used in conjunction with deep diving bells and transfer under pressure systems and are described in Chapter 3. Required to sustain much higher working pressures, they therefore differ from the lower-pressure chambers, with an increased chamber wall thickness and weight. There are much higher safety standards with regard to life-support instrumentation and, with the greater emphasis on diver comfort, health and safety, better sanitary arrangements are required and the diameter of the chambers needs to be sufficient to allow the occupants to stand up. This requires a chamber with a diameter of 2100 mm or greater.

Compression Chamber Components

The main components of compression chambers have been summarized. Safety requirements and technical innovations have increased to conform to the high operating standard now required by national regulations in the off-shore field. Most of the main components mentioned are similar to those for deep diving systems and diving simulators discussed in other chapters.

Doors

Doors are designed to sustain pressure from either one side or both sides and, although normally of circular shape, they can be of varying sizes and different design.

Doors for one-way pressurization

The basic designs in Fig. 2.15 are based on a simple flat frame door with various combinations of hinges and dogs. The use of rubber seals

Fig. 2.14. Double-hinged one-way pressure door.

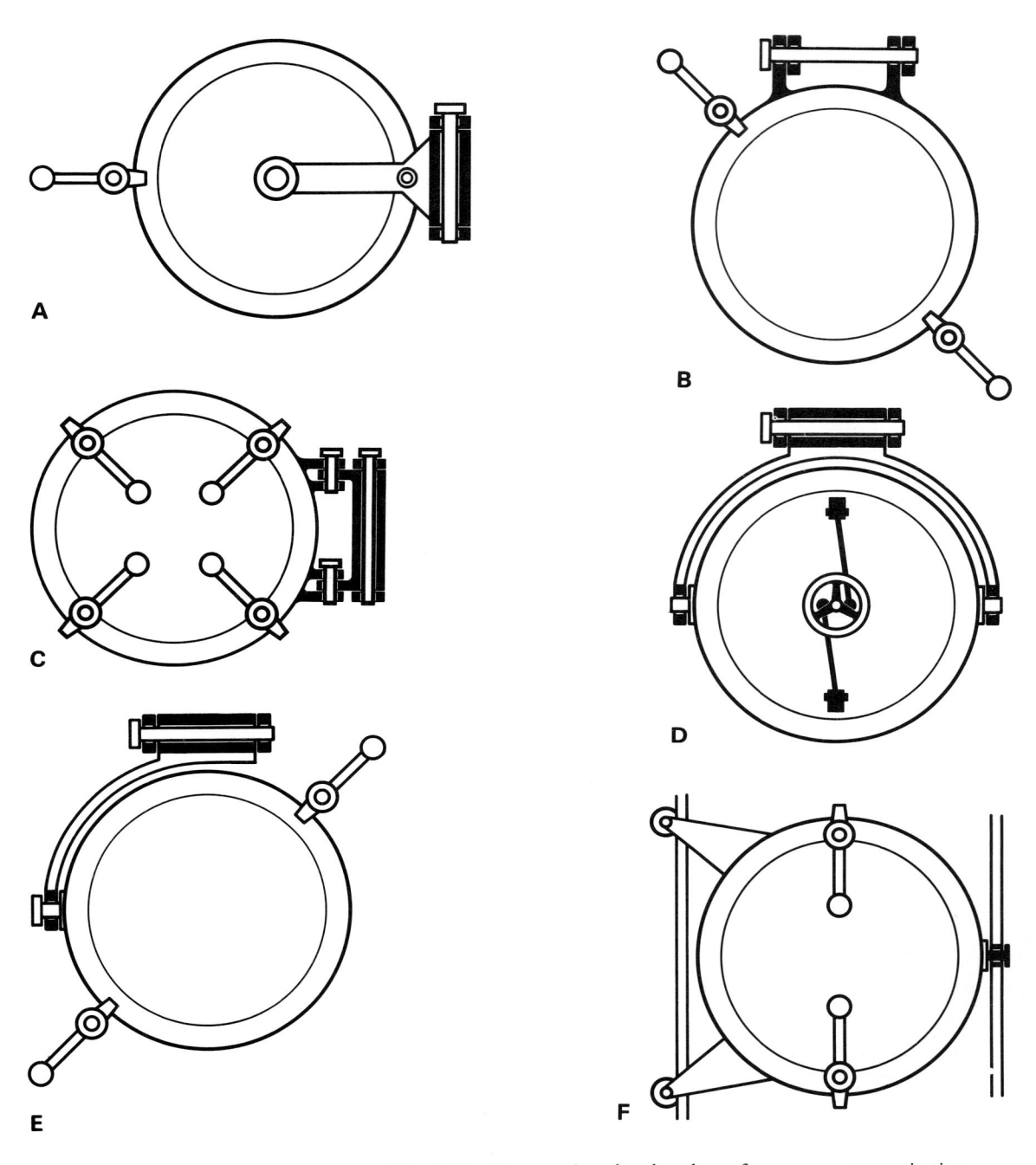

Fig. 2.15. Compression chamber doors for one-way pressurization.

    A   Central suspension, dog and pressing bolt
    B   Hinged suspension and two dogs
    C   Short double hinge and four dogs
    D   Double-hinged gallow suspension
    E   Gallow-hinge suspension and two dogs
    F   Three-point suspension and guide rail

to assist the pressure-tight seal permits small tolerances in the seatings of the doors and allows them to be used as a standard fitting. Spring-loaded dogs operated from the centre can save an additional penetration. The most common design in the past is shown in Fig. 2.15B. Since the door will be able to move axially during pressurization, the penetrations in the suspension must be elongated. To achieve an all-round pressure fit, two dogs are required. For external doors in saturation systems, which are not required to be used very often, there is no need for dogs if a crossbar can be fitted with a central screw bolt to exert initial pressure. In small chambers, where space is limited, a double-hinged door can be fitted, or a gallow hinge suspension, and these reduce the space needed for opening and closing. The doors can be held in the closed position by two dogs or cams, although damage to the alignment of the door can be sustained if the door is opened by force with the dog nearest the hinge in the retained position. To avoid damage to double-hinged doors by careless handling, simple guides and buffers can be fitted. Finally, a sliding door on rails can be used as in Fig. 2.15F with a three-point suspension and, carefully designed, is very suitable for vertical and spherical chambers.

Doors for two-way pressurization

More sophisticated chambers require the internal doors to sustain different pressure from both sides. If there is sufficient space, then two

Fig. 2.16 Two-way pressure door.

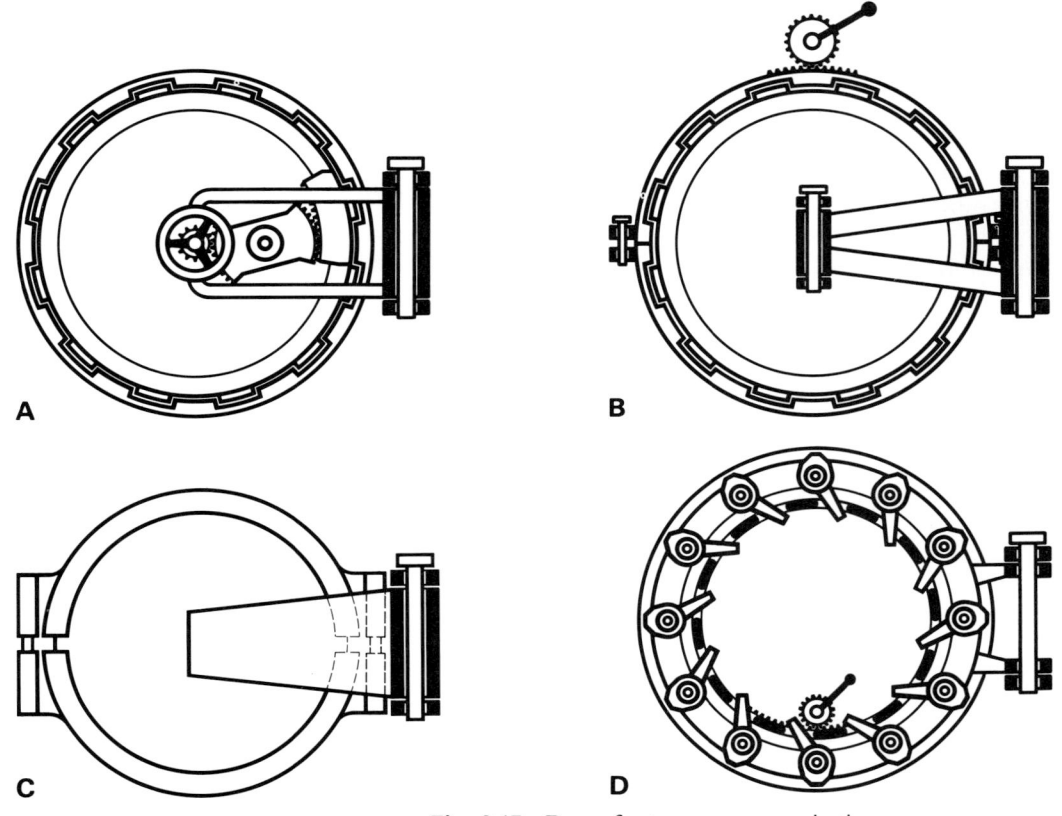

Fig. 2.17. Doors for two-way pressurization.

    A Bayonet lock with rack and pinion gearing

    B Bayonet lock with rotating bayonet ring (gear or hydraulic)

    C Flat form with a clamp ring lock (divided U ring with screw or hydraulic drive)

    D Multiple dogs (central drive with rack and pinion)

separate one-way pressure doors can be fitted with a deadspace between them, but if there are overall restrictions on space this is not possible. In many cases a single door is fitted and Fig. 2.17 shows the various options. In Fig. 2.17A the door is moved around with a hand wheel in the centre which rotates the door and engages the dogs in a bayonet joint. The seal is made by fitting a flexible sealing ring; as the door is moved, so also is the seal, which must be carefully preserved with powder and silicon grease to avoid damage and the danger of a gas leak. The design in Fig. 2.17B allows the rack and pinion to move the outer ring and the door remains stationary; therefore there is no damage to the seal which can be an O-ring. However, it is a complicated design to manufacture and is not generally favoured. Fig. 2.17C shows an end clamp ring locking device which may be operated by a gearing device or hydraulic cylinders. Fig. 2.17D shows a design where a rack and pinion on an inside guide ring moves a number of strong cams into a locked position, the disadvantage being that the door is heavy and expensive. The use of hinged doors to

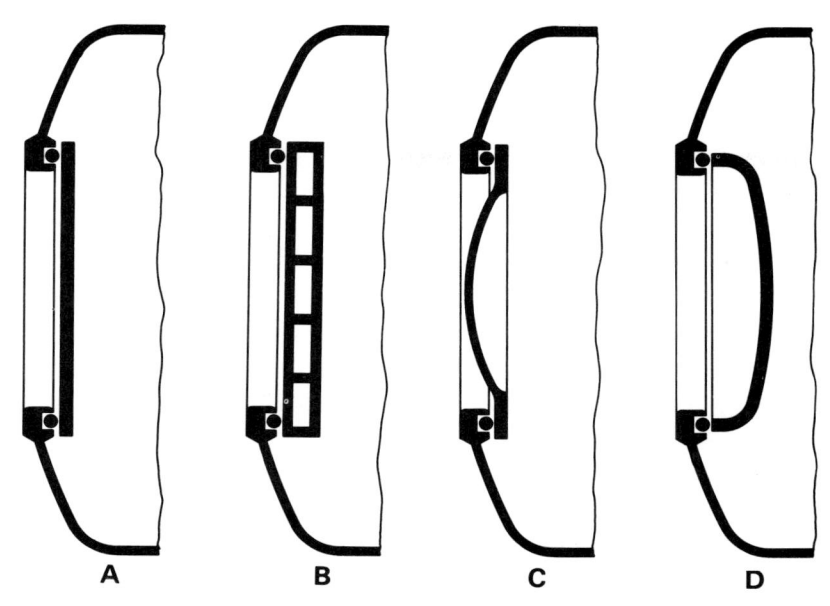

Fig. 2.18. Cross-section of doors commonly used in compression chamber design.

- **A** Flat plate, for small pressure loads and rectangular doors
- **B** Sandwich construction for large doors
- **C** Flat frame: the most common form
- **D** Dished head

sustain double pressure is not considered, owing to the reduced safety factor.

Door cross-sections

The favoured dished head design for doors is not the only type in use and other designs have certain advantages. The most common and simplest design is the standard flat form, in Fig. 2.18A, economical for rectangular and for circular doors. The design, although simple, needs to take into account the considerable stress sustained at the corners of rectangular doors. It is suitable only for small entry and low pressures. The sandwich design in Fig. 2.18B is interesting as a light-weight design and more suitable for large doors not required in diving compression chambers. A more common design is the calotte design in Fig. 2.18C, where a sphere is welded to a flat plate. The advantage is that it is simple to manufacture, particularly as the door can be pressed in one piece, and it is both light and well proven. The least expensive door in more general use is shown in Fig. 2.18D. Designed with a simple suspension system, it is unsurpassed. Depending on the wall thickness of the head, the sealing flange can be reduced to a relatively small thickness. This is a common design which, because of the increased width, is generally used in less sophisticated chamber design.

Recently, the introduction of titanium in pressure vessels has enabled this material to be used for flat doors (Fig. 2.18A) where weight and space savings can be achieved, but at some expense in terms of cost and difficulty in manufacture.

Door frames

Fig. 2.19 illustrates the main alternative designs for doors as fitted to pressure chambers. The most common door is, of course, circular. The design is straightforward and simple to manufacture, with the disadvantage that it is not the best shape for movement of the human body. The diameter for the door should under no circumstances be less than 600 mm and for both safe and efficient operations the minimum size should be 700 mm.

The oval design shown in Fig. 2.19B gives better access but is more complicated to manufacture. The advantage, apart from better access, is that the door, if damaged, can be unhinged from inside and removed to be replaced, which is not possible with a circular door. However, this is not a consideration that should influence the choice of design.

Finally, the rectangular door shown in Fig. 2.19C is a perfect design for access but it is difficult to achieve adequate strength as pressure requirements increase. It is therefore used for stretcher trolleys where

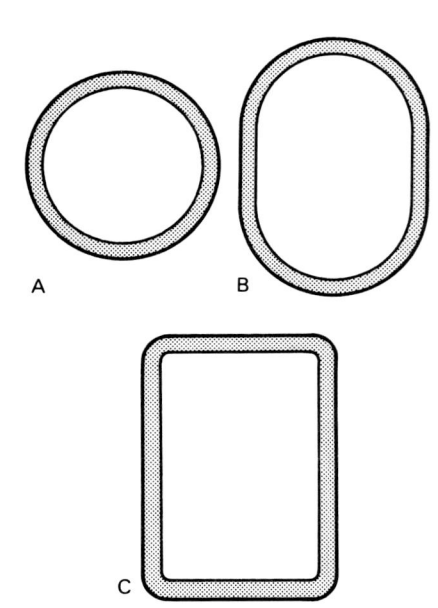

Fig. 2.19. Door configurations used in the construction of pressure chambers.

A Circular: standard design for maximum pressure
B Oval: easy access, expensive to manufacture
C Rectangular: excellent access, very expensive to manufacture, low pressure

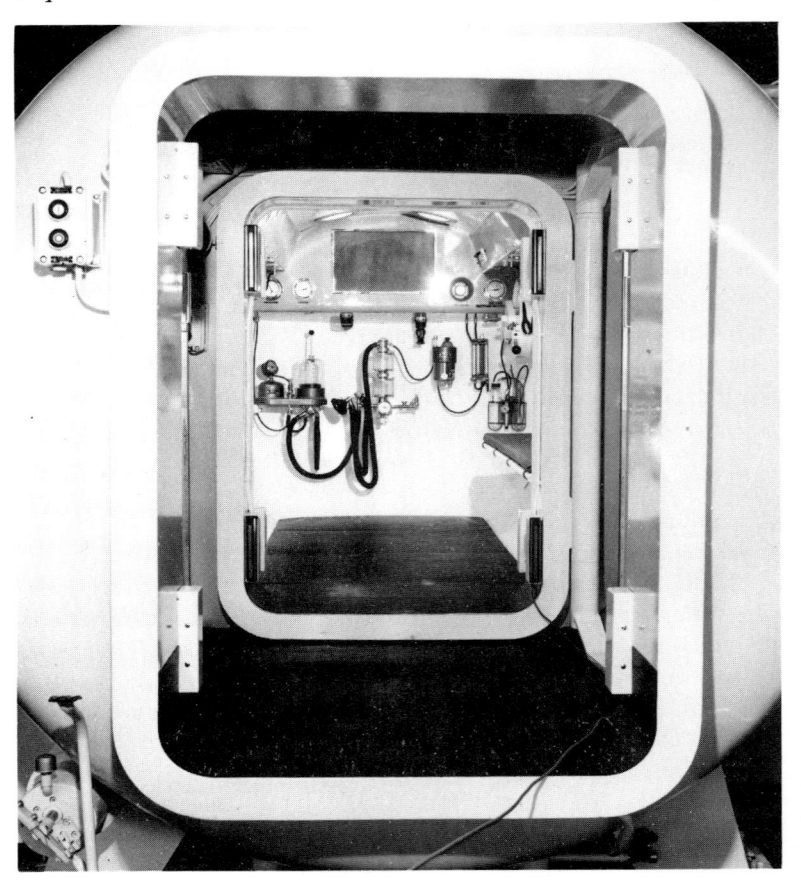

Fig. 2.20. A rectangular door.

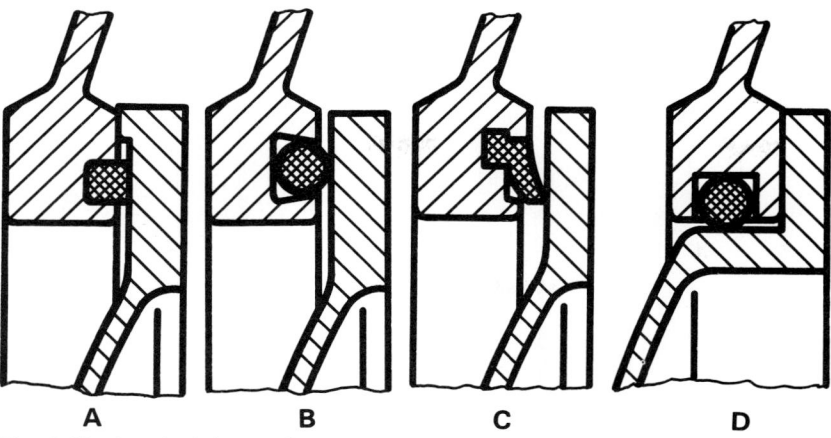

Fig. 2.21. Standard designs for door seals.
- **A** square seal
- **B** O-seal
- **C** Lip seal
- **D** O-seal

seriously injured patients need hospital treatment under pressure. This particular facility is rarely needed but these units are being used more for hyperbaric oxygen treatment in medical centres.

Seals

The need for a perfect pressure seal is paramount and is as much a requirement at higher pressure where any loss of gas can upset the balance of life-support as in very low pressures where accurate pressure is essential. Seals are made of high-elastic rubber, resistant to oil and ozone. One-way pressure doors under pressure will become stressed axially. Whether the seals are mounted into the door or into the seating of the chamber itself is immaterial and the only advantage of the latter is that in general it is less likely to be damaged.

The simple rectangular seals in Fig. 2.21A are still in use today. Basically, the same O-ring as in Fig. 2.21B is held in a V-shaped groove to prevent it from being misplaced. The lip seal shown in Fig. 2.21C is excellent for two-way pressurization and the design also allows for some movement to take up any irregularity in the mating flanges and maintain a good seal. Fig. 2.21D shows another two-way pressure seal. In this case the seal needs to be manufactured to exact size, for an error in shape or size may prevent an initial seal and, even if the pressure seal is made, the friction between the two parts will inhibit the axial movements of the doors.

General

An added advantage in entry systems is to fit small observation windows in the doors, especially between the main compartment and outer transfer compartments. Visual contact between occupants under pressure but in separate chambers can be useful. Two-way pressure doors must incorporate safety devices to prevent premature

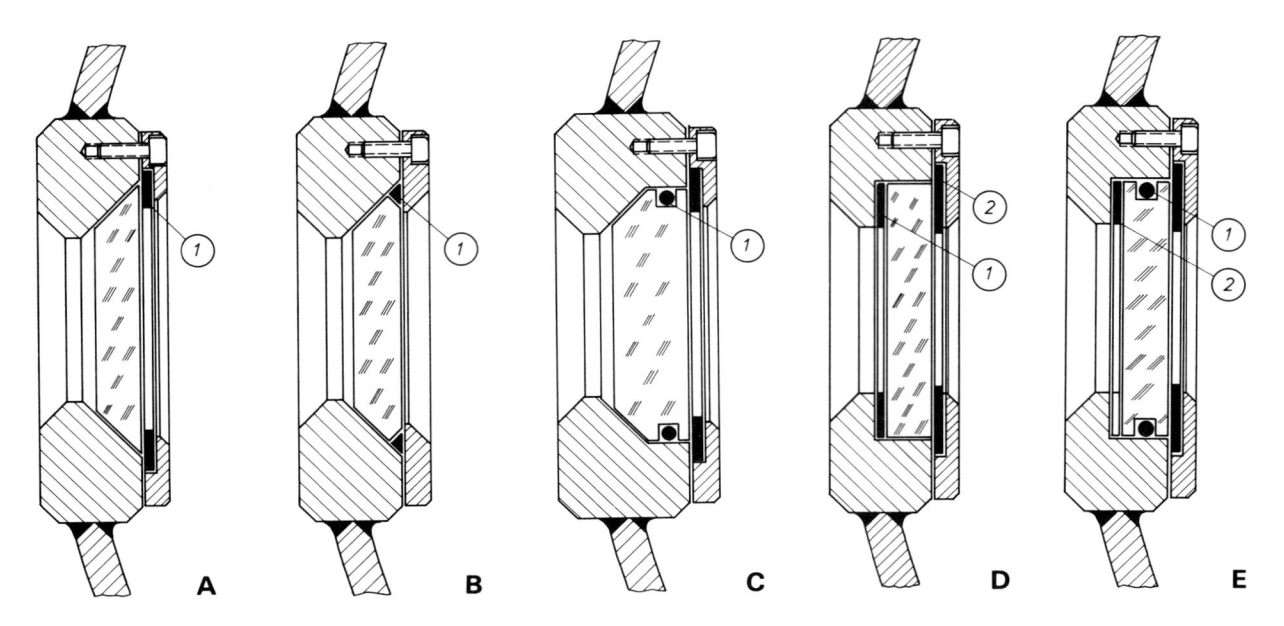

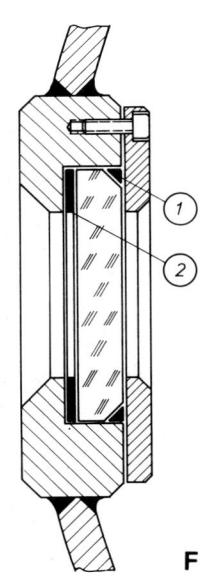

Fig. 2.22. Window designs and gasket types for one-way pressurization (by Det Norske Veritas).

- A1 Neoprene gasket
- B1 Neoprene O-ring
- C1 Neoprene O-ring
- D1 Soft neoprene gasket
- D2 Hard bearing gasket
- E1 Neoprene O-ring
- E2 Hard-bearing gasket
- F1 Neoprene O-ring
- F2 Hard-bearing gasket

movement. An equalizing valve with interlock must be fitted. Doors that are not hinged to allow them to move naturally by hand, such as those hinged from the top, usually need power assistance to open and close. Spring or weight compensation and hydraulic or pneumatic systems are therefore required.

Compression Chamber Windows

A chain is as strong as its weakest link and in the design and care of observation windows the greatest attention is needed to what is potentially the weakest part of the whole system. Basically, there are two main designs, the plain glass windows as illustrated in Fig. 2.22D,E,F and the conical window in Fig. 2.22A,B,C.

Conical windows are designed to stand the maximum pressure and manufactured in acrylic glass or high-grade thermoplasts with similar properties. They are an expensive item and the geometric fitting of the two cones is difficult.

Plain glass designs can be manufactured in either acrylic or mineral glass. Mineral glass is less sensitive to temperature, which is important if the window is being used for electrical illumination. However, the danger of fracturing limits the use of this material. Similarly, the possibility of fracturing and the poor optical quality of the finished product precludes the use of mineral glass melted into steel rings.

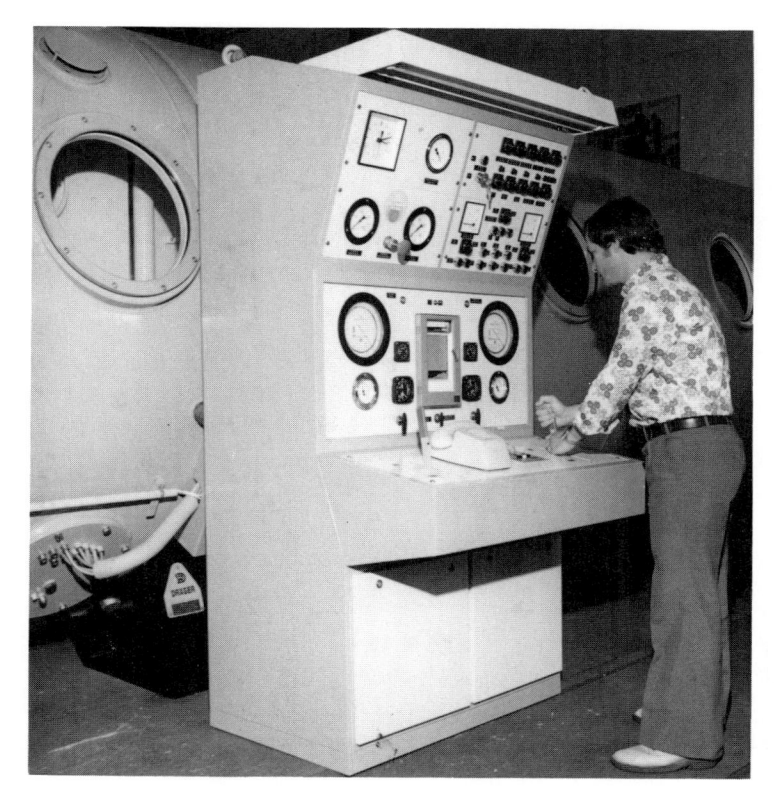

Fig. 2.23. Special large windows fitted in a compression chamber.

Plain windows with a radial groove and fitted with an O-ring are very common and suitable for the higher pressure range. Det Norske Veritas have issued good detailed specifications for window designs in compression chambers and diving bells, and these are found in *The Rules for the Construction and Classification of Diving Systems*, containing information on types, application, physical properties, geometry calculations and testing.

The number and position of the windows in a chamber must clearly achieve optimum coverage with the minimum number of windows. If television is used, much smaller windows, approximately 70 mm, are adequate if fitted in the dished ends. Sight windows are normally about 150–200 mm, but can be made considerably larger. The design safety factor must be higher than that of the pressure vessel itself, as it would be totally unacceptable for a window to fail with consequent rapid depressurization of the chamber. To prevent mechanical damage it is advisable that thin clear protective plates be fitted in front of the windows and these can also help to reduce the effect of heat on the acrylic. As a final precaution against the total failure of the window, blank flanges can be quickly fitted to maintain the internal pressure integrity of the chamber.

Medical Supply Lock

Originally designed for medical equipment, the supply lock is also used nowadays for the domestic and everyday needs of divers under

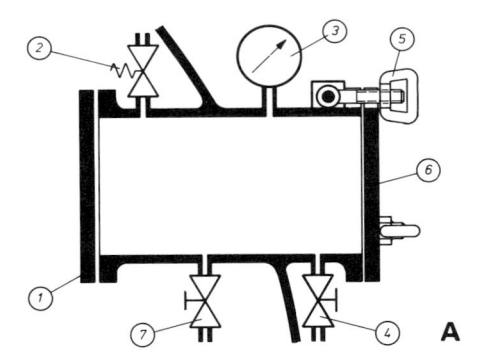

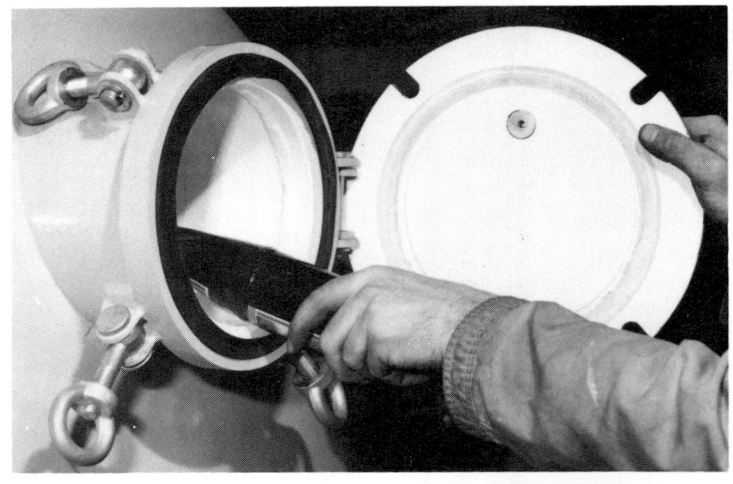

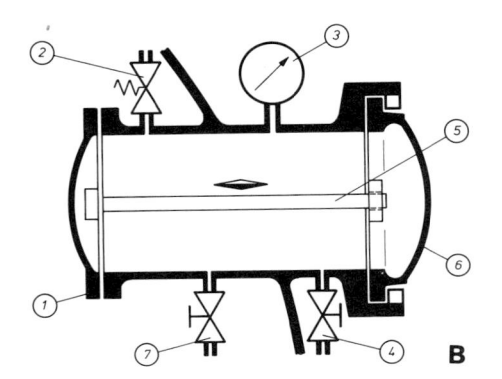

Fig. 2.24. Medical and supply locks for compression chambers.

A Clamped type	**B** Bayonet type
1 internal hatch	1 internal hatch
2 safety valve (internal)	2 safety valve (internal)
3 gauge for supply lock internal pressure	3 gauge for supply lock internal pressure
4 external relief valve	4 external relief valve
5 hinged bolts for external hatch	5 safety locking mechanisms
6 external hatch	6 external hatch
7 internal pressure-equalizing valve	7 internal pressure-equalizing valve

pressure for long periods. The supply lock is fitted to the main chamber and can be set either into the cylindrical trunking of the hull or into the dished ends, depending on the space available for the projection of the lock into the chamber. The other consideration is the best position for working both for inside and for outside operations.

Deck Compression Chambers

In Fig. 2.24 the two basic designs for locks are illustrated. The simple design in Fig. 2.24B has hinged bolts or butterfly clips to effect the pressure seal. It is used for low pressures and its cost is low. A bayonet lock is fitted for most standard chambers operating at higher pressures. Other possible methods of door-locking use spreading tappets. Divided U-rings are rarely used. To avoid the possibility of a differential pressure building up in the lock, relative to the internal pressure of the chambers, or similarly to the outside surface pressure, when the lock is opened for use, simple safety locking devices are fitted.

The normal clear diameter for locks fitted to standard compression chambers is between 200 and 300 mm and the overall length between 300 and 400 mm. Extra large locks are incorporated into saturation diving complexes and discussed in Chapter 3.

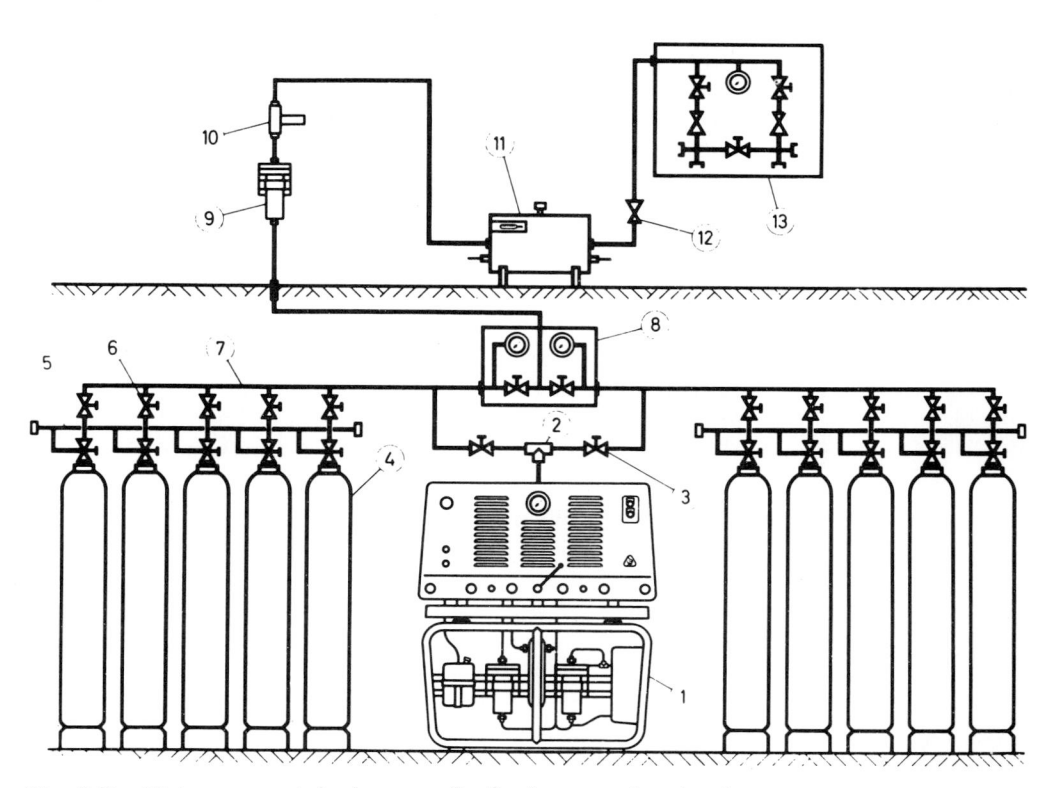

Fig. 2.25. High-pressure air bank storage for fixed compression chamber.

1. high-pressure compressor
2. outlet manifold
3. main outlet valve to designated bank
4. high-pressure air bank cylinders
5. dewatering line
6. inlet/outlet valve
7. inlet/outlet line
8. supply bank control panel
9. oil vapour-filter
10. dust particle filter (sinter metal)
11. heat exchanger
12. pressure reducer
13. diver supply control panel

Compressed-air Supply

Fixed compression chambers
The majority of under-water work is still in the air range of diving, although the increasing work off-shore is deep enough to need mixed gas supplies at increased pressure. However, with the main emphasis on air range diving which rarely exceeds 70 m, the largest commitment is to provide high-pressure compressed-air supplies. Fig. 2.25 shows the complete piping system for a static chamber. The selection of a compressor is determined by the type of operation to be carried out and the size of the storage bank to provide the air when required. This will determine the rate needed to replenish the storage bank and therefore the required delivery output of the compressor. A compression chamber used for training or installed in an institute will be in use more regularly and therefore a large storage bank with a medium-delivery compressor or a small storage bank with a high-delivery compressor is needed. A chamber for emergency and standby use can be supplied from a less powerful compressor. The choice of compressor and air should be based on the maximum anticipated air demand, but it is always good practice to install a compressor one size larger than needed, with the further option of expanding the storage capacity.

The usual drive for a compressor in a fixed installation is electric, with possibly diesel as standby. In a ship installation it is normal to provide a back-up compressor. Petrol-driven compressors are rarely considered except as portable units.

The storage bank must supply air to the highest specification and clear of impurities to a certified standard. No oil, carbon monoxide, water vapour, carbon dioxide or other impurities above the agreed standards are permitted. Therefore, proper filtration units must be placed in the system before the air is stored. Charcoal filters are frequently inserted between the bank and the compressor to remove all water vapour. The storage bank must be versatile, with cross-connections at least to allow the bank to be split so that one section can be recharged whilst the chamber is being supplied from the other section. The actual size of the storage cylinders is immaterial as long as adequate total capacity is provided. However, when planning ship installations consideration should be given to the need for reservoirs to be removed for tests every five years or as prescribed.

It was common practice for the air supply into the chamber to be reduced to about 40 bar but as compression now is carried out at a much faster rate, so this has led to the practice of pressurizing the chamber directly with air or mixed gas. An orifice in the chamber limits the flow which would normally reduce the temperature around the fitting rapidly. By fitting the orifice inside an injector the warm air in the chamber is passed around the orifice and mixed with the cold air. There is only a slight increase in temperature during compression where, without this arrangement, temperature increases of between 30° and 40°C are possible. By housing the unit inside a silencer, the noise level is within acceptable limits, generally considered to be

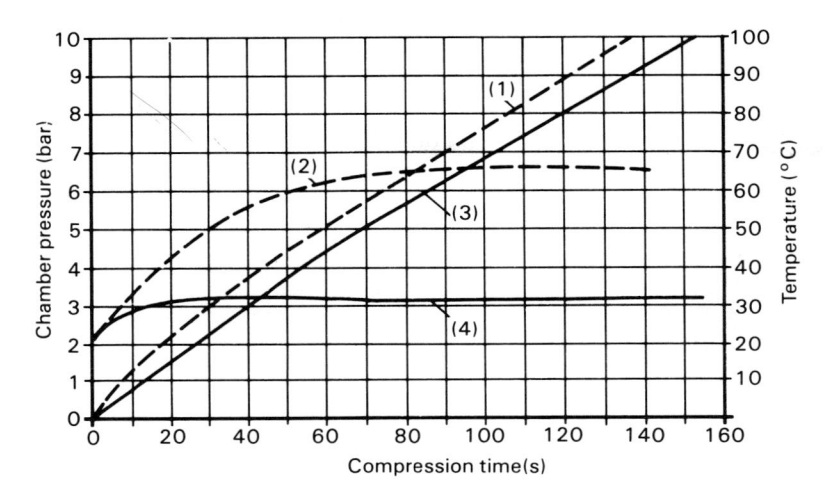

Fig. 2.26. High-pressure charging system, injector and silencer. Temperature rise in the chamber with high- and low-pressure charging systems.

1 Pressure rise (low-pressure charging system)
2 Temperature rise in the chamber during pressurization (low-pressure charging system)
3 Pressure rise (high-pressure charging system)
4 Temperature rise in the chamber during pressurization (high-pressure charging system)

below 50 dB. Vibration frequencies between 5 and 9 Hz should be avoided. Fig. 2.26 shows a cross-section of the high-pressure air inlet system and a graph showing the temperature curves of a conventional low-pressure charging system.

The injection of fresh air ventilation can also be integrated into the compressed-air supply system and this is discussed later. There are certain options in the selection of valves: stem valves, ball valves or even needle valves. Needle valves are very accurate and reliable, but it is difficult to measure their exact position. Ball valves are not easily adjustable but do have the advantage that the open and closed positions are easily identified and can be operated quickly in an emergency. The disadvantage is that the levers can be pushed over in error.

The use of an automatic control system, even linked to a computer program for decompression, is not considered here, although used successfully in controlled conditions in shore-based experimental facilities and in some operational systems.

Mobile compression chambers
Generally the same type of air supply system is used for mobile chambers as for fixed ones. The chamber must be robust and secure because it will need to be capable of being transported and operated in rough conditions. Fig. 2.28 shows an operational storage chamber with a storage bank fitted under the chamber; the control panel is additionally fitted with a diving panel for the supply of two surface-

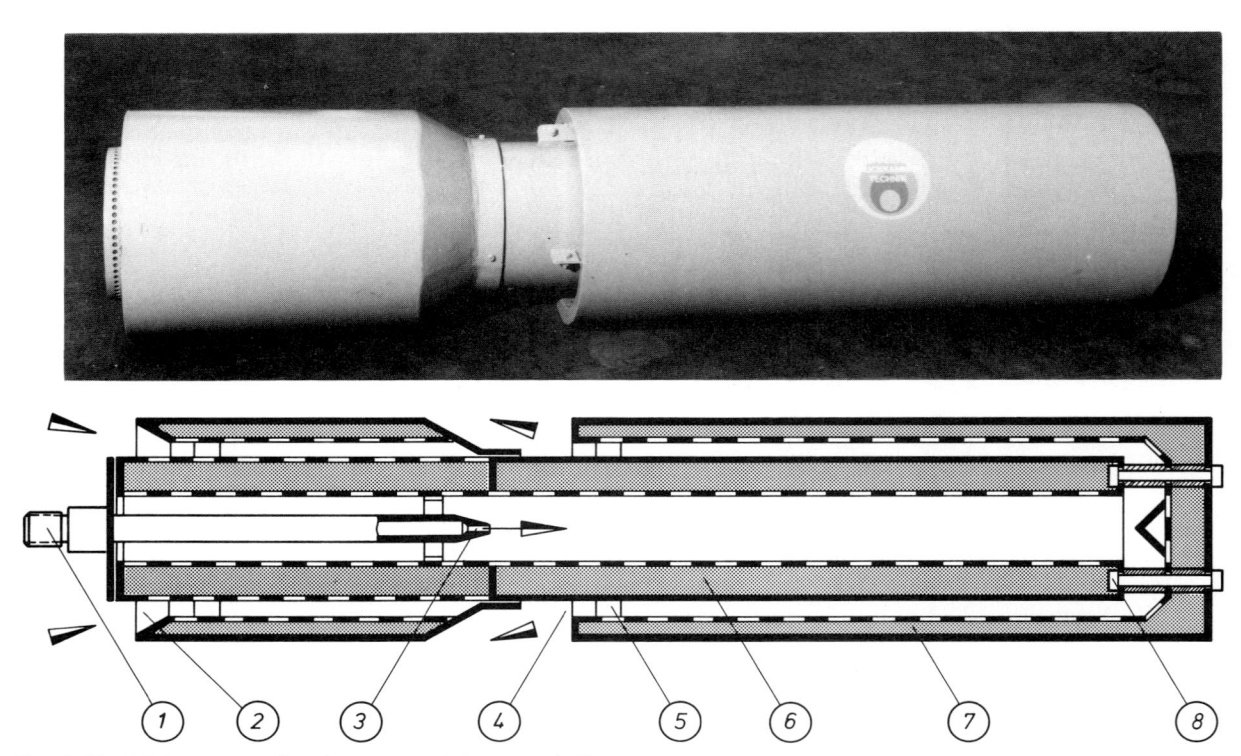

Fig. 2.27. High-pressure charging system, injector and silencer.

1 high-pressure connection
2 chamber air inlet
3 interchangeable orifice
4 silencer, air outlet
5 spacing piece
6 internal silencer
7 external silencer
8 spacing piece bolt

supplied hard-hat divers and, separately, of the chamber itself. This is the standard package for surface-orientated diving where the divers return rapidly to the surface on completion of their dive and undergo a marginally longer decompression in the chamber than they would normally do, carrying out their stops in the water.

Fresh Air Ventilation

A known product of breathing is CO_2 and in a confined space this will be dangerous unless steps are taken to ventilate and reduce the partial pressure to below acceptable limits. In larger systems CO_2 filtration units are incorporated into the system but these are not normal in the smaller compression chamber. It is bad practice, unless there is no alternative, to flush the chamber from time to time by opening the inlet and exhaust valves. Some variations of pressure occur and also unless the positions of the intake and exhaust are diagonally opposite there will be a most inefficient turnover of air. Also the noise level tends to be unacceptably high, even if silencers are fitted.

The following are some considerations based on the assumption that the chambers are continuously supplied with fresh air:

Fig. 2.28. A small mobile compression chamber with compressed air storage underneath.

Formulas 1 and 2 apply to conditions in chambers which are not ventilated:

$$P_{CO_2} = \frac{B}{v} \times t \times P \quad \text{(bar)} \quad (1)$$

$$C' = \frac{P_{CO_2}}{P} \times 100 \quad (\%) \quad (2)$$

where
P_{CO_2} = CO_2 partial pressure (bar)
B = CO_2 production (litres/min)
v = gas volume (standard, litres)
t = time (min)
P = atmospheric pressure (bar)
P_T = internal chamber pressure (bar)
v' = chamber volume (litres)
C' = CO_2 (%)
F = fresh air ventilation flow (litres/min)

When the chambers are ventilated with fresh air during use, the P_{CO_2} rise with time is calculated using formula 3:

$$P_{CO_2} = \frac{B}{F}\left[1 - \exp\left(\frac{1}{(F/v') \times t}\right)\right] \quad \text{(bar)} \quad (3)$$

On the assumption that CO_2 production B is 0.5 litres/min, fresh air ventilation F is 33.3 litres/min and chamber volumes are 1, 2, 3, 4 and 5 m^3, the CO_2 curves are plotted in Fig. 2.29 for ventilated and non-ventilated chambers. It shows clearly that the time at which a

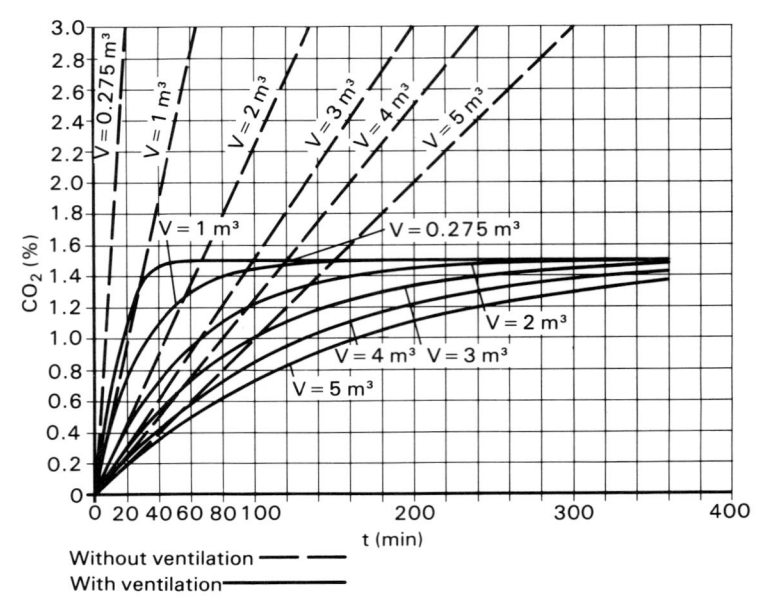

Fig. 2.29. Carbon dioxide rise in ventilated and non-ventilated chambers of different sizes at normal pressure.

stationary condition is reached in ventilated chambers depends on the chamber volume. The amount of CO_2 produced is of equal importance.

As $t \to \infty$ formula 3 is simplified to formula 4:

$$P_{CO_2} = \frac{B}{F} \quad \text{(bar)} \qquad (4)$$

If the internal chamber pressure P_T and the number of occupants n are introduced, one gets:

$$P_{CO_2} = \frac{B}{F} \times P_T \times n \quad \text{(bar)} \qquad (5)$$

and by rearranging formula 5 we arrive at the formula 6:

$$F = \frac{B}{P_{CO_2}} \times P_T \times n \quad \text{(litres/min)} \qquad (6)$$

With the help of formula 6 and the assumption of a P_{CO_2} of 0.015 bar and a CO_2 production of 0.5 litre/min Table 2.2 is arrived at.

The measurement of CO_2 can be effected with either an on-line analyser or a gas-detecting tube indicator taken into the chamber. The tubes may not function correctly at higher pressure where the filling becomes displaced after opening and are therefore recommended only in the lower pressure range.

For the latter stages of decompression, the use of pure oxygen at 18 m or oxygen-enriched air and mixed gases is standard practice to reduce the decompression time by reducing the intake of inert gas into the body. In air diving this inert gas would be nitrogen. Oxygen

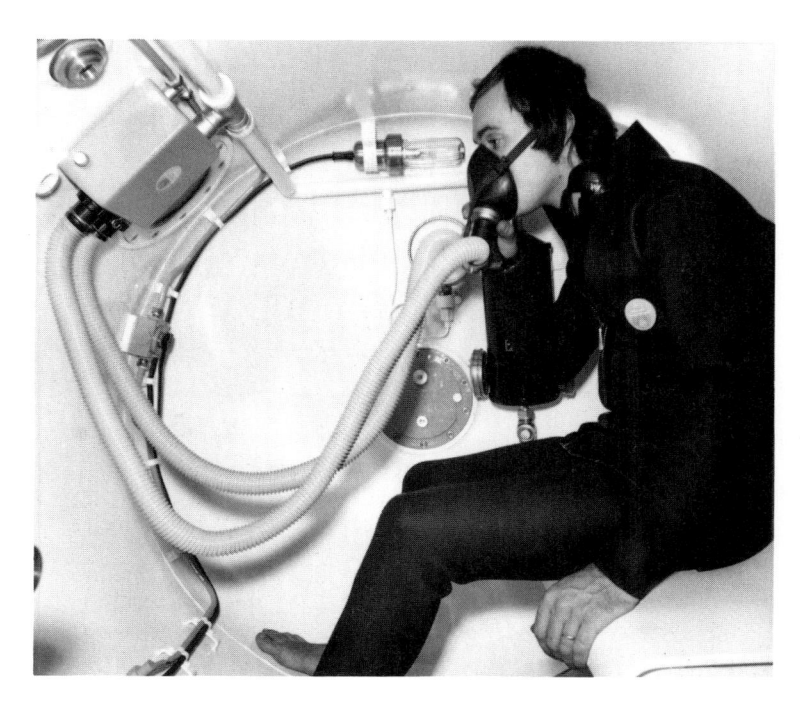

Fig. 2.30. Oxygen breathing unit in a stationary compression chamber.

Table 2.2. Ventilation air flows for transport chambers with operating pressures up to 10 bar*

Chamber pressure (bar)	Ventilation air flow (litres/min)			
	1 person	2 people	3 people	4 people
1.3	43.5	87	130	174
1.6	53.5	107	160.5	214
1.9	63.5	127	190.5	254
2.2	73.5	147	220.5	294
2.5	83.5	167	250.5	334
2.8	93.5	187	280.5	374
3.1	103.5	207	310.5	414
3.4	113.5	227	340.5	454
4.0	133.5	267	400.5	534
4.6	153.5	307	460.5	614
5.2	173.5	347	520.5	694
6.0	200	400	600	800
7.0	233.5	467	700.5	934
8.0	266.5	535	799.5	1066
9.0	300	600	900	1200
10.0	333.5	667	1000.5	1334
11.0	366.5	733	1099.5	1466

*For an open-circuit system, calculated on the basis of formula 6, with a maximum permissible CO_2 partial pressure of 0.015 bar and a CO_2 production of 0.5 litre/min.

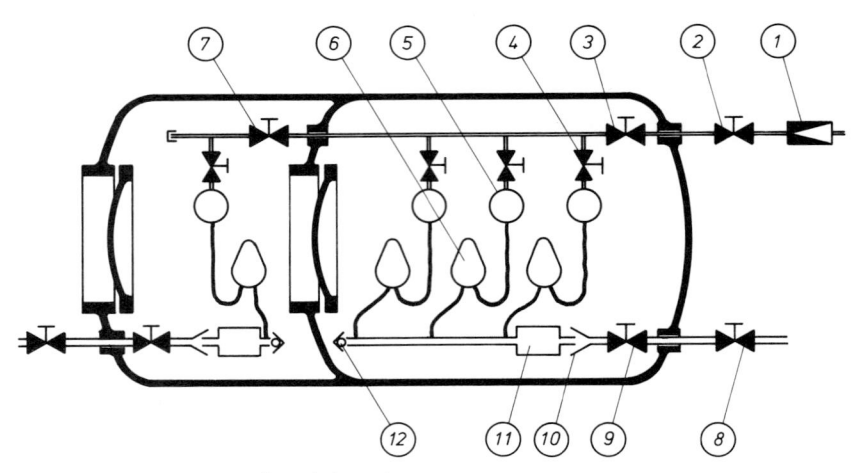

Fig. 2.31. Oxygen overboard dumping system.

1 oxygen regulator
2 external shut-off valve
3 internal shut-off valve
4 shut-off valve for breathing unit
5 breathing regulator
6 breathing unit with inhalation and exhalation hose
7 shut-off valve in outer chamber
8 shut-off valve for exhaust line
9 control valve for exhaust line
10 funnel
11 collection tank
12 one-way valve

breathing is also used extensively in treatment. Oxygen-enriched spaces are potentially explosive and hazardous and therefore totally unacceptable in modern diving operations. Fig. 2.31 shows overboard dumping systems to remove exhaled oxygen from the chamber completely. Breathing masks used to inhale the oxygen mixture are fitted with an additional exhalation hose which passes to a collection pipe and then to a central collection chamber which gathers all the exhaled mixture. The system is fitted with an evacuation injector, operated by chamber air and through control valves, and the oxygen mixture passes to the external surface pressure. By this method the build-up of oxygen is avoided and the fire risk reduced. All oxygen piping systems, however, have to be kept scrupulously free of oil or grease. Fig. 2.32 summarizes the various methods of gas ventilation and elimination.

A number of fires and explosions inside chambers have caused fatalities and serious injuries. A raised oxygen content of over 25% increases the risk of fire and a number of preventive methods are used. Fire-resistant material will radically reduce the risk. Electrical installations inside the chamber should be kept to a minimum and use low voltage. Lighting should be sited externally. Fire-retardant paint must be used for interior surfaces, applied to a minimum thickness. In spite of all these precautions, methods of fighting the fire need to be considered. Although the use of matches and smoking is universally barred in diving chamber practice, there may be other sources of ignition. For hand use inside the chamber the divers should have a

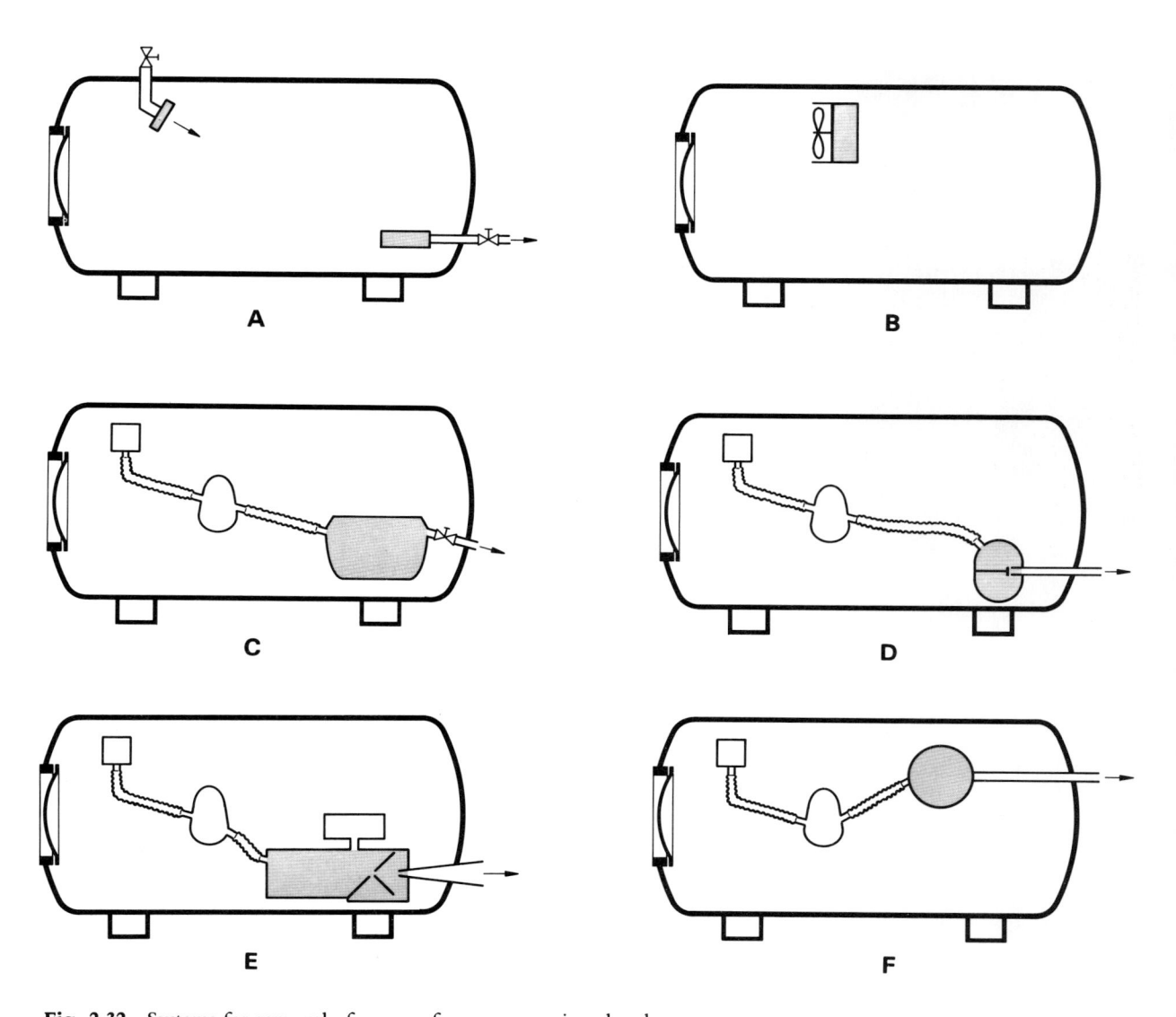

Fig. 2.32. Systems for removal of oxygen from compression chambers.

- **A** Fresh-air feed and removal of air enriched with oxygen; requires large quantities of air, has high noise level and temperature variation and is expensive
- **B** Catalytic burning of oxygen to desired partial pressure: a rare system for experimental units only
- **C** Collecting bag with manual removal of exhaled oxygen: a valve must be used and complicates handling
- **D** Gas removal controlled by a regulator: after partial filling a valve is opened and gas can be released
- **E** Oxygen removed from a collecting tank through an injector; a weak vacuum can be adjusted to facilitate exhalation
- **F** Oxygen removed by a special regulator with a large diaphragm area or a pneumatic regulation unit (cyclo-flow)

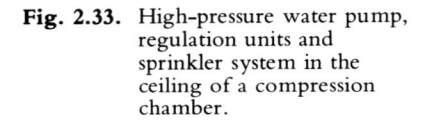

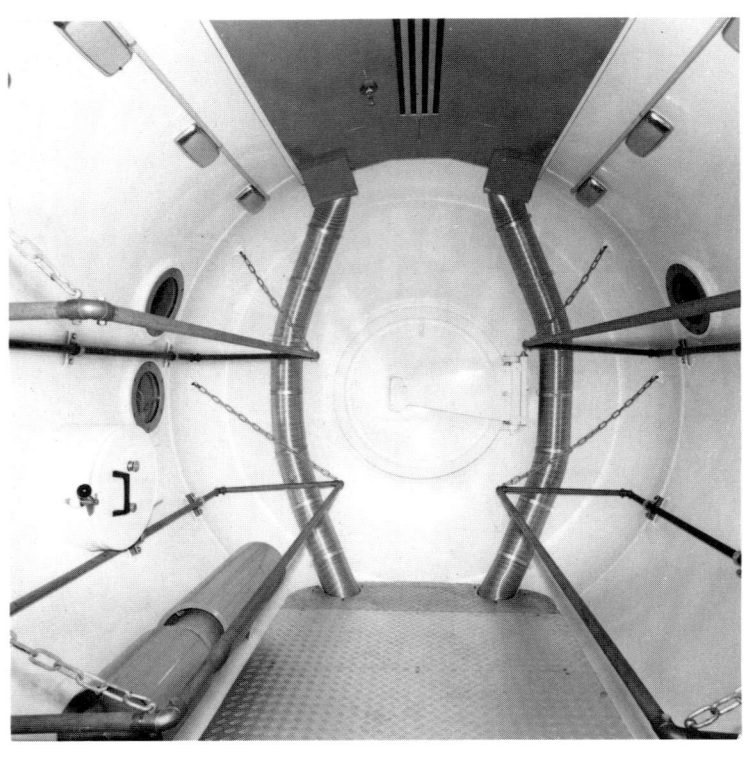

Fig. 2.33. High-pressure water pump, regulation units and sprinkler system in the ceiling of a compression chamber.

water bucket and fire-proof blankets. Also for consideration is the use of an inert gas cylinder which, effectively used, can blanket the source of fire and remove any oxygen. CO_2 and dry cylinder extinguishers cannot be used. Mechanical high-pressure water sprinklers, capable of delivering an omnidirectional spread over the entire surface area of the chamber hull, have been fitted.

Fig. 2.33 shows a high-pressure water pump externally operated from tanks. The sprinkler system is fitted in the ceiling of the chamber so that there is good coverage throughout the interior. The system can operate automatically, initiated by an infra-red sensor, or by hand. Some water systems recirculate the water where there is a limited water supply. The water is recirculated through the system by a pump at the bottom of the chamber. Sprinklers for deep diving systems are discussed in further detail in Chapter 3.

Some regulations insist on sprinkler systems not only inside chambers but also externally for gas storage areas and control rooms.

Lighting

Natural light penetrating through the windows of a chamber is insufficient for practical operations, except in an emergency. Some artificial light needs to be provided and there are advantages and disadvantages in the installation of internal and external lighting, and there are certain options in the choice of the light fitting. Table 2.3 clarifies in general terms the advantages and disadvantages of both.

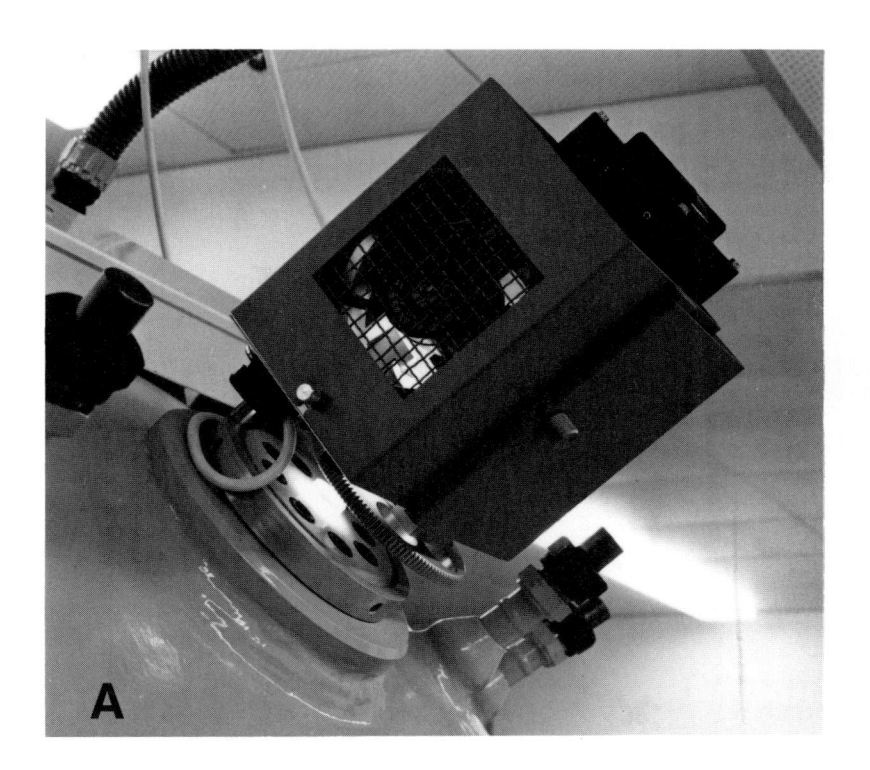

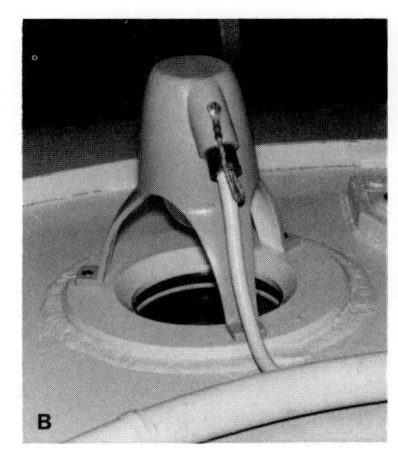

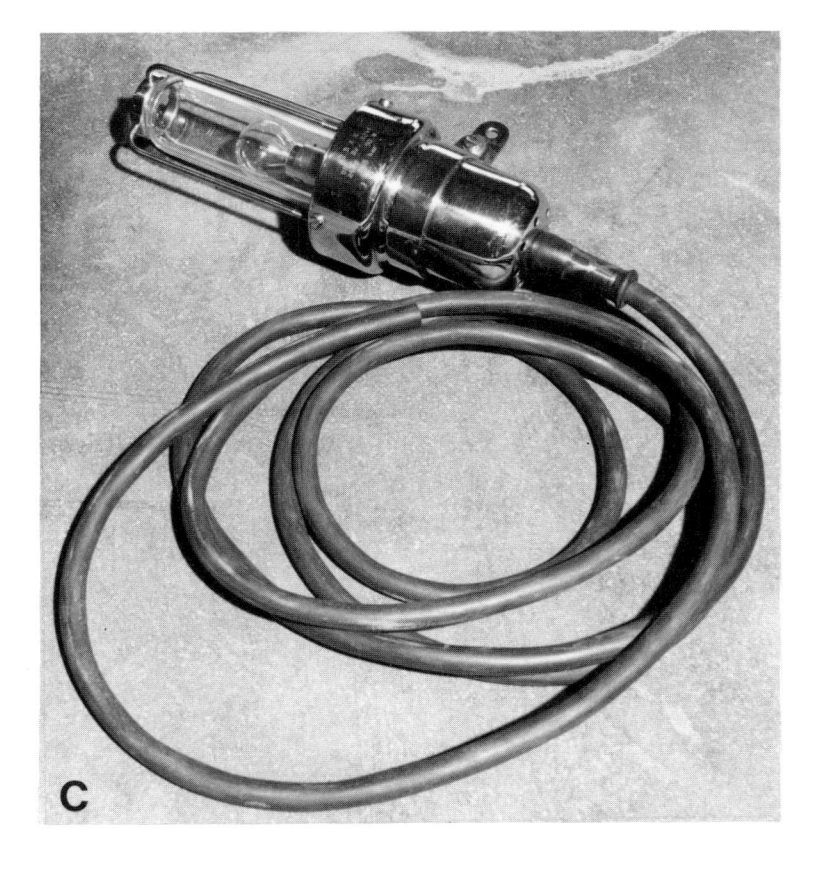

Fig. 2.34. Various compression chamber lights.

    A   Fibreoptic (cold)
    B   External
    C   Pressure-safe internal

Table 2.3. Advantages and disadvantages of internal and external light

	Internal lights	External lights
Light output	Excellent	Good
Heat dispersal	Poor	Good
Temperature effect on windows	None	Variable
Pressure seal	Required	Not required
Installation	Additional	Normal
Space requirement	Major consideration	Not relevant
Maintenance	Complicated	Simple
Costs	High*	High*
Safety	Reduced	Normal
Resistance to damage	Good	Poor

* The cost of internal lights is high due to the pressure-tight sealing requirements, but external lights, although inexpensive themselves, require additional windows and penetrations.

Whatever the choice of lighting arrangements, a low-voltage supply below 42 V must be used internally for safety reasons. Fig. 2.34 shows an external light, an internal light fitting rated for 50 bar pressure and a fibreoptic light. For general guidance a main chamber 2400 mm long and 1800 mm in diameter will require two lights each of 100 W. External lights can be hinged so as to allow the window to be used for observation and heat protection discs can be fitted over the top of the window with the light source set away to disperse the heat. Fibreoptic lights or cold-light systems are being installed in modern static chambers, notwithstanding the high cost, because they have many advantages. They require only a small penetration into the chamber, give good diffusion of light, are adjustable, have minimal heat output and have a high safety factor.

Heating and Cooling

Heating inside chambers is essential for the health and safety of the occupants. Electricity as a method of heat exchange is the most usual, although steam and hot water are acceptable. Normally the heating tubes are set underneath the bunks, with a control switch for adjustment (Fig. 2.35). If the heat is too localized explosion-proof blowers help to circulate the chamber air.

The measurement of temperature using bimetal thermometers will give the quickest electrical measurement on the control panel. For a standard chamber, with a volume of 5 m^3, 3500 W is sufficient power for heating. The sharp drop in temperature between decompression stops can be partially mitigated by increasing the chamber temperature just prior to the pressure change. With the use of oxy-helium mixtures the exceptional heat conductivity of the helium sharply lowers the chamber temperature and only on raising the temperature to about 32°C does the chamber atmosphere become comfortable again.

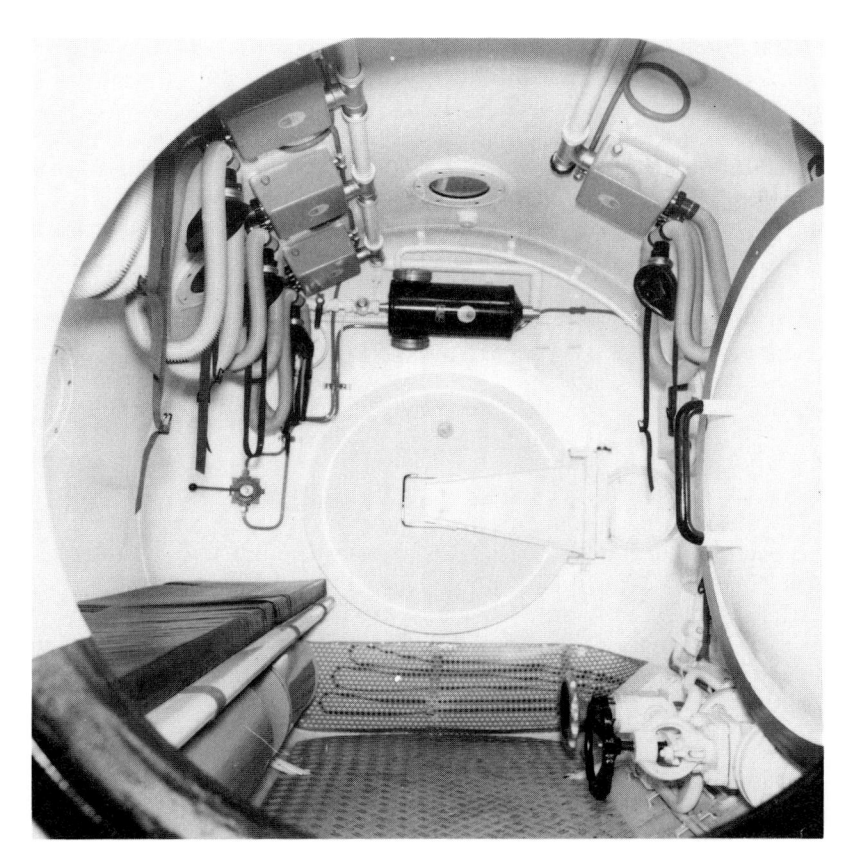

Fig. 2.35. Electric heating in a compression chamber. The heating tubes are covered by perforated metal gratings.

Fig. 2.36. Heat exchanger with an air circulation system (external unit).

The installation of cooling units is rarely needed except in very hot climates. They are often provided in test facilities for experimental purposes. Rapid compression, which is now normal practice, will raise the temperature significantly and the application of the injector system, described previously, will help cool the air. If cooling systems are installed they are designed with the cooling aggregate externally and the heat-exchangers placed either on the chamber ceiling internally or externally in a circulation tunnel, as shown in Fig. 2.36. In this case a blower is used to circulate the gases.

Carbon Dioxide Absorption

The ventilation of the chamber using the supply and exhaust for the removal of CO_2 has been discussed. Although effective for small chambers, the operation is crude and inefficient for larger chambers and unacceptable for mixed gas operations. In these circumstances a CO_2 absorption unit is installed. Such a system incorporating an electric blower attached to a CO_2 absorption unit is shown in Fig. 2.37. The CO_2 absorbent, usually soda-lime, is either prepacked or packed into the containers. The unit can be programmed to activate from a CO_2 analyser or manually. Other systems favoured for use in under-water habitats are described in Chapter 10.

Water Removal

The increase in humidity accelerates if there is no ventilation and water vapour is not removed. Apart from being unpleasant it is

Fig. 2.37. Carbon dioxide absorption unit in a compression chamber.

unhealthy and dehumidification systems are fitted for long decompression schedules. A CO_2 absorption system can be modified to contain silica gel or some other water-retaining chemical and the flow through the absorption unit reversed to blow the air from top to bottom. The blower can be controlled by a hair hygrometer. An alternative method is using a heat-exchanger with condensation plates to condense the water vapour.

Silencers

The effects of high noise levels are generally considered to be dangerous in any environment. As noise levels can be excessive inside chambers, especially during rapid compression where there are high flow velocities through gas supply orifices, the fitting of silencers is particularly important. Noise generation should be kept below 50 dB.

Communications

Good communications are fundamental to all operations. A communication failure significantly reduces the safety margin and, if not rectified, may jeopardize the divers and the mission. The selection of communication equipment with secondary and emergency back-up systems must have the highest priority, although the failure of communication systems is less likely in compression chambers than in diving bells; ultimately, if all else fails, the controllers and the occupants under pressure can still communicate visually through the observation windows.

Two main systems used are the intercom or talk-back and the telephone. The talk-back system is usually the primary system because it does not require push-buttons to initiate and, with the use of an override button on the control panel, any feed-back of noise level or multiple use of the system can be controlled. The system requires a very low voltage to conform to good safety practice. The use of the sound-powered telephone is an obvious secondary or emergency system. The link does not require power and therefore is ideal for emergency use in the event of a power failure or a defect on the primary system. The strength and clarity tend to be low and speech must be clear and precise. Another system in use is a call-up system based on one master station, which would be on the control panel, and a number of extensions. These are not entirely satisfactory due to the danger from salt water corrosion.

All primary communication systems need to be used in conjunction with helium unscrambler systems for communications where divers are breathing oxy-helium mixtures. The lightness and rarity of helium distorts the speech and makes interpretation difficult.

Television systems

The use of television systems is generally reserved for experimental facilities and operational deep diving systems. They are not usually fitted to smaller single compression chambers but Fig. 2.38 shows a

Fig. 2.38. A television unit in a laboratory compression chamber.

system used for a one-lock stationary system where the camera is conveniently mounted at the end of the chamber. By using a wide-angle lens a greater overall coverage can be achieved. The position of the monitor on the control panel is important to enable the supervisor to observe the interior without losing his concentration or his view of the rest of the control panel. The number of control staff may be reduced if there is well planned television coverage. Television cameras are not normally installed inside the chambers. Video-tape recorders are standard items to log important sequences.

Internal Fittings

Clearly the amount of internal fittings required to give adequate life-support and environmental control does not allow much space for additional fittings, which cannot be classed as essential for the safety of the occupants but which are nevertheless very important for the health and safety of the diver. Because space is so very limited in chambers, much more effort is needed in the design of the layout, to obtain the maximum space for the occupants. The many small irritations that affect a man under pressure for long periods need the designer's attention as much as essential life-support equipment. For example, an uncomfortable bunk with a painful projection can produce some minor side effects. Therefore, careful attention is needed to the design and comfort of bunks, bedding, cushions, mattresses, chairs and tables and, perhaps not least, to the use of colour to brighten up the chamber.

Deep Diving Systems 3

The use of diving bells and the application of deep diving techniques has, over the last 15 years, become an important part of off-shore engineering. Although this is the normal method of carrying out off-shore diving for oil and gas operations in the hostile and deeper water of north-west Europe, it should be noted that the use of diving bells and chambers accounts for less than 7% of commercial work world-wide. The conventional and practical method by which divers enter the water on the surface, either carrying their own supply of air (known as scuba diving) or being supplied by air through a hose (known as standard or surface-oriented diving), is still the primary method. These commercial diving operations are generally limited to 50 m, but in some areas of the world, such as the Gulf of Mexico, surface-oriented diving is used to 90 m, breathing mixed gases. World energy requirements have pushed the search for oil and gas into deeper waters; where it has been successful, production installations are built and the exploration probes further and into deeper water beyond the limits of the Continental Shelf. Today, diving to 200 m is normal practice and this is expected to extend, not without some practical problems, to 600 m. The practical depth limit for commercial diving cannot yet be stated. Although the ultimate practical depth will be constrained by the limitations of the human body, there may well be other inhibiting factors, not least the very high cost of operating divers at the great depths, and alternative methods are being developed which are in some cases less costly and safer. However, for the foreseeable future, divers will not be entirely replaced at these deeper depths, even though there is much scope for further development in unmanned vehicles and submersibles.

The introduction of the diving bell in depths in excess of 50–90 m of water allows the divers to be transported in a dry chamber to their work site and to enter the water close to their work site from the comparative safety of the bell. The diving bell will provide the required breathing gases and the energy to drive tools as well as warmth for the divers. For shallower depths and for shorter decompressions on air, the complete decompression schedule may be carried out without transferring to larger deck compression chambers.

As great as was the advance from scuba diving to the use of diving bells, described as intervention or bounce diving, so was the advance of keeping divers under pressure for long periods so that they would

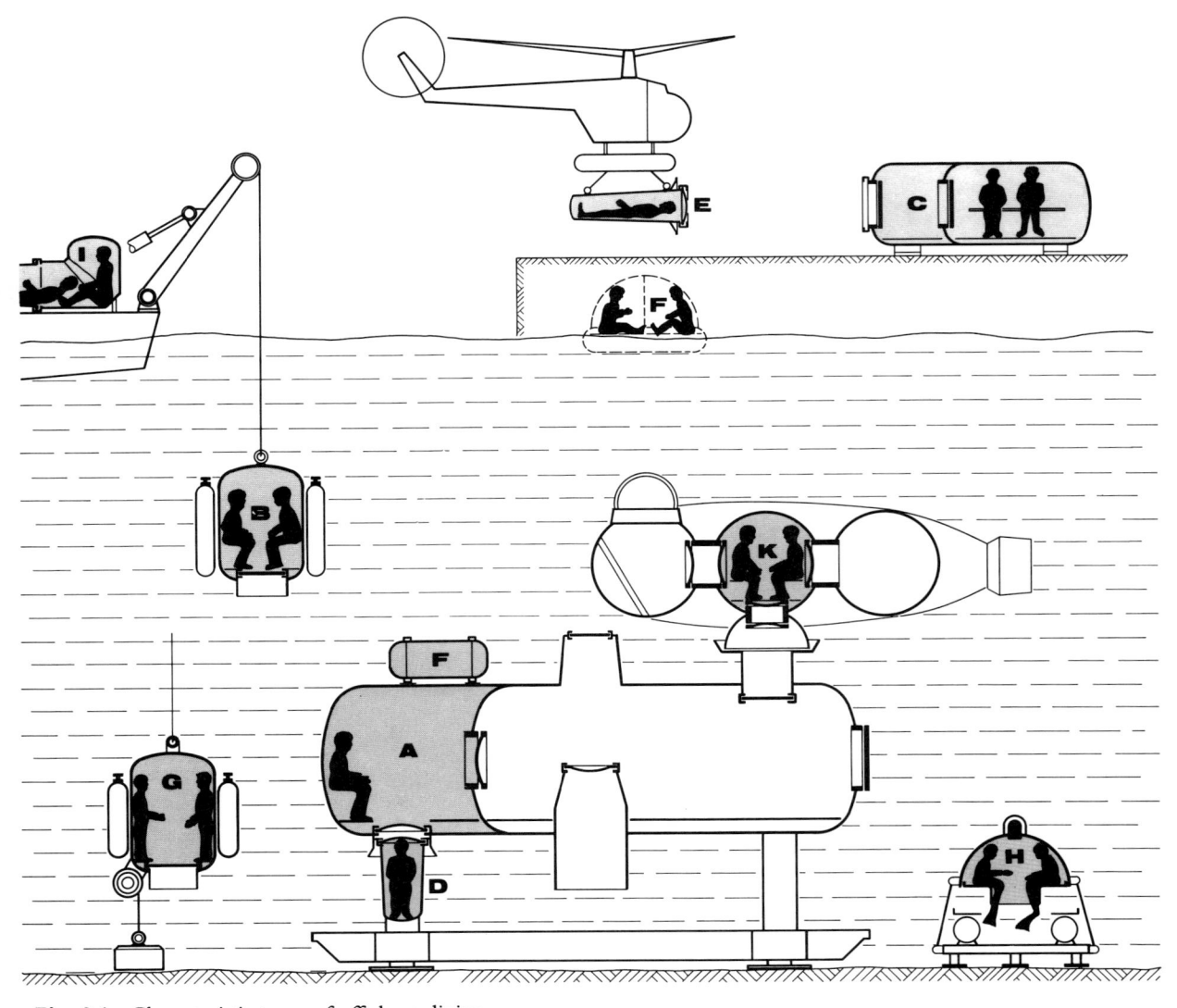

Fig. 3.1. Characteristic types of off-shore diving.

- **A**   habitat
- **B**   diving bell
- **C**   deck compression chamber
- **D**   lock-out
- **E**   air-borne transfer
- **F**   hyperbaric lifeboat
- **G**   ballasted diving bell
- **H**   habitat capsule
- **I**   transportable therapeutic chamber
- **K**   submersible transfer

not have to undergo constant pressurizing and decompressing, known as saturation diving. The technique eliminated the decompression schedule after every dive and consequently improved the efficiency of the diving operation. In other words the time actually spent on the bottom working, known as bottom time, as against decompression time, improved dramatically.

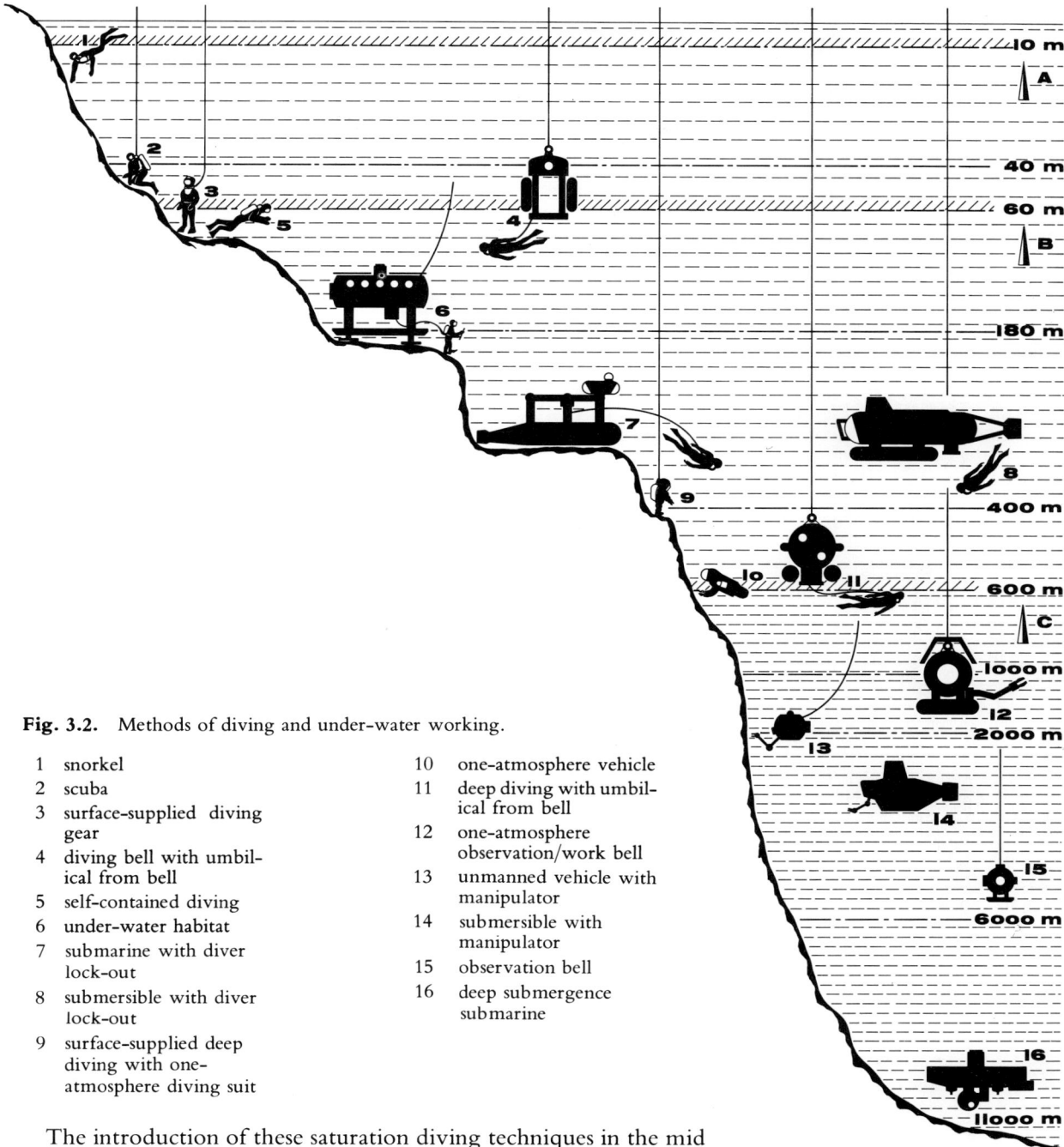

Fig. 3.2. Methods of diving and under-water working.

1. snorkel
2. scuba
3. surface-supplied diving gear
4. diving bell with umbilical from bell
5. self-contained diving
6. under-water habitat
7. submarine with diver lock-out
8. submersible with diver lock-out
9. surface-supplied deep diving with one-atmosphere diving suit
10. one-atmosphere vehicle
11. deep diving with umbilical from bell
12. one-atmosphere observation/work bell
13. unmanned vehicle with manipulator
14. submersible with manipulator
15. observation bell
16. deep submergence submarine

The introduction of these saturation diving techniques in the mid 1970s was surprisingly fast. Before the technique could be accepted for commercial use two factors had to be resolved:

1. Deep diving saturation diving schedules had to be calculated, tested and prepared for operational use.
2. Deep diving systems had to be enlarged and redesigned with additional safety factors due to the need to accommodate divers for long periods and cater for their long-term domestic needs.

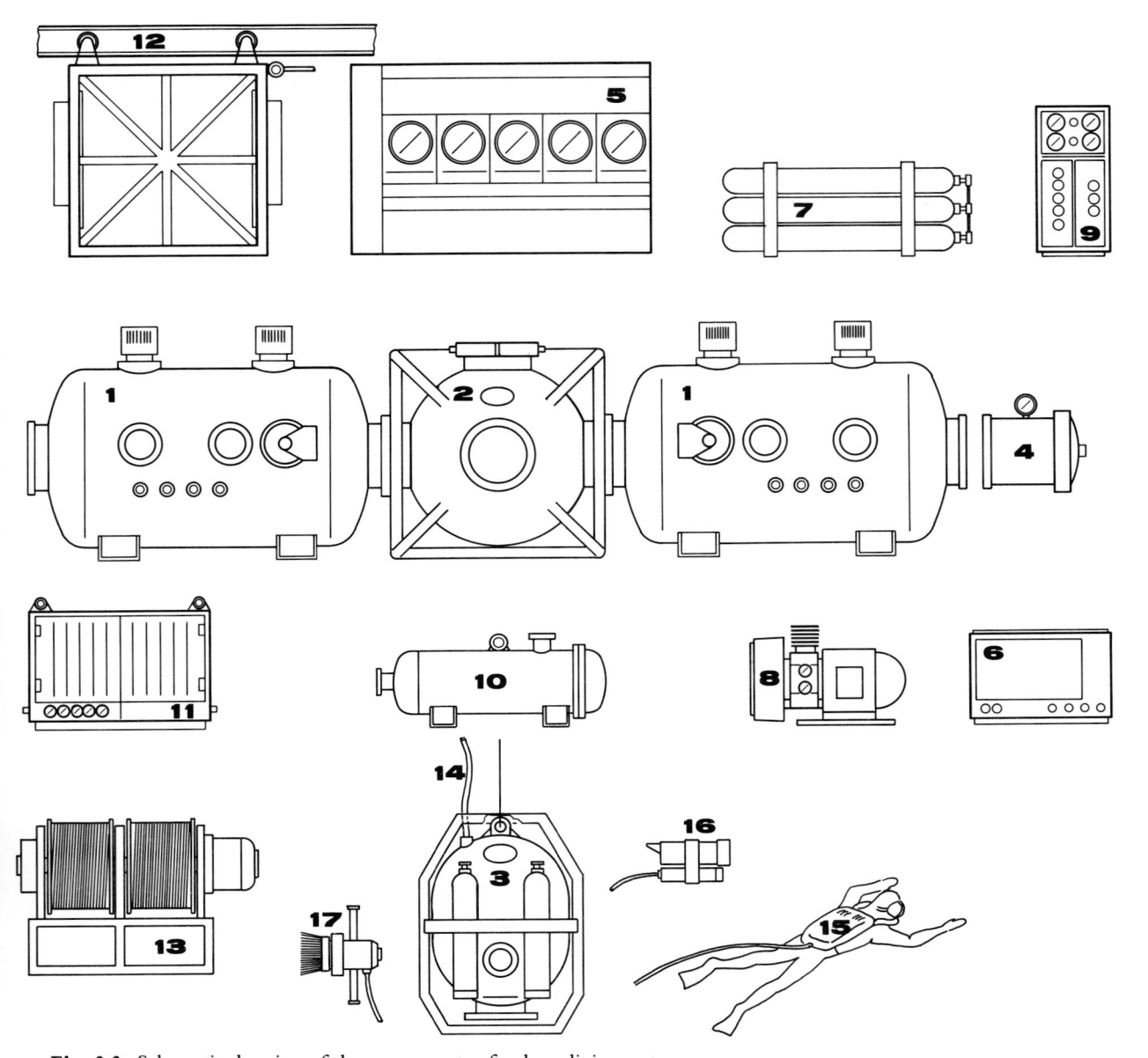

Fig. 3.3. Schematic drawing of the components of a deep diving system.

    1 deck compression chamber
    2 deck transfer lock
    3 diving chamber
    4 supply lock
    5 control panel
    6 air-conditioning unit
    7 gas storage bank
    8 compressor
    9 helium recovery
10 water supply and sewage
11 hot-water supply for divers
12 diving chamber trolley
13 winches
14 umbilical cord
15 diving gear
16 under-water television
17 under-water tools

Both these requirements were resolved and the operational techniques were introduced to meet the long work schedules under water.

The methods of modern diving are summarized in Fig. 3.2. Methods 1, 2 and 3, where divers enter the water from the surface, are not discussed. Methods 6 and 7 are discussed in detail in other chapters dealing with habitats and lock-out submersibles. Methods 4 and 11, which are discussed in this chapter, involve the function of decompression chambers, diving bells and the back-up equipment. The total package can be applied to many functions, either bounce diving or saturation; the components are listed in Fig. 3.3.

General Layout and Procedures

A safe and efficient deep diving system must be capable of working under the most adverse conditions. Therefore the many different components that make up the system must be carefully designed so that any one failure cannot stop the whole complex from continuing to function. Ideally the whole function of design, manufacture, fitting out and installation should be controlled by a single engineering team. Clearly this is rarely possible, but at least the design must carefully consider the choice of materials, the standardization of fittings and the implementation of the highest engineering standards needed for units which have to support human life.

Diving systems are designed either for permanent installation, for example in diving vessels, or for limited deployment on different craft, usually in drilling rigs and barges. In some cases the systems have been transported and assembled inland for work on dams and barrage walls. Therefore it follows that these systems must be capable of being dispersed, even interchanged with other systems and reassembled with different but standard component parts. The advantages of modular systems make them pre-eminent in efficiency and cost-effectiveness not just because of the ability to change defective units but also because the size of the complex may be expanded or contracted to meet specific operational needs. Good design will allow the smaller bounce diving system to be expanded into a larger saturation system. In Fig. 3.3 the main components of a deep diving system are shown.

The Observation Dive

The general arrangement for observation diving is shown in Fig. 3.4. Here the diving bell is being used as an observation chamber and, as part of a total system, the bell mates on the top of a deck chamber. The diving bell is used in an observation role and the inside is at normal atmospheric pressure. Technically this is referred to as a one-atmosphere system, a term used more in relation to systems designed to operate under water where occupants are not under any pressure. We see this concept utilized in the observation role with the use of submersibles and in the working role in subsea production systems. In

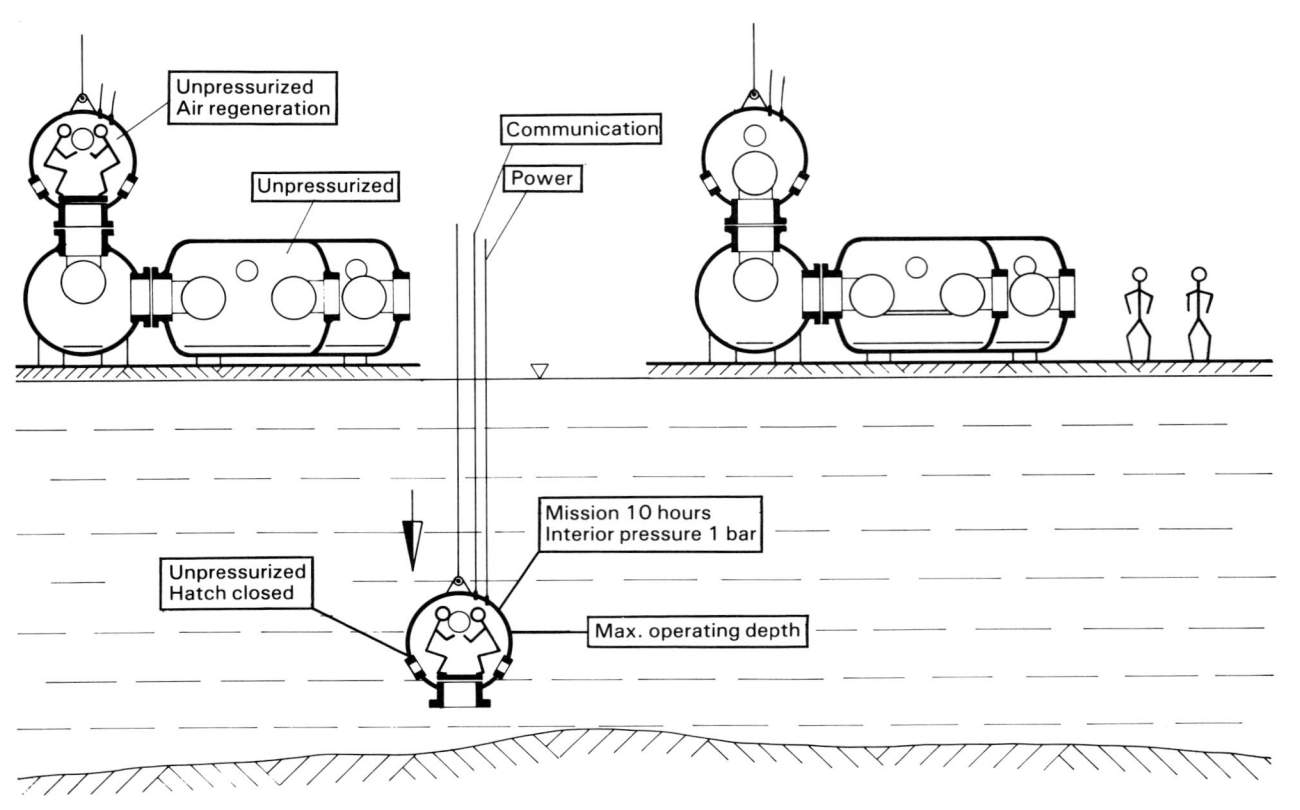

Fig. 3.4. Observation dive with diving bell.

Fig. 3.4 a diving bell is being used as an observation bell in a secondary role, but some bells are designed for observation only, being the forerunners of the modern diving bell and used for deep salvage work to identify and control the recovery of salvage. The diving bell can conveniently be used in this role and, whilst normally designed to accommodate two divers, up to four observers can fit in most bells. The maximum depth to which the bell can be lowered depends on the certified safe working pressure; if this is 50 bar the maximum depth will be 500 m. Due consideration must be given to adequate breathing arrangements, even for relatively short periods. Unless there is an umbilical cord capable of delivering fresh air, an internal self-supporting system must be considered. A circulation system through which air is passed will be needed and the carbon dioxide will be removed by absorption through soda lime or similar absorbents. The oxygen taken into the human body needs to be replaced from a source of pure oxygen. For long observation dives the measurement of oxygen and carbon dioxide content is necessary as well. With an efficient life-support system observation dives of ten hours or more are feasible, the limitations being imposed more by fatigue than by the capability of the system to provide an adequate ventilated atmosphere. With an oxygen consumption of 0.5 litre/min per person, 90 litres of oxygen are consumed by three crew members each

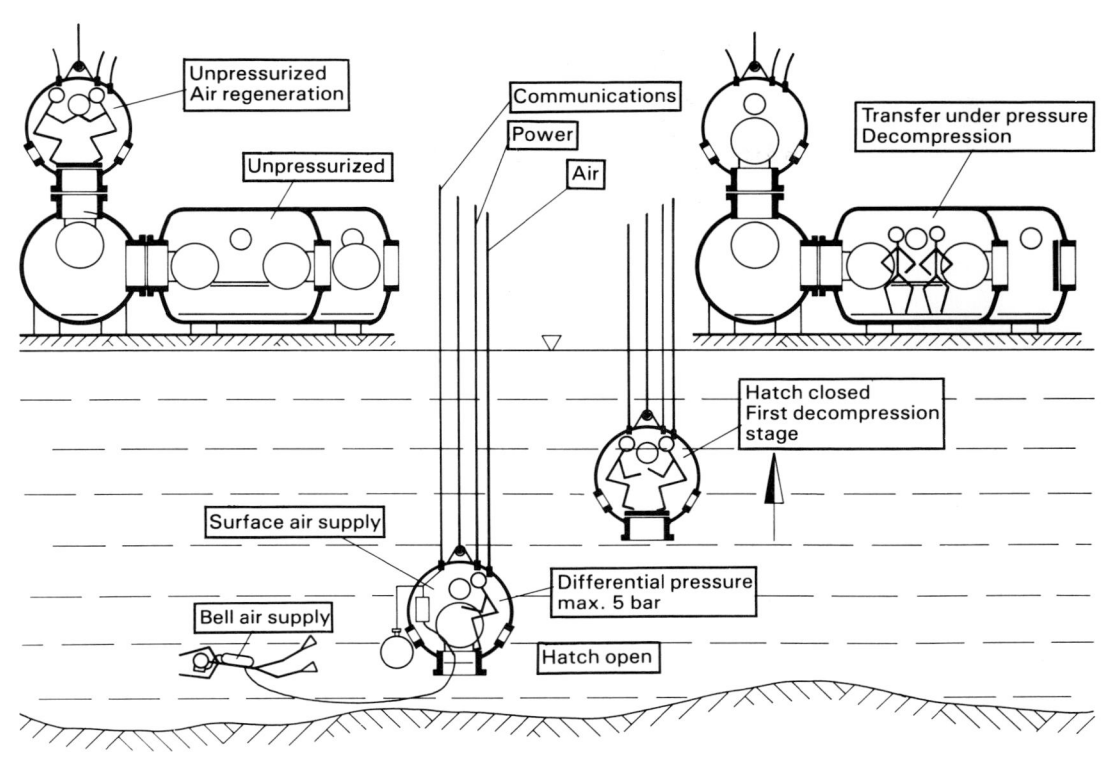

Fig. 3.5. Short duration dive to 50 m on air.

hour. To replace this 90 litres, storage capacity of only 0.45 litres at 200 bar pressure is needed. Measurement of the oxygen content will avoid an unnecessary build-up of oxygen, leading to a fire hazard, and extra care must be taken to avoid any naked lights near the bell after the observers have been evacuated. The observation bell must have good communication to the surface, a power supply for heat and lighting and a good range of observation windows fitted around the chamber.

A modern development of the observation chamber is to fit the unit with propulsion motors. These will give limited movement and, depending on the depth of the dive, can move the chamber over a radius of 20–30 m.

Short Duration Dive on Air (Fig. 3.5)

Under certain conditions a deep diving system can be used efficiently in depths to 50 m, or deeper in some areas, with air as the breathing gas. If a diving system is being used at deeper depths, where mixed gases are required, but there are under-water tasks to be performed at shallow depths where air can be breathed safely, it is economical and safer to use the diving bell. It is safer because the divers can work from the security of a diving bell. There is a greater exposure to risk when diving from the surface, using either scuba or surface-oriented diving directly, owing to surface conditions and the effects of surge and currents at the shallower depths. These exposures are reflected in shallow-water diving accidents and therefore the bell, if available, is more effective and safer.

For shallow-water bell dives there can be up to two divers and one tender in the chamber supervising the dive. The bell is submerged to the required depth at normal internal atmospheric pressure, using a procedure identical to an observation dive. When the divers are ready the inside pressure is increased to equal the external pressure using compressed air either from the surface through an umbilical cord or from the bell's own storage capacity. The bottom door, unlatched, will open when the internal pressure equalizes with the ambient pressure outside and the air supply is then closed. The chamber is ventilated by flushing through with fresh air, usually under the control of the occupants who open and close the air supply valve, but it can be controlled from the surface using a pressure-controlled air supply regulator. The chamber occupants, divers and tenders, can freely breathe the chamber air; for diving the divers may use scuba equipment but an umbilical cord to the diver, supplying air from the bell, is preferred. The umbilical supply is safer not only because it provides the necessary endurance for long diving exposures in the water but because the tender has more control over the position and condition of the diver. In the event of the umbilical cord being severed, the mandatory bale-out bottle carried by the diver will allow him sufficient air to return to the bell. The bale-out bottle is a breathing cylinder which can be turned on in an emergency by the diver and is usually carried on his back. For long exposures air is supplied from air banks installed around the bell but can also be supplied from the surface. At a depth of 50 m as much as 16 000 litres of compressed air are needed for 60 min diving by one diver but there is no problem in carrying 80 000 litres of compressed air on the outside of an average-sized bell.

On completion of the task the final sequence is for the diver and his equipment to be recovered inside the bell and the bell raised, with the bottom door open, to the depth of the first stop, thereby conveniently evacuating a large portion of the chamber gas with a corresponding reduction of pressure. The bottom door is closed and the bell is hoisted out of the water and mated to the main chamber with a pressure-tight connection. The decompression chamber and the diving bell are equalized for pressure and the divers transferred to the decompression chamber to complete their decompression in comfort.

Short-duration Dives Using Mixed Gases (Fig. 3.6)

Referred to as bounce or intervention diving, these dives are in excess of the acceptable limits of air diving and some national regulations make the use of deep diving systems mandatory below 50 m, although other national agencies do not impose any restrictions until depths of up to 90 m are reached. The physiological limit of air diving is 100 m but the rapid onset of nitrogen narcosis below 50 m requires a

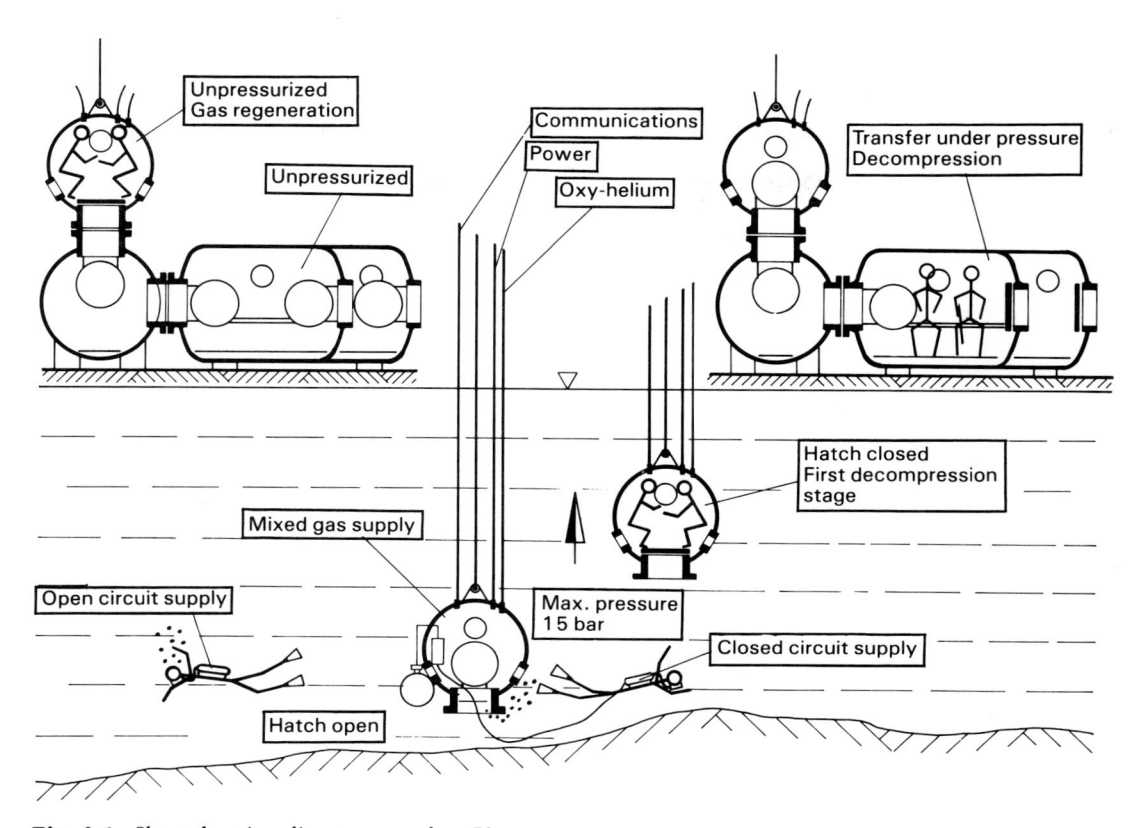

Fig. 3.6. Short duration dive to more than 50 m.

reduction in the nitrogen content in air using helium as a substitute or the total elimination of nitrogen. There are many variations in the proportional make-up of nitrogen, helium and oxygen (Trimix) and helium and oxygen (Heliox) depending on depth and the way in which the diving schedule has been calculated. The use of the much less expensive hydrogen as the inert gas has been found to have no practical application so far owing to storage problems and explosion hazards.

The different breathing mixtures can be used in any of the breathing systems currently in use and do not require any modification. The simplest type of breathing system is known as open circuit and used universally in air diving. Whether scuba equipment or umbilical supply is used, the exhaled air is exhausted naturally into the water. The reduction from high pressure to low pressure and finally to breathing gas is simple and dependable. Gas consumption is very high and, whilst perfectly reasonable in air breathing, open-circuit systems should be avoided, whenever possible, with mixed helium gases owing to the immense cost and the logistics of storing large volumes of breathing mixture.

Diving below 50 m in diving bells still uses open-circuit breathing systems despite the high consumption and cost but semi-closed- and closed-circuit breathing systems are also now in use off-shore. The higher cost of the equipment and the skilled maintenance needed for the integrated breathing systems are offset by the reduction in helium consumption. Furthermore, in diving systems in lock-out submersibles, open-circuit breathing systems are difficult to use because of the limited space for carrying breathing gases in the vehicles.

The diving sequence is similar to air diving except that the chamber is pressurized at the diving depth with the correct breathing mixture for that depth, allowing the occupants to breathe without special apparatus. The pressurization is rapid and the diver enters the water as soon as the bottom door opens when the internal and water ambient pressures are equal, thereby keeping the time on the bottom as short as possible. Even small reductions in bottom time will have an effect on the length of decompression. The bell is pressurized from the surface through an umbilical cord and the diver is supplied through his own umbilical either from the surface or, more usually, from the storage cylinders installed around the diving bell. The diver will have a line communication to the bell and to the tender, who will in turn have a communication with the surface supervisors.

A hot-water system or an alternative electrical heating system may be required below 50 m, depending on the water temperature, and this additional service hose will need to be combined with the breathing line and communication. The tender inside the bell, who is ready to enter the water as the standby diver to assist the diver in an emergency, continues to breathe the gas in the bell, which must be monitored for oxygen and carbon dioxide partial pressures. Emergency breathing masks are available should the gas become unsafe to breathe. The diving depths for this type of diving, bounce diving, is normally restricted to 150 m. Even for short bottom time in depths below 150 m saturation procedures become inevitable. In bounce diving, as soon as the diver has completed his work and entered the chamber, the door is closed and decompression to the first stage begins. Different mixtures may be used at various stages of the decompression, with the final stages on high-oxygen-content mixtures and pure oxygen. The diving bell is hoisted and mated to the deck compression chambers where the divers transfer to complete their decompression.

If the system has been designed to be flexible the procedures can be varied and used with a variety of breathing gases. If sufficient gas is not available or stored on the bell, the unit can be partially or completely pressurized before leaving the surface. In addition to the main gas supplies an adequate amount of emergency breathing gas must be available on the bell.

Saturation Diving

Long duration dives in depths down to 150 m or any dives to deeper depths require the use of saturation diving procedures (Fig. 3.7). At these pressures the saturation of the tissues of the human body with inert gas requires long decompressions lasting days and therefore it becomes economical to keep divers in a state of limbo at a holding saturation pressure for weeks at a time. This holding pressure, less

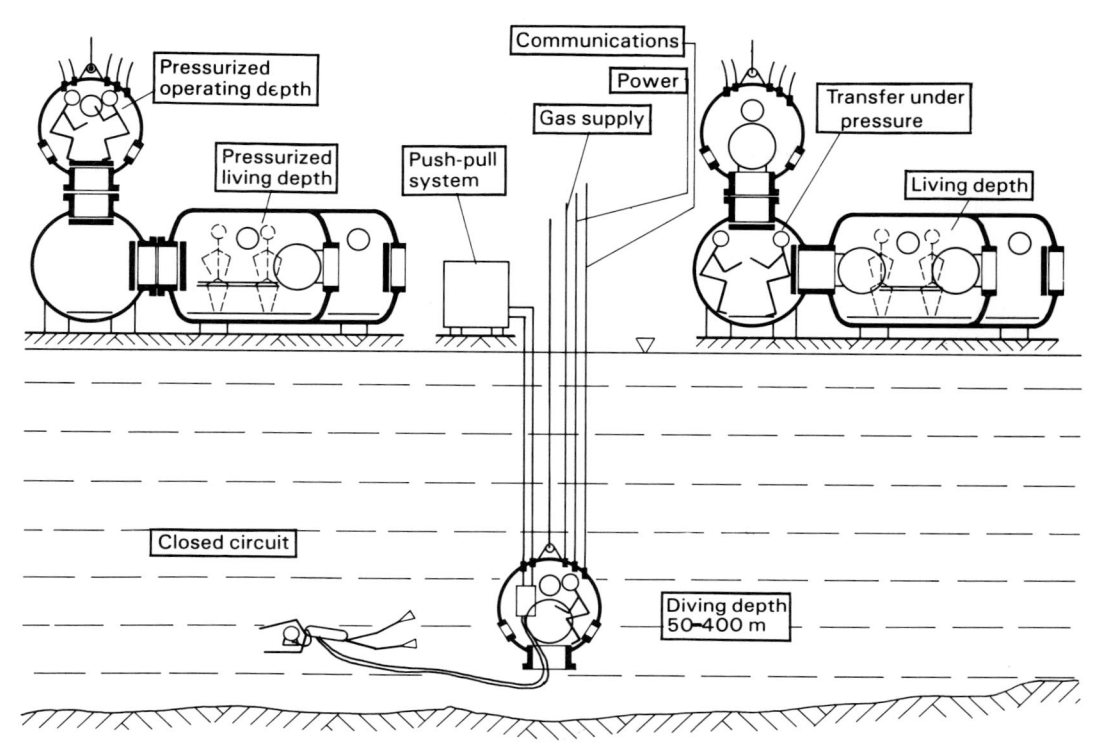

Fig. 3.7. Saturation diving with 'large closed circuit'.

than the diving depth, is maintained inside the surface compression chambers and the diving bell transports the divers to the required depth in the usual manner. Although open-circuit or semi-closed-circuit breathing systems can be used by the diver, the closed-circuit system is used to greater advantage.

The divers under saturation in the surface chamber are briefed for their work and transfer to the diving bell breathing the same chamber gas. The operating procedures are similar to bounce diving. The pressure in the bell is increased to the bottom depth and the bottom door is opened on pressure equalization. In the closed-circuit breathing system the diver connects the umbilical to the circulation line and enters the water. The life-support breathing system is circulated through a compressor and filter system and these are described in Chapter 10. The recovery procedure is also the same as in bounce diving with the diver being recovered, the bottom door closed, the bell hoisted and mated to the surface chamber and pressure reduced to the saturation level. The divers returning to the living chambers can be replaced by other divers also in saturation and a pattern of shift work can be introduced. On completion of the work all the divers can be decompressed or, if the work continues, teams of divers can be rotated into and out of saturation.

Design Criteria

Before a system is designed the operational requirements of that system need to be clearly defined. It is not necessarily cost-effective to design a system to undertake the most exhaustive diving missions if operations are only required for back-up or for an observation role in the exploration phase. These criteria may be defined as follows:

General
    Maximum work depth
    Maximum observation depth
    Diving procedures (bounce/saturation)
    Diving crew under pressure
    Certification by classification societies
    Electrical supplies

Diving bell (SCC; submersible compression chamber)
    Type of transfer lock (top, side, rollover or from below)
    Shape of diving bell (cylinder, oval, sphere or conic frustum)
    Hatches: locking system, number and diameter
    Windows: type, number, size and location
    Type of insulation
    Design of ballast weights (single, segments, pellets)
    Design of gas supply system
    Communication systems (telephone, loudspeaker, television, wireless)
    Type of life-support system
    Design of umbilicals for diving bell and divers
    Heating

Transfer chamber
    Shape and dimensions of transfer chamber (horizontal or vertical cylinder, sphere)
    Number of doors and connections for DCCs
    Number, size and location of supply locks
    Windows: type, number, size, location
    Insulation
    Lighting system (internal or external)
    Communication systems (telephone, loudspeaker, television)
    Monitoring units for chamber atmosphere, such as P_{O_2}, P_{CO_2}, CO and others
    Gas control panel
    Life-support system
    General furniture: berths, lockers etc.

Deck compression chamber
    Shape and dimension of compression chamber (horizontal or vertical cylinder, sphere)
    Design with or without sanitary lock
    Windows: type, number, size and location

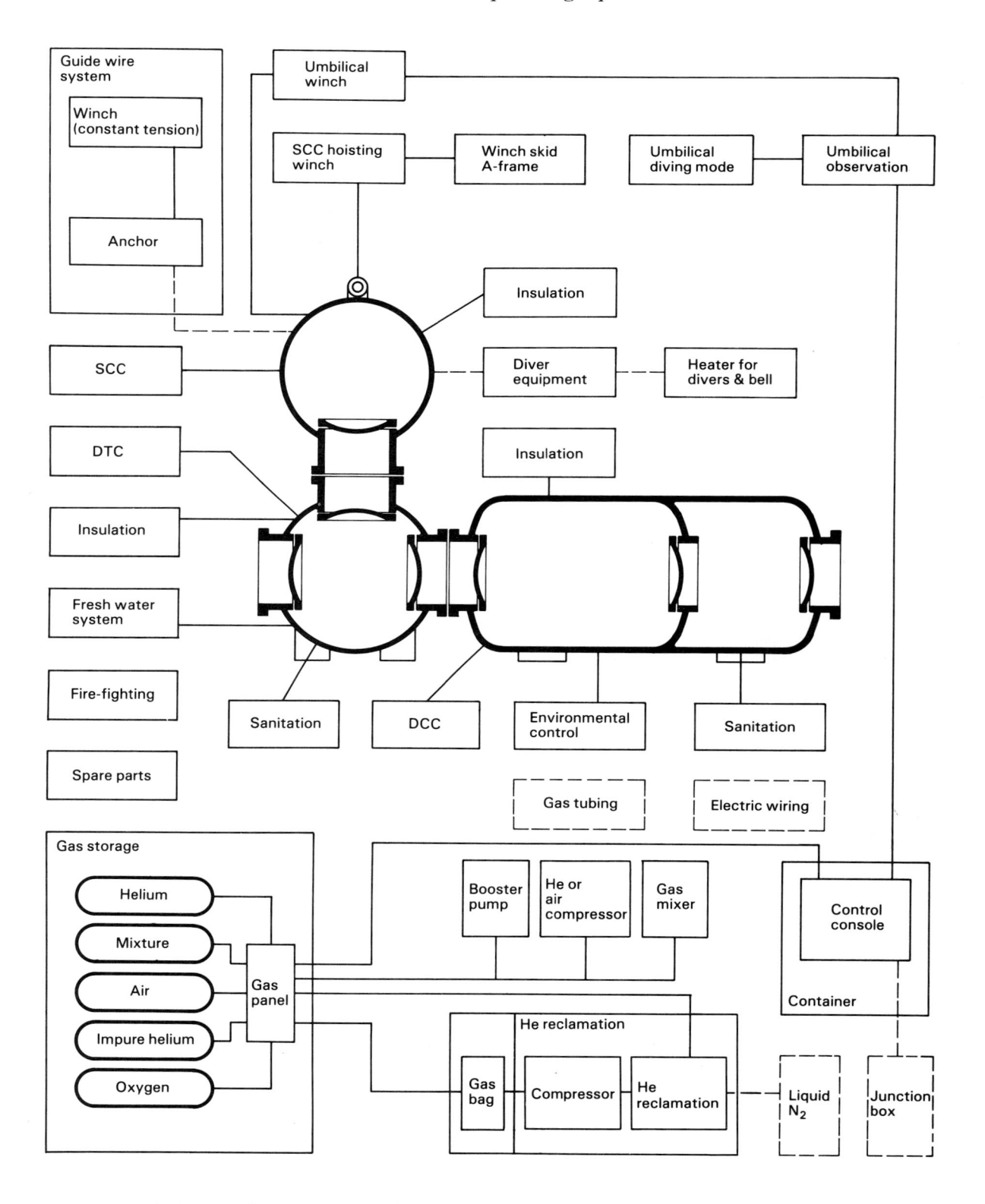

Fig. 3.8. Block diagram of the components of a deep diving system.

- Lighting system (internal or external)
- Communication systems (telephone, loudspeaker)
- Monitoring units for chamber atmosphere such as P_{O_2}, P_{CO_2}, CO and others
- Gas control panel
- Life-support system
- General furniture: berths, benches etc.
- Outfit of sanitary lock: WC, shower
- Supply lock
- Sprinkler system

Rescue chamber for abandon-ship procedure
- Additional equipment such as a hyperbaric lifeboat

Control panel
- Type of installation (container, ship compartment)
- Instrumentation
- Explosion protection

The size, volume and weight of the basic chamber construction will additionally determine the design criteria for the following:

- Handling system
- Gas storage
- Gas regeneration
- Heating systems
- Compressor systems
- Domestic services

The modern system becomes very complex and this chapter will examine the criteria and the different options that need further consideration.

Deck Compression Chamber Configurations

The factors that affect the shape and position of the various chambers used for compression and decompression are as follows:

1. Type of diving operation (bounce/saturation).
2. Number of divers under pressure.
3. The type of vessel, rig or barge.

The diving depth does not affect the configuration. The type of diving and the number of divers do, however, and whilst a system on board a drilling rig may have two or three separate compression chambers, a diving vessel employed on maintenance, repair or construction work may need to have as many as 24 divers under pressure at different pressure levels, covering compression, working, resting and decompression. Ideally the chamber configuration should be designed at the same time as the vessel. The majority of diving

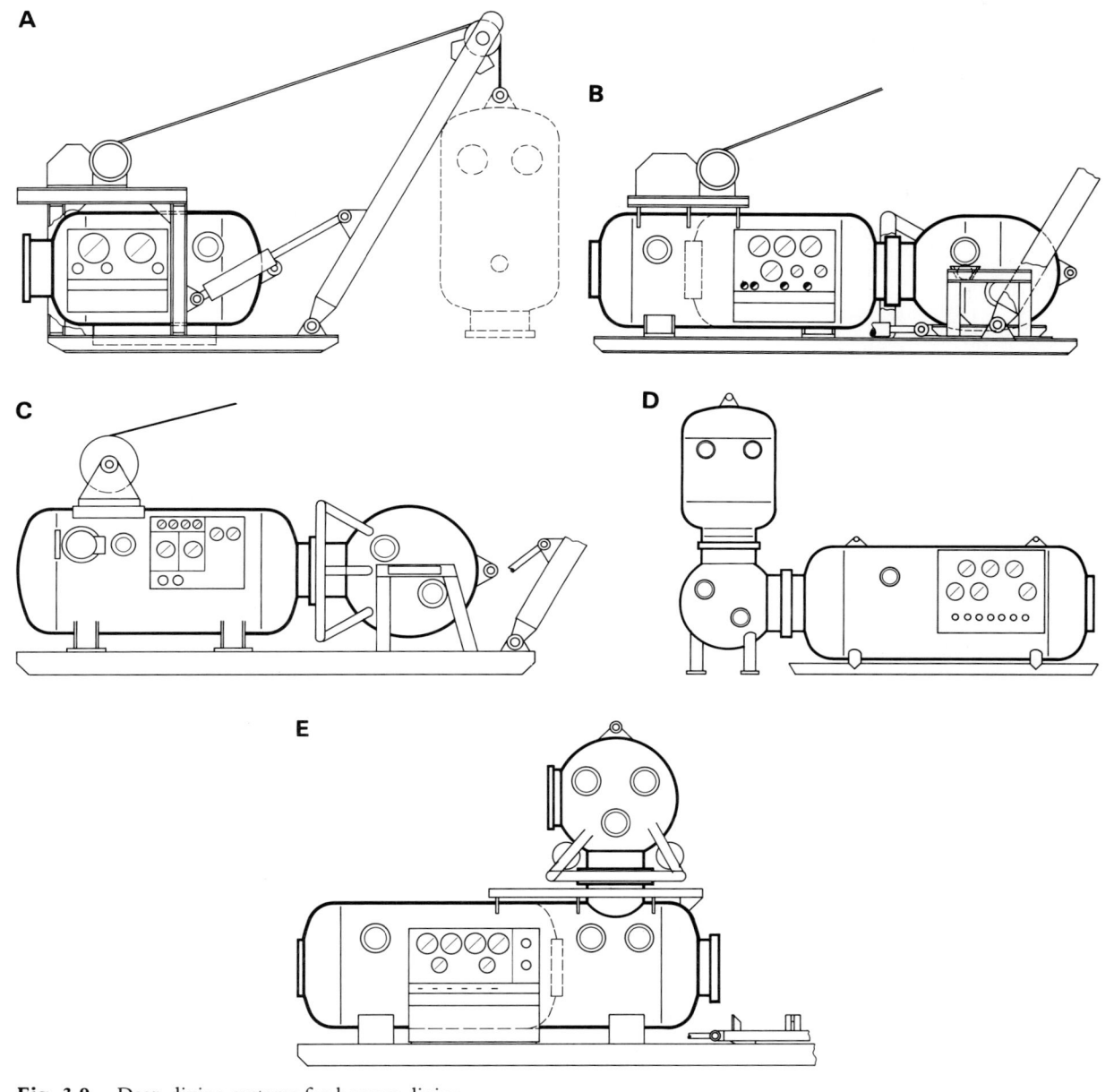

Fig. 3.9. Deep diving systems for bounce diving.

- **A** Dräger Subcom system for 200 m. DCC and SCC 1500 mm diameter. Rollover system. Two or three divers
- **B** Haux system for 100 m. DCC 1500 mm diameter, double lock. SCC 1500 mm diameter. Rollover system. Two divers
- **C** Perry deep diving system for 206 m. DCC 1500 mm diameter, double lock. SCC 1680 mm diameter. Two divers
- **D** Perry deep diving system for 122 m. DCC 1500 mm diameter, double lock. SCC top mating or rollover. Two divers
- **E** Dräger deep diving system for 200 m. DCC 2200 mm diameter, double lock. SCC 1900 mm diameter. Top or side transfer. Three divers

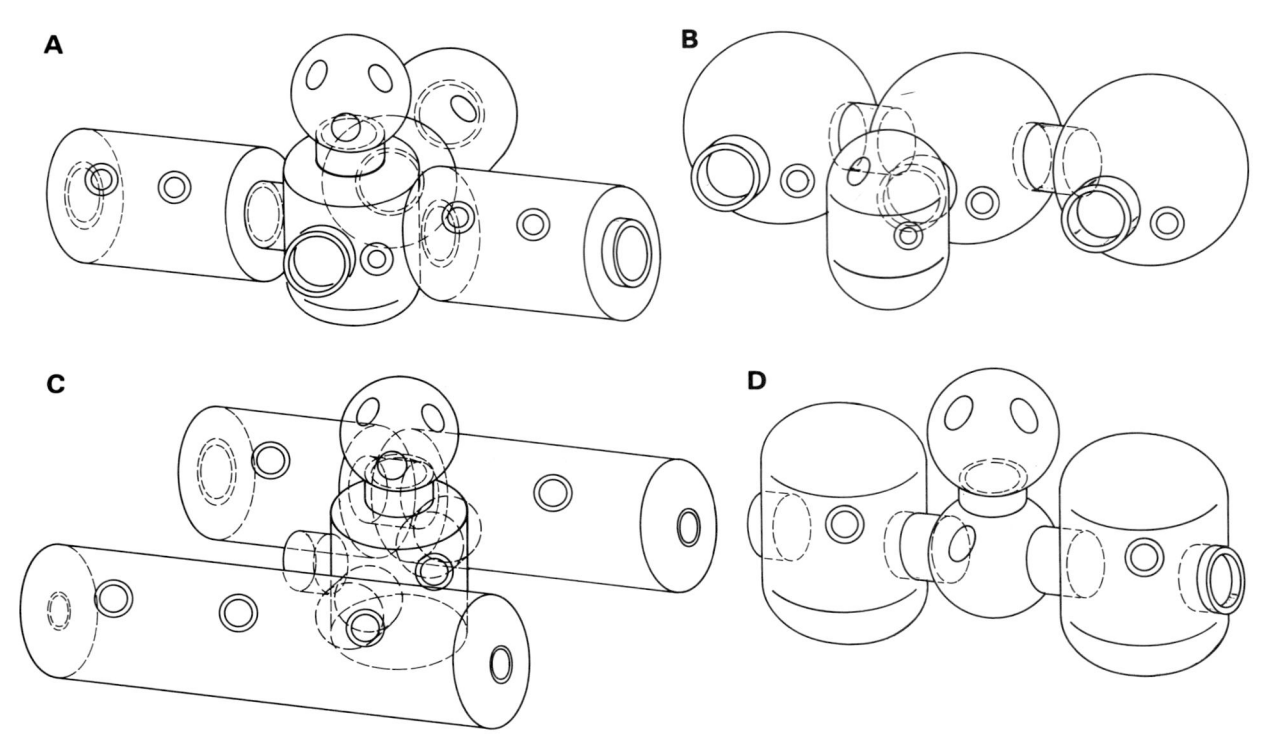

Fig. 3.10. Large deep diving systems for saturation diving.

- **A** Dräger module for 500 m. DCC 2200 mm diameter. DTC 2200 mm diameter. SCC 1900 mm diameter. Top or side transfer. Nine divers
- **B** Ray McDermott. Side transfer. Nine divers
- **C** Dräger system on the *Artic Surveyor* for 500 m. DCC 2200 mm diameter. SCC 1900 mm diameter. Top transfer. Twelve divers
- **D** Solus Ocean Systems International system for 500 m. Top transfer. Six divers. Can be enlarged in a modular manner

systems have had to be incorporated into an existing ship which has not been designed for diving. Even major conversions to fit a diving moonpool have tended to inhibit the layout of the diving system. However, special-purpose ships are now being built for diving where every possible advantage can be taken to design the ship to meet the diving requirements.

In Fig. 3.9 are chamber configurations for deep diving systems using bounce or intervention diving. Simplicity, compactness, minimum weight and relative ease of dismantling for mobilization on another rig are the main features. Systems A, B and C are mounted on skids with an integrated handling system. These systems are designed for rapid mobilization and some are even transportable by air. The installations shown in B and C are designed with side transfer with the diving bell in C designed so as to roll over into a position to allow transfer under pressure.

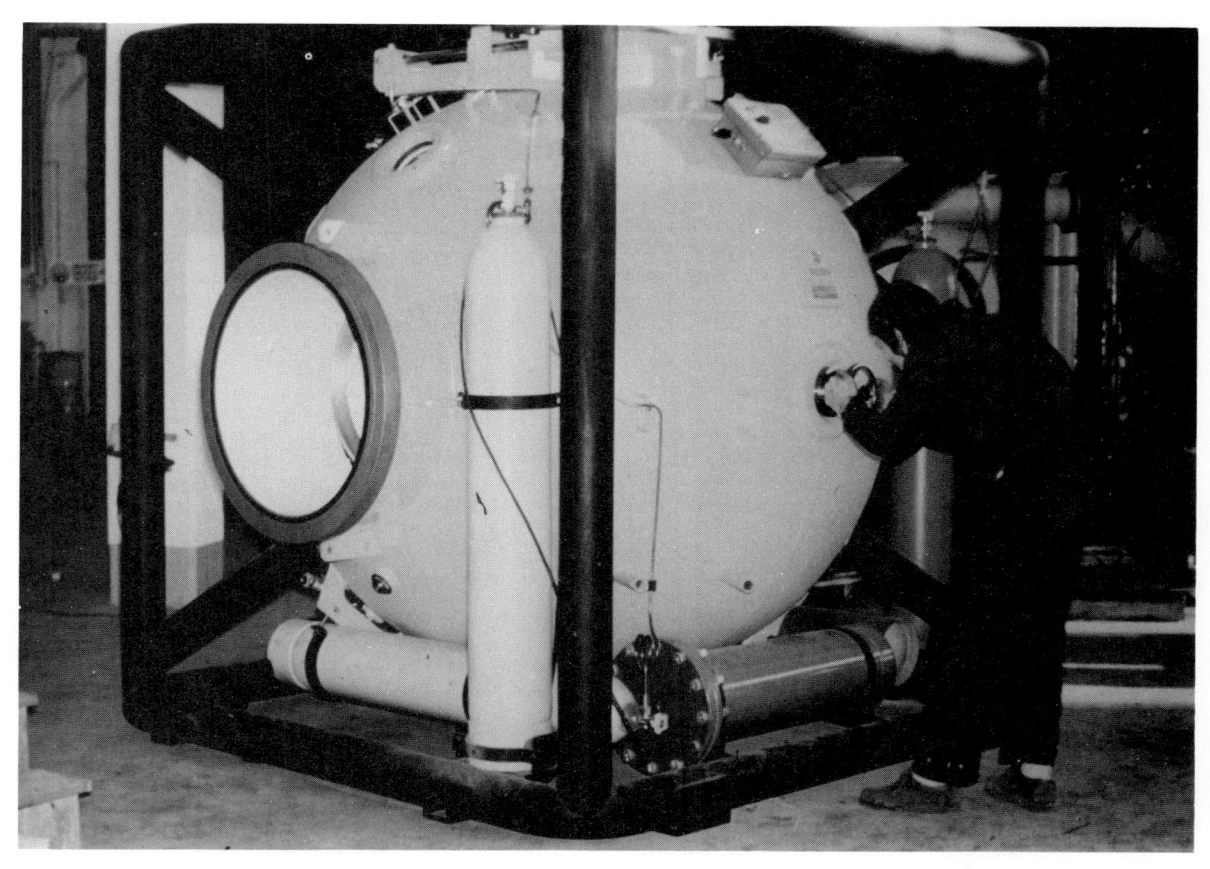

Fig. 3.11. Central transfer chamber of a modular deep diving system (turning 90°) (Dräger).

Fig. 3.10 gives a classification of some of the configurations used in saturation diving complexes. The variations in design layout are considerable and diving contractors and system designers have differing ideas. There are no hard-and-fast rules for system layouts. The layout in A is the most commonly used where one, two or three living chambers are grouped logically around a transfer chamber. The transfer chamber can be designed 90° over to one side, allowing a side transfer as shown in Fig. 3.11. One of the largest and most successful off-shore diving systems installed in the diving vessel *Arctic Surveyor* was built to the design in C. Designed with a top transfer, the main living chamber has eight bunks and there are a further four bunks in the other chamber. In addition there is a rescue chamber designed to be separated if a ship emergency necessitates the evacuation of the divers. The layout shown in D is based mainly on vertical chambers whilst A and C are essentially horizontal chamber configurations. Horizontal designs are economical for space and are assembled on construction barges where the diving area is restricted. There are problems to be overcome in the installation of bunks in horizontal chambers. In B the use of spheres gives maximum

SL

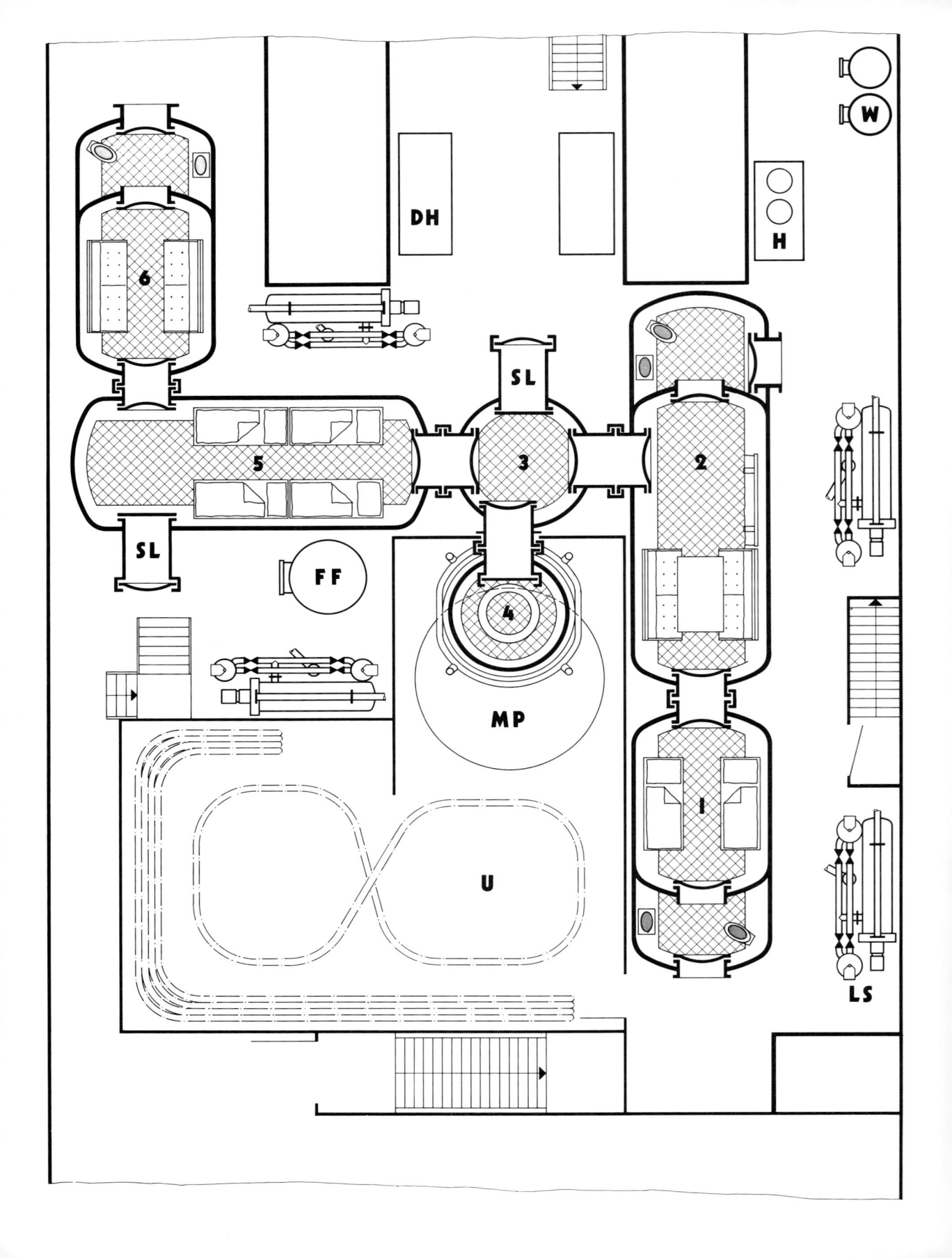

DH

W

H

6

SL

3

2

FF

SL

4

MP

1

U

LS

economy of space and the shape also allows for higher pressures if required. The American company Dick Evans Inc. was probably the first company to use the spherical layout.

The arrangement of the system in the diving vessel *Arctic Seal* is shown in Fig. 3.12, with the four independent living chambers set around the transfer chamber. Three of the living units have a separate sanitary compartment fitted with a WC, shower and sink and all four units can be operated separately, allowing teams to work in shifts over a period of 24 hours.

Component Parts of a Diving System

Many separate units with different functions need to be considered before they are integrated into a complete system. They can be listed as follows:

1. Deck compression and rescue chambers (DCC).
2. Transfer chambers (DTC).
3. Submersible compression chambers (SCC).
4. Large supply locks.
5. Control centre.
6. Life-support systems.
7. Gas storage for helium, oxygen, mixed gases etc.
8. Compressor units.
9. Helium regeneration systems.
10. Water and compressed air supplies.
11. Hot-water systems.
12. Handling systems for SCC and rescue chamber.
13. Winch units for SCC, umbilical, anchor and guide wires.
14. Umbilical.
15. Diving gear.
16. Communications including television.
17. Under-water tools.

Fig. 3.12. Configuration of the saturation diving system on the *Arctic Seal* (Odd Berg, Tromso).

1	DCC 1 (40 bar)	
2	DCC 2 (40 bar)	
3	DCC 3 (40 bar)	
4	diving bell (50 bar)	
5	DCC 4 (40 bar)	
6	rescue chamber (40 bar)	
DH	warm-water generator for diving suit heating	
W	hot-water system and cold supply for compression chambers	
LS	life-support systems	
U	umbilical	
MP	moonpool	
FF	water tank for fire-fighting system	
SL	supply lock	
H	heat-exchanger for life-support system	

Fig. 3.13. Transfer chamber, compression chamber and rescue chamber on the diving vessel *Talisman* (Comex).

No one component unit is any less important than another. A defective unit in the system, unless replaced or designed with a secondary back-up system, will usually render the whole system inoperable. Some of these component parts of the system merit further discussion.

Submersible Compression Chamber (SCC)

The SCCs which are used for deep saturation diving work vary in some respect from those used for shallow work. They are discussed in detail in Chapter 4. The options are to have the transfer under pressure (TUP) sited at the top of the transfer chamber or to have a side transfer. To give more flexibility to the system a transfer chamber can be designed with both a top and side transfer mating flange. Wherever possible side transfers are currently more favoured and the design must allow for either two openings (a bottom door to exit into the water and a side door to mate with the DTC) or a rollover operation. In the rollover operation the SCC is turned 90° on its side and the bottom door is mated to the transfer chamber, so that only one door is needed. In Fig. 3.14 a side transfer is shown. Consideration needs to be given to the type of locking flange used. In this case a bayonet locking ring is used because there is a good centering arrangement which does not put an unequal strain on the DCC flange. The horizontal trolley system is very precise and the three-point alignment can be adjusted for exact positioning. Bolts or hinged bolts and divided U-shaped ring segments are other TUP locking designs in current use.

Fig. 3.14. Deep diving system with side transfer on a drilling rig.

Some earlier SCCs were built with two internal compartments sited vertically one on top of the other. The upper internal compartment, most usually at normal one-atmosphere pressure but possibly at an intermediate pressure, was a control room. The supervisor monitored the dive from this compartment and effectively controlled the gas supplies. The lower compartment, from which the divers entered the water, was under pressure and the system had clear advantages with regard to controlled safety procedures. However, there were greater disadvantages in that, apart from the additional cost, the chambers were heavy and cumbersome, demanding large handling systems and hoist arrangements.

Except in ideal conditions where there are minimal weather factors affecting the sea and negligible currents, guidance wires are used to control and direct the movement of the bell. The most effective guidance system will have two wires secured to a constant mass anchor on the seabed. Although single wires are used, careful seamanship is needed to keep the umbilical hoist wire clear of the guideline. A single wire attached to an anchor is often used to traverse the bell away from the plumb position below the point of hoisting. Known as keel-hauling the bell, it is not considered to be a safe method for diving operations in many situations. Constant-tension devices are very often fitted to the guide wires to reduce or eliminate, depending on the efficiency of the compensator, the movement or surge in the lines caused by the vertical movement of the ship or platform.

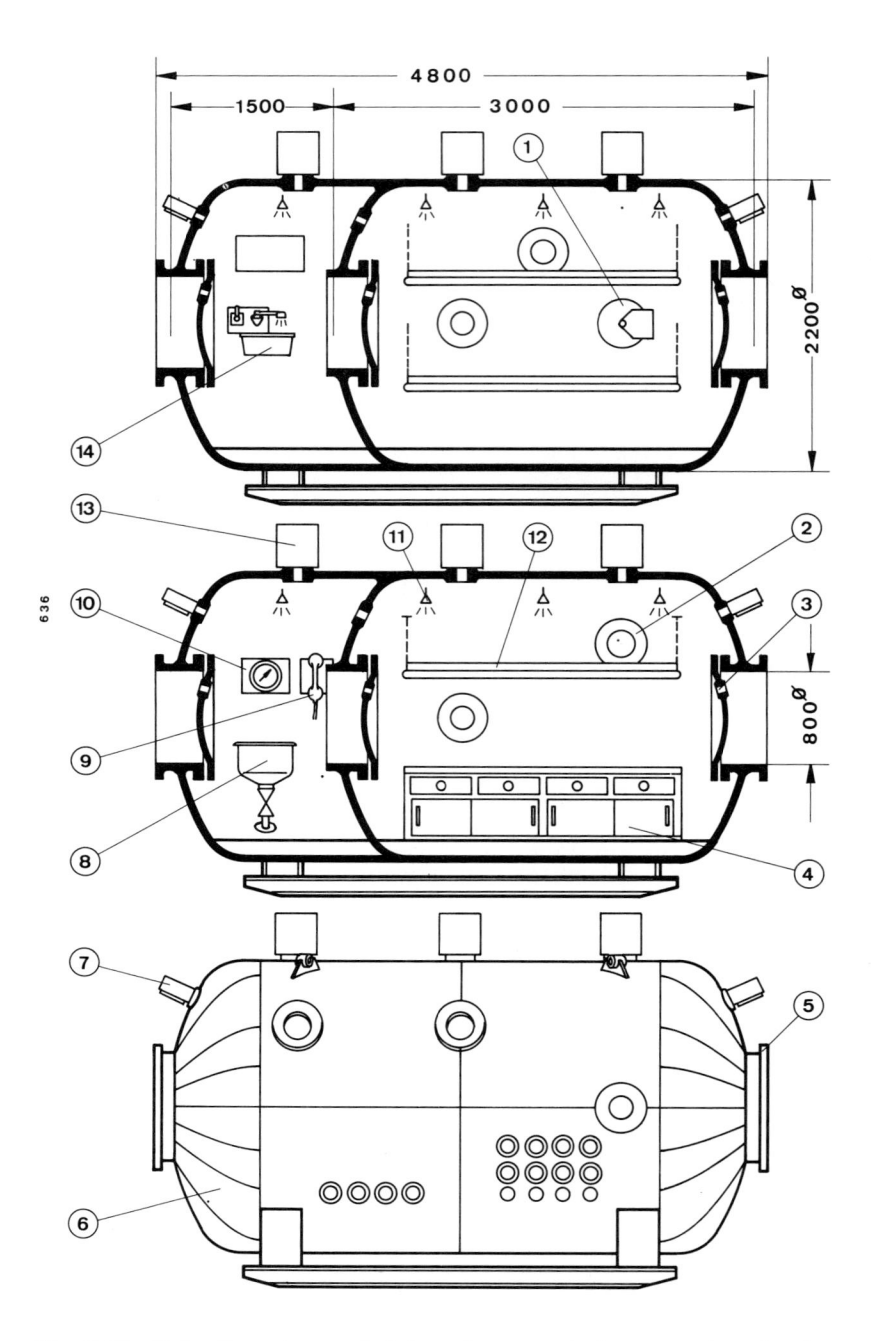

Fig. 3.15. Main dimensions and fittings for a standard compression chamber designed for deep diving systems.

1 supply lock
2 large window
3 small window
4 locker with bed
5 mating flange
6 insulation with cover
7 TV camera
8 WC
9 hand shower
10 gauge for internal pressure
11 sprinkler
12 hinged bed
13 fibreoptic light
14 hand basin

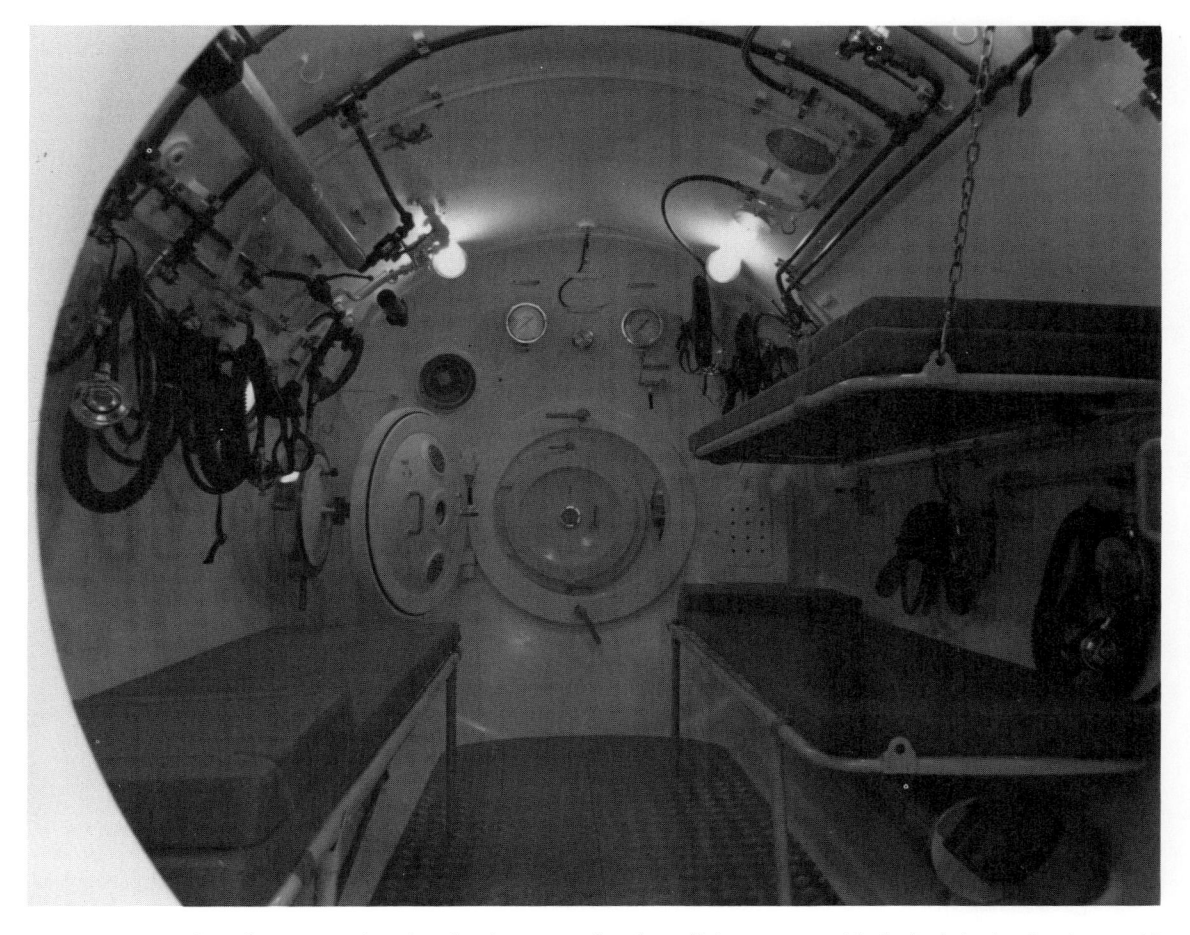

Fig. 3.16. Interior of a compression chamber in a saturation deep diving system with the beds in the sleeping position.

Deck Compression Chamber (DCC)

In Chapter 2 the DCCs are discussed in more detail. Some additional and important features need to be considered in DCCs used as part of a deep diving complex. If the chambers are horizontal they should be not less than 2200 mm in diameter to allow the occupants to stand up, particularly important in saturation diving. A minimum overall length of 3000 mm between the dished ends is required, adequate for full-length bunks to accommodate three to four occupants. At least a further 2000 mm in length is needed for additional berths. In Fig. 3.15 is shown the smallest unit which can be used for deep diving. Experience has shown that the sanitary arrangements and washing should be separate, for health reasons, from the living space. A hand basin, disposable or fixed shower and water closet are essential for long-duration dives. Safety valves must be fitted to the flushing system of the water closet and carefully positioned so that rapid evacuation of pressure through the system cannot take place whilst

Fig. 3.17. Large supply lock of the compression chamber in a deep diving system.

the system is being used. The separate sanitary compartment can be depressurized and disinfected as required. Fig. 3.18 shows a complete sanitary compartment and Fig. 3.19 a suitable layout.

Other aspects of chamber design and the fitting out of the chambers are covered in other chapters and Chapter 10 separately covers life-support systems.

Deck Transfer Chamber (DTC)

The transfer chamber is the central modular unit of any deep diving system, capable of operating to saturation levels. In smaller systems the transfer chamber can be a compartment within a main DCC as shown in Fig. 3.9E. In larger systems it must connect the diving bell to various deck chambers and is the focal point of the system. The transfer chamber also is used for maintaining the diving equipment, tools and accessories and to provide a place where divers can remove or put on their diving suits and carry out any number of tasks in preparation for and on completion of a dive. The size of the DTCs varies considerably, from the small sphere shown in Fig. 3.9D to large vertical cylinders greater in volume than the SCC shown in Fig. 3.21.

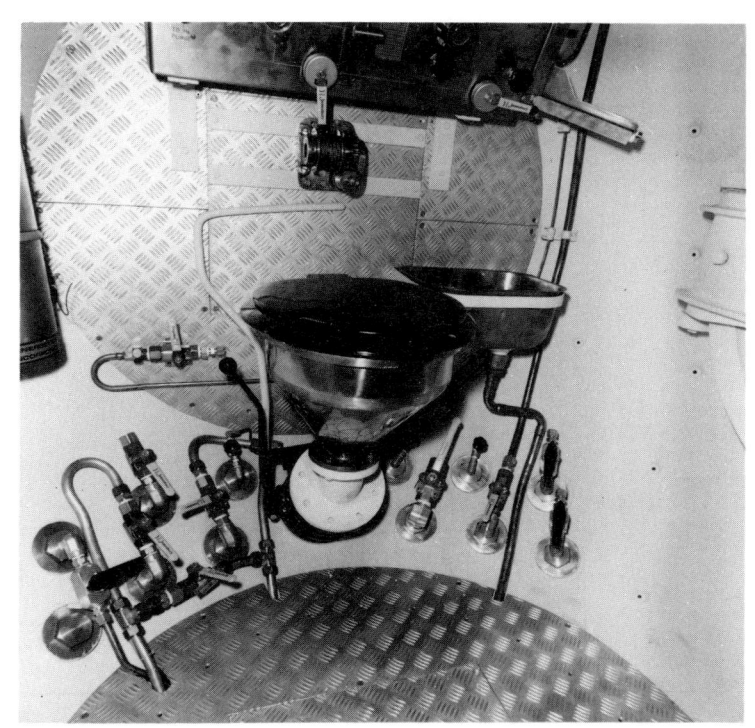

Fig. 3.18. Washing facilities in a side chamber with WC, hand basin and hand shower.

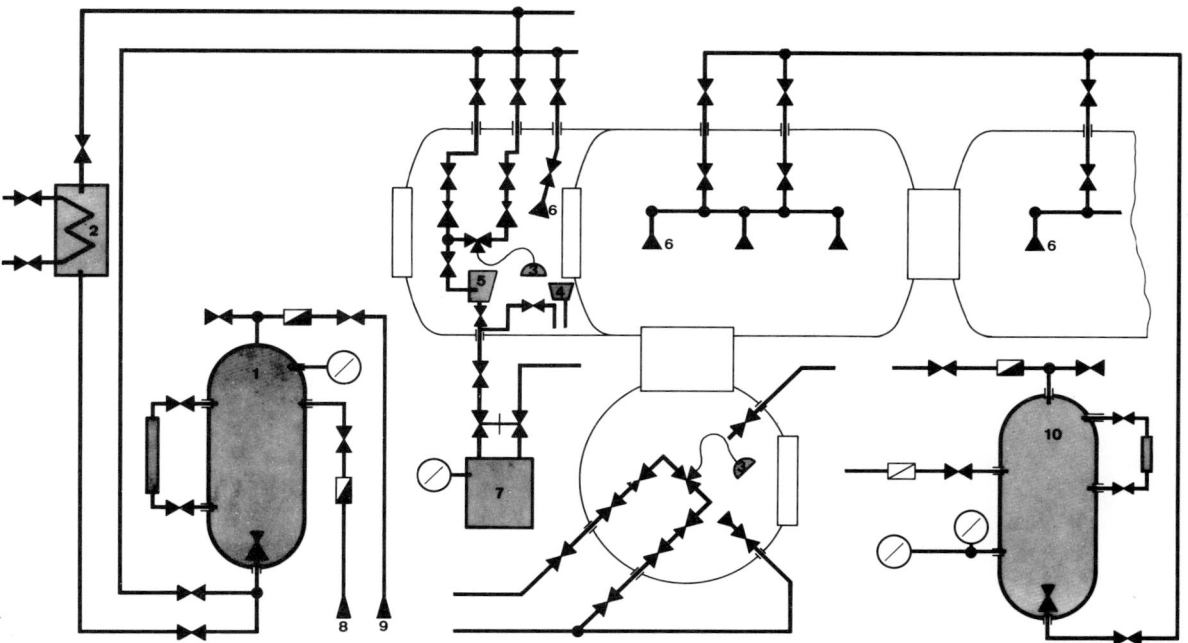

Fig. 3.19. Sanitary installations in a deep diving system.

    1 pressure water tank for fresh water   6 fire sprinklers
    2 water heater (heat-exchanger)   7 pressure waste disposal tank
    3 shower   8 fresh water connection
    4 wash basin   9 pressure gas connection
    5 WC   10 pressure water tank for fire sprinklers

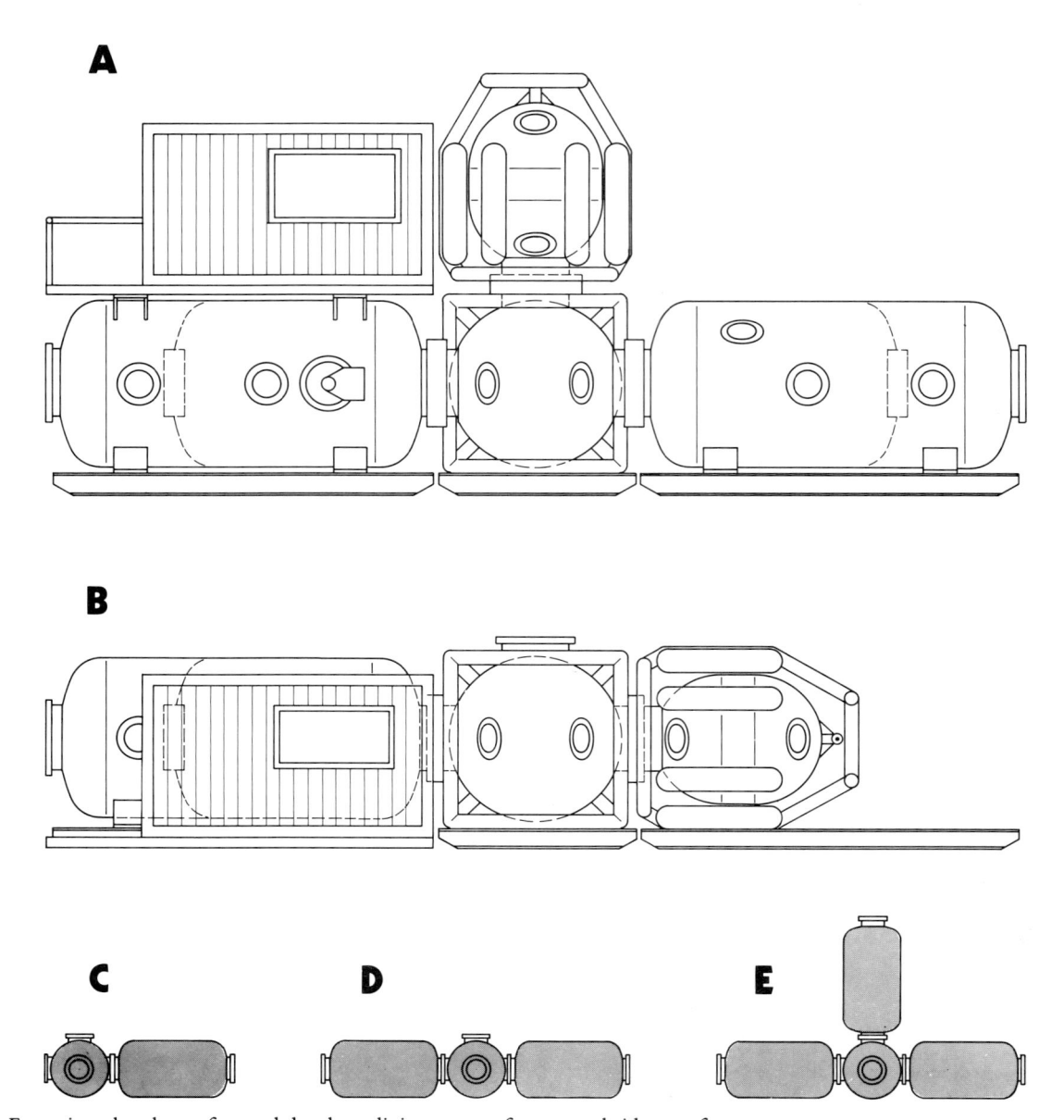

Fig. 3.20. Extension chambers of a modular deep diving system for top and side transfer.

A modular concept, whereby different units can be joined together and subsequently altered into various configurations, is a cost-effective method of adapting to different situations. A module complex developed by Drägerwerk extends the flexibility further by designing the DTC to be turned 90° for conversion to either top or side transfer. Fig. 3.20 illustrates the complete system in various alternative configurations. In A two or more chambers are connected to the DTC for top transfer with the SCC whilst in B the SCC is in a rollover position for side transfer. Types C, D and E show various possible completions.

Fig. 3.21. Deck transfer chamber of cylindrical design with top transfer connection (Dräger).

The vertical DTC shown in Fig. 3.21 is installed on the diving vessel *Arctic Seal* with a side transfer position and an option of two DCC connections. The complete layout of the system is shown in Fig. 3.12. This system is large in comparison to most contemporary DTCs; the diameter is 2200 mm and the height 2600 mm. The fourth quadrant of the chamber, which is not connected to a DCC, has a large door capable of transferring large items of equipment for use by the divers in the diving bell. The transfer chamber in effect becomes a workshop and store in addition to its other functions.

The rules affecting the interior fittings and the windows are similar to basic chamber described in Chapter 2. The locking devices will generally be U-segment rings, in either two segments or four, rather than the various types of bolted connections, as this arrangement has proved very successful in both top and side transfer. The mating arrangement for the DTC shown in Fig. 3.21 has a four-segment lock guided in around the flanges which are centered by four tapered tappets between the clamp segments. The device is operated with two hydraulic cylinders. Safety features which are installed allow for a lock to hold mechanically even without hydraulic pressure and a control valve on the control panel for pressurizing the internal shaft can only be activated when the lock is secure. Other types of locking systems sometimes used in American systems have a driven threaded spindle instead of the hydraulic cylinders.

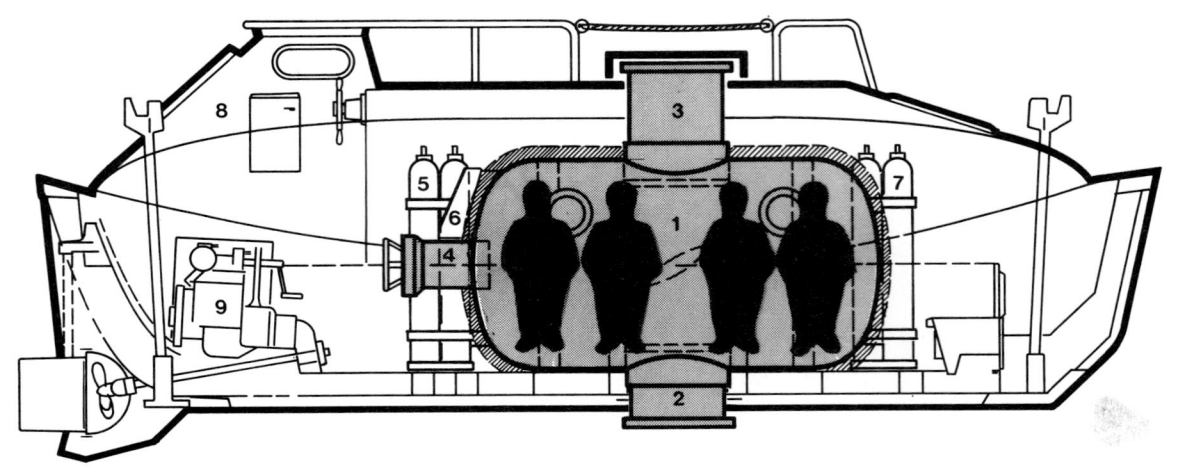

Fig. 3.22. Rescue chamber (hyperbaric lifeboat) for a crew of 12 divers.

1	hyperbaric chamber	6	control panel
2	entry pressure door	7	mixed gas
3	exit pressure door	8	lifeboat cockpit
4	supply lock	9	propulsion unit (engine)
5	oxygen		

Rescue Chambers (Hyperbaric Lifeboats)

Sometimes these chambers are referred to as hyperbaric rescue chambers and in certain situations are integrated with deep diving systems. They are designed to accommodate the divers under pressure, in one chamber, and to be launched overboard in an emergency.

The normal sequence of events leading to the crew abandoning the vessel because of fire, collision or for some other reason is a standard marine discipline. With divers under pressure, who cannot be decompressed in the time available to evacuate a vessel or rig, consideration has been given to finding a solution. Whilst the consensus is that the likelihood of such a disaster is remote and therefore that prevention is better than cure, the Norwegian regulations have declared that a rescue pressure chamber must be provided. The rescue chamber must carry and support all the divers under pressure and the chamber must be capable of being launched into the sea without sinking.

The main considerations are that the chamber, which can normally be used as a living compartment, must be quickly disconnected from the complex and from all shipboard services in an emergency and lowered into the water. The chamber must, of course, be buoyant and the insulation material resistant to the absorption of sea water. Figs 3.22 and 3.23 illustrate the rescue chamber of an off-shore diving system and Fig. 3.24 shows an operational rescue chamber built by

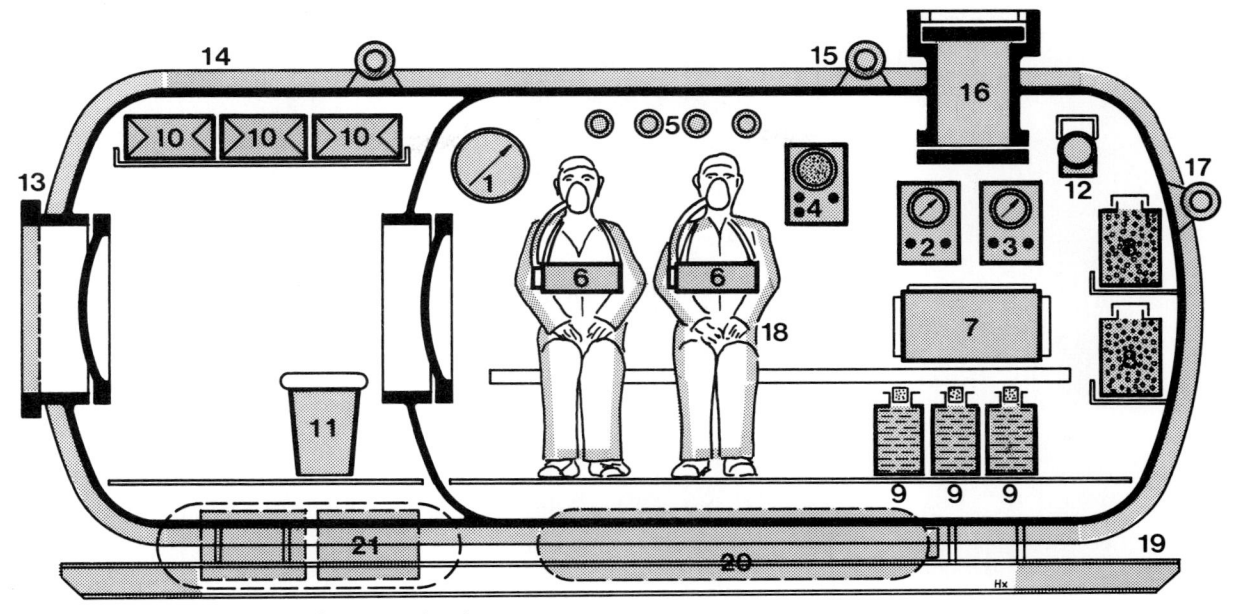

Fig. 3.23. Internal fittings of a rescue chamber.

1. internal pressure gauge
2. oxygen analyser
3. CO_2 analyser
4. communication set
5. windows
6. CO_2 filter (breathing sets)
7. CO_2 removal unit
8. CO_2 absorbent
9. water
10. food
11. WC
12. hand lamp
13. entry lock
14. main chamber with buoyancy/thermal coating
15. hoisting lugs
16. supply lock
17. towing point
18. bench
19. skid
20. life-support gas
21. battery power pack

Drass and installed in a diving vessel. Hyperbaric lifeboats have developed from a simple expedient of evacuating the divers in a hyperbaric chamber, either a capsule or a cylinder which floated and needed to be taken in tow by a boat. The natural progression led to the hyperbaric evacuation chamber being designed to fit into a standard lifeboat and finally to the lifeboat hull being designed around a purpose-built hyperbaric chamber complex. The design in Fig. 3.24 allows differential pressures, important if divers at separate pressures need to be evacuated. Differential pressures are quite common if two saturation teams are being used, since whilst one is working the other team may be decompressing. If all the divers can be evacuated at the same pressure then the additional chamber in the lifeboat may be used for the transfer of doctors. The two chambers are designed to accommodate six and four divers, a total of ten, with an additional three to crew the boat and supervise the divers. The total length of the pressure chamber is 2900 mm, divided into two

Fig. 3.24. A hyperbaric lifeboat with two chambers designed for different pressures secured aboard a diving vessel and mated to a deck compression chamber.

chambers of 1800 mm and 1100 mm. The emergency life-support system provides gas, analysing equipment, CO_2 absorbent and a heating system designed to provide adequate heat for at least 24 hours. Normal heating is supplied from the heat generated from the boat's engine.

The lifeboat is stowed on board in a conventional manner with regard to davits and lowering equipment but is also connected by transfer-under-pressure trunking to the ship-borne diving chamber complex.

Control Rooms

The control room is the operational centre for the whole system. All information is monitored at this position and controls are operated to activate all the systems on the DCCs and DTC. The handling system for the SCC is usually operated separately where the operation can be seen visually.

The control panels are divided into individual chambers with appropriate instrumentation for each system. Fig. 3.25 shows a control panel and Fig. 3.26 the various functions. This control room would operate a system as illustrated in Fig. 3.12 and, using Fig. 3.25 as a reference, each separate function can be seen.

Control panel for DCC
The panels marked 1 to 14 in Fig. 3.25 monitor and control each room of the various DCCs. The basis of the design for control panels is that they must present the information clearly and without straining the controller's vision or concentration. The most vital information, such as pressure gauge readings, must be prominently

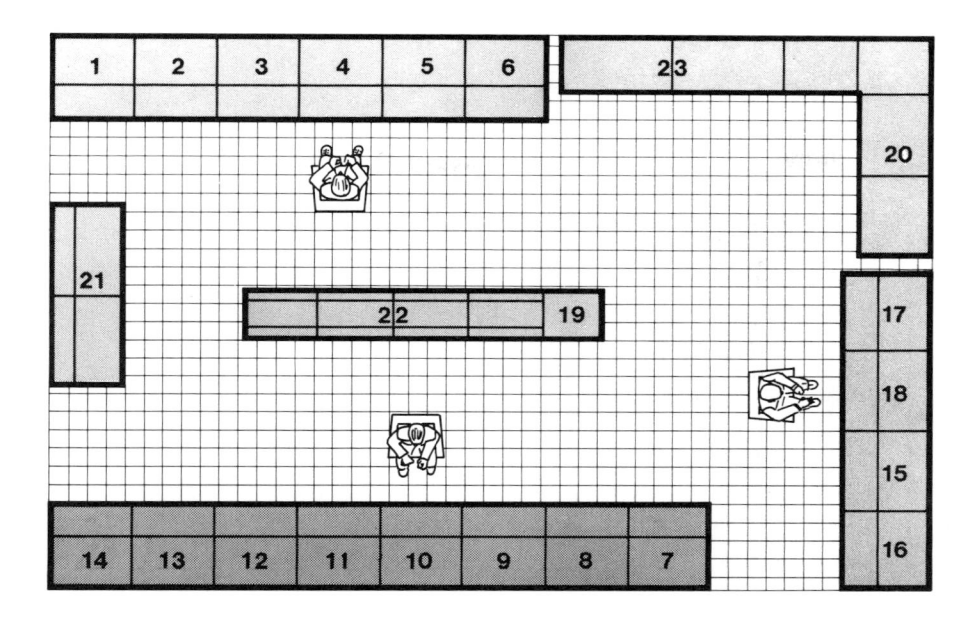

Fig. 3.25. The layout of the control centre of the deep diving system on board the *Arctic Seal*.

- 1–14 control panels for compression chambers, including pressure gauges, valves, communications and TV screens
- 15, 16 control panel for diving bell
- 17, 18 control panel for transfer lock
- 19 electrical manifold
- 20 electrical connection boxes
- 21 gas control panel
- 22 electrical switchboard and control panel
- 23 main electric power supply

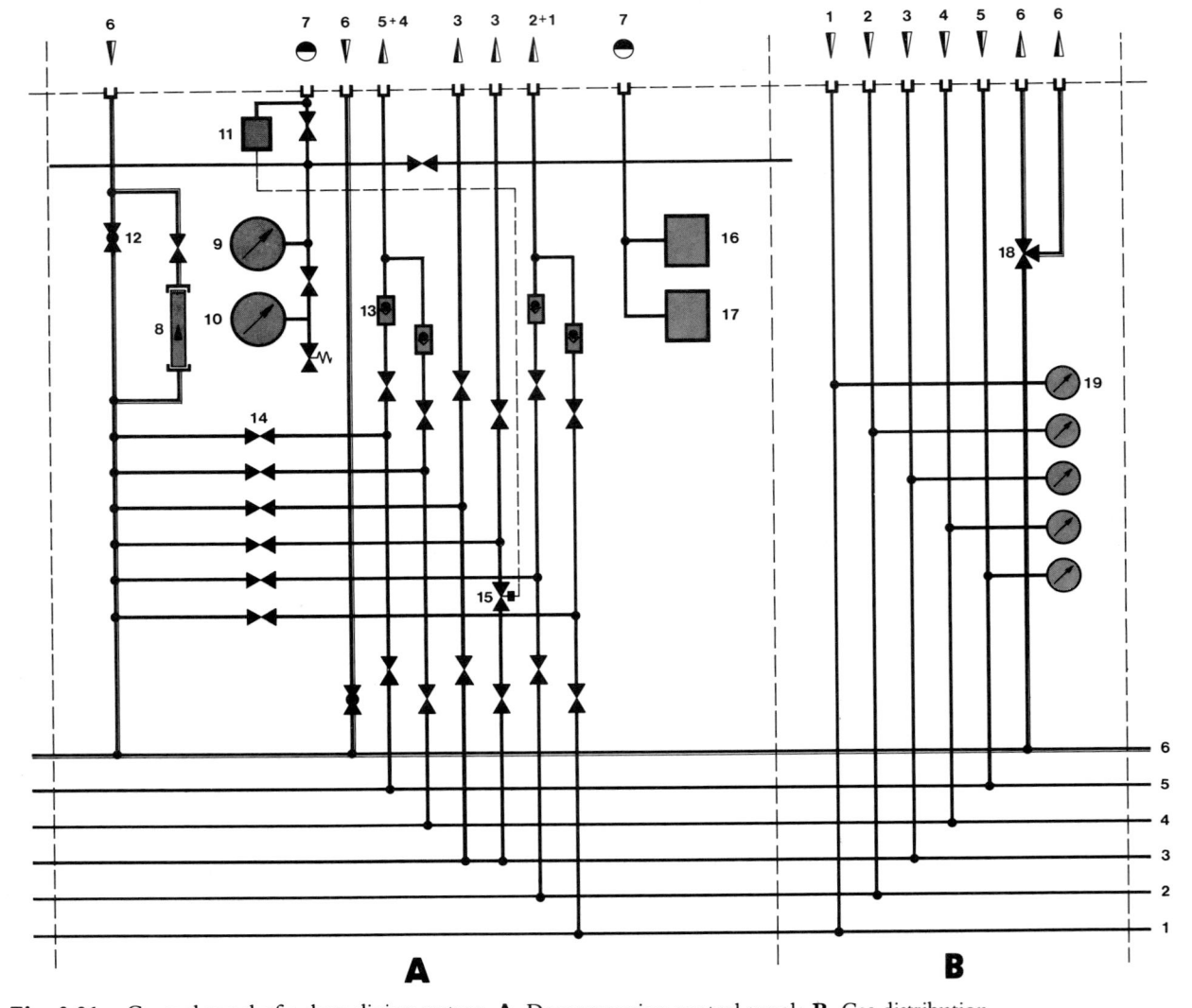

Fig. 3.26. Control panel of a deep diving system. **A**, Decompression control panel; **B**, Gas distribution.

1. oxy-helium 1 (200 bar)
2. oxy-helium 2 (200 bar)
3. oxygen (80 bar)
4. air (200 bar)
5. helium (200 bar)
6. exhaust 1
7. exhaust 2
8. flowmeter
9. precision gauge for max. operating pressure
10. precision gauge for low-pressure range
11. pressure sensor
12. shut-off valve (large diameter)
13. one-way valve
14. shut-off valve
15. solenoid valve
16. plotter
17. excessive pressure warning
18. three-way valve
19. gas storage pressure gauges

displayed. Fig. 3.25 shows the large precision gauges, in this case up to the maximum operating pressure of 40 bar. For more exact readings in the lower pressure ranges scales of up to 70 m are used. Precision gauges are designed to be unaffected by vibrations and are capable of fine adjustments.

In saturation diving in the later stages of decompression, fine adjustments of pressure are required between decompression stops and long periods where the same pressure has to be maintained. Referred to as linear decompression, the schedule has to be carefully controlled. Computer control units are used, but off-shore operators in the field prefer to control the decompression manually. To obtain a greater degree of accuracy and as a check of the precision gauges, the system can be fitted with a flowmeter. Based on the known volume of the chamber, the amount of sample gas drawn off and measured in a given time will accurately register the internal pressure. The timing units are fitted onto the control panel. The valves for the control of the gases are fitted on the flat portion of the panel. In the most straightforward deep diving operations the gas requirements at various stages of a saturation dive require compressed air, two oxy-helium mixtures, pure oxygen and pure helium. The gases selected must be designed to supply each of the chambers independently and each gas system must be designed with shut-off valves in series and with intermediate exhaust valves, so as to prevent residual and wrong gas mixtures entering the correct supply. Non-return valves are fitted to stop chamber gases from passing back into the manifold system. Pressure-relief valves and excess-pressure alarms are fitted. Gas and physiological monitoring systems, heating, humidity and temperature controls are displayed on the panel. There are communications and television coverage of all chambers. The detailed examination of life-support systems is discussed in Chapter 10. The complex design of a gas control manifold system integrated with monitoring equipment and communications into a control panel, with the additional facility to record all or selected data over a continuous period, must, as a prime design priority, consider the need to have quick access to all component parts for maintenance and repair work.

Control panel for DTC
The panels controlling the transfer chamber are indicated as 17 and 18 in Fig. 3.25 and they are similar to the DCC control panel. In addition there are two multi-purpose valves which can control the equalization of the two pressures when transferring the divers to and from the diving bell and the deck chambers.

Control panel for SCC
The panels controlling the diving bell life-support system are indicated as 15 and 16 in Fig. 3.25. In addition to the information displayed on the other chamber panels the SCC panel also indicates the internal pressure of the bell through a pneumo-fathometer and an additional gauge for the measurement of the depth. There is also

Fig. 3.27. Control panel for a deep diving system showing the internal piping (Dräger).

control over the open-circuit hot-water system which is designed to pass through the umbilical to heat the diver comfortably. Pressure-reducing valves are fitted to reduce large volumes of selected breathing gases from 200 bar to 40 bar.

Central gas supply panel

Indicated as 27 in Fig. 3.25, this panel indicates the different single supply pressures of the various storage banks and with a valve manifold can shut off the main supplies or supply as required to the chamber control panels.

Environmental control system

A separate panel measures the various gases in all the different chambers and is the heart of a total life-support system. These requirements are discussed in Chapter 10. A picture of the panel in Fig. 3.28 shows the measuring instruments for carbon dioxide and oxygen and the duplicate back-up systems. A gas chromatograph, not shown in the picture, records the analysis of the gases.

Electrical distribution panel

A separate panel controls the distribution of the main power supply to all parts of the complex including the large power requirements for the bell handling system. The essential emergency supply, usually provided by a separate diesel generator, is also controlled through the distribution box. Both main and standby power must be controlled directly from the source.

Gas Storage and Gas Distribution

The amount and variety of gas mixtures carried are determined by considering the following factors:

Fig. 3.28. Gas measurement panel of a modern deep diving system.

1. Maximum diving depth.
2. Total volume and maximum operating pressure of all pressure chambers.
3. Type of diving (bounce or saturation).
4. Type of equipment (open-, semi-closed- or closed-circuit, push/pull).
5. Maximum operational diving period.
6. Availability of space.
7. Logistics with regard to operational area and re-supply.
8. Emergency supply requirements.

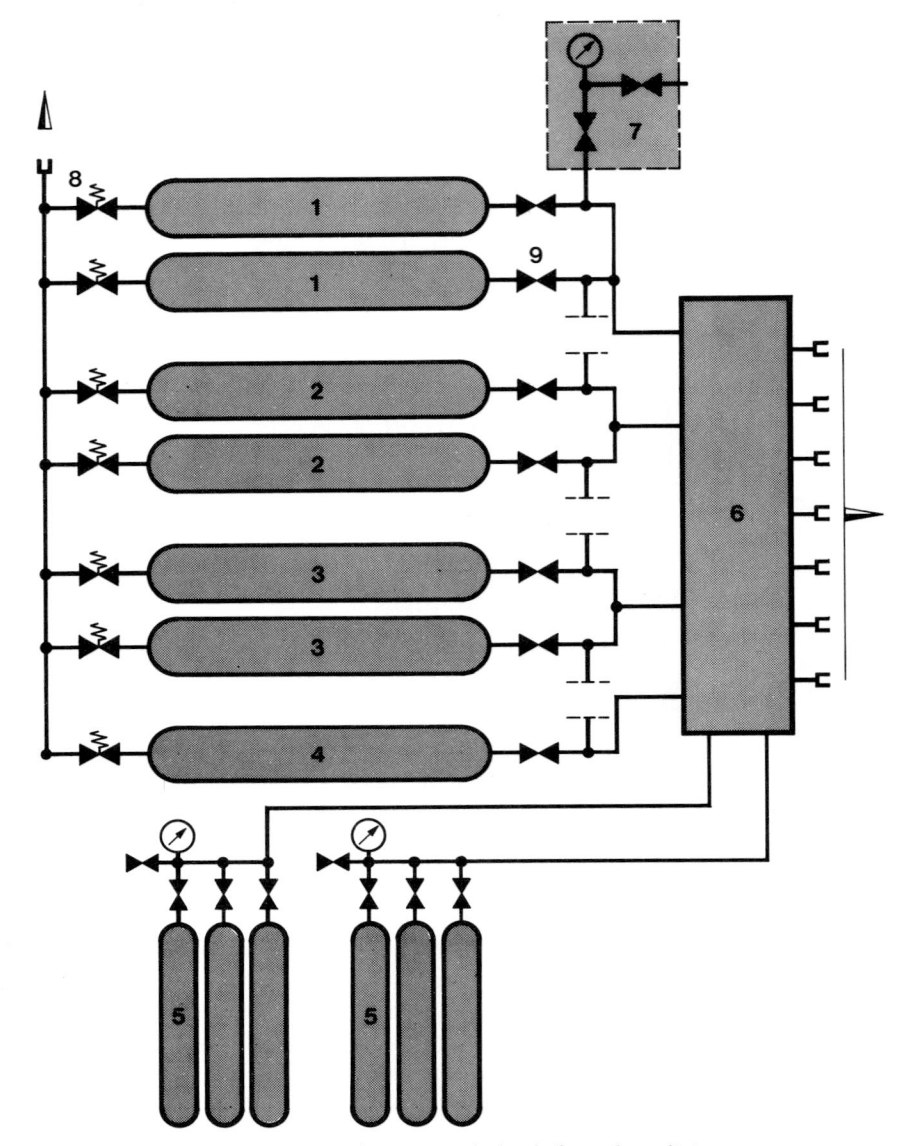

Fig. 3.29. Arrangement of a gas supply bank for a deep diving system.

1. pure helium
2. oxy-helium
3. compressed air
4. contaminated helium
5. oxygen
6. gas supply panel
7. gas bank panel
8. safety valves
9. shut-off valves

The size and arrangement of the gas storage system are determined by the type of diving operation envisaged, taking into account the same considerations that affect the choice of diving system. Diving operations in support of exploration drilling require short-duration bounce dives, whilst diving in support of the installation, maintenance and repair of production facilities requires saturation diving and this is reflected in larger gas storage systems. For bounce diving the gas supply can be contained in small cylinders of 50 litres made up conveniently into small banks which are easily transportable and stowed in any designated area. For saturation diving the gas cylinders are up to 2000 litres in volume to supply the larger volumes for breathing and for the pressurization of large chambers. All storage cylinders have a working pressure of at least 200 bar. The gas storage systems, whether for high- or low-capacity diving systems, are divided into at least five groups and Fig. 3.29 illustrates the layout of a typical gas storage system that would supply the system outlined in Fig. 3.12 or a smaller complex.

Compressed air reservoir volume tank

Although not used as a breathing gas in depths greater than about 60 m, air has many other uses in a deep diving system. As a carrier gas, air may be used as a base into which proportions of oxygen and helium can be mixed to make up a combination of N_2, O_2 and He, known as Trimix, for certain diving depths and decompression mixtures. For depths less than 60 m air is used in the DCCs, SCCs and breathing systems, and in surface-oriented diving it is supplied to the diver through an air hose using low-pressure air or, in scuba self-contained cylinders, high-pressure air. Most advanced ship-borne diving systems operate the diving bell through a moonpool and the injection of high-pressure air into the surge zone in the moonpool reduces the turbulence of the water. The detail of this is discussed in the section on handling systems in this chapter. Considerable quantities of air can be consumed but the capacity of the air reservoirs is proportionally small in relation to the output of the air compressors.

Oxygen storage

Oxygen is fundamental to all life-support gases; a separate pure oxygen storage provides the required O_2 content in the DCCs and SCC to maintain the correct partial pressure of O_2 (Po_2) mixed with helium or nitrogen. As a pure breathing gas, oxygen is also used in normal and therapeutic decompressions in the last stages above 18 m depth. When pure oxygen is breathed the oxygen is supplied directly to the divers at low pressure. Pure oxygen is a considerable fire hazard and requires additional precautions. It is normally supplied in small cylinders of 50 litres capacity and manifolded into groups because of the danger of supplying oxygen from a bulk carrier; the oxygen banks are preferably kept in the open away from other hazards. If it is necessary to install the oxygen below decks it must not be adjacent to other fire hazards and must have adequate ventilation. Further stringent restrictions apply to the use of materials, which must be compatible whilst in contact with pure oxygen or with mixtures with a high oxygen content of over 40% by volume. The oxygen must be reduced from high-pressure to low-pressure at the supply manifold so that no high-pressure oxygen is allowed to enter the life-support

Fig. 3.30. Oxygen storage bank on a diving ship.

system. No sharp bends are permitted in the oxygen piping runs, which should be of hard metal and routed separately from the other breathing gas lines and fire risk areas. No ball or quarter-turn valves should be fitted in the oxygen systems, to avoid the possibility of a leak. When it is necessary to dump pure oxygen overboard the piping runs should exhaust into the open air, downwind and away from other fire hazards. The accepted practice of using non-hydrocarbon oil or grease throughout all gas supply systems for lubrication is particularly important for oxygen or high-oxygen-content supplies. Recommended non-toxic cleaning agents only should be used.

Helium

Large quantities of this expensive and almost finite gas, in terms of overall world resources, are needed to support off-shore deep diving operations and it comprises at least 90% of the total gas volume consumed. Considerable economies can be made with the use of closed-circuit breathing systems, but the various chambers and the diving bell are pressurized with the oxy-helium gas which may not be recoverable. Pure helium is used to make up any required breathing gas by mixing with oxygen or air.

Oxy-helium

It is normal practice for the correct oxy-helium mixtures to be made up by the gas suppliers for a particular depth range for practical convenience. At least two separate mixtures are usually provided to cover the programmed depth range and the addition of pure He and O_2 supplies for mixing on board will provide additional mixtures for

Fig. 3.31. Part of the helium storage bank on an under-water construction vessel.

different depths. This will give greater flexibility and autonomy. Where a diving system is being used on a fixed installation where depths remain the same one mixture will be used.

Gas logistics and layout

When the pressures in the chamber are lowered, the excess gas can either be dumped overboard or passed to a temporary storage reservoir where considerable cost-effective purification systems can be used to remove the impurities and return the gas for analysis and further use.

In Fig. 3.32 a gas distribution panel is shown which coordinates the various reservoirs which are grouped together. The saturation diving system layout in Fig. 3.12 has a total chamber volume of 90 m^3 with a pressure rating of 40 bar (400 m) and a diving bell with a pressure rating of 50 bar (500 m). Using this as an example we can calculate the gas needs of an advanced and representative system. Using the operating conditions prevalent in the North Sea—30 days' saturation and a 24-hour work coverage using diving teams in shifts—the requirements for the various gases and storage capacity are shown in Table 3.1.

The basic layout of the gas storage system is shown in Fig. 3.29 and, except for the oxygen supply, the helium and oxy-helium gases are usually built into a diving vessel or barge and refilled by road bulk

Fig. 3.32. Gas distribution panel (Dräger).

transport whilst the vessel is alongside. The reservoirs in this instance are manufactured with a capacity of either 2000 or 1000 litres, and grouped together to provide the storage needed. The lengths are 10 m or 5 m, weighing 2000 kg or 1000 kg respectively. As varying pressures occur in the reservoirs the construction should allow for the differential expansion and contraction of the cylinders caused by fluctuations in temperature. The reservoirs are fitted with individual supply valves with a manual relief valve and gauges. When the reservoirs are refilled the supply system must have a non-return valve in the system and, if necessary, a blow-off valve in case the supply pressure should exceed the reservoir working pressure.

Other important features of a well designed storage system are a common colour code for marking the different gas flows in addition to the identity discs, resilient mountings to support the piping, pressure gauges to record pressure drops, with alarm signals for drops below minimum pressures, and easy access for cleaning and maintenance.

Table 3.1. Examples of requirements for various gases

Gas	Volume		Pressure bank		No. of banks
	m^3	litres	Quantity	Pressure (bar)	
Helium	158	2000	79	200	4
Air	2	2000	1	200	(1)
Oxygen	9	50	180	200	15
Oxy-helium	36	1000	36	200	4
Impure helium	4	2000	2	200	(2)

Gas Recovery

Whilst the partial pressure of oxygen remains constant, the proportion of helium increases with depth and in saturation diving the recovery of the gas during decompression is financially attractive, due to the very high costs of helium. Nowadays there is every incentive to re-cycle and re-use the gas rather than dispose of it to the atmosphere. Commercial diving has become very competitive and the financial benefits of using closed-circuit breathing systems in conjunction with a recovery system are being realized. The large volumes that are released from the chambers are collected in a gas bag whilst a compressor pumps the dirty gas into the contaminated gas storage. This dirty gas contains nitrogen, together with some carbon dioxide and minor impurities like methane, carbon monoxide and organic vapours. Once the gases have been collected there are a limited number of ways in which the helium can be extracted. One method is cryogenic purification, where the gas is cooled to about $-195°C$ and the gases and vapours, other than helium, condense or liquefy and are separated out mechanically. Since the process is carried out at high pressure there is no need to compress the gas after purification. Another method is to remove the other gases and vapours by selective absorption, using alumina and molecular sieves. Both processes will yield between 93 and 98% of helium which can be re-used with a purity of 99% or more.

SCC Handling and Winch Systems

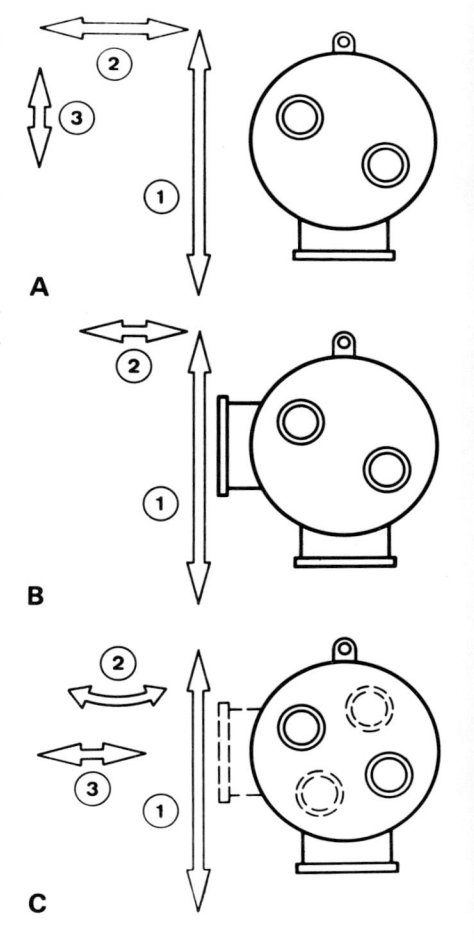

A handling system for a diving bell must be capable of controlling the depth of the SCC and also the position on deck for mating with the deck compression chambers or deck transfer chamber for transfer under pressure. The handling systems may be complex or very simple, with the basic rules of good seamanship applied to the use of wires, sheaves, winches and the static and moving parts. The type of system is influenced by the type of craft, the weather conditions and the type of SCC both in terms of size and the mating arrangement. The basic movements of an SCC on deck are summarized in Fig. 3.33 and these movements have to be translated into a handling design to

Fig. 3.33. The basic movements of SCC handling. For side transfer rotation about the vertical axis may be needed.

    A   Top transfer. (1) Lowering vertically over very long distances of several hundred metres. (2) Horizontal motion over several metres. (3) Mating procedure, locking, over a few decimetres

    B   Side transfer. (1) Vertical lowering over several hundred meters. (2) Horizontal motion over short distances of a few centimetres or metres

    C   Side transfer/rollover. (1) Vertical lowering over several hundred metres. (2) Rotation about 90°. (3) Horizontal motion over short distances of a few decimetres

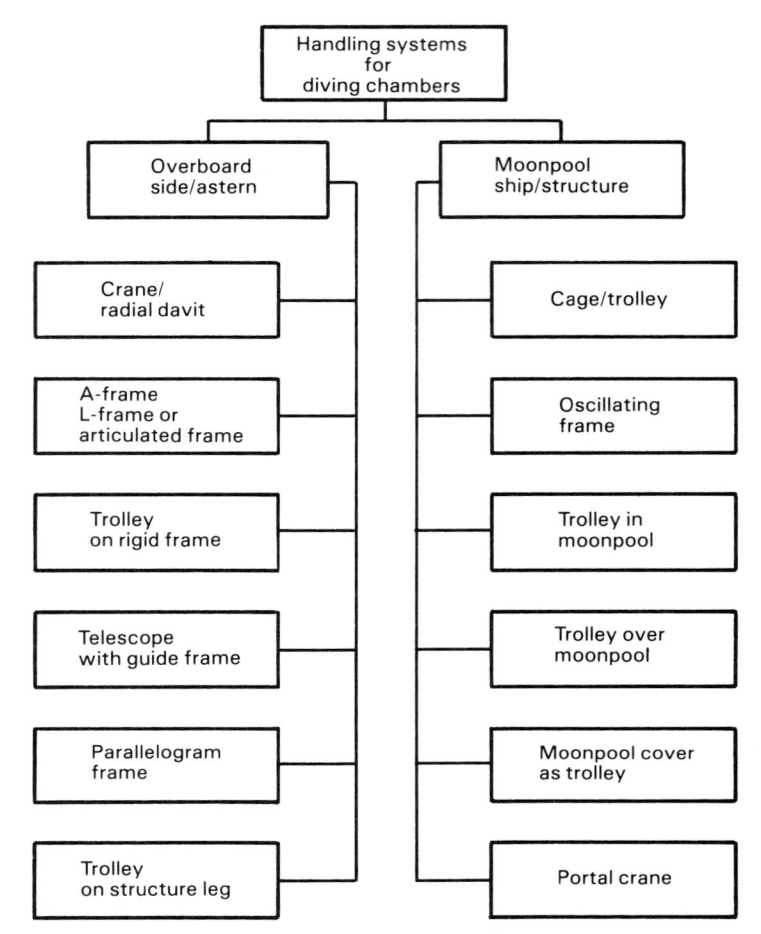

```
                    Handling systems
                          for
                    diving chambers
                    ┌─────────┴─────────┐
              Overboard              Moonpool
             side/astern           ship/structure
```

- Crane/radial davit
- A-frame, L-frame or articulated frame
- Trolley on rigid frame
- Telescope with guide frame
- Parallelogram frame
- Trolley on structure leg

- Cage/trolley
- Oscillating frame
- Trolley in moonpool
- Trolley over moonpool
- Moonpool cover as trolley
- Portal crane

Fig. 3.34. Handling systems for diving bells.

effect the transfer of the divers under pressure. The movements on deck are complex, variable and precise, and may be further complicated by the different layout of each ship or barge needing individual modifications. Lowering and hoisting the bell in the vertical plane is standard and straightforward. In the Gulf of Mexico, where sea and weather conditions are good, the SCCs are hoisted and lowered on a simple radial davit or derrick, quite unsuitable for systems operating off the east coast of North America and in the North Sea. The movement in the horizontal plane is small and precise for a side transfer under pressure and, even though roughly aligned to the transfer mating flange, the bell will need separate precise alignment over the vertical axis to centre the flanges. In the rollover design for mating the SCC is controlled by turning rods which rotate the bell, but some horizontal movement is also needed. The various designs are classified in Fig. 3.34 into overboard systems or moonpool systems. The use of guidewires and anchors can generally be adapted to all the systems.

Fig. 3.35. Under-water construction, diving and fire-fighting vessel *Stefanieturm*.

Overboard Systems (Side or Stern)

Until the advent of the moonpool, the overboard method was the only way in which diving bell operations could be undertaken. The moonpool design clearly has some advantages, which will be discussed later, but nevertheless for a number of technical reasons it cannot always be used. The design of the vessel may not be suitable for a modification to incorporate a moonpool and, further, certain diving systems are better handled over the side, such as welding habitats and subsea production systems which require the use of an SCC. Naturally in stable good weather conditions the overboard system is efficient as the surface vessel can anchor in a fixed position, but in bad weather conditions considerable forces can be applied to the SCC during the dangerous period when it is moving through the turbulence of the air and water interface.

Crane, derrick crane, radial crane

The use of standard cargo-handling cranes can only be considered if the platform is stable, as on fixed off-shore installations which are either jacked-up drilling rigs or production platforms. Other stable platforms are provided by the new generation of pipelaying and derrick barges and semi-submersible safety and work barges. The cranes must be certified for use for handling personnel.

Three ship-borne arrangements are shown in Fig. 3.36. The crane shown in A is installed in all off-shore structures in some form and is capable of handling SCCs for temporary deep diving systems; although capable of free movement around a single point, it is

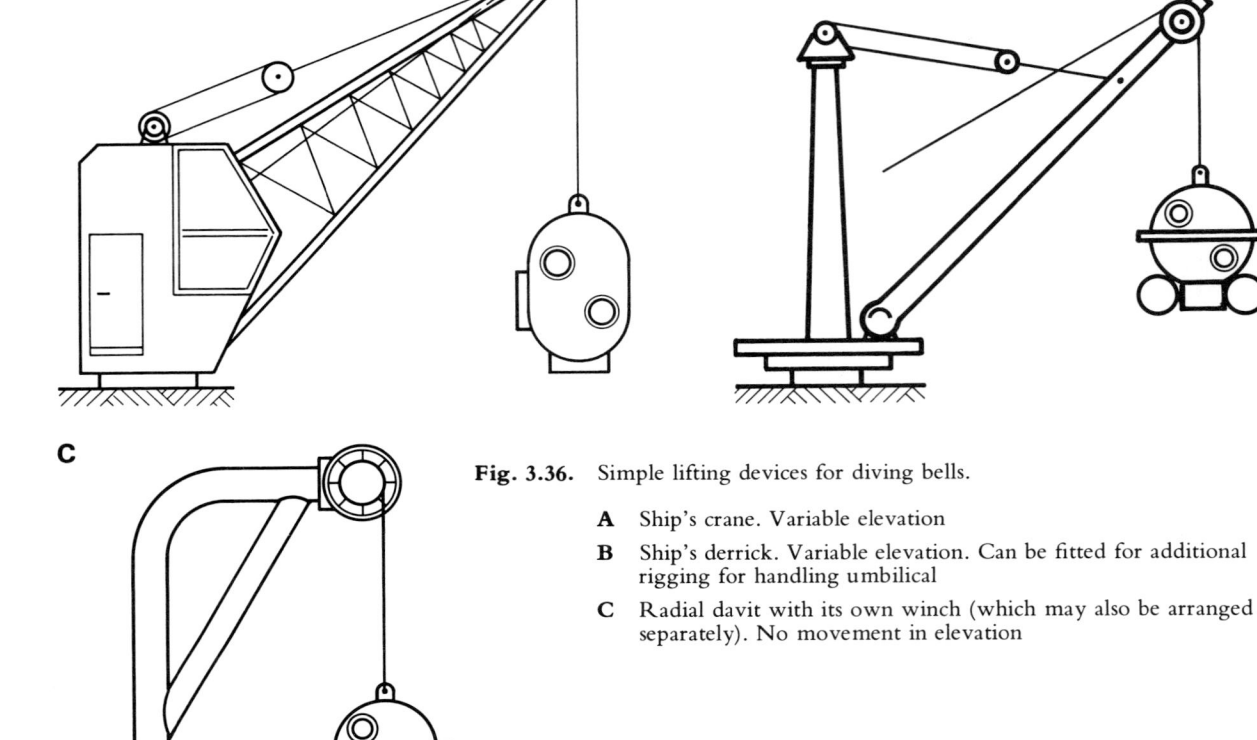

Fig. 3.36. Simple lifting devices for diving bells.

- **A** Ship's crane. Variable elevation
- **B** Ship's derrick. Variable elevation. Can be fitted for additional rigging for handling umbilical
- **C** Radial davit with its own winch (which may also be arranged separately). No movement in elevation

constrained by lack of mobility. In some construction barges, caterpillar cranes which can move more freely are used to handle the diving bell from the best position. Derrick cranes shown in Fig. 3.36B are commonly fitted in naval diving vessels, submarine rescue and salvage vessels and have different rigging for different operations. A separate hoist can be added to the derrick boom for handling umbilicals and the US Navy operates this method using shock-absorbers. In all other operations using these multipurpose cranes the umbilical cord may often have to be tended by hand, thus restricting the size of umbilical and the depth of the dive. In Fig. 3.36C the radial davit is very restricted and is usually purpose-built for a specific requirement with limited scope for depth. A specific requirement for the davit is shown in Fig. 3.37.

A-frame, L-frame, joint frame

The A-frame design for handling systems has the greatest application and is more commonly used than any other. The A-frame is commonly used for the launch and recovery of submersibles over the stern of motherships. The A-frame can be mounted on the stern or side of a vessel. The frame shown in Fig. 3.38 is constructed of box girders or tubular steel and fixed to two heel positions on the deck where it is allowed to pivot. The pivoting movement is controlled by two hydraulic rams and moves the SCC from the overboard launch position to the mating position onto the DCC. Top transfer is

Deep Diving Systems 149

Fig. 3.37. Radial davit with its own winch (Sub Sea International, USA).

Fig. 3.38. An A-frame with an H-frame for retaining the diving bells.

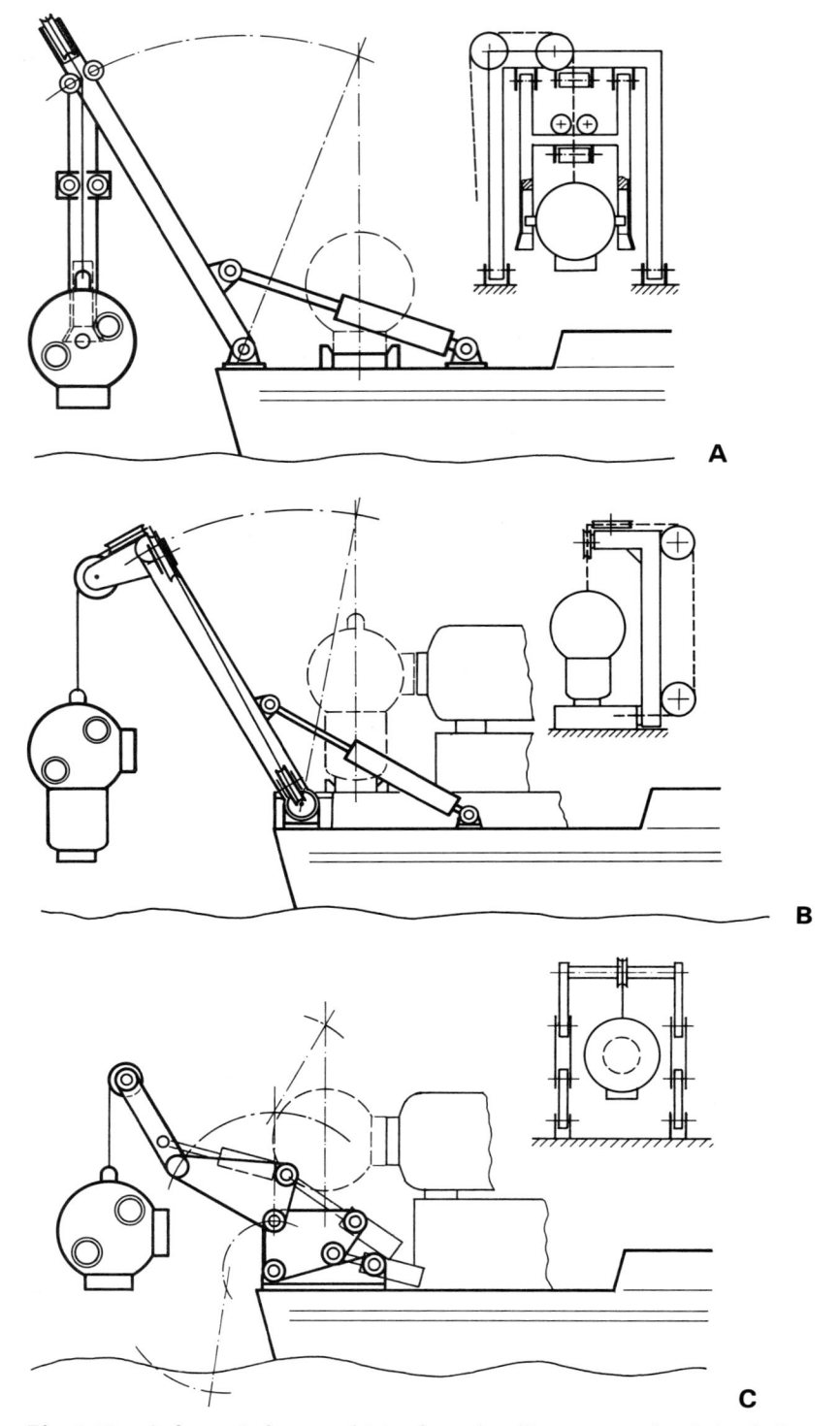

Fig. 3.39. A-frame, L-frame and joint frame handling systems for diving bells.

    A A-frame with hydraulic drive and H-frame guide. Suitable for launch over side or stern

    B L-frame for handling twin-chamber bells

    C Multiple joint for lowering the bell below the water surface (Babcock design)

preferable to side transfer, which is more complicated. The rigging of the hoist wire is conditioned by the position of the winch drum. If the winch drum is installed in direct line with the A-frame axis, any movement of the A-frame will result in a movement of the SCC and will have to be compensated. To avoid this movement the hoist wire can be rigged through rollers and sheaves along the A-frame and this arrangement is shown in Fig. 3.38. In addition, the A-frame can be fitted with guidewires to damp any movement of the bell swinging in air caused by movement of the diving platform. In Fig. 3.39A the bell is retained by bolts on the H-frame whilst inboard and this arrangement gives the control necessary for the subsequent mating operation. Hydraulic shock-absorbers give further protection. An alternative method of rigidly controlling the bell from swinging is with the use of a cage or crown frame.

The L-frame, shown in Fig. 3.39B, which is rarely seen, is designed for the additional height of the two-compartment bells. Designed for the *Seashore II* range of diving bells, it has not been used to any great extent. There are no great advantages in this design except for a marginal saving in space.

The proposed Babcock design (Fig. 3.39C) has yet to be proved and is designed for the large two-compartment chamber, more specifically for the handling of subsea production maintenance capsules. The system is designed to operate from a low freeboard, allowing the three-point frame to lower the capsule into the water and be released. Fitted with hydraulic heave compensators and controlled automatically to compensate for wave motion in the interface, the system has yet to be proved, but clearly with the new generation of subsea intervention capsules, much larger than SCCs, better systems of control are needed. The design is shown in Fig. 3.40.

Trolley and telescopic frames

Instead of using an A-frame, the diving bell can be launched and recovered from an extended frame, using trolleys to move the unit horizontally. In Fig. 3.41 tried arrangements of this diving spread are shown. In A, the simplest version, the bell is moved along rails suspended on a trolley and the main winch is mounted on the top of the rails. The trolleys are often fitted with a cage or crown to retain the bells firmly. In A the extension is rigid, and therefore only suitable for installation over the stern, whilst in B the projecting extension piece can be dismantled.

A telescopic arm can be designed which extends from a fixed guide frame and when fully retracted there are no projections over the side, so that it is suitable for operation from side or stern. In the Vetco Offshore Inc. system a large telescopic frame is fitted with a bell cage and the hoist is fitted with heave compensation.

Fig. 3.40. Design for the launch and recovery of large manned subsea systems. With the PTC on the seabed undertaking a task, the control chamber moves up and down with the motion of the sea, independent of the mothership.

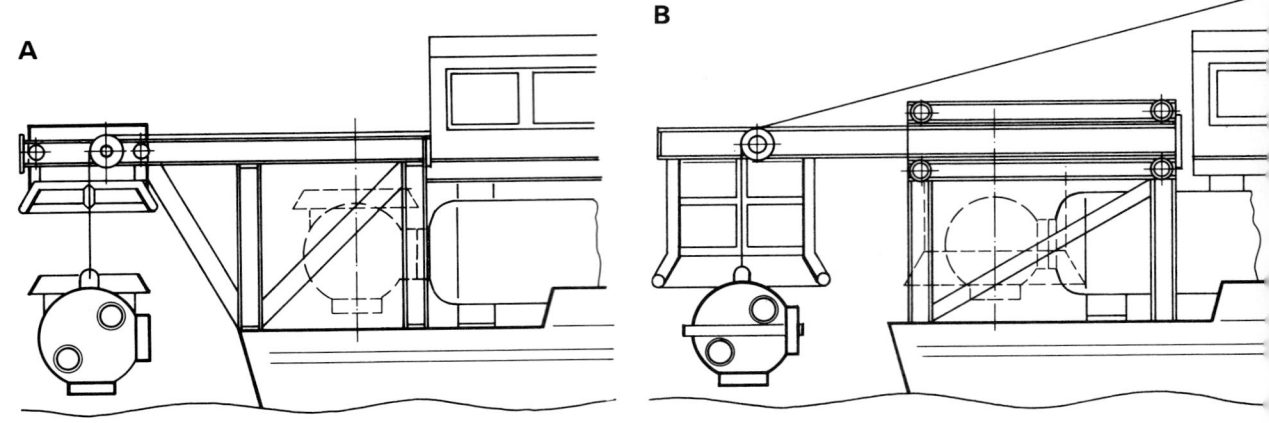

Fig. 3.41. Travelling trolley and telescopic frame.

A Travelling trolley with catching cage for SCC. Rigid or hinge guide frame construction. Mainly for stern launching

B Extendable telescopic arm or frame. Catching cage or holder rigidly attached to lifting point. Suitable for both stern and side launching

Fig. 3.42. Parallelogram and guide trolleys for SCC handling.

A Parallelogram for horizontal movement of the SCC

B Guide trolley and rails for the SCC and semi-submersible, fitted on a leg

Parallelogram frame and platform leg guide trolley

An extension of the A-frame design is the parallelogram frame (Fig. 3.42A), developed by the Dutch company SKADOC which has some advantages in being light. The hinged frame is best placed above the deck mating chamber to save space. The bell is rigidly retained by roller clamps whilst being handled and this allows for the rotation of the bell to the correct position for mating and transfer under pressure.

A more special use of a guide rail and trolley is for launching and recovery of the SCC up and down the leg of a semi-submersible craft.

The rails are part of the outside or inside leg of the semi-submersible and the trolley moves along the rails. Fig. 3.42B shows the diving bell moving outside the leg. There are considerable advantages in placing the bell inside the leg with the bell coming out of the bottom as it will not be affected by surface weather.

Although there will in the future be other designs for launching diving bells and subsea capsules they will not differ substantially from these basic designs.

Moonpool Systems

Theoretically the perfect moonpool and bell handling system would recover the bell and transfer the SCC to the DTC automatically and safely with the ship at any angle and the sea in any state. This is not yet possible, but certainly the use of a moonpool through which the SCC is operated is the most efficient method of handling and capable of further refinement. The use of the moonpool for diving came about with diving operations in drillships. As drilling was carried out through moonpools in drillships, so also were diving operations, and the advantages of using a moonpool became obvious when special diving vessels were built or converted. The main considerations for moonpool design are as follows:

1. The angle of the moonpool from the vertical.
2. The seawater/air interface.
3. The surge zone turbulence.
4. The rigidity of the bell and its cursor or frame.
5. The vertical speed of the bell.
6. Rise and fall of the waterline.

The angle of the moonpool should ideally remain vertical at all times, but this is not always possible. The stability can be improved by fitting stabilizing fins and passive stabilizing tanks and by dynamic positioning to weathercock the vessel to the most favourable heading.

The interface of seawater and air is traditionally the most dangerous area of bell handling, with the transition from a denser medium of water to air. The use of guide wires and anchor systems to some extent damps the effect of waves passing through the interface, but in most cases the use of guide wires in moonpools has been overtaken by the use of moonpool aeration and the fitting of a cursor. Moonpool aeration is the injection of high-pressure air into the surge zone, which reduces the density of the water and allows the bell to sink more rapidly through the interface, reducing time and ballast. Air acting on the water will tend to act as a shock-absorber.

To reduce the turbulence in the surge zone the combination of aeration and baffle tubes will modulate the horizontal movement of the sea. The combination of baffle tube and aeration is most effective.

The rigidity of the bell using a fitted cursor is illustrated in Fig. 3.48 and described later.

The speed of the bell downwards through the interface is significantly greater than upwards through the aerated zone. The

Fig. 3.43. Single travelling cage for SCC top transfer on board the diving vessel *Arctic Surveyor*.

proper design of the aeration system is important to achieve maximum efficiency and the smoothest transition of the bell from the waterline to inboard.

The rise and fall of the waterline can produce unacceptable shock loading forces on the bell hoisting wire as the sea level in the moonpool falls away before the winch can take up the slack on the hoist wire. Aeration of the interface helps to keep the wire hoist taut, but other methods, although expensive, are possible. They include expansion tanks at the bottom of the moonpool or some form of bottom door. Alternatively, the entire moonpool compartment may be made pressure-tight to reduce the rise and fall of the water.

Trolley cages (for top transfer)

SCC handling systems are greatly influenced by the availability of space especially with moonpool systems in ships, where buoyancy

Deep Diving Systems 155

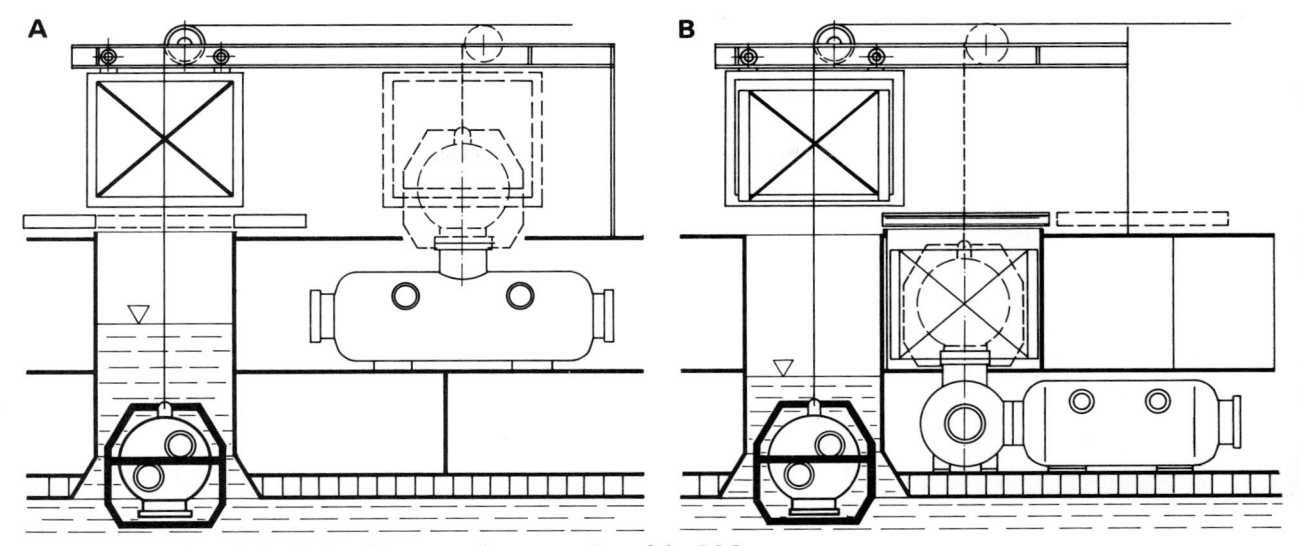

Fig. 3.44. Single and double handling cages for top mating of the SCC.

    A Single handling cage. Moonpool cover and DTC mating flange for bell on one level. Separate winch system

    B Double handling cage. Moonpool end and mating flange for DTC differ by one deck height

Fig. 3.45. SCC handling system with double cage on board the diving ship *Seaway Falcon*.

and stability considerations are fundamental to the integrity of the ship. The bell may need to be moved horizontally over relatively large distances and downwards to mate with the deck transfer chamber (DTC). Where the DTC is on the same level as the moonpool deck the movement of the SCC inside the handling cage is straightforward. Fig. 3.44 shows the different conditions; in B the added complication of lowering the bell onto the DTC requires a second frame or cage to position the mating flanges correctly which can be seen in Fig. 3.45 showing the operation prior to transfer under

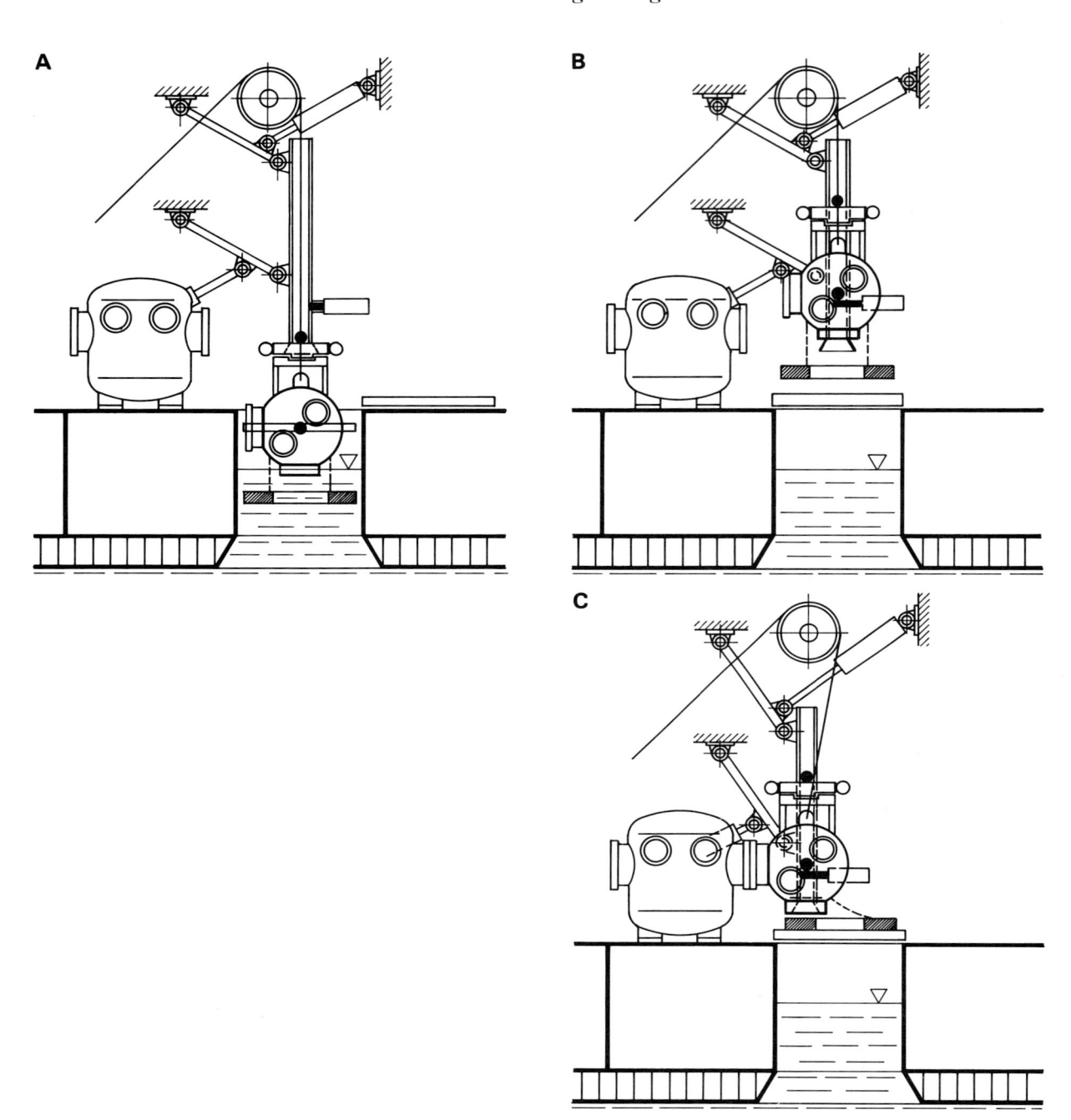

Fig. 3.46. Parallelogram arm with rotation mechanism for side transfer of the SCC.

A The SCC is moved into the rotating unit after leaving the moonpool. The flange position is oriented with respect to the guide rails by rope pulley and hydraulic cylinders

B The SCC is inserted into the guide frame. The moonpool cover is closed and the SCC lowered on guide blocks. The anchor weight is now resting on the moonpool cover

C The swinging arm is lowered and the SCC brought into mating position. The SCC is locked to the deck chamber complex by a hydraulically operated U-clamp lock

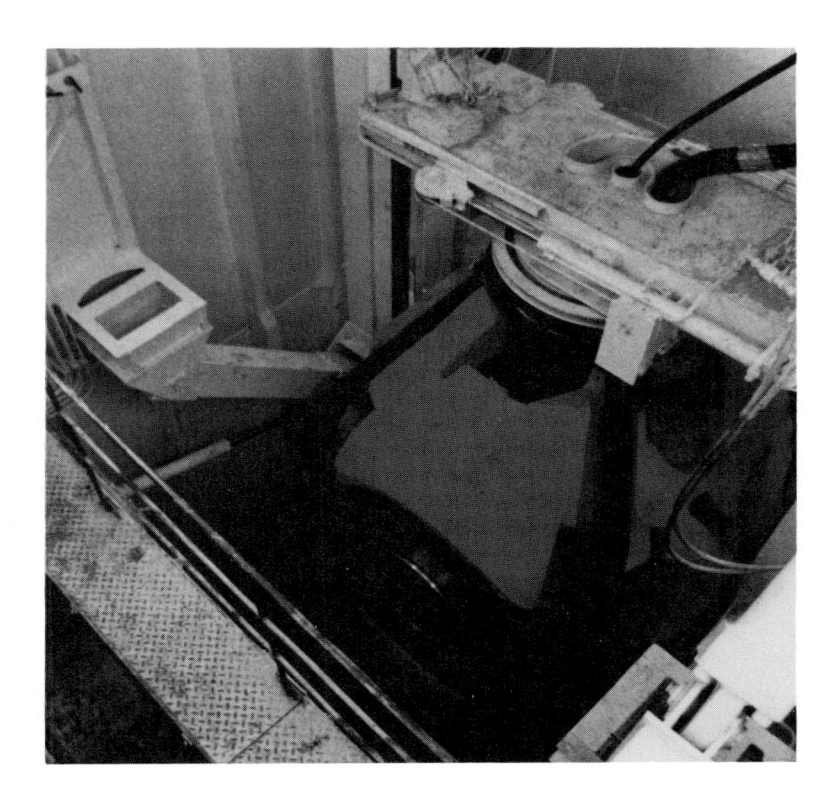

Fig. 3.47. SCC in locking position with parallelogram arm for side transfer, on the diving vessel *Arctic Seal* (Odd Berg, Tromsø).

pressure on board the Norwegian diving vessel *Seaway Falcon*. The cables are operated hydraulically.

The use of an anchor and guide wires for the diving bell requires a suitable storage position, either secured in the moonpool itself or on top of the moonpool cover or in some adjacent position. The weight of these heavy loads on decks needs careful consideration, so as not to exceed the deck-loading factors.

Rocker arm

The advantages and disadvantages of side transfer have been discussed. The handling system for side mating and transfer does require more complicated handling to orient the SCC correctly for mating. All the methods of handling can be used for side locking transfer, but a special technique is described here and shown in Fig. 3.46. The sequence of movement is shown in three stages using a parallelogram rocker arm and rotation mechanism. In the first stage the bell is rotated so that the mating flange is correctly positioned. In the second stage, the bell is hoisted and lowered onto the guide rails. After the guide bolts have been activated, the bell is lowered to rest on them and released from the ballast weight. In the final stage the parallelogram is swung into the mating position and the bell locked onto the DTC. The whole operation can be controlled remotely.

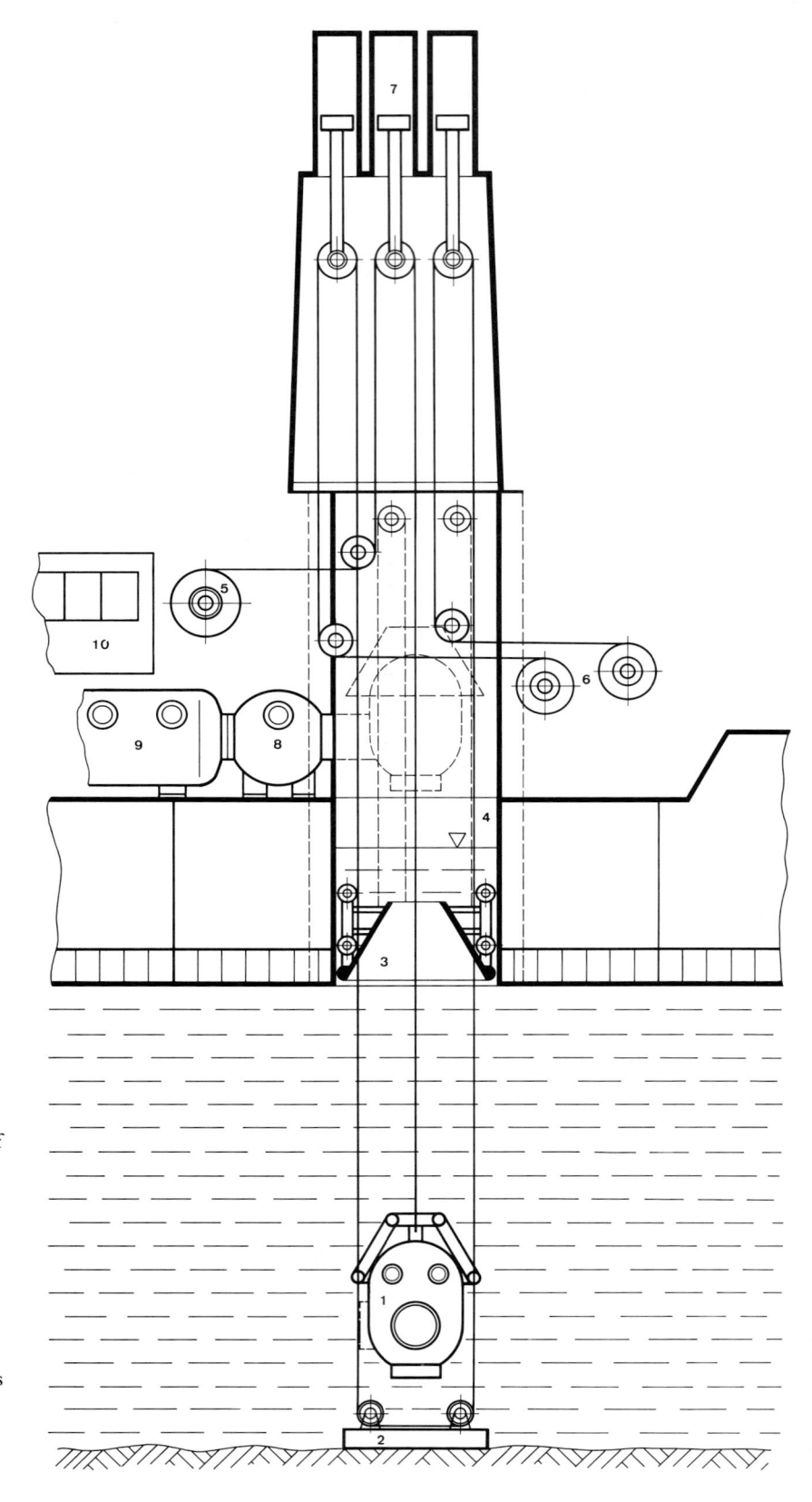

Fig. 3.48. The moonpool, lift and SCC guidance system of the diving vessel *Kattenturm*.

1. diving bell
2. anchor
3. moonpool cursor
4. moonpool
5. bell winch
6. anchor winches
7. motion compensators
8. lock
9. DCC
10. diving control cabin

Moonpool cursors

An additional modification to a moonpool allows for the fitting of a cursor, which is a trolley moving inside the moonpool. The cursor is designed to retain the diving bell and avoid any contact and possible damage to the bell by interaction with the sides of the moonpool. Fig. 3.48 shows the arrangement fitted to the diving vessel *Kattenturm*. The moonpool cursor has a centering cone which guides the fendered guide bars on the SCC into a rigid position before being hoisted through the moonpool. The reverse procedure applies in the launching operation. For mating with the DTC in side transfer a radial davit is used and heave compensators are fitted for the anchor and bell hoists.

Similar moonpool cursor systems are installed on some semi-submersible vessels, where the diving bell uses the inside of a support leg as a moonpool, and could be used on any appropriate floating installation.

Where the vessel has an exposed moonpool with a clear through deck, not normal in ships but sometimes to be found in special lifting craft, the bell can be operated from an overhead crane.

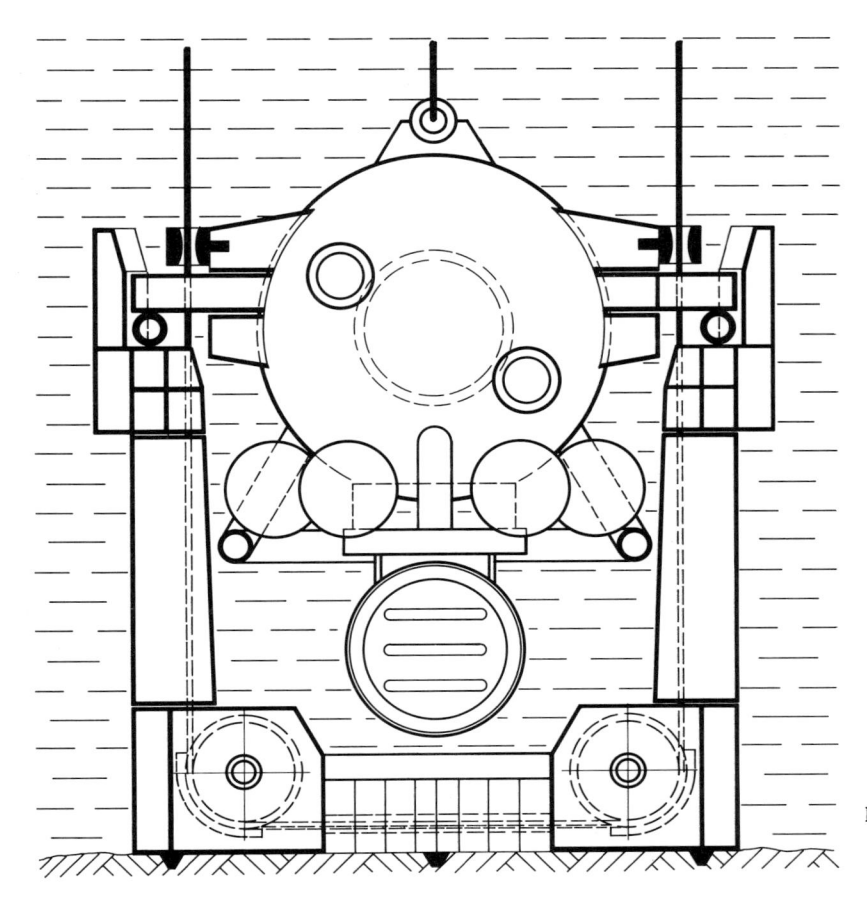

Fig. 3.49. Bottom anchor with double guide cable (Gusto, Netherlands).

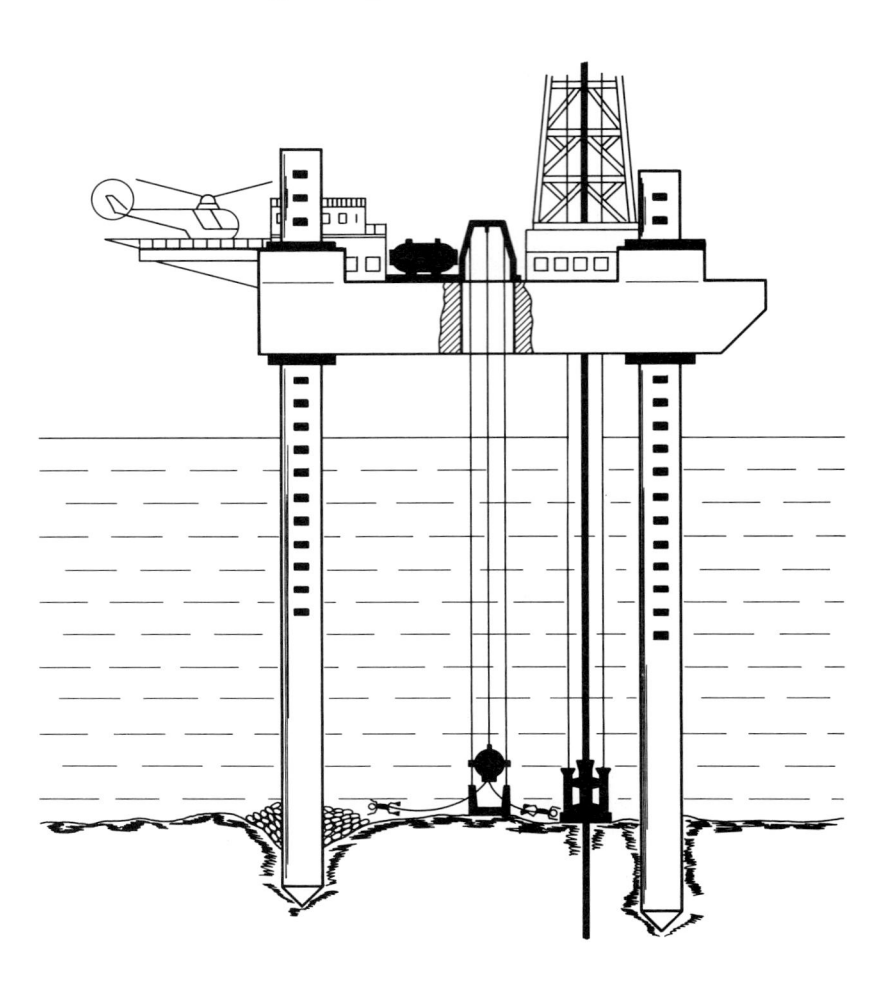

Fig. 3.50. Deep diving complex with guide wire system for SCC.

Guidance Systems

The subject of guidance systems is covered in Chapter 4, but the integration of the guidance system into the overall diving system needs some specific comment. For some diving operations a single guide wire is sufficient where the accurate position of the SCC is not the priority. Where accurate placing of the bell is needed, in most cases where bottom currents are strong and where there is clearly an advantage in positioning the diver close to the work, the use of double guide wires and anchor gives some clear advantages. In Fig. 3.49 a double guide wire system is illustrated, where the guide wire is passed through the rollers of the anchor. With one guide wire secured to a fixed point on the diving platform the anchor can be lifted and furthermore the bell can be lifted in the event of the failure or parting of the main hoist wire. Compensation for vertical movement of diving platforms can be achieved by slackening the main hoist wire and resting the bell on the anchor with sufficient clearance for the divers to pass under the bottom hatch. Heave compensators can be fitted to the main hoist wire and the guide wires to damp the vertical movement.

Fig. 3.51. Diving bell with hydraulic drive.

Winch Systems

Diving bell winches

The lowering and hoisting of SCCs are in most cases carried out using winches and, as the safety of divers is at stake, safety regulations attach great importance to this requirement. National regulations generally state the following requirements:

1. The normal operation of lowering the bell must be controlled by the main drive and not by the brake.
2. The control of movements and the speed must be smooth and not put any excess loads on the system.
3. In the case of power failure the brake must act automatically and hold the position of the bell.
4. The winch must be designed to carry 1.5 times the static load with the brakes on.
5. An automatic stop cut-out must be installed for the maximum permitted height of the SCC in the frame.
6. In addition to the normal lifting winch there must be a secondary system for recovery of the bell to the surface in case of failure of the primary system. This could be the guide wire system or the umbilical.
7. The controls must be fitted with a dead man's handle.
8. The lifting winch should be designed for a working load calculated on twice the operating weight, this weight to be considered as the larger of the following:
   a. The maximum weight of the bell in air.

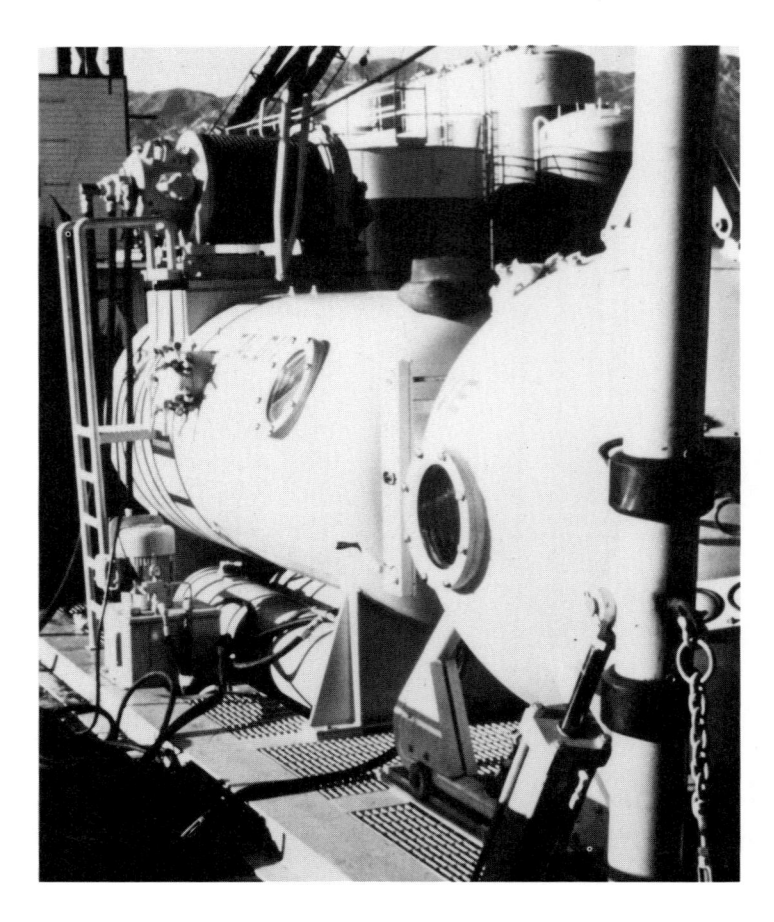

Fig. 3.52. Deep diving system compactly designed with an integrated winch system.

  b. The combination of the maximum negative buoyancy of the SCC submerged plus the weight of the lifting wire for the maximum diving depth.
9. The safety factor of the hoist wire should be eight.

  The technical specification for winches will vary and it will be sufficient for them to meet the standards of the classification societies and any national regulations. Systems designers do need to give special attention to the correct positioning of the winch, which must have a good foundation. This may not allow the most efficient lead for the hoist, which ideally is direct from the winch to the overhead lifting point. The tendency nowadays is for diving systems to be fabricated in one large unit capable of being transferred to and from a diving vessel or rig or installation in one single lift with minimum installation work to mobilize the system. Fig. 3.52 shows a complete system where the winch is conveniently sited on top with a direct wire lead. In systems operating in shallow water, the winches may be fitted directly at the lift point where the recovery system is either a radial davit or a travelling trolley. There are a few systems where the diving bell is fitted with a haul-down winch. The winch on the bell pulls the bell down on a cable secured to an anchor. The bell has therefore an additional safety factor in that it is buoyant at all times

Fig. 3.53. Gusto winch system with umbilical winch for a deep diving installation.

and this arrangement is used in manned intervention capsules for transferring to subsea production cellars.

If guide wires are fitted in the system, drum winches are required, similar to the main hoist winches, and are often fitted with constant-tension devices to dampen any movement caused by the rise and fall of the sea. The guide wires and anchor can be used as an emergency hoist arrangement for the bell by lifting the bell on the anchor (see Fig. 3.49) and the selection of the winch should allow for the additional weight of the bell in the water, at least to the surface, but not necessarily out of the water.

Umbilical winches

There are divided opinions as to whether the various eventual life-support services should be inside sheathing to make a compact unit or taped together with secure fittings. A sheathed umbilical is as much as three times more expensive than a bundle of loose services, due not only to the additional cost of sheathing but also to the additional expense of fitting an umbilical winch drum, which is large, because of the size of the umbilical and because it requires expensive slip rings (Fig. 3.53). For diving systems operating in relatively shallow water the loose umbilical is generally preferred, so that the taped umbilical can be hoisted inboard by hand with the assistance of a powered drum. Fig. 3.54 illustrates different methods of handling umbilicals.

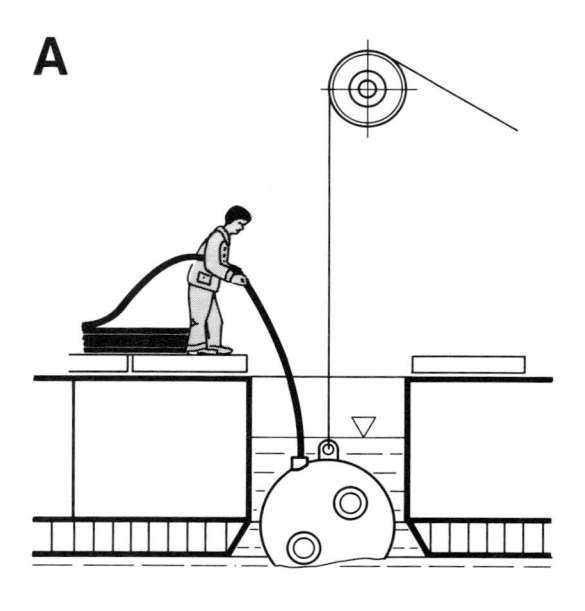

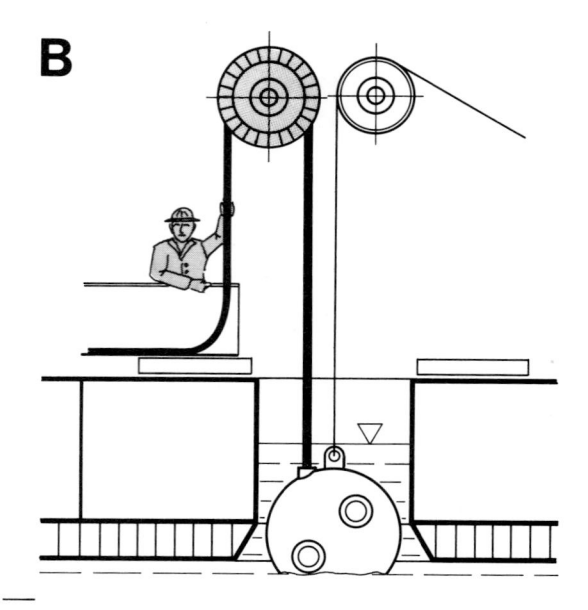

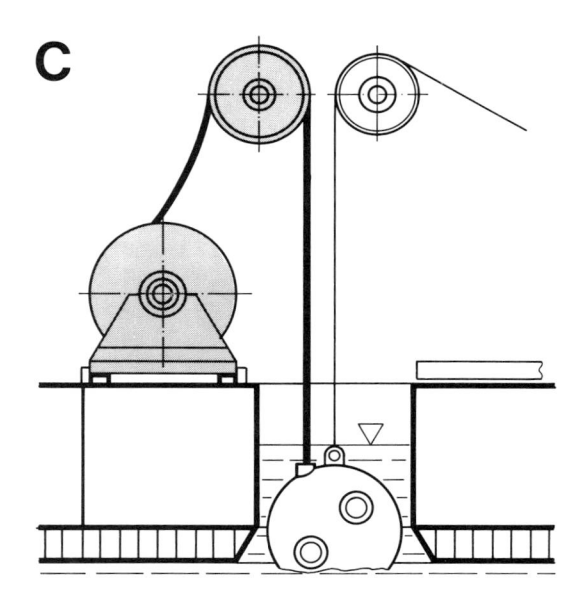

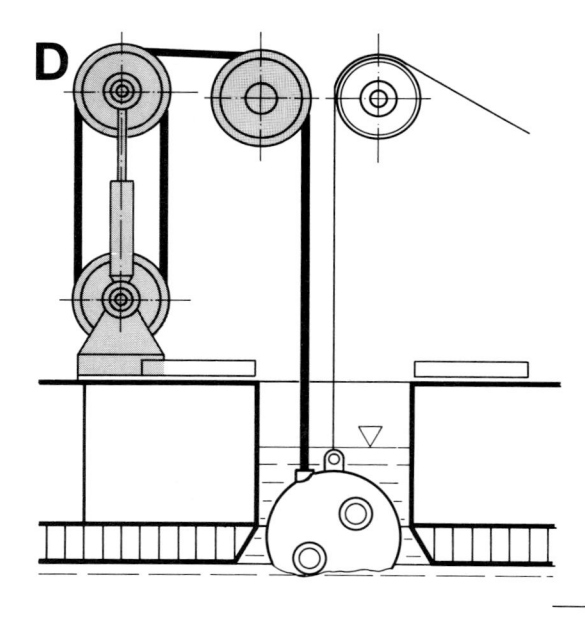

Fig. 3.54. Methods for umbilical handling.

- **A** Manual only. For medium depths and light unsheathed umbilicals. Low cost, but requires personnel for operation and large space for stowage
- **B** Power drum. Suitable for umbilicals with and without sheathing. Low cost. Little space needed for stowage. Personnel needed only for stowage
- **C** Umbilical winch with slip ring. Suitable only for sheathed umbilicals. High cost. Little space needed for stowage. Minimum personnel required
- **D** Block and pulley ring. Additional length of umbilical needed but requires few personnel. Rarely used

Fig. 3.55. A 'stacked' saturation diving system by Taylor Diving enables two teams of divers to operate independently at different depths. Both DCCs use the same submersible diving chamber.

Sanitary Systems

Every complex will need adequate sanitary arrangements, including the domestic hot and cold water supply system for the divers. The fire-fighting system for a saturation diving complex is usually incorporated in it.

Fresh Water System

The fresh water is supplied from the central water tanks, in this case two 500-litre pressure-proof tanks, and the internal pressure is maintained with the oxy-helium breathing mixture. With an appropriate pressure regulator, the water pressure is maintained at slight over-pressure to the internal chamber pressure where the water will be used and water level indicators are fitted. The hot water is supplied by passing the cold water from the tank through a non-pressurized heat-exchanger, through double valves and pressure regulator to the internal chamber manifolds. Cold water is plumbed into the chamber in the same way. Hot and cold water are supplied to the basin and shower and cold water only to the lavatory closet.

Sewage Fluids

All fluids, both washing water and lavatory fluids for disposal, are poured into a pressure-proof collecting tank outside the main chamber with a capacity of 30–50 litres. The used water from showers and hand-basins is passed to a bilge inside the chamber and then, with the WC fluids, is passed through a double valved pipe to outside the chamber to a collecting tank which drains to a common tank for discharge overboard at normal pressure. A mechanically interlocking pair of valves is fitted to avoid premature discharge.

Hot Water Supply

Hot water for diver heating and for heating the SCC is also supplied from the central domestic services and may be either fresh or sea water. Sea water is normally used for heating as it is not recirculated. After passing down the umbilical in insulated hoses, it is dispersed into the sea after use by the divers in heating their suits and by the radiator inside the SCC. The overall water system should be cross-connected to allow any deficient systems to be supplied by other systems.

Fire-fighting Systems

Little is known about the physiological effects of the common fire suppressants if used in hyperbaric chambers under pressure. It must be assumed that, although effective in putting the fire out, they will contaminate the chamber atmosphere and be dangerous. The use of inert gases, such as helium, to suppress the chamber gas has been proposed, but there are certain problems. If the inert gas is not helium, a proportion of it will dissolve in the tissues of the divers, inducing unknown physiological problems including possibly narcosis, and also it can itself be toxic. The use of inert gas will also increase the pressure.

Fire in a hyperbaric chamber requires a source of ignition and fuel and the degree of risk is relevant to the density of oxygen molecules present. When the volume percentage of oxygen is substantially below the normal atmospheric percentage of 21% the risk decreases and may in some cases be almost non-existent. However, when the partial pressures increase, so do the risks of fire, to an extent that spontaneous combustion may occur if the fuel is available. Therefore, although in mixed gas diving the risks of a fire are low, the use of high-oxygen content or pure oxygen for normal or therapeutic decompression needs most careful monitoring and the use of BIBS (built-in breathing systems) with overboard dumping. Should a fire occur in a chamber where helium is being used as the inert gas, there will be swifter propagation due to the high heat conductivity of helium.

In compressed-air chambers the risk is therefore considerably higher than in mixed gas chambers and the occupants will usually be unable to do anything to fight the fire or even call for help. It is therefore essential that a fire detection system should be virtually instantaneous in activating a safe fire suppression system and should not be sensitive to any other environmental change except that caused by incipient fire. The development of infra-red scan equipment to detect temperature rises, although expensive, will produce an effective means of fire detection.

The most effective fire suppressant is water and the best available technique is to force water at high pressure through fog nozzles, causing a super-saturated atmosphere. The water should be as cold as possible. Sea water should not be used as, being conductive, it may well initiate an electrolytic reaction with the source of the fire, producing a dangerous gas, hydrogen, for example. Sea water can also complicate the treatment of burns sustained by the divers. The design should allow for a 2000-litre pressure vessel for water kept at 10 bar pressure above the maximum chamber-operating pressure and activated by a fire detector. The system should also be capable of normal operation both internally and externally. Ideally, the suppressant should be selective for use in various chambers. In the event of fire in the SCC the shower, if available, can be used.

Diving Equipment

The choice of diving equipment depends on the size and function of the deep diving system. The considerations that apply to the design of the complex are in most cases the same as in the selection of diving equipment. The ultimate task requirement, the depth of water, the environmental conditions, the dive profile and the number of divers are all factors to be considered. In the final analysis the divers' equipment will need to be compatible with the diving complex to become part of the total system. A complete set of equipment normally comprises the following items; the breathing system is considered in detail in Chapter 10.

1. Diving suit, preferably heated, with hood, socks and gloves.
2. Boots or fins, depending on the task.
3. Weight belt with interchangeable weights.
4. Breathing system (open, semi-closed or closed).
5. Diver heating system for breathing gas and water.
6. Umbilical, comprising connecting gas hoses for supply and recovery, hot-water hoses and communication cables.
7. Divers' watches, knives, torches, compasses, etc.

Under-water Television Systems

Hand-held television systems are sometimes carried by the diver or fixed onto his helmet. Fitted with lights and possibly small display monitors at depth in addition to the surface monitors, these systems are marketed by a number of companies.

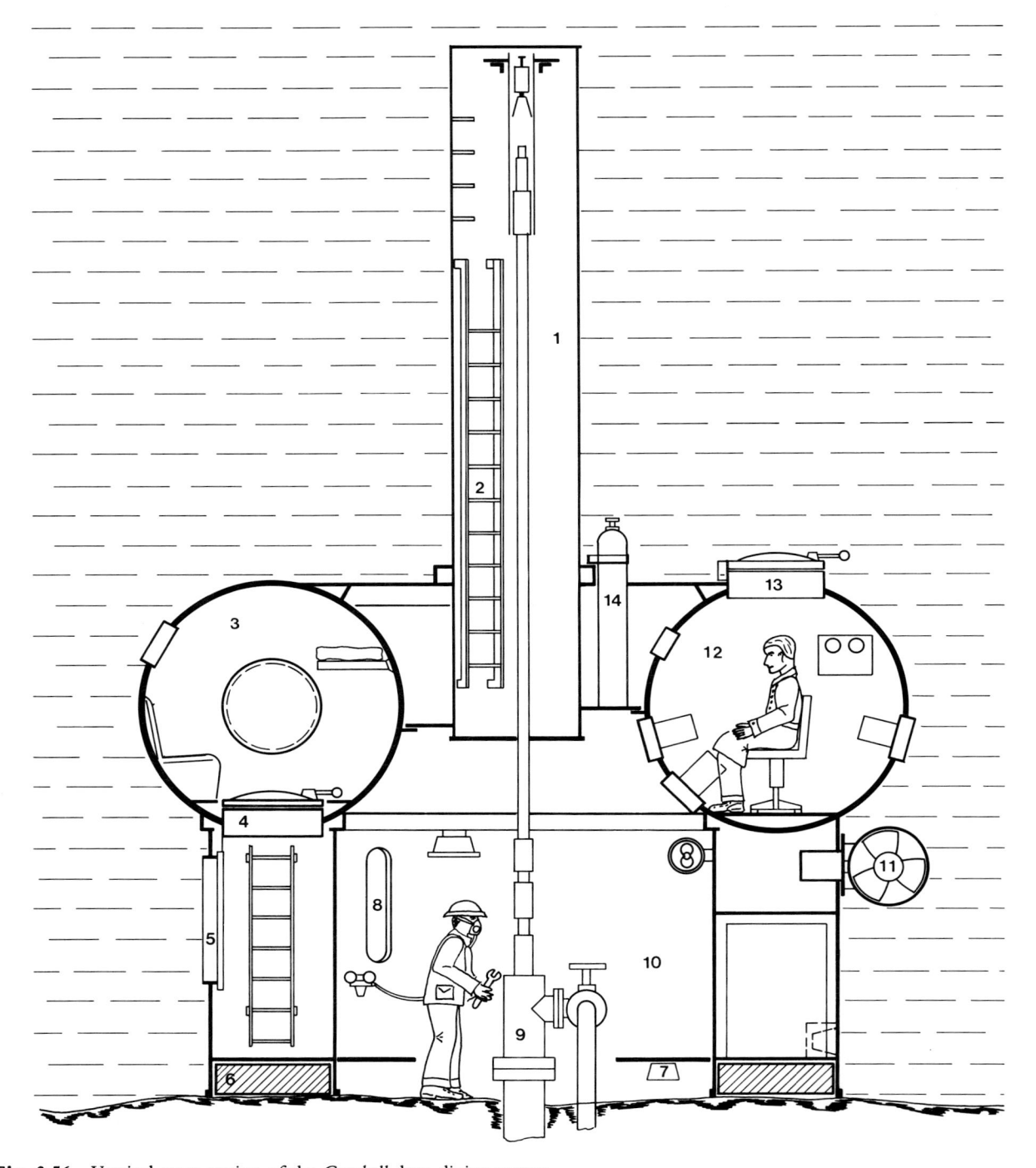

Fig. 3.56. Vertical cross-section of the *Capshell* deep diving system.

1 shaft for pipe assembly
2 ladder
3 pressure hull
4 exit hatch, bottom
5 exit hatch, water
6 solid ballast
7 external lights
8 hatch to caisson work chamber
9 drilling unit
10 caisson work chamber
11 propulsion unit
12 observation room
13 exit hatch, top
14 gas storage

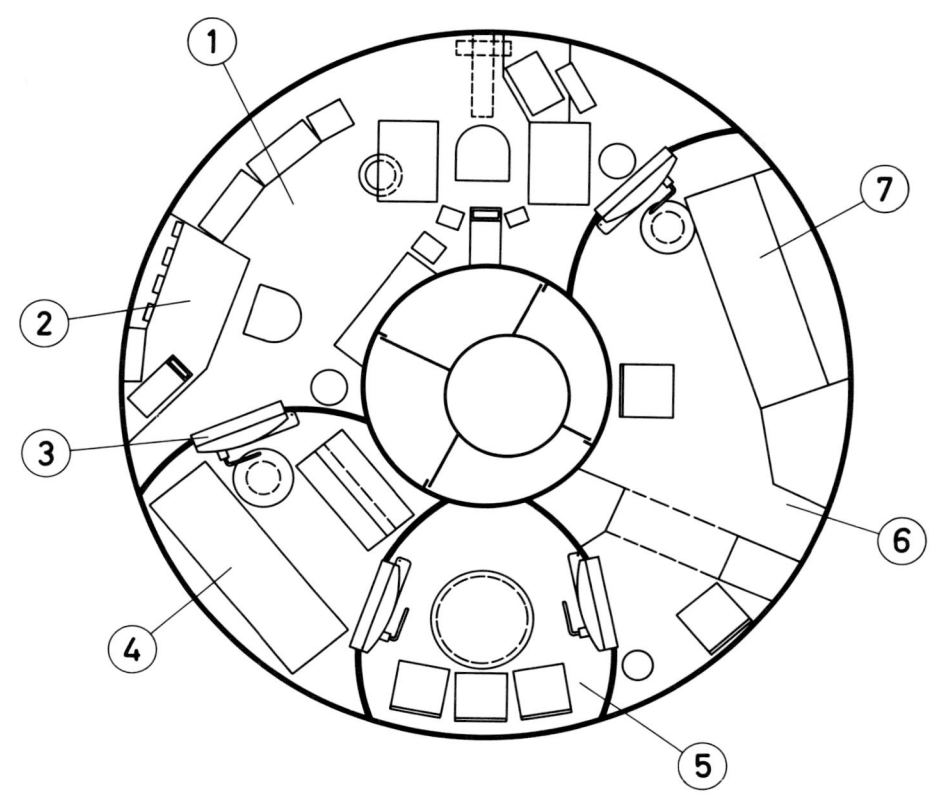

Fig. 3.57. Horizontal cross-section of the *Capshell* deep diving system.

1 monitoring compartment
2 control panel
3 transfer hatch
4 decompression room
5 transfer compartment to caisson
6 beds
7 living chamber

Under-water Tools

Apart from general-purpose tools used on the surface, a considerable number of specially adapted tools are used in the off-shore industry depending on the task. Similar provisions of compatibility with the diving system that apply to diving equipment are relevant. Compatible power sources and the size and compactness of the tools are vital considerations.

Capsule Systems

Most deep diving systems conform to the design principle of a deck decompression chamber and a separate diving bell. A number of deep diving systems have been built which incorporate into one unit the two functions of working at depth and decompression. Here we examine two such systems, *Capshell*, a development of Shell, and a much smaller unit, *Subcom*. It is difficult to know whether to classify *Capshell* as an under-water habitat or a tethered vehicle.

Fig. 3.58. Combined decompression chamber and diving bell *Subcom*.

Capshell

In Figs 3.56 and 3.57 the total deep diving work system *Capshell* is illustrated. The torus-shaped pressure vessel is subdivided into several pressure compartments. Below is a double-walled skirt, the centre being a work site, with gratings on the bottom, allowing the area to be flooded or dewatered in similar fashion to a caisson. A tower extends above the level of the pressure compartment to house well servicing wire line equipment. *Capshell* was designed with an operating depth of 200 m and, with breathing gases, air and power supplied from the surface, it theoretically has unlimited endurance. With side thrusters as shown in Fig. 3.56, it could manoeuvre over a work site. The operations and living level is shown in Fig. 3.57. The operations compartment has a closed-circuit television system covering all chambers. There is a DCC for living and a further DCC to decompress divers. A transfer chamber separates the two chambers and leads down into the work chamber.

Capshell was built in 1967, a concept well ahead of its time. Although the unit was never used as fully intended, the concept is as valid now as then, which is to get maximum endurance on the seabed with unlimited power resources and avoid the surface interface. The limitations of the *Capshell* design—small pressure compartments, heavy weight and dependence through an umbilical on a mothership—will need to be overcome. The commercial submarine concept in the 1980s will overcome these limitations to a great extent and *Capshell* has recently been converted to a submarine.

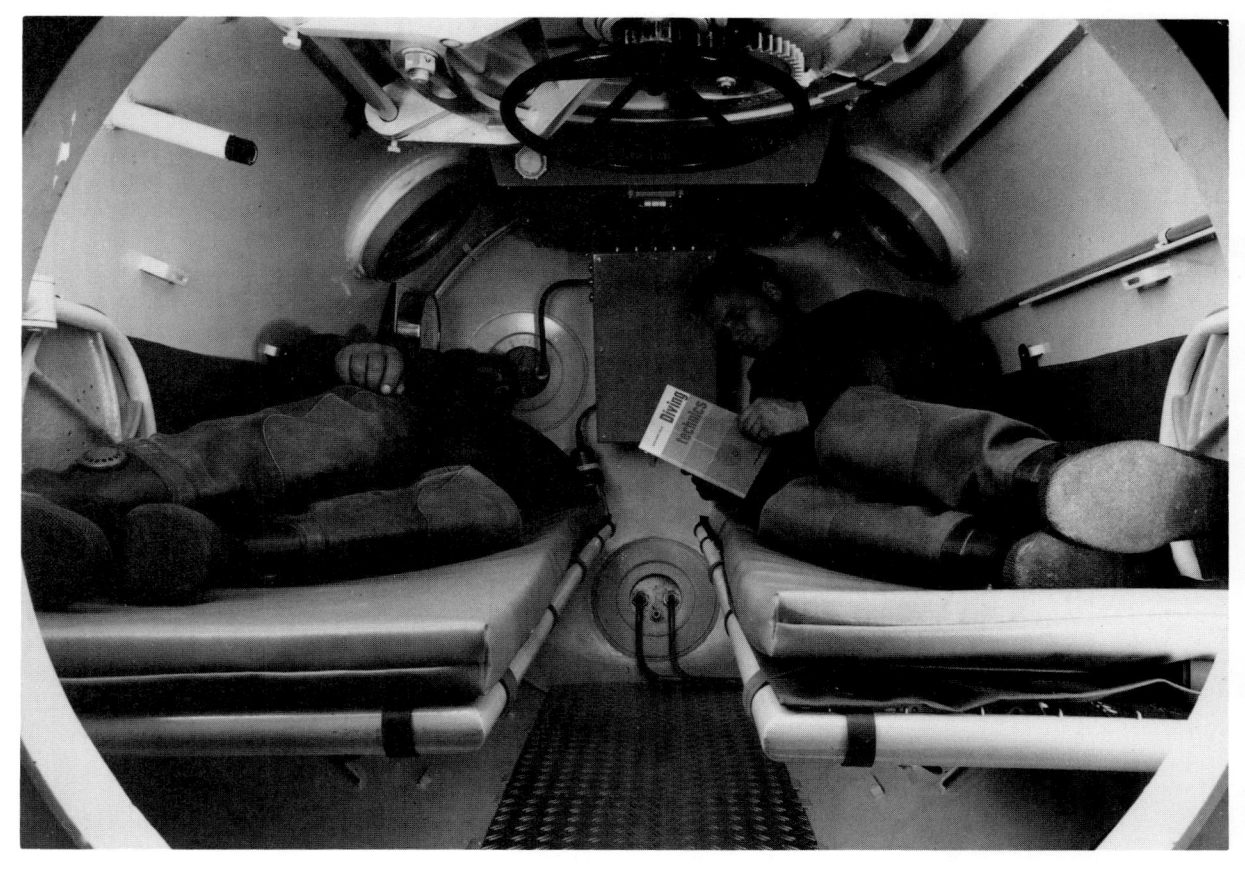

Fig. 3.59. *Subcom* combined decompression chamber and diving bell during the decompression of two divers.

Combined DCC and SCC

For limited, short-duration dives, a *Subcom* design as shown in Fig. 3.59 can be used. For diving the unit is operated vertically and for decompression it is used horizontally. With a diameter of 1300 mm and a length of at least 2200 mm the very restricted living space limits its capability to short-duration dives only. The gas supply cylinders are fitted around the cylinder and there is a small separate control panel. Two unfolding bunks are fitted internally for decompression and a supply lock is also fitted. Electrical connections are provided for heating. The system can be modified to accept a one-man decompression chamber for transfer of divers.

4 Submersible Compression Chambers, Open Diving Bells and Observation Chambers

Submersible Compression Chambers (Diving Bells)

Deep diving techniques have developed with great speed in recent years and this has necessitated an increased use of improved diving bells. Bells are an essential component of all deep diving systems that include one or more compression chambers, the diver's equipment and such peripherals as the gas supply system, winches, trolleys etc.

In this context the definition of a submersible compression chamber (SCC) or bell is a water- and gas-tight vessel (usually) without a propulsion system which is lowered by winch or crane into the water and from which a diver can lock out. Sometimes small electric or hydraulic thrusters are fitted to give limited horizontal, radial motion. The purpose of the bell is to provide vertical transport for the diver to and from the work site and to act as a refuge for the diver when there.

With the introduction of saturation diving the use of the SCC became essential since it permits the vertical movement of the diver at any desired pressure irrespective of the ambient hydrostatic pressure. The SCC provides the diver with a haven which is warm, dry, light and relatively comfortable. These features, together with its ability to transport him effortlessly to the vicinity of his task, reduce both his physiological and his psychological load. It is normal for the diver to be supplied with gas and heating, either electrically or by hot water, from the SCC. The bell also supplies light and visual observation and supervision of the diver from it is possible.

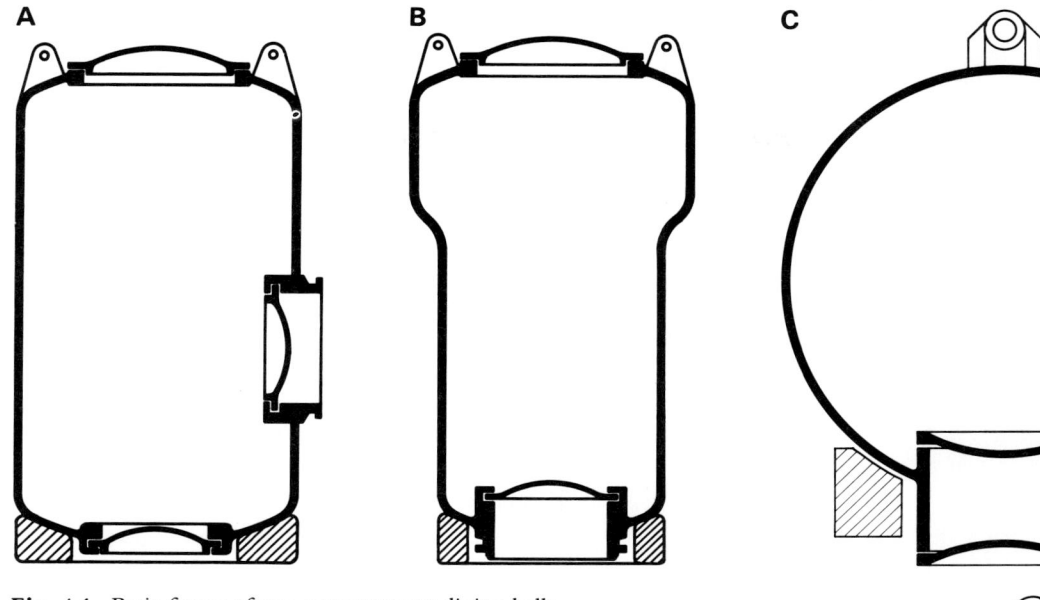

Fig. 4.1. Basic forms of one-compartment diving bells.

- **A** Cylindrical one-compartment bell with top entry, side transfer flange and permanent or loose ballast. Generally used up to 200 m
- **B** Cylindrical one-compartment bell with enlarged upper third. Bottom exit, bottom flange and top entry. Permanent or loose ballast. Rarely used
- **C** Spherical one-compartment diving bell with bottom exit, side hatch, side transfer flange. Permanent or loose ballast. The commonest type
- **D** Oval one-compartment bell with bottom exit, side hatch, side transfer flange. Permanent or loose ballast. Increasingly common

The economic advantage of the SCC is most obvious when successive teams of saturation divers are working. It is, however, still economic on most other deep diving tasks and it always increases the diver's safety. For these reasons it is regularly specified and sometimes legally required for all jobs deeper than 50 m, whether the task is salvage, in support of the oil industry or working on a dam.

The SCC has been proved satisfactory when operated from such varied surface support platforms as ships, rigs or barges. It is an added protection when passing through the sea/air interface in rough weather or tidal conditions and when free ascent would be dangerous. Lastly, it ensures that satisfactory decompression procedures are used.

Survey of Different Types

When studying the various forms the SCC can take it is useful to consider the surface compression chamber which also can have several varieties. In both cases the construction is dictated by the number of compartments and crew and by the pressure strengths, mating possibilities and types of gas supply specified.

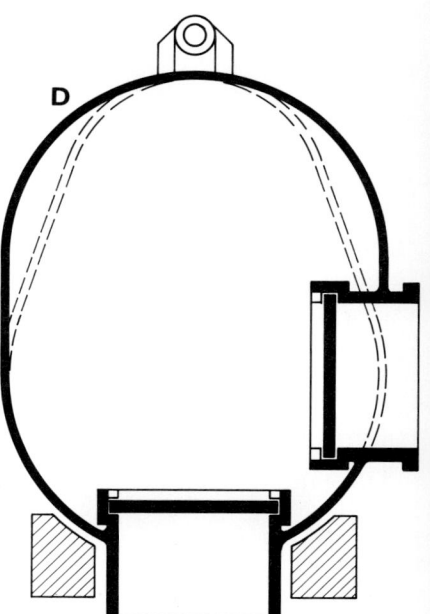

Fig. 4.2. Dräger diving bell TK 100 ready for operation in the German research vessel *Friedrich Heinke* at the Biological Institute, Helgoland.

One-compartment diving bells

The simplest and least expensive is the one-compartment diving bell where the external dimensions can be kept reasonably small and thus produce a reasonable weight. Operationally this type is very popular. The only possible disadvantage is that the tender is subjected to the same pressure as the diver, but it must be appreciated that the diver may require immediate assistance and consequently this is not a significant disadvantage. The common basic designs are shown in Fig. 4.1.

Type A is suitable and normal for low pressures. The vertical cylindrical vessel is made with dished caps at both ends. The drawing shows it fitted with a side transfer flange and top entry, although the simplest type might have just a bottom hatch with only one-way pressurization. A diameter of 1300 mm would provide the minimum chamber for divers and tenders. Any reduction of this diameter would lead to a lack of safety in handling diving gear and internal equipment. It is sufficient for two divers and a third could join them if necessary.

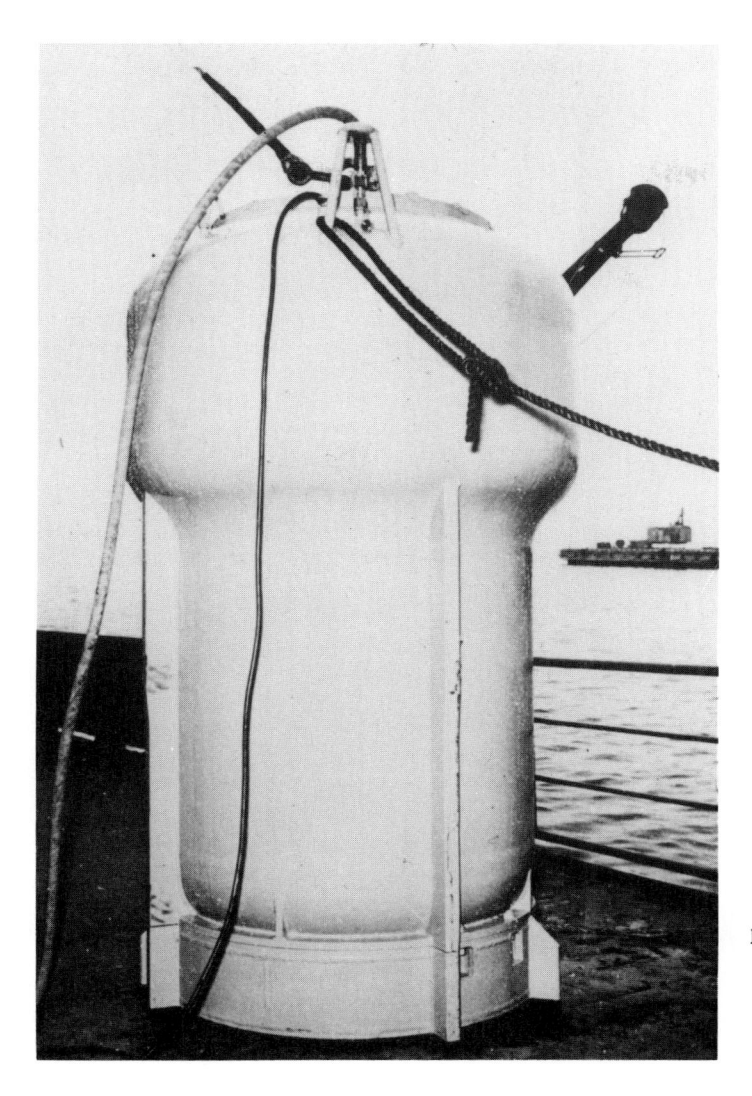

Fig. 4.3. One-compartment diving bell with the upper part of the cylindrical pressure hull enlarged, on board the diving ship *Belos* of the Royal Swedish Navy.

The height of the bell should allow an adult to stand upright. From this one would get a fully equipped bell weighing 3.5–5 tonnes. The ballast problem will be discussed in detail later in this chapter. The maximum operating pressure for cylindrical vessels of these dimensions is about 25 bar when using a high-grade boiler steel for construction. The operating range could be increased by stiffening frames, but as positive buoyancy after the release of the ballast weight is essential, weight considerations limit this solution. Fig. 4.3 shows a typical one-compartment bell.

More complicated and therefore more expensive to manufacture is *Type B* in Fig. 4.1. Better utilization of space is provided by this shape as all instruments, fittings and units necessary for operating can be installed in the upper large diameter. It is a feature of this design that there are no fittings externally, but consequently the amount of gas

Fig. 4.4. One-compartment diving bell in spherical form, Dräger model TK 500, designed for a maximum internal and external pressure of 50 bar, corresponding to a diving depth of 500 m.

that can be stored internally is severely restricted. Fig. 4.3 shows this unique design which was built by the Royal Swedish Navy.

A hybrid design consisting of a conical vessel with hemispherical ends which might be advantageous for use with a moonpool is shown by the dotted line in *Type D* in Fig. 4.1.

The spherical shape in *Type C* in Fig. 4.1. is the best solution when considering pressure stresses from inside or out and provides the minimum surface area and wall thickness for the maximum internal volume. A sphere constructed of boiler steel H1 with a thickness of 15 mm and 2000 mm diameter will provide 4.67 m^3 volume and is suitable for a pressure differential of 20 bar. To meet the same pressure requirements a cylinder of 1500 mm diameter and 2000 mm height produces a volume of only 3.5 m^3 but requires a wall thickness of 18 mm. Consequently for all pressures in excess of 20 bar a spherical design should be used. Unfortunately it is more difficult to manufacture these curved shapes and in the above example the ratio of pressure vessel costs is about 1.4:1. Spherical vessels are normally constructed from hemispheres, except for the larger sizes where it is possible, and sometimes necessary, to use segments because they provide a better control of wall thickness and thus save weight.

Fig. 4.5. One-compartment diving bell with oval form (Comex).

Fig. 4.4 shows a spherical diving bell designed for a maximum internal or external pressure of 50 bar. It is compact, with gas storage in spherical tanks. Recent trends have produced bells with hemispherical ends and a short cylindrical centre section which is also both compact and economical in space. A chamber of 1800 mm diameter and 2100 mm height has proved ideal for *Type D* in Fig. 4.1. The two bottom doors are made of titanium alloy with pressure sealing on one side only.

Fig. 4.5 shows a modern oval-shaped diving bell, insulated and fitted out. The doors of the system, which are made of high-yield titanium, are much easier for the divers to handle as they are only one-third of the weight of those made with high-grade boiler steel.

Two-compartment diving bells

Very few of this type have been made in recent years. Their disadvantages of high initial price, large size and weight and

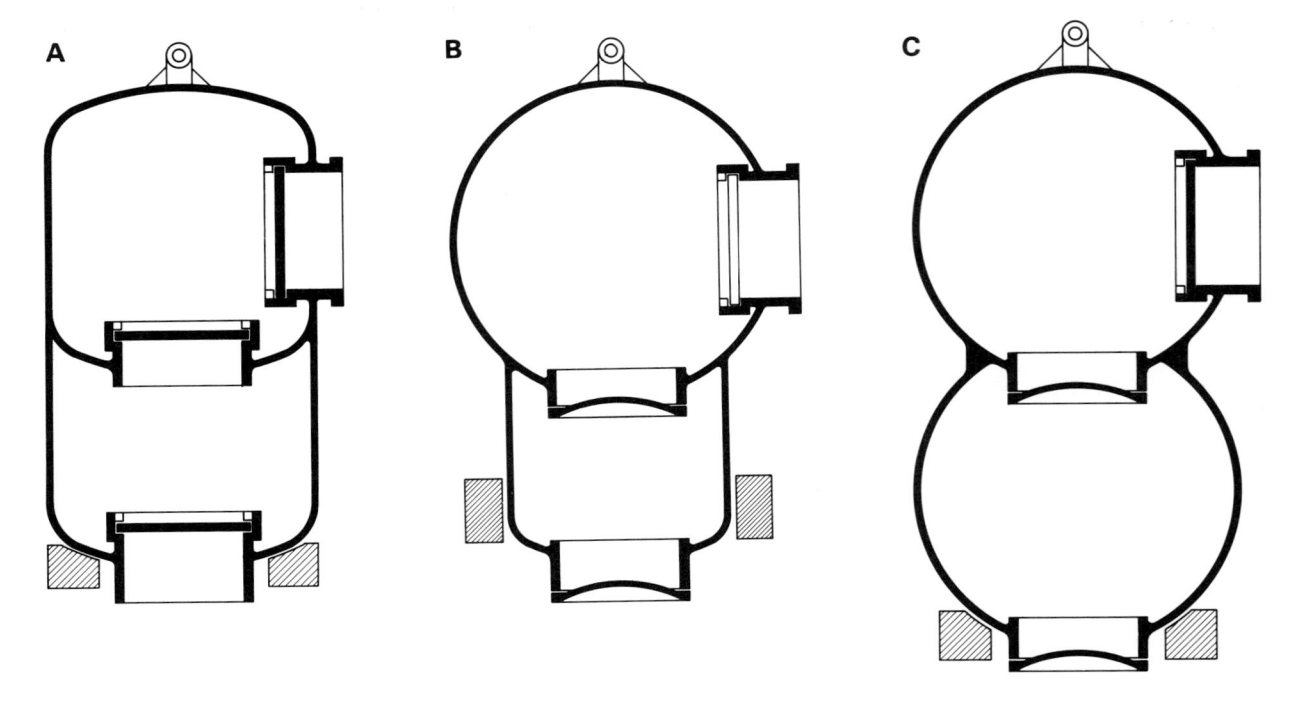

Fig. 4.6. Basic types of two-compartment diving bells.

- **A** Cylindrical bell with bottom exit, side hatch, side transfer flange and ballast
- **B** Sphere/cylinder combination with bottom exit, side transfer flange, side hatch and ballast
- **C** Spherical bell with bottom exit, side hatch, side transfer flange and ballast

awkwardness to handle are not balanced by their advantage of close one-atmosphere supervision of the diver by the supervisor from the upper compartment. There is no doubt that the system does provide some increase in safety but in no way sufficient to overcome the disadvantages and the increased operating costs.

Fig. 4.6 shows three types of this design. *Type A*, with its cylindrical shape, is reminiscent of a one-lock compression chamber but has the added disadvantage of very large total height in addition to its total size and weight. *Type B* is a better design, giving the supervisor or supervisors a better view of the working diver and with a more convenient shape for the arrangement internally of monitoring equipment and other fittings. The lower part is sufficient for two divers. Using high-grade boiler steel a pressure rating of 40 bar can be achieved with this design. Flanging can be either on the side or underneath; providing both types of flange gives a better safety factor and allows more varied applications. *Type C* meets all requirements, particularly maximum operating pressures, but the same disadvantages of price, weight and height still apply and consequently it has only limited application. Also a sphere is a wasteful shape for the wet compartment. If the lock-out shaft can be used for standing, a minimum diameter of 1600 mm is acceptable.

Pressure Strength (Internal–External)

SCC differ from open diving bells in that they can be hermetically sealed. All modern ones can be pressurized both internally and externally. A few old systems were designed for internal pressurization and can withstand only slight external pressure. This double pressure requirement presents problems for pressure vessel construction, especially for cylindrical shapes where stiffening rings may be required. The designs of bulkheads, penetrators and doors are all influenced by this problem. For doors it is necessary to choose mechanically simple but large double doors or else some form of bayonet or ring lock.

Fig. 4.7 shows the space requirement of both types. Although in recent times price and simplicity have led to the predominance of double-door solutions, there are some advantages of safety and reduced space in the single-door solution. It is still, however, largely a matter of individual company preference.

Window construction and the need for penetrators must be taken into account when calculating the strength requirements of the chamber wall.

Fig. 4.8 shows the three different pressure conditions to which an SDC is subjected. These are:

1. *Internal pressure* occurs when the divers are under pressure in the chamber, when the internal pressure will be greater than the external ambient pressure. This will occur either when the divers are pressurized on the surface, before being lowered to the working depth (at which pressures will be equal), or when they are returning to the surface to be recompressed or returned to saturation pressure.

2. *External pressure* occurs when the bell is used in the observation mode and internal pressure remains at atmospheric pressure whilst the external pressure corresponds to the water depth.

3. *Equal pressure* occurs when the SCC is depressurized on deck or is being used by a diver at depth when locking out.

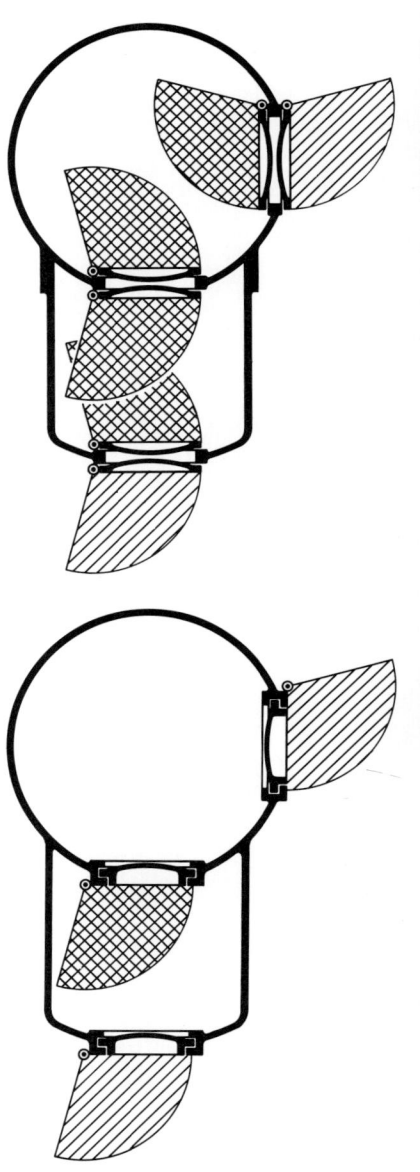

Fig. 4.7. The space requirements in diving bells for opening and closing different types of doors.

Mating Flange Systems

The method of mating the SCC to the DCC will dictate the type of flange system to be fitted. The SCC can be put on top of the DCC, alongside it or underneath it. The last has been studied theoretically only.

Table 4.1 shows the relative advantages and disadvantages of the two methods. Technically, top transfer is advantageous for reasons of cost and ease of making the initial seal between the two chambers.

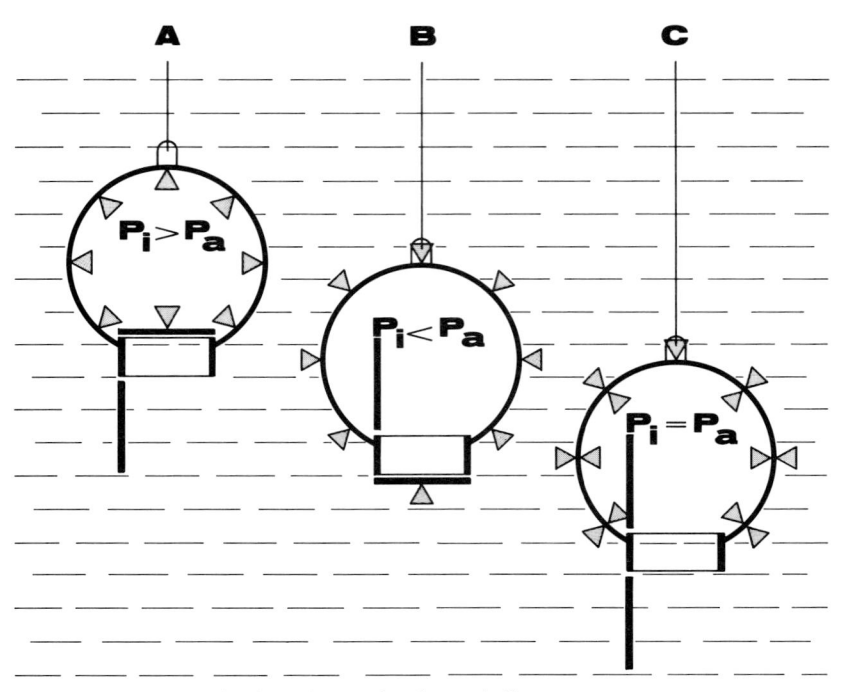

Fig. 4.8. Pressure load conditions for diving bells.

    A Internal pressure greater than external. Diving bell operating as a transfer capsule

    B External pressure greater than internal. Diving bell used as an observation chamber

    C Internal and external pressure equal. Diver locked out from bell under water

Fig. 4.9. Spherical diving bell with side transfer flange and bayonet lock for two-way pressurization.

Table 4.1. Comparison of side and top transfer

Symbol	Criterion	Top Transfer	Side Transfer
	Threading into guide mechanism	Easy with special guide mechanism. Increased danger of swinging due to greater crane height	Easy by special guide mechanism. Procedure can be automated
	Making seal at transfer flange (plane position)	Excellent plane position is reached by own weight. No adjustment necessary	Precise adjustment necessary to attain plane position of transfer flange
	Handling of SCC	Long transport distances due to horizontal motion. Flange position discretionary	Short horizontal distance. Flange must be positioned correctly
	Shifting of centre of gravity	May become critical for upward motion with arrangement on deck	Minimum influence
	Location below deck	Large deck height necessary in area of deep diving system	No problems with moonpool system
	Transfer DCC/SDC	Vertical transfer somewhat troublesome	Horizontal transfer easy
	Water restriction	Water easily carried into transfer compartment	Good. Only a little water carried into transfer compartment
	Safety	Rescue of divers may be very difficult. They may be lying on bottom hatch	Facilitates rescue of divers
	Cost	Small. Bottom hatch doubles for transfer to DCC	Large. Additional hatch must be inserted in SCC (except for rollover systems)

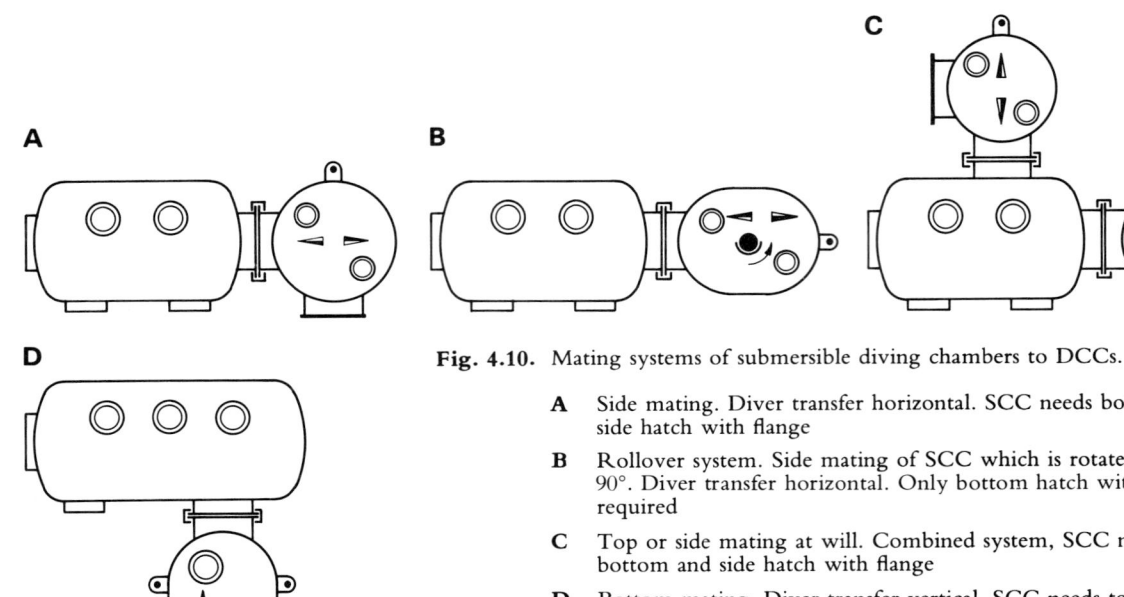

Fig. 4.10. Mating systems of submersible diving chambers to DCCs.

- **A** Side mating. Diver transfer horizontal. SCC needs bottom and side hatch with flange
- **B** Rollover system. Side mating of SCC which is rotated about 90°. Diver transfer horizontal. Only bottom hatch with flange required
- **C** Top or side mating at will. Combined system, SCC needs bottom and side hatch with flange
- **D** Bottom mating. Diver transfer vertical. SCC needs top hatch with mating flange and bottom hatch (rarely used)

Side transfer has advantages with regard to safety. The residual water in the chamber after the dive is retained and divers and equipment can be more easily transferred, particularly injured divers. This has led to a preference for the latter system recently.

There are also a few combined systems and others where the bottom flange mates on the side of the DCC in a horizontal position (rollover systems).

Diving Bell Components

As with SCCs there are several varieties of component which can be used in each type of bell. The basic features remain the same but details are constantly changing to deal with increasingly severe requirements, new materials and new methods of manufacture. The following examples are all taken from one-compartment diving bells but are equally applicable to other types.

Doors (hatches)

The same basic design in DCCs is used for side-transfer doors and intercompartment doors in bells except that, due to even greater restrictions on space, doors of 600 and 700 mm diameter are used instead of the standard 800 mm.

Fig. 4.12 shows a modern side-transfer door of titanium alloy with a bayonet lock which can be pressurized and operated from both sides. Operation is by a mechanical tappet drive and as it is only required to move horizontally the expensive hydraulic drive is omitted. The O-ring seal faces are preferably produced with a coating of stainless steel.

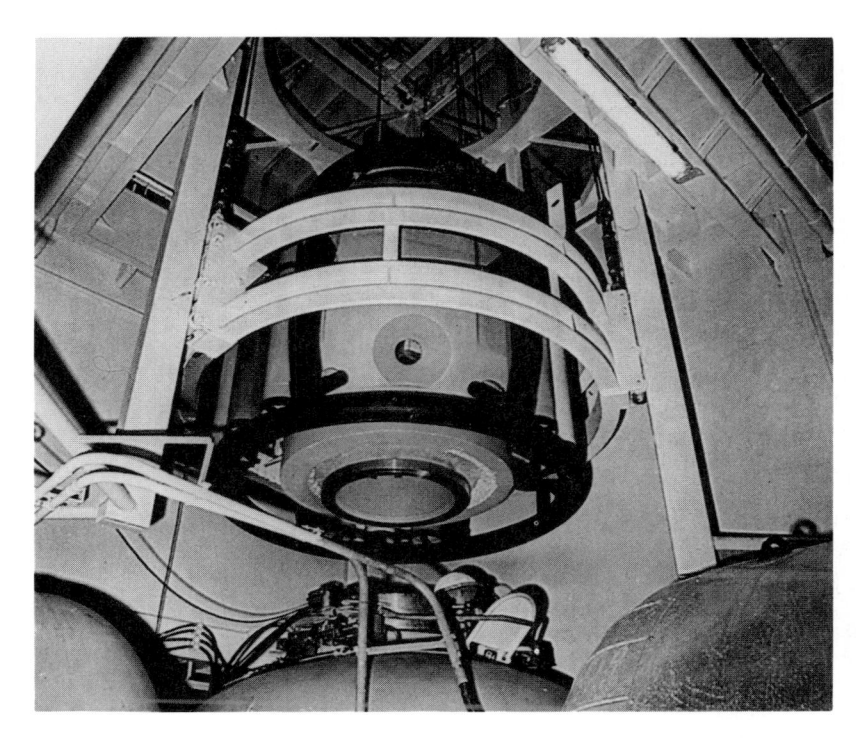

Fig. 4.11. Diving bell for top transfer in a travelling cage on board the *Seaway Falcon* (Stolt Nielsen).

Fig. 4.12. Side door of a diving bell with a bayonet lock and a tappet drive for rotation.

184   Subsea Manned Engineering

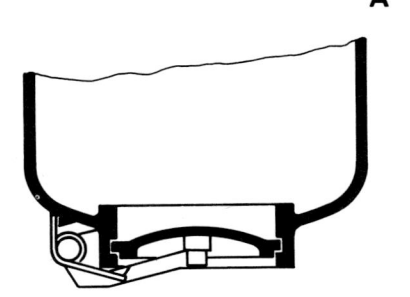

Fig. 4.13. Bottom exit systems on diving bells.

    A   Bayonet lock door opening outward. May use either spring or weight compensators or hydraulic cylinder and hinge

    B   Bayonet lock or sliding lock door opening inwards, with hydraulic or mechanical rotation and lifting

    C   Double-door bottom hatch. Depending on weight, may be with or without lifting appliance. Double joints at the outside

Where space conditions permit, a double door can be fitted. It requires a double-hinge arrangement for the outer door to allow space for mating. Automatic mating is not possible.

The bottom exit requires special attention because it must be easily operated by divers under pressure and, as the materials are thus exposed to ambient sea conditions, they require careful selection. In addition it must be possible to open the door from the outside in an emergency if the operating mechanism fails. There are three basic types: the two-way pressurized door, usually with bayonet lock, which can be made to open either inwards or outwards and the double door system. The three types are shown in Fig. 4.13.
and the double door system. The three types are shown in Fig. 4.17.

Type A is a bayonet lock outward-opening door requiring no internal space. Either springs or weights can be used to compensate for the door weight. Neither system is completely satisfactory as compensation can be chosen for only one position of the door, usually 45°. It is advisable, therefore, to have tackle available to ensure closure under all conditions. Alternatively either hydraulic cylinders or rotary units can be fitted, the linear motion of the piston being transformed into the swinging motion by a joint.

B

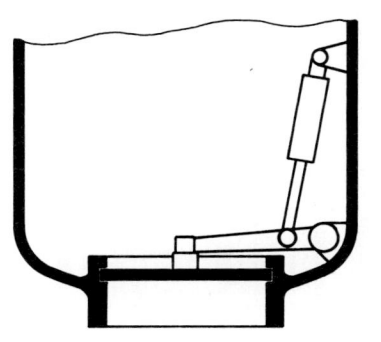

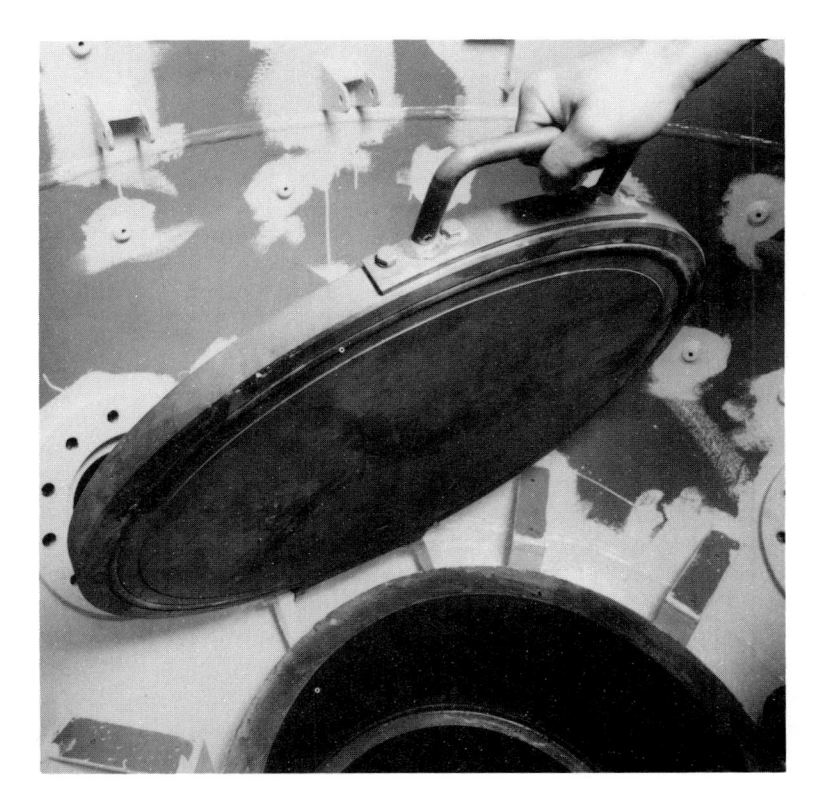

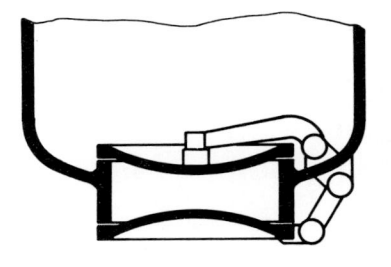

C

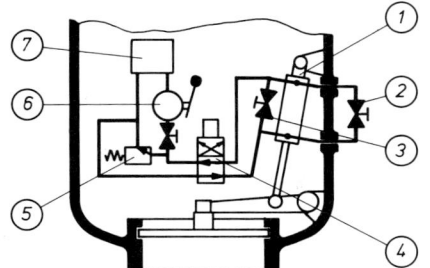

Fig. 4.14. Hydraulic drive for door (lifting and lowering).

1 hydraulic cylinder
2 external short-circuit valve
3 internal short-circuit valve
4 selection valve
5 safety pressure-equalizing valve
6 hydraulic hand pump
7 hydraulic fluid container

Type B is similar but in this case it is fitted with a slide lock and opens inwards. Both bayonet and slide locks can be rotated hydraulically, but provision must be made for the connection of a pump externally in order to open the door in an emergency. The use of a mechanical tappet drive allows the door to be opened both safely and simply from either side. When hydraulic fluids are used care must be taken to ensure that they are neither flammable nor toxic.

Type C is the double-door design. Depending on the pressure conditions, only one door need be shut at any one time. The relative simplicity is paid for by a larger space requirement and some reduction in safety. Heavy doors will still require weight compensation but those manufactured in titanium alloy may be plane plates requiring no compensation. The only disadvantage of titanium is the cost of the material and the difficulty in working it.

The decision on which type of system to use is dependent on the many parameters involved which have been discussed here only briefly and no one system can be recommended categorically.

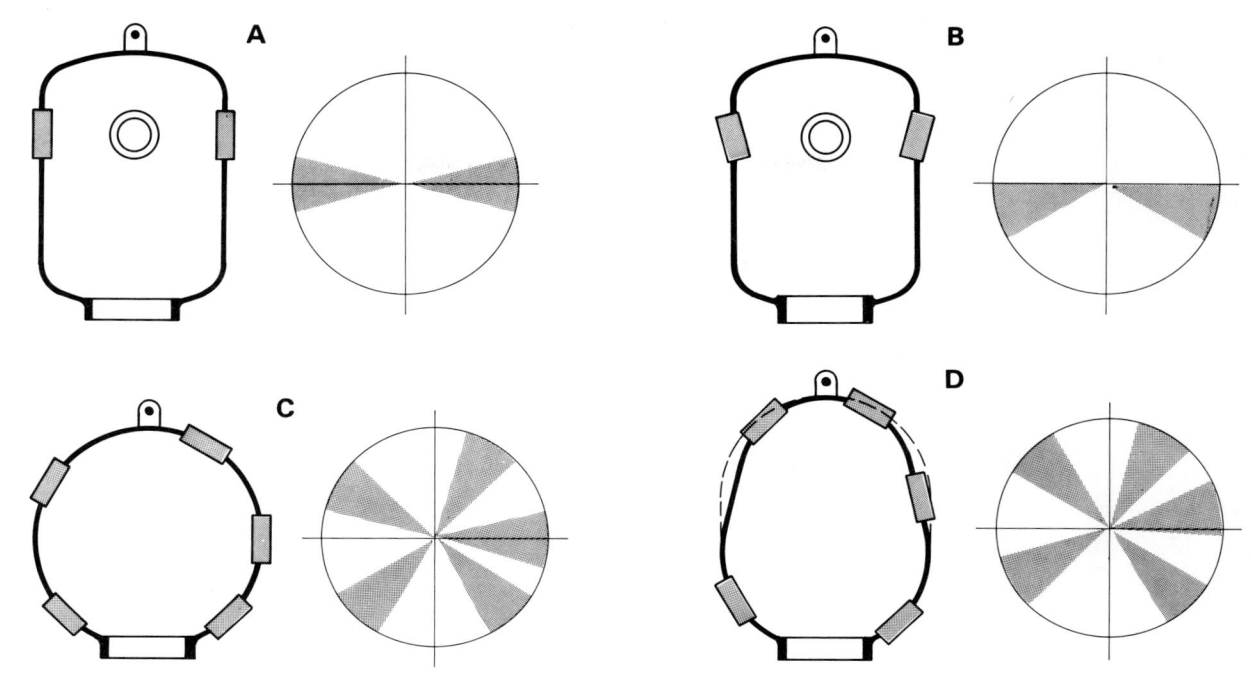

Fig. 4.15. Typical siting of windows on diving bells.

- **A** Simplest arrangement. Visibility is considerably restricted upwards and downwards
- **B** Improved arrangement. Little sight upwards, but better in downward direction
- **C, D** Ideal visibility is possible in spherical, oval or conical bells in spite of simple framing

Windows

Windows are required almost exclusively for observation from inside. Their number, size and position are dictated by the need to avoid blind arcs. This is easiest to achieve with a spherical or oval SCC. As pressure is exerted on both sides, care must be taken to ensure that the external ring is bolted to take the full internal pressure. Protection is required against mechanical damage by projecting rings, plates, grills or the fendering itself.

Acrylic, as opposed to silica glass, is preferred both for its machining qualities and for its resistance to mechanical impact damage. Extensive and thorough testing by Dr Igor Stachiw has proved its superiority over all other materials. Over-dimensioning in respect to strength appears to be necessary and normal. Usually the window is made from a cylindrical plate or disc, although some are single or double conical plates. There are only a few curved dished plates in use. The whole tendency is towards more and larger windows.

Fig. 4.15 shows typical window positions. Vision is obviously restricted in Types A and B, although less so in the latter case. While good visibility is obtained with Types C and D, it must be

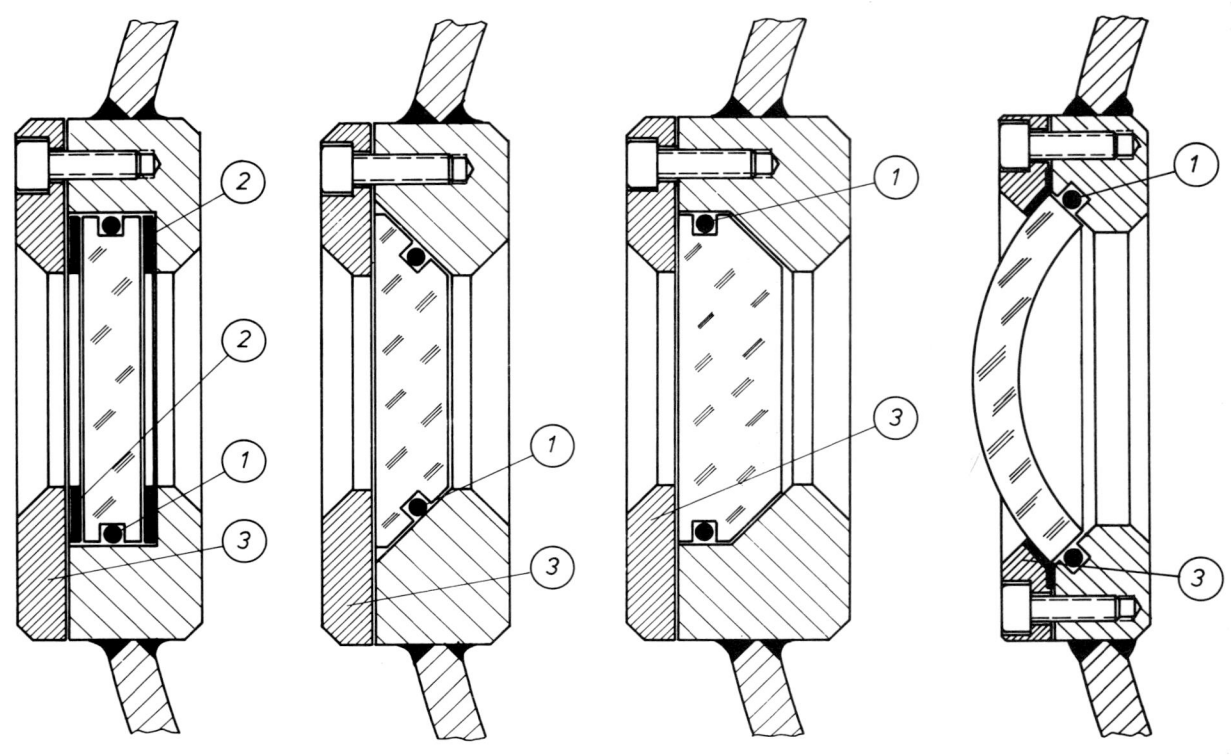

Fig. 4.16. Types of window for diving bells with two-way pressurization (modified from Det Norske Veritas).

1 neoprene O-ring
2 hard-bearing gasket
3 support ring with high-strength bolts

remembered that this will be reduced by the external fittings on the SCC. In Fig. 4.16 the different methods of securing the glass are shown.

Flanging system for SCC and DCC mating

A transfer or mating flange is provided to allow the transfer under pressure of divers between the SCC and DCC. The type depends on whether side or top transfer is used or a capability for both is required. The four most common systems are summarized in Fig. 4.17.

Type A was very common but is now rarely used due to the time taken in screwing up the nuts, no matter whether hinged bolts or studs are used, and because of the increased pressures currently in use. Small radial or angular misalignment is unimportant and the system is cheap.

Type B was normal for top transfer in the British off-shore areas but the small tie rods are not suitable for large pressures. Some radial misalignment is acceptable.

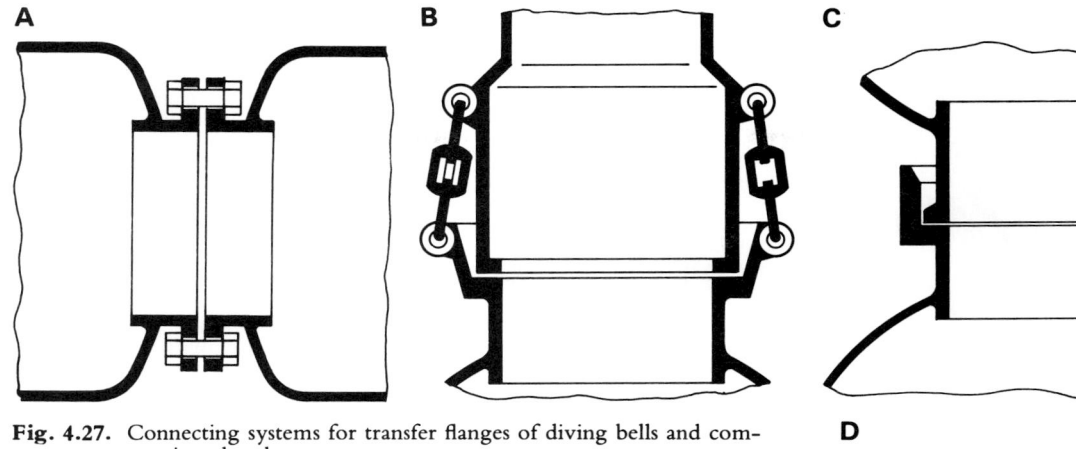

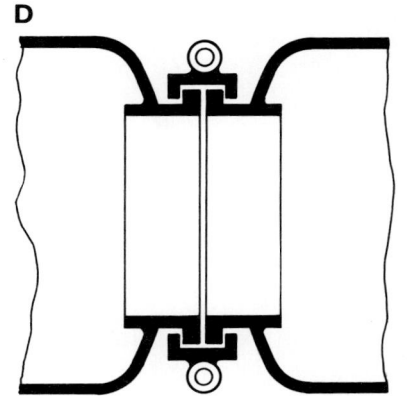

Fig. 4.27. Connecting systems for transfer flanges of diving bells and compression chambers.

- **A** Locking by hinged bolts or studs. Small radial or angular deviation acceptable
- **B** Locking by tie-rods. Precise centering not necessary. Suitable for low pressure only
- **C** Locking by tapered bolts and conical ring. Simple and inexpensive
- **D** Lock with bayonet ring or U-ring segments. Precise centering required. Suitable for maximum pressures

Type C is mainly used in Sub Sea International's bells. The conical bolts are slow to screw up over the conical flange but it is reliable, easy to operate and cheap.

Type D is a locked bayonet ring or a two or four part U-profile clamp ring. Provided centering is precise, especially with side mating, this form of mating is unsurpassed. The bayonet ring can be rotated manually by a toothed gear or operated by hydraulic or pneumatic power. For high-pressure systems this method is increasingly common, with either conical or parallel flange rings and power operated. The Americans commonly use spindle gears. It is essential that either the bell should be swung into position or the support should be adjusted to prevent excessive misalignment, which would either prevent mating or place unacceptable loads on the connecting parts. Some systems provide self-correction for a limited amount of misalignment.

Ballast

Ballast is necessary to ensure negative buoyancy when the SCC is lowered to the work site. After dropping in an emergency the bell must have residual positive buoyancy in order to return to the surface unassisted, even if fully loaded with crew and equipment. Depending on the size of the chamber, the type of operation and the safety regulations in force, a minimum buoyancy of 0.2 tonnes is required. If there is no system of jettisoning the umbilical at the bell, allowance is required for its weight.

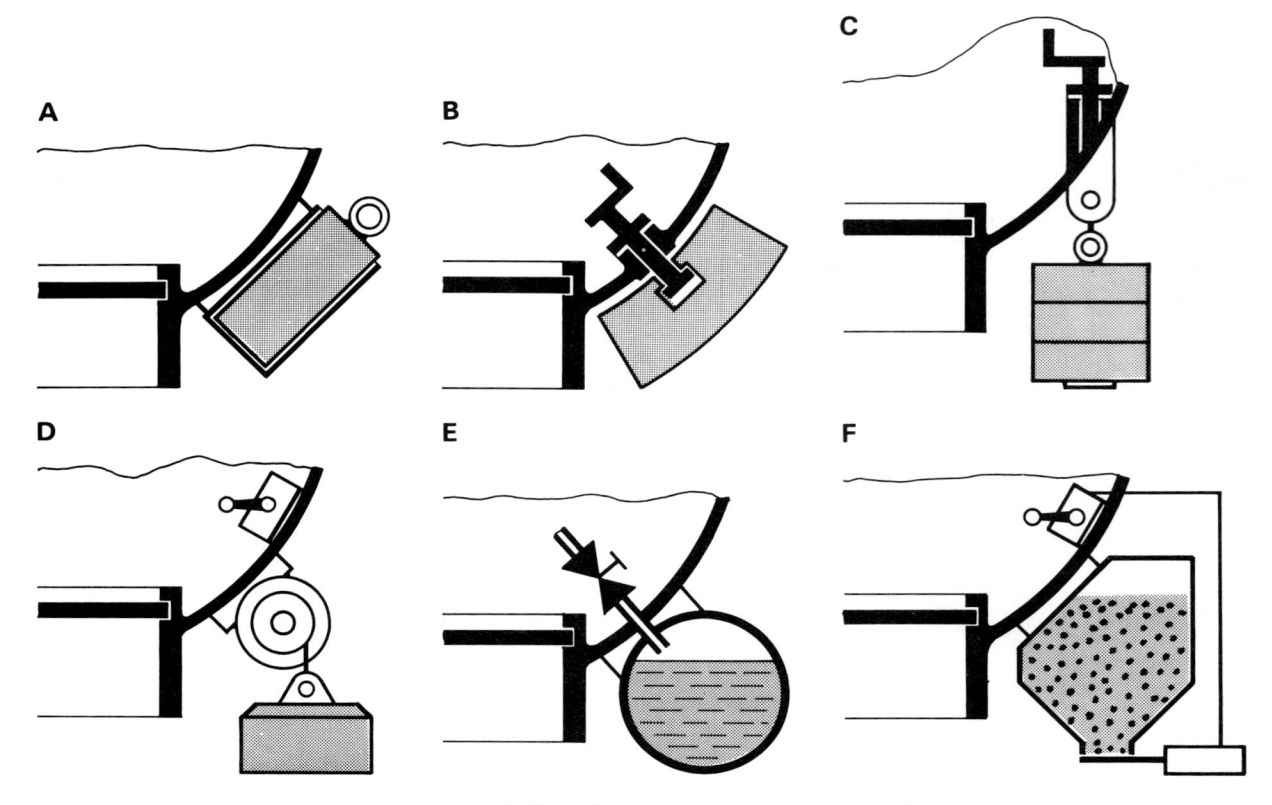

Fig. 4.18. Ballast arrangements on diving bells.

- **A** Permanent ballast which can not be jettisoned by crew. This system should not be used
- **B** Ballast ring or single weights can be released from the inside. For an example see Fig. 4.19
- **C** Hanging ballast. Length adjustable, weight changeable. Can be released from the interior. For an example see Fig. 4.4
- **D** Ballast on a winch. Diving bell descends with the help of the winch
- **E** Ballast tanks can be flooded and emptied for regulation of the buoyancy of the bell
- **F** Ballast pellets can be released in a controlled manner. The container is kept closed mechanically, hydraulically or electrically

Fig. 4.18 shows a few examples of different types of ballast system.

Type A is the cheapest and simplest system. The weights are either placed loosely or bottled into a tray. They cannot be released from inside the bell and consequently the system is unacceptable on grounds of safety.

Type B is typical for a bell fitted with a bottom anchor or base frame. The ballast is in the form of divided rings, spherical segments or suspended cylinders and can be jettisoned quickly and easily from inside the bell. The release mechanism must be fitted with a safety device to prevent unintentional operation. By fitting it in two parts

Fig. 4.19. Submersible diving chamber with ballast ring.

the release of one will reduce the negative buoyancy and allow the bell to be hoisted by the umbilical.

Type C allows the bell to remain floating the correct distance above the bottom to allow the diver to lock out if the bell system is designed without a bottom frame or used without an anchor. Again the weights can be released easily and quickly internally.

Type D is a rare system which allows the bell to be hauled down to the correct distance from the bottom by the internal winches and prevents the ship's motion being transmitted to the bell during operations.

In *Type E* the ballast tank is flooded or emptied as in a submersible and provides a variable control at considerable technical cost.

Another rare system is *Type F*, where the ballast is chopped scrap metal retained and released by a mechanical or electromagnetic arrangement.

Most modern systems allow the weight to be changed to conform with the operation requirement.

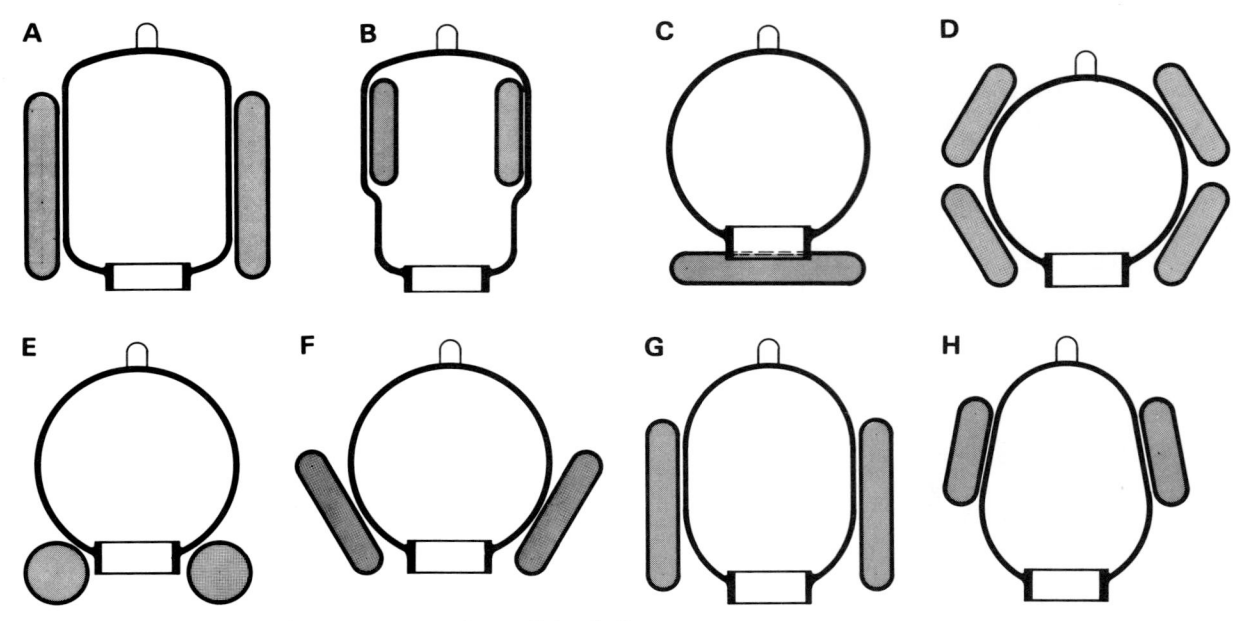

Fig. 4.20. Arrangements for gas storage tanks on diving bells.

- **A** Cylindrical bell with large vertical storage cylinders
- **B** Cylindrical bell with enlargement containing medium-sized storage tanks inside
- **C** Spherical bell with storage cylinders at the bottom
- **D** Spherical bell with storage cylinders at top and bottom
- **E** Spherical bell with spherical storage tanks
- **F** Spherical bell with horizontal storage cylinders on the frame
- **G** Oval bell with similar vertical storage cylinders
- **H** Pear-shaped bell with vertical storage cylinders in the conical section

Gas supply

The gas supply of a DCC provides two functions. It provides life-support for the occupants and ambient pressure at the work site. Basically three types are possible:

1. Bulk stowage on the bell.
2. Surface supply through an umbilical.
3. A combination of (1) and (2).

In Type 1 the supply is limited by the need to pressurize the bell and the restricted stowage available. Type 2 provides unlimited capacity but increases the risk due to possible damage to the umbilical. Consequently Type 3 is the accepted method.

In Fig. 4.20 eight methods of storing gas on a SCC are shown. The rare two-compartment bell is not covered. In *Type A*, the main consideration is not to restrict the view from the windows by the vertical storage cylinder. *Type B*, an infrequent solution, severely restricts the gas storage capacity but leaves the outside clear. *Type C* is a spherical bell with standard 50 litre bottles and *Type D* a spherical bell with greater number of bottles which could be scuba size. *Type E*

Fig. 4.21. Fendering system of a modern diving bell.

offers the most compact solution, with a favourable weight ratio due to shape. A typical American solution is *Type F*. In *Type G*, owing to the size of the bell, 50 litre cylinders have to be replaced by 20 litre bottles near the windows. In *Type H* small scuba bottles can be fitted. Types E and F permit a saddle-shaped frame design which allows easy mating to the DCC and sufficient ground clearance for locking out. In all cases mechanical protection must be fitted and straps and clamps stressed against shock, which is inevitable.

To protect storage tanks and other external fittings, fendering is necessary. This should have rubber supports and covering to dampen shocks. Fig. 4.21 shows the fendering of a spherical bell which is conical at the top to fit entry into a ship's moonpool. The four large sliding fenders are made from heavy tube and are cushioned by elements of rubber bonded to metal.

Penetrations of the pressure shell must be kept to a minimum and all gas penetrators must be fitted with a valve either side of the shell for safety purposes.

Umbilical cables

In order to minimize the risk of entanglement, it is advisable to have as few connections as possible between bell and surface in addition to the lifting cable. Practice shows that the interconnections for the following functions are necessary:

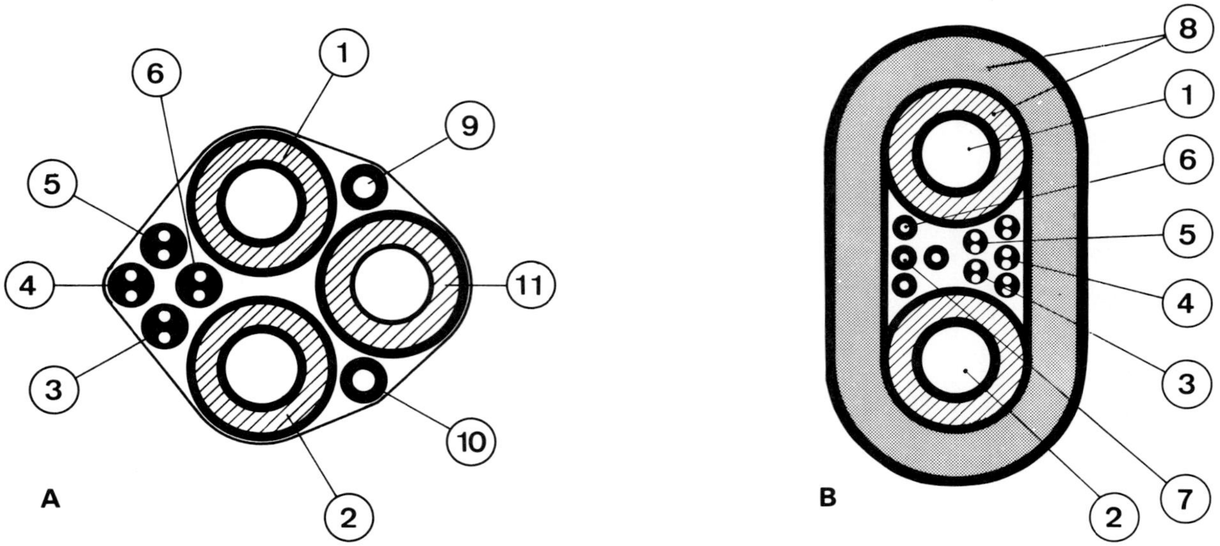

Fig. 4.22. Cross sectional drawings of taped (A) and coated (B) umbilical cables.

1 gas supply hose
2 gas return hose
3 signal system
4 telephone system
5 intercommunication system
6 energy supply 1
7 energy supply 2
8 coating
9 pneumogauge
10 spare
11 diver heating

1. Supply of gas to the bell.
2. Removal of gas from the bell.
3. Supply of electrical power.
4. Supply of hot-water heating.
5. Measurement of diving bell pressure and depth.
6. Communications by telephone, loudspeaker, television etc.
7. Measurement of bell gas (O_2 partial pressure and CO_2 partial pressure).
8. Physiological data on the divers.

This will result in a large bunch of wires and hoses, some of which may require duplication for safety.

Fig. 4.22 shows the cross-section of the 550 m long umbilical cable in the diving ship *Arctic Seal*. For reasons of safety all the wires and hoses must be combined into one bundle. The sheathing of the umbilical makes handling easy and gives protection, but repairs are impractical, modification impossible and the price exorbitant. Therefore most umbilicals are formed by bunching together the cables and binding them with strong adhesive tape at 2-m intervals. Manual handling is not easy and there is little protection, but the disadvantages of the moulded solution are overcome. The umbilical must be supported at the bell to prevent tension at the entry point. A cutter will allow the user to release the cable if free ascent is necessary or entanglement necessitates it. The handling of umbilicals and related appliances are discussed in detail in Chapter 3.

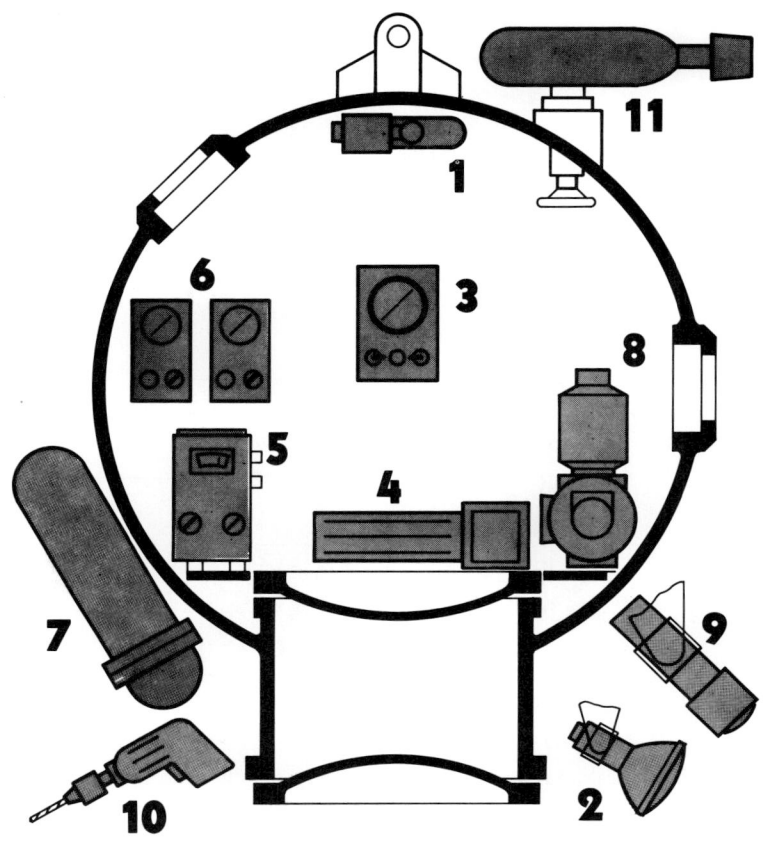

Fig. 4.23. Consumers of electrical energy in diving bells. The approximate number of Watts required is shown in brackets.

1. internal lights (50–100)
2. external lights, fixed or moveable (1000–2000)
3. communication systems (50)
4. electrical heating (2000–2500)
5. hot-water generator for divers' suits (5000–10 000)
6. gas measuring instruments
7. circulation compressor for closed circuit (5000)
8. blower for CO_2 scrubber (200)
9. television system, internal/external (750)
10. electrical tools and testing devices (1000)
11. electric propulsion (5000–20 000)

Power supply

Electric power is required in SCC for all or some of the following systems:

1. Internal lighting.
2. Fixed and movable external lights.
3. Communication systems (intercommunications, internal television) and signal systems.
4. Chamber heating (unless by surface-supplied hot water).
5. Hot-water supply for diver suit heating and perhaps a shower.
6. Measuring systems for general and individual monitoring.

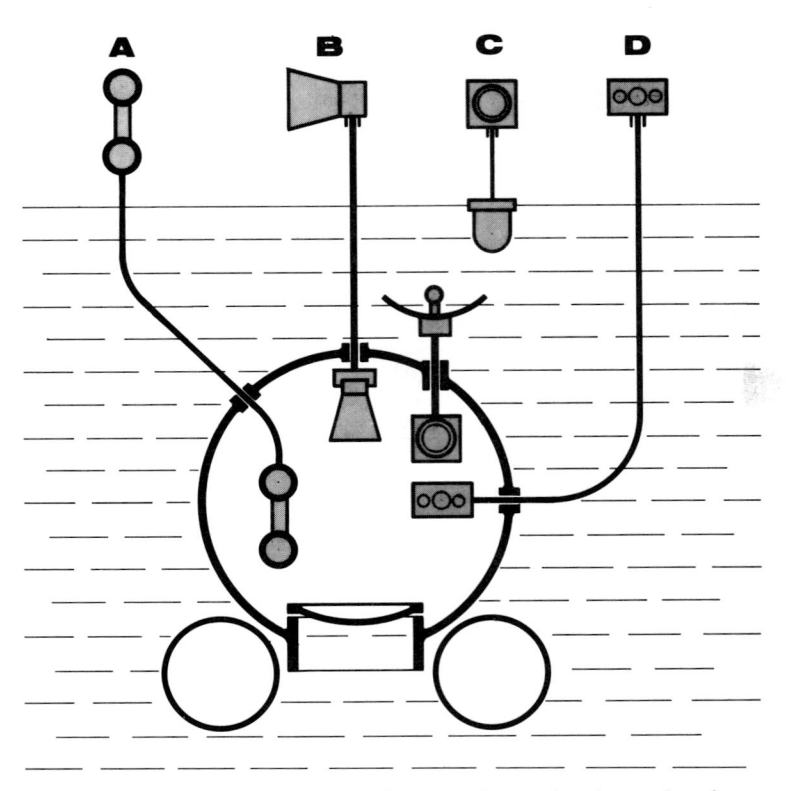

Fig. 4.24. Communication systems between diving chamber and surface.

- **A** Telephone. Generally a dynamic system without external power (sound powered)
- **B** Loudspeaker system, either press-to-talk or talk-back
- **C** Through-water system (sonar)
- **D** Signal system for transmission of messages when visual communication fails

7. Power for circulating compressors of closed-circuit systems for the breathing gas supply of the divers.
8. Blower motors for CO_2 scrubbers.
9. External television system.
10. Electric under-water tools and NDT equipment.
11. Propulsion motors for limited motion of the bell.

Electric power can be provided locally or through the umbilical cable. The former would be preferable, but is impractical in all except the simplest system due to the amount required. The batteries can be placed inside or outside the bell; if they are placed internally, care is essential to prevent the escape of harmful gases and consequently nickel–cadmium accumulators are preferred.

Batteries are always required for emergencies. Some countries require bells to be capable of operating all essential systems for 24 hours with the umbilical severed. This dictates the battery capacity

Fig. 4.25. A sound-powered telephone installed in a diving bell.

and therefore size. Experience shows that this size will necessitate the battery being fitted externally.

The normal umbilical supply can be by either high or low voltage. Low voltage leads to large losses in the cable, while with high voltage a transformer is needed at the bell to reduce the voltage. Both 42 and 24 volts are used in SCCs.

Fig. 4.23 shows the electrical systems of a bell. The total power will vary according to the operating conditions. The power requirements must be calculated before the umbilical is designed.

Communication Systems

Diving bell to surface (voice)

Reliable communication between the bell and the surface control is essential under both normal and emergency conditions. Through-water systems and communication by wire through the umbilical cable are both available for this and for safety reasons both should be continuously available.

There are four basic systems which are completely independent and these are shown schematically in Fig. 4.24.

Telephone. Sound-powered telephones (Fig. 4.25), in spite of their lack of volume, are efficient because of their ruggedness, simplicity, ease of maintenance and independence from an external power source. The call is made with a magneto inductor, which acts both audibly and visually at the receiver. Switching arrangement will allow communication with a variety of out-stations including the DCC. They are unsuitable for deep diving as they are not fitted with helium unscramblers.

Loud-speaker Intercommunication. It is useful to be able to communicate without having to use a handset and a loud-speaker system also provides group communication. When helium–oxygen mixtures are used, a voice unscrambler is essential and is normally provided. There are several types on the market, varying markedly in price and efficiency. The system is wired to provide permanent communication from bell to surface, and the reverse, by pressing a button at the amplifier control panel. Voice discipline is necessary but easily acquired. Talk-back systems with voice-operated switching are also available but rarely used as they are more expensive, less reliable and more difficult to maintain.

Through-water Communications (Ultrasonics). This system ensures communication in the event of failure of the umbilical. It is also possible to speak direct to the diver, but a reliable system must be chosen.

Signal Systems. These provide audio and visual communication when voice contact fails. A typical system might consist of a green light with no sound to indicate 'Everything OK', a yellow light and a bell to indicate 'Stop' and a red light with a hooter to indicate 'Hoist bell immediately'.

Communications between diver and SCC

The minimum crew of a SCC is two, with one working and the other tending and acting as communication link to the surface. Communication is by telephone or ultrasound but may suffer from helium distortion.

Under-water television systems

Television can be used both as a safety method of monitoring the diver and also to supervise his work. It is essential for inspection and survey work. They are easy for the diver to operate and the results are recorded on video tape at the surface. A local monitor is sometimes provided.

Gas System Instrumentation

The bell designer has the same problem as the naval architect, in that the overall dimensions are decided first and the instrumentation must then be designed to fit the space available. This requires an instrument engineer who is experienced in this field and can therefore produce a compact layout. Fig. 4.26 shows the gas functions needed:

1. Monitoring the chamber pressure.
2. Monitoring the ambient hydrostatic pressure.
3. Monitoring and controlling the internal gas atmosphere.
4. Monitoring the pressure in the gas storage tanks.
5. Controlling gas supply to the diving gear.
6. Controlling the emergency breathing system.

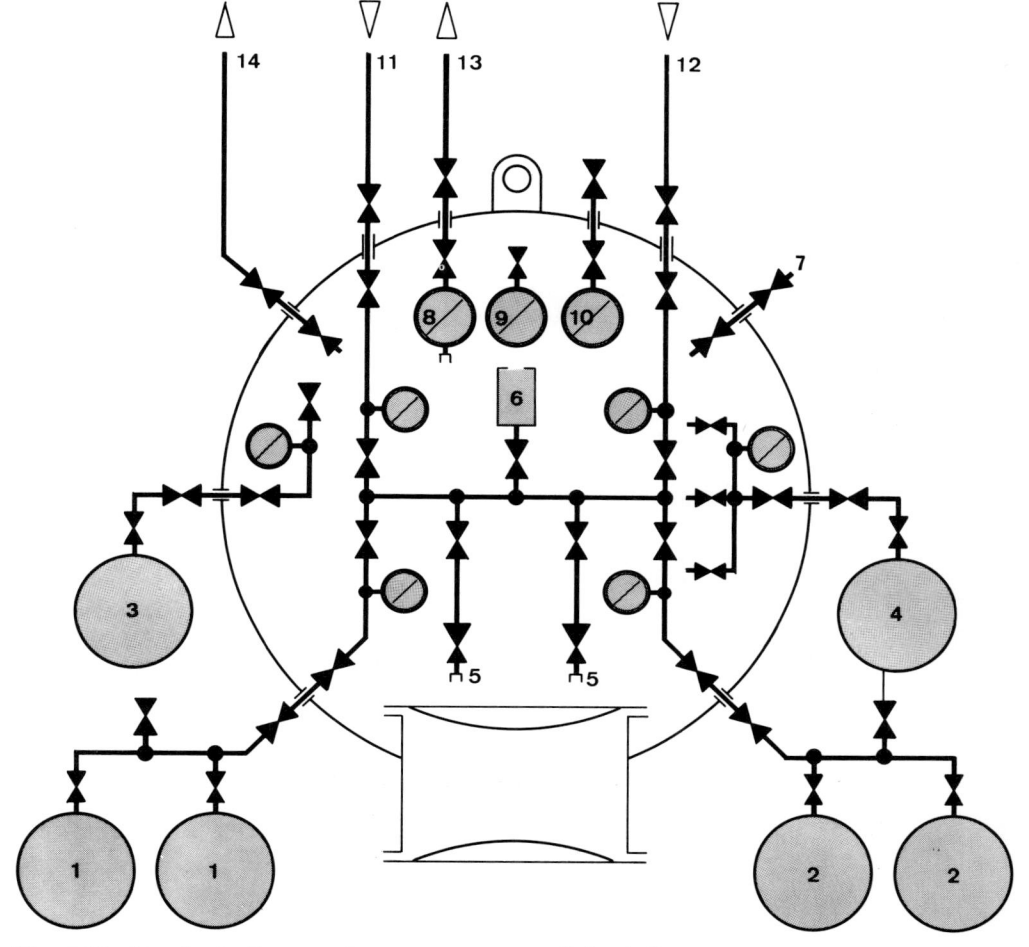

Fig. 4.26. Gas circuit diagram of a one-compartment diving bell

    1 external emergency breathing gas bank 1
    2 external emergency breathing gas bank 2
    3 oxygen emergency bell supply
    4 oxygen emergency breathing supply
    5 diver and attendant main breathing panel
    6 bell gas supply
    7 bell exhaust
    8 pneumo pressure depth gauge
    9 internal pressure depth gauge
  10 external pressure depth gauge
  11 surface umbilical gas supply
  12 surface umbilical gas supply (additional)
  13 pneumo pressure depth gauge to surface
  14 exhaust umbilical gas supply to surface

To design the system the bell designer must know the following parameters:

1. Maximum depth for the bell.
2. Maximum number of divers and tenders in the bell.
3. Type of supply (autonomous or by umbilical).
4. Breathing system (open-, closed- or semi-closed-circuit or a combination of these).
5. Applications (observation chamber, diving bell and mating system, provision for decompression).
6. Design rules and criteria as laid down by classification societies and national authorities.

There are too many different systems available for it to be worth while describing any one. It is, however, necessary, owing to the restricted space available, to consult an ergonomic specialist to ensure the practicability of the final design.

Diving Bells, Insulation and Buoyancy

Insulation is necessary to keep the divers warm, when breathing a helium–oxygen mixture, and reduce the power consumption required by heating. Insulation could be fitted either internally or externally, but by placing it outside added buoyancy is achieved simultaneously. Internal insulation also produces hygiene problems.

The criteria for the insulating material should be:

1. Good and lasting insulation properties.
2. Low specific weight.
3. Good durability in salt or fresh water.
4. Good durability in sunlight (ultra-violet radiation).
5. Pressure resistance.
6. Good mechanical properties and abrasive strength.
7. Fire-resistant and non-toxic (must meet local legal requirements).
8. Easy to work.

Few materials meet all these requirements.

Insulation with glass or mineral foam, polyurethane foam, glass-reinforced polyester, epoxy resin and rubber plating have all been used. Eccofloat is now normally employed. It is made with gas-filled microballoons and macrospheres from epoxy embedded in a resin binder and can be formed to any desired shape. These moulds are then glued to the hull with a two-component cement and smoothed over. It is not cheap, but in all other respects is satisfactory. Fig. 4.27 shows a SCC during the application of Eccofloat insulation. On this 500 m bell approximately 3.5 m^3 is fitted, helping to attain a net buoyancy of 300 kg.

Sometimes gas-filled containers are provided for additional buoyancy which can be used simultaneously as ballast tanks. Another method of providing buoyancy is by inflatable balloons stowed on top of the bell until required.

Fig. 4.27. Submersible compression chamber during application of Eccofloat insulation material.

Guide Wires

The bell must be placed as close to the work site as possible in order to increase the diver's safety, keep his umbilical as short as possible and ease the monitoring problems of the tender. Not only is the bell liable to drift with current, but also the surface craft, from which it is lowered, may move with wind and sea. If the SCC is fitted with guide wires these problems can be overcome.

Fig. 4.28 shows a bell with the usual double guide system on board a drilling rig for work in deep water. The wires are moored on the bottom in the desired position relative to the work site. This is achieved with the use of a bottom anchor. A suitable design of anchor frame will support the bell at the correct distance from the bottom for locking out. If the bell's lift wire is slacked away surface movement will no longer affect the bell.

The anchor winches are fitted with constant-tension devices to prevent surging of the guide wires and are capable of hoisting the bell to the surface in an emergency, thus providing additional safety. The guides on the bell are fitted with hinges to release the wires during transfer procedures on deck. Special clamps (as shown in Fig. 4.28), which are operated hydraulically from inside the chamber, enable the bell to be moored safely at any desired depth.

Fig. 4.28. Double guide wire on a submersible diving chamber.

Different Tasks for Bells

If a bell is designed for several different types of work it becomes both complicated and uneconomic, but equally it will be inefficient to have a different bell for each task. The solution to this problem is to have a single pressure hull with replaceable frames as shown in Fig. 4.29.

In *Type A* the frame will be fitted to carry a television camera and other photographic equipment. Additional lights are essential and will probably necessitate extra battery power.

In *Type B* the work will be carried out using manipulators as in a submersible. Manoeuvrability is essential and will necessitate thrusters. The hydraulic power unit will be fitted externally but additional controls will have to be fed into the bell.

In *Type C* the bell is used for diving or personnel transfer. The frame is fitted to carry gases and to allow lock-out when sitting on the sea bed. It must also be fitted to carry tools and equipment for maintenance and inspection.

Open Diving Bells

Unlike the bells described in the previous section of this chapter, open bells are vessels with the bottom end open to the sea water. Only by keeping the internal pressure equal to the external pressure will water

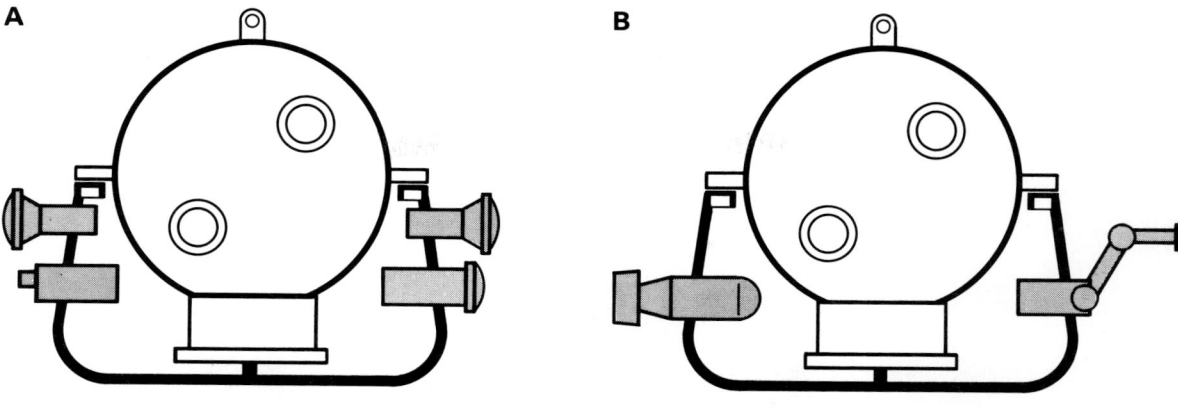

Fig. 4.29. Diving bell with exchangeable frame as a system carrier for different equipment.

- **A** Observation, television, photography. Illumination TV cameras and film or still cameras may be mounted on the frame. Power units may be installed. The pressure hull remains at atmospheric pressure
- **B** Working, not pressurized. A frame with suitable manipulators can be fitted for underwater work with the occupants at atmospheric pressure. A certain amount of manoeuverability can be obtained with one or more thrusters
- **C** Diving, working under pressure. The pressure hull is connected to a frame primarily designed for the installation of gas supply. Whether the gas is stored in spherical or cylindrical tanks is of secondary importance. At the same time the frame may be used to carry inspection equipment and tools

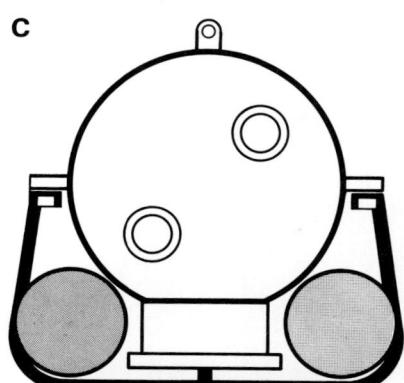

be excluded. These open bells are rarely used for conventional commercial work and never for deep diving.

The technical design is simple, consisting of a water-tight dome with a few windows, or made completely of acrylic glass, and a frame structure, which is closed off by a grating for standing on and a weight at the lower end, and in some cases a gas supply. Open diving bells provide additional safety in shallow water work, particularly when taking the diver through the air–water interface in rough weather.

During scientific diving operations open bells are sometimes moored at different depths to act as decompression stages and for storage of reserve diving gear. They are also used in the vicinity of large under-water habitats, particularly if fitted with acrylic domes.

Open Observation Diving Bells for Training Towers

Free ascent from submarines is a normal escape method for which special training is required. This is done in diving towers ashore with a 20- or 30-m column of water. Facilities are provided to allow instructors to give immediate assistance to divers at any depth. Fig. 4.30 shows an open bell being lowered with two instructors on board.

204   Subsea Manned Engineering

Fig. 4.30. An open diving bell in the training tower of the German Federal Navy at Neustadt.

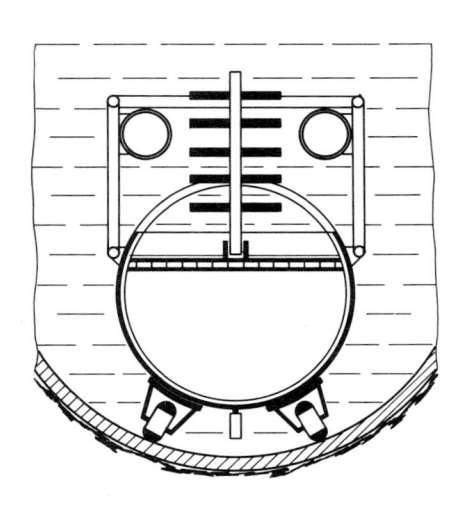

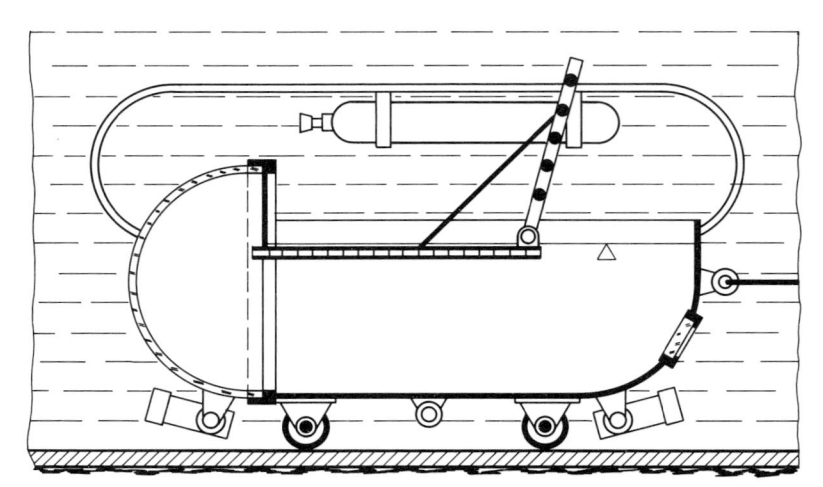

Fig. 4.31. Open work and rescue bell for diving in horizontal pipelines.

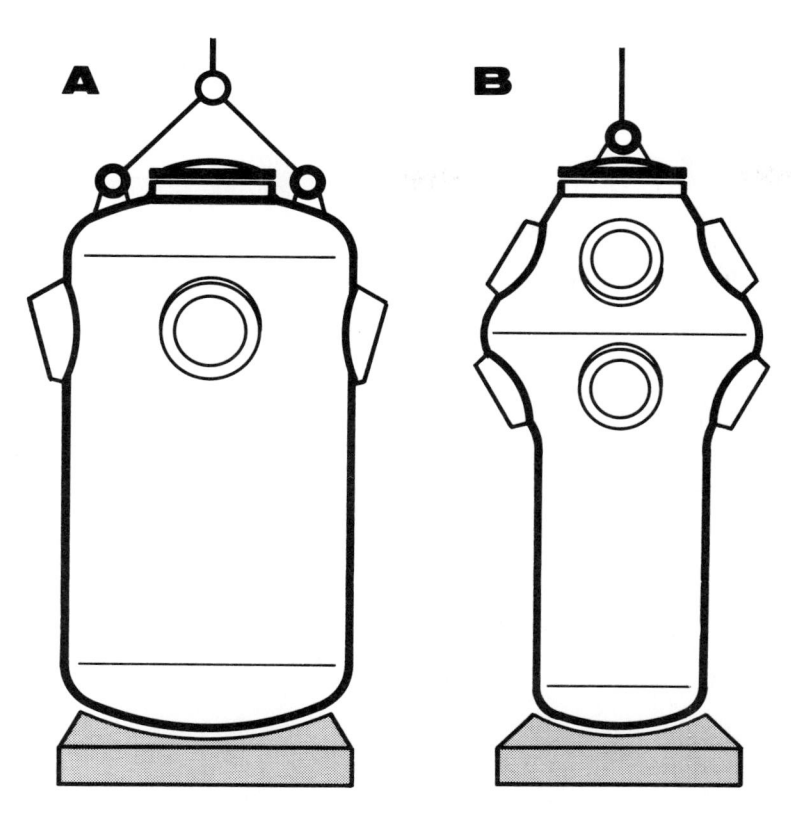

Fig. 4.32. Constructional forms for under-water observation chambers.

- **A** Cylindrical
- **B** Modified cylindrical
- **C** Semi-cylindrical trunking, capped spherical
- **D** Spherical

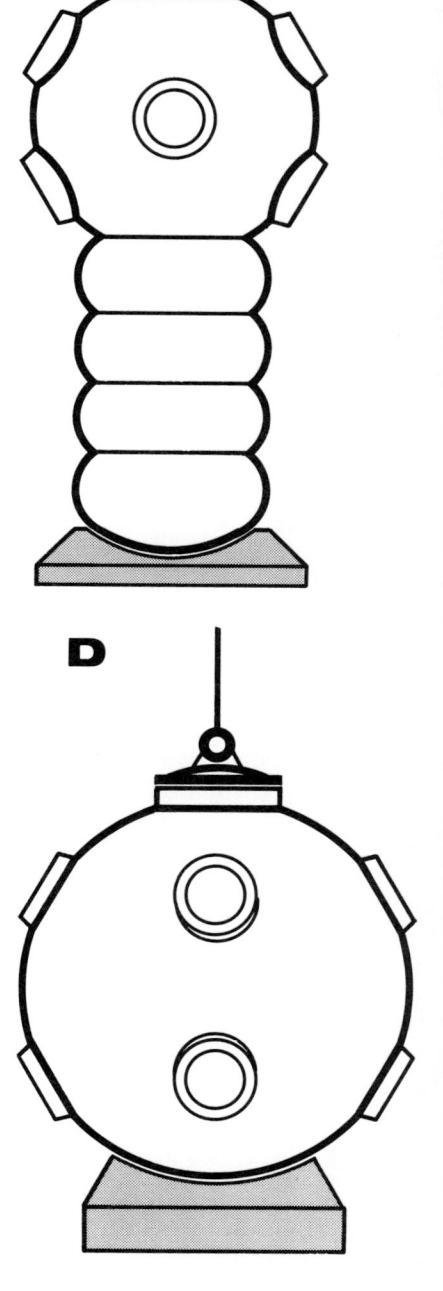

The bell top is small and the divers are submerged to their chests. The air is regulated by an inlet–outlet system similar to those fitted in 'hard hat' diving systems. Communications are provided and the grating on which the divers stand also provides ballast. A guide wire system is fitted. The bell is buoyant and is pulled down on reverse rollers, vertical motion being variable and controlled.

Open Rescue Bell for Pipeline Diving

Diving in horizontal water-filled pipelines is extremely dangerous, especially if the pipe is long. Not only is there great psychological stress but also it is exceptionally hard work for the diver. The use of a bell allows the diver to rest as well as providing a refuge. Fig. 4.31 is a schematic drawing of an open bell for work inside pipelines. Basically it is an upside-down water trough running on overhead wheels and filled with air. The diver lies on a grating with sufficient space for a

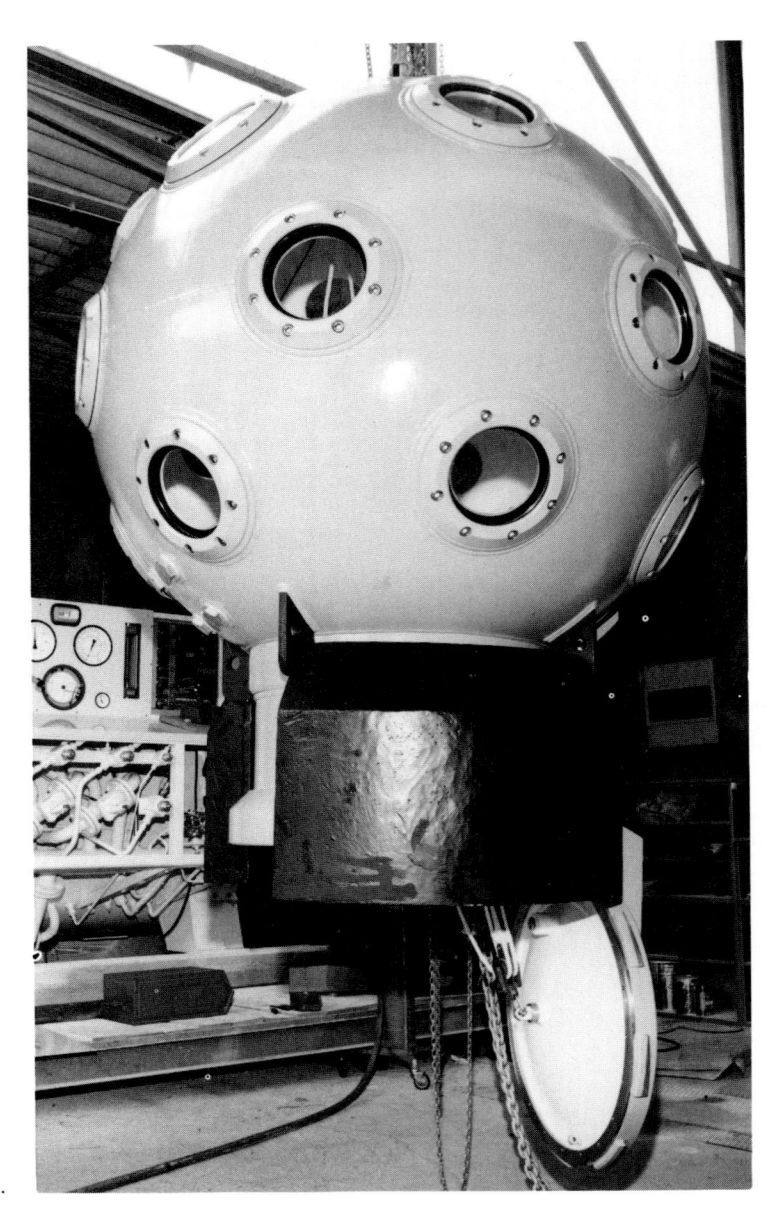

Fig. 4.33. A spherical under-water observation chamber for diving to a depth of 500 m.

second diver in an emergency. Equipment would consist of lights, jetting equipment, a gas supply, emergency breathing units, batteries and communications. A thruster might be fitted but a rope to pull the system back to the mouth of the pipe is essential.

Observation Chambers

A number of under-water tasks such as search, inspection and salvage do not require the diver to be exposed to ambient pressure. Fig. 4.32

summarizes the types of one-atmosphere bell available. *Types A and B* are suitable for depths down to 200 m but viewing is restricted in Type A. *Types C and D* are designed for greater pressures with special attention to windows, access locks and penetrators. The windows, normally made of acrylic glass or similar thermoplast, are almost exclusively shaped as conical frustra.

Internal equipment is relatively simple, consisting of:

1. An air regeneration system consisting of an oxygen supply, a carbon dioxide scrubber and sometimes a dehumidifier.
2. Communications by wire or ultrasound.
3. Internal and external lights and a heater.
4. Monitoring instruments for external pressure, oxygen and carbon dioxide partial pressures, chronometer etc.
5. Devices for the operational tasks such as film cameras, television, thermometers and salinometers.

Under-water Observation Chamber

Salvage tasks are assisted by having visual guidance rather than chance for their surface-operated grabs. Unmanned television systems can sometimes be used but they are not always satisfactory and the alternative is an observation chamber. Fig. 4.33 shows a system operable to 500 m. The spherical chamber has a diameter of 1800 mm and is fitted with many viewports to provide all-round visibility. The cylindrical shaft hatch is closed by a bayonet lock which opens to the outside. This allows the occupants to stand upright for comfort and allows later conversion to a SCC. The ballast weights on the shaft can be released internally for free ascent. Internal fittings are as described above. 144 man hours of life-support (oxygen and carbon dioxide scrubbers) are provided and this chamber was used for the salvage of an American F14 fighter lost in the summer of 1976 from an aircraft-carrier off Cape Wrath in 459 m of water.

5 Transportable Recompression Chambers for Divers

Both one- and two-man transportable recompression chambers are widely used. They differ from static chambers solely by reason of their relatively small size and weight and consequently their price. Owing to their size they can be moved from site to site by different methods as shown in Fig. 5.2. The disadvantage of the one-man system is that once the diver is inside and pressurized he cannot be given any further assistance. The two-man chambers overcome this disadvantage and are therefore becoming more common. This latter type is receiving increased attention with the need to transport

Fig. 5.1. A flexible one-man recompression chamber for divers, constructed in 1913.

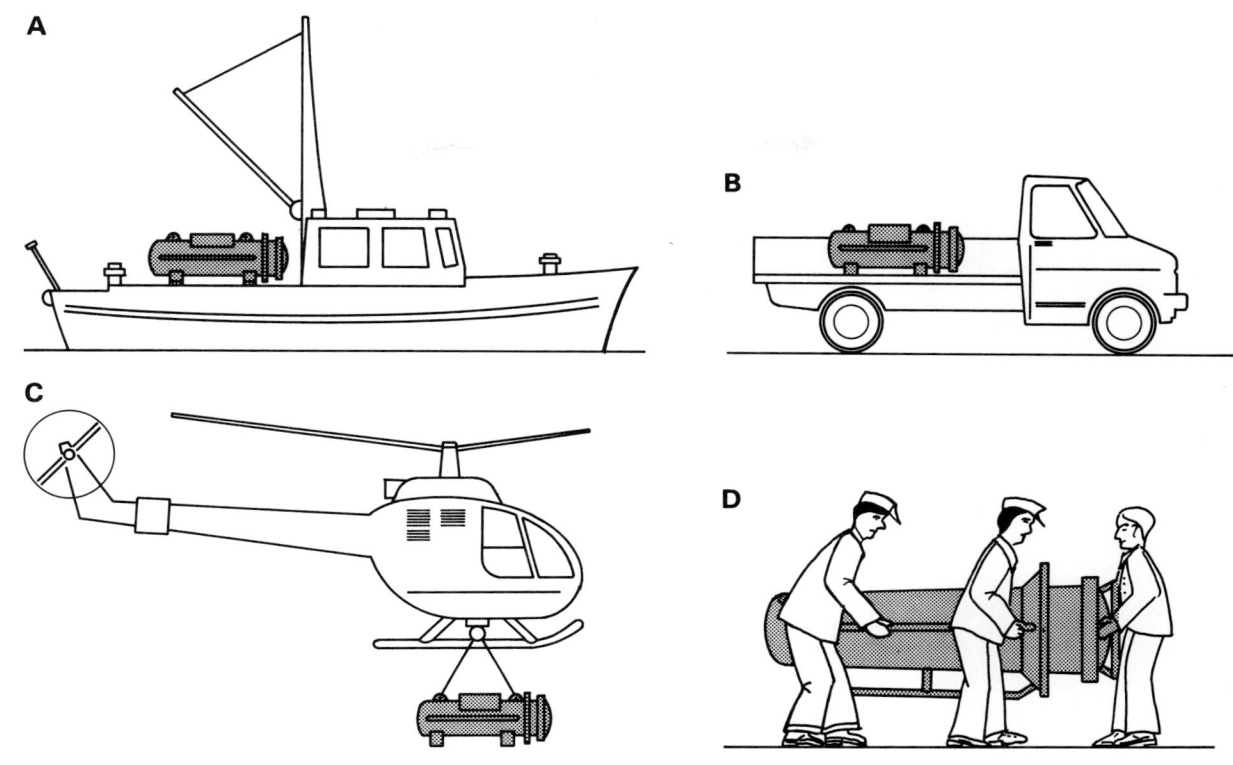

Fig. 5.2. How a transportable chamber can be moved.

- **A** From the diving location by fast boat to the nearest shore facility. Mainly for naval operations
- **B** To the nearest hospital treatment chamber after on-shore operations in lakes, rivers or harbours
- **C** Over long distance or in inaccessible areas, or for quick assistance, by large helicopter inside the cargo hold or suspended
- **D** Over short distances using four to six men

injured divers under pressure from off-shore rigs, pipe-laying barges and diving ships to a hyperbaric medical treatment centre ashore. Because of the use of very high pressures and the need for easy handling in restricted spaces or by helicopter, a very high standard of design is required. The use of special materials such as titanium and high-alloy special steels is also essential.

Many chambers are fitted with flanges to allow mating under pressure with static treatment chambers. These flanges have not been standardized and consequently compatibility is restricted to chambers made by the same manufacturer. It is hoped to reach agreement on standardization for the new off-shore high-pressure transport chamber system. One transfer system, described later, gives some hope of compatibility regardless of type or manufacturer.

Transportable One-man Recompression Chambers

Fig. 5.3 reviews the main basic types of pressure hull. These types can

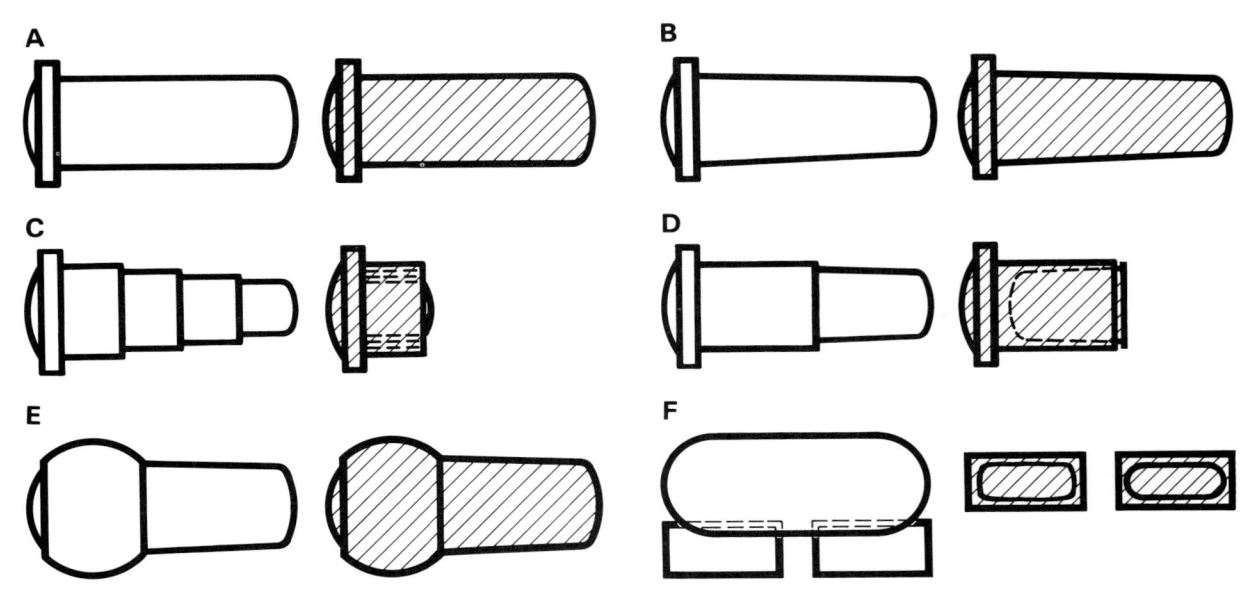

Fig. 5.3. Basic types of pressure hull for one-man chambers.

- **A** Cylindrical. Large volume, large weight. High gas consumption for pressurization. Simple to manufacture
- **B** Conical. Smallest volume, small weight. Low gas consumption for pressurization. Medium difficulty to manufacture
- **C** Telescopic segments. Small volume, large weight. Many seals. Smallest storage requirement. Difficult to manufacture
- **D** Telescopic element. Medium volume, medium weight. Medium gas consumption for pressurization. Small storage requirement
- **E** Sphere/cone combination. Large volume, large weight. High gas consumption for pressurization. Difficult manufacture from glass-reinforced plastic
- **F** Flexible cylinder. Large volume, medium weight. Large gas consumption for pressurization. Difficult to manufacture and problematic material

be divided into two families, the one rigid and requiring the same volume for stowage as for operations, and the other semi-rigid, telescopic, foldable or assembled and requiring less storage space. Fig. 5.1 shows a folding type designed in 1913, made of heavy fabric from a diving suit and reinforced with chains. It was never actually used as some of the technical problems were unresolved.

Telescopic Chambers

Fig. 5.4 shows one such telescope type that has been used successfully for dry decompression of divers for decades. As no immediate medical attention is possible, arrangements may have to be made to place the complete telescopic chamber inside a large static treatment chamber.

The pressure hull of these chambers consists of four telescopic cylindrical rings with a dished head welded to the last ring and the other end fitted with a hatch with a bayonet lock. Some hatches were fitted with 10 to 16 studs or swing bolts but locking is slow and sometimes unreliable. Note should be taken of the extendible rods on

Fig. 5.4. Telescopic recompression chamber in operational condition.

Fig. 5.5. Telescopic recompression chamber retracted and transport box for its storage.

either side which provide the initial sealing pressure and also provide general stability during pressurization.

As the diver will not necessarily be able to enter unassisted, a stretcher is provided and fitted with a double roller at the foot to roll over the hull segments as it is inserted. When dismantled, the stretcher is kept in the chamber transport box (Fig. 5.5).

Except for the communications, all the fittings required for operational use are on the hatch and protected against damage by a circular tube frame. These fittings are:

1. A depth gauge for reading internal pressure.
2. An air inlet connection.
3. A compressor connection.
4. An adjustable venting valve for fresh air ventilation.
5. A relief valve for depressurization.
6. A spring-loaded safety valve to prevent the safety pressure being exceeded.
7. A pure oxygen connection (but oxygen breathing in one-man recompression chambers is prohibited by some national regulations).

The oxygen breathing system is described later in this chapter. A transistor-amplified voice intercommunication system is fitted on the first hull ring in addition to the two windows.

It is vital in these small one-man chambers that there is sufficient fresh air to keep the CO_2 partial pressure within acceptable limits; this would otherwise rise quickly as the volume is only about 350 litres, of which about 75 litres are displaced by the diver. As the operating pressure increases the total quantity of air flushing through the chamber will increase and metering is therefore necessary. Flowmeters are too expensive, fragile and unwieldy. Control in Dräger one-man chambers is obtained by fitting a venting valve which is set to allow the correct amount of air to be exhausted according to the pressure. Constant pressure is maintained by adjusting the amount of fresh air entering. Fig. 5.6 shows the relationship between ambient pressure in the chamber, CO_2 partial pressure and ventilation air flow. Although the air flow rises with pressure, it is not directly proportional and therefore some rise of CO_2 partial pressure has to be accepted. Telescopic chambers were originally made for a maximum pressure of 3 bar. In recent years this has been raised to 5 bar in order to allow the use of the latest therapeutic tables for treating injured divers.

Modern chambers of this type are made of high-grade aluminium alloys but still weigh about 120 kg, which makes them awkward to handle particularly when locking on to a stationary chamber. To reduce this, the chamber is set down on rollers and pushed into the larger chamber on rails. The whole operation is slow and requires skill and considerable physical strength. After pressure equalization the diver is removed from the transport chamber which is then telescoped and placed in the transport box. This also contains such accessories as an oxygen pressure regulator mask with demand regulator and

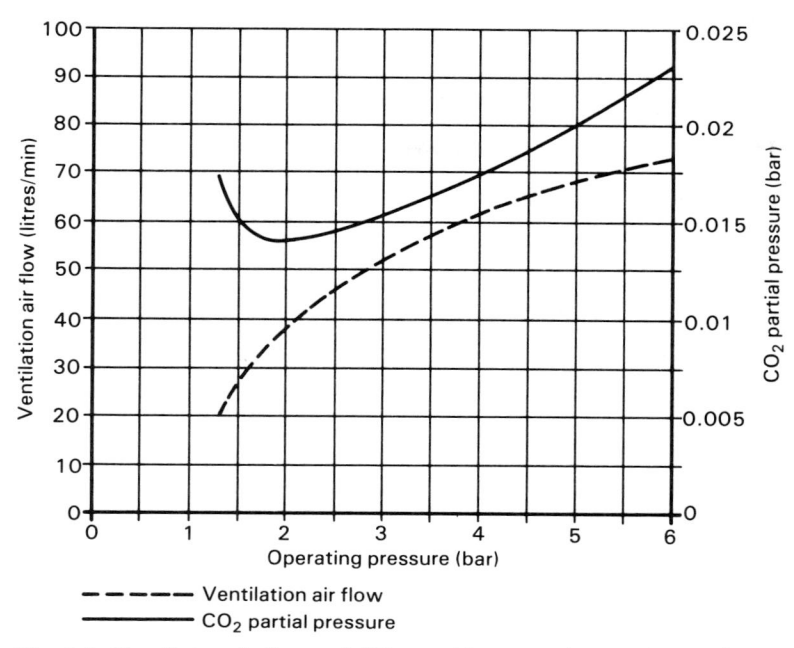

Fig. 5.6. Ventilation air-flow and CO_2 partial pressure in a one-man telescopic chamber expressed as a function of the operating (stationary) pressure.

necessary tools and spares. This type is rarely used today as its advantages do not out-weigh its disadvantages when compared to rigid chambers.

Rigid One-man Recompression Chambers

These are the accepted normal type and there are several thousand in use world wide. The pressure hull may be cylindrical in shape but is usually a conic frustrum with the small end fitted with a dished head. Fig. 5.7 shows a typical example. The conical shape fits the natural form of the body and the chamber volume will be about 350 litres. 1375 litres of air are required to pressurize to 5 bar, allowing for a diver displacement of 75 litres.

The chamber is closed with a bayonet lock hatch that can be sealed very quickly. A safety device is fitted which prevents pressurization if the hatch is not correctly locked and unlocking if the internal pressure has not been completely vented. The diver is pushed into the chamber on a stretcher running on rails and then locked to prevent movement during transportation. The fittings are the same as with the telescopic chamber with two viewports and the controls on the hatch. Fig. 5.8 shows schematically all the functional elements required for the operation of a chamber.

These chambers are made for operating pressures up to 8 bar. Aluminium alloy is used for construction and a chamber of this type would weigh about 70 kg. Without a mating flange they have the major disadvantage that diver transfer to a stationary treatment chamber is feasible only in a few cases and this restricts their employment.

214　*Subsea Manned Engineering*

Fig. 5.7. Rigid transportable one-man recompression chamber.

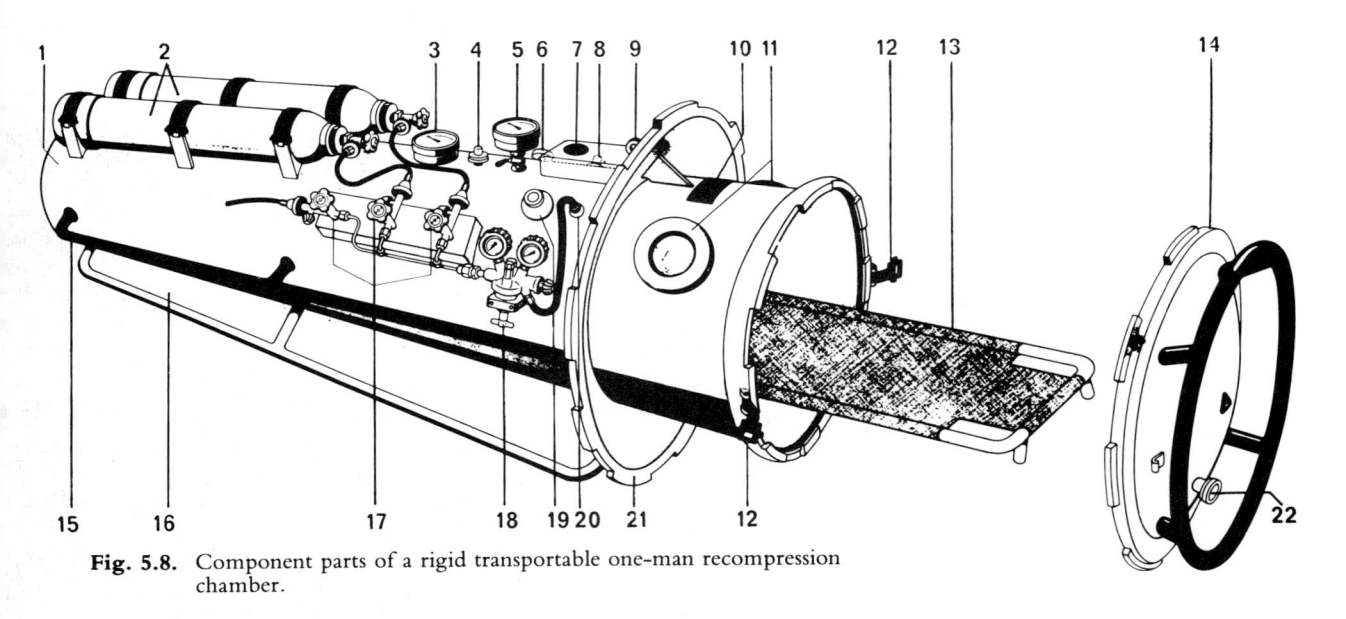

Fig. 5.8. Component parts of a rigid transportable one-man recompression chamber.

1. pressure hull
2. compressed air cylinders
3. pressure gauge 0–100 m
4. safety valve
5. pressure gauge 0–30 m
6. headset
7. intercommunication
8. oxygen connection
9. lifting eye
10. data plate
11. viewports
12. tightening strap
13. stretcher
14. hatch cover
15. handle bar
16. skid
17. valve
18. pressure regulator
19. venting valve
20. compressed air inlet
21. bayonet mating flange
22. pressure equalization valve

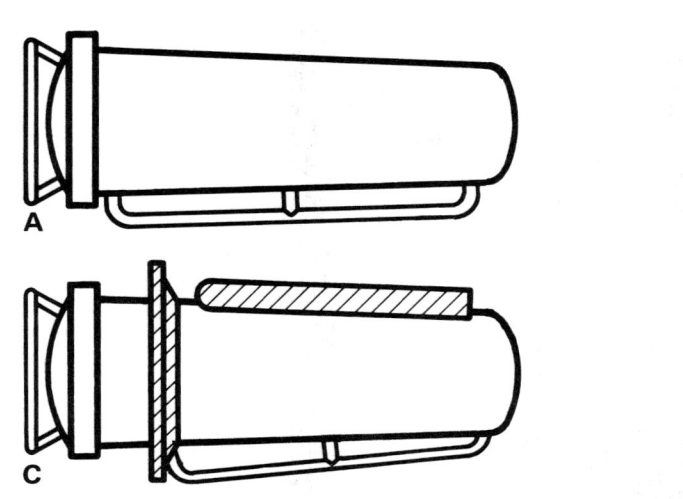

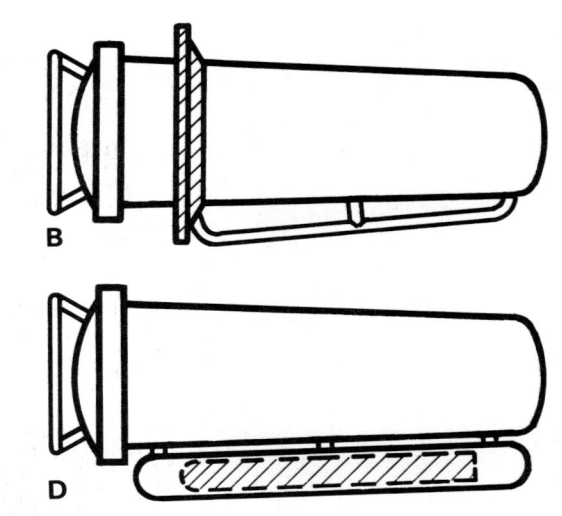

Fig. 5.9. Standards for rigid one-man recompression chambers.

- **A** Simplest chamber model, without gas supply or mating flange. For fixed use and transportable only under certain conditions. Transfer of diver into chamber is very difficult
- **B** Simple chamber model without gas supply but with mating flange. For fixed use and transportable only under certain conditions. Transfer of diver into fixed chamber easy provided systems are compatible
- **C** Complete one-man transport system with gas supply and mating flange. Suitable for both fixed use and transport. Simplest diver transfer provided systems are compatible
- **D** Most modern one-man transport system with complete gas supply inside the frame. Excellent for both fixed use and transport. Transfer is possible without flange system provided the treatment chamber is appropriate

Fig. 5.10. Rigid transportable one-man recompression chamber with mating flanges.

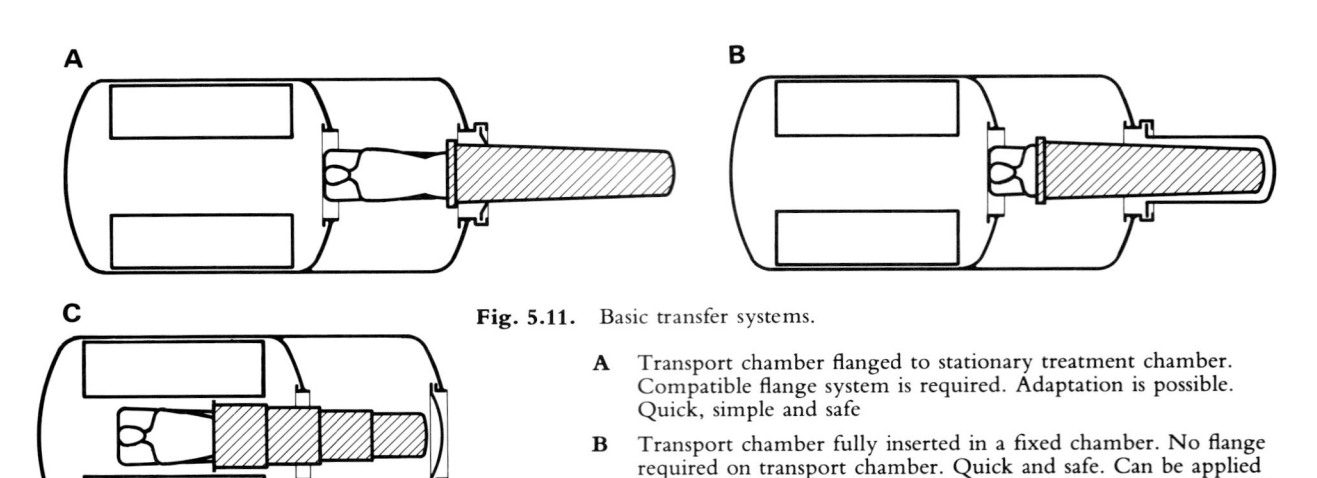

Fig. 5.11. Basic transfer systems.

A Transport chamber flanged to stationary treatment chamber. Compatible flange system is required. Adaptation is possible. Quick, simple and safe

B Transport chamber fully inserted in a fixed chamber. No flange required on transport chamber. Quick and safe. Can be applied to many chambers provided certain dimensions are not exceeded

C Transport chamber placed totally inside the fixed treatment chamber. Generally no specific preparations are necessary. Time-consuming and strenuous

Fig. 5.9 shows the different standards of rigid chamber from the simple cylinder without gas to a complete system with a mating flange for connection to a stationary treatment chamber. The mating flange requires a complementary flange on the fixed chamber so that a pressure-proof connection can quickly be achieved (Fig. 5.10). Unfortunately flanges have not been standardized although a ring of 850 mm with 10 bayonet sections is most common. It is used by the German navy and many others and is standardized within NATO. Adaptor pieces can be provided for dissimilar flange systems but must be supplied in advance. Fig. 5.11 evaluates the basic transfer systems: Type C has obvious advantages but is not in general use.

The complete transfer procedure is shown in Fig. 5.12. In A the doctor is in the static chamber's treatment compartment and the transfer lock is unpressurized. In B the transfer chamber has been mated to the DCC and the transfer chamber's pressure has been equalized. In C the patient has been moved to the treatment compartment on his stretcher. All that remains is to depressurize the transfer lock and remove the transfer chamber (D). With a well-trained team this will take about three minutes. None of the transfer chambers so far described has been completely autonomous as gas supplies are also required. This is not a serious problem if only one vehicle is used for transport, but where the transport is in stages, such as by helicopter, an autonomous chamber is preferable. If the chamber has to be operated after it has been mated to a static chamber then all the fittings and controls must be on the side and not, as previously described, on the door. With autonomous chambers the following additional fittings are required:

1. A manifold for connection of the air storage cylinders.
2. A pressure regulator to reduce the high pressure.

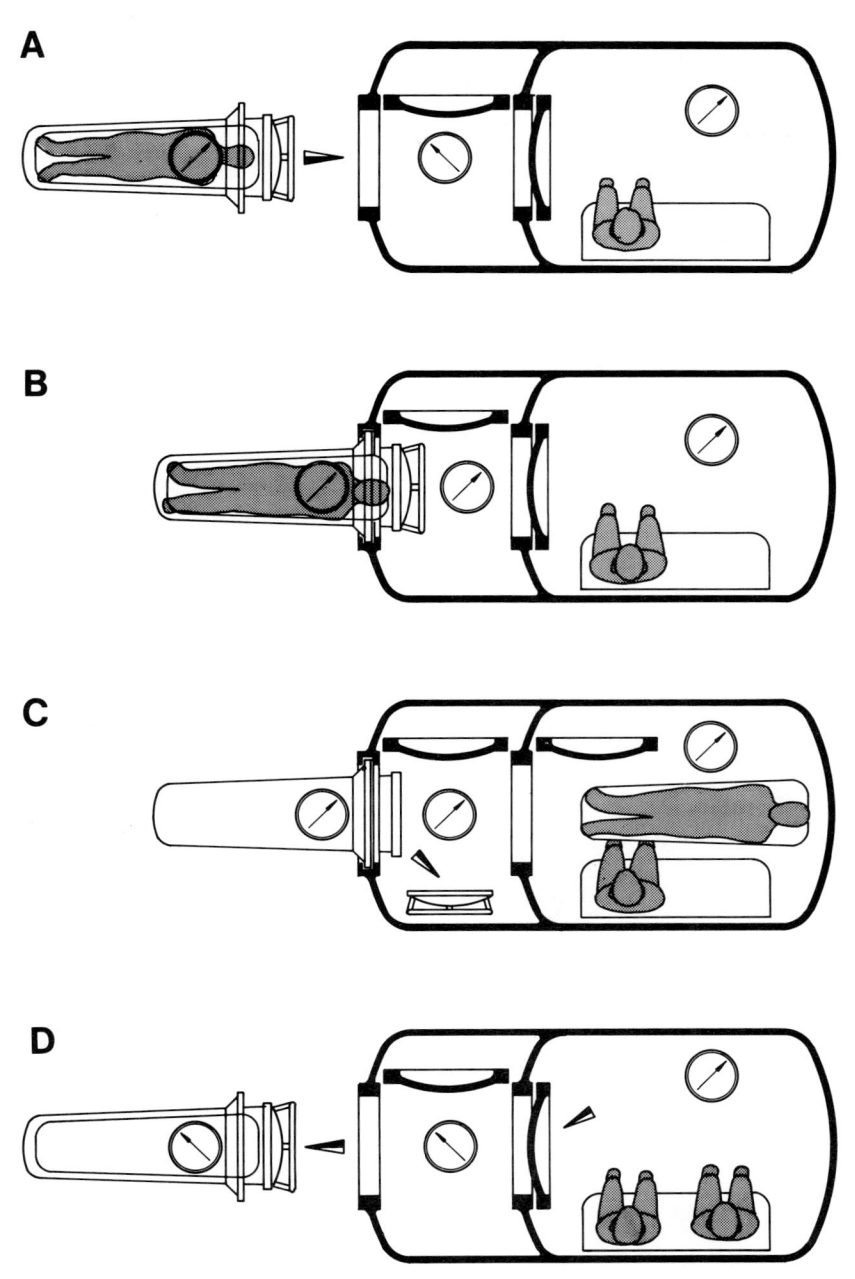

Fig. 5.12. Schematic drawing of the transfer of a diver from a transportable one-man chamber into a fixed treatment chamber.

Figs 5.13 to 5.15 show the transport of a sick diver to a final destination in a stationary treatment chamber. In the design of these chambers the door lock is critical, in view of its effect on speed, safety and cost. In Fig. 5.16 five different examples of lock with their uses and advantages are shown.

Fig. 5.13. A diver laying on a stretcher in a rigid one-man recompression chamber.

Fig. 5.14. Once inside the helicopter the chamber will be flown to a navy hospital where it will be connected to a large treatment chamber.

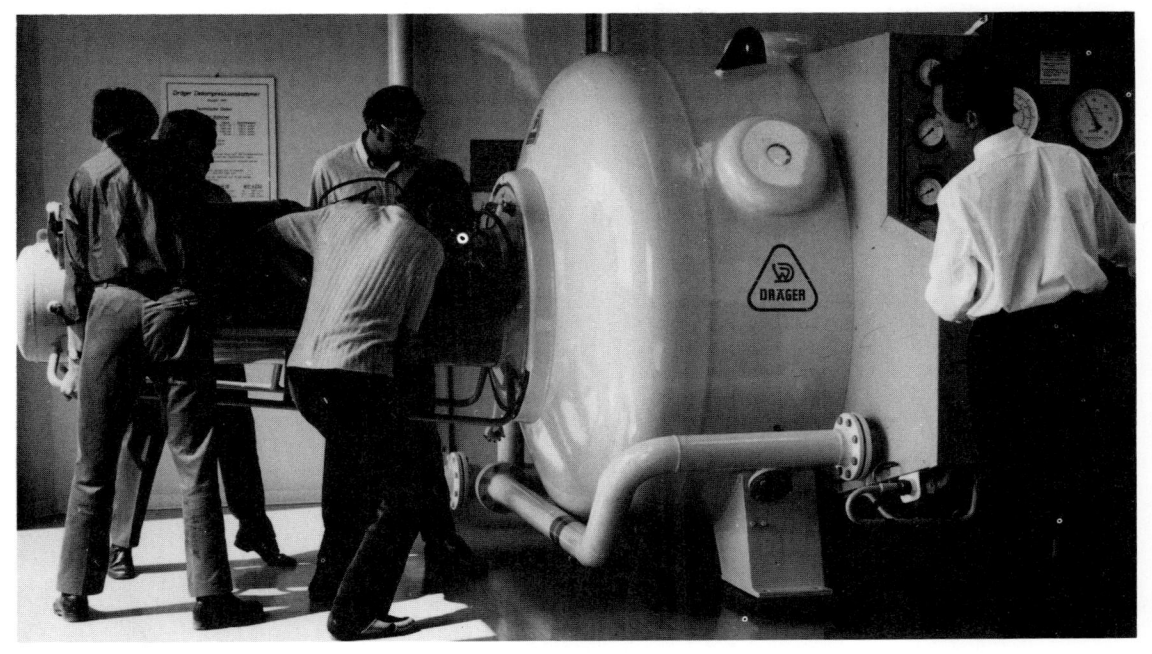

Fig. 5.15. Connection of a one-man transport chamber to the treatment chamber.

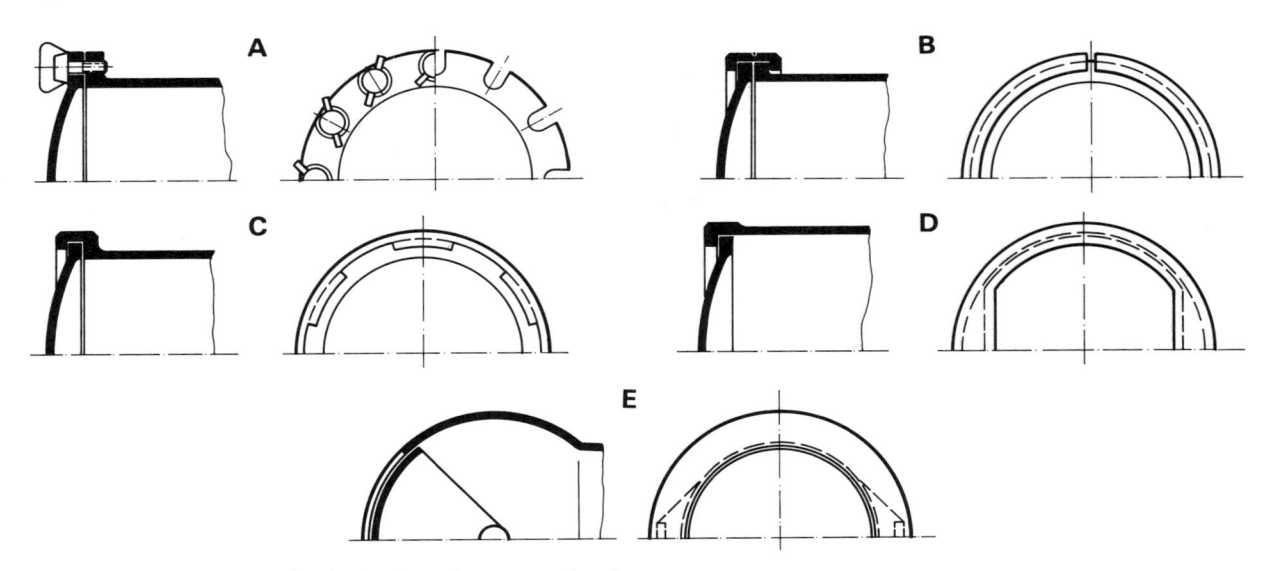

Fig. 5.16. Lock systems for the hatches of one-man chambers.

- **A** Bolted lock with plugged-on hinged bolts. An out-dated system. The locking procedure is very time-consuming. Medium technical effort
- **B** Clamp lock with divided U-ring. Specially suitable for high pressure. Operation requires some physical strength or mechanical assistance. Medium to large technical effort
- **C** Bayonet lock. A very common system with quick, safe and easy operation. Large technical effort
- **D** Oval hatch supported on the inside with downstream seal. Simple manufacture but needs space. Medium technical effort
- **E** Rotating hatch supported on the inside with downstream seal. Suitable for GRP chambers. Very high technical effort

Fig. 5.17. Semi-rigid one-man recompression chamber, the Haux Transcom III, with its own external air supply and trailer.

Semi-rigid One-man Recompression Chambers

The characteristics of rigid chambers are simple construction, good functional safety, easy readiness for use and comparatively low weight but they occupy considerable storage space. This is the exact opposite of telescopic chambers. The example shown in Figs 5.17 and 5.18 combines the good features of both types. The two pressure halves have approximately equal lengths and when combined form a rigid transportable one-man chamber. The upper half is cylindrical, giving good freedom around the head and shoulders, while the lower conical half fits the general shape of the body and keeps the internal

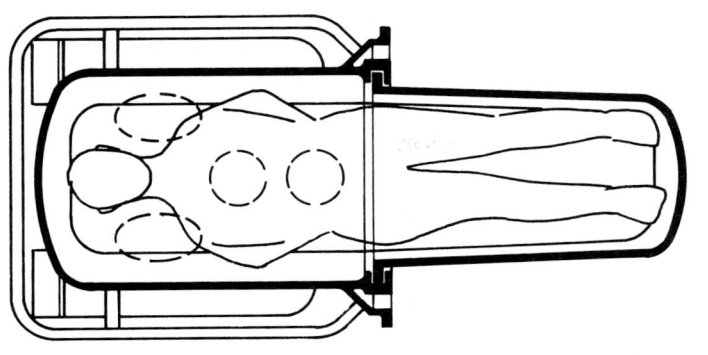

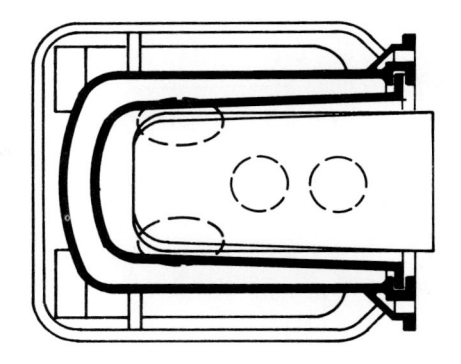

Fig. 5.18. The chamber in Fig. 5.17, showing the storage mechanism.

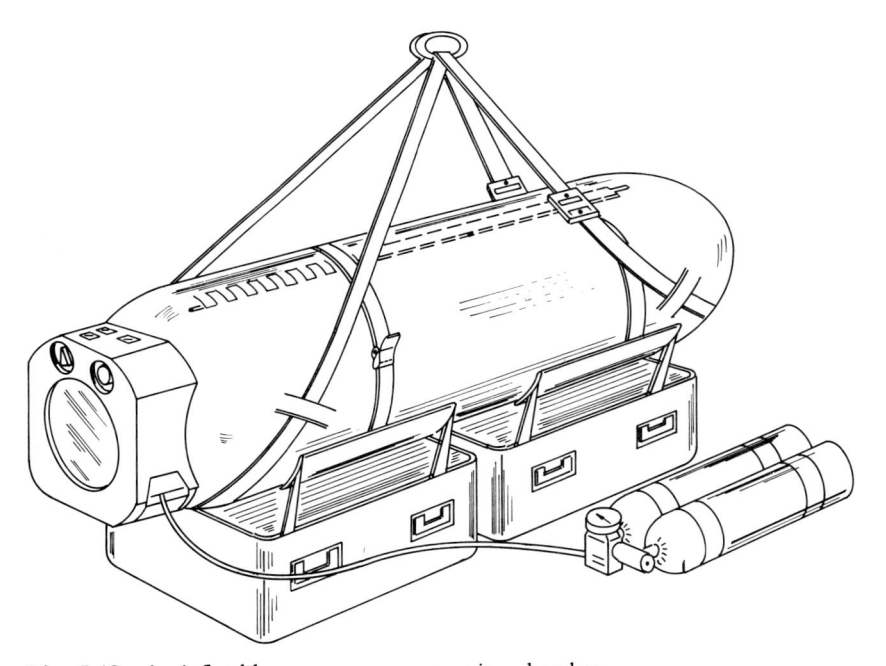

Fig. 5.19. An inflatable one man recompression chamber.

volume small. A rugged tube frame obviates the need for a transport box and acts as a base. Two scuba-type cylinders of 10 litres volume can be installed inside the framework. To enter, the diver is placed on a stretcher and slid in head first. The conical lower half is then slid over the stretcher and attached to the upper half by a bayonet lock. A flange ring at this point provides a method of securing the transport chamber to the stationary chamber by bayonet lock. Fittings and controls are similar to other autonomous chambers. The conical shape allows the bottom to be placed inside the top half for storage which results in a compact unit of 880 × 880 × 1260 mm. A chamber of this type for a pressure of 5 bar would weigh about 165 kg. Possible improvements to this chamber are a supply lock and fully automatic air ventilation.

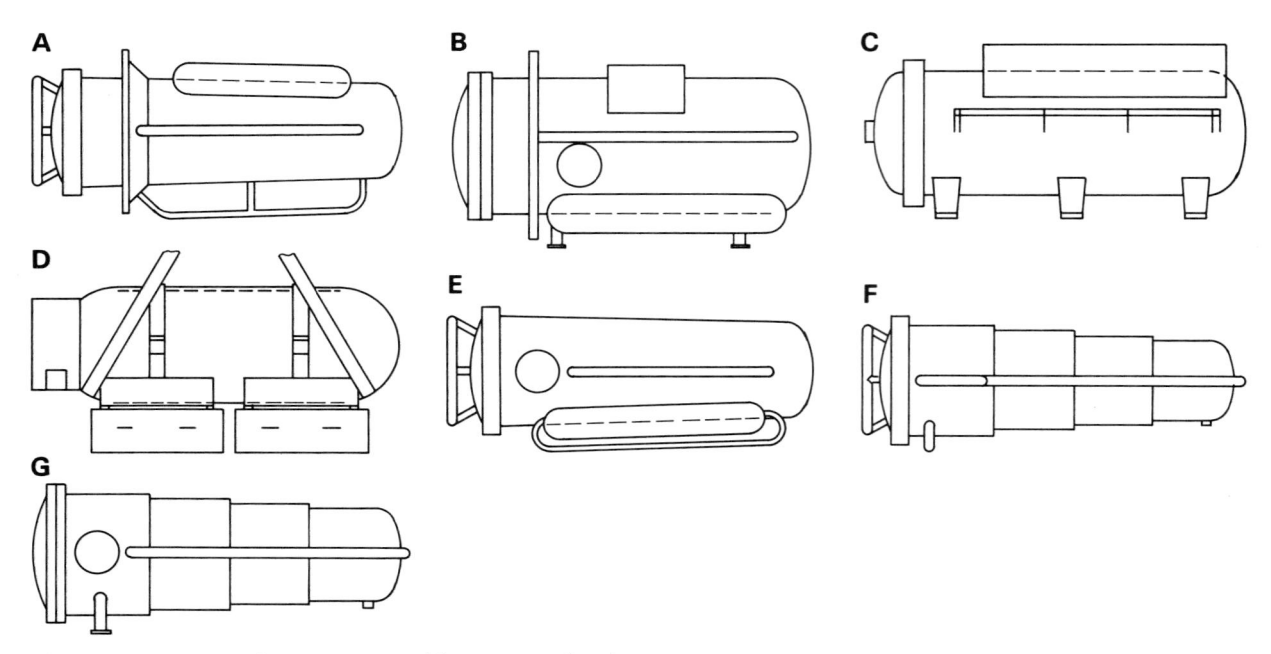

Fig. 5.20. A review of some transportable one-man chambers.

- **A** Dräger 'piggy-back' model in aluminium alloy. Internal volume 350 litres; weight 127 kg, operating pressure 5 bar, gas supply 2 × 11 litres at 200 bar. No supply lock, bayonet hatch lock
- **B** Galeazzi model 35/cag 2 in aluminium alloy. Internal volume 700 litres, weight 280 kg complete, operating pressure 5 bar, gas supply 2 × 40 litres at 200 bar. Supply lock. Six hinged bolts on hatch lock. Transfer requires operation of 16 bolts
- **C** Cammell Laird model type 4 in aluminium alloy. Internal volume 880 litres, weight 263 kg, operating pressure 7 bar, no gas supply. No supply lock, bayonet hatch lock. Complete transfer is possible under certain conditions
- **D** US Navy model in coated fabric. No gas supply. No supply lock, zip fastener hatch lock. Complete transfer is possible
- **E** Haux Eco-transfer 1 in aluminium alloy. Internal volume 400 litres, weight 130 kg complete, operating pressure 5 bar, gas supply 2 × 11 litres at 200 bar. Supply lock and bayonet hatch lock. Complete transfer is possible
- **F** Dräger Telescope chamber in aluminium alloy. Internal volume 350 litres, weight 110 kg, operating pressure 5 bar, no gas supply. No supply lock, bayonet hatch lock. Transfer difficult as not foreseen
- **G** Galeazzi model 33/b in steel. Internal volume 600 litres, weight 230 kg, operating pressure 4 bar, no gas supply. Supply lock and hatch lock with six bolts. Complete transfer possible under certain conditions

Inflatable One-man Recompression Chamber

Fig. 5.1 shows an inflatable chamber dated 1913 which failed. Sixty years later the US Navy produced a modern version for emergency use. The chamber is 2200 mm long and 760 mm in diameter. It is made of high-strength fabric with a rubber coating. The diver enters through a slit which is closed with a pressure-tight zip fastener. There is a viewing port at each end but the controls are all at one end. The diver is supported in a type of hammock in the chamber which in turn rests on the two transport containers (Fig. 5.19). The life-support is exceptional in that it is a semi-closed-circuit system with an injector-driven CO_2 absorption unit. Detailed information is not available and consequently comparison with other types is not possible.

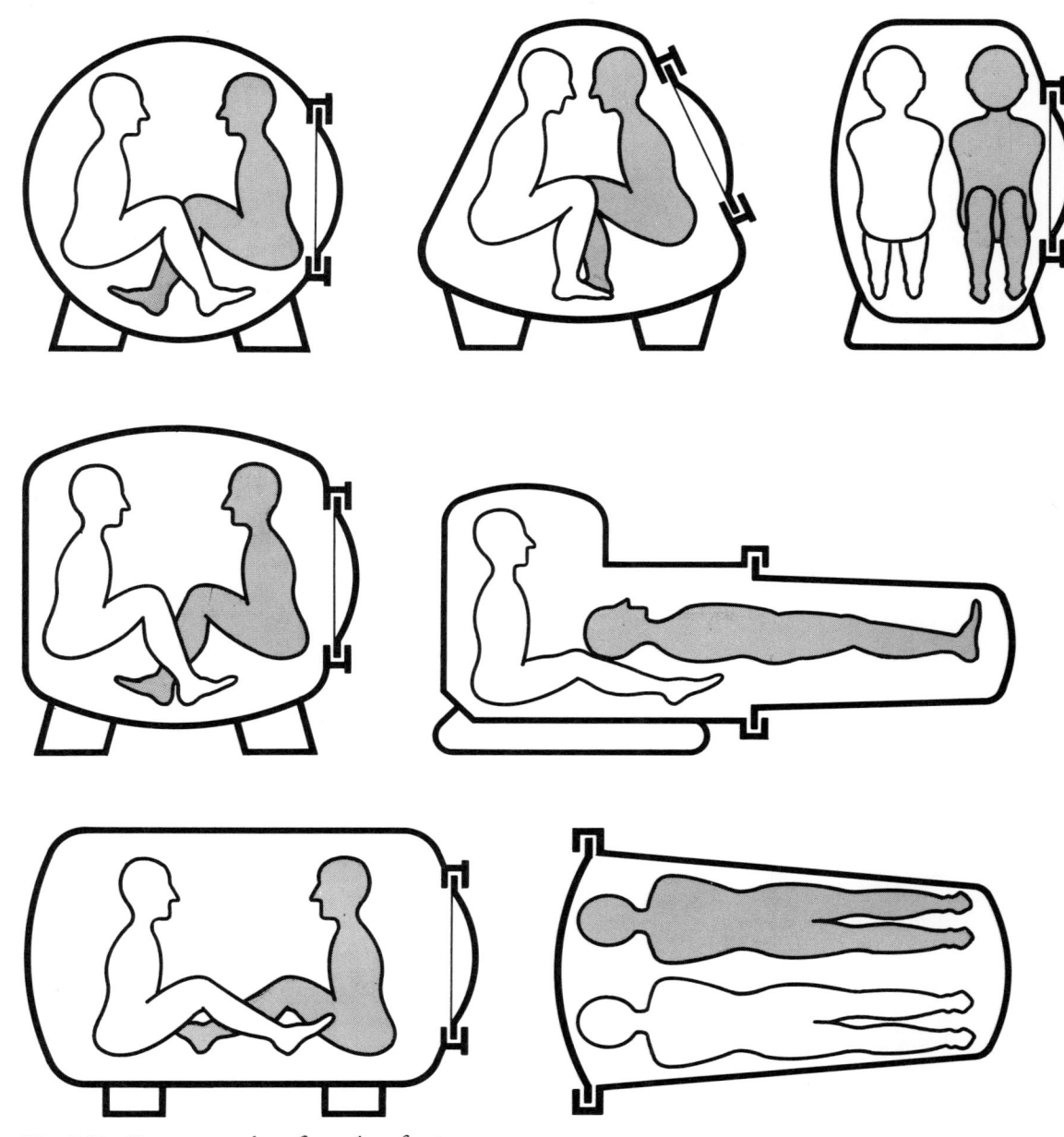

Fig. 5.21. Pressure vessel configurations for two persons.

Transportable Two-man Recompression Chambers

All one-man chambers have the serious disadvantage that once the diver has entered and been pressurized, direct access is impossible and no assistance can be rendered to the man. For this reason the use of two-man chambers is sometimes favoured.

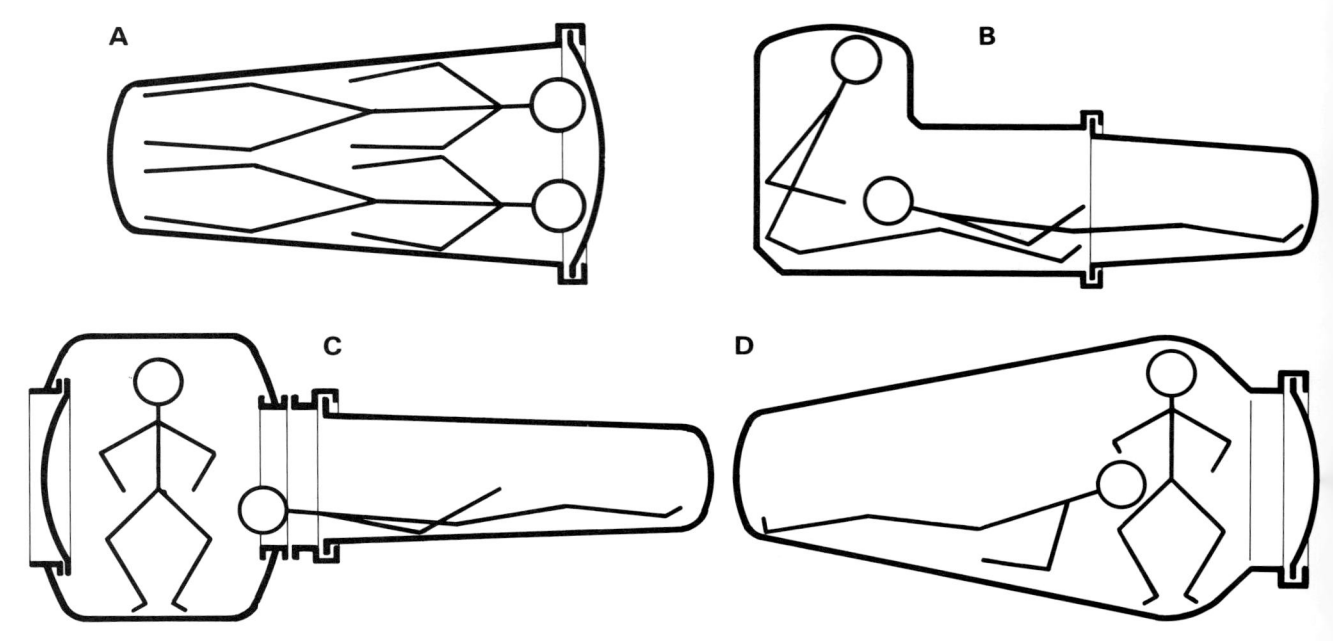

Fig. 5.22. Types of transportable two-man recompression chamber.

- **A**   Rigid conical two-man chamber
- **B**   Split two-man chamber
- **C**   Two-man chamber assembled from modules
- **D**   Rigid double-cone two-man chamber

Design Evaluation

There are many ways of placing two people in a chamber: horizontally, vertically or a mixture of the two. For obvious reasons the vertical possibility is ignored. Fig. 5.21 shows possible configurations. As it must be assumed that the diver under treatment is in the prone position, only those designs where at least one person is horizontal need be considered. The comparative volumes are shown in the drawing and it can be assumed that weights will vary in a similar manner. The attendant can give much better assistance from a sitting position as he can easily reach the man's arms, head and chest but movement is very restricted if he is lying down.

Construction

Development of two-man chambers is of recent origin and consequently experience is limited. Fig. 5.22 shows four types with practical applications. A small number of *Type A* have been made but are not popular. Although the conic frustrum shape leads to low cost, the parallel frame position prevents the attendant carrying out his task satisfactorily. *Type B* is most common and is described in detail later. *Type C* consists of two modules which can be used separately but it is

Fig. 5.23. A two-man chamber assembled from modules and a standard one-man chamber.

heavy and extremely difficult to move by hand. An example is shown in Fig. 5.23. *Type D* is specially designed for rescue missions off-shore and is capable of withstanding very high pressures. It is made of a high-strength titanium alloy to save weight and due to its very high price only a few are available at central locations for possible emergencies.

Semi-rigid Two-man Chamber

The following is a description of Type B in Fig. 5.22. It is comparatively light, the relative position of diver and attendant is good and it has a well-designed life-support system. The pressure hull consists of two cylinders at right angles which produces the minimum volume, and therefore weight, for two persons, one sitting and one lying. The diver's foot end is a conical frustrum segment which is attached by bayonet lock and can be inserted in the main portion to save space during storage. Two large viewports are fitted for observation of the occupants and to provide light internally. A medical lock is fitted in order to pass small articles to the occupants. The chamber is fitted with a flange to allow mating to a stationary chamber as with one-man chambers. Externally there is a rugged tubular framework on which it stands or is stored after turning through 90° to save space. It is designed for a differential pressure of 5

Fig. 5.24. A semi-rigid transportable two-man chamber.

bar and is made of high-strength seawater-resistant aluminium alloy to save weight. Fig. 5.25 shows the life-support system which can be either open-circuit or semi-closed with an injector-driven scrubber. The air supply is from two 11-litre cylinders mounted below the pressure hull. Pure oxygen breathing is also available with overboard dumping to prevent a fire risk. Communication is provided by a battery-powered amplifier and both a loudspeaker and a head set are provided externally in case the ambient noise level is high. Fig. 5.26 shows diagrammatically how the system is brought into use, loaded and used to transfer a patient to a static chamber. Additional refinements are a flat disc in lieu of the conical frustrum if it is required for one person and a pedestal of three 50-litre bottles for additional gas storage.

Life-support in Transport Chambers

Life-support in these chambers is generally restricted to maintaining a sufficiently high level of oxygen partial pressure and an appropriately low level of CO_2 partial pressure.

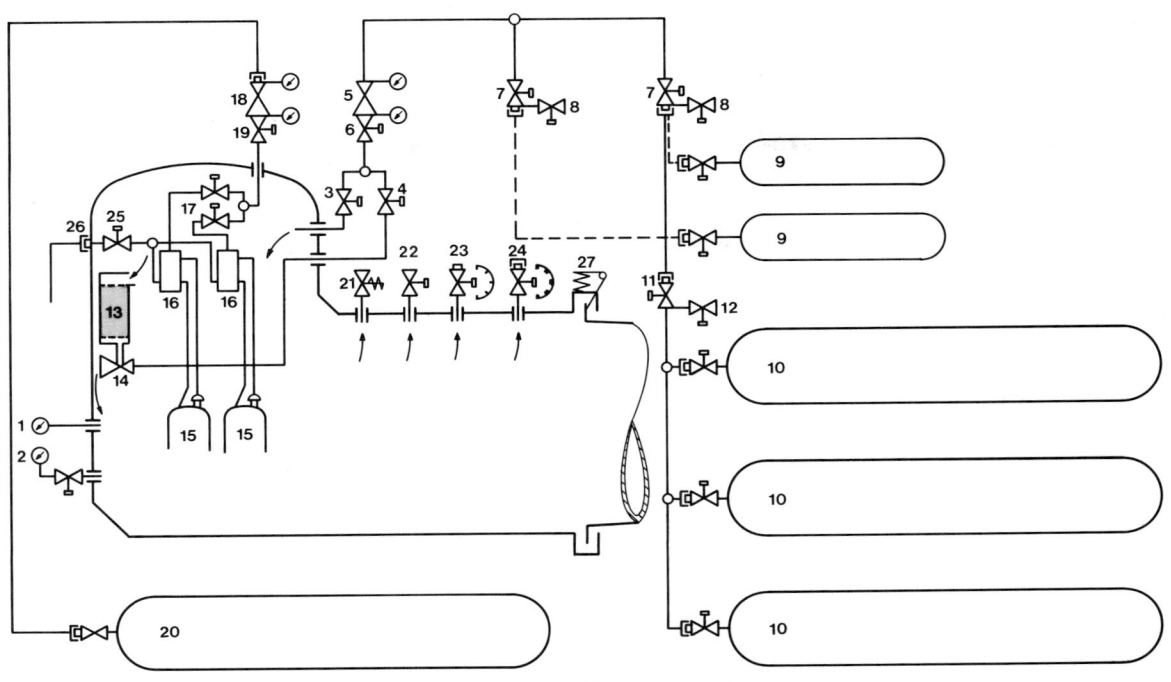

Fig. 5.25. Gas supply and life support for the transportable two-man chamber.

1. pressure gauge 0–50 m
2. pressure gauge 0–18 m
3. filling and flushing valves
4. shut-off valve for injector
5. pressure reducer for compressed air
6. shut-off valve
7. high-pressure shut-off valve
8. discharge valve
9. compressed air cylinders
10. compressed air cylinders
11. high-pressure shut-off valve
12. discharging valve
13. refillable soda lime cartridge
14. injector (for semi-closed circuit)
15. full vision mask with demand regulator
16. cyclo-flow control for O_2 breathing
17. low-pressure shut-off valve (O_2)
18. pressure reducer for O_2
19. shut-off valve
20. high-pressure O_2 cylinder
21. relief valve
22. exhaust valve for decompression
23. adjusted flushing valve
24. adjusted exhaust valve
25. shut-off valve for O_2 exhaust
26. hose coupling for O_2 outlet
27. safety device on bayonet lock

Some chambers have facilities for breathing pure oxygen and, exceptionally, methods of controlling humidity and temperature. A medical lock is sometimes fitted. Since operating pressure of chambers, except for the North Sea evacuation chamber, is low the life-support systems are simple, controlling the oxygen and CO_2 levels only. In Table 5.1 three basic types are sketched. Temperature and humidity are not considered. The carbon dioxide removal is controlled by adjustment of the exhaust. The formula which is applied to determine the necessary exhaust air flow for a stationary condition is described in Chapter 2. Table 2.2 gives the ventilation air-flow required for transportable chambers up to 10 bar and is based on the assumption that inside the chamber a maximum CO_2 partial

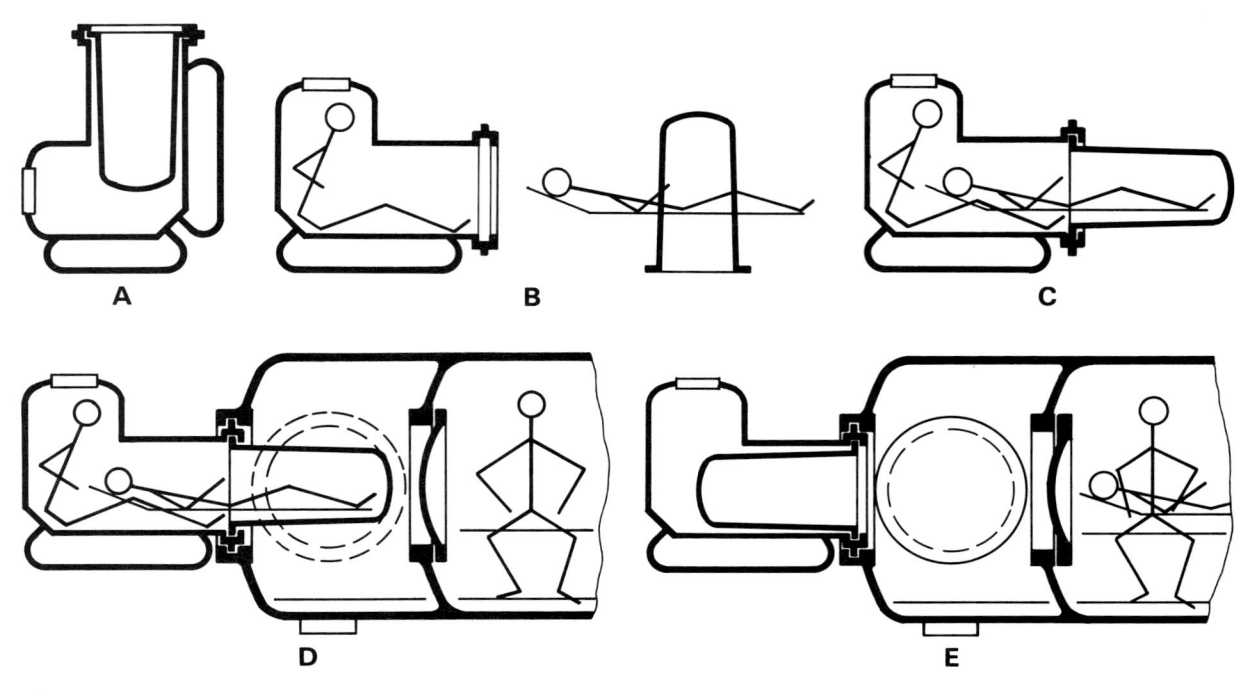

Fig. 5.26. Operation scheme for semi-rigid transportable two-man chamber.

- **A** Storage condition showing the small space requirement, about 1.3 m³. The closing segment is inserted into the main chamber in the reversed position
- **B** Transport chamber being prepared for use. Physician or medical assistant enters the chamber. The diver is placed on a stretcher and pushed inside the main chamber section
- **C** The chamber is closed with the conical end. Pressure treatment can start. If necessary the chamber may now be transported to the next static treatment chamber
- **D** Transport chamber connected to the static treatment chamber. The transfer compartment is pressurized
- **E** After pressure has been equalized in all chambers the diver and attendant are transferred to the main chamber. The closing segment is inserted into the main section in reversed position. The transfer chamber is depressurized and the transport chamber disconnected

pressure of 0.015 bar can be tolerated and that B is 0.5 litres/min of CO_2 produced per person. In the open-circuit system in Table 5.1 it is best to measure the air flow on the exhaust side but it is immaterial whether a flowmeter is fitted in series with the exhaust valve or a metered regulation valve is fitted. No additional power is required but gas consumption is considerable with high pressures. The semi-closed-circuit system overcomes this consumption problem. The CO_2 absorption unit, which can be internal, is usually driven by an injector supplied from the fresh air supply. The fresh air feed is dependent on the efficiency of the injector. As oxygen consumption for a man at rest is only 0.5 litre/min, independent of pressure, little fresh air is needed. It is cheaper to fit the CO_2 absorber internally but if it is fitted externally in a pressure pot it is easier to change when exhausted. Intermittent measurement is advisable to check the

Table 5.1. Life-support systems in transport chambers

System	O_2 feed	CO_2 removal	Additional power
Open circuit	Fresh air ventilation	Exhausting air adjusted quantitatively for number of occupants	Not required
Semi-closed circuit	Fresh air ventilation	Injector-driven CO_2 absorber, cartridge. Intermittent CO_2 measurement required	Not required
Closed circuit	Oxygen feed. Constant O_2 partial pressure measurement required	Absorber with gas circulation by electric blower. Intermittent CO_2 measurement required	Electric power

efficiency of the absorbent. Fig. 5.27 shows a CO_2 absorber as fitted in a two-man chamber. The cartridge is sufficient for two men for four hours and can be changed by the occupants. The lowest gas consumption is achieved with the fully closed system, once pressurization has been achieved. This system requires continuous monitoring of internal oxygen partial pressure. CO_2 is normally removed by externally powered blowers working in tandem and requires intermittent monitoring as well, so consequently the technical effort is considerable. Compared with the open-circuit system the result is both more complicated and more expensive and the maintenance effort is not small. With high-pressure systems using helium–oxygen mixtures and where transport by helicopter is normal closed-circuit systems are inevitable.

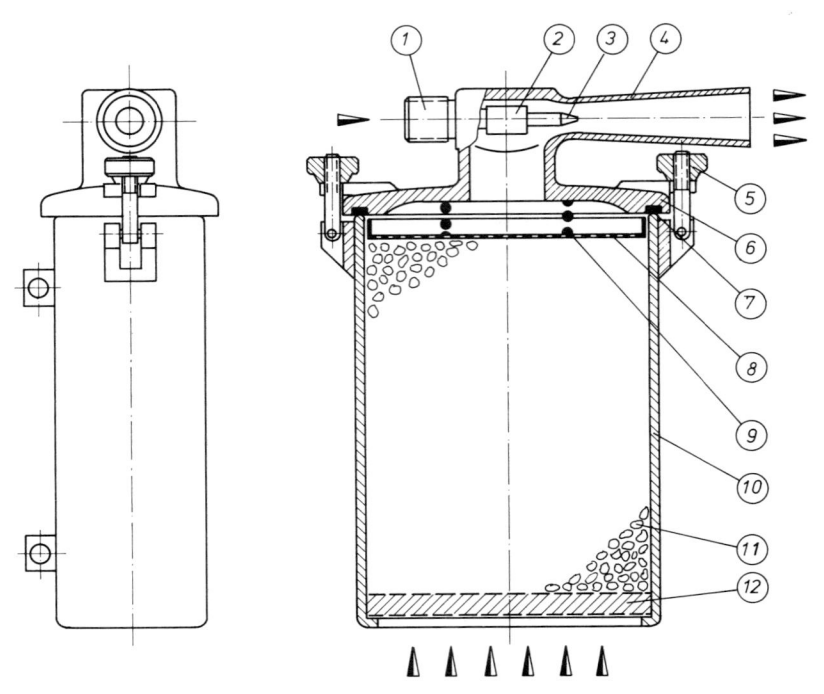

Fig. 5.27. CO_2 absorption unit for transportable one-man and two-man recompression chambers.

1 compressed-air inlet
2 ejector body
3 ejector nozzle
4 ejector tube
5 hinged screw
6 closing cap
7 gasket ring
8 pressure plate (sieve)
9 pressure spring
10 absorbent cannister
11 absorbent
12 dust-filter

Evacuation of Divers Under Pressure

For several years discussions have centred around what action should be taken to safeguard divers who are in saturation or in long diving schedules, particularly with regard to those areas where there is a concentration of off-shore diving such as the North Sea. The thought of divers being locked in a chamber and unable to assist themselves in the event of a blow-out, fire or collision presents a horrifying picture, but the reality of the situation should not be distorted by emotion. The chances of these accidents happening are very small and there is no certainty that divers would be under pressure at the time. In fact there is only one case recorded where it was considered necessary to evacuate divers and, in retrospect, they would have been safer had they remained on board. In many other cases studied, in which divers were not involved, premature evacuation has resulted in unnecessary casualties. The response to an emergency situation will never be as effective as prevention of the situation. The three methods that need to be considered are air, crane and hyperbaric life raft.

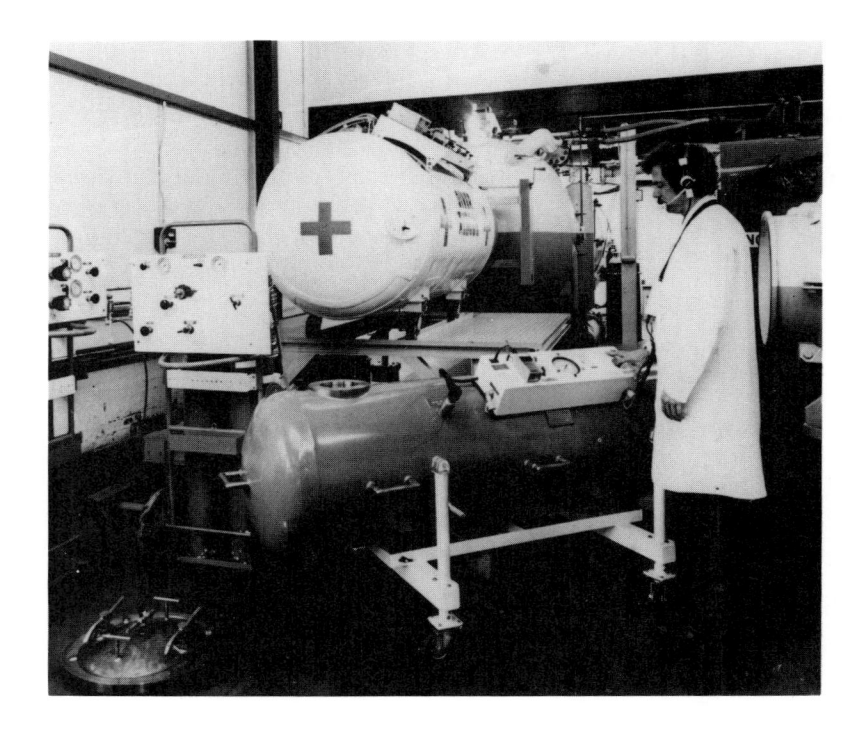

Fig. 5.28. Transportable titanium chamber by International Underwater Contractors.

Air-borne Transfer

The evacuation of divers by helicopter using small one- or two-man chambers has already been discussed, but this operation is more relevant for an injured diver who requires transport to a hyperbaric chamber for treatment because either there is no DCC on site or the nature of his injuries prevents proper treatment at sea. Most diving systems at sea are equipped so that injuries can be treated on site and the transfer of specialist medical personnel to the injured diver under pressure should always be considered first, rather than moving the diver in a transportable chamber to a shore hyperbaric rescue centre. However, in serious cases, where perhaps major surgery is required, a transfer may be advised, in which case a single one-man chamber is unsuitable. Also it does not meet the requirement of divers under pressure, as well as the crew, in the event of a blow-out, fire or sinking. Larger chambers are needed and Fig. 5.28 shows the first large chambers designed to be integrated into a North Sea Hyperbaric Rescue Centre at Aberdeen. The facility, designed and operated by International Underwater Contractors with the assistance of the Continental Oil Company and with the support of major diving and oil companies in the North Sea, can use the emergency diver transfer system for injured divers and has facilities for subsequent post-mortem and for up to ten divers in the rig abandonment role.

The two chambers used in the system are made of titanium; the larger chamber remains fitted in the helicopter and the transfer chamber is used to transfer the injured diver or divers from the DCCs.

The system is designed to be carried in the Sikorski S61 helicopter. The diameter of the mating flange of the transfer chamber is 600 mm and adaptor spool pieces are needed for deep diving systems that are not complementary. Both chambers have lifting pads at either end and in the middle. The transfer chamber can be manhandled. Full life-support facilities are provided with this sophisticated system, including CO_2 scrubbers, molecular sieve, chamber heating, lighting, two-way communications, independent gas supplies and monitoring, a BIBS system with overboard dump for use with pure oxygen therapy, a medical lock and emergency battery-power supplies. A specially designed oval hatch is used on the transfer chamber to enable the last man out in an evacuation operation to secure himself in the restricted space of this one-man chamber. The maximum working pressure of both vessels is 22 bar, with a safety factor of 6 bar. Maximum power requirement from the helicopter is 32 A and 28 V. The weight of the transfer chamber is 250 kg and the helicopter chamber 793 kg.

Crane Transfer

Off-shore regulations require a safety vessel to be stationed near the installation in the event of the evacuation of the crew of the installation. To enable any divers under pressure to be evacuated there should also be crane facilities to lift a DCC on board the safety vessel. The deep diving complex should be designed to allow a chamber to be detached and the safety vessel to supply essential life support once it has been transferred.

Hyperbaric Life Raft

The concept of a pressure chamber committed to the sea has not gained favour in the off-shore industry although it is a mandatory requirement in Norwegian waters. Therefore a considerable number of vessels and rigs may need to be modified to attach a specially designed rescue chamber to the deep diving system. Capable of being launched into the sea, the chamber must float and have a separate life-support system with 24 hours duration. The rescue chamber is discussed in detail in Chapter 3 as part of a deep diving system.

Diver Lock-out Submersible

If the vessel is operating diver lock-out submersibles, a submersible can be used in an emergency to evacuate the divers under pressure. Most submersibles can accommodate only two divers owing to the severely limited space inside the diver lock-out chamber, and operations in certain situations and areas may be limited by the number of diver lock-out submersibles available for emergency evacuation.

In general therefore prevention is better than cure and further consideration should be given to the termination of diving and the decompression of divers when the risk of accidents occurring are greater. Higher-risk situations occur whilst drilling vessels are under tow or diving vessels are passing through congested waters, in poor conditions or when hurricane warnings are in force. Drill ships operating in iceberg zones need to be able to implement safety procedures.

6 Under-water Habitats

Manned under-water stations have already played an important role in the study of the continental plateau. In the future it will not always be possible to carry out operations from the surface either by diving, which will become severely limited as the depth increased beyond 300 m, or by manned intervention in the form of submersibles. It is probable that production systems and manned stations on the sea bed will be required in order to produce hydrocarbons from deeper depths or in adverse surface conditions such as ice. In this case operators will have to remain on the seabed unattended for long periods with the need to be resupplied and the crew changed. Many projects are being formulated to meet these needs in the future and, whilst the many habitats that have been installed over the last two decades have been non-commercial, designed primarily for research, they are invaluable for the experience that has been gained. This chapter discusses the development of habitats and the essential considerations that need to be taken into account, of which energy to meet the power requirements is among the most important. If this is solved many of the limitations disappear. Risk areas are reduced to acceptable proportions and the concept becomes cost-effective. Properly conceived and designed, the habitat can give the operator a number of options when fulfilling a work task which are not necessarily available to the surface-orientated operation. The possible work tasks where using a habitat may provide a solution are listed below. In certain circumstances it may be the only solution.

1. Salvage of ships, aircraft, missiles, submarines in hostile areas and in deep water.
2. Salvage of precious or dangerous cargo in hostile weather areas and in deep water.
3. Extended repairs on dams and reservoirs.
4. Submarine supply.
5. Subsea production.
6. Subsea drilling.
7. Oceanographic, biological and geological observations and investigations.
8. Site preparation prior to installation/construction, i.e. concrete structures.
9. Research and development into marine biology and associated subjects.

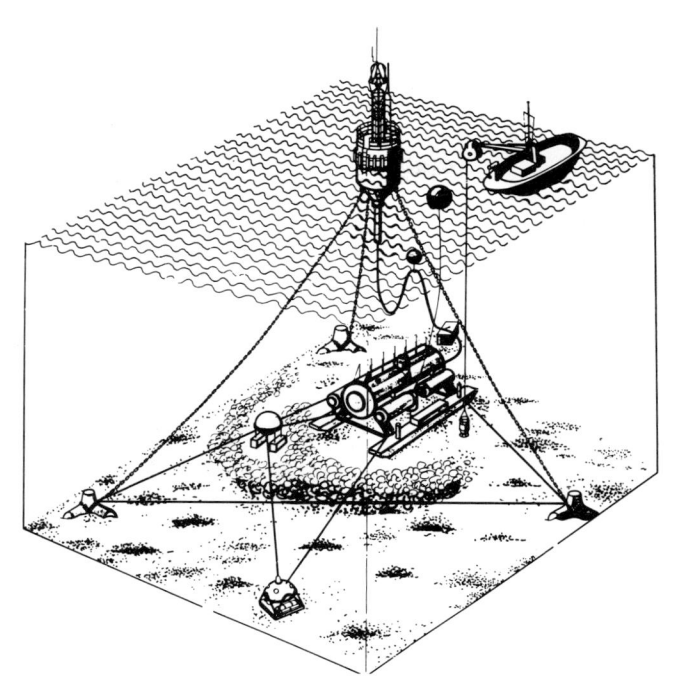

Fig. 6.1. Under-water installation of the under-water laboratory *Helgoland*.

10. Research and development of divers' equipment and work tools.
11. Welding.

The scope of the habitat will vary considerably depending on the requirement. Whereas a short intervention in shallow water may demand little more than an inflatable open-ended bag or tent, another deeper and sophisticated requirement may need to accommodate large numbers of technicians and scientists. Many problems are identical and basic whatever the depth and requirement. In this chapter the aim is to identify the different features of habitats and show in practice how some have been overcome and how other problems will be met in the future.

Conventional Designs

The size and shape of a habitat are determined on much the same basis as those of a surface hyperbaric complex. The size is governed by the number of personnel using the facility and the shape is dictated by external parameters. In this latter case the diving system as well as the habitat may be designed for permanent emplacement or be capable of being moved from one position to another. Unlike diving systems, however, there are a number of conceptual variations in habitat systems with satellites. Figs 6.2–6.5 show the use of these satellites, not unlike igloos, which can fulfil the functions of observation and

Fig. 6.2. Designs for under-water shelters for short use.

communication posts centred around and dependent on a master station. There are a number of options based on the free movement of divers and not in these cases deploying one-atmosphere systems. In much the same way as modern surface diving complexes have standardized on the use of modular chamber construction which allows for any number of chambers to be mated in a suitable configuration, so also does this practice lend itself to the construction of a habitat complex to support different tasks with different configurations, for example in salvage and marine research. The main requirement stipulates that the habitat should embody its own life-support system, unlike a diving bell. This life-support system must be common to all configurations.

Satellites are dependent upon a central habitat and can only be considered for short duration. Therefore the materials and fittings do not all necessarily have to meet the same requirements of the habitat. The satellites can be used for a number of purposes and Fig. 6.2 summarizes the different current designs.

Type A is a simple 'telephone box' used for communication, with clear reception, to the central habitat base. It is in the form of a simple hemispherical design made of acrylic glass, for good visibility, and with a diameter rarely exceeding 600 mm. The correct breathing gas is maintained by flushing the air space through with new gas in preference to using a removal system for CO_2 and other various gases. If the bottom currents are not strong, the cell can be kept in position by the attachment of a bottom weight. In strong currents the ballast weights need to be increased.

For longer duration, possibly for the use of two divers, the single cell, or igloo, is not suitable and a large hemispherical igloo (*Type B*) can be used. An optimum size would be 2000 mm bare diameter giving minimal drag when exposed to bottom currents. The space inside would be sufficient for two divers to sit or lie down for short periods and a gas supply is provided. The inverted T-shape support at the base carries both the breathing gases for normal and emergency use and the ballast tanks for recovery. A small life-support system inside provides a CO_2 scrubber, oxygen at required partial pressure, lighting and communication. The unit can be either self-contained or, if close to the central habitat, supplied with life-support and power from there. The overall capacity of the main habitat can determine the number of igloos that can be maintained. Because of limited instrumentation and life-support fittings needed, this allows more efficient utilization of space. Stores needed for the main habitat, such as CO_2 absorbent, can be stored in these units.

Type C. Small vertical cylinders can be used for short periods but are very restrictive, with diameters of less than 1 m, and therefore are more effectively used in the transport role. In this role they can transport divers to and from the main habitat in the same way as a diving bell and also provide an eventual safety function for use in an emergency evacuation. The UWL *Helgoland*, whilst operating in north-west Europe, had two rescue chambers permanently operational, adjacent to the habitat.

Whilst spherical, hemispherical or cylindrical designs in acrylic or steel are usual, other box type structures can be installed using flexible rubber materials spread over metal frames and secured (*Type D*). To alleviate the tension load on the surface netting can be spread over the inflated structure and directly secured to the ballast weights. Larger units can be fabricated to accommodate two to four people. The inflated fabric has very poor insulation properties and is suitable only for warm waters or brief stays. By the nature of their construction they are modestly equipped.

The main habitats have greater space for additional fittings as distinct from cells or igloos which are only used for short durations. Even if supplied with power and life-support from the surface, the additional secondary life-support systems will impose space limitations. Illustrated in Fig. 6.3 are the different geometric forms suitable for straightforward habitats capable of equalization.

For the deepest depths the sphere (*Type A*) is the most favoured form because its construction can more easily allow differential internal and external pressures. With the change in depth, whilst ascending and descending, the pressure is equalized internally and externally. A sphere will utilize space economically if split into different floor levels. With an overall diameter of 6–8 m several floors can be installed with a crew of up to ten.

The horizontal cylinder (*Type B*) is by far the most usual design for a habitat with up to three separate compartments. One compartment can be designed for differential pressures and used for diver lock out operations not possible with the sphere. Normal dimensions range from 1.20 to 4 m in diameter for the hull form and from 4 to 17 m in length, with a minimum crew of two and a normal maximum of ten. One of the great difficulties of the pressure equivalent design is the controlled lowering onto the site with all the dangers inherent in this type of operation.

Fig. 6.3. Simple designs for under-water laboratories suitable for longer stays.

The advantages of the ellipsoid (*Type C*) for an under-water habitat are not due merely to the aesthetic value of this shape but also to the fact that it has minimal drag characteristics and greater overall strength. However, the constructional problems would be reflected in the very high cost, although the shape is economical in terms of meeting the maximum space requirements for a given volume. An ellipsoid with a minimal internal diameter of 4–5 m would be practical, given that the higher costs of the habitat were acceptable.

Advanced Designs for Habitats with Integrated Pressure Hulls

For practical reasons the use of integrated modular hull forms is more favoured. Surface compression and decompression chambers have been designed in modular form to facilitate transport and assembly, and with the option to extend or decrease the overall capacity to suit the requirement, and the same disciplines will apply to the design of habitats. Also, by separating the units, certain safety requirements are met should some sections sustain damage or become unserviceable, allowing evacuation into safe areas. In Fig. 6.4 three basic configurations are described.

Type A consists of a parallel arrangement with two vertical cylinders connected by a horizontal shaft in the upper portion. This

Fig. 6.4. Designs for under-water habitats with integrated pressure hulls.

was the basis of the American *Tektite* design, allowing the space to be divided into two levels, whether they were for work or living. In this configuration the machinery can be isolated in one chamber and the controls and living space in the other. The design allows for longer missions than other designs but is severely restricted in use due to the large hull area exposed to the currents whilst on the seabed, and basic instability in shallow waters and during launch and recovery through the interface of air and water, imposed by the limitations of the sea state on the surface.

A centralized design with peripheral compartments installed around the central chamber is shown in *Type B*. This was first put into practice in Captain Cousteau's French-designed *Starfish* house. The central hull may be cylindrical or spherical and several compartments for different functions can be connected to this nucleus, housing the central control, life-support and monitoring functions. Certain advantages lie in the possibility of increasing or decreasing the number of peripheral compartments, perhaps even whilst under water.

Type C is a modular concept establishing the American *Bottom Fix* theoretical design and allowing different sized spheres to be combined together. The present Underwater Test Range at Hawaii using the same concept is very modest as shown in Fig. 6.4C with two cylinders connected to a centre sphere, on the same axis and the whole resting on a pontoon. The pontoon allows the complex to be towed

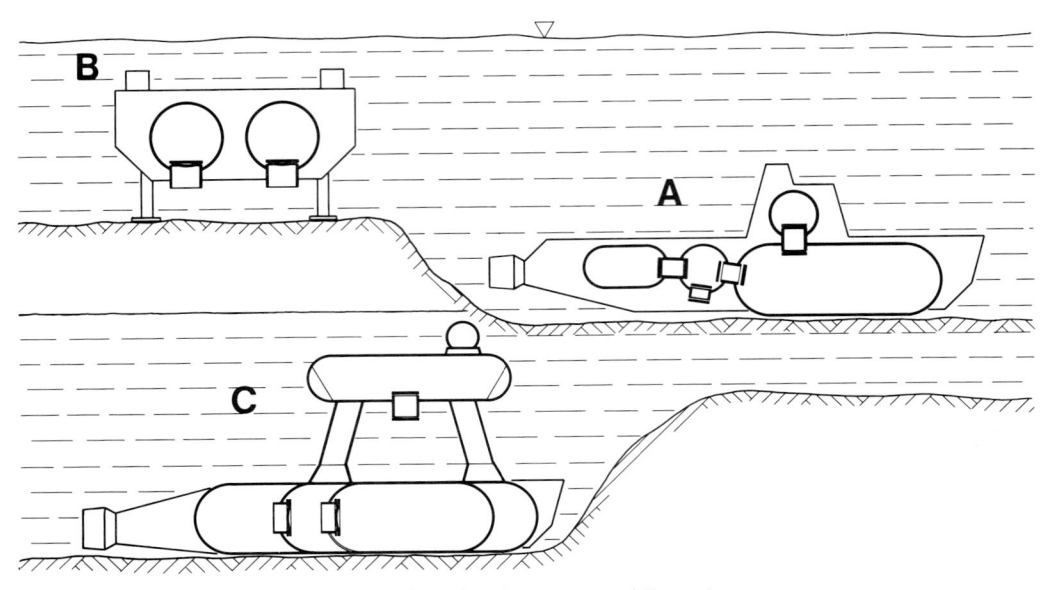

Fig. 6.5. Examples of under-water mobile stations.

to and from the site in sea states which preclude similar transport for other systems with reduced stability. The advantage of designing the overall system for safe towage is considerable, as the only alternative is launch and recovery which demands heavy lift cranes and barges. Another design which incorporated towage facilities was the habitat design by Perry Oceanographics known as *La Chalupa* where two horizontal chambers forming the habitat were designed into a pontoon.

Mobile Under-water Habitats

Except for habitats designed as part of deep sea production systems where they can be considered permanent and provide oil and gas separation, water injection and other requirements, the modern concept of the habitats demands that it should be capable of being moved from location to location and able to undertake research and investigation. The latest concept, *Ocean Lab*, planned by the National Oceanographic Atmosphere Administration, has incorporated an integrated pressure chamber complex which comes close to being a submarine. However, with its ability to operate aquanauts and remain in one position for relatively long periods of time, it should continue to be classified as an under-water station or mobile habitat.

The main constructional forms for these mobile habitats are shown in Fig. 6.5.

The concept of the submarine hull enclosing a habitat (*Type A*) was advanced by Captain Cousteau in the design of the *Argyronete*. The hull was in fact built before the high cost of completing the vessel and

Fig. 6.6. Under-water *Igloo* before operations in the North Sea.

the limited commercial return at that time put an end to further work. However, the principle is valid and as the commercial opportunities are realized for this configuration, the design will be updated and the autonomous submarine habitat will finally be built.

A less conventional but in many ways more practical approach to the problem is in the submersible catamaran design (*Type B*). The catamaran can meet the basic requirements of a habitat, which is to provide a work base on the seabed from which to operate divers and carry out investigation in a one-atmosphere environment, and also undertake other missions. By transporting and supporting welding habitats and small submersibles to the work place, other tasks could be carried out. The sea-keeping qualities of the catamaran design in a semi-submerged condition will give additional flexibility whilst stationary or underway on the surface. An additional feature is the use of the catamaran as a deep diving vessel where a diving bell can operate from a transfer under pressure system inside the hull and below the waterline. Operating diving bells and submersibles from a position below sea level overcomes the inherent dangers and limitations when operating caused by wave motion and possibly surge near or on the surface.

Construction of Habitats

The various designs already discussed, some theoretical and unproven, now lead to actual constructions based on those basic designs.

For short missions the under-water shelters or igloos need to be relatively small. A good example of this is shown in Fig. 6.6, either

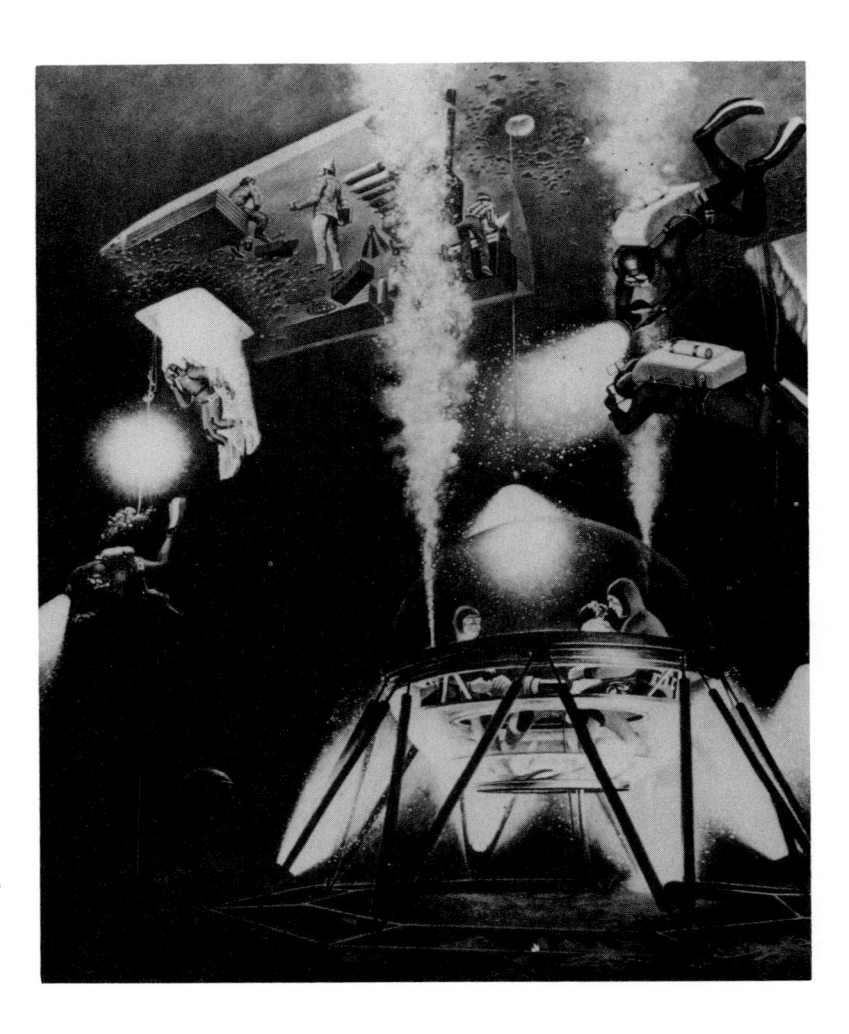

Fig. 6.7. *Sub-Igloo* (Canada) was successfully employed in Antarctic exploration programmes in 1972 and 1974.

used autonomously or connected to a central habitat supplying certain life-support functions and direct line communications. The hull is a hemispherical shell, made from corrosion-proof, well insulated glass-reinforced polyester resin, and closed towards the bottom with a flat dished shell with a central shaft for lock-out made of the same material. The lock-out shaft has no door and is open to the water. The gas or air inside is at ambient pressure to prevent the water from flooding the interior.

Large viewports are installed for good observation. A flashlight on the top will indicate the position of the igloo in poor visibility.

To some extent the internal fittings of the igloo will reflect the proposed use of the shelter. The use of the unit in an emergency, whilst in transit or occasional shelter, will demand more modest fittings than if it is used as a forward-operating base from which to undertake a task. Generally the interior will have an electrically driven CO_2 scrubber, an oxygen supply unit adjustable for the number of occupants breathing the air or gas mixture and an air supply or gas mixture for keeping the water level constant, and for ventilation by flushing should this be necessary. The gas supply is stowed in two 50-litre cylinders which are mounted on the base frame. Communication and appropriate lighting are provided inside the igloo which can be connected to the central habitat. At least two closed-circuit or scuba breathing sets are provided with each igloo in this case.

Even with these small units, very careful ballasting is needed. With a radius of 0.9 m and an overall volume of 1.5 m^3, the displacement of the water has to be compensated with weights. The base frame was built with additional steel bars for ballast and two large buoyancy tanks were used to control the descent, without a crane. This allowed the igloo to be towed out to a coastal site by a small boat and placed on the seabed in shallow water using divers. On land it is easily transportable by road.

Acrylic glass can be used for this type of igloo in addition to the smaller 'telephone box' shown in Fig. 6.2A. In the larger installation by Dr MacInnis, known as *Sub-Igloo* and pictured in Fig. 6.7, the use of acrylic for the hemisphere, although considerably more expensive than glass-reinforced plastic, allowed scientific observations to be made with exceptional all-round observation in Arctic waters. In this case the diameter of the acrylic dome is 2.5 m. The use of under-water tents, where only short and temporary operations are contemplated, requires durable waterproof materials.

For large habitats designed for the deployment of satellite igloos or other variations of small habitats, the construction clearly becomes very complex. Common to most habitats that have been built there is the horizontal cylinder. Fig. 6.8 shows a plan and section drawing of *Sealab III* built for the U.S. Navy and Fig. 6.9 shows *Sealab* suspended on a crane, shortly before its tragic first operation off California. The cylindrical main body has a length of 19.4 m and an internal diameter of 3.65 m. There is no internal pressure-proof subsection and the working and living areas are separated by flexible bulkheads. Additional compartments are connected at each end and below the main chamber. One compartment is the diving chamber with the main diver lock-out and the other is built with large viewports for under-water observation. An additional lock-out is fitted in this observation compartment as an emergency lock out. The ballasting arrangement incorporates an unusual design in that the main horizontal chamber is not secured rigidly to the ballast frame but suspended on cables, in much the same way as a balloon. The ballast frame carries all the gas supplies, which are considerable. The habitat has to be launched and recovered by a crane using a pontoon on which the habitat is towed to the site and therefore is very dependent on weather and surface conditions. The first operation, off the west coast of California at a depth of 183 m, resulted in a fatal accident and further operations were promptly ended due to some basic technical problems.

Spherical under-water stations are rare in spite of the advantages already discussed. The best known was Cousteau's habitat deployed in the Mediterranean in 1965 at a depth of 100 m. Also deploying a

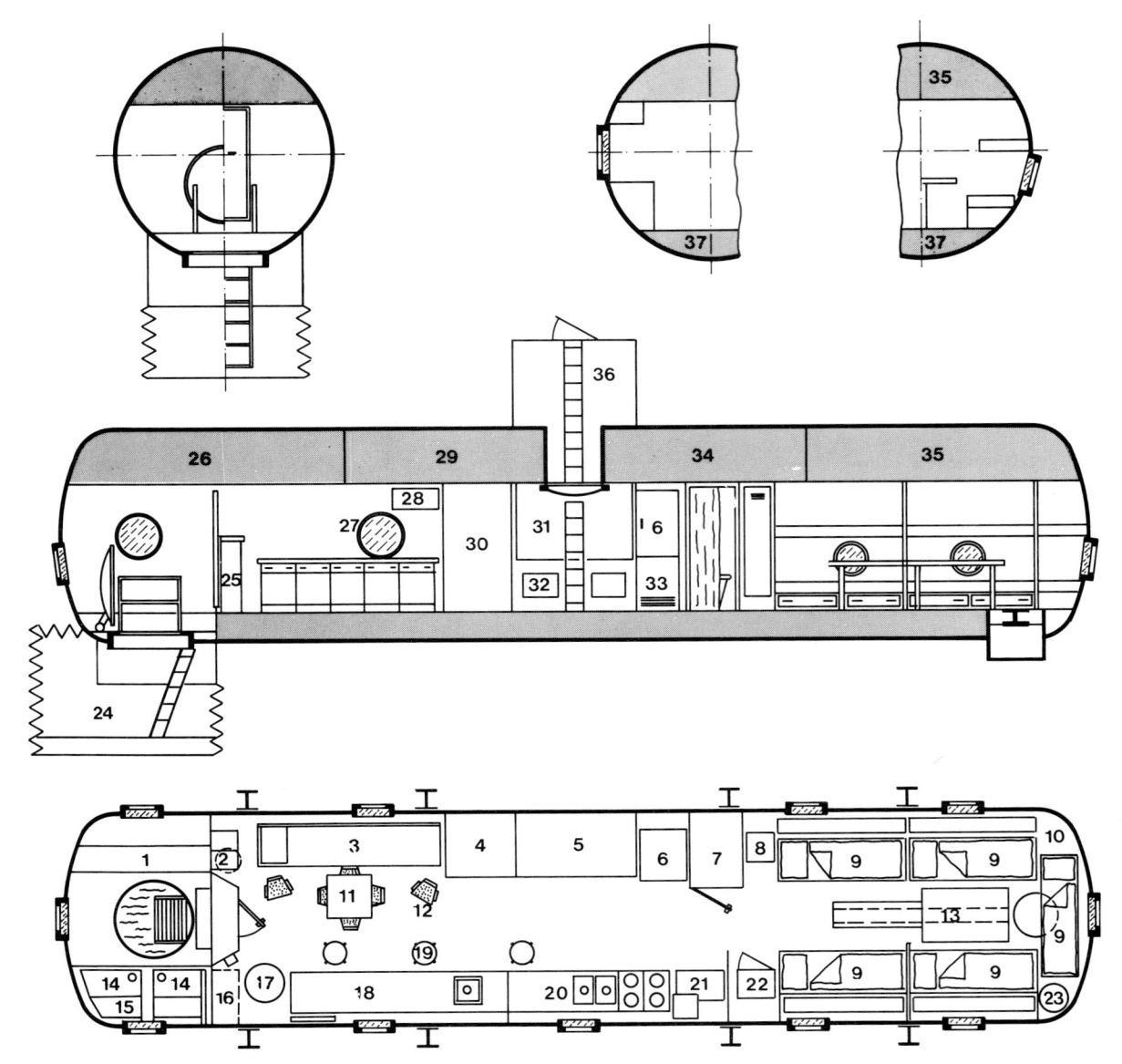

Fig. 6.8. Scheme of *Sealab III* (side and top view)

1	swim gear stowage	14	bath	26	water ballast
2	TV	15	shower	27	window
3	work bench	16	canister stowage	28	O_2 monitor
4	fan room	17	water heater	29	water ballast
5	electric power and light	18	work bench	30	ventilation machinery
6	refrigerator	19	stool	31	power panel
7	WC	20	galley	32	stowage
8	locker	21	laboratory	33	fridge-freezer
9	berths	22	locker	34	water ballast
10	stowage	23	CO_2 canister	35	water ballast
11	table	24	anti-shark cage	36	upper access
12	chair	25	cable locker	37	concrete ballast
13	table				

Fig. 6.9. *Sealab III* suspended on a crane shortly before its unlucky first operation.

satellite, a considerable depth and area was covered. Some Eastern European countries have built spherical habitats and in the Baltic Sea the *Sadko 1* was built, enlarging the vertical axis by incorporating a second sphere.

Under-water habitats with integrated separate chambers are less common than the 'monocells' described. Best known are the *Precontinent II, Tektite One, Sadko II, Aegir, La Chalupa* and the under-water laboratory *Helgoland*. Especially of interest is the *Aegir* at the Makai Underwater Test Range in Hawaii. Shown in Fig. 6.10 is a picture of the *Aegir* with two cylindrical chambers and an intermediate sphere on the same axis, with two rescue chambers, each for four people. Finally the two ballast chambers and gas storage cylinders are mounted with the main chamber on a catamaran pontoon. The sea-keeping qualities of the pontoon are good, up to sea state four whilst under tow, and generally the design is considered most successful, holding the record for the deepest depth of 158 m, achieving a duration of 14 days in 1970. The ability of the habitat to control its descent and ascent without the need for a crane rates it as an advanced design. The habitat can support four to six people, with separate chambers for saturation diving, and decompression can be completed whilst allowing the whole unit to come to the surface. The life-support system on board allows for 20 days operation without surface support. An unusual feature of the system allows for some recovery of the cost of the habitat by making it available to other

Fig. 6.10. The under-water laboratory *Aegir* and the *Holokai* at the Makai Range Pier (Makai Undersea Test Range, Oahu, Hawaii).

interested scientific bodies to carry out their own programmes. A similar arrangement was later offered for the lease of the under-water laboratory *Helgoland* for scientific research.

The integrated pressure hull concept incorporated in the *La Chalupa* in 1972 went further in perfecting the pontoon arrangement by designing the pressure hulls into the contours of the vessel.

Most habitats have been designed for operation in sites on the seabed without any ability to move except in the vertical mode for lowering, emplacement and recovery, using controlled buoyancy systems but without any propulsion units. Usually the movement of the habitat has been by crane onto a barge and subsequently from the barge into the water. The under-water laboratory *Helgoland* was transported suspended under a crane 90 miles from Hamburg to the launch area for its first operation (Fig. 6.11). As an alternative method the Dutch company Skadoc proposed that the habitat should be slung underneath a working submersible and moved from the base to the operating site where they would be lowered together, releasing the habitat on the bottom. The delicate handling of the habitat in this final stage of manoeuvring on the seabed is covered later in this chapter.

Stationary habitats without the ability to change position and lacking any form of self-propulsion tend to be used for scientific research where they are required to operate in the same place for long periods. In the future it is likely that production of oil and gas will

Fig. 6.11. The under-water laboratory *Helgoland* during transport from Hamburg to Helgoland.

take place on the seabed, probably in depths of water between 200 and 1000 m. By the nature of this requirement and the scope of the services that are needed it seems likely that the habitat will be separate from but connected to the main complex. The larger complex will need to undertake some or all of the tasks of oil and gas separation, water and gas re-injection into the well and the servicing of the well and be a permanent structure for the life expectancy of the field. In the small under-water laboratories the depths are very shallow and they usually have power supplied from the surface or from shore if the distances are not too great. Therefore it is unlikely that these habitats will be autonomous, particularly with regard to energy needs. The large habitats currently being considered as part of deep sea hydrocarbon production systems will need to have their own energy sources, refuelled over long periods. Mobile habitats strive to be to some extent autonomous and early concepts in this flexible role envisaged the use of conventional submarines refitted to withstand internal as well as external pressures and to provide lock-out facilities for divers. Nevertheless the constraints of limited energy sources, which usually required recharging, restricted the time spent on the bottom whilst also remaining mobile. However, the development of

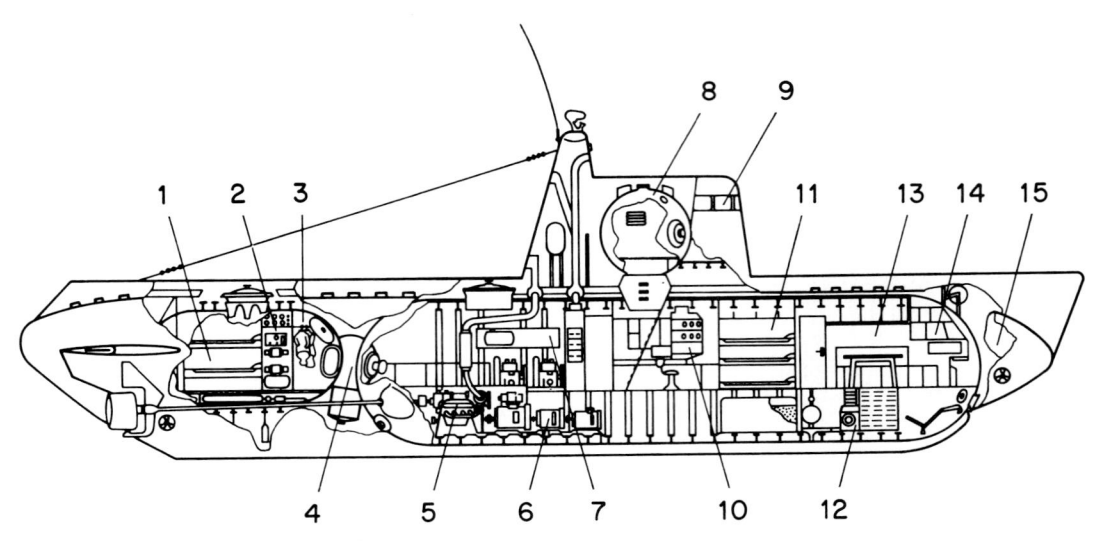

Fig. 6.12. The mobile under-water laboratory *Argyonete*.

1. sleeping space
2. electrical switchboard
3. diver compartment
4. two transfer chambers (transfer and lock-out)
5. diesel engine and main propulsion
6. generators
7. engine room
8. large pressure (rescue) sphere
9. surface bridge
10. control centre
11. sleeping areas in submarine
12. air circulation and purification
13. living room
14. oceanologists' room
15. trimming tanks

fuel cells and closed-circuit diesel engines and the design of commercial as distinct from military submarines has recently opened up many possibilities for the 1980s. The role of the autonomous submarine is discussed in Chapter 8.

The concept of a habitat contoured within a submarine hull is shown in Fig. 6.12. The *Argyronete*, as already discussed, was never completed beyond the hull but many of the ideas associated with the design were later incorporated in the American NOAA Habitat project, the *Oceanlab*.

Some designs have tried to incorporate an umbilical cable for the supply of energy from the surface to self-propel the habitat. Such a design was the *Seabed Vehicle* built by Cammell Laird with considerable government funding. Designed with large surface area wheels operating separately for movement across rocky or soft sea bottoms, the project was scrapped at a late stage. Basic design parameters that could not be met during the initial trials could have been foreseen at the early design state. Had the vehicle ever progressed into operation one of the greatest drawbacks of the surface-supplied concept would have been the sheer weight and drag of the umbilical. Mobile habitats must as a general rule aim to be autonomous. The diver lock-out technique is the same in stationary units as in mobile units.

Logistics Support Systems

In whatever circumstances man finds himself operating under water the need for life-support is fundamental. Habitats have a greater permanency than other under-water systems, such as diving bells and submersibles, in that they are not designed to be launched and recovered at short notice. Submersible and diving operations are surface-orientated with decompression, living, maintenance and repair all carried out onboard a vessel. Habitats therefore require a much higher standard of safety, particularly with regard to life-support and secondary back-up systems than submersibles and diving bells.

Support of habitat operations means supplying the following:

1. Energy (usually electrical).
2. Gases (oxygen, nitrogen, helium and air).
3. Water (drinking and for domestic use).
4. Food (prepared and deep frozen).
5. Stores (spare parts and consumables).
6. Mail.

Other support factors not directly associated with the logistics of supply are as follows:

7. Waste disposal.
8. Communications.
9. Medical.
10. Rescue.

Undoubtedly the energy requirement is paramount since without sufficient energy the endurance of the habitat is either reduced or terminated. Experience with stationary habitats indicates that power of at least 25 kW is required for an under-water team of four and this precludes the use of just battery sources.

Water in sufficient quantity is another major need. If not supplied from the surface support vessel, fresh water can be made from sea water but considerable electrical energy is needed to make the conversion.

In Fig. 6.13 the various options for stationary habitats are illustrated. If the habitat is close inshore a cable may be laid from shore to habitat as shown in Fig. 6.13A. The power cable from a shore generator needs protection, particularly on the beach and above and below the surface. For semi-permanent sites consideration should be given to trenching cables into the seabed and covering them with concrete or with fastenings. Other services that can be supplied along the same route are gas, water and communication and data lines, making up a composite umbilical. This option can be very expensive because of the danger to the umbilical from trawlboards, anchors and other intrusions and may not be acceptable particularly if the distance off-shore is considerable. Food and stores are carried out by supply boat from the surface as and when needed. Another disadvantage is

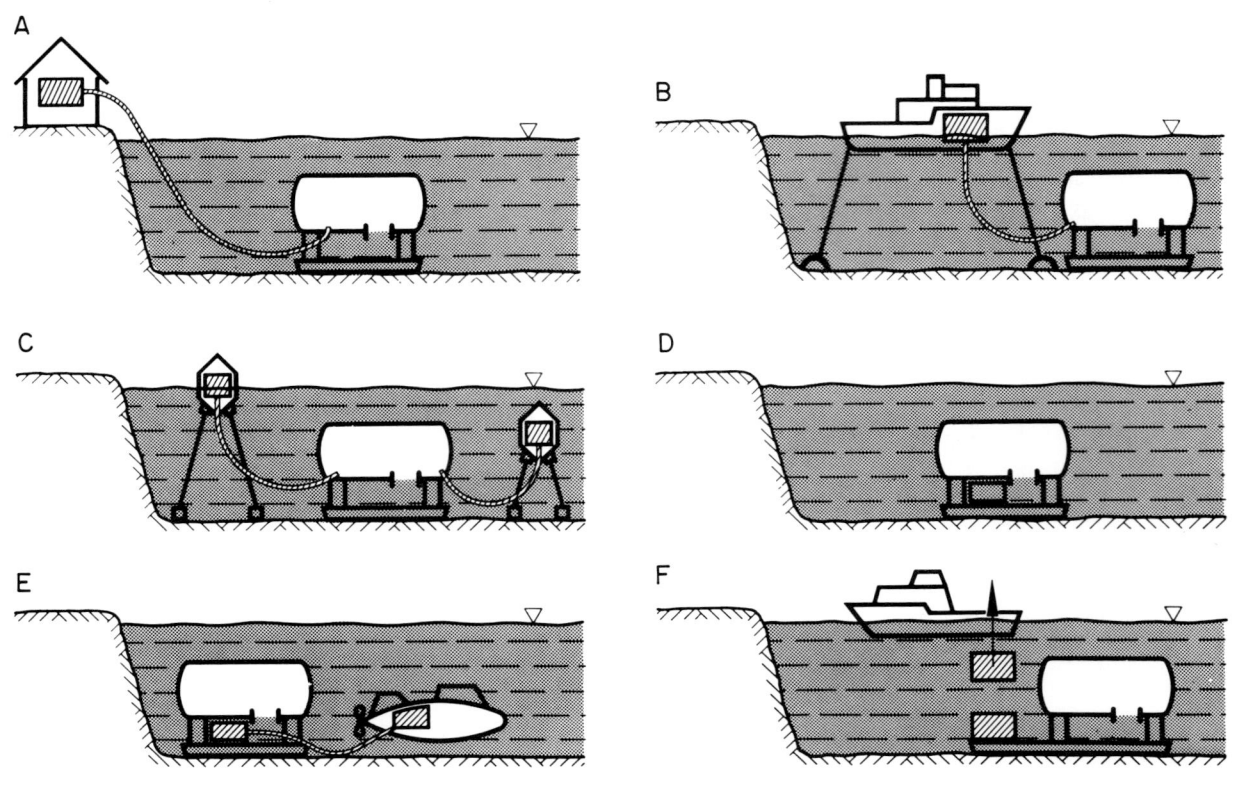

Fig. 6.13. Support systems for stationary under-water habitats.

    A   Energy supplied from shore. Suitable only where the distance between shore and habitat is short
    B   Energy and water supply from a moored ship or pontoon
    C   Energy and gas supply from surface or under-water buoy
    D   Autonomous habitat with nuclear energy supply or source, i.e. batteries or fuel cells
    E   Periodic support from surface ships or submarines
    F   Periodic supply of a complete life-support package

that, should the habitat subsequently need to be moved to a different site, an alternative shore supply would be required. The remaining options in Fig. 6.13 therefore need to be considered.

All the services can be supplied from a moored or dynamically positioned vessel but with two fundamental disadvantages: the limitations of weather and the disproportionate number of personnel manning the vessel to the number of personnel in the habitat, a ratio of as much as 20 to 4. Generally this method of surface support is for short periods of days or a few weeks. For longer periods the method in Fig. 6.13C has proved very successful; the power source is contained in a buoy either on the surface or below sea level to avoid contact with surface vessels. This solution presupposes that in all such operations it is essential to designate an exclusive zone and prohibit

Fig. 6.14. Support buoy for the under-water laboratory *Helgoland* in the North Sea (DFVLR system).

all shipping and submarines from entering the area. The buoy can be left unmanned and operate for up to about 20 days before resupply and maintenance. The submergence of the buoys beneath the sea level does present air intake problems. These were investigated in an experiment for an under-water village in a lake in northern Italy. Diesel generators in large cylinders were fitted with snorkels to the surface. The most outstanding example of the buoy technique was that of the surface buoy used several times to supply the UWL *Helgoland* in the North Sea, the Baltic Sea and finally off the east coast of America, near Boston. The buoy is pictured in Fig. 6.14 in calm conditions in the North Sea. This buoy, one of the largest floating sea marks in the North Sea, was moored to three concrete blocks, each weighing 6 tonnes, and secured with anchor chains. Fig. 6.15 shows the mooring plan with the additional scope of umbilical to allow for any slight lateral or horizontal movement and designed with additional buoyancy. The umbilical is led through a gooseneck fitting to avoid any damage and to allow for free movement. Carefully adjusted, the buoy maintains position in prevailing sea states and tidal movements in both the horizontal and the vertical position. The overall weight of the buoy is about 16 tonnes with an external diameter of 3 m and an overall height of 13 m. Fig. 6.16 shows the inside of the unit with very much the same fittings as one

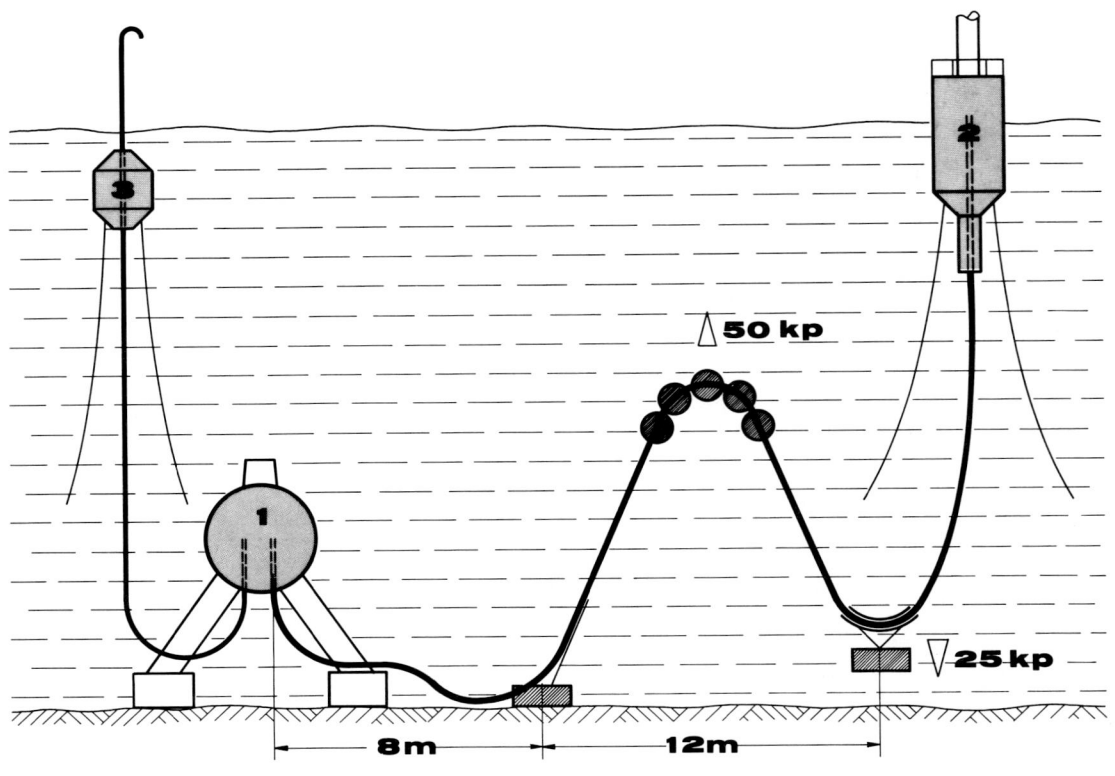

Fig. 6.15. Support buoy with goose-neck faired lead-in for umbilical from the habitat.

1. Under-water habitat
2. Supply buoy
3. Decompression buoy

would expect in a ship's engine room. The centre of the internal space is taken up by the diesel generator with an output of 25 kW. By redesigning the generator with a larger oil sump maintenance was reduced to periods in excess of 1000 hours. The fuel tanks contained 3200 litres and fitted into the bottom of the buoy, giving an endurance of at least 20 days.

The power was not only supplied direct to the habitat but also used to drive two high-pressure air-compressors sited inside the buoy. The compressor with intakes of 120 litres/minute compressed air into two banks on the habitat itself. These air reservoirs each had a capacity of 3000 litres. The habitat drew on the air reservoirs for maintaining the air pressure inside and for recharging scuba bottles as required for excursions into the water. The compressors were fitted with automatic start and stop switches to keep the air reservoirs within preset pressure levels, cutting in and out as required to keep the pressure not more than 200 bar and not less than 120 bar, allowing for sufficient air in an emergency. The compressors were carefully designed to operate without maintenance within the 20-day period and to achieve this had automatic water drainage valves. The alternate use of the two units spread the work-load over the operating period.

An axial blower was fitted to the top of the buoy for the necessary intake of air into the engine space supplying the required 3200 m³/hour. The additional engine fittings were the oil pumps, fuel and bilge pumps. The compressors and generator had to meet the strict requirements imposed by the movement of the buoy in bad weather with inclinations of up to 45° and accelerations of $2g$.

Also installed inside the buoy were the other life-support requirements of oxygen, nitrogen and helium, as required, contained in 14 gas storage cylinders, each with a capacity of 50 litres. With a crew of four in the habitat the oxygen supply is sufficient for at least 14 days without having to use the emergency supply in the habitat. For depths down to about 30 m the helium and nitrogen supplies are not needed but as the site becomes deeper the use of these gases, either in a tri-mix of helium, nitrogen and oxygen or for deeper depths in oxy-helium mixtures, becomes necessary.

In addition to its purely logistical function, the buoy is fitted as a relay station providing a communication link to the habitat and if necessary also a television link. Using radio for the external link to the outside world from the buoy, the communication link is through direct line to the habitat. This line communication and all the other sources of gas, power and water are passed through 16 hoses joined together to form the composite umbilical protected by a non-abrasive plastic sheath. For the UWL *Helgoland* the length of the umbilical was 60 m. Marine growth was eliminated by the use of anti-fouling paint, an important consideration in all buoyancy design calculations. The buoy was also used for landing supplies, mail and other essentials including the transfer of crew.

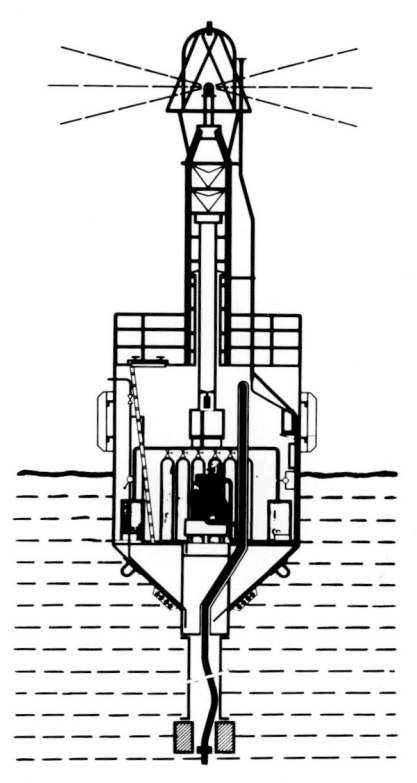

Fig. 6.16. Cross-section of the support buoy for the underwater laboratory *Helgoland*.

The buoy technique has been used with other habitats notably the *Aegir* off Hawaii and the much frequented *Hydro Lab* in the Bahama Islands where the buoy housing the diesel generator was designed as a monohull. A later system using the autonomous energy buoy was the Perry-built *Prinul*. Much of the background study of various competing systems has been taken from the work of Dr P. A. Borovikov.

Energy Supply

The three systems already discussed are all in some way dependent on surface support, whether ashore or to a ship or buoy, and there is an inherent vulnerability in total reliance on outside sources. The more difficult solutions involve maintaining some measure of autonomous survival without recourse to the surface. The fundamental problem lies in creating an energy source at the site. If this can be satisfied other needs for life-support, such as gas supplies and the elimination of noxious or toxic gases, are relatively uncomplicated. The following are the possible sources of energy which need to be considered.

Batteries

Lead–acid, nickel–cadmium and silver–zinc batteries will all, to a greater or lesser degree, provide power to a habitat. Careful

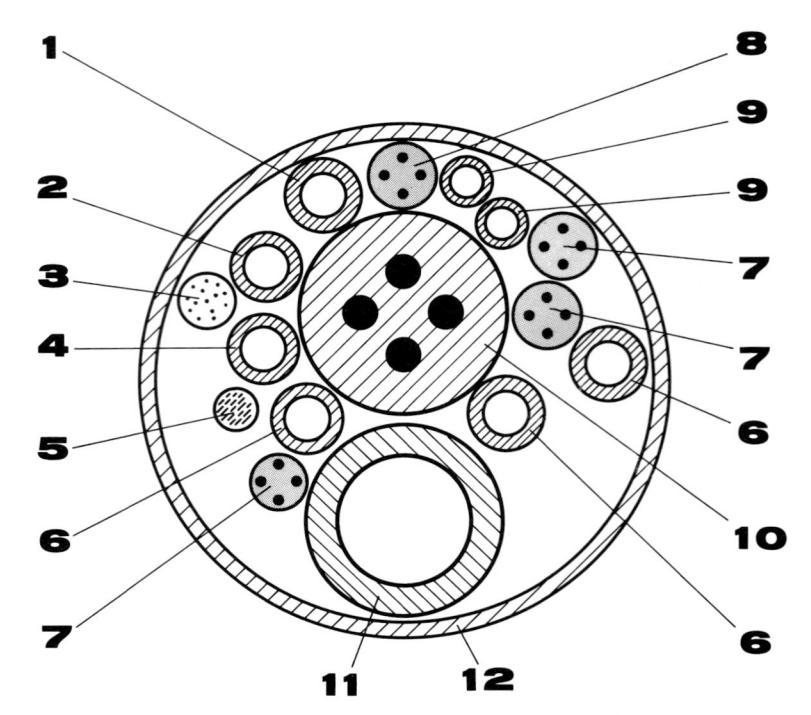

Fig. 6.17. Cross-section of the umbilical of the under-water laboratory *Helgoland*.

1	nitrogen	7	electrical control system
2	oxygen	8	electrical control system
3	communications	9	compressed air
4	helium	10	power cable
5	television	11	fresh water
6	exhaust air	12	protective plastic sheeting

insulation is needed in a seawater environment where it is necessary to surround them with oil or nitrogen. Clearly the main disadvantages are the high weight-to-output ratio and the requirement for recharging. For long missions or where there is an increased demand for power, such as may be needed for heating, the battery source may not be able to provide this power. Depending on the tasks being undertaken from the habitat a power supply of between 1 and 10 kW per person is needed, with more under special circumstances.

Fuel cells

Fuel cells are being seriously considered as the ultimate solution to the question of energy in habitats and submersibles. In these units the energy is not stored as in a battery but initiated as a product of a chemical reaction, usually with a high measure of efficiency. The fuel sources considered are mainly hydrogen and methanol but other hydrocarbons may be possible in the future. Water produced in the process could possibly be used for domestic purposes. The whole fuel cell concept is very expensive and still in the trials development stage.

A 30 kW fuel cell has been tested down to depths of 1700 m in the Lockheed *Deep Quest* submersible.

Internal combustion engine
By recycling the gases within a closed-circuit system made possible by resupplying the engine with oxygen a system was developed for use in military submarines during World War II. Theoretically very high powers can be generated but currently it is limited to a few hundred kilowatts. As power increases the oxidant storage and exhaust disposal requirements become greater in addition to the fuel tanks needed in the habitat.

Nuclear energy
The use of nuclear reactors may provide the best solution as the refuelling period can be extensive, allowing for extended missions. Theoretical design work is being carried out on the feasibility of using mobile nuclear reactors, profiting from the experience of nuclear plants fitted into military submarines. It is beyond our scope to examine the possibility of using nuclear power except to say that it does offer very real possibilities for use in large habitats connected to permanent subsea hydrocarbon production systems, particularly in areas of ice where surface-supplied power is not possible and where a great deal of energy, to supply water injection, gas separation and compression and other systems in addition to those of the habitat, is necessary.

Other sources
Other sources of energy are radio-isotopic, heat reservoirs, converters for thermal energy, thermionic converters and magnetic hydrodynamic converters. Perhaps in the future ocean thermal energy conversion will be possible.

The power requirements of the habitat depend on its purpose and tasks that are to be undertaken and, as variations are considerable, it is not possible accurately to assess and compare the respective costs and the sizes and weights of the optional power sources. The need for a power supply as technically secure as possible is greater than in a surface vessel or production platform where a power failure in most cases will be an inconvenience until restoration of power or the arrival of outside assistance. A power source for total submergence demands the highest possible integrity. A failure of power supply may require a shutdown of the complete system and in most circumstances the emergency battery system cannot provide the same power output to continue normal services. To avoid having to evacuate the habitat, a secondary power supply is necessary. Batteries are power storers rather than power sources and although essential for emergency use should only be considered, in the long term, in conjunction with true power sources.

In Fig. 6.13D the power source is part of the habitat, whether battery, fuel cell or nuclear reactor. With regard to future

Fig. 6.18. Recovering a supply container.

development clearly the use of a nuclear reactor is expensive. In Fig. 6.13E the power source is being recharged by a submersible but this facility is now likely to be carried out from a surface vessel or a submarine because of the small power resources of submersibles in general. For smaller habitats with short mission cycles the arrangement illustrated in Fig. 6.13F has been used successfully with the exchange of used for new life-support packages containing a CO_2 absorbent cannister with blower, an oxygen supply, drinking water, hot-water generator, food and lights and batteries. In this particular project the units were exchanged every 24 hours.

Replenishment

In addition to energy, gases, water, food, stores and mail have to be delivered on site. In the event that water cannot be produced in the habitat, a sufficiently large water tank needs to be provided, the capacity being dependent on the frequency of supply. Where a vessel is on station supplying through an umbilical, there is no need for a large tank in the habitat but with a buoy connected to the umbilical a larger tank is needed to hold water long enough to cover a maximum period of bad surface weather when a supply vessel cannot approach and service the buoy. Should the habitat be supplied by submarine there are normally no limitations imposed by weather, assuming that the submarine is autonomous and can move from base to the site in any weather state.

For the transfer of stores, mail and food, both fresh-prepared and frozen, pressure-compensated water-tight containers need to be

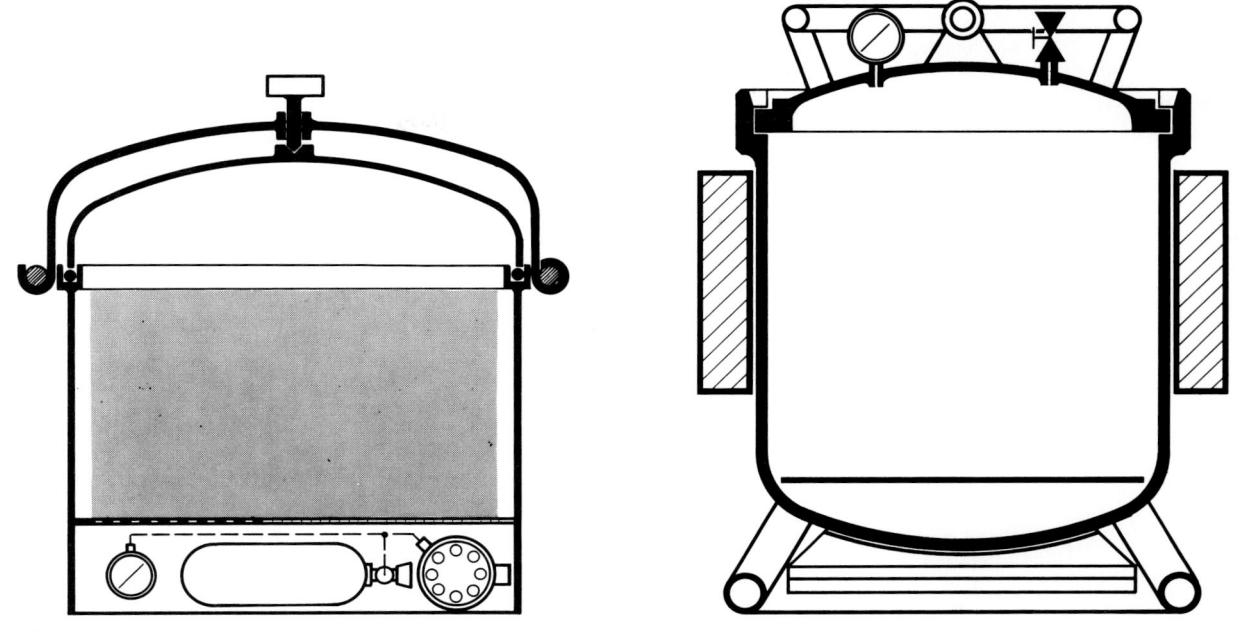

Fig. 6.19. Design of a pressure-compensated and pressure-resistant supply container.

provided. Sometimes known as stock pots, the containers have in the past had a capacity of between 50 and 100 litres. The sealed unit must, of course, be designed for external and internal pressure and equal pressures and because the transfer at sea needs to be carried out quickly and efficiently, the sealing design must be foolproof but capable of a quick operation. The use of bolts and butterfly nuts to maintain a seal, in preference to a bayonet flange and seal, is not advised. The procedure is for the container, filled with the required stores, to be pressurized on the surface to the same pressure as the habitat on the bottom. The control system for this includes a charging inlet, a pressure gauge, a relief valve and a blow-off safety valve. Buoyancy is controlled on the descent by weights or enclosed ballast tanks. However, at greater depths the units tend to become too heavy for efficient handling on the surface, in which case an alternative method can be designed using automatic pressure-compensating control systems. In conjunction with light-weight containers, open-ended at the bottom similar to a diving bell, the pressure control automatically vents air into the chamber commensurate with the increase of pressure during the descent. The gas supply is either from the surface or from cylinders attached to the unit and the design is naturally simplified by avoiding expensive sealing locks.

The containers are lowered to the habitat either manually or by surface winch and a convenient pick-up arrangement on the habitat can pull the slightly buoyant container from the surface into the habitat. A straightforward way is for the divers from the habitat to enter the water, collect a negatively buoyant container and return to the habitat. However, wherever possible divers should not be employed to do this work if alternative methods can be used. The pick-up method was used in *Sealab III* operations and subsequently applied several times for operations from UWL *Helgoland*. For the transfer of bulky stores, bigger containers have to be used or alternatively a diving bell. If the equipment is not sensitive to contact with water plastic bags to wrap up the stores are quite acceptable for the transfer from container or diving bell to the habitat. If this method is not possible because the stores and equipment are sensitive to contact with water, the use of the pressure- and water-tight rescue chamber can overcome the problem.

For the transfer of equipment from depth to the surface in open-ended containers, waterproof plastic bags are ideal as they will automatically blow off as the depth of water, and consequently the pressure, decreases, with little chance of water penetrating the inside.

Support of a Habitat in an Emergency

The supply of services and the operation and replenishment of an under-water habitat is not exceptionally difficult if properly planned and designed in the first place. This chapter has covered some of these aspects but the planning and design stage needs to carry out a risk analysis and evaluation of the risks to the personnel in the event of unknown design failure for any factors outside the control of the designers and operators. Habitat operations involving personnel working on the seabed demand higher standards of safety than other subsea operations involving personnel either in one-atmosphere normal pressure conditions or under pressure in hyperbaric conditions. Other subsea operations involving personnel, such as diving and submersible operations, are eventually surface-orientated, in that the aim is to inject the diver and craft to a work site and return to the surface after a given time. In habitat and autonomous submarine operations the design and capability allow for continuous uninterrupted operations and these are dependent on the logistics of re-supply. As long as supplies of the various items can be continued within the framework of a reasonable mission cycle, and within the bounds of accepted technology, advances will be made but the ability of habitats to survive under emergency conditions where no re-supply is immediately forthcoming is a primary design factor. This, as previously stated, involves electrical energy, food and drinking water, oxygen and other gases for pressure maintenance and the absorbent materials for life-support.

Emergency Electrical Supply

The needs of lighting and heating, important analysing equipment, communications and the operation of the primary life-support system are all demands on the emergency power supply. The importance of an autonomous power supply has been discussed and

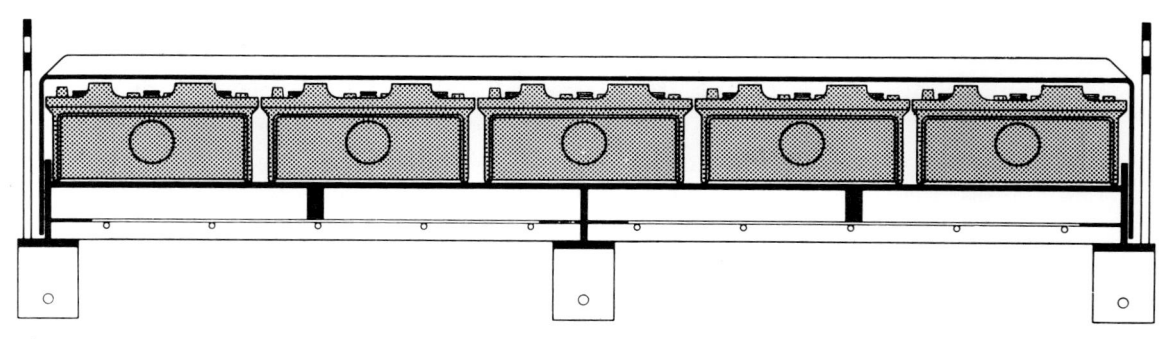

Fig. 6.20. Cross-section of an under-water battery pack.

the same considerations apply to emergency supplies. As standby units they should ideally be autonomous but smaller habitats will need to rely on power stored in emergency batteries similar to those provided in submersibles. Standby units in the future may well use recycled diesels or fuel cells, separate from the main power source. These standby power units are essential for any proposed subsea production system which involves personnel working in a habitat as part of the total complex and without surface or shore power supply. The continuous running of main services and machinery without any significant reduction, except for maintenance and repair, demands the installation of standby units which will also provide emergency power. In the event of the standby power sources failing, emergency batteries can only be expected to provide emergency life-support and communications; all other services will probably be shut down prior to an emergency evacuation.

An emergency battery pod for the under-water laboratory *Helgoland* is shown in Fig. 6.20. The batteries will function in the habitat at the ambient pressure with the bottom part placed in water. Relatively inexpensive car batteries are used and as long as the terminals are protected with acid-proof grease against the effects of humidity, they are a dependable power source. To maintain air space around the terminals the batteries are covered with a water-proof insulated housing, such as glass-reinforced plastic, placed over the whole assembly. To keep the water inside the battery cells at a constant level during pressurization whilst descending to the site, air or nitrogen can be blown inside the housing controlled automatically by a supply pressure valve. The build-up of explosive gases is prevented by periodically purging the free space above the batteries with nitrogen. The explosive gas mixtures which are formed in the process are dispersed by the periodic purging of the space above the terminals with pure nitrogen. Battery pods can be designed as a permanent part of the habitat. They require inspection and maintenance and the design must allow for easy access to carry out these routines so as to avoid the premature removal of the batteries and replacement. Battery cells will, in any event, discharge slowly without being used and a charging system is needed to maintain their capacity. Apart from free flooding cells, an alternative battery design

Fig. 6.21. Cylinder stowage on the support leg of the underwater laboratory *Helgoland*. On the ballast is a 300 litre reserve tank for compressed air.

is the oil-filled battery unit, with the advantage that the danger of seawater coming into contact with the terminals is excluded. Another alternative is the encapsulation of the batteries in pressure-proof vessels as used in submersibles and described in Chapter 7.

Emergency Water Supply

The technical problems of producing fresh water from sea water preclude the use of desalination plants in habitats, at any rate for the foreseeable future. Water for drinking and for general domestic use has to be carried in or around the habitat in quantities which will suffice should the regular supply from the surface or from shore be interrupted or terminated. Rather than using pressure-proof vessels outside the habitat, which are expensive, flexible containers or bags secured to the outside of the habitat do fulfil the requirement to some extent, but there is a danger that the water bags may develop leaks, caused by the damaging effects of strong currents and the interaction against the structure, or, worse, they may be swept away. A logical solution is to place the water bags inside the rigid buoyancy tanks of the habitat and to compensate for the weight and volume of fresh water consumed by filling the area between the tank and the container with sea water. The buoyancy characteristics of the habitat will not vary sufficiently to alter the stability. On the *Helgoland* 6000 litres of fresh water were stored in this way with a sight glass to indicate the water level inside the tank. A further fresh water supply was carried for special missions and this was fitted between the support legs and resting on the seabed where the weight was taken. This additional water supply considerably increased the mission cycle.

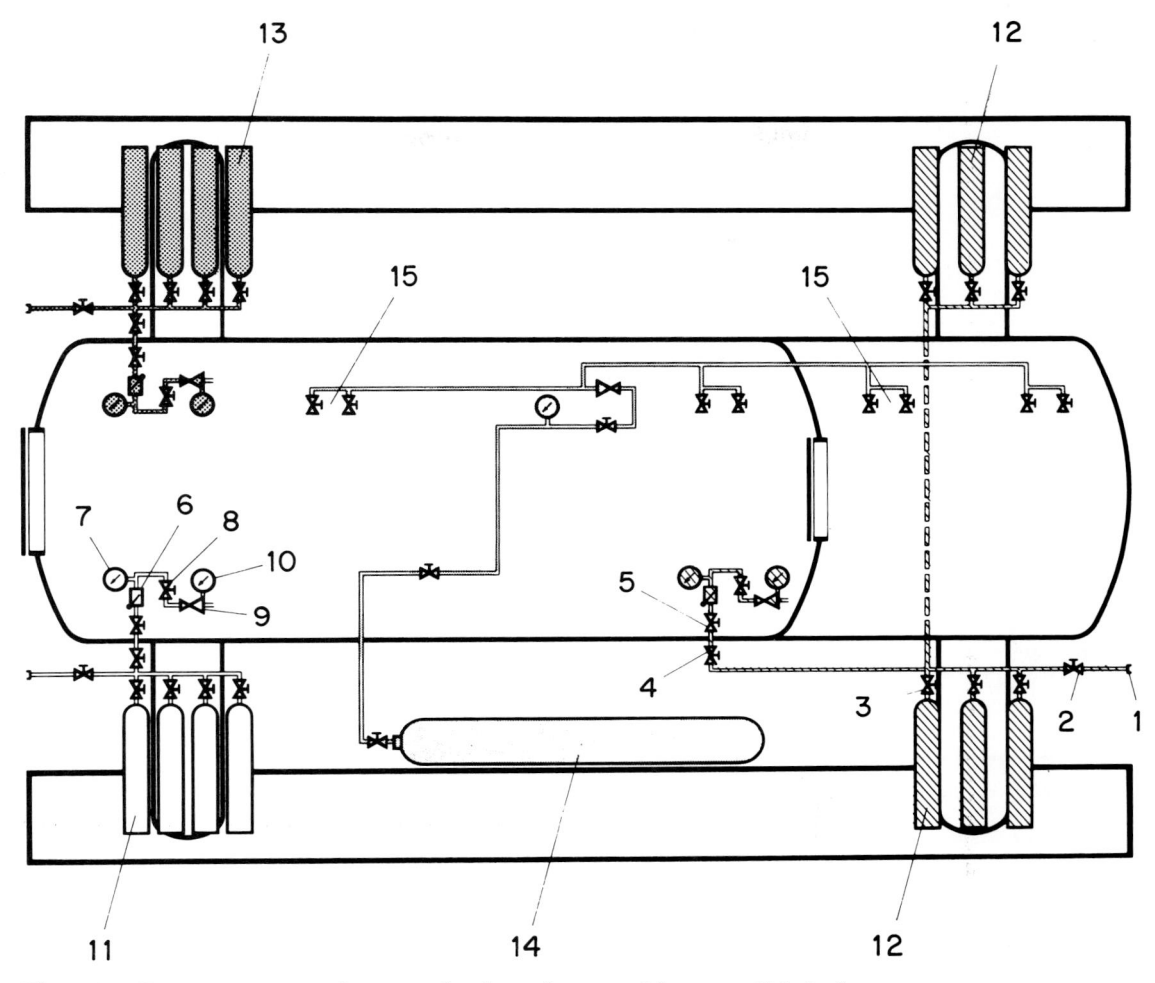

Fig. 6.22. Emergency gas supply system for the under-water laboratory *Helgoland*.

1 charging connection	9 pressure regulator
2 charging shut-off valve	10 operating pressure gauge
3 cylinder valve	11 nitrogen storage (30 m^3)
4 shut-off valve, external	12 oxygen storage (60 m^3)
5 shut-off valve, internal	13 helium storage (30 m^3)
6 one-way valve	14 air storage (120 m^3)
7 supply pressure gauge	15 breathing connections
8 outlet valve	

Emergency Gas Supplies

The additional supplies of gas needed in the event of an emergency, should the re-supply be terminated or the main supply be contaminated, are clearly dependent on depth and physiological requirements. In the most complicated situation all the breathing gases will be stored separately, these being oxygen, nitrogen, helium, air and possibly some prepared gas mixtures as well. Separate storage

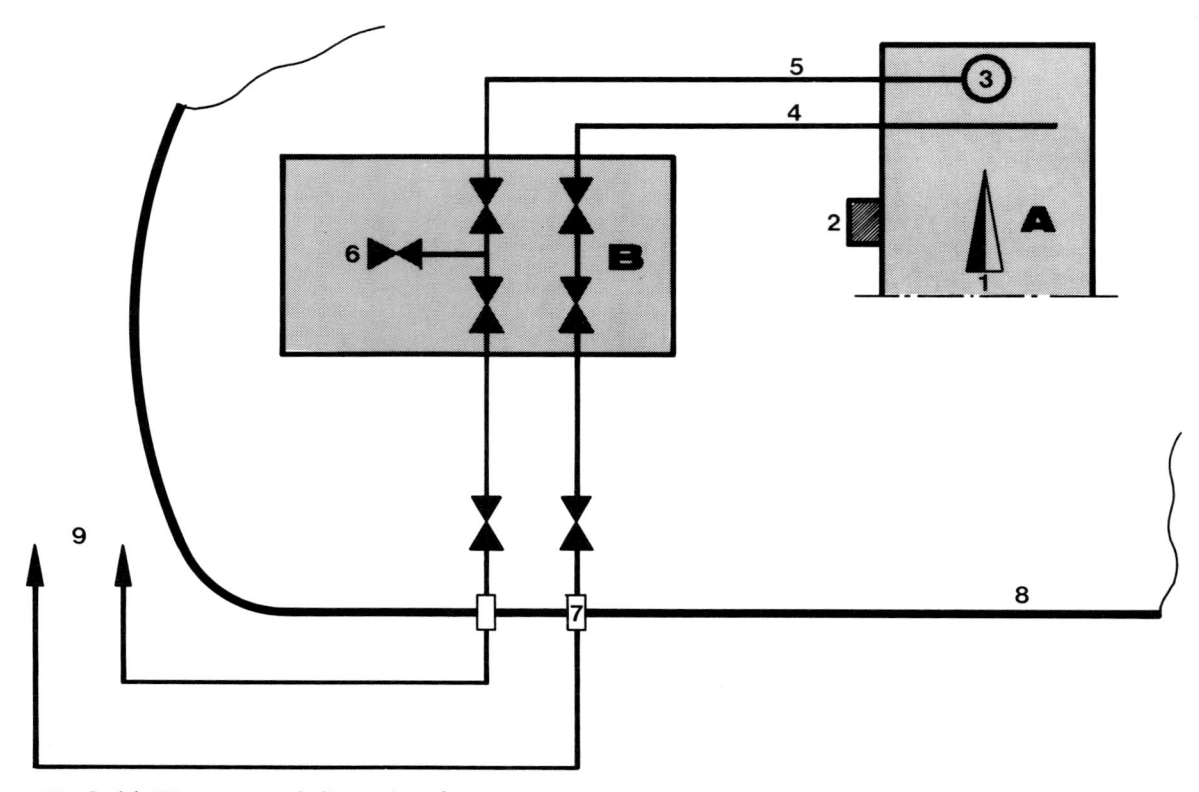

Fig. 6.23. *Sealab III* emergency helium, air and oxygen system.

- A scrubber/filter exhaust plenum
- B gas control panel
- 1 gas flow
- 2 P_{O_2} sensor
- 3 distribution duct
- 4 helium and air, charging and make-up
- 5 oxygen make-up and gas sampling
- 6 gas sampling hose
- 7 stuffing tube
- 8 bottom of hull
- 9 to umbilical connections topside

space to accommodate these has to be designed around the habitat's main chamber and be interchangeable to meet the requirements of depth and task. The gas supply arrangement for the *Helgoland* is shown in Fig. 6.21. It is preferable to position the cylinder connections inside the air or gas pocket within the dome of the habitat so that these cylinders can be exchanged without sea water entering the system. Fig. 6.22 shows the emergency gas system of the *Helgoland* for the initial trials. Subsequent alterations are made at later stages to conform to national certification as these are liable to change in different countries. The gas supply arrangement for the U.S. Navy *Sealab III* was such that the emergency supply was linked to the surface whilst the normal consumption was met from onboard supplies. There are clearly different views as to how to provide satisfactory emergency cover.

Emergency Food

The diet of habitat dwellers is dependent on the type of food that can be stored for long periods under pressure or in moist conditions. If the supply of food is interrupted to the extent that emergency rations need to be breached, food must fulfil the minimum dietary and energy requirements. As power supplies in an emergency will be very restricted, cooking will be limited to heating pre-cooked food either deep-frozen or canned if the latter is possible under ambient pressure conditions. Power may not be sufficient to maintain deep-freezers. Vacuum-dried food needs less storage and by adding water and heating nutritious food can be served.

Emergency Re-supply of Stores

An emergency plan to provide additional stores, should re-supply from the surface become impossible, is needed because the consumable items such as food supplies and CO_2 absorbent are needed in large quantities, depending on the number of occupants. They are bulky in volume and space is severely limited inside the habitat. If the life-support system is on closed circuit the CO_2 filtration system will greatly increase the demand for CO_2 absorbent. With the possibility of emergency periods without re-supply or evacuation in excess of 20 days, the bulk requirements can be met by locating the stores in under-water store depots placed near the habitat. Fig. 6.24 shows the use of a storage depot in conjunction with other systems that may be part of a total habitat operation. The storage can be a construction of reinforced polyester resin and has the shape of an under-water igloo. No life-support or other equipment is needed except shelves to make use of the available space. The water-tight hemispherical shell with a diameter of 2 m floats like an umbrella secured by two chains attached to two concrete weights, about 1.5 m above the seabed to allow good access for the divers when recovering the stores.

Safety and Rescue

An evaluation of the risks to personnel, based on the design of the habitat, needs to be undertaken. It cannot be overstressed that the standards of safety and the integrity of rescue facilities need to be far greater than other undersea systems which are based on intervention only from the surface. In the final analysis a straightforward recovery system is needed for the evacuation of all personnel. This has not always been the case and consequently there have been fatal accidents although in most cases these have been caused by human error. Financial considerations should not influence the design for safety and rescue and if the project cannot be adequately funded then its concept should not be implemented.

In Fig. 6.24 a number of important aspects are shown diagrammatically. They are not all essential to the overall plan but

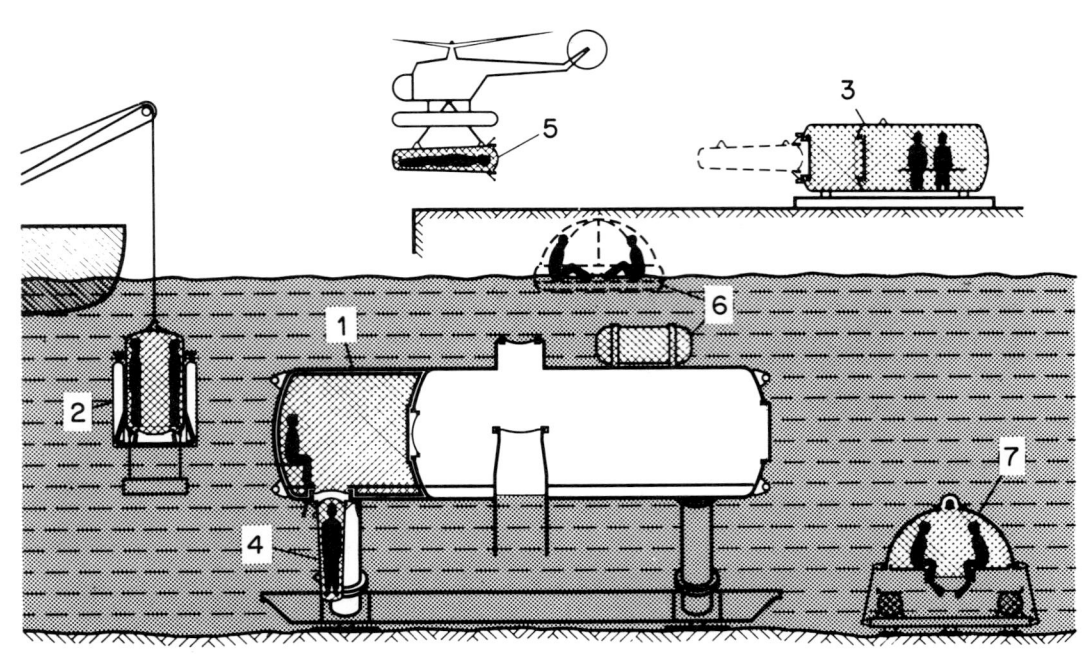

Fig. 6.24. Safety installations for manned under-water stations.

1. decompression compartment inside the under-water laboratory
2. personnel transfer chamber
3. stationary recompression chamber
4. one-man rescue chamber
5. transportable one-man chamber
6. rescue float
7. under-water igloo

should be considered on their merits to fulfil a rescue plan for all known eventualities. If the 'aquanauts', as they might be described, need to be decompressed on completion of their mission cycle, the ability to decompress inside the habitat whilst it is being recovered to the surface is clearly a major safety factor. This means that the habitat must have an internal decompression chamber. Conversely, manned under-water stations which need to be in pressure equilibrium are not suitable except in very shallow water or if transportable one-man chambers are designed which are capable of transporting divers under pressure from the habitat to the surface to transfer under pressure into a surface compression chamber. Unlike transportable chambers used on the surface, for instance to transport an injured diver from an off-shore installation to a medical chamber ashore, the chamber may need to withstand an external pressure as great as the internal pressure. The use of free ascent is practical for occupants not under pressure, based on the experience of naval submarine crews. It requires training beforehand and is not an established practice outside certain navies. The Russian attitude is not to consider free ascent for commercial or scientific operations.

Fig. 6.25. Diving superviser's control panel in the under-water laboratory *Helgoland*.

In Fig. 6.25 a diving supervisor's control panel is shown inside the habitat. The layout and fittings are standard and do not differ significantly from a control panel on the surface. In certain situations where all the occupants may be under pressure the control panels are by necessity inside the diving chamber and controlled directly by those under pressure. Therefore any decompression requiring a reduction in pressure, change of gas mixtures and the continuing need to control and monitor the atmosphere, will be done by the divers or others similarly under pressure. During the recovery phase of the operation the responsibility and control of these factors will remain with the occupants until connected to a surface control system. To reduce the decompression period and so avoid exposing the divers continuously to the maximum depth at the seabed, the chamber for living may be maintained at marginally less pressure. This technique, known as excursion diving, is used extensively in deep diving operations from the surface. Excursion diving effectively limits the amount of inert gas that is absorbed by the tissues of the body by returning the body to a lesser pressure for living and sleeping, exposing the body to the greater pressure only for the work periods.

It is probable that a personnel transfer system will be used and essential if there are no decompression facilities contained within the

Fig. 6.26. One-man rescue chamber of the under-water laboratory *Helgoland*

habitat. Even where there are such internal pressure chambers a transfer system is usual. The recovery phase of the habitat will be conditioned largely by other factors such as tidal conditions and weather on the surface and these can cause delays. Also if the decompression period is long, and bearing in mind that any long exposures to pressure will effectively have saturated the divers' body tissues, the de-saturation period of decompression will run to some days. Conveniently, and for safety, the personnel can be transferred to the surface compression chamber to complete the decompression. This transfer is made by a diving bell or submersible with the ability to mate with a surface unit on board a vessel and transfer personnel

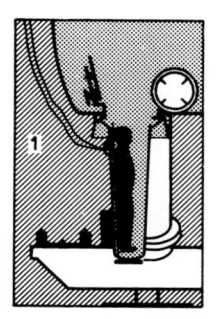

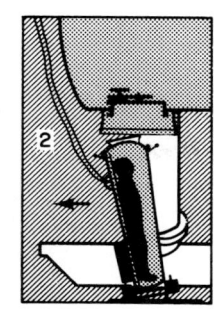

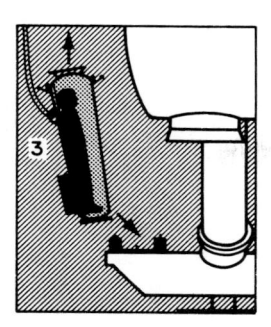

Fig. 6.27. Releasing procedures for the one-man rescue chamber of the under-water laboratory *Helgoland*.

1 diver being placed in the one-man rescue chamber
2 ballasting and shift of the chamber to the side
3 dropping the ballast and surfacing the chamber

under pressure. This is already standard operating practice and presents no great technical difficulties. This method of transfer was used during the *Sealab*, *Helgoland* and *Tektite* operations.

For the stand-by emergency use SCC or diving bells are frequently stationed permanently near the habitat for emergency evacuation. Recovery may be by hoisting from the surface or, alternatively, it is technically possible for the occupant to control the winch from the bell. The surface compression chamber is required to be of sufficient size to cater for therapeutic decompressions and with a compatible medical transfer chamber for evacuation ashore.

A one-man rescue chamber of the type shown in Fig. 6.26 allows for a dry transfer of an injured person from the habitat to the surface. On the surface the chamber is recovered by a support vessel, rescue launch or helicopter depending on the conditions and circumstances. The skids attached to the chamber facilitate the pick-up operation on the surface. The sequence of disconnecting the chamber from the habitat is illustrated in Fig. 6.27 in three stages. The initial pressure needs to be adjusted to equalize the pressure inside the transfer capsule and the main chamber allowing the pressure-tight doors to be opened. The injured person is placed in a supporting stretcher which slides down retaining rails inside the capsule. A CO_2 scrubber is the main life-support fitting, filled with new absorbent. The three retaining bolts are released, securing the capsule to the main chamber trunking of the habitat, and the attending divers in the water compensate to achieve a negative buoyancy. A guide wire pulls the capsule clear and releases the ballast frame. The capsule will become positively buoyant and rise to the surface. The capsule can be used for the transfer of larger dry stores by the same method. Although this method of evacuation is based on a bottom transfer, recent submarine rescue techniques are being perfected by submersibles and recovery

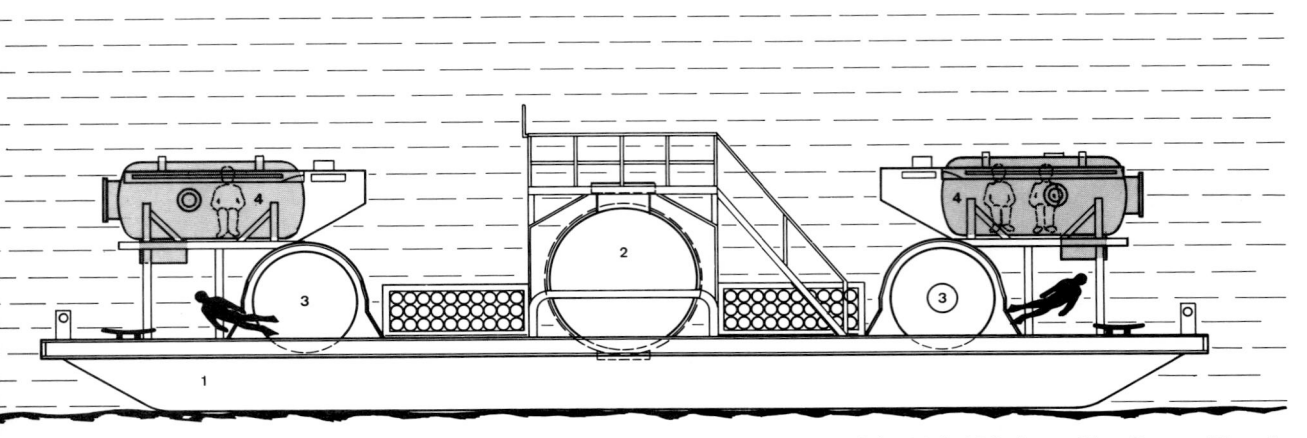

Fig. 6.28. Arrangement of rescue chambers on the under-water station *Aegir* of the Makai Undersea Test Range, Hawaii.

1. pontoon
2. habitat pressure hull
3. ballast tanks
4. rescue chambers

vessels using a mating collar on the top of the submarine casing. This same technique can be successfully applied to a habitat, with the advantage that the habitat is a stable and flat platform.

Another interesting variation on evacuation techniques is designed into the *Aegir*, the habitat at the Makai Undersea Range in Hawaii. The general arrangement is shown in Fig. 6.28. Two small emergency life boats are fitted separately on each side of the main chamber as part of the buoyancy chambers. Each life station can accommodate two people normally but four people for short periods. Each carries its own life-support system and is positively buoyant, the buoyancy being restrained by a special winch system. On surfacing they are either towed to a sheltered area or recovered immediately by a surface vessel, depending on the weather conditions. For long decompression the chamber can be mated to larger chambers as required. This concept of a lifeboat is a forerunner of the hyperbaric lifeboat designed and favoured by the Norwegians and French for the evacuation of divers under pressure from surface vessel or structure and designed to surface and then operate as a boat. This is described in Chapter 3.

There are many under-water operations other than habitats where surface decompression is not suitable for lengthy and complicated therapeutic treatments possibly involving surgery. The use of one-man transfer chambers and larger chambers for several people, constructed with titanium alloy for minimum weight and maximum pressure, and with helicopter attachments, is covered in Chapter 5.

In an extreme situation where the emergency standby chambers are not available and an immediate recovery is needed, an ultimate safety plan could allow the aquanauts to remain inside the habitat, if decompression is still possible, and allow the habitat to achieve positive buoyancy with the release of ballast weights and gain additional buoyancy. Theoretically it would be possible for the ascent to allow the habitat to remain below the surface, secured to floats on the surface allowing for the subsequent location and recovery by surface vessels and divers. If the habitat has to be evacuated because it is flooded or the main services have been destroyed, the only alternative if transfer chambers are not available may be temporary refuge in the satellites or igloos described earlier in this chapter.

The use of fire-resistant materials and the careful selection of materials is clearly of great importance for the same reasons as apply to any manned pressure chamber. These considerations cover the need for alarm systems and methods of fire control such as sprinkler systems. Using separate emergency breathing systems a dangerous explosive atmosphere or an actual fire or explosion can be controlled by purging the whole atmosphere with an inert gas such as nitrogen or helium.

Lowering Procedures, Ballast and Trim Systems

There are certain technical difficulties which need to be taken into account when designing a system for placing on the seabed. In the past in some cases insufficient attention has been given to this aspect and where difficulties have been experienced they have not been caused solely by weather problems. Equal-pressure systems, as distinct from closed systems, are the most difficult to control during their descent from the surface. Basically there are five methods of placement for habitats that do not have their own propulsion and these are illustrated in Fig. 6.29.

In *Type A* the habitat is placed by a crane and is at its most vulnerable if there is movement of the crane or the barge and is clearly very vulnerable to weather and the sea state. This procedure was used for *Sealab III* (see Fig. 6.9). As the off-shore construction industry has acquired lifting barges capable of a 1000 tonne hoist to lift production modules with pin-point accuracy and control, so comparative technology has lessened the risks of using the straight lift technique.

In *Type B* a more sophisticated approach allows the habitat to be towed to the site and secured to the bottom area with a ballast weight. Ballast tanks are flooded to a trim condition where the remaining buoyancy is less than the negative lift of the bottom weight and the habitat is winched to the bottom. There are a number of variations on this method.

A descent controlled entirely by buoyancy and trim is illustrated in *Type C*. It is particularly suitable for a closed habitat since the crew can control the descent with precision. However, with open-ended habitats the variable volumes which need to be taken into account may lead very quickly to an unstable condition. Experience has confirmed this in practice.

In *Type D* the placing of the habitat presupposes that the position is known and allows for a weight to be placed on the seabed

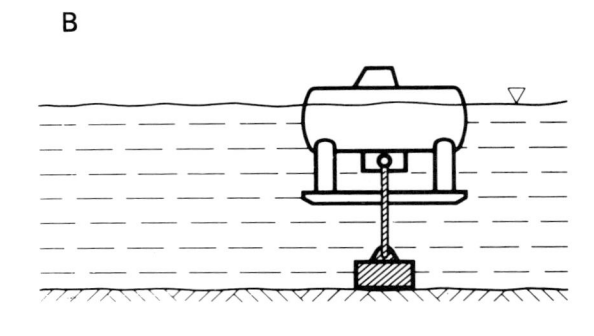

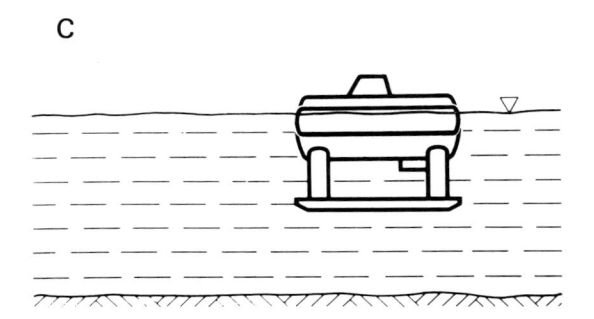

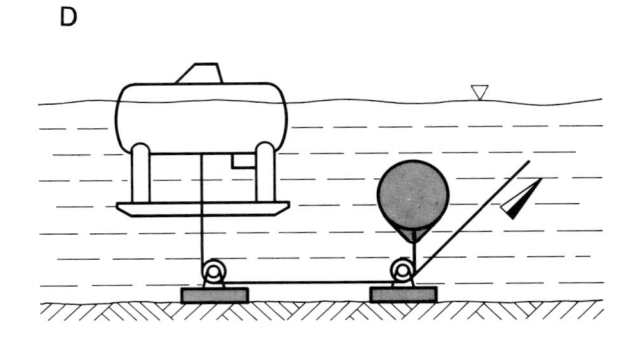

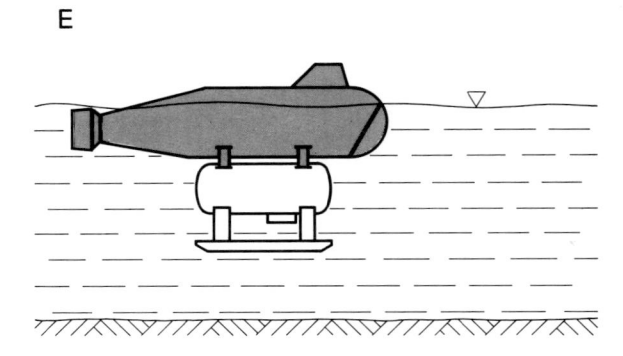

Fig. 6.29. Lowering procedures.

- **A** The habitat is totally ballasted on the surface and then lowered by crane. Requires support by ship or pontoon and good surface conditions

- **B** From the floating habitat a floatable ballast tank or weight is first lowered. The habitat is then hauled down

- **C** Free descent of the habitat by controlled flooding of buoyancy and trimming tanks

- **D** Use of cable rollers which are mounted on bottom weights and by lifting ballon or surface winch

- **E** Submarine brings the habitat to the operating area and places it on the seabed

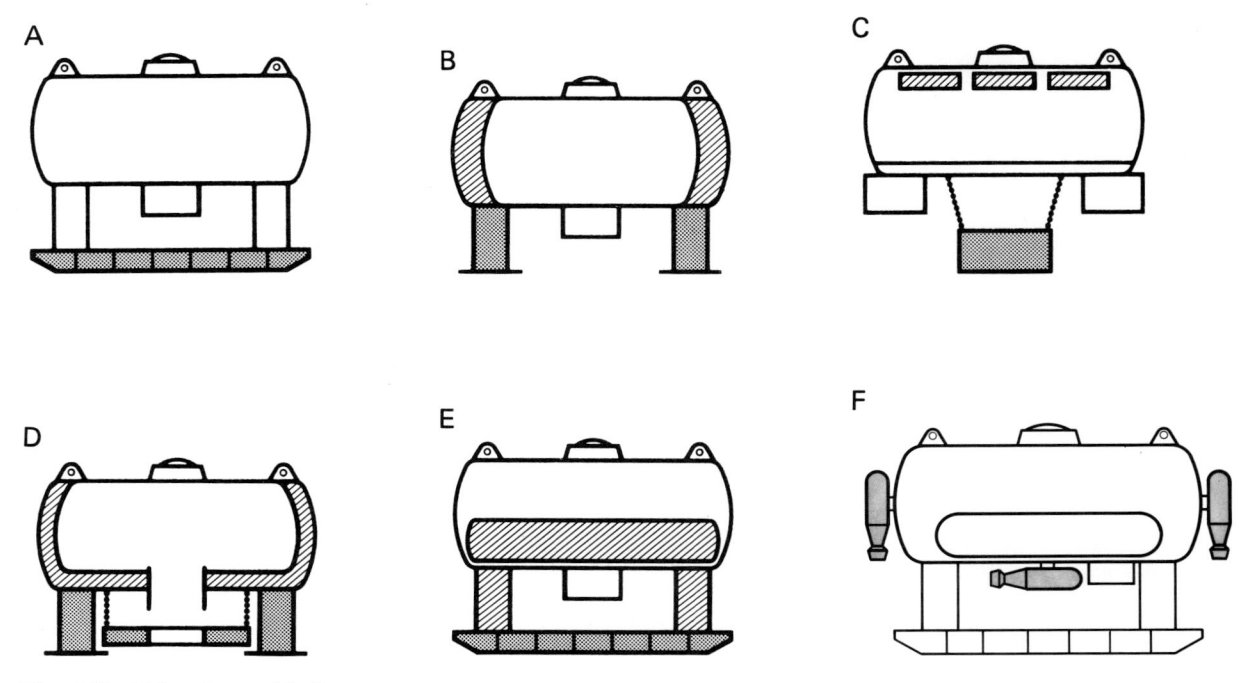

Fig. 6.30. Trimming and ballast systems.

- **A** Ballast in the support legs is adjusted in such a way that sufficient negative buoyancy is obtained to ensure stability. The ballast can be in the form of iron-filled concrete blocks. Descent and ascent are possible only with use of appropriate lifting gear
- **B** Solid ballast is mounted in the four support legs in the form of metal or concrete. For lowering, the tanks on both front ends can be flooded. These tanks are blown with air for ascent
- **C** The complete habitat is suspended on the bottom weight like a balloon. The bottom of the habitat is filled with concrete. For final descent the tanks in the ceiling are flooded
- **D** Permanent solid ballast hangs below the habitat in the form of a concrete plate. The support legs may be filled as well. Ballast tanks are located at both ends around the hull
- **E** The legs are filled with solid ballast in the form of iron-filled concrete blocks. The support legs are constructed as trimming tanks which can be flooded for lowering. Stability on the seabed is obtained by flooding the side ballast tanks
- **F** Basically the same construction as in E. Additional propulsion units mounted on the habitat provide a certain mobility in the vertical as well as horizontal planes

accommodating a roller through which the down-haul line is passed and secured to a buoyancy device with a defined buoyancy. The movement upwards of the buoyancy device can be assisted with a surface hoist. As in Type B, the habitat is trimmed to a slight positive buoyancy and is suitable for use as a closed chamber.

In *Type E* a submersible to lock on to the habitat using its own propulsion and buoyancy can transport the personnel to the bottom. This method is only suitable for very small habitats, such as welding habitats.

Submersibles conceived in a catamaran design will be more suitable for this, with the catamaran astride the habitat.

Whereas trimming tanks are mainly used for the controlled descent, integral ballast systems are fundamental for the ultimate stability of the whole to achieve a large negative buoyancy for a given volume. The different trim and ballast systems are summarized in Fig. 6.30.

The simplest procedure shown in Fig. 6.30A demands a solid ballast tray fitted with ballast. The support legs may support ballast as well. Sufficient negative buoyancy will maintain stability and the choice of ballast is limited to lead, scrap iron or concrete blocks and is usually dependent on local conditions. Lead is expensive, although weight-for-volume it is preferable, and is not used because of the cost. Scrap iron is generally available at low cost but the corrosion of iron in the water may not be compatible with biomarine ecology. Concrete mixed with scrap iron and set into blocks is the most practical method. Scrap rivets, for example, have proved most successful. Special weights for size can be made and designed to handle well. By adjusting the number of concrete blocks the habitat can quickly achieve a floating position. To achieve a low centre of gravity the position of the ballast will need to be as low as possible. For habitats that are required to float or be towed the ballast carried needs to take into account the safe surface trim of the whole. Where ballast tanks are incorporated to control the descent as in Fig. 6.30B the partial flooding of the tanks at both ends will achieve a negative lift which can be controlled for a slow descent and is suitable for a closed system. For open systems a retaining lifting wire from a crane is usually needed for additional security. In Fig. 6.30C the use of a concrete weight will reduce the amount of ballast needed on the habitat. By flooding trimming tanks located in the upper part of the pressure hull the descent is made. This system was used in *Sealab II* and *Sealab III*. The trimming arrangement in Fig. 6.30D incorporates a concrete weight hanging below the habitat in addition to the support weights being filled with ballast. The trim tanks assisting the descent and recovery of the habitat surround the pressure hull.

In Fig. 6.30F a basic design similar to Fig. 6.30E illustrates the use of a thruster providing limited propulsion vertically and horizontally. If the crew has good visibility the habitat can be manoeuvred in the hovering position over short distances. Greater propulsion is possible in the future, moving towards the submarine concept.

The whole procedure of trimming and ballasting is shown in Fig. 6.31 for the under-water laboratory *Helgoland*. A buoyant situation is shown in A without ballast. In B solid ballast in the form of concrete blocks and scrap iron is fitted and a lower floating profile is reached. A good floating position without rolling and a stable position during descent requires the solid ballast to be placed very low. For precise trimming on the surface containers on the ends can be filled with small amounts of scrap. For a soft landing a chain was suspended below the ballast tray to relieve the moment of impact by reducing the negative buoyancy gradually. A greater relieving effect was found by using the surface buoy shown in C and pulling it under water at the moment of impact. The legs were then flooded. The different

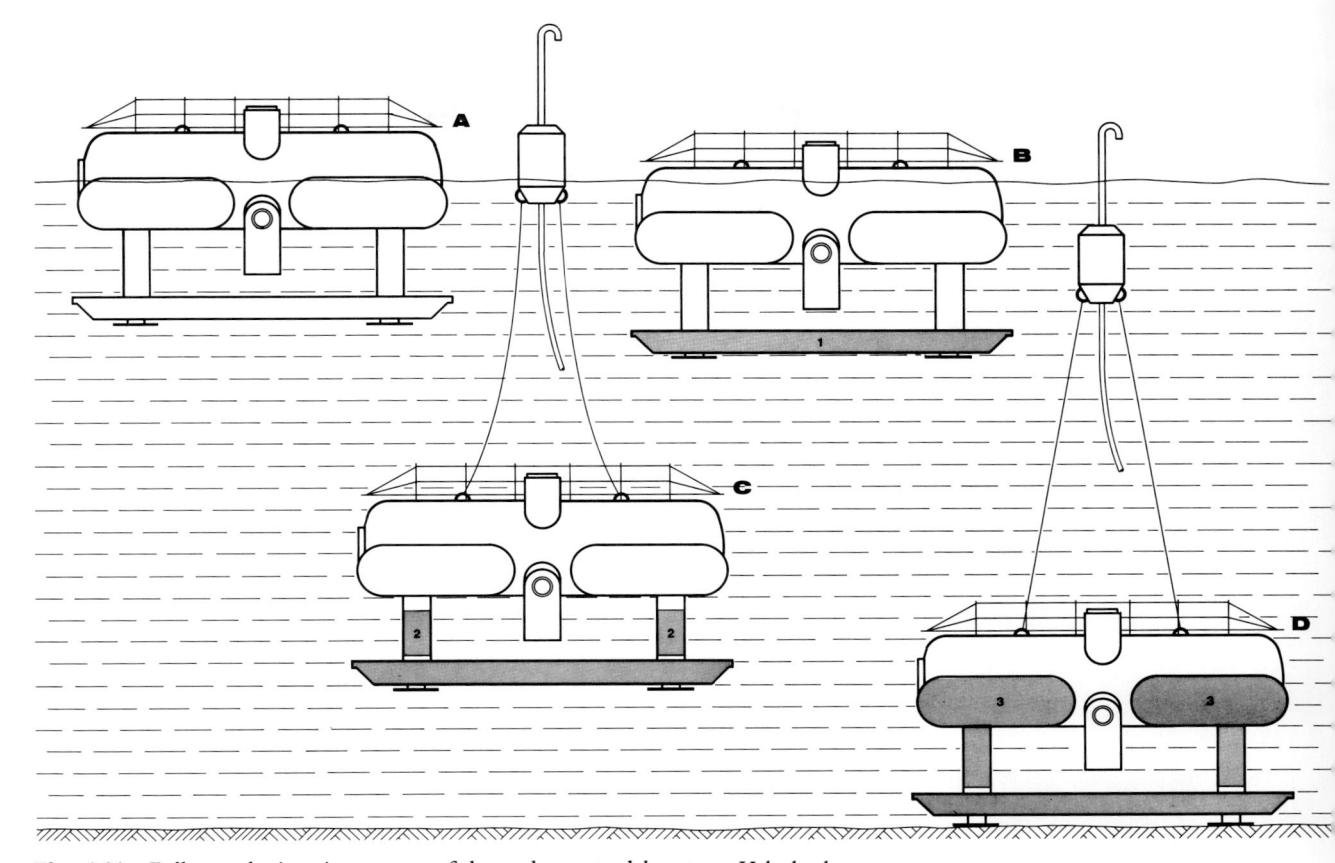

Fig. 6.31. Ballast and trimming system of the under-water laboratory *Helgoland*.

densities of sea water and fresh water need to be taken into account as variations are considerable for relatively large volumes. Before the descent starts the pressure hull and side buoyancy are pressurized to the depth in which the habitat is placed. Then the support legs are flooded crosswise until a minor negative buoyancy of a few kilograms is achieved and the habitat begins to sink. At this moment no more water is put into the trim tanks so as not to increase the descent rate. The descent is controlled by the crew inside the habitat and the control system with valves and gauges is underneath the flooring for economy of space as they will not be used again except for recovery.

When the habitat reaches the sea floor the effect of the chains and the surface buoy is felt. If the negative buoyancy is minimal and the scope of the chains and the surface buoyline adjusted, the habitat hovers over the seabed. When in position the trim tanks are quickly flooded achieving negative buoyancy. To obtain the maximum required negative buoyancy for stability the ballast tanks are flooded and the telescopic legs are extended. For the first operation the negative buoyancy of the *Helgoland* was 16 tonnes and was sufficient

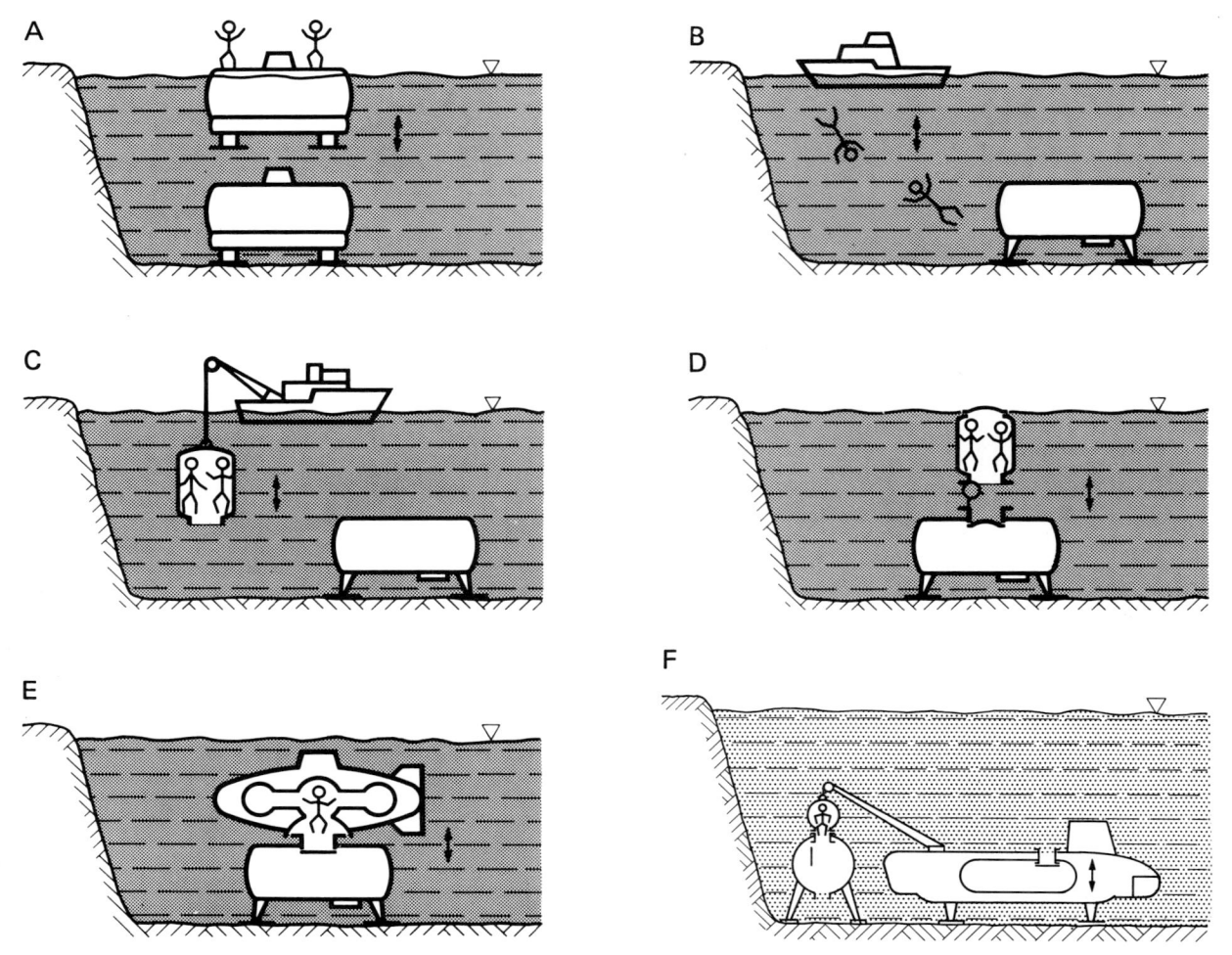

Fig. 6.32. Personnel transfer to and from manned under-water stations.

- **A** The habitat itself is mobile and ascends for crew changes. Decompression is inside the habitat
- **B** Divers ascend or descend freely. Final ascent is after decompression inside the habitat
- **C** Divers are transferred to the habitat by a submersible decompression chamber. Entry is through-water. Decompression is in a deck compression chamber
- **D** The habitat itself is supplied with a submersible decompression chamber for dry transfer. Divers decompress in the habitat
- **E** Divers are brought to and from the habitat by a submersible which mated to the habitat
- **F** Divers are transferred to and from the habitat by bell from an autonomous submarine

to keep a firm position during heavy storms passing over head. The correct distribution of the ballast weights, the calculation of the buoyancy contained within the hollow volumes beneath the pressure chamber and skirt and the scope of the telescopic legs gave the maximum stability so that even in strong currents no damage or movement was experienced. Even if the habitat tilts it will always right itself on the tumbler principle. After the experience of carrying out hoisting and lowering, lowering to 20 m was done in less than five minutes.

Personnel Transfer to Manned Underwater Stations

Transfer of personnel in an emergency situation has been discussed. Fig. 6.32 summarizes the methods which are available for transfer. Clearly the important factors—frequency of crew change, depth, average weather conditions, sea state, distance from shore base and not least the financial resources of the enterprise—determine the method. An acceptable safety factor is common to all.

In Fig. 6.32A the crew descend and ascend in the habitat after the mission has been completed or the endurance of the crew is exhausted. For multiple missions in the same position this will need a special anchoring and positioning system. Although generally a safe approach, there are disadvantages in that any permanent connections and installations on the seabed require disconnection and subsequent reconnection. In a closed habitat the decompression is carried out normally, but with an open habitat a controlled ascent has to be made to different levels to complete the decompression. As far as is known the Russian *Chernomore* missions were performed using this technique. In B the habitat is reached from the surface by free-swimming divers and crew changes are carried out in this way. This is in very shallow water, in all probability where no decompression is needed. If decompression is needed it has to be carried out in the habitat, with divers returning to the surface along a buoyline. This guideline is important in strong currents. The surface boat should have a compression chamber and be prepared for all emergencies. This free ascent method is not used, for example, in Russia, where it is considered to be too hazardous. The method in C is currently the most practical because it uses the conventional diving bell to transfer the personnel from surface to habitat and back. The diving bell may be a compression chamber on the surface where divers can either be decompressed or held in saturation pending a crew change by transferring under pressure. This method was used in the *Sealab III* operations and Fig. 6.33 shows the American surface support vessel *Elk River* in this role. The disadvantage of the method is that it is dependent on weather and to close this gap larger surface vessels are needed to operate successfully in marginal conditions. The divers are obliged to transfer to the habitat by swimming, unless an overhead lock-on is available, a method illustrated in D. There are a number of technical difficulties in this solution but these are being overcome with experience in submarine rescue techniques. The use of submersibles for submarine rescue has proved that the concept illustrated in E is quite feasible and overcomes some of the problems of keeping a surface support vessel over the position in bad weather conditions to effect a transfer. The same weather restrictions will

Fig. 6.33. Diver transfer installation on the American support ship *Elk River* (U.S. Navy).

affect the hoist and recovery of the submersible but possibly not so severely. The use of wet submersibles can be considered more as a transport from one station to another where there are no great variations in depth.

A sophisticated and somewhat unlikely concept which has been considered in France was to place a transfer shaft from the surface to the seabed with intermediate locks to enable divers to exit. The supporting leg of a structure connected to a seabed habitat would fulfil the same function.

Materials and Equipment

The numerous alternatives already discussed regarding the shape, size, operating depths, mission requirements and methods of transfer will lead to many options in the type and selection of materials and equipment.

The materials which are used in the hull will naturally depend on the configuration and the depth. To date in most cases boiler steel has been used. For equal-pressure systems a rubber-coated fabric can be used, supported and retained by a net or grill to reduce the stresses,

Fig. 6.34. Under-water station being insulated with glass foam.

particularly at the seams. Usually balloon-shaped, the habitat has an entrance trunk underneath the air–water interface. Glass-reinforced polyester resin is a good material to work in and is more durable than rubber-coated fabric. It needs no surface protective coating and has relatively good insulation properties. Boiler steel, on the other hand, needs most careful protection. After preparing a clean surface several layers of paint are needed, which must not be incompatible with marine life, especially where the purpose of the research is in this field. For recognition a good colour is yellow, orange and sometimes white.

Insulation is particularly important as energy is at such a premium in any event and heat losses through the walls of the chamber must be reduced. Cork applied internally is resistant to sea water but apart from having an uneven surface the adhesives used to secure the material may be toxic and frequently have an unpleasant smell. External insulation would appear to be better and a number of materials may be considered. They must all be seawater-resistant, pressure-proof for the depth, easy to form and apply, not toxic, a good volume-to-weight ratio and economic. The use of plastic-based materials has proved the most successful. For instance, polyurethane foam (Fig. 6.34) has been sprayed on to the external surface to a thickness of about 50 mm with excellent results, particularly if the steel is well prepared before the application, and this also will prevent

Fig. 6.35. Under-water habitat *Helgoland* just prior to its first descent in the North Sea. The author is on the right.

corrosion for many years. The application process is dirty but with a further application of glass-reinforced plastic the result is strong and effective. More expensive applications are Ecofloat and, separately, rubber strips. Unvulcanized rubber has been used as insulation on some smaller habitats. After applying the rubber, carefully treating the seams, the whole chamber is placed inside a vulcanizing boiler. This process can produce reasonable coatings of between 15 and 20 mm. The use of glass-reinforced polyester resin as the only coating will provide limited insulation although it gives a rugged finish.

The design and construction of lock-out trunking, doors and windows will vary, particularly with regard to whether the habitat is open or pressure-proof. The upper entrance trunking and door shown in Fig. 6.36 are used for preparation prior to immersion. If the missions are likely to be short between launch and recovery a single double-acting bayonet-locking door should be considered, allowing quick and easy through access. The door should be capable of being opened from both sides and the height of the trunking should be sufficient to stop spray and the surface movement of seawater from entering the habitat. Ideally view ports set into this column will give all round coverage in good visibility before the descent from the surface and whilst on the seabed. This column shown in Fig. 6.36 may be modified for a mating with a diving bell or submersible requiring a support and guide frame.

It is essential that the observation viewports give the crew the best possible coverage dependent on the visibility conditions. A very large window incorporated into the *Hydrolab* habitat in the Bahamas gives a panoramic view. Special observation compartments have been built into the habitat with either large windows or even observation domes

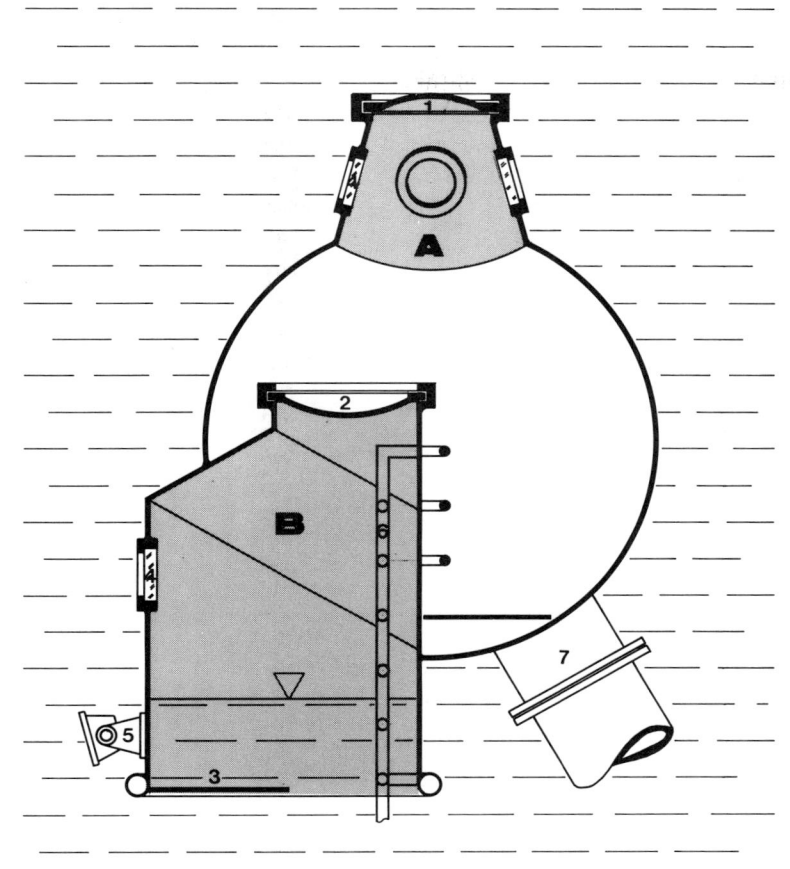

Fig. 6.36. The diver lock-out and trunking for a habitat allowing tidal movement.

- A Upper escape trunking
- B Lower escape compartment
- 1 one-way pressure door
- 2 diver lock-out compartment
- 3 floor boards
- 4 windows
- 5 external light
- 6 ladder
- 7 support leg

such as in the *Tektite* habitat. In the *Helgoland* an observation dome was fitted to the wet laboratory compartment which extended sufficiently to enable it to rotate through 360°. The same criteria of design and selection of materials that apply for windows in hyperbaric chambers and diving bells also apply to habitats. Acrylic glass is used almost exclusively to meet all these requirements.

The bottom lock-out will normally face directly downwards although there is no technical problem in having the lock-out position on the side using the principle incorporated into the Buffalo hyperbaric simulator described in Chapter 1. There may be more than one lock-out position but in any design consideration will need to be given to tidal differences in order to avoid losing any gas inside the compartment by calculating the correct length of the trunking,

Fig. 6.37. Inner hatch of the connection domes and below-deck installation of instruments and pipework.

taking into account the cross-section of the trunking and the maximum tidal lift. As in the upper access the door should be a single double-acting door opened and closed with a hydraulic drive. The trunk shaft should preferably be large enough for two divers and their equipment with the facility to remove their equipment and possibly have a shower to clean off dirt and debris brought in from the worksite. The space offers a dry shelter for resting between working. Fig. 6.36 shows a lock-out trunking system designed to operate in a tidal movement of about 3 m. The trunking is set off centre to gain the maximum economy of space and not so high as to make it difficult for the divers to re-enter the compartment with their equipment. In some lock-out arrangements the trunking becomes a compartment capable, as in *Sealab III*, of supporting a team of several divers and designed to be used for temporary storage of equipment. Protective cages are sometimes necessary in the water around the trunking to keep out unwelcome and dangerous fish. These cages were fitted to the *Tektite* and *La Chalupa* habitats.

Connections for the main services, such as gas, power, water, sanitation and communications are better situated in the lower portion of the pressure hull as there is the least danger of leakage. In Figs 6.37 and 6.38 the penetration can be seen with the various services combined into a single connection point. The domes around the

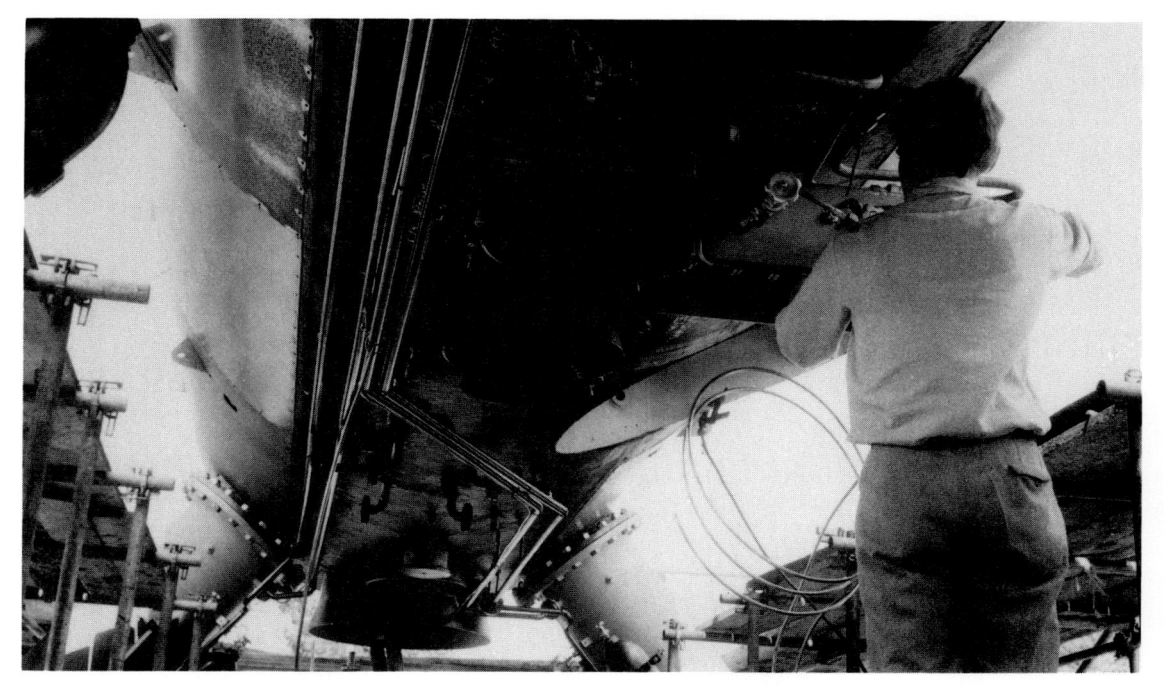

Fig. 6.38. External connection domes of the under-water laboratory *Helgoland*.

connection are filled with nitrogen after the habitat is placed on the bottom so as to remove any likelihood of sea-water contact. At a later stage the dome was replaced by a right angle shaft, filled with gas and large enough for the divers to operate.

Life-support Systems

In Chapter 10 the whole subject of life-support is discussed in some detail. The same requirements for life-support have to be met in the design of habitats to control the partial pressures of oxygen and the amount of inert gases and also the monitoring of carbon monoxide, hydrocarbons, hydrogen sulphide and other toxic substances. There is also the constant need to control the temperature and humidity. There are, however, some particular points that are relevant to habitats depending on their size and shape.

Air as a breathing gas is only used if the habitat is positioned in shallow water. If it is assumed that the oxygen partial pressure should not exceed 0.3–0.4 bar for long periods, normal air as we breathe it would limit the depths to about 10 m if the air is passed through an open circuit. Using a closed circuit, where the CO_2 is absorbed and removed, the O_2 partial pressure is controlled and the oxygen content can be lowered to the desired level. For approximate calculations the average oxygen consumption per person is about 0.5–0.6 litres/min. The supply of the correct amount of oxygen into the system may be controlled automatically or manually.

Fig. 6.39. Control and monitoring panels in the under-water laboratory *Helgoland*.

Air is also needed to charge scuba diving bottles as well as for filling buoyancy tanks and for trimming. Air will be needed for pneumatic tools and for pressurizing the lock-out trunk and other services. These services may not require air to the purity required for breathing standards. Part of the central gas control panel of the *Helgoland* is shown in Fig. 6.39 and illustrates the large number of regulators, valves and gauges that are needed to support the system. The actual means of compressing air and the storage of the air has been covered previously in the chapter including the need for emergency cylinders on the habitat itself.

With regard to oxygen, it is usual for a closed-circuit system to be installed, reducing the amount of air needed to service the chambers and maintain the correct oxygen content. For oxy-helium mixtures the partial pressure of oxygen has to be very carefully controlled with accuracy between 2.7 and 3.6% for depths of about 100 m. Because there are less constraints on space inside the compartments than in lock-out submersibles and diving bells, this allows for accurate monitoring; analysis and control systems are either automatic or manual, or both. To ensure a blanket distribution of oxygen the

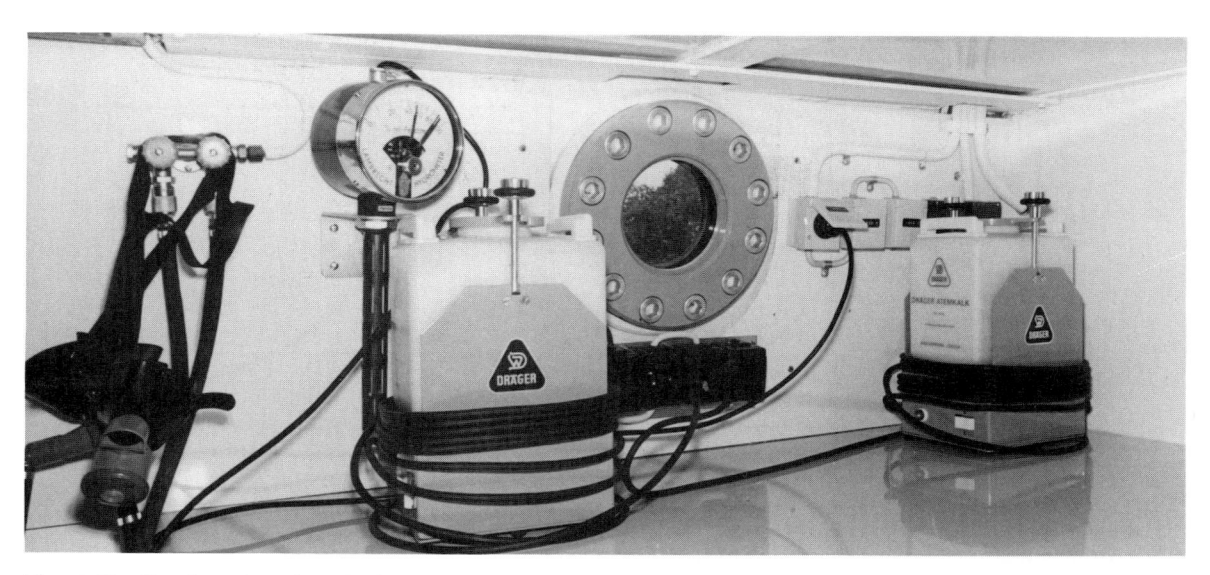

Fig. 6.40. Simple carbon dioxide absorption systems for an under-water habitat. These units can also operate from emergency batteries.

supply is best fed into the blower of the CO_2 absorption unit. An alternative standby position is needed to keep a sufficient quantity of oxygen in reserve for 14 days emergency supply, based on a four-man team using 3000 litres of oxygen per day.

The carbon dioxide content in air at atmospheric pressure should not exceed 1.5%, equal to a partial pressure of 0.015 bar; lower values are preferable. If air supply is on the open-circuit principle, sufficient ventilation flows are necessary for the removal of CO_2 and these flows are discussed and laid down in the tables in Chapter 2. The amount of CO_2 produced is clearly related to the oxygen consumption of the crew of a habitat. For a rough calculation it may be taken that 0.9 litre of CO_2 is produced per litre of oxygen consumed. Therefore with an average consumption of 0.5 litres/min, about 650 litres of carbon dioxide need to be removed from the atmosphere per day for each person. The method of ventilating or flushing through has been mentioned but it is only suitable for shallow depths and where supplies of air are plentiful. The other methods—freezing the CO_2 or washing out the CO_2 in the seawater—can be considered but the most usual method is for the CO_2 to be absorbed by passing through soda lime or lithium hydroxide. Fig. 6.40 shows a simple electric blower connected to an absorbent container. Careful design of these systems is needed in regard to the motors for safety reasons in view of the risk of electric fires and explosions. Pressure-proof casings and purging with inert gases need to be considered. A closed ventilation system is usually designed for large systems. Such a system which absorbs the CO_2 in a two-compartment habitat occupied by two to four people, is shown in Fig. 6.41. Two blowers with a total input of 200 W provide the

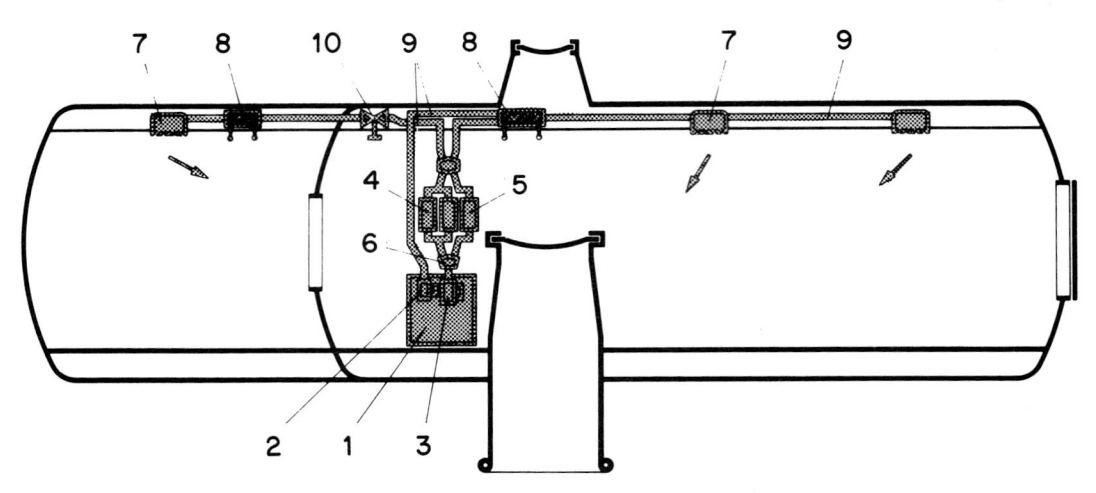

Fig. 6.41. Central carbon dioxide removal system in a two-compartment under-water habitat.

1 inlet filter
2 blower I
3 blower II
4 CO_2 absorption filter
5 fine dust/odour filter
6 air distribution box
7 air outlets in ceiling
8 heating elements
9 distribution line
10 shut-off valve

necessary circulation. To reduce the noise level the blowers are installed inside a grill casing which is filled with sound insulating material and filters. These filters act to trap dust particles. Six 4-litre containers are sited in a frame designed for easy replacement and connected in parallel. Assuming that 1 litre of absorbent absorbs 100 litres of CO_2 under normal conditions of humidity, temperature and a set constant flow, a total capacity of at least 2400 litres of CO_2 is achieved. For example, if there are four people in the habitat, theoretically, after 20 hours of operation, the container will need to be refilled or replaced. A special filter can be mounted in the circuit which will temporarily remove carbon monoxide, fine dusts, odours and oil vapours but it is important that the flow characteristics are the same. The cleaned air is passed through distribution piping to adjustable exhaust louvres set over the deckhead which can be regulated. An air heating system with an input of 2.5 kW is sufficient to heat the clean air and may be regulated for a comfortable temperature.

In an oxy-helium atmosphere where the helium content is high a comfortable temperature is between 30 and 36°C. Electrical heating is the only known method of providing heat. Excessive waste of power can be avoided by using insulating material. Local heating can be provided by individual blowers and infra-red heaters are especially welcomed by divers in the lock-out and changing compartments.

In warm waters where habitats are in temperate or tropical regions, good insulation only may be sufficient and in certain circumstances, due to the heat generated from electrical equipment, it may be necessary to cool the atmosphere. Air conditioning systems which

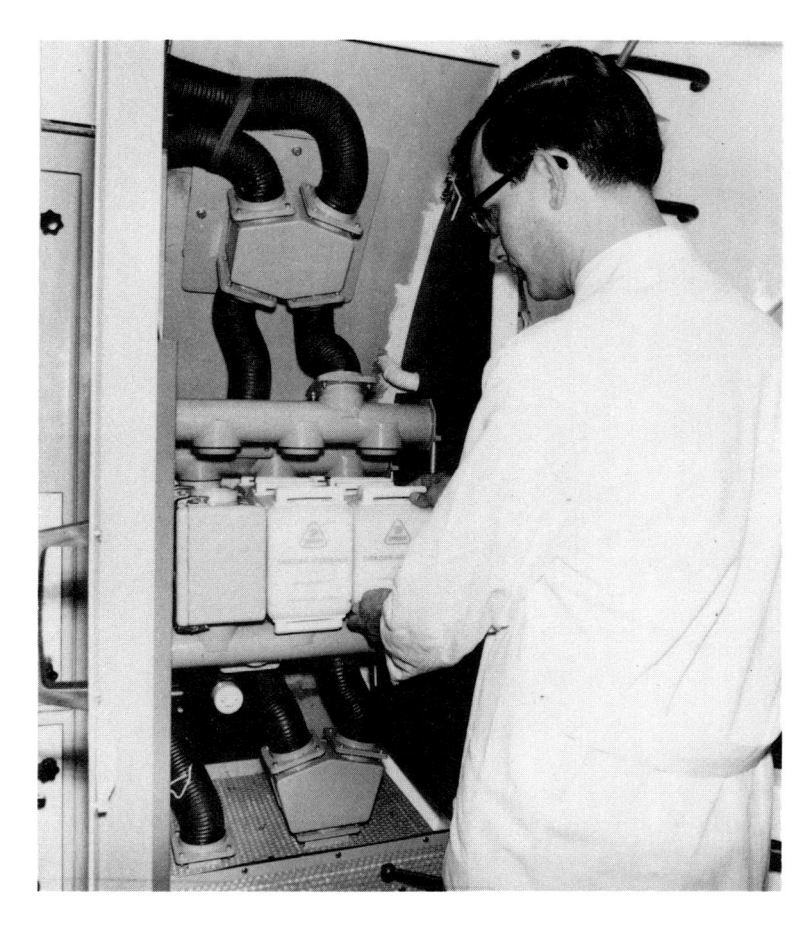

Fig. 6.42. Air circulation system of the under-water laboratory *Helgoland*. The two central blowers are located inside the bottom grill box which is covered with dust filter plates on the inside.

also dehumidify the system work well but special attention needs to be paid to the correct insulation of the units.

Humidity control is always a major problem, particularly in habitats. If possible the lock-out compartments which are exposed to the water should be separate, though this is not always possible in smaller designs. A relative humidity of 55–60% is comfortable for the crew but if soda lime is used for CO_2 absorption, a better efficiency is achieved with an increase of relative humidity to 70%. If there is no central dehumidification unit, separate units can be sited in areas of high humidity. Depending on the limitations imposed by the power requirements humidity can be controlled by cooling aggregates. An alternative method requiring less power is the use of chemicals, for example silica gel. A basic method is to install cooling coils with sea water passing through them, or even exposing a chamber wall, not insulated, which allows the water vapour to condense if there is sufficient difference in temperature each side.

The monitoring of the life-support inside the habitat is clearly vital. Measurement and recording require very high precision instruments which need to be capable of operating to their maximum efficiency in high pressures at depth. The life-support may be monitored from the surface or from the habitat itself. A monitoring unit is shown in Fig.

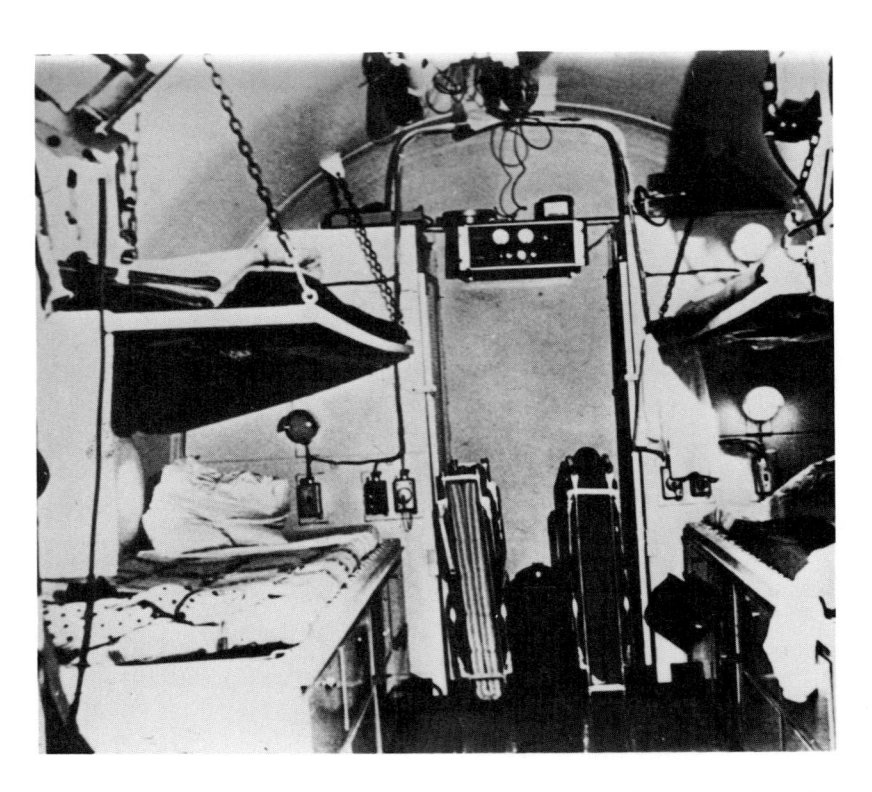

Fig. 6.43. Sleeping accommodation of the under-water station *Aegir*. Oxygen and carbon dioxide sensors are at the end of the chamber.

6.39 where measurements and recordings are made in situ, but the information is transmitted visually by television to the surface. The basic requirements are an oxygen analyser for measuring the partial pressure of O_2. Alarm systems can be fitted for an increase or decrease of O_2 partial pressure set within adjusted limits. A further refinement is to actuate a solenoid which controls the input of oxygen. A carbon dioxide analyser can also be fitted with an alarm when reaching an upper level. A CO_2 partial pressure of 0.015 bar is normally considered to be the maximum permissible level. The actuation of the CO_2 absorbent blower may be controlled by the alarm or at a lower setting. A CO meter to sense and measure carbon monoxide is important as its source cannot always be ascertained. A high warning is usually set when CO reaches 50 ppm. A temperature gauge can be incorporated to measure and to control the temperature automatically by controlling the heaters. An hygrometer will measure the relative humidity of the atmosphere; pressure gauges give the precise measurement of internal pressure and possibly will also determine the differential pressure in the collar of a lock-out. If the gas can be analysed on the surface, very accurate measurements can be taken using gas chromatographs which can be used in normal atmosphere conditions. In the chamber an instant measurement of contaminants and gases can be obtained using chemical test tubes. They are also useful in an emergency as they do not use power.

If the chamber atmosphere becomes toxic in an emergency where there has been a fire, or the oxygen supply has been cut off and the normal filter and absorbent systems are unable to contain the

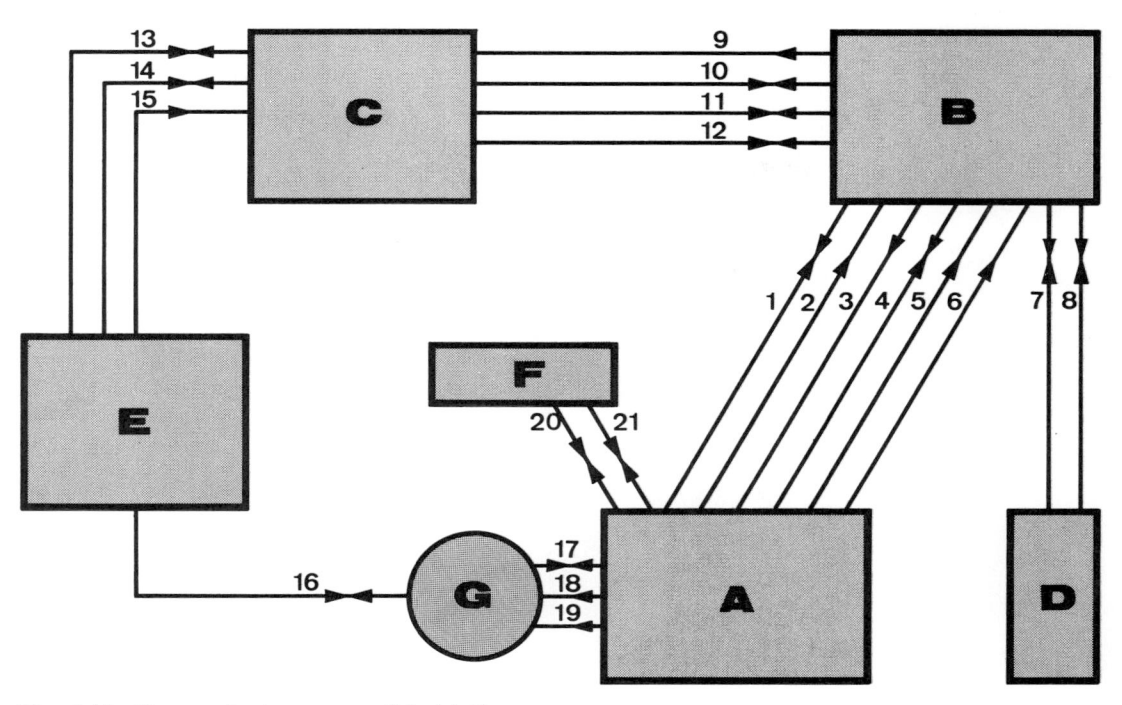

Fig. 6.44. Communication system of *Sealab II*.

A	habitat	8	wire audio
B	support	9	closed-circuit TV
C	shore control	10	telephone (3 lines)
D	PTC	11	battle phone
E	benthic control	12	radio
F	swimmers	13	telephone
G	benthic laboratory	14	audio
1	electrowriter	15	TV
2	closed-circuit TV	16	coax multiplexed link
3	entertainment TV	17	audio
4	audio	18	TV
5	oxygen partial pressure	19	data
6	wedge spirometer	20	sonic audio
7	sonic audio	21	wire audio

contamination, an emergency breathing system will provide the necessary life-support. A careful design will provide for a breathing system to be available at every station. A BIBS which has independent supplies of breathing mixture will also have sufficient oral-nasal masks or mouth pieces at the various positions. If decompression is being undertaken closed-circuit breathing units will be required if pure oxygen or breathing gas rich in oxygen content is being breathed to reduce the fire risk. A closed-circuit system will need its own CO_2 absorption unit and breathing systems used in mine rescue work may be adapted for this use.

Communications are vital for the transmission of data and no operation can succeed without good clear speech. The communicat-

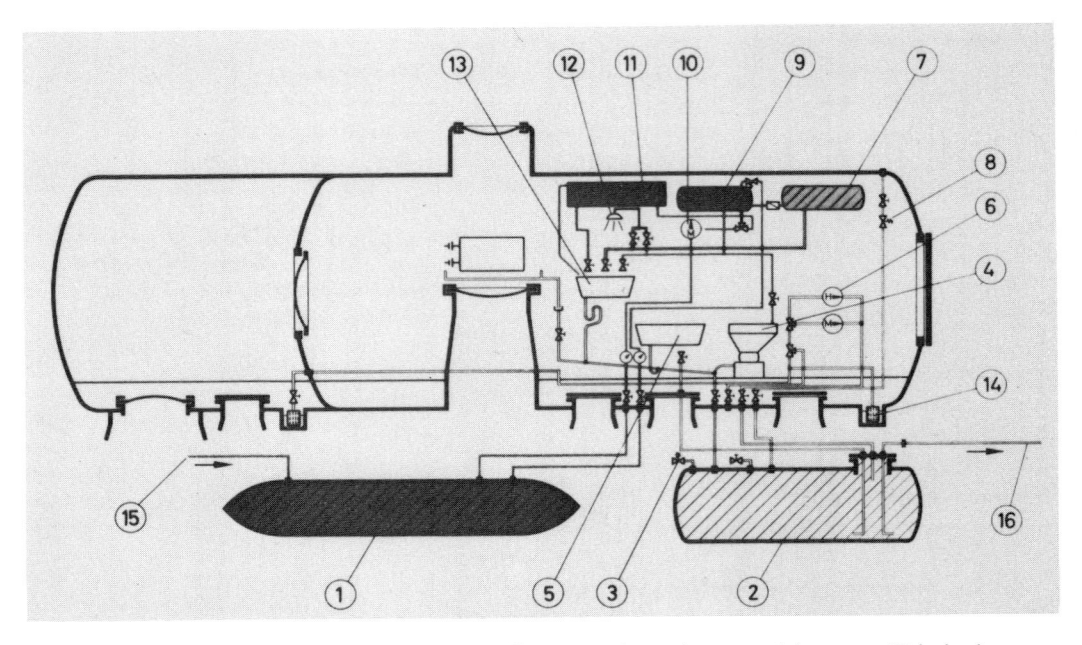

Fig. 6.45. Sanitary installations in the under-water laboratory *Helgoland*.

1. fresh water tank
2. sewage water tank
3. overpressure valve
4. WC
5. basin
6. sewage water pump
7. hot-water boiler
8. air exhaust valve
9. pressure tank
10. fresh water pump
11. ready-use water tank
12. shower
13. bidet
14. bilge drainage
15. fresh water connection
16. sewage water drainage hose

ion layout is shown in Fig. 6.44 for the *Sealab* project. Hard line wire systems are preferable for communication with the surface. A push-button talk-back system is preferred using loudspeakers. A radio telephone buoy on the surface is an essential back-up system should the support craft have to be released. If it incorporates a receiver the buoy can provide the essential link between the habitat and the surface support or shore base. Telewriters are a most useful development as they are not influenced by pressure and can transmit drawings as well as written messages. They can be used with line or wireless communication. Television links to the surface and within the system are normal. Apart from monitoring the behaviour of the crew they can pass visual information.

Proper sanitary and domestic arrangements are essential and require detailed planning. The arrangement in the *Helgoland* is illustrated in Fig. 6.45. The supply is carried in flexible bags placed in containers where they are immersed in sea water. The fresh water bags will tend to float and withdrawal pipes are set low in the containers to pump out the maximum amount of water. It is not

Fig. 6.46. WC compartment with water lavatory, water pumps and control valves on the under-water laboratory *Helgoland*.

always possible to design a natural differential flow and pumps are needed in most cases. Washing facilities should include a shower and bidet. Because showers increase the humidity they are better confined to the wet compartments. If this is not possible additional dehumidification units may need to be installed.

Adequate and safe WC facilities require sufficient water for flushing and also a waste disposal unit to shred the waste and avoid a blockage (Fig. 6.46). The sewage is discharged either into a tank or direct into the sea. There are certain advantages in integrating the bilge and sewage tanks.

The appetites of habitat dwellers are not diminished by being under pressure, perhaps the contrary, even though the quality and taste of certain foods diminish under pressure. Fig. 6.47 shows the kitchen in the *Helgoland*. Careful design of the fittings within the

Fig. 6.47. The kitchen of the underwater laboratory *Helgoland*, with deep freezer, refrigerator, stove, sink, cupboard and water tank for daily consumption.

available space will need to take into account the food that is suitable for cooking. Baking and roasting are unacceptable because of contamination. Prepared frozen food is ideal and therefore deep-freezers and refrigerators are essential. Heating arrangements for solid and liquid foods are shown in the *Helgoland* which catered for four people. Small habitats will have few facilities, confined perhaps to a heating facility or food provided from the surface in containers.

Electrical systems may be complicated and the needs of a well equipped habitat can be summed up as follows:

1. Internal lighting, external lights, search lights, indicator lights and emergency lighting.
2. Measuring instruments and recording devices.
3. Air circulation blowers, fresh water pumps and sewage water pumps.

Fig. 6.48. Electrical switchboard on the under-water laboratory *Helgoland*.

4. Communication systems, such as radio and television, telewriter and loudspeaker systems.
5. Refrigerators, freezers, stoves, hot water generator, cooling aggregates.
6. Compressors, hydraulic pumps, bilge pumps.
7. Winches.
8. Push/pull diving pumps.
9. Electric blankets.
10. Instrumentation.

A central switchboard (Fig. 6.48) shows a distribution box connecting up the various services. A typical power requirement based on the experience in the *Helgoland* was 20 kW whereas the power requirement for *Sealab II* was 75 kW.

With regard to furniture and general fittings, careful design to make use of available space must take into account comfort, lighting and decor, particularly for longer missions. The small comforts of life may become more important than the more obvious ones and a practical consideration is to have a practice run on the surface before installation so that, as far as is possible, nothing is forgotten.

Brief Descriptions

Man in Sea I (USA)

In September 1962, just about the same time as the *Precontinent I* (*Conshelf*), the American scientist E. A. Link carried out the first under-water laboratory project. This experiment proved that humans could live and work under water, even in cramped conditions, for long periods of time. Although there were difficulties it was confidently predicted that these would be overcome.

Precontinent I (France)

Jacques-Yves Cousteau's *Precontinent I* project was started only a few days after Link's successful under-water laboratory experiment had been carried out. The first location was only 10 m under water, but for the first time two divers, Albert Falco and Claude Westy, were a whole week under water. The station was equipped with two one-man chambers, so that under-water decompression could be carried out if necessary. However, decompression was dispensed with and instead the divers were given a breathing mixture of 80% O_2 and 20% N_2 over a period of two hours, whereby the nitrogen was successfully eliminated.

Precontinent II (France)

In June 1963 the first steps of the previous year were followed by Cousteau's great success. His *Starfish-House* and *Rocket* as well as the 'under-water shed' for the diving saucer *Denise* created together what could be called the first small under-water community. Cousteau did not choose the Mediterranean as a location this time but instead installed the habitats in the Red Sea. In these ideal conditions they were able to live a full month under water for the first time.

Man in Sea II (USA)

Now it was the Americans' turn. Edwin Link operated his *Man in Sea II* project near the Bahama Islands at a water depth of 132 m. Two divers lived and worked at this depth for 49 hours, which was a major step forward. The under-water laboratory was a flexible, cylindrical balloon covered with a net.

Sealab I (USA)

The *Sealab I* project was carried out by the US Navy in July 1964 under the direction of George Bond who was responsible for much work in saturation diving. The under-water house with a long profile was constructed out of naval pontoons. It was designed to be pressure-compensated so a crane was necessary to help lower it. This caused many difficulties and Dr Bond described the seemingly endless problems they faced in his report.

Sealab II (USA)

The former astronaut Scott Carpenter took part in the *Sealab II* project. This under-water laboratory, weighing about 200 tonnes and 17.4 m long, was lowered to the seabed off the Californian coast at a depth of 60 m in August 1965. Carpenter spent 29 days in the habitat. Again, as in the previous *Sealab I* project, there were technical difficulties.

Kitjesch (USSR)

The Russians entered the experimental under-water field for the first time in summer 1965 with their under-water laboratory *Kitjesch*. The pressure hull was made out of a locomotive boiler and divided into three chambers. The two end rooms were used to live in, and the middle chamber served as command centre and bathroom facilities. Twelve windows were used for observation and two hatches for entrance and emergency exit.

Precontinent III (France)

In this project Cousteau designed and built a two-storey under-water laboratory. In October 1965 six divers dived to 60 m to live in a sphere of 7.5 m diameter in the Mediterranean for three whole weeks. 70 tonnes ballast was necessary to launch the under-water habitat.

Permon II (Czechoslovakia)

The *Permon II* project was plagued by misfortune from the beginning. Two trials of the habitat were aborted one after the other due to bad weather. The first launch took place near the Yugoslavian coast near Split where waves pounded the ballast tanks under the habitat until the cables finally broke and the ballast tanks sank. Eventually the habitat was recovered. The second time was worse; heavy waves again pounded the ballast tanks and broke the cables. The cable securing *Permon II* to the shore parted as well. Because the habitat itself began to drift into a congested sea area, the sea cock valves had to be opened and the *Permon II* sank. This marked the last trial at sea. The next trial took place in a local lake.

Ikhtiandr 66 (USSR)

In 1968 the Russians installed their *Ikhtiandr 66* for the second time during the summer. No details are available.

Sadko I (USSR)

In 1966 the Russian habitat *Sadko I* was launched. This one-room spherical chamber with an external diameter of 3 m was very basic, with space for two divers. Both electricity and air supply came from the surface (either from a support ship or from land) and the laboratory was lowered by a winch and block system. The first trials involved the accurate measurement of water currents and temper-

Table 6.1. Technical data on under-water habitats

Project name	First trial	Country	Dimensions	Crew (number, time)	Depth	Respiration gas	Supply	Pressure ratio	Remarks
MAN IN SEA I (E. A. Link)	1962 (Sept.) Mediterranean, France	USA	Length 3.2 m Diameter 0.9 m	1 person 1–4 days	61 m	3% O_2; 97% He	From ship energy + gas	Positive pressure inside–outside possible	Double chamber Weight 1.9 tonnes
PRECONTINENT I (Conshelf I, Diogenes)	1962 (Sept.) Mediterranean, France	France	Length 5.2 m Diameter 2.45 m	2 persons 1 week	10 m	Air		Balanced pressure	
PRECONTINENT II (Conshelf II, Star House, Deep House)	1963 (June) Red Sea	France	Diameter uncertain, about 11 m	5 persons 29–31 days 2 persons 1 week	11 m 27 m	Air (5% O_2; 20% N_2; 75% He)	From ship energy + gas		Ballast 90 tonnes
MAN IN SEA II (Spid)	1964 (June/July) Bahamas	USA	Length 4.2 m Diameter 1.2 m	2 persons 49 hours	132 m	4% O_2; 5% N_2; 91% He		Balanced pressure	Rubber tent
SEALAB I	1964 (July) Bermudas	USA	Length 12.2 m Diameter 2.7 m Height 4.5 m	4 persons 11 days	59 m	4% O_2; 17% N_2; 79% He	From ship energy + gas	Balanced pressure	Double chamber
SEALAB II	1965 (Aug.) Pacific, Calif.	USA	Length 17.4 m Diameter 3.65 m Height 4.5 m	28 persons (3 teams 10 days each) Carpenter 29 days	60 m	4% O_2; 25% N_2; 71% He	Ship energy, own gas	Balanced pressure	Total weight 200 tonnes. Decompression time about 33 hours
KITJESCH	1965 (summer) Crimean coast	USSR	Length 5.6 m Diameter 2.55 m	4 persons	15 m		From land		Volume 30 m³. Three chambers
GLAUCUS	1965 (Sept.) Plymouth	UK	Length 3.7 m Diameter 2.1 m	2 persons 7 days	10 m	Air (closed-circuit)	Electrical energy from surface	Balanced pressure	Ballast 13 tonnes
PRECONTINENT III (Conshelf III)	1965 (Oct.) Mediterranean, France	France	Length 14 m sphere Diameter 7.5 m Height 8 m	6 persons 3 weeks	100 m	1.9–2.3% O_2; 1% N_2; rest He	From surface gas Autonomous		Total weight 130 tonnes. Ballast weight 70 tonnes
PERMON II	1966 (July) Yugoslavian coast at Split	Czechoslovakia	Length 2 m Width 2 m	2 persons	30 m. planned		Autonomous	Balanced pressure	Water displacement 5 m³ Abandoned
IKHTIANDR 66	1966 (Aug.) Black Sea, Crimean coast	USSR	Width 1.8 m Height 2 m	2 persons 3 days	11 m	Air	From land		Single-chamber laboratory Weight 1.1 tonnes Volume 6.8 m³
HYDRO-LAB	1966 Bahamas	USA	Length 4.9 m Diameter 2.4 m	4 persons, 14 days/crew	20 m	Air	Surface-supply buoy	Balanced pressure	Many crews since 1966
SADKO I	1966 Black Sea Caucasus coast	USSR	Sphere 3 m diameter	2 persons, 6 hours (1 month at 25 m Oct. 1966)	40 m		From land, From ship	Balanced pressure	Volume 14 m³, Ballast weight 13.5 tonnes

Name	Country	Dimensions	Crew	Depth	Atmosphere	Supply	Pressure	Remarks
CARIBE I	Cuba	Length about 3 m, Diameter about 1.5 m	2 persons, 3 days	15 m		From ship, gas partly autonomous	Balanced pressure	
PERMON III	Czechoslovakia	Length 2 m, Width 2 m	2 persons, 4 days	10 m		Energy from land. Gas autonomous		Ballast weight 5 tonnes. Weight of station 1.5 tonnes
1966 (end of year)								
1967 (March) Bruntal								
MEDUSA I	Poland	Length 2.2 m, Width 1.8 m, Height 2.1 m	2 persons, 3 days	24 m	37% O_2; 63% N_2	From land	Balanced pressure	Weight of station 2.95 tonnes
1967 (July) Lake Klodno								
HEBROS I	Bulgaria	Length 5.5 m, Diameter 2 m	2 persons	10 m				No details
1967 (July) Bay of Varna								
OCTOPUS	USSR		3 persons, (Several weeks?)	10 m	Air	From land	Balanced pressure	Collapsible Hemispherical
1967 (July) Black Sea, Crimean coast								
IKHTIANDR 67	USSR	Length 8.6 m, Height 7 m	2–5 persons	12 m				Three chambers Weight 27 tonnes
1967 (Aug.)								
SADKO 2	USSR	Ball diameter 3 m	2 persons, 10 days	25 m (50–60 m)		Energy from land-ship. Gas autonomous	Exterior positive pressure, 4 bar	Buoyancy of laboratory 12 tonnes. Ballast weight 27 tonnes
1967 (summer) Black Sea, Caucasus coast								
KOCKELBOCKEL	Netherlands	Height 4.6 m, Diameter 1.9 m	2–4 persons. Short period	15 m	Air	Gas and energy autonomous	Balanced pressure	Ballast weight 9.5 tonnes
1967 Sloterplas								
UWL-ADELAIDE	Australia		Several persons			From pontoon		No further details
1967–1968								
ROMANIA LS 1	Roumania		2 persons			From ship		
1968? Bicaz Lake								
KARNOLA	Czechoslovakia		5 persons	8–15 m				Data incomplete
1968?								
CHERNOMOR	USSR	Length 8 m, Diameter 3 m, Height 6.1 m	4 persons. Several crews 1 month in total	5–14 m (poss. 30 m)		From surface (ship)	Balanced pressure	Water displacement 62 tonnes. Autonomous for three days
1968 (June) Crimean coast								
MEDUSA II	Poland	Length 3.6 m, Width 2.2 m, Height 1.8 m, Total height 2.5 m	3 persons, 14 days	30 m	Air	From ship		Autonomous up to 50 hours
1968 (July) Baltic								
ROBINSUB I	Italy	Length 2.5 m, Width 1.5 m, Height 2 m	1 person	10 m	Air	From land	Balanced pressure	Wire cage, rubber tent, volume 5 m^3
1968 (July) Ustica Island								
HEBROS II	Bulgaria	Length 6.7 m, Diameter 2.5 m	2 persons	30 m (10 days?)		From surface		Effective volume 30 m^3
1968 Cape Maslennos								
SPRUT	USSR	Height 1.5 m, Diameter 3.0 m	2–3 persons 14 days	10 m				Flexible net-enclosed ball
1968 Crimean coast								

Table 6.1. Continued

Project name	First trial	Country	Dimensions	Crew (number, time)	Depth	Respiration gas	Supply	Pressure ratio	Remarks
BAH I	1968 (Sept.) Baltic	Federal Republic of Germany	Length 6 m Diameter 2 m	2 persons 11 days	10 m	Air	From ship	Balanced pressure	
IKHTIANDR 68	1968 (Sept.) Crimean coast	USSR		Several crews Total 8 days	12 m		From land		'Glass chamber' Water displacement 15 m^3
MALTER I	1968 (Nov./Dec.) Malter Dam	German Democratic Republic	Length 4.20 m Diameter 1.80 m Height 3.50 m	2 persons 2 days	8 m	Air	From land and autonomous	Balanced pressure	Effective volume 10 m^3 Weight 14 tonnes
TEKTITE I	1969 (Feb.) Virgin Islands	USA	Cylinder height 5.5 m Cylinder diameter 3.8 m	4 persons 59 days	12.7 m	8% O_2; 92% N_2	From ship	Balanced pressure	Ballast 175000 lb Negative buoyancy 20000 lb
SEALAB III	1969 (Feb.) St Clemente, Calif.	USA	Length 17.4 m Diameter 3.65 m Height 4.5 m	5 × 12 persons	183 m	2% O_2; 6% N_2; 92% He	From land and ship	Balanced pressure	Project suspended indefinitely
ROBIN II	1969 (March) Genoa, Mediterranean	Italy		1 person 7 days	7 m			Balanced pressure	Transparent plastic hull
AEGIR	1969 Hawaii	USA	Length 2 × 4.6 m Diameter 2.75 m Ball diameter 3 m Total length 15.2 m	4–6 persons 14 days	147 m	Variable gas mixtures	From land, buoy or ship	Internal pressure 18.3 bar	Ground pressure 40 tonnes. Ascent and descent totally controlled from inside
UWL-HELGOLAND	1969 (July) North Sea, Baltic Sea, USA, East Coast	Federal Republic of Germany	Length 9.0 m Diameter 2.5 m Height 6 m	4 persons 10 days each up to 30 days	23–31 m	Air	From buoy	Internal pressure 10 bar External pressure 10 bar	About 64 tonnes (First unit)
SUBLIMOS	1969 (June) Lake Huron		Diameter 2.4 m Height 2.7 m Total height 6.4 m	2–4 persons	10 m	Air	From land via umbilical	Balanced pressure	Weight 8 tonnes Ballast approx. 5 tonnes
BAH II	1969 (June/July) Lake Constance	Federal Republic of Germany	Length 6 m Diameter 2 m	2 persons. Several days	10 m	Air	From surface	Balanced pressure	
SD-M 1 (SD-M 2)	1969 (August) Malta	UK	Length 2.9 m Width 1.85 m Height 1.85 m	2 persons 1–7 days	9 m (6 m)	Air	Autonomous	Balanced pressure	Rubber tent with steel frame
CHERNOMOR-2	1969 (Oct.) Black Sea	USSR	Length 8 m Diameter 3 m Height 6 m	4 persons Several weeks	25 m, 35 m	O_2–N_2 mixture	Autonomous		With rescue chamber. Water displacement approx. 75 tonnes

Name	Country	Dimensions	Crew/Duration	Depth	Atmosphere	Support	Pressure	Remarks
ATLANTIDE	Italy 1969 (Sept.) Lago di Cavazzo	Length 7 m Diameter 2 m (Two rooms)	12 persons 25 days (three houses)	12 m	Air	Under-water machinery house		Under-water village with three houses and one machinery house
SADKO 3	USSR 1969 (Oct.) Black Sea	Diameter 3 m Height 7 m	6 persons 6 days	25 m	15% O_2; 85% N_2	Autonomous	Balanced pressure	Ballast 39 tonnes
TEKTITE II	USA 1970 (April) Lamashur Bay	Height 5.5 m Diameter 3.8 m	5 persons 11–30 days	12.7 m	N_2–O_2 mixture	From land		11 crews, 5 persons each
SHELF 1	Bulgaria 1970 (autumn) Black Sea	Length 6 m Diameter 2.5 m	3 persons 7 days	21.5 m	Air	Surface support ship	Balanced pressure	
EDELHAB	USA 1970 Alton Bay, New Hampshire	Length 3.7 m Diameter 2.4 m	4 persons 36 h	7.6 m	Air	From land		
MINITAT	USA 1970	Height 3.5 m Diameter 2.4 m	3/2 persons 7 days 14 days	26 m 56 m	N_2–O_2 mixture	Surface		Not used owing to technical difficulties
ASTERIA	Italy 1971 Lake Garda							
SEATOPIA	Japan 1971	Length 11.9 m Diameter 2.3 m Height 6.5 m	4 persons 30 days?	design diving depth 100 m	O_2–N_2–He mixture	Surface support vessel	Internal pressure-resistant	
HUNUC	South Africa 1971							Abandoned during launching
LAKE LAB	USA 1971 Lake Michigan	Width 3 m Height 2.1 m	2 persons 2 days	10 m	Air from land			
SUBIGLOO	Canada 1972, 1974 Arctic waters	Sphere diameter 2.5 m	2 persons 1 day	13 m	Air	From surface	Balanced pressure	Designed as acrylic work station
LA CHALUPA	USA 1972 Puerto Rico	Length 5.8 m Width 2.4 m Height 2.4 m	5 persons 2 weeks	33 m	N_2–O_2 mixture	Surface vessel or supply buoy	Internal pressure resistant	Autonomous for 48 hours
LORA	Canada 1974 Newfoundland		3 persons 24 h	8 m	Air	Surface		
GALATHÉE	France 1977	Length 7 m Width 6.6 m Height 4.75 m	5 persons 2 days	approx. 18 m	Air	Surface vessel	Pressure compensated	Weight 7 tonnes
NERITICA	Federal Republic of Germany 1977 Red Sea	Length 2 m Width 2 m Height 3.4 m	3 persons	10 m	Air	From shore	Pressure compensated	Volume 14 m^3 Ballast 18 tonnes

ature. The habitat went down to between 10 and 40 m depth and divers made excursions into 45 m depth. The system was only meant for short-term habitation as the available documentation refers only to under-water exposures not exceeding six hours.

Caribe I (Cuba)

About the end of 1966 Cuba's first under-water laboratory was installed at a depth of 15 m off the north coast near Havana. From all reports this habitat was primitive and small, a fore-runner of the larger more sophisticated project *Caribe II*.

Permon III and IV (Czechoslovakia)

In March 1967 Czech divers installed the laboratory in 10 m depth in a quarry lake. Conditions on the surface created more difficulties than those below: the intense cold and high winds almost halted the underwater work. A further experiment, *Permon IV*, was also successfully completed. Two divers lived at 25 m depth for 102 hours and carried out a wide range of psychological tests and practical tasks.

Medusa I (Poland)

Whereas between 1962 and 1965 only about two or three underwater laboratories were set up a year, after 1967 there was an increase in the use of these stations. The Poles entered the field with their *Medusa I* sited in Lake Klodno in July 1967. Two divers worked for three days at 24 m depth with the experiment serving as forerunner for the *Medusa II* and *Medusa III* stations which were to follow later.

Hebros I (Bulgaria)

In July 1967, the Bulgarians installed their *Hebros I* under-water laboratory. Other than that the laboratory body was 5.5 m long, with a diameter of 2 m, and operated at a depth of 10 m, not much else is known.

Octopus (USSR)

In July 1967 the Russians installed flexible, hemispherical underwater laboratory called *Octopus* in the Black Sea off the Crimean coast. It was reported that a three-man team spent several weeks at a depth of 10 m under water.

Ikhtiandr 67 (USSR)

It is not clear whether this project was a new under-water laboratory or simply a modification of the previous year's attempt. The under-water team was increased from two to five persons. Trials were held in the Black Sea off the Crimean coast with the object being to gain more detailed information concerning human gas exchange and to carry out psychological studies while living under water for long periods of time.

Sadko II (USSR)

After gaining experience with *Sadko I*, scientists at the Leningrad Hydrometeorological Institute, cooperating with the Institute of Acoustics at the Russian Scientific Academy, designed and developed the *Sadko II* station. This construction was a double-sphere arrangement with one sphere on top of the other. The first trials were reported to have taken place in the summer of 1967 in the Black Sea. The aim was to study long-term human habitation under water as well as certain physiological studies.

Kockelbockel (Holland)

A simple design and construction limited for use by amateur sport divers.

UWL Adelaide (Australia)

Not many technical details are known about this habitat except that it had a number of compartments including separate living accommodation, pressure chambers and laboratories. Installed in September 1967 it was supplied from a surface raft.

Roumania LS I (Rumania)

The Rumanians designed the *Rumania LS I* and installed it in the Black Sea. With a diameter of 1.8–2 m and about 5 m long, it accommodated two people.

Karnola (Czechoslovakia)

Karnola was the third under-water laboratory produced by the Czechs. Not much is known about this project. Apparently it served to house five people in 8–15 m water depth, and was probably installed in 1968.

Chernomor (USSR)

Gelendshik, a blue bay in the Black Sea, was the location for the first installation of *Chernomor*, a relatively large Russian under-water station. The laboratory was installed in June 1968 and accommodated up to 30 divers for a month at a time at 14 m depth with teams of six exchanging in succession. The purpose of this project was oceanographic investigations in coastal areas, where biological and geological processes are particularly interesting. Marine life was abundant. The habitat's internal fittings were limited. The crew changes took place on the surface, the habitat surfacing every five or six days. Decompression time was limited to about ten hours.

Medusa II (Poland)

Poland's second under-water laboratory, the *Medusa II*, was completed in July 1968. A square habitat with about 14 m^3 internal capacity was launched from a ship, for the first trials to a depth of 30 m in the Baltic Sea. The habitat served as dwelling for three divers for 14 days.

Robinsub I (Italy)

During the tenth international Diving Sport Week on Ostica in July 1968, a small under-water house was sunk just off the island in 10 m water depth. The house was more or less a wire cage covered in plastic and the Italian Italo Ferraro lived in it for 48 hours.

Hebros II (Bulgaria)

The Bulgarians made considerable technical progress with their *Hebros II*, compared to their *Hebros I*. In contrast to *Hebros I*, *Hebros II* was designed not only to carry out purely scientific activities but also for economic studies. The main considerations were physiological and psychological studies under 4 bar pressure.

Sprut (USSR)

No metal was used in the construction of this habitat in 1968, even the floor was made of fabric and was flexible. A development of the *Octopus*, the project was for hydrochemical tests in which sea water samples were studied for their dissolved gas content, particularly oxygen.

BAH I (West Germany)

In September 1968, the West Germans installed the *BAH I* habitat in the Baltic. It was a simple straightforward design but unfortunately the project was over-shadowed by the death of Dr Horst Hartmann, who was part of the project, as a medical specialist. He died during a survey dive from the surface without having entered the habitat.

Ikhtiandr 68 (USSR)

The *Ikhtiandr 68* was installed in September 1968 off the Crimean coast, a construction with 15 m^3 water displacement. The station was 12 m under water and several teams lived there for eight days, mainly concerned with testing precise depth measuring equipment and geological equipment as well as studying ergonomics and the movement of humans under water.

Malter I and II (East Germany)

The first East German under-water dwelling called *Berlin I* was not developed until there was sufficient funds and personnel for it. A group of sport divers installed the *Malter I* in the Malter dam basin in November 1968. This habitat had room for two persons, sited at a depth of 8 m under water, and was very basic. On the other hand, the construction of the *Malter I* did prove that a small group of divers with limited funds could, with sufficient motivation and energy, design and install a basic dwelling.

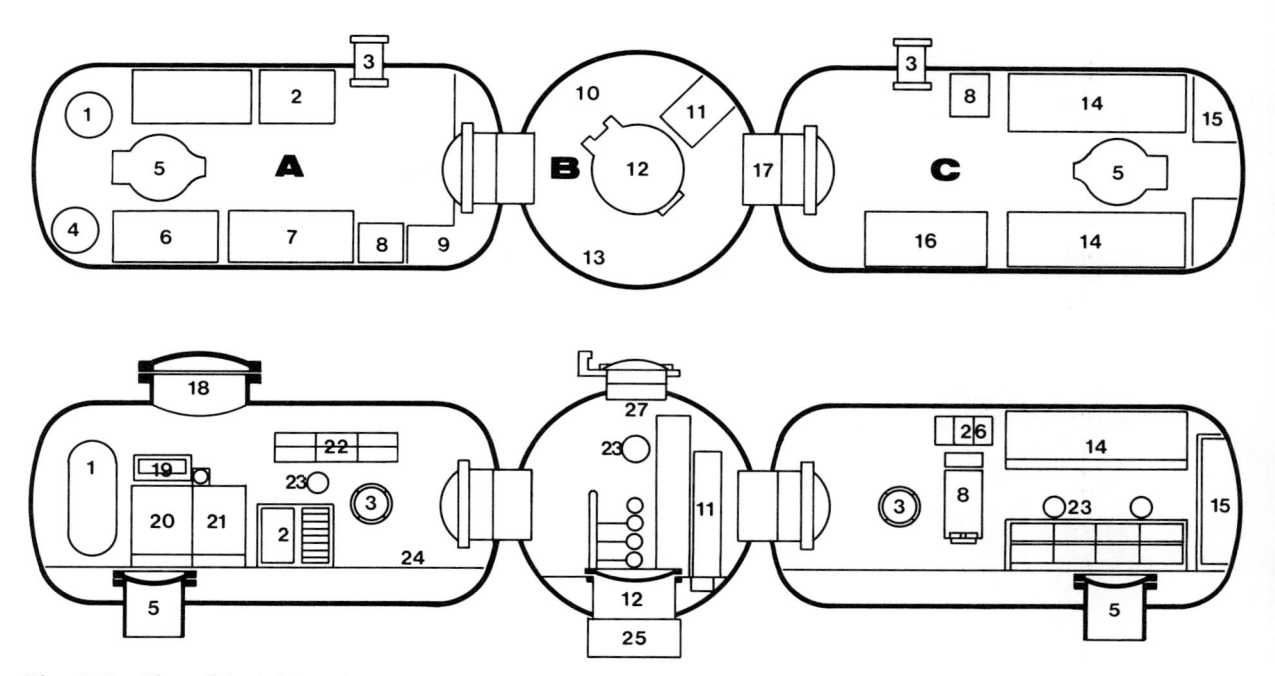

Fig. 6.49. Plan of the habitat *Aegir*.

1. hot water storage
2. galley
3. tool lock
4. cold water trunks
5. escape hatch
6. communications
7. laboratory sink
8. communications and dehumidifier
9. wet suit storage
10. shower
11. shower room
12. diving entry hatch
13. hookah breathing equipment
14. bunks
15. linen storage
16. WC
17. connecting tunnels
18. refitting hatch
19. infra-red oven
20. freezer
21. refrigerator
22. bulkhead storage space
23. observation port
24. deck plating
25. diving skirt
26. environmental control system
27. central sphere

Tektite I (USA)

This project was financed and supported jointly by General Electric Co., NASA, and the Ministry for the Interior. Four aquanauts lived for 59 days at a depth of nearly 13 m. The main purpose of the project was not to set up a record but rather to study human behaviour when subjected to living for long periods in relatively cramped quarters. The experiment was successfully brought to a conclusion without any major difficulties.

Sealab III (USA)

The biggest and most expensive under-water experiment of all times was ended before it really got started. Whereas many of the American

Fig. 6.50. The habitat *Aegir*.

space projects were carried out with incredible precision, this third *Sealab* programme seemed to be beset by bad luck. After various postponements, it was finally launched in February 1969. Technical problems required a four-man team of divers to dive down to the *Sealab* which was sited 183 m under water to carry out repairs. On the way from the diving bell to the habitat one of the divers, Berry Cannon, got into difficulties and died shortly afterwards in the bell. It was reported that his CO_2 absorbent container had not been filled. After this tragic accident, the project was terminated.

Robin II (Italy)

A successor to the *Robinsub I* project, this under-water station was very simple, being simply a transparent plastic container.

Aegir (USA)

One of the largest American under-water research centres located on the island Oahu in the Hawaiian Islands, the Makai Undersea Test Range incorporates a considerable installation on land including a big sea aquarium and a large under-water laboratory completed in early 1969 for working at depths down to about 150 m. This well designed

Fig. 6.51. The under-water laboratory *Helgoland* after recovery from the sea.

system has carried out successful projects and still holds the depth record of 158 m for known habitat installations. The facility is available for outside research.

UWL Helgoland (West Germany)

Ever since its first successful mission in 1969, the *Helgoland* has undertaken successive trials and experiments and also improved the general state of the art. Successive operations in the North and Baltic Seas as well as off the USA coast in 1976 have made *Helgoland* probably the most successful habitat to date. Scientists and technicians from all over the world have lived and run their experiments in this habitat for weeks and months. Although this habitat is now becoming outdated it has served its purpose by adding much to the knowledge of habitat operations.

Tectite II (USA)

The *Tektite II* programme used the same double cylinder habitat as the *Tektite I*. In 1970 the project involved 11 separate teams each of five aquanauts carrying out a large number of projects and tasks.

Shelf I (Bulgaria)

After *Hebros I* (1967) and *Hebros II* (1968) Bulgaria installed its first UWL, *Shelf I*, in the autumn of 1970. The laboratory was sited 21.5 m under water in the Black Sea. The experiments lasted seven days.

Edelhab I and II (USA)

Edelhab I was first sited in a fresh water lake at a depth of 10 m in 1968. It was designed and constructed by engineering students. After modifications and improvements in 1971 the laboratory was renamed *Edelhab II* and sited off the Florida coast south of Miami. For nearly three months oceanographic studies were carried out at 17 m depth by the Florida Aquanaut Research Expedition.

Asteria (Italy)

The Italian company, Galeazzi, installed a tower-shaped under-water habitat in Lake Garda in 1971. The main objective was diver training and testing technical instruments.

Seatopia (Japan)

Japan's interest in under-water technology was surprisingly limited when one considers its large coastal area. Except for a few brief reports about observation towers, small submersibles and under-water bulldozers, nothing much else was heard from Japan. Then in 1971 a large-scale habitat was announced and finally set up after some technical difficulties. The laboratory's shape was very similar to the American *Sealab II* and various features were also similar to other known designs.

Hunuc (South Africa)

Major difficulties arose while the habitat was being lowered and ballasted and before the habitat was occupied a storm destroyed it.

Lake Lab (USA)

The *Lake Lab* was a large igloo although a five-cornered shape. This small laboratory was designed for shallow waters at depths to 10 m and to be occupied by two divers for up to 48 hours. A mobile van on shore provided the support and to decompress the aquanauts surfaced and transferred to a decompression chamber.

Sub Igloo (Canada)

First installed in 1972, the *Sub Igloo* accommodated two or three people at a shallow depth of 13 m. The unit was made in the form of an acrylic dome, giving all-round visibility and designed for use under the ice pack.

La Chalupa (USA/Puerto Rico)

The use of portable pontoons with the under-water station was part of the Perry Oceanographics design with the advantages of quickly changing location by rapid launch and recovery. This compact laboratory consisting mainly of two chambers was first installed in Puerto Rico in 1972. The diving depth was 33 m with a team of five persons for two weeks. The safety installations and procedures were particularly good.

Galathee (France)

In 1977 a new beautifully shaped installation was designed. The *Galathee* was an elliptical house with huge observation panels for studying the under-water life in the Mediterranean.

Projects Being Designed and Constructed

One major project is currently progressing. It is the enormous *Chermomor 3* project now being developed by the Russians, a conventional laboratory as far as design goes but with a weight of about 300 tonnes In the USA NOAA had been planning to build the *Oceanlab*, a highly manoeuvrable submarine habitat, but the project has been abandoned.

7 Submersibles

This chapter deals with the development of the submersible and in particular with that of the diver lock-out which exposes the diving crew to ambient pressure. Whilst man's endeavour to build a true submarine goes back over a century, starting with manual propulsion and progressing to steam, diesel, electric and finally nowadays nuclear power, the addition of the lock-out facility is relatively new. The development of the submarine from the previous century to the present day has been designed for naval use, either in an attack role, armed with torpedoes, mines and recently with nuclear missiles, or in a defence role, with anti-submarine weapons and detection equipment. The fundamental requirement is always to achieve the maximum endurance under water, to the greatest depth possible without having to surface. The constraints of having to surface in order to recharge the batteries, a requirement for all diesel or electric boats, whilst not reducing the boat's autonomy, necessarily increased the risk that it would be detected by surface vessels and aircraft, thereby increasing its vulnerability. The recent introduction of nuclear power into submarines has increased the endurance of the submarine under water to complement its autonomy so that it may remain submerged for a complete mission. The development of the submarine is almost unique in that the prime considerations in its design are motivated by its use solely for military application, unlike other types of ship. Two major world wars in this century developed the military submarine without any serious commercial application and only after the Second World War was a commercial role considered for it.

Man's recent enthusiasm for outer space gave considerable impetus to the research and discovery of Earth's hydrospace, which covers two-thirds of the Earth's surface. Apart from the bathyscape and observation chambers, both severely restricted in movement, the tools for investigation were limited to probing, sounding, cameras and the collection of samples. Research and development is always severely inhibited by lack of funds unless there is a foreseeable commercial application. Research into the sea in the past was no exception to this. Whilst the prestige of the super-powers motivated probes into outer space, supported technically by military requirements for missiles and commercial requirements for satellites, no such condition supported research into hydrospace until recently. The extraction of hydrocarbons from below the seabed developed in shallow waters after the Second World War and moved into deeper and more hostile waters of north-west Europe in 1965. The ever-increasing energy requirements of the world and the need to find further supplies of oil and gas were to provide the financial resources to develop more sophisticated tools to explore and ultimately extract the hydrocarbons under water.

The development of the submarine and the submersible for research use was limited by financial considerations until 1970. As many as 100 vehicles of one sort or other were designed but only a few were actually successfully operated. Their size varied between 2 and 30 tonnes and their maximum diving depths varied between 30 and 10 000 m. They ranged from the primitive to the advanced, but all suffered in that they were built for research purposes with little regard for commercial requirements or financial constraints. By 1970 off-shore drilling was moving into deeper waters of 200 m, mainly in north-west Europe, and by 1975 drilling depths were in excess of 300 m and moving deeper. By 1980 drilling had been carried out to depths of 1400 m. The energy crises resulting from the continuing rise in oil prices have accelerated the search for off-shore hydrocarbons and led to the funding and development of submersibles. These vehicles have assisted in the construction and production phases as well as the maintenance requirements of structures, platforms and pipelines throughout the life of each oil field.

Until about 1970 the under-water tasks required in both the exploration and the production phases of the off-shore oil industry were almost entirely carried out or assisted by divers. The development of diving techniques and equipment, based only on the needs of naval, salvage and shallow water mine countermeasures, advanced rapidly, extending the depth and the endurance to meet the objectives of the oil industry. By 1970 the use of diving bells had advanced to the stage where the limitations were to a greater extent those of man's physiology. The development of surface-oriented diving, using a bell to transport the divers to the work site and on completion return them to the surface under pressure for a transfer to a deck compression chamber, has become a safe and efficient procedure. The use of these saturation techniques, together with improved life-support facilities, has given greater capability to the diver. Purpose-built dynamically positioned diving ships, fitted with moonpools through which the diving bells are operated, have refined the procedure and allowed operations to be carried out in bad weather conditions. The main limitations are man's reduced capacity to operate in the deeper depths required and the limited freedom of movement possible at the work site. The diver operating from a bell is limited to the length of his umbilical, not normally exceeding 30 m, whilst the diving bell is maintained in a stationary position and should not be moved. It was therefore logical to consider using submersible craft to carry divers, giving them the flexibility of being able to move along such installations as pipelines and to some extent inside production installations.

At this stage it is important to differentiate between a submarine and a submersible. The difference lies in the relative autonomy of the design. A submarine carries fuel to generate its own power and subsequently uses batteries to operate under water, recharging as needed. A submersible, on the other hand, does not generate its own power but relies on batteries that require recharging from an external source, namely a surface support ship. This use of a mothership, to which submersibles of about 25 tonnes and 10 m length are recovered for crew changing and battery charging etc., makes operation weather-dependent for launch/recovery, which is an operational restriction. However, a submarine is a single autonomous unit unlike the submersible. Except for a few notable exceptions submarines have been designed solely for military use whilst submersibles have been designed solely for commercial use. Clearly a purpose-built commercial submarine will be designed to carry out many of the tasks now being performed by diving bells, unmanned vehicles, submersibles and the lock-out submersible. This may be expected in the early 1980s. In the early 1970s submersibles were designed with manipulators to perform simple tasks, including detailed visual recording, for the oil industry at all required depths. Simultaneously surface-oriented diving was being evolved to carry out the same tasks. Later the lock-out submersible was also developed, allowing divers to lock out from the submersible and, on completion of their tasks, to be transferred back under pressure to the decompression system in the mothership. This provided competition for bell diving systems. Both the diver lock-out submersible and the diving bell have advantages and disadvantages which can be quantified, but the very high operating cost in terms of manpower, equipment and surface-support vessels is common to both. The high cost of putting man in the water with either of these systems was in the main the impetus that led to the development of the unmanned vehicle systems with their long endurance and ability to carry out inspection and limited physical tasks using manipulators.

Contemporary Submersible Development

Table 7.1 lists the diver lock-out submersibles built up to 1980 which have been operated successfully.

The *Shelf Diver* and *Deep Diver* were based on a cylindrical pressure hull with semi-spherical ends. The conning tower through which the crew enters is fitted with windows. The pilot's compartment is connected to the diving compartment by trunking. A sphere at the rear contains the life-support gases for the divers and a single cylindrical battery pod is housed underneath the forward pilot's one-atmosphere compartment. The stand-off distance from the diver lock-out hatch to the seabed is minimal, conditioned by the height of the battery container on which the submersible rests. Early trials of the *Shelf Diver* involved a lock onto the *Hydrolab* habitat in 15 m of water. In 1973 the *Shelf Diver* carried out the first important commercial operation in the Bay of Biscay. Divers were locked out at

Table 7.1. Diver lock-out submersibles to 1980

Name	Builder	Owner	Year	Depth (m)	Weight (tonnes)	Length (m)	Energy capacity (kWh)	Crew: pilots/divers	Life-support (hours)
Shelf Diver	Perry	French Navy	1968	244/244	8.5	7.1	37	2 + 2	48
Deep Diver	Perry	Museum	1968	420/420	8.5	7.1	22	2 + 2	48
Beaver IV	North American Rockwell	IUC	1968	620/310	17.0	9.0	44	3 + 2	360
SDL-1	HYCO	Canadian Navy	1970	620/310	14.2	7.6	68	3 + 3	204
Johnson Sea Link I	Harbour Branch Found. Inc.	Smithsonian Institute	1971	330/330	9.5	6.9	32	2 + 2	480
L1 (VOL-1)‡	Perry	British Oceanic	1973	360/360	14.0	9.9	39	2 + 2	300
Mermaid III	Bruker		1975	260/260	13.5	7.5	36	2 + 2	600
PC 1202	Perry	British Oceanics	1975	310/300	13.6	9.6	53	2 + 3	120
Johnson Sea Link II	Harbour Branch Foundation	Smithsonian Institute	1975	330/330	9.5	6.9	32	2 + 2	204
PC 16*	Perry	Saipem	1976	915/915	14.0	7.8	52	2 + 2	700
Mermaid IV	Bruker		1976	260/260	13.5	7.5	36	2 + 2	600
PRV 2	Pierce	Pierce Submarines Inc.	1976	300/200	8.5	6.4	46	1 + 2	360
Taurus‡	HYCO	British Oceanics	1977	400/400	24.0	10.7	134	2 + 3	500
PC 1801†	Perry	British Oceanics	1977	300/200	10.9	6.7	31	2 + 2	120
PC 1802†	Perry	British Oceanics	1977	300/200	10.9	6.7	31	2 + 2	120
PC 1803	Perry	Supersea Transp. Ltd	1978	300/200	12.2	7.3	41	2 + 2	172
PC 1804†	Perry	Fred Olsen	1978	300/200	10.9	6.7	31	2 + 2	120
LR 4†	Vickers Slingsby	British Oceanics	1978	457/457	20.0	10.3	52	3 + 2	600
LR 5†	Vickers Slingsby	British Oceanics	1978	457/457	20.0	10.5	52	3 + 2	600
SM 358	Comex	Romania	1978	300/200	12.5	7.5	45	2 + 3	360
Mermaid VI A ‖	Bruker	Mediterranean Navy	1979	600/300	19.5	8.0(6.5)	52	2 + 3(DLO) 2 + 8(SAR)	660
SM 358	Comex	China	1979	300/200	12.5	8.0	45	2 + 3	360
Mermaid VI B ‖	Bruker	Mediterranean Navy	1980	600/300	19.5	8.0(6.5)	52	2 + 3(DLO) 2 + 8(SAR)	660
Mermaid VI C	Bruker	no information	1981 und. constr.	600/300	19.5	8.0	52(70)	2 + 3(DLO) 2 + 8(SAR)	660
Mermaid VI D	Bruker	no information	1981 und. constr.	600/300	19.5	8.0	52(70)	2 + 3(DLO) 2 + 8(SAR)	660

* Dry transfer facilities only.
† Dry transfer facilities and diver lock-out.
‡ Diver lock-out and rescue facilities.
‖ Rescue submersible with diver lock-out facilities.

100 m to loosen a connecting link retaining a platform tower. Whilst *Deep Diver* is out of commission, *Shelf Diver* is still operated by the French Navy.

The *Beaver Mark IV*, designed and built by North American Rockwell primarily as a deep diving vehicle for nuclear submarine rescue for the US Navy, was a very sophisticated craft. The submersible had two spheres connected by trunking, the forward one being the command sphere at 1 atmosphere and the rear sphere for diver lock-out. The degree of sophistication of the equipment made the craft difficult for commercial use and personnel, including lock-out divers. Two submersibles of the *Beaver IV* type were designed but the second craft was not built. The pressure spheres were used in the *SDL 1*. Built for the Canadian Navy and based on Hyco designs, the submersible was used by the Canadian Forces. The configuration of the spheres and trunking were similar to the *Beaver IV*.

The main feature of the *Johnson Sea Link* was the pilot sphere made entirely of acrylic glass, at the rear of which was the cylindrical diving chamber with dished ends. The diving gases were carried in a spherical pressure container similar to *Shelf Diver* and *Deep Diver*. The stand-off distance from the diver lock-out hatch and the sea bed was achieved by the battery pod under the pilot's sphere. The submersible had little or no exostructure, having no hull fairing. A tragic accident led to the loss of two crewmen when the craft was caught in the rigging of a sunken ship. Before the submersible was freed two crew members in the divers' compartment died as a result of CO_2 poisoning and hypothermia due to insufficient heating.

The *VOL 1*, built by Perry, was designed using the experience gained from the *Shelf Diver* and *Deep Diver*. It differed in three important characteristics. Greater weight and size, two cylindrical battery pods instead of one on which the submersible was supported and a large acrylic window set into the pilot's compartment to give greater visibility. The diving chamber was large enough for the divers to stretch out and be more comfortable. Hydraulic legs were fitted on which the submersible could rest whilst on the seabed and these were long enough to provide easy access for the divers in and out of the diving chamber.

A further development of the *Mermaid I* and *II* which were built for inspection only, the *Mermaid III* was designed to operate divers in water depths of 200 m. A cylindrical pressure body with dished ends provides space large enough for the divers to stretch out and they can also stand in the exit trunking. A large acrylic dome is fitted in the pilot's compartment. Breathing gases are carried in cylinders fitted around the pressure hull. As with most diver lock-out submersibles, the diving compartment can be mated to a deck compression chamber on board the mothership, the divers transferring under pressure to remain under saturation or decompressed.

The *PC1202* is similar to the *PC15* but shorter and capable of operating divers using mixed gas and with a transfer under pressure

Fig. 7.1. *Mermaid IV* submersible with diver lock-out.

capability to a deck compression chamber on board the mothership. The *PC16* was designed for a greater diving depth of 1000 m and has three pressure spheres with an overall length of 7.6 m in a very compact design. It is designed for dry transfer under water in addition to transfer under pressure on board the mothership.

In the *PRV2*, the diver-lock out compartment, a cylindrical chamber, was separated from the remainder. The battery pod on the centre line could be moved along the fore and aft axis for trim and the correct stand-off distance of the diver exit to the seabed.

Weighing 24 tonnes, the *Taurus* is the largest lock-out submersible at present capable of operating divers. As submersibles are operated from motherships the size and weight limitations of the craft are to a great extent conditioned by the capacity of the ship's handling system to hoist and recover it on board. Designed for a diving depth of 400 m, outside current operational diving, the diving compartment can accommodate up to four divers with a command crew of three. In addition to commercial diver lock-out operations, the craft is designed for dry transfer for submarine rescue. It has a cylindrical pilot's compartment linked to a spherical diving compartment.

Additionally there are four spheres for ballast and to contain the breathing gases.

The successful development in the use of high strength glass-reinforced plastics in sail planes led to it being applied to submersible pressure hulls. The design, manufacture and testing of small reinforced plastic vessels had shown that a marked reduction in weight could be achieved in comparison with steel. Larger glass-reinforced plastic pressure hulls were successfully tested and incorporated in *L2*, an observation only submersible, followed by *L3*, a similar vessel. *L2* was the first commercially used submersible with a glass-reinforced plastic hull. *L4* and *L5* were later built with an additional module for a diving chamber and commissioned as lock-out submersibles. The use of glass-reinforced plastic has advantages in that it allows a higher payload and increased battery power; it is also non-corrosive, which results in an improved operating life.

The *Comex SM 358* is constructed around two pressure hulls connected by a pressure door but no transfer compartment. There are four thrusters and, in place of the usual single acrylic observation window for the pilot, there are three separate spherical windows. The diving system is designed for 200 m although the class of submersible is capable of 300 m depth in an observation role.

The *SM 351* (URF), although not a commercial submersible, was designed and built by Comex and Kockums Shipyard for the Royal Swedish Navy. It is designed to rescue 25 crew from a submarine to a maximum depth of 450 m. Equipped with a diver lock-out compartment for diving operations to 300 m the craft has a displacement of 49 tonnes with a length of 13.5 m. It has a crew of five including two divers.

Mermaid III and *IV* were similar in design with a diving depth of 260 m and a weight of 11.5 tonnes. These were built in 1975 and 1976. Improvements were later incorporated in *Mermaid VI* A and B with a weight of 19.5 tonnes in air and a lock-out depth of 300 m. It was also designed for dry transfer with an operating depth of 600 m. The pressure hull has a diameter of 1.8 m, whereas the cylindrical hull diameter for *Mermaid III* and *IV* was 1.25 m. All the submersibles have electrohydraulic propulsion.

The difficulty of obtaining the correct balance between optimum operating characteristics in the submersible and optimum diving performance, within the constraints of the limits imposed by handling systems on size and weight, has made the development of these craft slow and expensive. About half the diver lock-out submersibles built between 1968 and 1978 have been used commercially. These better-designed craft have proved their ability to operate divers safely and efficiently.

The development of the lock-out submersible did not evolve from the wet submersible but rather from the advance in diving techniques using diving bells. The wet submersible has little or no commercial application as it is limited to about 50 m by depth and pressure on the occupants and also by the very short periods during which operations

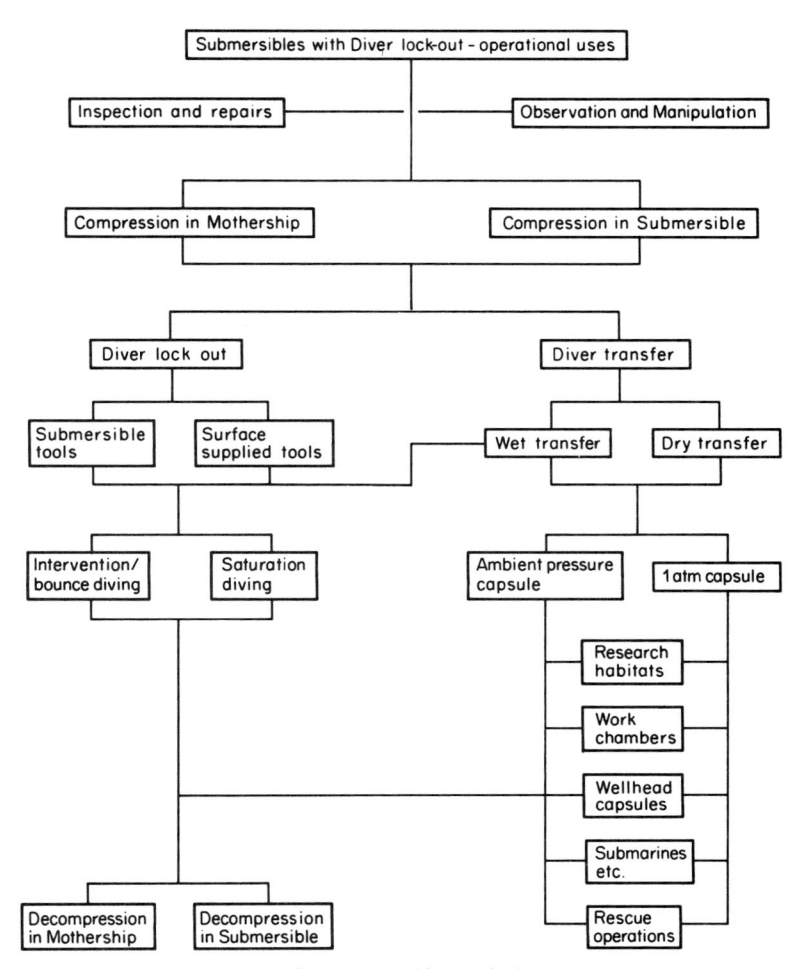

Fig. 7.2. Operational uses for submersibles with diver lock-out.

can be carried out. Probably the only application of wet submersibles is in shallow temperate calm waters and in good visibility. Lock-out submersibles become cost-effective in depths below 50 m and increase in effectiveness as depth and manoeuvrability are required. Fig. 7.2 illustrates the main types of operation which can be undertaken by lock-out submersibles and in different operating modes. All operations are conducted from a mothership and the same constraints apply to all types of work.

A wet lock-out by the diver may be for a short exposure, the time under pressure being short enough for the tissues of the body not to have absorbed the breathing gases to the extent that they become saturated. The decompression period is relatively short, perhaps even non-existent in lesser depths where a bounce dive is carried out. A diver entering the water will do so when the submersible is resting on the seabed and stationary. Only under exceptional circumstances will the diver exit whilst the submersible is in midwater and then only if the submersible is attached to a structure. Whilst on the bottom the diver carries out the task and is at all times connected by the umbilical to the diving chamber, being supplied with breathing gases and heating and in communication with the stand-by attendant diver in the diving chamber. Under certain circumstances the submersible may move slowly along the bottom with the diver in the water but in this potentially hazardous situation the diver must be visible to the pilot and in front of the command sphere. This technique, known as live boating, is discussed later.

Whilst it is possible in a bounce dive, or an intervention dive requiring a short decompression period, for the diver to remain inside the diving sphere for the complete period of the dive, any longer periods of decompression and, separately, whilst the diver is under saturation require a deck compression chamber on board the mothership with a transfer under pressure facility onto which the submersible can mate and effect a pressure-tight seal. The procedure is identical to a diving bell transfer under pressure system described in Chapter 4. There is, however, greater urgency to transfer divers from the submersible to a ship-borne chamber because of the limitations on gas supplies which can be carried by the craft. A diving bell has none of these restrictions, as life-support can be supplied continuously through an umbilical.

Apart from these wet lock-out operations the submersible can be used in the transfer mode by either wet or dry transfer under the ambient pressure at depth or at one atmosphere. Habitats have already been evaluated on the seabed, including the first seabed systems for oil and gas production. These installations are described in Chapter 6 and they will be common to the deeper depths over 300 m where fixed surface installations become impracticable. The simplest form of wet transfer is where the diver leaves the submersible and passes through an entry hatch into the habitat. The diver can either continue to use the submersible life-support system or, if available, transfer to a similar supply from the habitat. A more efficient, but of course technically more difficult, method is for the submersible to physically lock on and mate with the seabed structure. By mating the flange of the diver exit hatch to a collar on the installation, a similar procedure to that carried out on the surface when transferring divers under pressure to the chamber on board the mothership, divers and personnel can pass into the installation chambers. The seabed chambers may be dry with a pressure of one atmosphere, the same as on the surface and often referred to as a 'shirt sleeves environment', or filled with water also at one atmosphere or under the prevailing pressure outside either dry or partially dry. Each of these options has its advantages. A dry transfer carried out at surface pressure is clearly preferable in most cases, and most of all for submarine rescue where the crew are at about one atmosphere surface pressure. There are clearly complications in the design of the trunking or collar between the submersible and the installation, depending on whether a wet or dry transfer is being carried out. For instance facilities to pump out the water in the trunking will be necessary for a dry transfer and if the lock-out chamber has two pressure doors through which to exit the

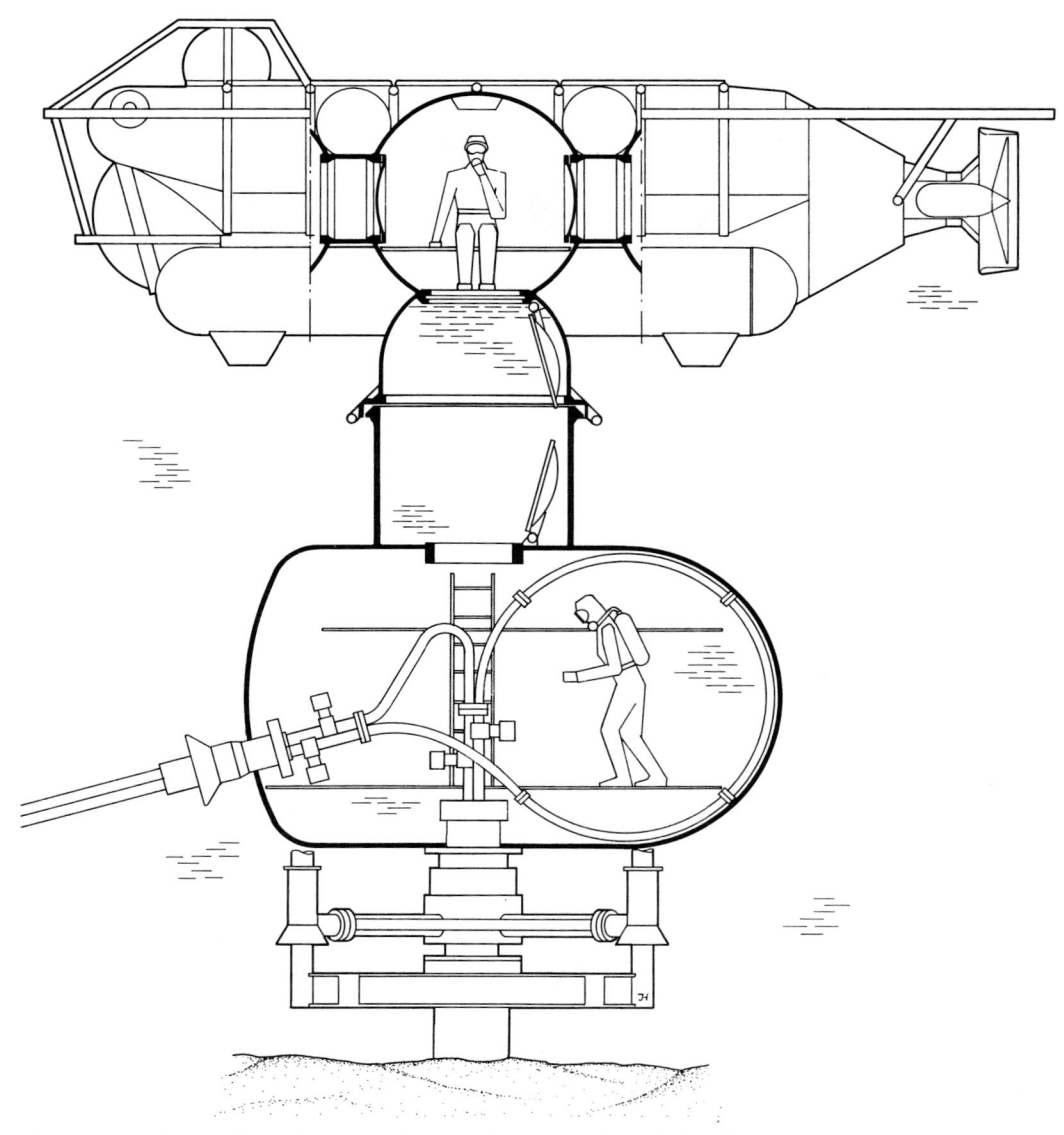

Fig. 7.3. A submersible with diver lock-out and wet transfer, suitable for use at 1 bar.

lower door will have to open inside the trunking. A wet transfer at one atmosphere will overcome this as no pumping will be required.

A 'shirt sleeves environment' is not always suitable and where welding habitats are placed over pipelines for repair, usually requiring cutting, grinding and welding, a dry ambient environment may be needed.

For rescue operations involving the recovery of crews in habitats or submarines, there may be variable pressures from one atmosphere to the ambient pressure at the depth of recovery, caused by damaged bulkheads and the ingress of water raising the internal pressure.

Table 7.2. Body metabolism

Input	
Oxygen	25 litres/hour*
Total breathing air	510 litres/hour*
Drinking water	2.7 kg/day
Nourishment (dry)	0.74 kg/day
Output	
Carbon dioxide	22 litres/hour*
Water vapour	1.5 kg/day
Urine	1.6 kg/day
Faeces	0.3 kg/day
Heat	120 kcal/hour

* At 760 mmHg.

Submersibles operating in rescue mode must necessarily be capable of operating in dry and wet transfers at different unknown pressures. If the crew of a habitat are breathing air at surface pressure of one atmosphere, for any increase in pressure over 6–8 bar, they will need mixed-gas life-support systems.

Life-support Systems

With the limitations of space both inside and outside the pressure hulls of submersibles, a careful balance has to be established between all the competing factors which need attention. The human body requires some periodic and some continuous input of solid, liquid and gaseous matter. Over a period of 12 hours, about the maximum time of a submersible mission, the body's metabolic requirements and output are as shown in Table 7.2. The same considerations apply to divers working from a diving bell as to those working from a lock-out submersible. The physiological needs for a diver to function efficiently and with safety through the three stages of compression to the working depth, undertaking actual work at the site in the water and finally the decompression, do not alter and these are covered in Chapter 10. The alternative operation of using a diving bell is covered in Chapter 4 where much of the equipment is similar to that fitted into the diving chamber of a lock-out submersible. However whilst the diving bell is relatively unrestricted in terms of working space and size, which are ultimately determined by the capacity of the hoisting system and the efficiency of the handling system for recovering the bell to the surface, these constraints are less severe than those which are relevant to the design of a diving chamber within the pressure hull of a submersible. The lock-out diving system has to compete with the primary design considerations of an efficient overall hull form, through-water speed, handling characteristics and, not least, acceptable endurance. Whilst the diving bell is supplied with power, breathing gases and heat from the surface by means of an umbilical, as described in Chapter 4, the lock-out submersible needs to carry all the essentials of life-support on board. All these requirements are limited by the overall weight of the submersible and the ability of the handling system in the mothership to recover the submersible in reasonable weather conditions.

The design of the life-support system to allow the diver to achieve at least a reasonable working time in the water at the worksite is largely determined by the amount of breathing gas which is used and, effectively, the endurance of the life-support system carried onboard. It is unlikely that air will be used or carried for breathing as this normally restricts diving to a maximum depth of 50 m. Submersible operations are not cost-effective at this depth and therefore helium gas is introduced as the inert gas and the oxygen content limited usually to 1.8 bar for short duration and much lower for longer durations. For short duration dives in which the tissues of the body do not become saturated, sometimes referred to as intervention diving, the compression should be as fast as possible and the pressurizing system should be capable of pressurizing the diving sphere at a rate of up to 70 m per minute. Breathing the atmosphere inside the dry chamber does not significantly increase the consumption of clean replacement gases if the atmosphere is being continually monitored for CO_2 and oxygen, with the removal of the former and the replacement of the latter. However, the type of breathing equipment used by the diver whilst in the water can affect the amount of breathing gas used and, consequently, the endurance of the submersible. The three types of breathing systems used, the open circuit, the semi-closed and the closed push–pull system, are described in Chapter 10. Clearly the open-circuit system, whereby the diver exhausts his expired gases into the water, whilst simple, is uneconomical. Much favoured for use from diving bells and surface-oriented diving, where the gas is supplied from the surface, this type of breathing system is frequently ruled out in lock-out operations because of the restrictions set by the limited storage facilities on board and the high gas consumption of the diver which, depending on depth, may be up to 60 litres/minute at ambient pressure. In semi-closed systems a small amount of gas is released but most of the exhausted gases is recirculated through a CO_2 absorber and the oxygen content made up by injecting clean gas; consumption can be reduced, depending on depth, to a constant gas flow of between 20 and 50 litres/minute at atmospheric pressure. Whilst the recirculation of the gases in a semi-closed system is carried out inside the breathing apparatus worn by the diver, in the fully closed or push–pull system the recirculatory systems are sited inside the submersible. Whilst the gas lost and the size of the breathing equipment worn by the diver are substantially reduced, these compensations are balanced by the need for an exhaust as well as a supply gas hose to the diver, a control unit to circulate the gas, CO_2 absorbers, analysers and O_2 regeneration units inside the submersible. The pressure of the gases needs to be at least 3 bar above the ambient pressure at the working depth and capable of maintaining pressure to the working diver even when above the level or depth of the submersible. The submersible must carry sufficient CO_2 absorbent and the partial pressure of CO_2 must not exceed 0.015 bar.

For diving cycles inside the submersible of less than six hours, which is usual, there is not normally any need for food. However, some concentrated food for emergency use should be carried, in addition to sufficient drinking water. Cooking facilities are not available in submersibles and any hot food must be prepared elsewhere and carried in vacuum containers. No normal facilities exist for the removal of human waste but plastic containers can be used. If a supply lock is fitted between the one-atmosphere control chamber and the pressure chamber it should be designed to meet these requirements.

No diving operation can be carried out unless the minimum heating needs for divers are met. In most cases the temperature of the water will be less than 10°C. In the control sphere in which the pilots live the breathing air at surface pressure will need to be not less than 15–20°C to be bearable and to avoid reducing the efficiency of the pilots. Inside the diving chamber the heat loss from divers breathing helium in place of nitrogen is six to seven times greater than from divers breathing air, if the breathing gases are not pre-heated. Respiratory helium gases must be heated to about 32°C, with an upper limit of about 36°C. The gas heaters will need a power supply of 0.8–1.5 kW per diver working in a water temperature of 6°C breathing an oxy-helium mixture and based on the diver heating a dry suit fitted with closed-circulation warm water. There are therefore two demands on the limited power supplies of the submersible as supplied from the batteries, gas heating and body heating by means of hot water circulated around and inside the diver's suit.

The ultimate aim is to keep the diver's body in thermal balance and thereby reduce any danger of hypothermia. In cold water conditions, for example in north-west Europe including the North Sea, it is normal to incorporate external body heating for diving at depths in excess of 50 m and respiratory gas heating in addition to body heating for diving in excess of 150 m. Both systems therefore need to be incorporated in lock-out submersibles under most situations.

The constraints set by the overall size and weight of the submersible and therefore the size of the pressure chambers lead to severe restrictions. To enable the divers, and there are at least two for every diving mission, to be reasonably comfortable, with space to sit and recline, the chamber should have a minimum diameter of 1250 mm and a length allowing them, as near as possible, to lie down when the bottom exit is closed. The hatch door should be not less than 650–700 mm, which allows the diver to move freely through the hatch without having to remove any personal diving equipment.

It is normal practice to limit submersibles to 8-hour mission cycles, whether they be diver lock-out or observation. These limitations are related to the pilot fatigue and battery capacity. Diver operations are normally restricted to less than six hours, which is similarly related to the capability of the divers and capacity of the life-support systems.

Other factors which determine the design of a submersible are the sea state and weather factors in general. Whilst the submersible is not affected by sea conditions during diving, other than current which affects speed, direction and control when stationary, surface conditions determine the overall operation. The submersible is limited by the capacity of the batteries and must always be recovered on board the mothership, and similarly the mothership can only launch and recover within set weather conditions. These will vary marginally between different motherships and submersibles but are more often determined by the experience of the crews and the efficient design of the handling system.

Although the water temperature is not likely to be lower than 4°C, except in Arctic conditions, the selection of materials in this respect is most important. High temperatures, on the other hand, will have a detrimental effect on acrylic domes and windows so that a safety factor of six for acrylic should be considered for water temperatures of 10°C, increasing to eight when water temperatures rise to 24°C.

Submersibles will not normally be permitted to operate in water where the maximum depth is greater than the designed safe working depth. The usual safety factors for the pressure hulls are from 1.5 to 2, with initial and periodic pressure tests carried out at 1.15 to 1.35 times the safe working pressure.

Currents on the seabed will limit the effectiveness of the diver and, if in excess of 1.5 knots, may stop diving altogether. The submersible will normally counteract the effect of current by settling on the seabed, supported on legs high enough for the diver to pass into and out of the diving hatch beneath the submersible. The submersible will remain steady by ballasting, by achieving negative buoyancy, and will therefore not use thrusters or propellers, a necessary safety precaution whilst operating divers in case they or their umbilicals become caught up and damaged. Where the work is to be carried out in a fixed position, such as a wellhead, a subsea production system or other fixed installation, this is the most practicable method, but where the submersible can use its manoeuvrability to advantage, such as moving along a section of pipeline which requires a diver in the water, a technique known as live-boating is used. In this operation the submersible is slowly manoeuvred along the pipeline with the diver walking alongside in full view of the pilot and therefore at least ahead of the beam of the submersible. This operation is restricted to good visibility and generally stable conditions.

Deck Compression Chamber Installations

For short decompressions it is quite possible for the diver to be decompressed inside the diving chamber of the submersible and in an emergency, where the submersible is forced to remain in the water, a controlled decompression could be initiated. However, the minimum diameter of a diving chamber is 1250 mm and the restrictions on space and comfort are not conducive to a successful decompression. Although the correct Po_2 could be maintained, it is less likely that the essential heating of the chamber and gases, and the continuous removal of CO_2, could be satisfactorily maintained, owing to the severe limitations of power. Diver lock-out operations are normally limited to the diver lock-out time and therefore mission cycles are under six hours; problems of human waste disposal and food are therefore not encountered and not considered except in emergency conditions. The limitation on size and weight of lock-out submersibles, determined by the ability of the mothership to launch and recover, will severely restrict the mission cycle of any submersible, and particularly the diver lock-out submersible where divers need to transfer under pressure to the compression chambers on board the mothership. Only with the introduction of the autonomous submarine, where the compression chamber is sited within the pressure hull, will the total sequence of pressurization, saturation, lock-out and subsequent decompression be carried out inside the pressure hull, irrespective of whether the craft is on the surface or submerged.

The compression chamber layouts are identical to those used with diving bells and the general arrangement of the chambers is determined by the general design of the ship. The chamber complexes are described in detail in Chapter 3, in relation to diving bells. In fact it is quite feasible for both diving bell and submersible to be operated from the same vessel, though not, of course, concurrently because of their different operating procedures. In this case the submersible lock-out divers and the bell divers would use the same compression chamber, mating to the same flange. The position of the transfer-under-pressure flange is critical. In diving bell transfers there are a number of options for mating. The basic shape of the bell may be spherical, oval or a vertically suspended cylinder. The coupling of the bell to a deck compression chamber can be either through the side of the chamber above or, in some specific instances, beneath the chamber. The bell handling systems for operations over the side or through the moonpool can be varied to allow a wide range of movements. Ingenious contortions allow the bell to be rotated and moved in a variety of ways which are not possible with a submersible. The most effective and standard handling system for launch and recovery of submersibles, described in detail later, is with an A-frame over the stern on the centre line. Ideally the transfer flange should also be on the centre line. This gives some measure of control over the movement of the ship. The design of the transfer flange coupling is more complicated than that of a diving bell connection because of the considerable weight of the submersible and because the lock-out transfer hatch is not at the centre of gravity. The unequal strains have to be compensated for in the support frame in which the submersible rests. The frame and the mountings on which the compression chambers rest must be rigid to avoid any displacement between the two and this poses difficulties in a vessel which is always flexing its internal structure as it moves in the water.

As stated before, the operational limitations of submersibles are set by the degree of efficiency of the handling system in launching and recovery. As the weather deteriorates so does the capacity of the handling system, particularly in recovery. As life is at risk, safety rules will terminate operations in certain sea states. Therefore, in general, it is fair to say that the submersible is only as efficient as its handling system. The submersible is a fragile craft on the surface and although the pressure hull is usually protected by an outer exostructure it cannot sustain contact with the mothership except where controlled by the handling system. The recovery has to be carried out quickly and therefore single-point suspension lifts are used. The point of suspension should be at the centre of gravity to reduce any movement of the submersible when hoisted clear of the water. In heavy seas there are serious problems caused by sea states with varying factors of amplitude, frequency and time interval. The normal procedure is for the submersible to surface well clear of the mothership which then manoeuvres her stern up to the submersible, both keeping headway into the wind and sea. To do this safely and well the mothership must be fitted with thrusters, propulsion and steering control which gives variable but fine control.

The recovery procedure in the water is in two parts prior to the actual hoist. A rubber dingy is launched from the mothership with a crew which includes a swimmer diver whose role is to board the submersible to make the recovery attachments. He is equipped as a diver in case he should be forced into and under the water. The first stage is to attach a towing rope to the bow of the submersible and whilst the mothership keeps a heading into the direction of the prevailing sea; the tow rope is hauled in, reducing the distance to a point where the swimmer can attach the hoist rope which is suspended beneath the extended A-frame over the stern of the mothership. In perfect weather conditions, where there is no surface movement on the sea, the towing rope can be dispensed with.

Hoisting out of the water must be steady and quick. With acceleration of up to $3g$ the system must be heave-compensated so that, as the submersible is lifted on waves, the slack on the rope is taken up to avoid excessive loads and stresses on all the moving parts and on the point of suspension. The submersible is hoisted into a semi-rigid position at the end of the A-frame which is then brought back over the stern of the mothership by hydraulic rams. Ideally the submersible should be in a rigid position after recovery from the sea, thereby ensuring that any movement is the same as that of the ship and that further movements to lower the submersible into its frame, and subsequently move over and onto the transfer coupling, are controlled.

The control position for launch and recovery, the launch being a reverse sequence of the recovery operation, is on or near the stern in full view of the operation over the stern. Whilst the ship movements are controlled by the Master the launch and recovery is controlled from the stern and there must be good coordination between the two positions. Clearly an operating procedure must be most carefully laid down, defining the precise responsibilities of the submersible crew and the diving crew and the various functions of surface support which cover ship control, launch and recovery and diving chamber control. Because of the risk of power failure the launch and recovery system should have a separate power supply alternative to the ship's main supply. Emergency diesel generators not used for any other purpose should be installed.

In the event of the ship having to be abandoned, the submersible can be launched as a hyperbaric lifeboat containing at least the complement of divers transferred from the deck compression chamber; the remainder, if any, may use the hyperbaric liferaft, if fitted, or air-transportable chamber.

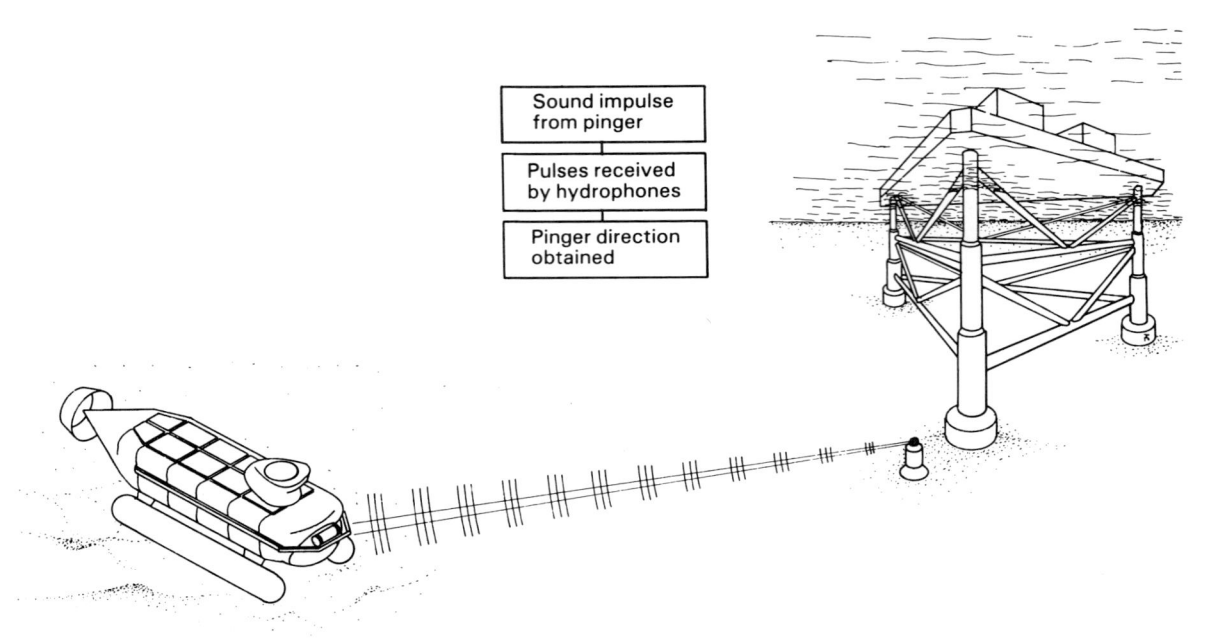

Fig. 7.4. Submersible navigation using the pinger.

Operational Procedures and Control

Although the submersible pilot has operational control and command of the submersible he is subject to overall control from the surface exercised via through-water communication. Similarly the diving supervisor on board the submersible, who remains with the pilot in the one-atmosphere capsule, is responsible for the way in which the diving operation is carried out and for the safety of the divers but is ultimately responsible to the pilot in command. The chain of command and the competence and responsibilities of the diving supervisor, the pilot and the operations supervisor on board the mothership need careful definition and should be set down in an operating procedures manual allowing the maximum flexibility compatible with safety. The control of the submersible is dependent on the quality of through-water communication and the positioning system used for navigation.

Navigation

Fig. 7.4 illustrates the simple arrangement whereby the submersible homes onto a transponder or 'pinger' which marks a known site. The equipment to establish accurately the depth and course of military submarines is fitted to submersibles but there is always the basic problem of calculating distance and position due to the free movement of water. Inertial navigation systems which give updated positions, and which are already used in military submarines, can be installed and they are invaluable for positioning whilst travelling over relatively long distances, such as surveying a pipeline route.

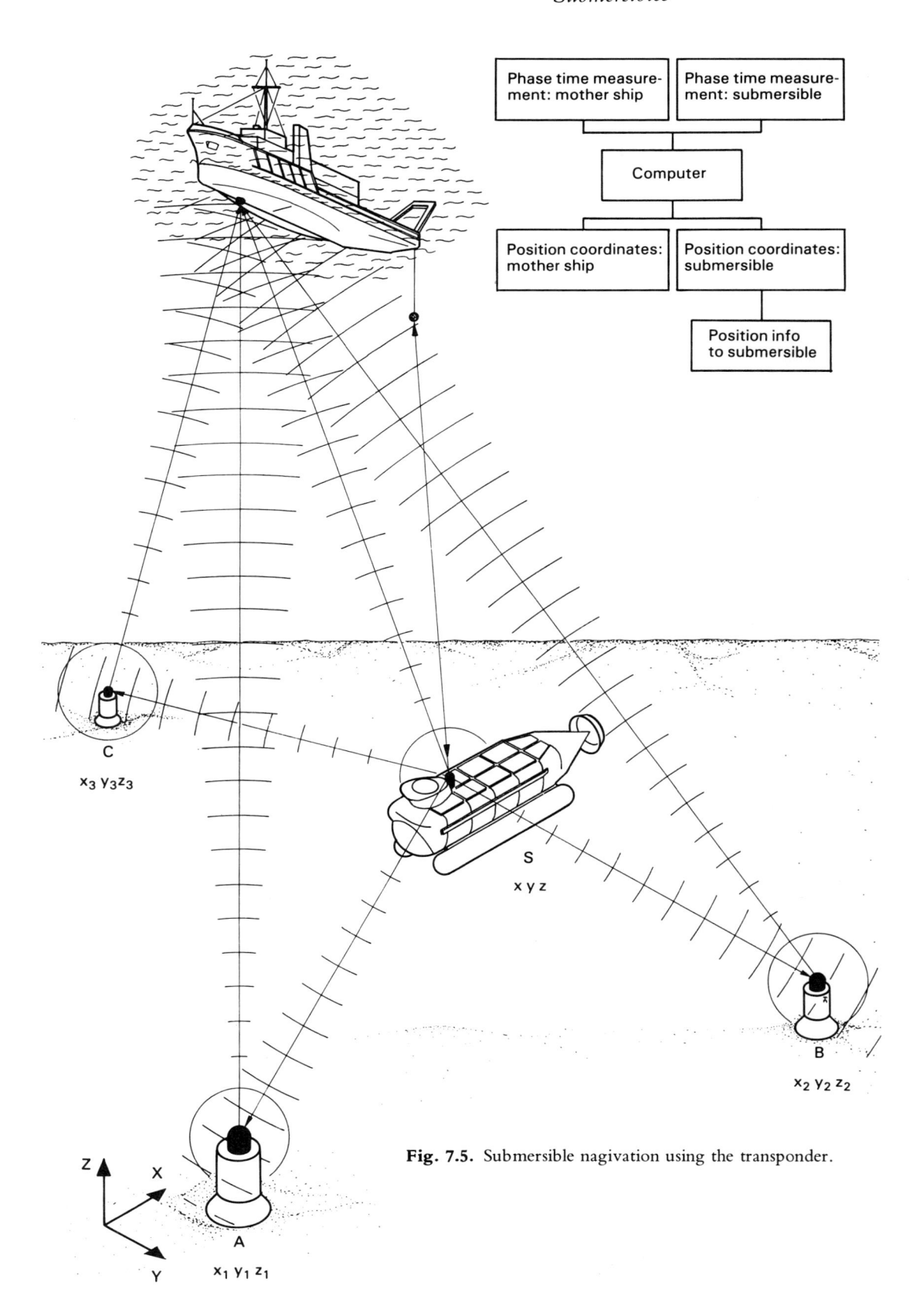

Submersibles 323

Fig. 7.5. Submersible nagivation using the transponder.

However, the bulk of submersible diver lock-out operations will be directed at specific work sites where the diver can operate from the submersible resting on the seabed. Therefore the submersible needs to navigate accurately within a small area in the certain knowledge of the position of seabed structures. The structures that are clearly relevant to this type of mission are seabed production units, platforms and flowlines, where collisions could be catastrophic. The use of selected transponders on the seabed can give the position of the submersible directly to the pilot as illustrated in Fig. 7.5. Alternatively the position of the submersible can be calculated in the mothership from the individual transponder transmissions and from the pinger beacon on the submersible itself. This information can be passed to the submersible with a course to steer to a target work site from the known position of the work site authenticated by a transponder on the target work site.

Communication

The communication plan illustrated in Fig. 7.6 is typical for a diver lock-out operation. Primary communications (shown in straight lines) are command lines and cover the direct through-water link between ship, submersible and diver. On the surface the direct communication is between the operations supervisor, bridge control, deck handling station and inflatable craft. Secondary lines of communication are used internally but may also carry separate primary communication for information. In the case of the primary command link between ship and submersible this information is useful to the handling personnel to coordinate the recovery of the craft.

Communication between the lock-out diver and the supervisor and standby is by line passed through the umbilical. The umbilical is normally restricted in length to about 20 m and in many cases the pilot can position the craft so that he can see the diver from the command sphere. Unlike the diving bell the diver can be seen and visual communications through hand signals and signboards can be used, assuming that there is good visibility. Heliox breathing mixtures are certain to be used and signals therefore have to be passed through an unscrambling unit to eradicate the voice distortion associated with breathing lighter helium gas.

Submersible Support Requirements

Gases

Compressed air, oxygen and diver breathing gases are carried aboard a submersible. Submersibles not fitted with a lock-out need to be stocked only with compressed air and oxygen. Compressed air is primarily needed to change the buoyancy of the submersible, to achieve the correct depth by blowing air into the ballast tanks and, ultimately, to surface the craft through controlled positive buoyancy.

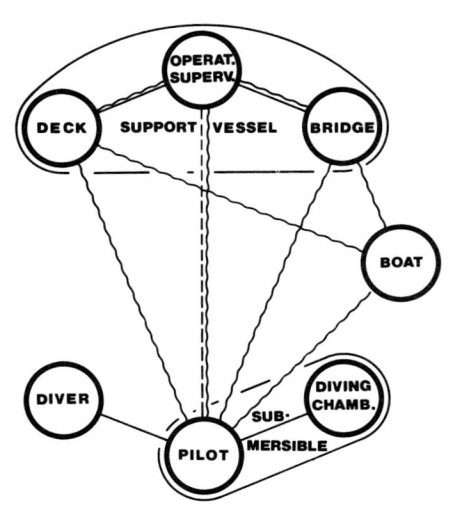

Fig. 7.6. An operational communication plan linking the submersible and its surface support stations.

The compressed air needs to comform to a laid down standard of purity for breathing with no trace of noxious gases or contaminant particles because it supplies air to the primary and emergency life-support systems for breathing in the one-atmosphere command sphere. Unlike military and autonomous commercial submarines, the submersible does not carry compressors to recharge whilst on the surface and must carry limited supplies in cylinders at pressures up to 300 bar. The endurance of the submersible is, as we have seen, limited effectively by battery power and gas. The recovery of the submersible between missions is followed by recharging of the air cylinder through a single manifold connection from ship's supply.

Oxygen is carried to maintain the content in the command sphere, together with a comparable supply of CO_2 absorbent to remove carbon dioxide. The amount of oxygen to be carried in cylinders is not substantial as the amount needed to support life is relatively small and emergency life-support systems are designed to provide sufficient oxygen and CO_2 absorption for at least 96 hours. The oxygen storage, piping and resupply whilst on board the mothership need to be carefully designed, taking into account the explosive nature of oxygen. A special transfer pump on board the mothership recharges the oxygen cylinders on board the submersible, also through a single charging manifold.

For pressurization of the lock-out chamber it is normal to carry sufficient gas to fill the chamber for a known depth and carry an additional reserve of 50%. As the depth is known the amount of gas needed is also known and, apart from flushing the chamber with clean breathing mixture where recovery on board is delayed for some reason before the divers are transferred to the deck compression chambers, there is no need to use the reserve except in an emergency. For short duration dives, where the divers are operating a bounce dive and the decompression period is short enough to be carried out inside the submersible diving sphere, the additional requirements to flush through with breathing gas need to be carefully considered taking into account any built-in CO_2 absorption unit and the breathing system used.

The selection of the breathing system for the diver and standby will have a very considerable effect on the gas supplies. The gas supply selected will be helium–oxygen or a mixture of helium, nitrogen and oxygen with the critical oxygen content predetermined. Although breathing gases can be mixed in the submersible by special mixing valves, the limitations of space and personnel normally preclude this method. Preset mixtures are provided through breathing masks. The breathing or life-support system can be open circuit, semi-closed or closed circuit. The open circuit, whereby the diver inhales and exhausts into the water, is very wasteful and will usually put an unacceptable demand on the supply from the submersible through the umbilical. With open-circuit breathing systems, the diving time will probably be reduced below an economically viable level owing to the need to keep within acceptable safety margins and maintain adequate reserves in the event of an emergency. In some cases very large gas tanks were installed in submersibles to overcome this problem. In semi-closed breathing systems all but a small proportion of the expired gas is recycled through CO_2 absorption units and blended with clean gas to maintain the correct oxygen content. A fully closed circuit, as its name implies, achieves the maximum recovery of all expired gases. These breathing systems are dicussed in more detail in Chapter 10.

For decompressing the divers over short schedules the control panels are outside the diving sphere and controlled by the supervisor. If the submersible is recovered on board the mothership before completion of the decompression the supply of gases for flushing should be switched from the submersible's own supply cylinders to a direct bypass from the ship's supply. This is a simple convenience to reduce the amount of recharging required.

Battery Charging

All conventional submersibles use battery-supplied electric power for propulsion and most ancillary services. For reasons of economy lead–acid batteries are used and mounted externally. The batteries require recharging after each mission and recovery but to achieve a quick turnaround used batteries can be exchanged for a fully charged set. If the batteries are charged in situ the maximum permissible charging current should be applied but the batteries should be pressure-ventilated to avoid a dangerous build-up of hydrogen and oxygen. If batteries are charged whilst out of the submersible and on board the mothership the same precautions must apply and it is usual to have a special battery-charging compartment. An important design consideration should be the quick and safe transport of the batteries to and from the pods on the submersible. Batteries constitute a very large proportion of the weight of the submersible and batteries weighing several tonnes need careful handling, especially on a moving deck. If divers are under pressure inside the submersible the ship's electrical power should be fed directly into the heating system to keep the divers warm and avoid using battery power until it is essential to do so.

Fresh Water

Sea-water has a damaging effect on nearly all materials and, even with the most careful selection of compatible non-corrosive metals for use in the building of a submersible, there will always be the danger of deterioration in a complex structure. Washing down with fresh water will help to avoid this and a suitable fresh water supply should be available for hosing down the submersible when recovered onto the deck of the mothership.

Ship Maintenance Facilities

Most motherships designed to operate submersibles will have a hangar or enclosed space to which the submersible is moved for all inspection, maintenance and repair work and also for stowage whilst on passage or otherwise out of use. Ideally the hangar workshop should allow at least 1 m, preferably 1.5 m, of working space around the hull. The hangar should be fitted with charging connections for air, life-support gases, fresh water and power. If the hangar is large enough the work benches and repair facilities can be arranged around the submersible with adjacent spare part stores. Well equipped clean workshop areas are essential for the repair and servicing of electronic equipment and life-support equipment. To reduce corrosion the hangar and workshop space should be well ventilated and heated. Careful attention paid to the design of the hangar, workshop and back-up services will have a very direct influence on the manpower needed to support submersible operations and not least on the serviceability and efficiency of the submersible.

Motherships

The relatively swift introduction of submersibles into off-shore use precluded the development of specially designed ships. Initially, in the early 1970s, the most suitable vessel was the deep water stern fishing trawler which was large enough to be capable of operating in all but the worst weather conditions. Although the submersibles are not intended to be capable of operating in poor weather conditions the ships were large and strong enough to accommodate a large crew and to launch and recover the submersible from a relatively stable platform. The launch and recovery of heavy fishing gear over the stern was comparable to the launch and recovery of a submersible over the stern using an A-frame. Off-shore support vessels have been adapted as motherships using the large deck area aft for the hangar and workshop area and an A-frame over the stern.

Diver lock-out submersibles require a considerable area owing to the size and complexity of the compression chamber complex with all the ancilliary requirements and additional personnel. A saturation diving complex to support submersible lock-out operations will increase the manpower by up to 20 to include the divers, supervisors and technicians. With this additional load it is difficult satisfactorily to convert stern trawlers or off-shore support vessels to carry out the dual function of submersible operations and diving operations. If a diving bell, making use of the compression chambers on board and thereby adding another useful dimension to the overall capability of the vessel, is added a large vessel, preferably purpose-built, is essential.

Submersible Propulsion and Power Requirements

A submersible is a tool operating within a small area rather than over a large area and the design of the propulsion unit takes this into account. The poor visibility usually experienced at deep depths on the bottom restricts the speed of the submersible to the extent that it must be able to stop within visibility distance, particularly vital when operating in the vicinity of under-water obstructions, whether natural or man-made. The visibility conditions in the North Sea limit the speed over the ground to about 1–1.5 knots. In addition, reserve performance is

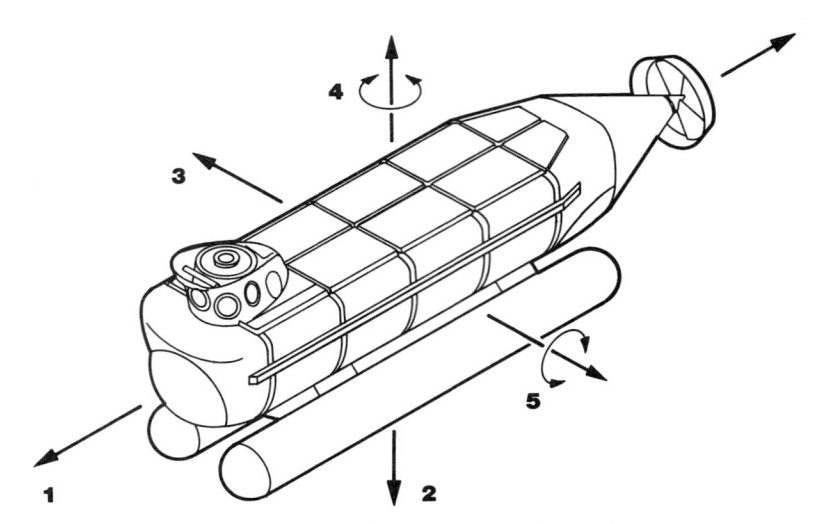

Fig. 7.7. Directional movement using thrusters and propellors.

required to overcome bottom currents and manoeuvre in these conditions whilst operating at a work site. Furthermore, the power required for propulsion escalates rapidly with a modest increase in speed. To double the speed may demand an eight-fold increase in driving force.

A submersible hull can be designed for minimum resistance to water, but without any of the exostructure and equipment that is essential to the submersible in order to fulfil its function as a workboat. By fitting the essential equipment, such as manipulators, lighting, navigational and recovery equipment, the resultant resistance to water flowing over the submersible is considerable. The lock-out submersible must be able to move freely in all planes both fore and aft and transversely. Fig. 7.7 illustrates the various propulsion units and thrusters. A single propellor is designed to move the submersible in a direct line and is not suitable for manoeuvring. The precise control needed for operating the submersible inside or near off-shore structures demands additional thrusters or two propellors as illustrated in Fig. 7.8. Whilst movement ahead and astern can be achieved by the configurations A, B and C in Fig. 7.8, sideways movement can only be achieved by using side thrusters. The Bruker *Mermaid* submersible shown in Fig. 7.9 has a main propellor which can swivel, in addition to thrusters, to give greater control and manoeuvrability. In addition to the main propellor, itself capable of a 180° swivel action, the submersible may have transverse thrusters on the bow and stern and vertical thrusters on the bow and possibly in the midships section.

Battery power driving electric motors is the conventional source of energy in small submersibles. Although most submersibles incorporate the electric motor inside the pressure hull, there are certain drawbacks in designing efficient propeller shaft seals and the space taken up by the motor inside the pressure hull. The design of pressure-tight electric motors outside the pressure hull driving propellers which can also swivel, as shown in Fig. 7.9, opens up new possibilities.

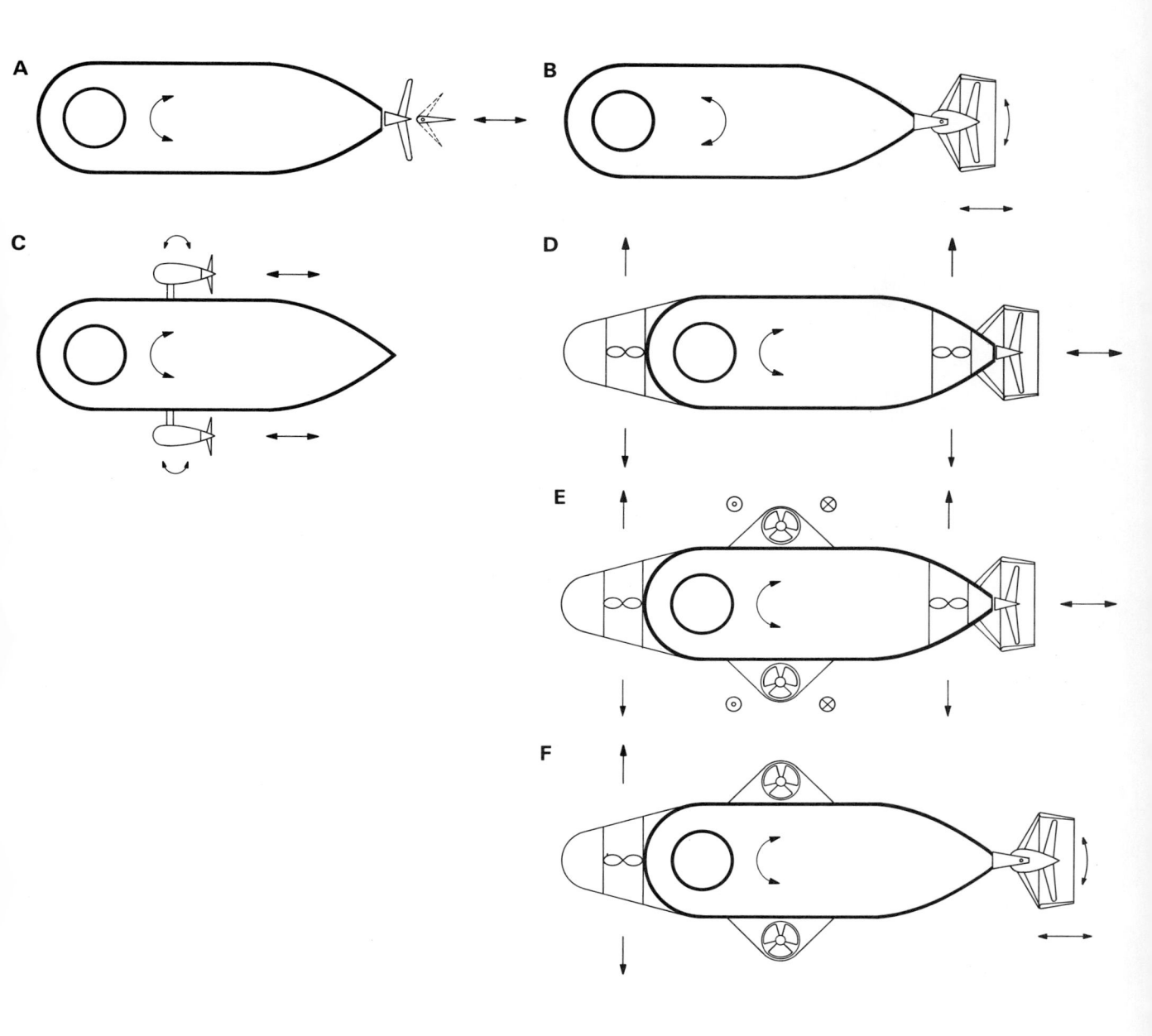

Fig. 7.8. Design considerations for propellors and thrusters to allow submersible manoeuvrability.

- **A** Main propulsion, rigid stern-mounted propellor. Movement is in the fore and aft axis only
- **B** Main propulsion, stern-mounted swivel propellor adjustable by up to 180° in the horizontal plane, allowing propulsion and steerage
- **C** Two side-mounted rotatable and reversible thrusters
- **D** Main propulsion, stern-mounted propellor. Bow and stern horizontal transverse thrusters
- **E** Main propulsion stern-mounted. Bow and stern horizontal transverse thrusters. Port and starboard midships thrusters
- **F** Main propulsion stern-mounted swivel propellors adjustable by up to 180° in the horizontal plane, allowing propulsion and steerage. Bow horizontal transverse thruster. Port and standard midships thrusters

Fig. 7.9. The Bruker *Mermaid* class submersibles.

To prevent the water getting into the motor the units are filled with oil. Attenuating current motors are much simpler to build and strong. Filled with water, these motors must be driven by rotary current. Hydraulic drive motors can be very satisfactory. They have some advantages over electric motors, for instance smaller size, simpler control and faster response, but also disadvantages. Commercial hydraulic motors are generally unsuitable for use under water as they have to be modified to withstand pressure differences.

Electric power is compatible with nearly all propulsion and for all lighting and instrumentation and is the exclusive power source in all deep submersibles. As hydraulics are effectively used for many exterior functions such as manipulators, they are also used to provide steerage. Fig. 7.10 shows the hydraulic plan for a modern lock-out submersible with various functions controlled by hydraulic power including manipulators, pan and tilt units, main propulsion, jetting and power tools, steering motors, trimming, retractable support and the movement of the diver lock-out hatch.

Pressure Hulls

Submarine hulls are designed primarily to protect the boat's crew and equipment and, with their displacement volume, provide the necessary buoyancy. As depths increase the proportion of hull deadweight increases and the boat progressively loses its inherent buoyancy. Pressure hulls may be designed spherically or cylindrically. By a weight factor of two the spherical is more economical than the cylindrical. The sphere, however, is more expensive to construct. In submersibles the limit for cylindrical design is about 500 m, although in most cases submersibles are built around spherical pressure hulls owing to their higher payloads. High-quality steels are normally used but also aluminium, titanium, acrylic and glass-

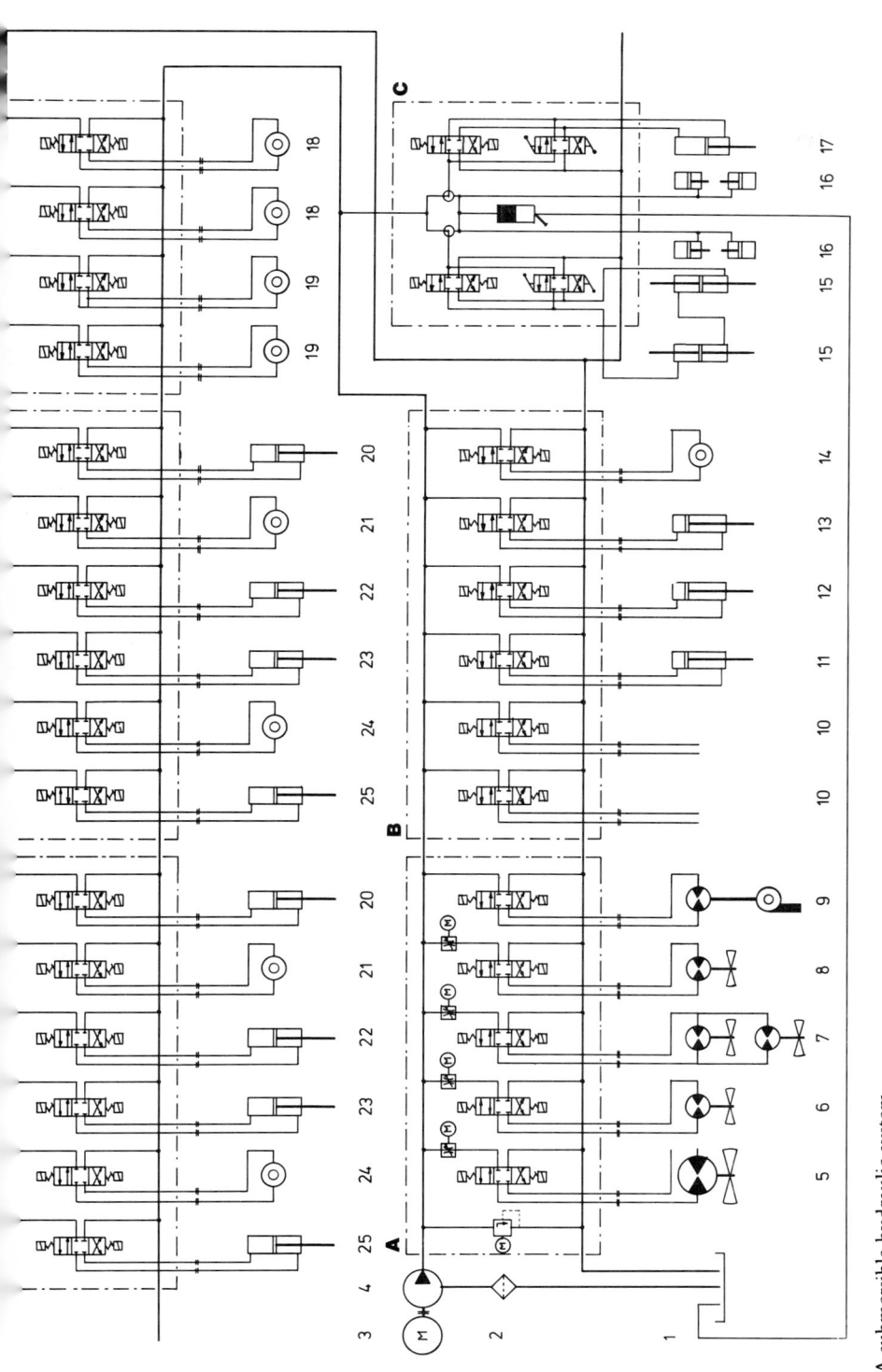

Fig. 7.10. A submersible hydraulic system.

A Valve block for propulsion units and water-jet pump, hydraulic pressure adjustment
B Valve block for hydraulic equipment
C Valve block for emergency operation of the trimming system and hydraulic releases
D Valve block for rotary drives

1 hydraulic fluid tank
2 filter
3 electric motor
4 hydraulic pump
5 main thruster
6 lateral thruster
7 vertical thrusters
8 lateral thruster
9 water-jet pump
10 spare connection
11 lifting cylinder for jet
12 rotary drive for jet
13 anchor winch
14 steering gear
15 trimming cylinder
16 release cylinders
17 hatch actuator
18 pan and tilt, search light
19 pan and tilt, TV camera
20 manipulator, upper arm
21 manipulator, elbow joint
22 manipulator, lower arm
23 manipulator, wrist
24 manipulator, claw rotation
25 manipulator, claw opening

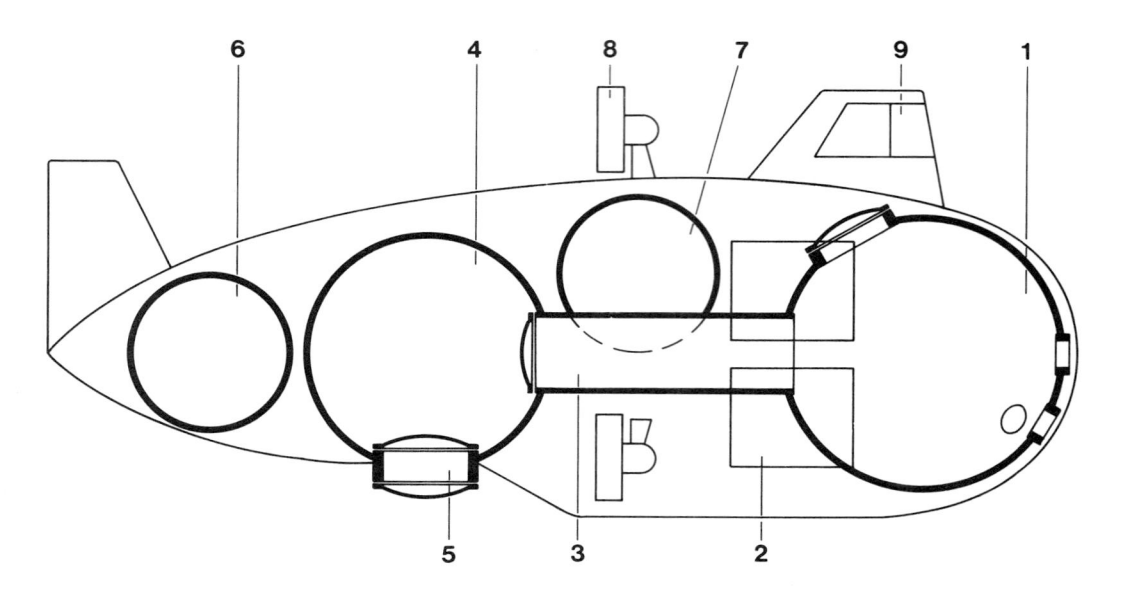

Fig. 7.11. Hull configuration of the *Beaver* Mark IV, SDL-1 submersible.

1. observation and control capsule
2. hydraulics
3. connecting trunk
4. diver lock-out chamber
5. diver lock-out hatches
6. trim tank
7. variable ballast and trim tanks
8. three propulsion thrusters: ports, starboard and topside
9. floodable sail

reinforced plastic. Acrylic domes are used for observation windows in the control sphere.

In lock-out submersibles, because of the need for the diver to operate in water at the ambient pressure, there is a pressure compartment, which is separate from the pilot's control capsule, which is always at atmospheric pressure. The diving pressure chamber needs to be capable of operating at a greater or lesser pressure than the outside ambient pressure, depending on different circumstances and, when designing doors, trunking and windows, this needs to be taken into account. Although the pilot's compartment can be separate and have no access to the diving sphere, relying entirely on communications, it is usual and preferable for the two compartments to be attached or connected by trunking and pressure-proof doors. By connecting the two compartments the diving supervisor and pilot have more control over the diving operation. If divers are not embarked and the submersible is being used in a non-diver role the additional space can be utilized with additional personnel or equipment or both. Some general hull configurations of up-to-date lock-out submersibles are briefly described.

Beaver Mark IV/SDL-1 (Fig. 7.11)
The pilot's capsule and diving chamber are spherically connected by a

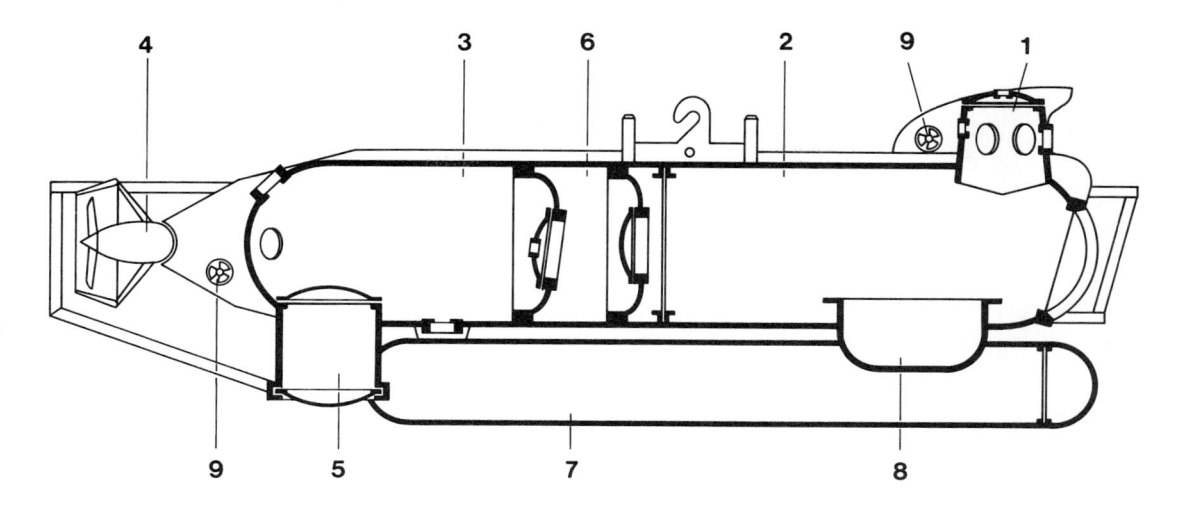

Fig. 7.12. Hull configuration of the *Mermaid* III and IV submersibles.

1. conning tower
2. observation and control chamber
3. diver lock-out chamber
4. stern-mounted swivel propellor·adjustable 180°
5. diver lock-out hatches
6. transfer chamber
7. battery pods
8. electro-hydraulic pump
9. lateral transverse thrusters, bow and stern

trunking. A one way pressure-tight door closes on the inside of the diving sphere, retaining atmospheric pressure in the pilot's command capsule. The diving compartment has two one-way pressure-tight doors through which the divers lock out and both, for safety reasons, need to be secured irrespective of the prevailing pressure conditions. The *SDL-1* is fitted for, but not with, a mating skirt at the lock-out point to lock onto a damaged submarine and rescue the crew.

Mermaid III, IV (Fig. 7.12)

A single cylindrical pressure chamber with a dished end at the stern and an acrylic observation dome at the bow is divided into three compartments. A small inter-lock separates the diving compartment from the pilot's compartment. This small lock allows personnel to be locked into the diving compartment without changing the pressure of that compartment but this procedure is only considered in an emergency to enable help to reach the divers. The diameter of all the compartments is 1250 mm and the length of the inter-lock compartment is determined by the space needed for one person and the need to close the door to maintain pressure integrity. A medical lock is fitted into the bulkhead between the diver's compartment and the inter-lock.

The diving compartment is designed to accommodate two divers who can stretch full length in reasonable comfort, a great advantage of the cylindrical design over the spherical design, particularly in an emergency where divers are unable to transfer under pressure to a

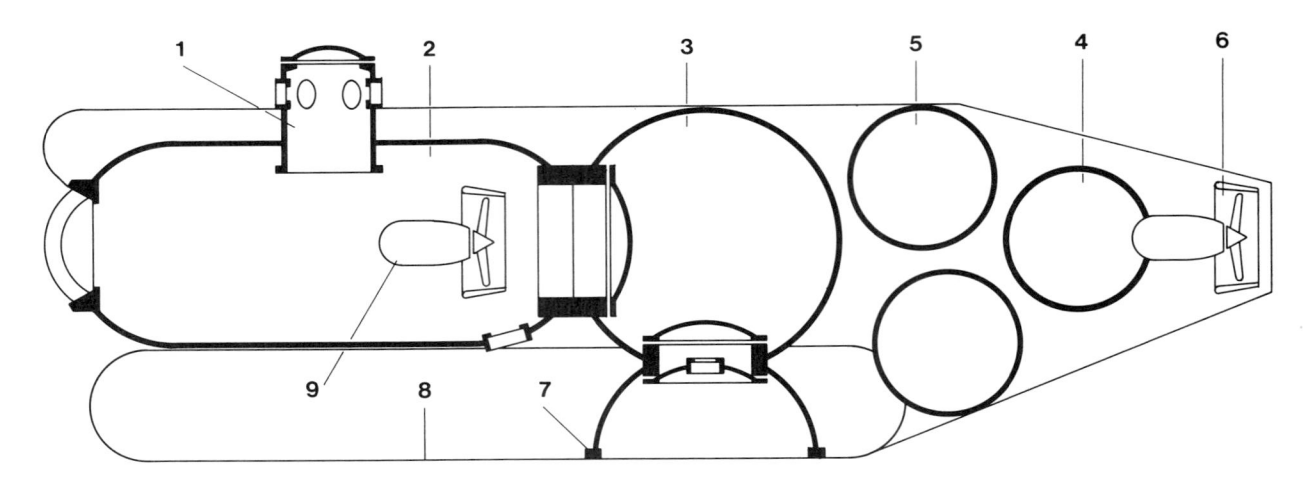

Fig. 7.13. Hull configuration of the *Taurus* submersible.
1. conning tower
2. observation and control chamber
3. diver lock-out chamber
4. propulsion chamber
5. sea water trim tanks
6. propellor
7. mating skirt for dry or wet transfer
8. battery pods
9. two side-mounted thrusters

Fig. 7.14. The interior of a diver lock-out submersible, with the pilot's command position in the foreground with instrumentation and electrical controls. In the rear is the hydraulic system. Beyond is the transfer compartment to the diving chamber.

Fig. 7.15. The diver lock-out chamber viewed through the transfer lock with two pressure doors.

mothership compression complex and are obliged to decompress inside the submersible. The lock-out hatch and cylindrical trunking are sited in the stern. The trunking is fitted with two pressure doors and designed to mate onto a ship's compression chamber for the transfer of the divers. The outside door, being a double-sided pressure door, is heavier than a one-way pressure door and facilitates a quick connection onto a compression chamber. Five observation windows, each of 170 mm diameter, are fitted in the conning tower. In common with other submersibles the large acrylic window with a diameter of 1100 mm allows the pilot very good observation and in diving operations allows the supervisor to see the diver working if the submersible is correctly positioned.

The hull is made in sections flanged together with O-ring seals and this modular concept allows alterations and modifications to be made to equipment and even to the modules themselves.

The hydraulic electric motor is inside the pressure hull, allowing access for the maintenance of the electric motor and partially set into the space below the pilot's compartment. Whilst allowing access to the motor from inside the hull, it does not take up any of the limited space inside the compartment.

Two battery pods are fitted directly onto the hull.

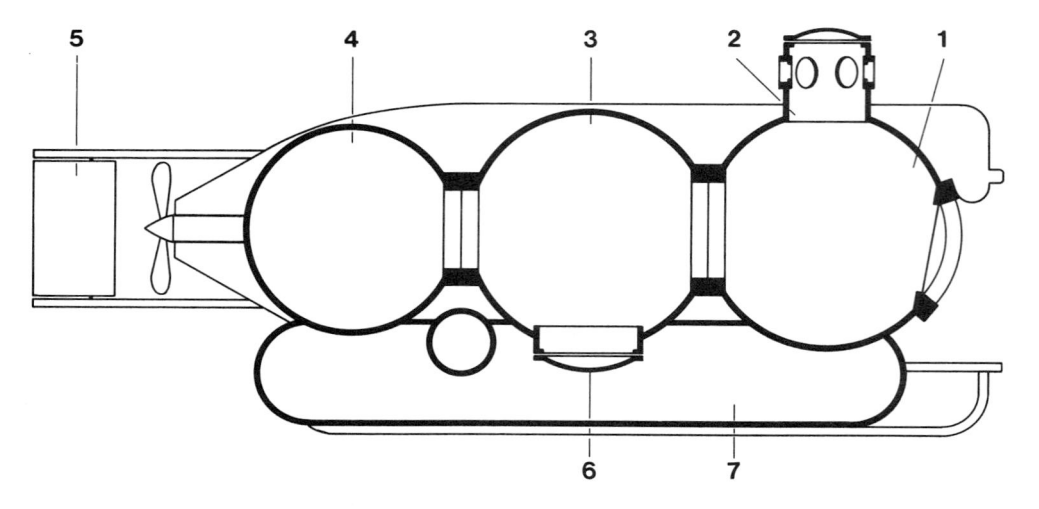

Fig. 7.16. Hull configuration of the *PC16* submersible.

    1 observation and control capsule
    2 conning tower
    3 dry transfer chamber
    4 propulsion chamber
    5 rudder
    6 dry transfer mating hatch
    7 battery pod

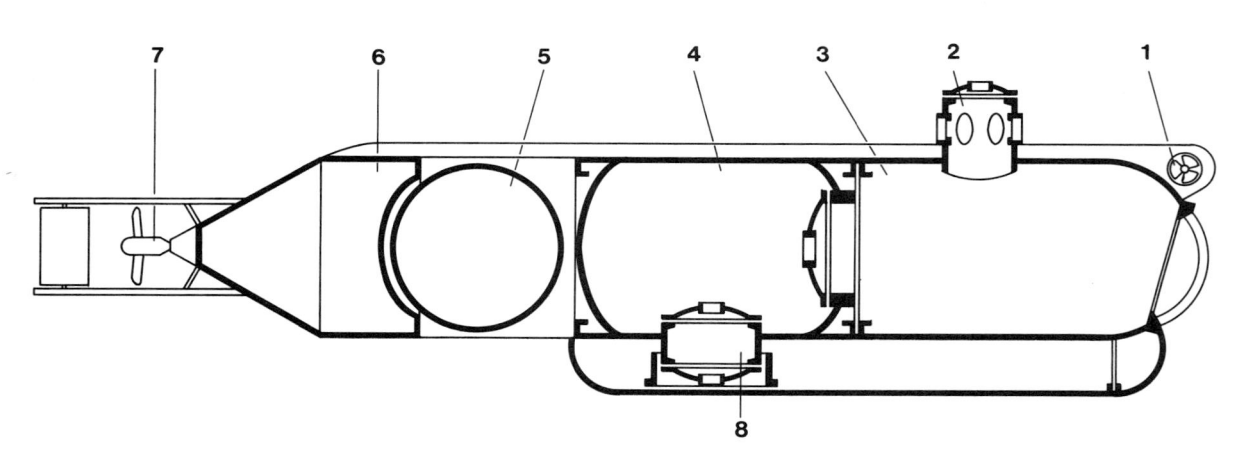

Fig. 7.17. Hull configuration of the *PC15/LR1* submersible.

    1 bow lateral/transverse thruster
    2 conning tower
    3 observation and control chamber
    4 diver lock-out chamber
    5 mixed gas sphere
    6 propulsion compartment
    7 propellor
    8 diver lock-out hatch

Taurus (Fig. 7.13)

The *Taurus* lock-out submersible is the largest of its generation, weighing 24 tonnes and combining a cylindrical pressure hull with a spherical diving chamber. The cylindrical compartment can accommodate three command personnel, including the diving super-

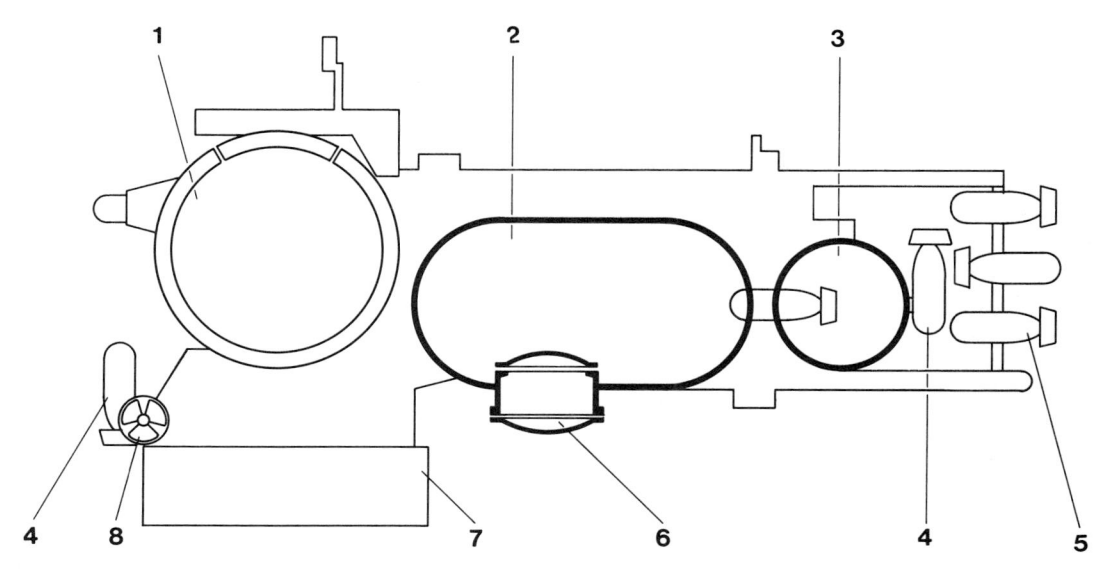

Fig. 7.18. Hull configuration of *Johnson Sea Link* submersible.

1. observation and command capsule
2. diver lock-out chamber
3. mixed gas sphere
4. bow and stern vertical thrusters
5. three propulsion thrusters
6. diver lock-out hatches
7. battery pod
8. bow lateral thruster

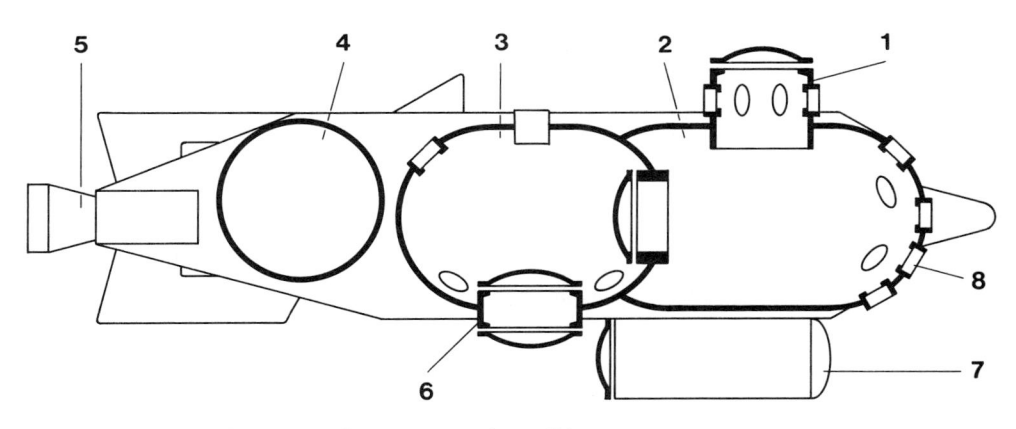

Fig. 7.19. Hull configuration of *Deep Diver* submersible.

1. conning tower
2. observation and command capsule
3. diver lock-out chamber
4. gas storage sphere
5. 180° main propulsion unit
6. diver lock-out hatches
7. battery pod
8. viewports

visor, and the life-support controls for the diving chamber. The lock-out sphere has a diameter of 2150 mm and is connected to the control compartment through a one-way pressure door. The lock-out hatch has two one-way pressure doors and can be fitted with a skirt which is designed to mate with a subsea capsule or submarine to transfer personnel either under pressure or at atmospheric pressure.

PC 16 (Fig. 7.16)

The design is based on three spheres, of which the centre sphere is the diving compartment. The spheres, each 1800 mm in diameter, are flanged together and separated by doors. Although designed for dry transfer the submersible can be operated for diver lock-out. The *PC 18* was more specifically designed for lock-out diver operations as well as dry transfer operations.

Buoyancy Control

On the surface the submersible must be able to keep a stable trim with sufficient reserve buoyancy. It must allow at least two swimmers to ride the submersible for the purpose of launch and recovery. Stability is also important when the submersible is towed on the surface.

Whilst submerged, the craft must be able to achieve positive, negative and neutral buoyancy. Defined buoyancy under different load conditions, depending on the mission and water density, will require variable system with water ballast tanks.

Ballast tanks maybe either non-pressure-proof, often referred to as soft ballast tanks, or pressure-proof, frequently called hard ballast tanks.

Soft ballast tanks are mainly used on the surface and will add considerably to the submersible's reserve buoyancy and stability. They are usually constructed with openings on the bottom through which water can enter or be discharged. To flood the tanks it is sufficient to open vent valves on top of the tanks. Owing to the hydrostatic pressure difference between bottom slots and vent valves, the air escapes and is replaced by water. To blow the tanks, compressed air is forced into the tanks and displaces the water through the openings on the bottom. The interior of soft ballast tanks must always be at ambient pressure since any larger differential pressure would lead to the rupture or collapse of the tank body. They are totally unsuitable to adjust buoyancy at depth as the air volume inside varies strongly with the ambient pressure according to Boyle's law. As a rule, soft ballast tanks are completely flooded before the submersible descends and care should be taken that no air remains inside. They should not be blown before the submersible has surfaced except in an emergency, when an uncontrolled fast ascent is acceptable. In this respect it is interesting that soft ballast tanks have been designed for automatic blowing if the submersible should exceed its maximum work depth so that positive buoyancy for surfacing is achieved. The same system is also automatically blown if a dead-man's handle is not operated periodically. The soft ballast tank system should be designed to consist of several separated tanks so that in the event of damage only one tank is lost. To avoid damage the ballast tanks, where exposed, should have

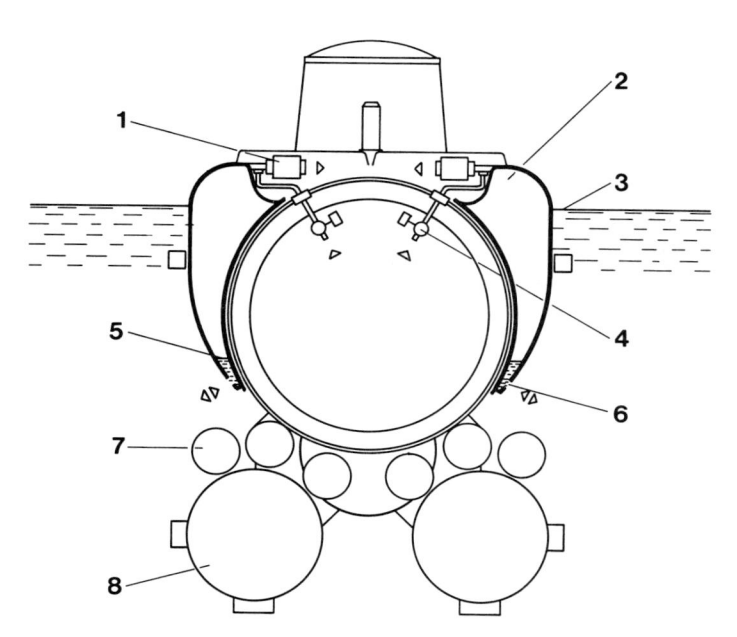

Fig. 7.20. A typical arrangement for main free-flooding ballast tanks, as fitted to the *Mermaid* class submersibles.

1. main ballast tank vent valves
2. main ballast tank, port side
3. water level when surfaced
4. main ballast tank blow valves
5. water level in tanks when blown
6. inlet/outlet valves
7. gas cylinders
8. battery pods

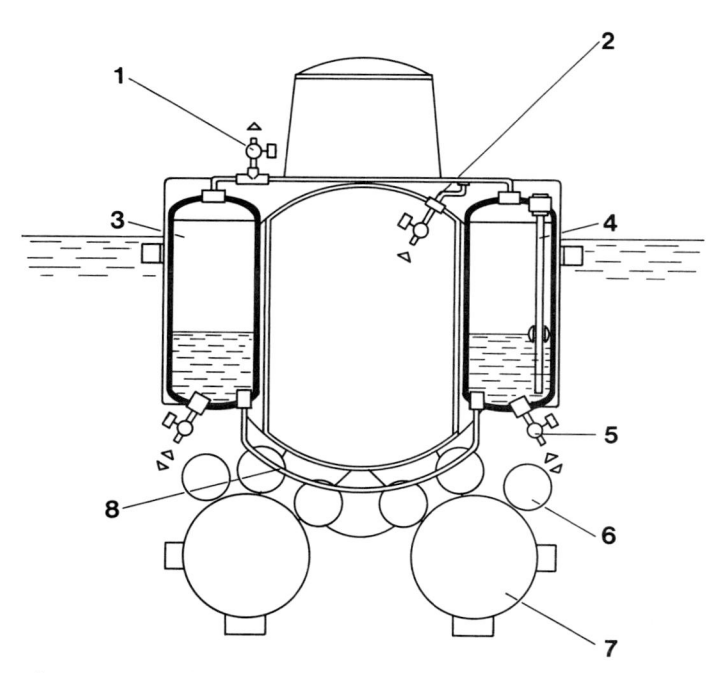

Fig. 7.21. Hard ballast pressure tanks with common vent valve and cross-equalization.

1. main ballast vent valve
2. main ballast blow valve
3. hard ballast tank
4. water level indicator
5. inlet/outlet valves, solenoid and manual
6. gas cylinders
7. battery pods
8. cross-connection for equalization between ballast tanks

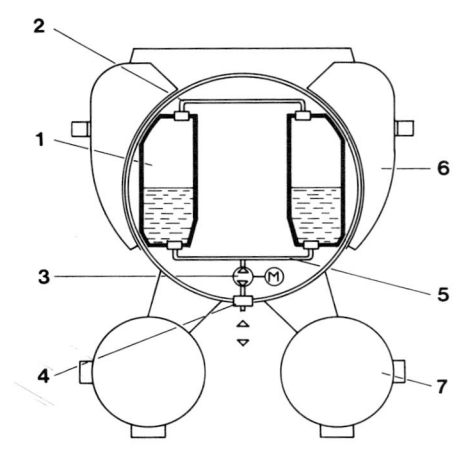

Fig. 7.22. Alternative design for a hard ballast system. Ballast tanks are located inside the submersible's pressure hull. They can be drained and flooded by a pump.

1 ballast tank
2 equalizing line
3 drain pump
4 water inlet/outlet
5 connection line
6 soft ballast tank
7 battery pod

some structural protection wherever feasible. The tanks themselves should be strengthened as far as is possible. Glass-reinforced plastic has been used successfully as a construction material.

Hard ballast tanks have an internal pressure which can be different from the ambient pressure and the amount of water ballast will not vary as long as the valves are kept closed. They are therefore utilized to adjust and maintain a desired buoyancy condition when the craft is submerged. The tanks can be either inside or outside the hull and are emptied for ascending or flooded for descending. To reduce the water ballast, compressed air is blown into the tanks and as soon as the pressure is above ambient, water can be discharged through an outlet valve. It is also possible to pump ballast, but the disadvantage is in the use of power which is restricted. In this case, however, internal ballast tanks do not have to be pressure-proof as no pressure is required inside the tank to force the water out. Pumping will become an advantage at greater depths where the volume ratio of air storage tanks relative to ballast tanks becomes less favourable. Pumping rates tend to be slow unless greater power sources are used and this may not be economical. Conventional hard ballast tanks have vent valves on top and inlets on the bottom which are actuated to permit water to enter the tank, very much in the same way as in the case of the soft ballast tanks when pressure is near ambient. Obviously the vent valve will also work as water inlet as long as the external pressure is higher.

Ballast tanks can be pressure-proof, without any outlet except to allow oil to be pumped into a bladder against the ambient pressure, thus creating variations in buoyancy. This method can be adapted for operating in very deep depths.

Thorough consideration should be given to the design of piping, valves, pumps and other components. Ballast control is vital for the safety of the submersible and a satisfactory degree of reliability and redundancy must be ensured.

Uneven distribution of water ballast can affect the trim of the submersible. The tanks should therefore be placed close to the submersible's centre of gravity to keep this effect small and water levels should be adjusted equally. Cross-connection of tanks will automatically lead to water level equalization but also reduces redundancy in case of leakage unless the tanks can be separated by in-line shut-off valves.

It is advisable to install water level gauges in hard ballast tanks. The precise negative or positive buoyancy can be calculated from the water level readings and this may be indispensable when manoeuvering in neutral or near-neutral buoyancy. One proven design works on the basis of a float with an integrated permanent magnet which is moved up and down a rod by the water level. The rod contains a chain of magnetically operated miniature switches and the level is thus transmitted to a read-out.

The ability to ballast and stabilize a submersible in one position, usually on the seabed, is generally not critical even when operating in a current, as the ballasting arrangements are normally more than adequate to compensate for any alteration of buoyancy and movement of weight. However, in diver lock-out operations the weight of a fully dressed diver would be in the region of 110–150 kg and the sudden exit of a diver considerably lightens the submersible. There may also be a gradual increase in buoyancy due to the consumption of gas, especially if an open-circuit breathing system is used. To exclude the danger of the craft ascending when the diver leaves the lock-out chamber, compensating flooding tanks can be fitted near or around the lock-out hatch. This is preferable to allowing the water level to rise inside the diving compartment, thereby reducing even further the very limited space. Another good solution is illustrated in Fig. 7.23 using the volume inside the lock-out trunking which can be flooded to certain levels. In combination with the variable ballast, this is sufficient to compensate for any increase in buoyancy. It also has the further advantage of facilitating exit and re-entry of the divers.

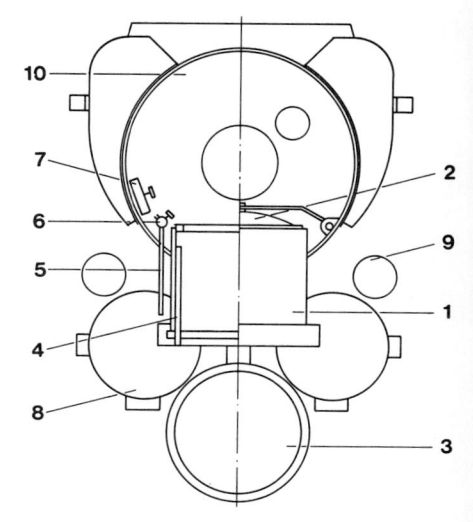

Fig. 7.23. Diver lock-out trunk at the rear end of the lock-out compartment, with internal one-way pressure hatch and external two-way pressure hatch with bayonet. The trunk is flooded for buoyancy compensation before the diver locks out.

1. lock-out trunk
2. internal hatch
3. external hatch with bayonet lock
4. water level sensor
5. pressure equalizing line
6. shut-off valve
7. controls for external hatch
8. battery pod
9. gas storage tanks
10. diver lock-out compartment

Solid Ballast

In the case of the surface vessels the displacement of the under-water section produces a buoyancy which is equal to the weight of the ship. When additional weight is added this simply leads to an increase in draught. In a submersible the regulation of the states of positive, neutral and negative buoyancy can be controlled up to a point by the variable ballasting systems but they are limited in their capacity to operate and maintain this balance from positive to negative condition without becoming unstable. To utilize the buoyancy tanks to their full capacity in controlling positive and negative buoyancy, correct amounts of solid ballast are necessary. The solid ballast is either stowed inside the hull or mounted externally and can be altered whilst in board to take account of the addition or removal of equipment and crew. Additional heavy equipment may need a reduction of solid ballast, bearing in mind that any ballast and other weights must be positoned to keep an even trim throughout the boat. If the solid ballast is mounted externally it should be capable of being released on command from the pilot as an emergency device.

Trimming Systems

An unequal weight distribution along the longitudinal axis of the submarine will affect the inclination of the craft and therefore its trim. This alteration of trim may be intentional or unintentional and a trimming system is incorporated, with a variety of methods, to transfer weight forward or aft and thereby alter the inclination. In a neutral hovering attitude the submersible centre of gravity is vertically below its centre of buoyancy. The trim of a submarine is effected by altering the centre of buoyancy as well as shifting the centre of gravity. The usual trimming system effectively moves the centre of gravity, as being the centre of mass, by moving weights along the centre line or longitudinal axis, either externally or

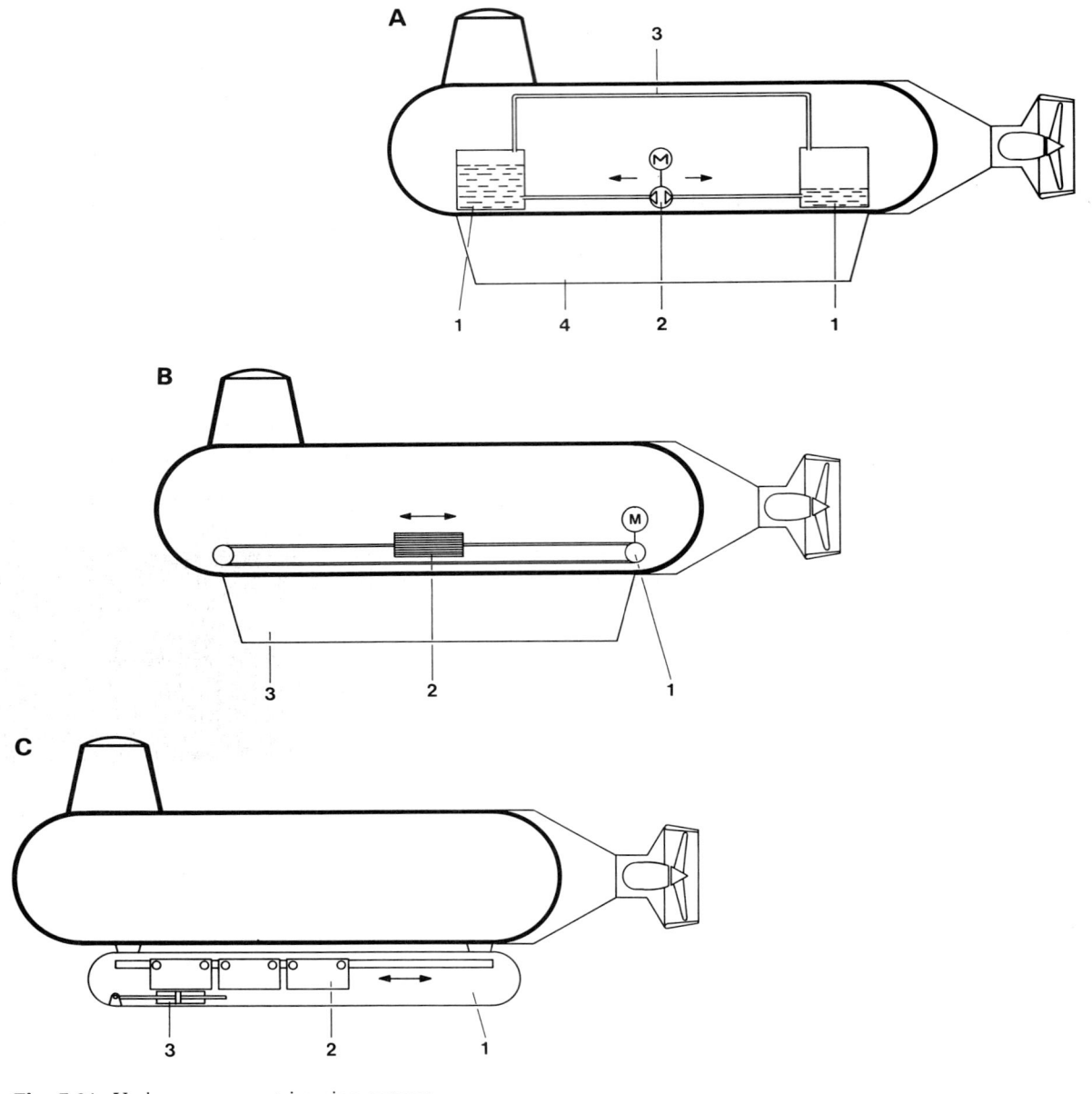

Fig. 7.24. Various common trimming systems.

    A Internal trimming tanks. Water is pumped from fore to aft. This system takes up valuable space inside the submersible

        1 trimming tank   3 equalizing system
        2 trimming pump   4 battery pods

    B Moveable trim weight activated by a chain, spindle or hydraulic cylinder. Also takes up considerable space

        1 chain track   3 battery pods
        2 trimming weight

    C The main batteries inside the battery pods are moved by hydraulic cylinders, also inside the pods, to allow trimming. Large trim loads can be achieved without losing payload or space. Batteries can be exchanged quickly

        1 battery space   3 hydraulic trimming cylinder
        2 moveable batteries

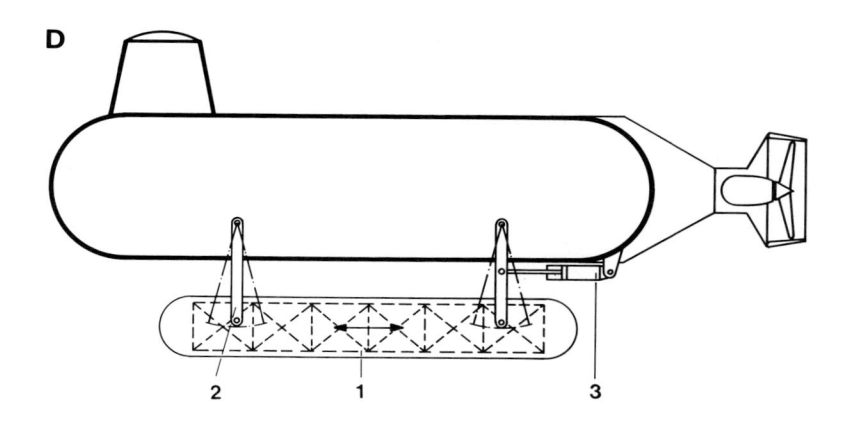

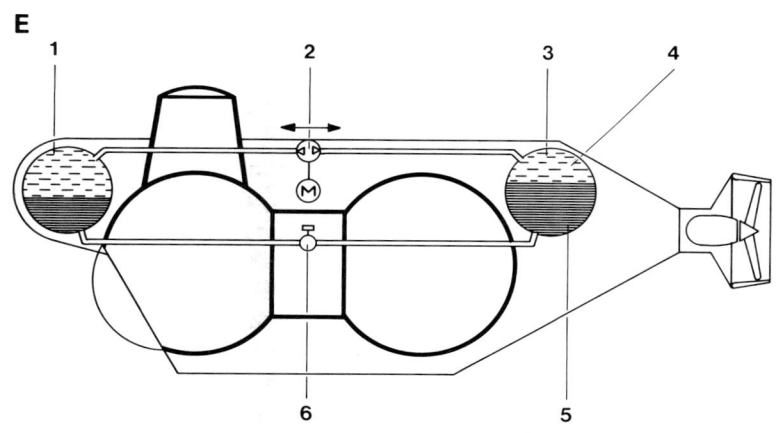

Fig. 7.24. *continued*

D Battery pods are hinged and can be moved by hydraulic cylinders or other means. No payload or internal space is lost, but the system is relatively complicated as heavy hinge mechanisms are required

1 battery pod
2 hinged supports
3 hydraulic trimming cylinder

E Trimming tanks are located outside the pressure hull at both ends of the submersible. They are partially filled with mercury. The remaining volume and the equalizing lines are filled with oil which can be pumped to the fore or aft tank. No space is required inside the hull but payload is lost owing to the additional weight of the mercury. Mercury is also toxic

1 forward trim tank
2 trimming pump
3 rear trim tank
4 oil
5 mercury
6 isolating valve

internally. Crudely this can be done by a crew member moving his position in the submersible. Most trim systems, however, function either by moving solid ballast or by pumping liquids as illustrated variously in Fig. 7.24.

Trim tanks, using liquids as the movable weight, are usually sited as far forward and aft as possible, either externally or internally. The liquid is pumped from one tank to another. Water, oil and also mercury, because of its high specific gravity, are used. If mercury is

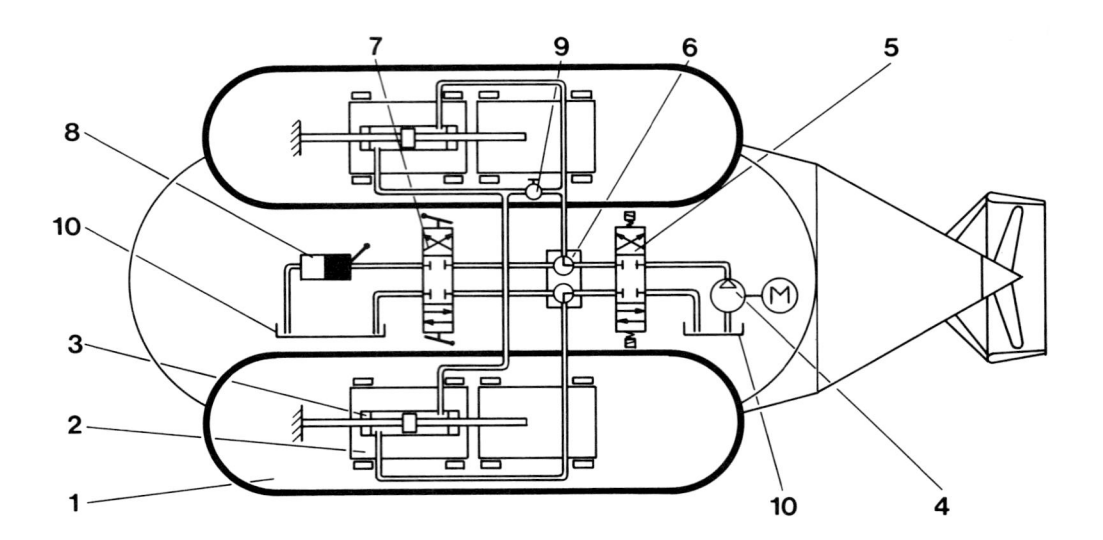

Fig. 7.25. A trimming system using hydraulic movement of the main battery.

1 battery pod
2 battery container
3 trimming cylinder
4 hydraulic pump
5 solenoid directional valve
6 selection valve motor/manual operation
7 manual directional valve
8 hand pump
9 bypass valve
10 hydraulic tank

used special consideration must be given to containing it safely in the event of damage or leakage because of its toxicity. This is normally done by displacing the mercury with oil and not compressed air. Trim tanks can be used as variable ballast tanks in a dual capacity.

Although some builders prefer liquid ballast as a trimming weight, others' designs use solid ballast. A lead or similar ballast weight is moved along the centre line by a spindle, hydraulic cylinder or chain mechanism. These and other methods are illustrated in Fig. 7.24. A feature of the *Mermaid* class is the use of batteries as the trimming movement, thereby effectively increasing the payload of the craft. The batteries are fitted in boxes which can be moved by hydraulic cylinders inside the battery pods. This method is illustrated in Fig. 7.25. As the batteries amount to between 10 and 15% of the total weight of the average submersible, this is ample to cover the trimming needs. With this type of trim system the alterations to trim caused by diver lock-out operations can be easily adjusted and the inclination of the submersible can be accentuated to conform to abnormal inclinations whilst connected to capsules and submarines in rescue operations.

The stability of a submersible on the surface both longitudinally and athwartship is dependent on the metacentric height. As with a surface ship, the centre of buoyancy is below the centre of gravity; once the

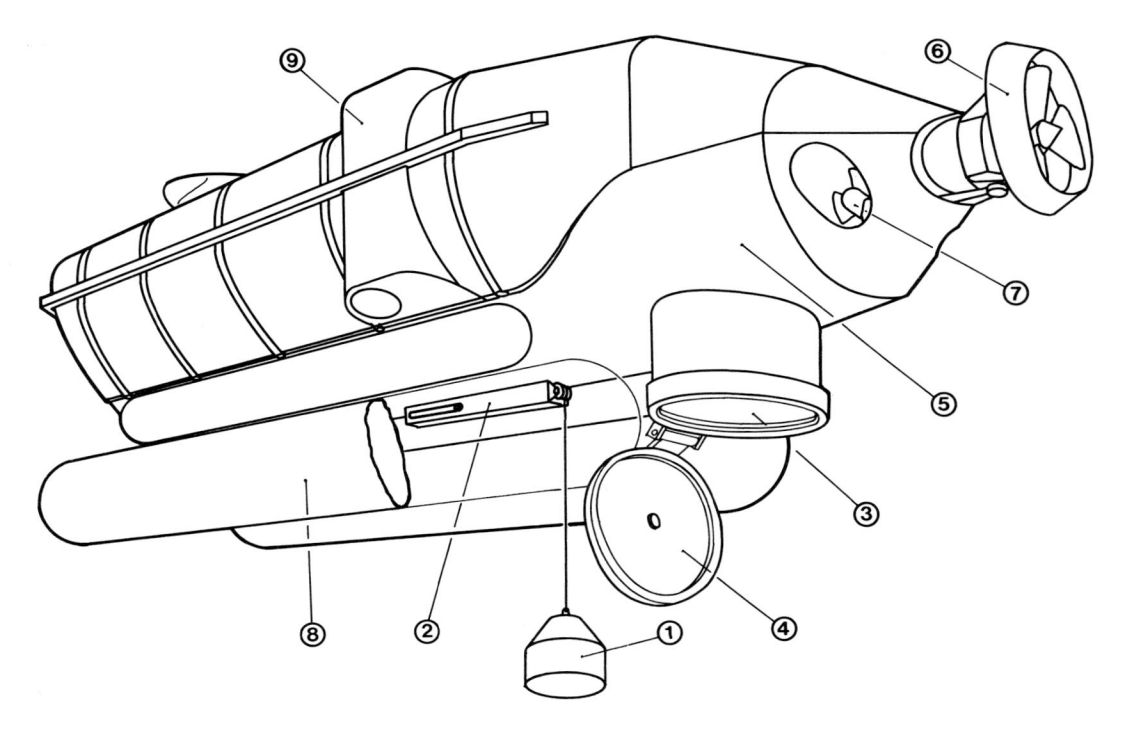

Fig. 7.26. Anchor weight on a diver lock-out submersible. The vehicle is suspended above its anchor weight. The length of the anchor wire determines the clear height above ground level. The system has been tested successfully and is especially suited for rocky terrain. The anchoring system can be jettisonned.

1	anchor weight	6	main thruster
2	hydraulic anchor winch	7	control thruster
3	diver lock-out trunk	8	battery pod
4	bayonet hatch	9	vertical thruster
5	diver lock-out compartment		

vessel is submerged the centre of buoyancy moves above the centre of gravity and stability is maintained by a pendulum-type action. During both diving and surfacing there is a moment when the centres of buoyancy and gravity coincide and stability is minimal. The design needs to consider the various effects and interactions between variable ballast compensation, the trim system and the overall stability of the craft together with alterations in movable weight, including ballast and the trim system.

Anchoring Systems

It is not considered safe, and therefore not recognized practice, to operate divers from a lock-out whilst the submersible is in a hovering position, and thus using thrusters and main propulsion. There is also the difficulty of synchronizing an immediate trim to compensate for

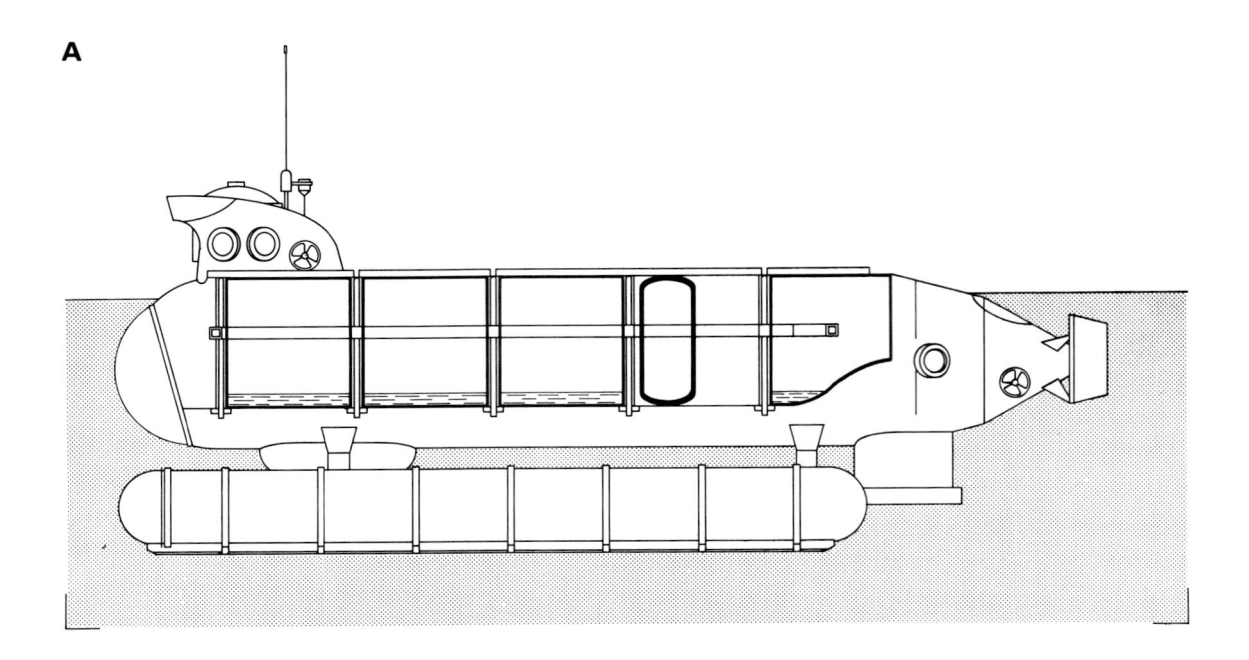

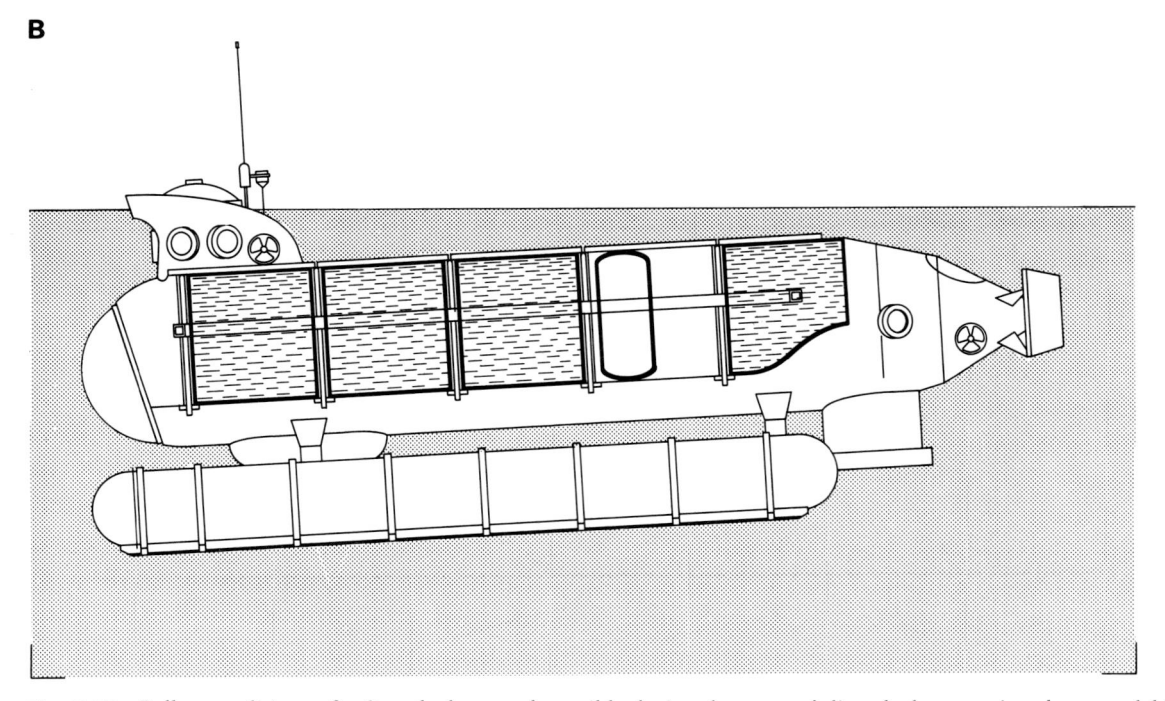

Fig. 7.27. Ballast conditions of a diver lock-out submersible during descent and diver lock-out, using the extendable legs.

- **A** The submersible is on the surface with both soft and hard ballast tanks empty
- **B** Before it submerges, the soft tanks are flooded completely. The hard tanks are still empty and the submersible still has some positive buoyancy
- **C** Negative buoyancy is achieved by partial flooding of the hard ballast tanks and the submersible descends
- **D** The legs are extended and the hard ballast tanks completely flooded. The submersible must remain negatively buoyant with both divers outside and with all breathing gas and compressed air consumed. The lock-out trunk is also flooded

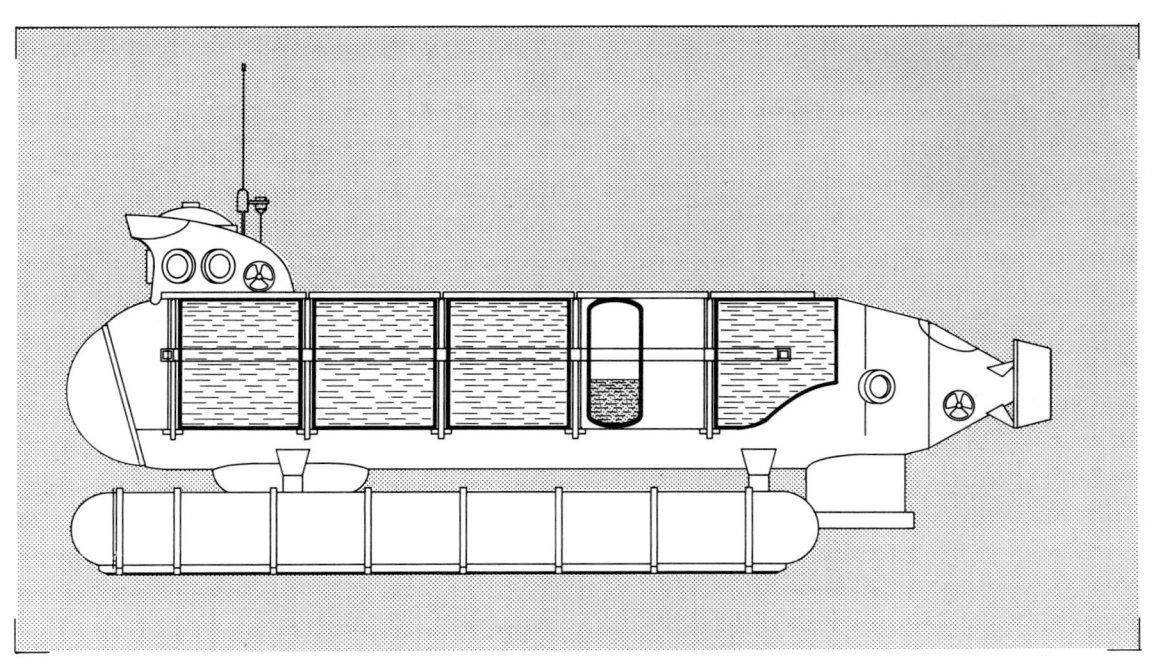

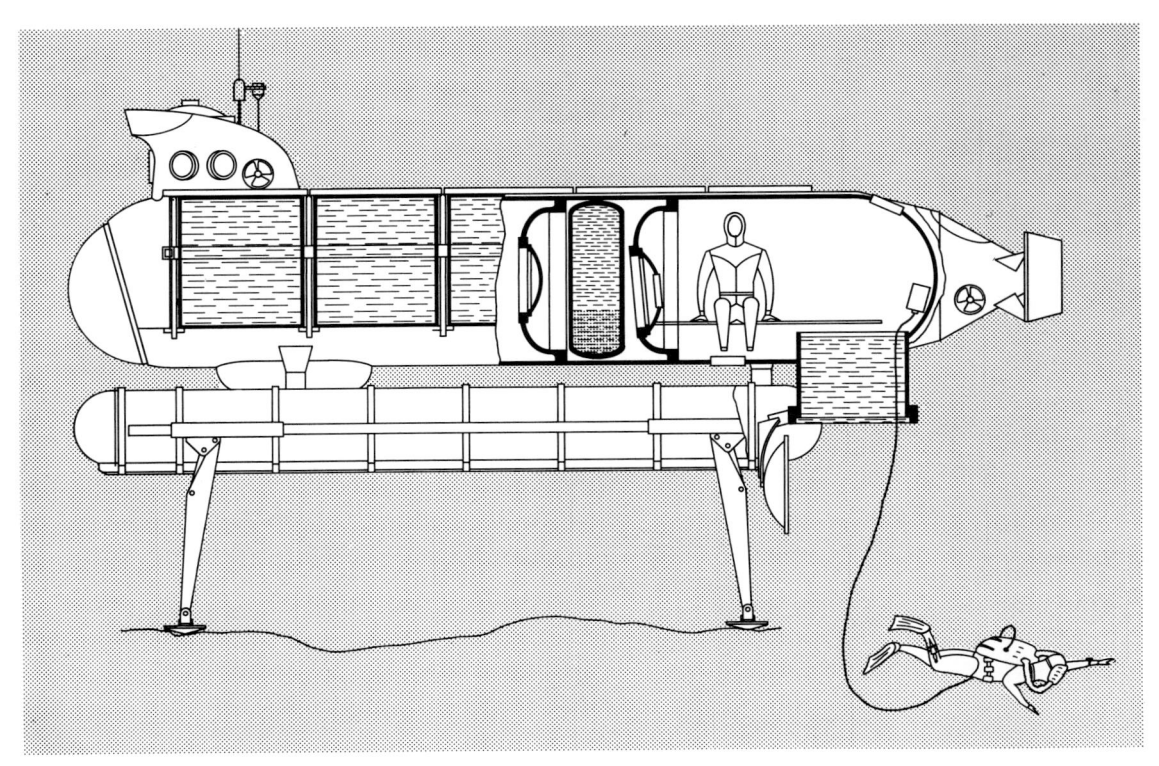

C

D

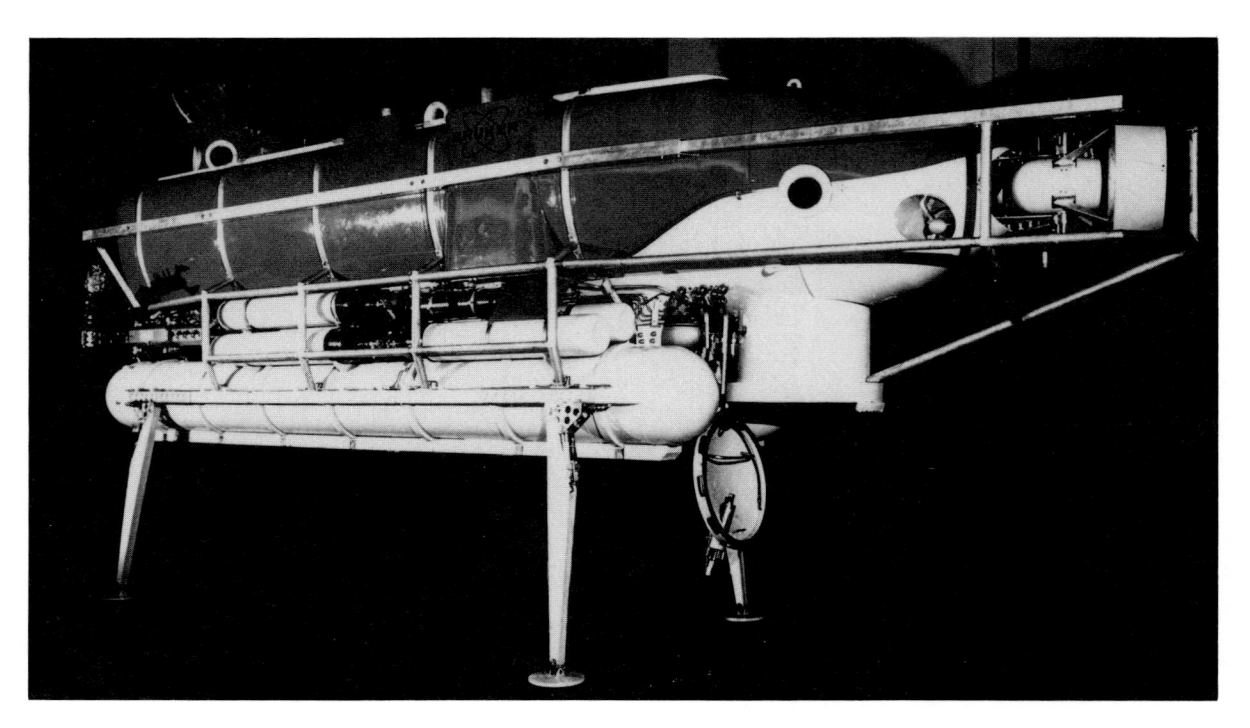

Fig. 7.28. Retractable legs for a diver lock-out submersible. In this case they are attached to the outside of the battery pods and swung out with hydraulic cylinders. The lock-out trunk at the rear end of the lock-out chamber is clearly visible.

the weight of the diver in this attitude and an undesired movement could endanger the diver. Therefore lock-out operations are carried out only whilst the submersible is resting on the bottom or, if in midwater, when it is physically attached to a midwater structure; in both cases thrusters and main propulsion are not required except in an emergency.

The use of an anchor has been considered on the same basis as for diving bells where, in some designs, there are anchor or ballast weights to which the bells ride in a positively buoyant manner on a wire rope. The same concept was considered in the system designed for the *Mermaid* to meet the possible requirement of anchoring the submersible above the seabed in areas of rock and strong currents where landings are difficult or impossible. The weight is attached to a wire rope and lowered to the bottom; the submersible rides on the weight using the variable ballast to compensate for strong currents by increasing the buoyancy to overcome the current's effect in pushing the craft towards the seabed, bearing in mind that divers cannot operate in currents in excess of 1.5 knots. The anchoring position on the submersible is aft so that the stern points into any current and provides less resistance to the water than if the more conventional forward attitude was adopted.

Extensive trials proved that the anchoring system does work provided the weight of the diver and equipment is known, but this method is not favoured because of the inherent risk of the cable wire parting, in which case the divers would be in extreme danger from the immediate buoyancy of the craft which would cause it to ascend rapidly without any chance of immediately achieving stability. Psychologically divers prefer working from the security of a submersible resting on the seabed.

Rigid and Extendable Legs

The distance of the seabed from the lock-out hatch is usually so small that the divers find it difficult, sometimes impossible, to exit from the submersible. There should be a clear space of at least 1.0 m. A rudimentary way of achieving this stand-off distance is to attach a frame underneath the submersible on which it rests at the required height. Whilst conceivably practicable for occasional lock-outs, the drag effect in water and the additional weight, particularly in air whilst the craft is being hoisted, makes it unsatisfactory. Further problems arise whilst on board the mothership and transfer under pressure procedures are made more complicated. Generally lock-out submersibles are designed to rest on extendable and retractable legs. Extendable legs, activated by hydraulic pistons or rack and pinion, tend to be bulky and complicated. Hinged legs that can be retracted on a swivel are more practical and shorter than the extended design. The hinged legs can be moved together or individually and are usually fitted with pads or shoes so as to spread the load on the sea bottom, particularly in soft material. With sufficient inherent stability the submersible can be supported one leg at a time. With all the legs swivelling in opposite directions one extended leg can support the craft whilst the others extend fully. Extending the legs is usually carried out when the submersible is in the working position and slightly negatively buoyant, i.e. with ballast tanks partially flooded. The legs must, of course, withstand the full negative buoyancy of the submersible with ballast and compensation tanks full and divers in the lock-out compartment. This weight should not normally exceed about 600 kg.

Transfer Under Pressure to DCCs and Under-water Capsules

Transfer under pressure is more usually carried out by divers transferring from the pressurized diving compartment of a submersible to the surface compression chambers in the mothership on completion of diving operations and the subsequent recovery inboard of the mothership. Here an internal overpressure is the major design factor for the transfer under pressure arrangement. However, the reverse situation has also to be considered, particularly for the future, for transfer to and from under-water chambers inside capsules or

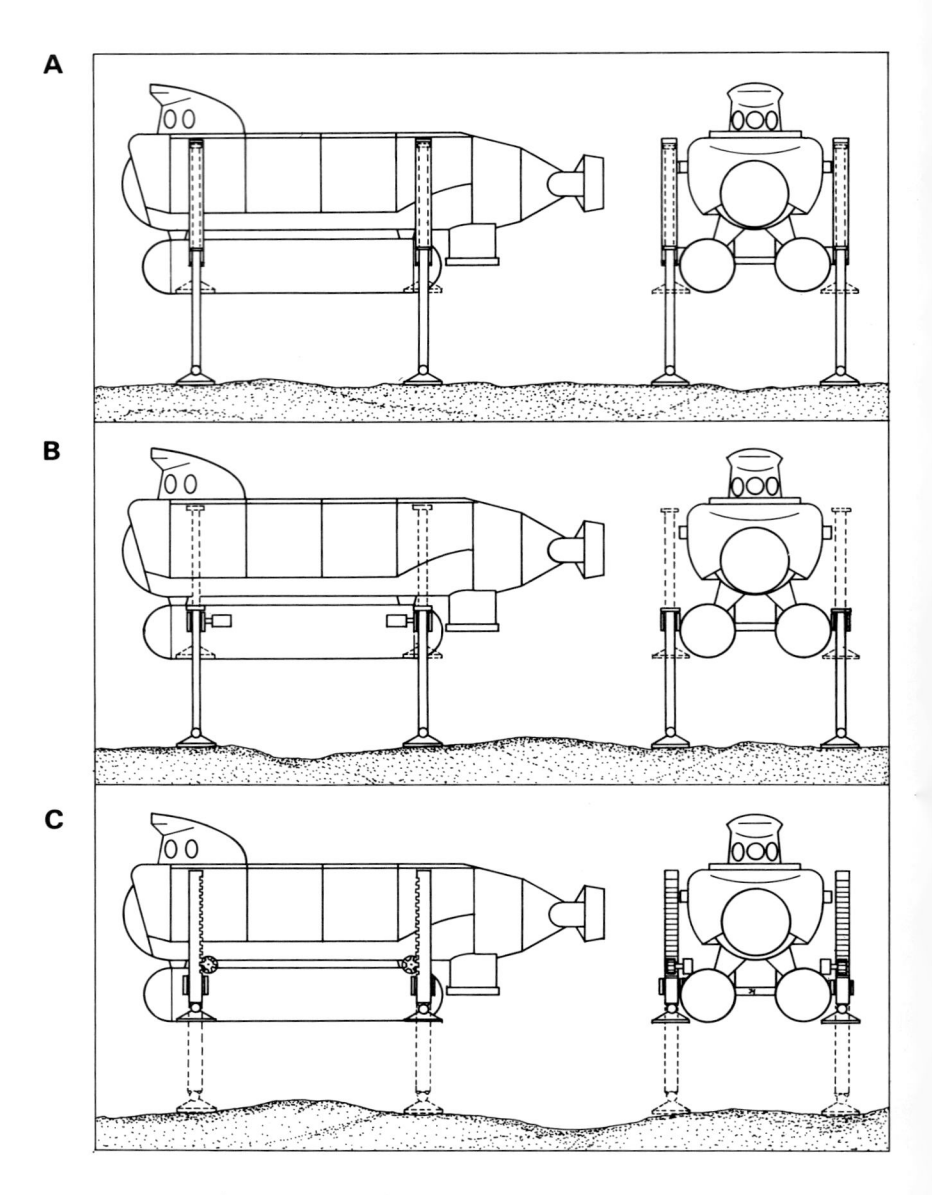

Fig. 7.29. Examples of the type of legs required for submersibles with diver lock-out.

- **A** Legs extended by hydraulic cylinders. Bottom unevenness can be compensated for easily. The weight is relatively large if the design is rugged
- **B** Legs pulled down by gravity after actuation of hydraulic or other release mechanism. To retract the legs, releases are actuated and the legs pushed back, so that the submersible sinks to the bottom
- **C** Extendable legs with rod and pinion. Compensation for uneven ground is possible. Great mechanical force is needed and the structure is heavy

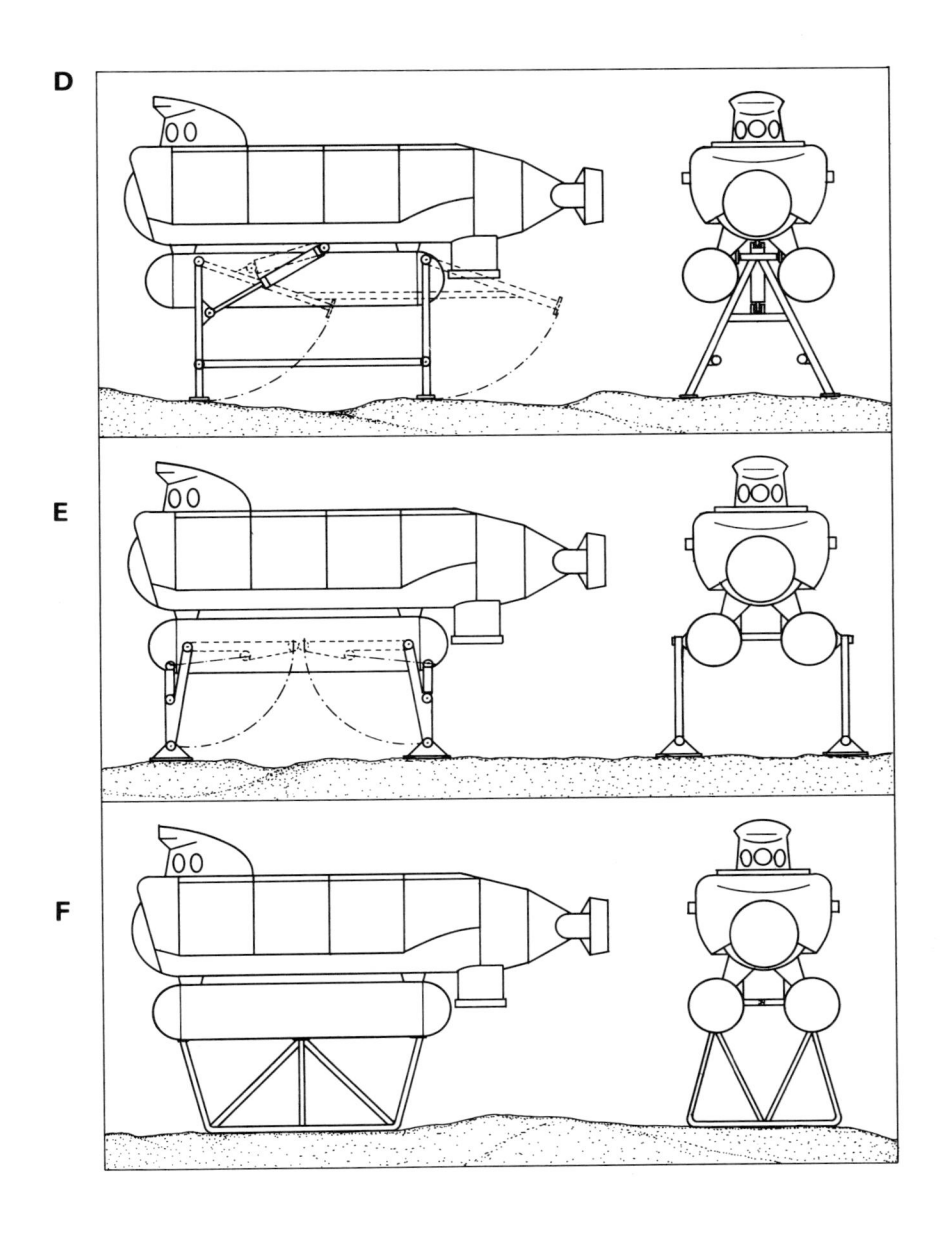

- **D** Legs designed as parallelogram with joints. Operation is possible with only one hydraulic cylinder. A light and rugged structure, but not always feasible
- **E** Legs with individual hinges and actuating cylinders for extension and retraction. Less suitable if the submersible is intended to move along the bottom with the legs extended
- **F** Rigid structure. Relatively high drag. The large distance from the ground is not favourable for inspection dives. Simple rugged construction

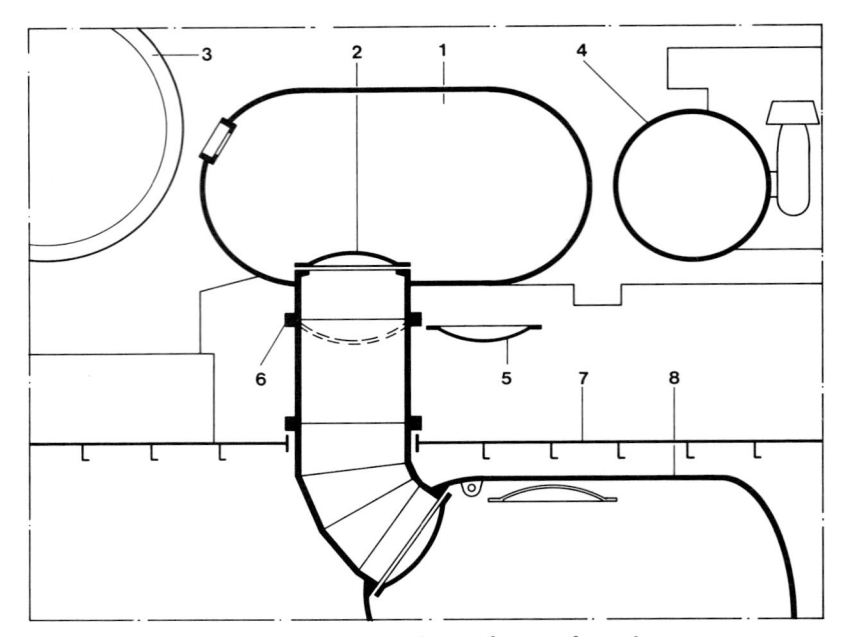

Fig. 7.30. Rigid connection by bolted flanges for transfer under pressure.

1	lock-out chamber	5	outer hatch
2	inner hatch	6	bolt flange
3	pilot compartment	7	deck
4	breathing gas tank	8	deck compression chamber

habitats, where there is an external overpressure. The development of the subsea completion systems for the production of off-shore oilfields will require the transfer of personnel (not divers) who will be at atmospheric or near-surface-atmospheric conditions. The design of the submersible transfer system needs to take both into account.

The mating of a submersible to a DCC is basically the same as that of a diving bell to a DCC. The difference is that, whilst the diving bell has an optional design factor in that the transfer hatch may be at the side or at the bottom, in a submersible, there is no reasonable alternative to having the transfer hatch fitted on the bottom. A major factor is the need to contain the stresses in a submersible whilst locked to a transfer chamber as the point of connection is rarely near the centre of gravity and the corresponding loads need to be contained by supports. The submersible is, of course, much heavier than a diving bell and this also has to be taken into account in regard to loading factors.

Whilst the entrance to the transfer compartment on board a mothership's compression chamber needs to have only one pressure door, because the internal pressure is always greater, the submersible must always have doors capable of acting against internal and external pressure. The transfer hatch of a submersible must have either a flange that can connect directly with a mating flange on the compression chamber or an adaptor in order to do so. The sealing arrangements on the flanges must be capable of taking the heavy load of a submersible.

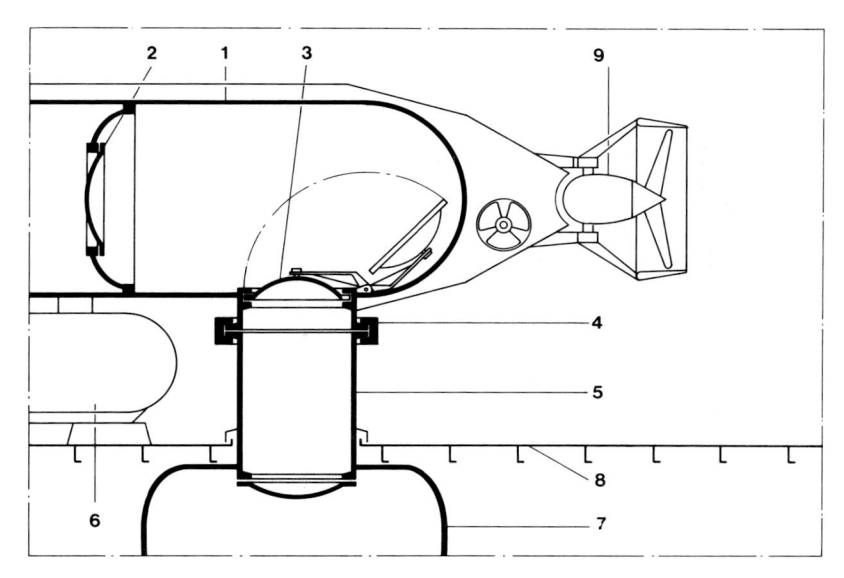

Fig. 7.31. Rigid connection by clamping ring for transfer under pressure.

1 lock-out chamber
2 hatch to interlock
3 inner hatch
4 clamping ring
5 transfer trunk
6 battery pod
7 deck compression chamber
8 deck
9 propellor

Various methods of connecting the submersible to the compression chamber are illustrated in Figs 7.30 to 7.35. Fig. 7.30 illustrates a flanged trunk with an internal and external hatch. The external hatch in the submersible is removed before the connection is made with the trunking. After pressure has been equalized inside the trunking and between the submersible and the surface compression chamber, both the doors in the lock-out and the compression chamber are opened to allow the divers to pass through. A single two-way pressure door with a bayonet action can be fitted to the submersible as shown in Fig. 7.31. The bayonet hatch opens inwards and the connection can be made quickly to allow equalization in the trunking with one less door to operate, there being two doors to open instead of three. In Fig. 7.32 the lock-out trunking extends downwards with a one-way pressure door in the diving sphere and a two-way pressure bayonet door on the outside. The connection to the transfer lock of the surface compression chamber is by a bayonet fitting around the counter flange and a clamping ring. The alternative to the bayonet connection is smooth flanges faced together. The submersible flange and the flange of the transfer lock are mated and a pressure seal is achieved by the use of a clamping ring.

There are a number of ways to overcome the possibility of misalignment of the submersible and the transfer lock. In Fig. 7.33 one solution is to incorporate diaphragm rings, each fitted with internal and external seals, which will allow for some misalignment of the two axes. Tension rods take up the vertical loads due to the

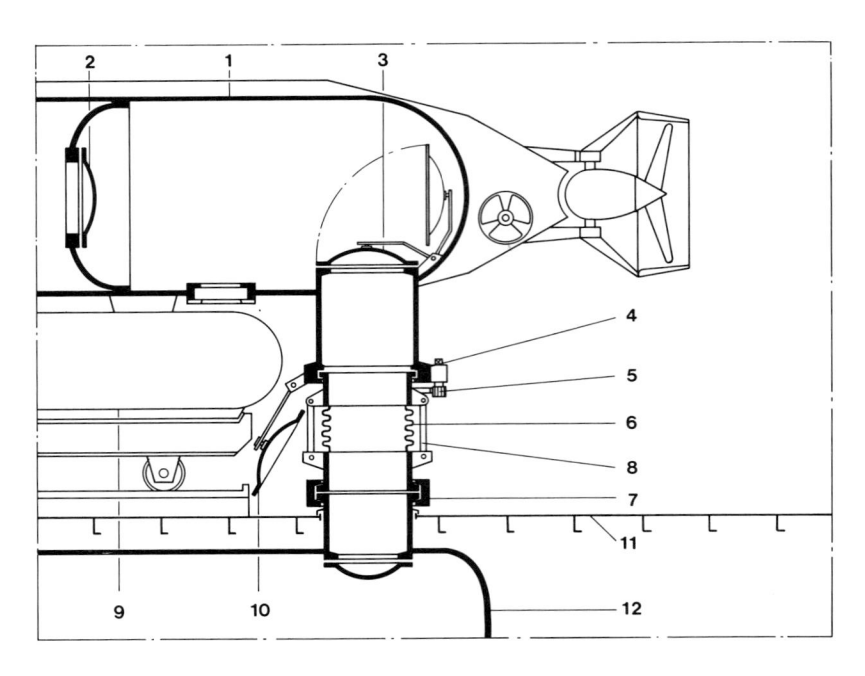

Fig. 7.32. Flexible connection by compensator/bellows.

1	lock-out chamber	7	clamping ring
2	hatch to interlock	8	tension rods
3	inner hatch	9	battery pods
4	bayonet lock	10	external hatch
5	rotary drive	11	deck
6	compensator/bellows	12	deck compression chamber

internal pressure rising on equalization. If a sufficient number of diaphragm rings are incorporated then it is possible to allow for some radial movement as well. The flanges will be held by one of the methods discussed, i.e. bayonet connection, bolts or clamping rings.

An alternative to the diaphragm ring method of alignment is illustrated in Fig. 7.34. Three cylindrical trunkings are fitted together and sealed with gaskets. Some misalignment can be taken up by the flexibility in the gaskets in addition to the centre segment. Lip seals are better for this purpose than O-seals.

For large displacements, particularly in rough weather, a 'bellows' design can be used. Illustrated in Fig. 7.35, the bellows compensates for axial and radial movements with a relatively short length of trunking. The bellows is constructed with individual layers of thin non-corrosive steel. The ends are welded to provide a seal. If the inner layer cracks and allows the oxy-helium gas to leak, the leakage will be reduced as it has to penetrate all the layers that make up the bellows. The labyrinth of metal surfaces will tend to produce a large pressure drop if there is a leak and the consequent slow leak can be measured on a leak gauge. Because the layers of steel that make up the bellows are susceptible to damage they need to be protected. The end of the compensating trunk can be welded to a bayonet flange which fits the

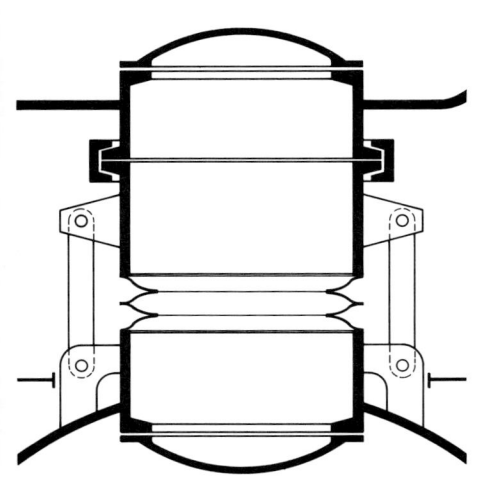

Fig. 7.33. Closely fitting diaphragm rings interconnected with internal and external seals allow for angular misalignments. Tension rods take up longitudinal loads.

submersible flange on the lock-out trunking as fitted to the *Mermaid* class of submersibles. The lower flange can slide and rotate on the transfer flange of the compression chamber and be rigidly secured with a divided clamp ring. Two tension rods are fitted to the upper and lower segments of the compensation trunking. A common procedure using bellows transfer compensation will be initiated by the recovery of the submersible on board the mothership, usually bow first but in some configurations stern first, and the submersible is lowered onto a trolley where it can be correctly positioned by guide plates. The trolley is moved by hydraulic power, usually by means of a pinion rod, along rails. The trolley can be moved vertically up to 100 mm, also hydraulically. The towing and hoisting wires are removed and the trolley moved over to the transfer under pressure position above the transfer lock. The flanges are positioned correctly by means of stops and the submersible is lowered hydraulically until the bayonet ring on the connection piece is inserted in the counter-flange and can be rotated. The trolley is then locked firmly and the transfer lock equalized as previously described. The divers then transfer from the submersible to the deck chamber. The procedure is reversed for the movement of divers from the chamber to the submersible.

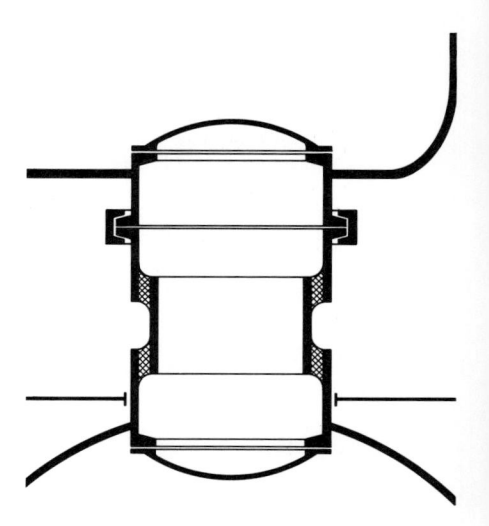

Fig. 7.34. Cylindrical trunks sealed by lip gaskets.

Transfer to and from Under-water Chamber Capsules

In Chapter 6 the use of habitats is broadly discussed and the need in the future for the off-shore oil and gas industry to introduce the subsea production system in certain situations. As the depths at which oil and gas are produced increase and the cost of permanent steel or concrete platforms becomes prohibitive, not least because of the technical considerations of designing such structures, the introduction of subsea wellheads and production systems, encapsulated within pressure chambers to allow personnel to be transferred for essential work, will become normal. The rise in oil prices will also determine that oilfields previously uneconomic or marginal, in terms of both quantity of reserves and depth of water, will become economic, particularly through the use of subsea completion systems. In Chapter 6 the distinction was made between wet and dry transfers either at ambient pressure, i.e. the pressure on the seabed, or at atmospheric pressure, sometimes referred to as a 'shirt-sleeves' environment. The use of a submersible to carry out dry transfers is feasible and logically best. The complete docking manoeuvre is carried out by the submersible crew, either because the subsea capsule is unmanned or, in the case of a submarine in distress, because it is assumed that the survivors are unable to assist. The design of the docking arrangement is determined by the type of hatches used in the same way as with a submersible transfer under pressure with a deck compression chamber in the mothership. In subsea transfer two alternatives are considered, either one hatch on the submersible or the capsule opens outwards or both hatches open to the inside. In Fig. 7.36 the arrangement whereby both hatches open into the chamber is illustrated. Both hatches must be pressure-resistant in both directions or at least under external

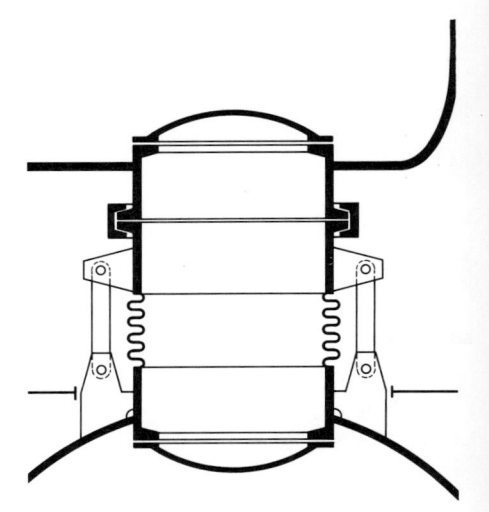

Fig. 7.35. Multi-layer bellows compensate axial, radial and angular misalignments. The loads due to internal pressure are taken up by tension rods.

Fig. 7.36. Transfer to an underwater chamber using hatches, both opening inwards.

1. submersible lock-out chamber
2. submersible bayonet hatch
3. transfer trunk which has to be drained
4. flange with gasket
5. guide ring
6. bayonet hatch of under-water chamber
7. under-water chamber
8. battery pod

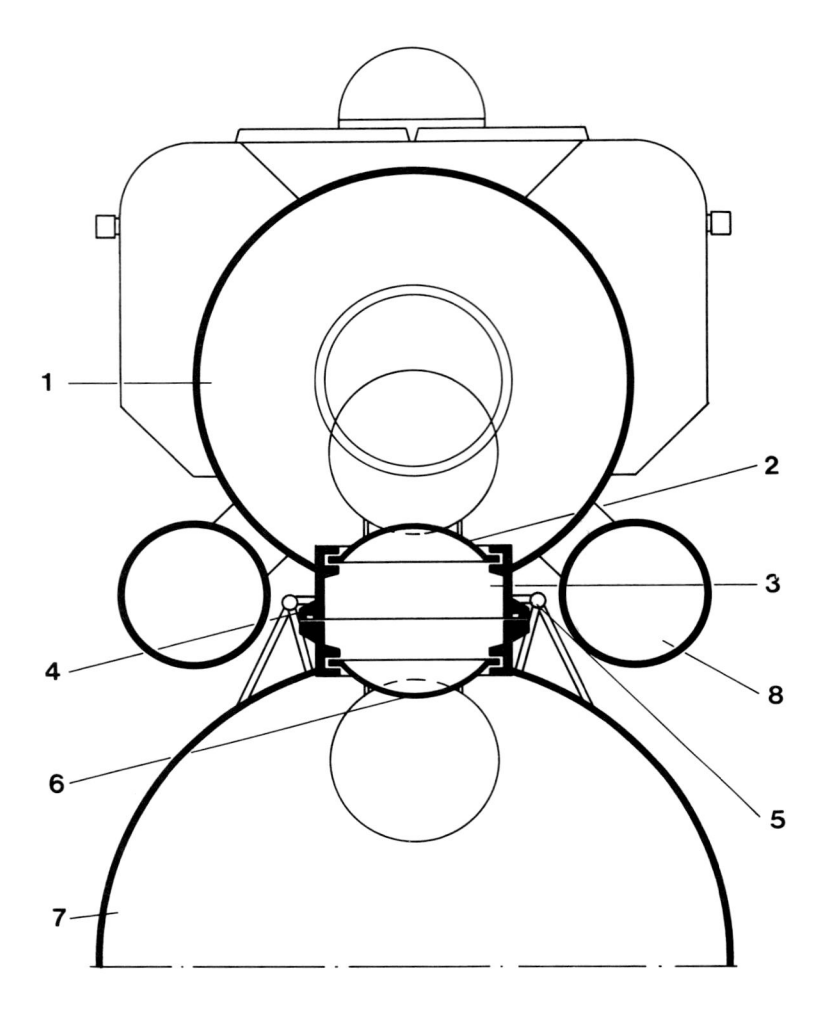

pressure. The flange on the submersible lock-out has to be fitted with a sealing gasket so that when it is centred onto the plain flange of the capsule a good seal is made. The seal is enforced when the water is pumped out of the transfer lock against the ambient pressure outside or into containers as shown in Fig. 7.3.9. As the water is evacuated the flanges are forced together and a pressure-tight seal is achieved, the total force being determined by the area of the flange. After the water has been completely drained from the trunk and the pressure equalized the lock-out hatch can be opened first and then the hatch of the subsea capsule, after the atmosphere inside the capsule has been tested for toxic gases. This arrangement, although economical in weight and energy for evacuating the water, because of the minimal size of the dome, is not popular. The limited development to date in undersea habitats, subsea capsules and lock-out submersibles has not incorporated two-way pressure hatches, but has favoured the one-way pressure hatch opening into the mating dome which is

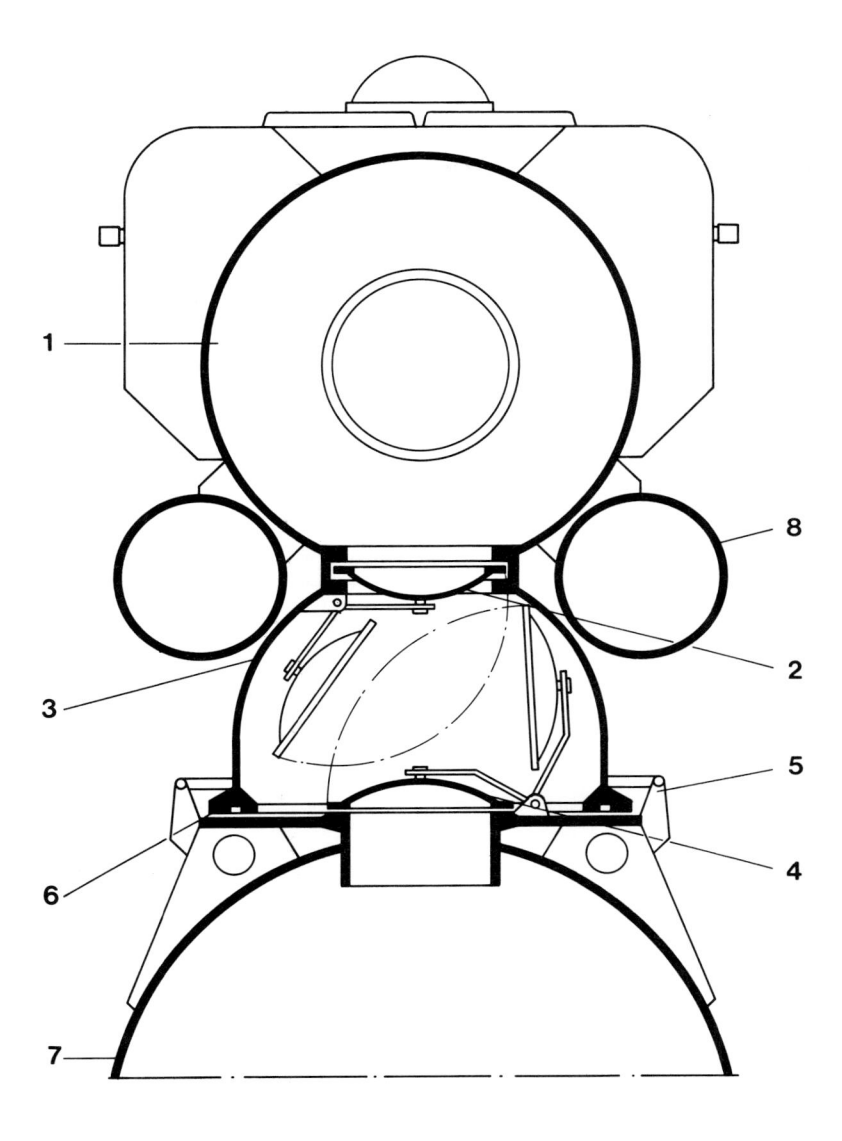

Fig. 7.37. Transfer to an under-water chamber using a mating dome.

1. lock-out chamber of submersible
2. outward-opening bayonet hatch
3. mating dome
4. outward-opening hatch of under-water chamber
5. guide ring
6. mating flange
7. under-water chamber
8. battery pod

simpler and lighter. The sealing arrangement illustrated in Fig. 7.37 is the method preferred using two separate inward-opening hatches. A large skirt has to be designed to allow both hatch doors to open inwards at one atmosphere. The skirt or dome large enough to take the open hatches is open-ended and flanged at the bottom with a sealing gasket to seal onto the flange of the subsea installation. The bottom diameter of the skirt would have to be in the order of 1500 mm to mate over an entry hatch of 600 mm which is the minimum size for normal access. The dome or skirt therefore cannot be fitted to small submersibles owing to the additional weight, volume and drag. The operational procedure is similar to the previous system but there are additional problems due to the greater volume of water that needs to be pumped out against ambient pressure or into containers. There are a number of solutions.

Fig. 7.38. Drainage of the mating dome into the underwater chamber. No energy is required, but the procedure can be used only if the chamber is specially designed.

1. submersible transfer chamber
2. soft ballast tank
3. battery pod
4. mating dome
5. drain valve
6. working chamber

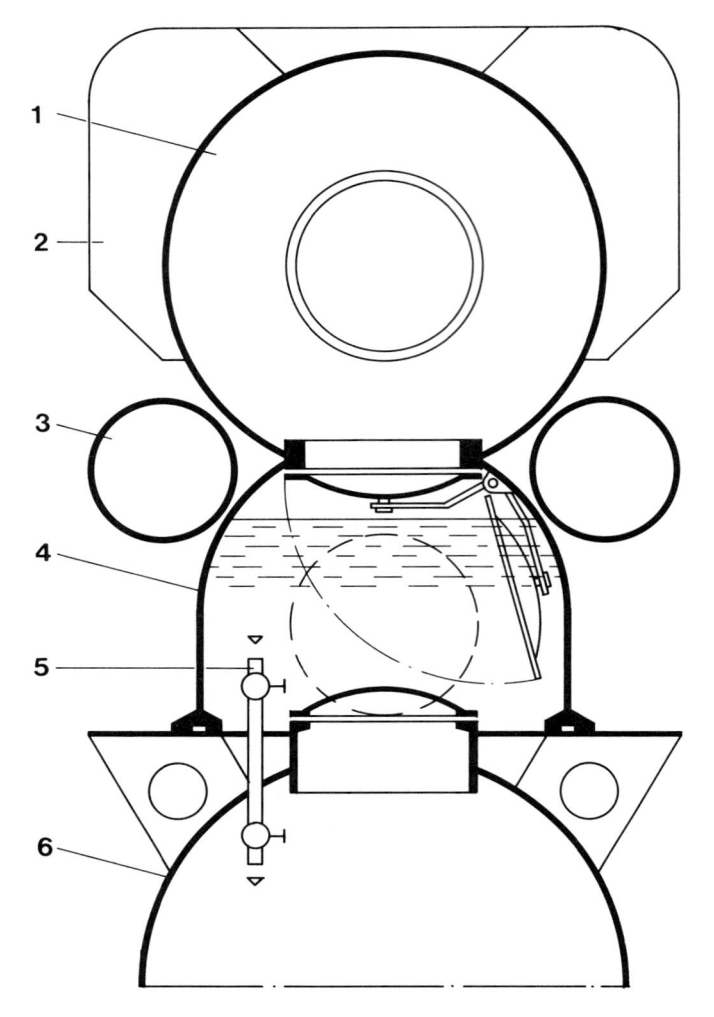

Evacuation of Water in Dry Transfer Systems

Drainage into the seabed chamber (Fig. 7.38)

The simplest solution is to drain the water into the chamber as illustrated in Fig. 7.38. The obvious limitation is in the number of times this can be done without a means of disposing of the water inside the chamber. This method is not considered except in emergency evacuation, particularly a submarine rescue, or for a single transfer where the water can be discharged into a bilge.

Draining into pressure-proof tanks (Fig. 7.39)

This solution uses one or more pressure-proof vessels, mounted on the submersible, whose volume is greater than the volume of the dome and which are at one-atmosphere pressure when empty. The water can be pumped into the vessels initially with little power but increasing as the pressure builds up. Being pressure vessels they are heavy and the additional weight factor has to be considered in relation to the small amount of energy needed for pumping.

Fig. 7.39. Drainage of the mating dome into pressure-proof water tanks. The pressure in the tanks is initially one atmosphere. The energy required for pumping is much less that for pumping against ambient pressure, depending on the volume of the water tanks. The tanks themselves, however, are large and heavy.

1 submersible transfer chamber
2 soft ballast tank
3 mating dome
4 water tank
5 drain pump
6 one-way valve
7 working chamber

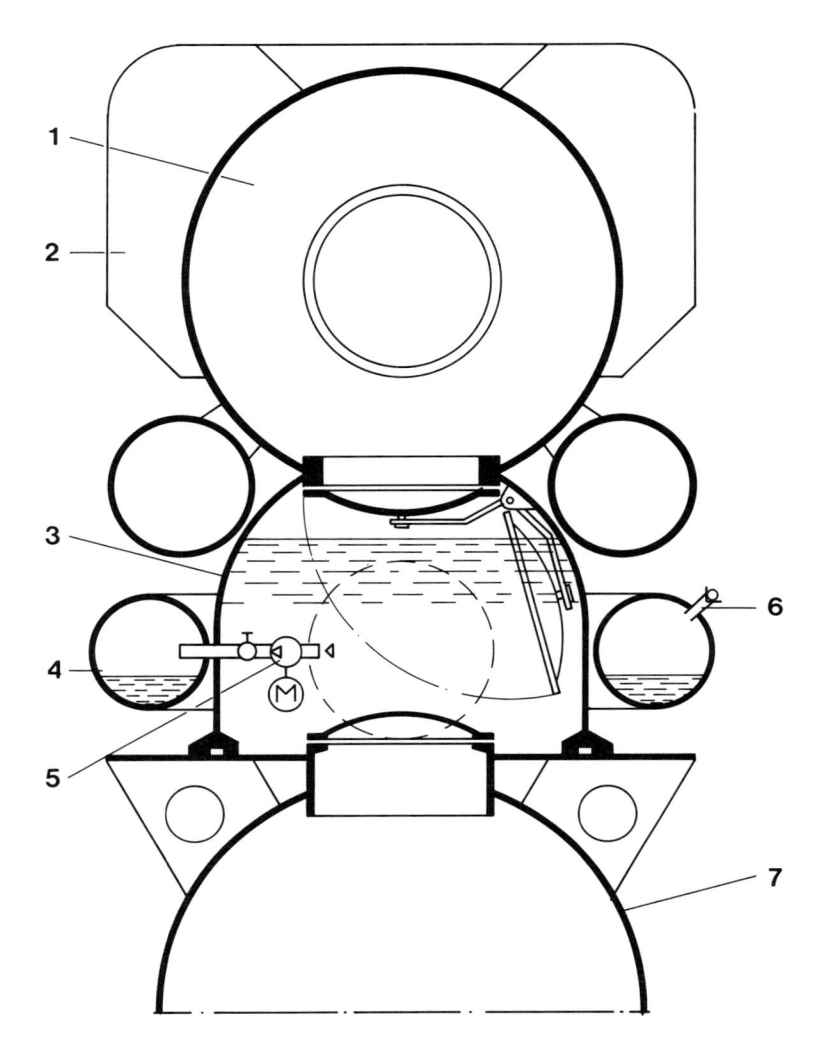

Drainage by high-pressure pump (Fig. 7.40)

Piston pumps are preferable for pumping out the water into the surrounding sea. However, the energy requirements as a proportion of the battery capacity are considerable. Assuming a 1 m³ volume of water to be discharged into the sea at 50 bar, equal to 500 m approximately, the energy requirements will be in the order of 10% of the battery power of an average submersible.

An hydraulic unit with piston drive is preferable and is capable of evacuating the same volume in about five minutes.

Blowing down the mating dome (Fig. 7.41)

This method is only possible in hyperbaric conditions under pressure. The dome has an inlet for high-pressure gas, the same as the submersible diving chamber and the habitat or capsule. Unlike one-atmosphere systems which rely on the pressure difference inside and outside the dome to help achieve pressure- and water-tight integrity, the blowing down of the chamber with gas will increase the

Fig. 7.40. Drainage of the mating dome by a high-pressure water pump. The energy required is proportional to the ambient pressure and the internal volume of the dome.

1. submersible transfer chamber
2. soft ballast tank
3. mating dome
4. battery pod
5. high-pressure drain pump
6. working chamber

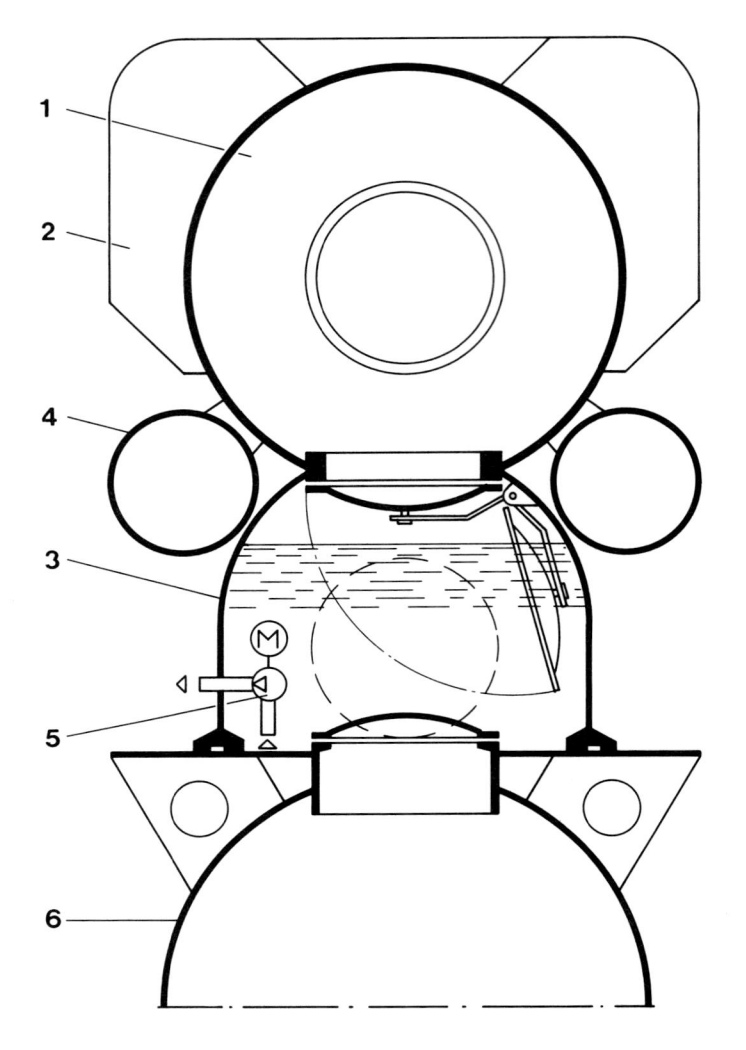

buoyancy of the submersible due to the buoyancy of the dome. It is therefore necessary to overcome this by locking the submersible onto the flange at the same time as positive pressure is achieved on the flanges and thereby achieving a seal.

Gas Supply Systems for Different Deep Diving Procedures

Life-support systems in general do not differ from those developed for other under-water operations, notably for use in diving bells where great advances have been made with safe and efficient systems. Life-support systems are described in Chapter 10 but not all these systems are suitable for use in submersibles which are limited by weight to under 20 tonnes. Systems will also vary to meet the designed mission cycle of the submersible. Bounce diving will require

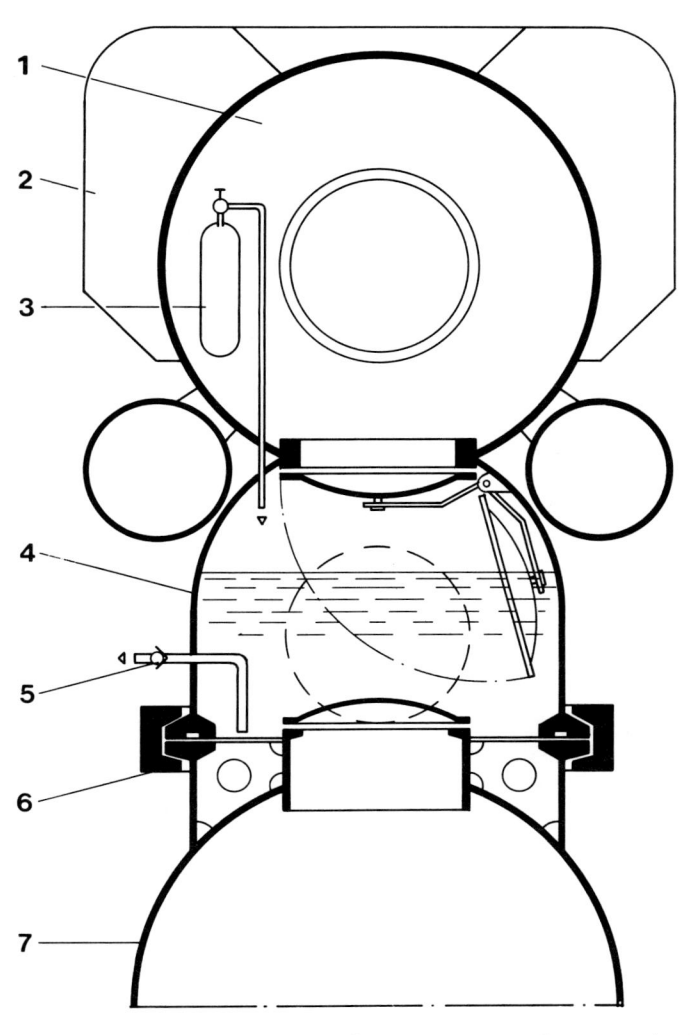

Fig. 7.41. Drainage of the mating dome by blowing down with compressed gas is suitable only for hyperbaric dry transfer. The mating dome has to be locked to the chamber. Electrical energy is not needed but gas is consumed instead.

1. submersible transfer chamber
2. soft ballast tank
3. gas storage tank
4. mating dome
5. one-way valve
6. clamping ring
7. working chamber

different gas supply systems from saturation diving and other factors in a mission cycle will need to be taken into account.

The choice and design of a life-support system for a submersible, compared to a diving bell system which is supplied with virtually unlimited supplies of gas from the surface, has to be very precise owing to the limited autonomy of the craft. Life-support systems, which of course include gas supply, are based on mixed gases and not air because the submersible is not cost-effective in the air range.

A basic requirement of any life-support system is that the partial pressure of oxygen (Po_2) must not exceed 1.8 bar for short exposures and that the Pco_2 must be contained to within a non-toxic limit of 0.015 bar or lower and related to exposure. Nitrogen, which at 79% is the major constituent of air, is replaced by helium. Helium is a lighter inert gas than nitrogen, easier to breathe but with seven times greater thermal conductivity than air, creating further problems of heating and speech deformity. Mixed gas therefore usually consists of oxygen and helium but can include nitrogen to make up what is known as tri-mix, the exact composition of any mixed gas being determined by the operating depth range.

Open-circuit Systems

Using the same principle as conventional scuba equipment with a demand valve that exhausts all the expired gas into the water, the amount of gas supply required as depth increases is considerable. For example breathing 45 litres of gas per minute at 200 m depth would exhaust a 50 litre gas cylinder charged to 200 bar in a mere 10 minutes. Thus this type of breathing system cannot be considered for normal use at depth in a lock-out submersible. Because the open-circuit system is so simple and dependable it may be considered in an emergency or for other urgent uses, where the cost of unreclaimable helium is not significant and there is no need for sustained endurance. An umbilical diving hose to the diver's mask, supplying gas from a large very-high-pressure storage tank with, for example, 500 litres at 300 bar, will be sufficient for 80 minutes work for one diver in 200 m.

Semi-closed Systems

Whereas in open-circuit systems the carbon dioxide produced by the human body is exhausted with the breathing gas into the water and with each breath the respiratory tract is supplied with fresh gas not containing any carbon dioxide, in semi-closed systems the harmful carbon dioxide is absorbed chemically and the oxygen partial pressure kept at the necessary level by adding fresh breathing gas. For this purpose the exhaled gas is passed through a CO_2 absorbent cannister and filtered before reinhalation. Since a constant gas flow greater than the actual oxygen consumption is supplied into the system, surplus gas is led out through an excess-pressure valve. The gas input is constant depending on depth and in the magnitude of 20–50 litres/minute increasing with depth. Gas consumption is therefore considerably less than with open-circuit systems. Endurance and therefore working time is increased accordingly. This advantage is balanced by the need for more sophisticated equipment, comprising CO_2 absorber, counterlung and fresh gas injection. Not only the gas storage but also the capacity of the CO_2 absorber are limiting factors with respect to possible working times.

Self-contained semi-closed breathing apparatus
Breathing gas is carried in the apparatus itself although an umbilical supply is needed for emergency use. The operating time may be very short depending on the diving depth. The units are bulky and heavy, require careful maintenance and are not required for use with diver lock-out submersibles because of the ability of a submersible to manoeuvre close up to the work site and within the scope of an umbilical supply.

Umbilical-supplied semi-closed breathing apparatus

These are suitable for short diving operations. The storage of the necessary breathing gas on the submersible does not present any great problems. The construction of the diving apparatus is rugged and relatively simple. Dependable systems are available. With umbilical lengths of 20–40 m most working sites can be reached easily by a diver operating from the submersible. Permanent control and supervision of the gas mixture is not necessary. In case of an interruption of the gas supply through the umbilical, gas stored in an emergency cylinder carried by the diver will ensure an emergency endurance of about eight minutes and allow sufficient time for the diver to return to the diver lock-out chamber of the submersible. The gas in the storage tanks can be either pre-mixed according to the diving depth range or mixed as required according to the operating depth by means of mixing units in the submersible. These mixing units are preferably installed in the dry lock-out chamber; otherwise they may be integrated in the gas control panel of the diving supervisor in the pilot's compartment. With this system the CO_2 absorbent cartridge and the counterlung are also carried as part of the diver's breathing pack. The umbilical contains a single gas supply hose, communications and possibly sensors for monitoring the diver. The umbilical will also carry the essential heating systems discussed later.

Closed-circuit Systems

When carbon dioxide is removed from the exhaled gas and oxygen is added this mixture of oxygen and inert gas can be used again for breathing. The oxygen consumption rate averages at about 0.9 litres/minute and is so small that the endurance of such a closed-circuit apparatus usually depends only on the capacity of the CO_2 absorbent cartridge. This system is clearly ideal for diving, especially when working from diver lock-out submersibles. However, a problem arises in the need for precise measurement and control of the oxygen partial pressure which depends on the diving depth and the individual gas consumption. Incorrect measurements will have disastrous consequences. This type of breathing apparatus is equipped with complex electronic measuring, regulating and monitoring devices. It has been successfully used in diver lock-out submersibles but its use for off-shore operations is restricted in some countries.

Where electronic sensors are used most careful consideration must be given to preventing interference from other electrical supplies such as electric motors and solenoid valves.

Closed-circuit systems can be supplied either from within the diver's back pack (a small circuit system) or from a large circuit system where the gas is passed back to the diver's compartment for processing and re-supply, sometimes referred to as a push–pull system. The system is based on breathing gas being circulated by a pump through an exhaust line and forced through a regenerative system which includes the CO_2 absorbers, sensors, oxygen injection and finally heating before being passed back to the diver through a separate supply line in the umbilical. Whilst conventional submersibles under 20 tonnes are unlikely to have the capacity to carry a push–pull system, a commercial submarine will and in the future this may become more usual.

A detailed description of a small circuit breathing system is given in Chapter 10 and in the context of submersible lock-out it is a practical system. Apart from communications, the umbilical will have heating and possibly diver monitoring sensors and one gas line for emergency use which will supply the diver should the closed-circuit system in the diver's back-pack fail. Such a system was used without failure for operations from a lock-out submersible in 1977.

Therefore it can be reasonably concluded that the two most suitable systems for use in diver lock-out are semi-closed-circuit supplied through an umbilical and a fully closed small circuit carried by the diver but with an umbilical connection for use in an emergency.

Gas Storage Systems

The following gases need to be carried in sufficient quantities: compressed air, oxygen and mixed gas or pure helium. As liquidization is not feasible all gases are stored in high-pressure containers, usually cylindrical but sometimes spherical, at pressures up to 300 bar. Cylindrical storage tanks are preferred as they conform to the overall hull form of the submersible; they must conform to very high standards of manufacture and maintenance tests as laid down by classification societies. To achieve sufficient redundancy the gas systems are split and cross-connected with shut-off valves to reduce the effect of any damage or leaks in accordance with good engineering safety practice. An emergency life-support system should be capable of sustaining the lives of the full crew, including divers, for a minimum of 96 hours over and above the planned dive time.

Oxygen systems

Additional oxygen supplies are required not only by divers under pressure but also by the remainder of the crew in the command module. The amount of oxygen required is determined largely by the consumption of the divers; the needs of the remaining crew, including the pilot, in their one-atmosphere compartment are modest in comparison. A typical oxygen supply system for a lock-out submersible is illustrated in Fig. 7.42 where, for example, an oxygen bank of 12-litre cylinders is installed in the recesses of the external ballast tanks. Four storage tanks are connected in parallel with individual charging manifolds or together. The supply lines from the external tanks are passed through the pressure hull to the diving supervisor's control manifold in the command module, suitably protected with shut-off valves. The high-pressure oxygen supply is reduced to low pressure at the control panel before entering the breathing system for the divers. For safety reasons the oxygen storage

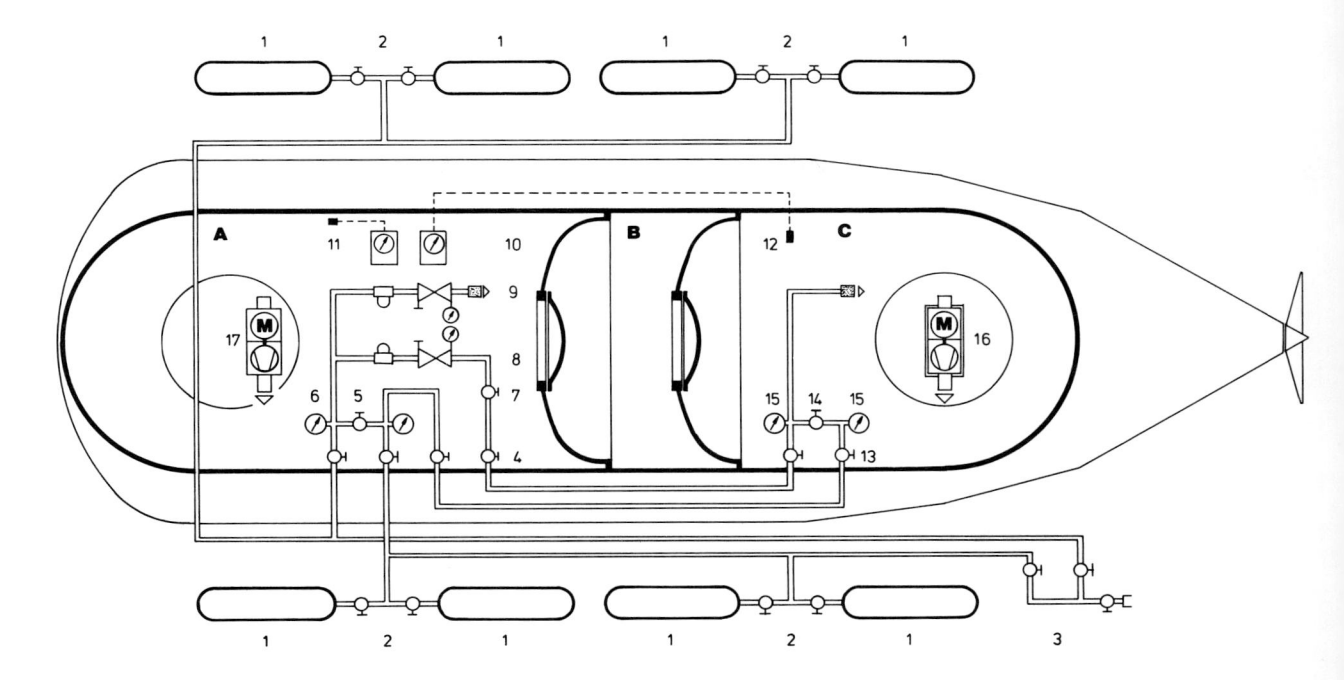

Fig. 7.42. An oxygen system for a diver lock-out submersible. Reliability of the supply is ensured by installing two independent subsystems. A = pilot compartment; B = inner lock; C = lock-out chamber.

1. oxygen cylinder
2. cylinder shut-off valve
3. charging manifold
4. pressure hull shut-off valve
5. cross-connection valve
6. pressure gauge
7. oxygen valve to lock-out chamber
8. oxygen dosage valve to lock-out chamber
9. oxygen dosage valve to pilot compartment
10. oxygen measurement, lock-out chamber
11. oxygen measurement, pilot compartment
12. oxygen sensor
13. pressure hull shut-off valve
14. cross-connection valve
15. storage pressure gauge
16. CO_2 scrubber, lock-out chamber
17. CO_2 scrubber, pilot compartment

system is divided into two branches and distributed from the supervisor's control panel to the pilot and diving compartments. The oxygen control panel will have high-pressure gauge and a pressure regulator reducing the oxygen to low pressure with a needle valve or fine adjustment in order to regulate the correct flow. The flow, in litres per minute, is measured by a flowmeter and set to between 0.3 and 0.5 litres/minute/person; it can be altered by fine adjustment to achieve the correct partial pressure of oxygen. Automatic control of Po_2, as in surface diving complexes, can be fitted in submersibles but is not generally in use.

Carbon dioxide produced at about 0.35 litres/minute per diver needs to be removed, the permissible levels being determined by pressure and exposure. For long exposure, exceeding five days, the CO_2 content should not exceed 0.5% at atmospheric pressure; for

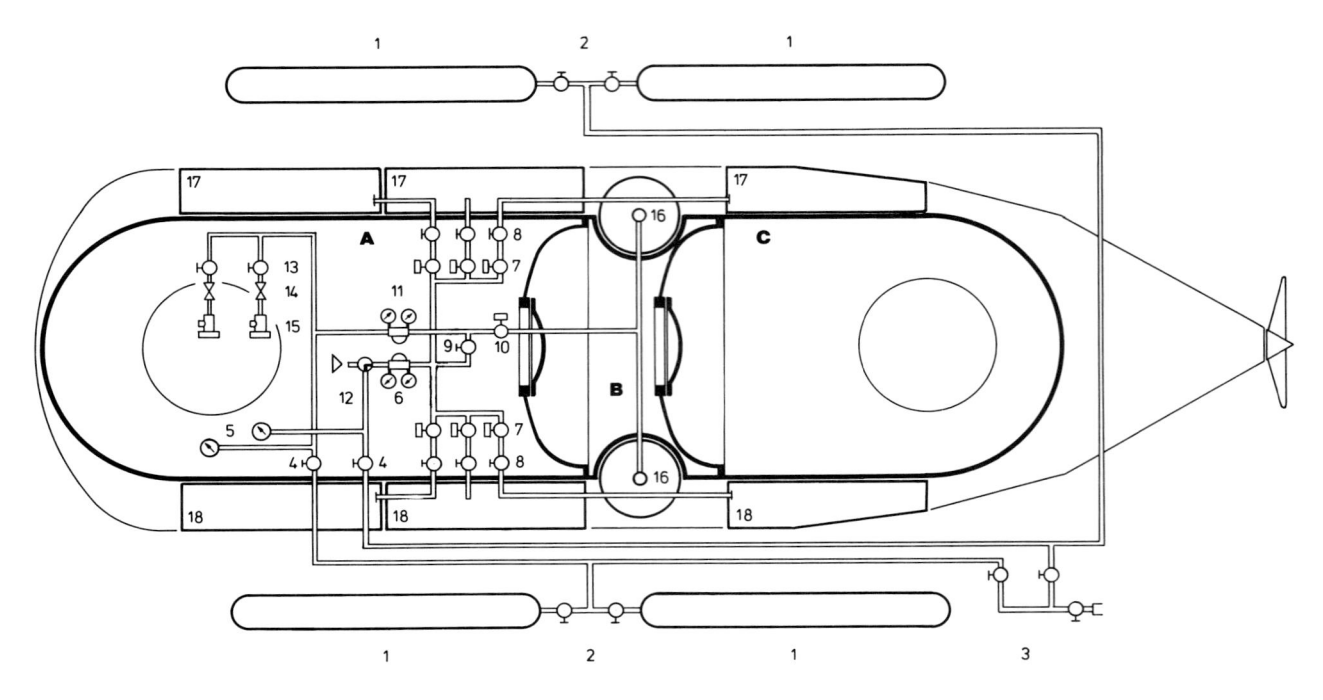

Fig. 7.43. Compressed air system for hard and soft ballast tanks and built-in breathing system. Two separate storage banks are installed but may be cross-connected. A = pilot compartment; B = inner lock; C = lock-out chamber.

1	air cylinders	8	pressure hull shut-off valve
2	cylinder shut-off valve	9	cross-connection hard/soft ballast tank systems
3	charging manifold	10	hard ballast tank blowing valve
4	pressure hull shut-off valve	11	pressure regulator for hard ballast tank system
5	storage pressure gauge	12	three-way valve cross-connection to mixed gas
6	pressure regulator for soft ballast tank system	13	shut-off valve for BIBS
7	soft ballast tank blowing valve	14	pressure regulators
		15	demand regulators
		16	hard ballast tank
		17	soft ballast tank, starboard
		18	soft ballast tank, port

shorter periods, 1.5% is considered acceptable. CO_2 is removed by chemical absorbents, the gas usually being forced through the chemical by a fan or blower. The chemicals which are currently used are lithium hydroxide (LiOH), Baralime (80% calcium hydroxide $(Ca(OH)_2)$ with an activator) and Sodasorb. The endurance of the chemicals differs and varies with the amount of CO_2 produced by the crew, the relative humidity of the air and the temperature. A 4-litre cannister of Sodasorb is expended in about eight to ten hours by a crew of two men. To ensure a 96-hour life-support in an emergency about eight 4-litre Sodasorb cannisters will be required, with an additional 12 kWh of power for the blowers. For an 8-litre cannister fitted with lithium hydroxide the manufacturer specifies an endurance of 60 man hours, so that at least three cannisters are required for emergency support for a two-man crew. Lithium hydroxide is considerably more expensive than Sodasorb. The installation of the CO_2 scrubber units, which include blower/fan and absorbent, needs to take certain factors into account. The density of the breathing gas passing through the absorbent will increase with pressure and will demand more power to achieve the same blower effect. If electric motors are installed inside the compression chambers they will need to be pressure-proof, in accordance with most classification society requirements, to avoid any danger of sparking and ignition when the oxygen content is increased as the pressure in the chamber is lowered.

Compressed air systems

Submersible operations demand considerable amounts of compressed air to blow their external and internal variable ballast tanks; at the same time provision for the breathing needs of the crew demands high standards of purity. The total volume of air storage is entirely dependent on the intended operating depth of the submersible and the size of the ballast tanks. Fig. 7.43 illustrates a typical system. For the same reasons of practical redundancy and safety, the system is separated and cross-connected, one system perhaps supplying the internal hard ballast tanks and the other the external soft ballast tanks. In this illustration each part is supplied from a 50-litre cylinder each with a charging manifold. A pressure reducer will reduce the air to a working pressure of 40 bar, sufficient to blow the tanks at diving depth. In this illustration the external tanks will produce about 1 tonne of positive buoyancy and be capable of blowing tanks 15 to 20 times on the surface. Internal tanks could be discharged and flooded about three times at maximum depth.

The emergency breathing system consists of breathing mask connected to the high-pressure compressed air system and reduced to breathing pressure. They can be used by the crew in the event of the atmosphere becoming contaminated, for example by fire or CO_2 build-up.

Mixed gas systems

Fig. 7.44 illustrates the life-support mixed gas system based on ten 50-litre storage bottles. The type of breathing system used by the divers determines the mixed gas capacity required. In the diagram the system has been designed for short excursions into the water using semi-closed breathing apparatus, a standard procedure; an additional role for bounce diving, where the divers are pressurized in the diving chamber using the gas from the storage tanks, imposes extra demand. The two parallel gas banks with four 50-litre cylinders are sufficient to pressurize both the lock-out chamber and the inner lock to 20 bar. A reserve of about 50% is left for further requirements and emergency use. The breathing gases are supplied from the remaining two cylinders which will provide breathing gases for the diver for about six hours lock-out time at 200 m at a constant flow of 50 litres/minute.

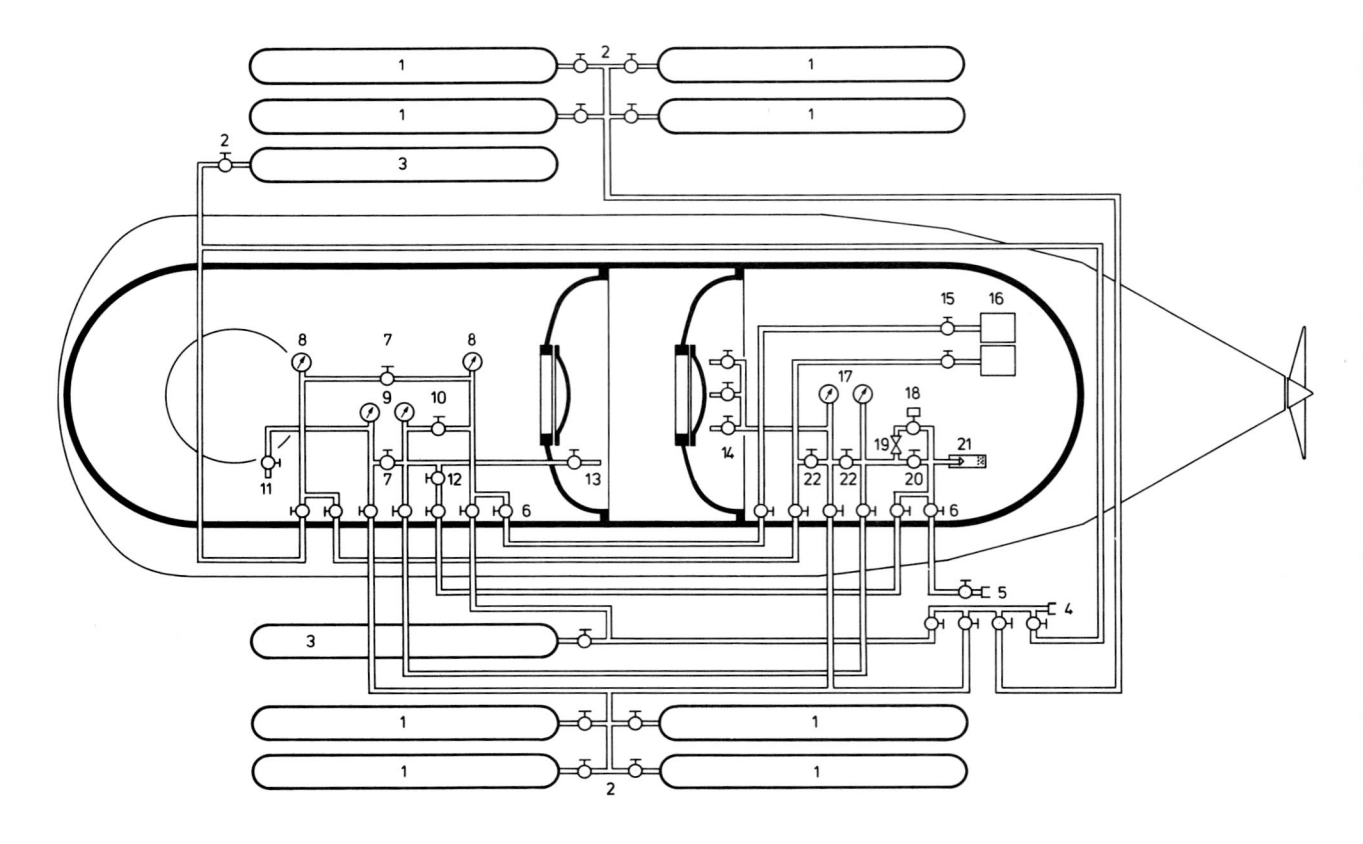

Fig. 7.44. Mixed gas system for a submersible with diver lock-out. There are two seprate systems for lock-out chamber pressurization and diver gas support.

1. mixed gas tank for lock-out chamber compression
2. cylinder shut-off valve
3. mixed gas tank for breathing system
4. charging manifold
5. connection for external support of lock-out chamber
6. pressure hull shut-off valve
7. cross-connection valve between storage banks
8. storage pressure gauge for breathing mixture
9. storage pressure gauge for lock-out chamber gas supply
10. cross-connection between breathing and chamber gas supply
11. cross-connection to high-pressure air system
12. lock-out chamber compression valve
13. inner lock compression valve
14. shut-off valve for BIBS
15. shut-off valve for diver mixed gas supply
16. diver mixed gas supply
17. storage pressure gauge for chamber gas supply
18. automatic chamber pressurization valve
19. pressure regulator
20. lock-out chamber pressurization valve
21. silencer
22. cross-connection valve

If the divers are in saturation the diving chamber is already pressurized on board the mothership prior to the transfer of the diving crew from the deck compression chamber and the gas storage on board the submersible will be full. In this case the supply can be almost entirely used for breathing apparatus, apart from adjusting the pressure at depth if required and, of course, retaining an emergency reserve. Two cylinders can supply gas for pressure adjustments and the remaining eight can theoretically provide 25 hours on semi-closed breathing equipment, although such equipment is naturally impracticable and unrealistic for that length of time. However, 80–90 minutes working time can be achieved using an open-circuit system.

If closed-circuit breathing systems are used the gas capacity can be reduced and more compressed air carried instead. Most gas storage systems carry pre-mixed gases for convenience as the mission cycles are generally known in advance, as are the maximum depths on the basis of which the oxy-helium mixture is calculated and prepared. However, it is feasible for the oxy-helium to be mixed in the submersible from pure O_2 and the supplies in the storage tanks, but this is time-consuming and requires additional mixing equipment. Helium recovery systems are not fitted because of the relatively short mission cycles and, more important, the relatively high cost in terms of weight and space.

Diver Monitoring Equipment

Because the divers are operating under pressure, probably in poor or nil visibility and experiencing currents and cold, even with efficient heating systems, the crew in the submersible must be in communication with them and keep them under close surveillance, with their performance and condition being monitored by instrumentation. The extent of this monitoring or surveillance needs to be kept in perspective and confined to essential information directly related to the diver's performance and safety in an operational mission; it should not extend to excessive use of medical monitoring. Advanced medical monitoring is possible but should be limited to research and development projects, not operations. The basic information required is the same as that needed from bell divers. However, the great advantage of submersible lock-out operations is that the supervisor is on site and the pilot and supervisor can very often observe the diver through the viewport by positioning the craft bows-on to the work site. A number of aids are essential for the supervision and monitoring.

Visual Communication

Subject to good visibility, visual communication through the viewport between the diver and the supervisor can be further enhanced by writing on message boards. Television systems can be used to monitor the diver in certain situations. In poor visibility a strong light on the submersible can help guide the diver back to the craft in addition to his umbilical. In the absence of voice communication between the supervisor and the pressure chambers, pre-arranged signals can be passed on coloured panel lights.

Voice Communication

Sound-powered telephones provide a standard means of communication between the pilot's compartment and the lock-out chamber in the event of the powered intercom system failing. Helium unscramblers are fitted but, despite the advances made since speech processors became available, the intelligibility of processed speech from divers breathing oxy-helium mixtures still needs further development. Communication lines are incorporated in the umbilical. In addition visual display units are now being incorporated inside the helmets of divers handling television cameras so that they can see what information they are transmitting. Through-water ultrasonic equipment can sometimes be used efficiently but its quality may deteriorate in poor under-water conditions. It can operate efficiently at close range and operation at up to 300 m is possible in good conditions.

Instrumentation

Both the stand-by diver and the diver should be relieved from having to watch or operate any instrument unless it is impossible for it to be done by the supervisor, e.g. operating the equalizing valves on the lock-out hatches prior to opening. The supervisor's instrument panel will have all the relevant gauges and valves needed to operate the system including pressure gauges of the storage tanks in banks with supply valves to the chamber and locks. Gauges to give the ambient pressure and the pressure in the diving chamber are fitted, with an additional gauge for the last 25 m for greater control and finer adjustment for the last stages of decompression should this need to be carried out in the submersible. The oxygen partial pressure read-outs are vital, both from the lock-out chamber and from the diver's helmet if closed-circuit systems are in use. The P_{O_2} is normally displayed as a digital read-out on the control panel. Also displayed will be the P_{CO_2}. An additional feature of advanced closed-circuit systems is for the partial pressure of oxygen and carbon dioxide to be projected on a visual display unit inside the diver's helmet. A simple arrangement could be a coloured signal, green for normal, yellow for change and red for a dangerous condition or malfunction.

The requirements for the pressure control valve differ with the type of diving mission being undertaken because of the varying compression and decompression rates. For saturation diving there may be little or no need for major adjustments but minor adjustments in the order of 1 m per 45 minutes will demand a very fine exhaust valve to bleed off at the required rate. For bounce diving, where minimum exposure to pressure is aimed at, decompression rates may be in the order of 18 m/minute and will demand larger valves. For compression the rate may vary by as much as 70 m/minute. Adjustable stem valves are used, not ball valves, because of the finer control they provide. Although primary control over compression and decompression is exercised by the supervisor through exhaust and supply valves, these may be duplicated inside the diving chamber so as to allow the divers local control, but in this case they are usually fitted with an override valve so that ultimate responsibility rests with the supervisor. Oxygen injection is always controlled by the supervisor as it demands most careful handling in a closed environment.

The temperature has to be regulated to heat the pressure chamber to take into account the temperature of the water and the chamber atmosphere. Breathing gases to the diver have also to be heated in most situations. The chamber temperature is easily read from a remote thermometer. It is useful to know the temperature of the breathing gases, particularly as the gas heat exchangers are not entirely predictable or efficient and ideal gas temperature at various depths is not always achieved. The temperature of the suit heating water is relatively straightforward to measure. However, with chamber gas, breathing gas and suit heating the objective report of the divers is the best form of monitoring, rather than information, which may be misleading, displayed on somewhat remote instruments on the control panel.

A supply lock is usually fitted to allow small articles, food and replacement cannisters of absorbent to be passed through. Gauges and equalizing valves are therefore required to pressurize or equalize the lock. Safety features which lock the doors mechanically if the pressures are unequal are well established precautions.

Diver Heating

Diver heating is as yet not entirely resolved and is severely restricted by the limited power available in a submersible. However, it is vital for the diver and many accidents and fatalities are caused by inadequate heating, particularly in an emergency. The human body can sustain its thermal balance for long periods, even without external insulation, in air of 22°C. In water the heat loss is about 25 times greater than in air. Insulating garments and diving suits can compensate for this fairly well at shallow water depth. The heat loss due to the exhalation of air is only one-seventh of the heat flow into the water and is therefore usually neglected. When breathing helium mixtures the heat transfer to the breathing gas is about six to seven times greater than with air and reaches the same order as the heat loss to the water. A considerable amount of heat is thus drawn from the body internally through the respiratory tract unless the temperature of the breathing gas or the atmosphere is kept consistent at about 32°C. The energy consumption for heating alone can be as high as 10 kW. This factor can represent a serious limitation in diver lock-out submersibles which carry a limited energy supply in their batteries and also provide energy for propulsion, lights, tools and electronic equipment. Thermal insulation can reduce the amount of power needed to supply heating. The thermal insulation of the lock-out chamber presents relatively few difficulties and needs to be considered at the design stage. Internal insulation may have the advantage that it can be fitted more easily and that it is not exposed to water. Both

A

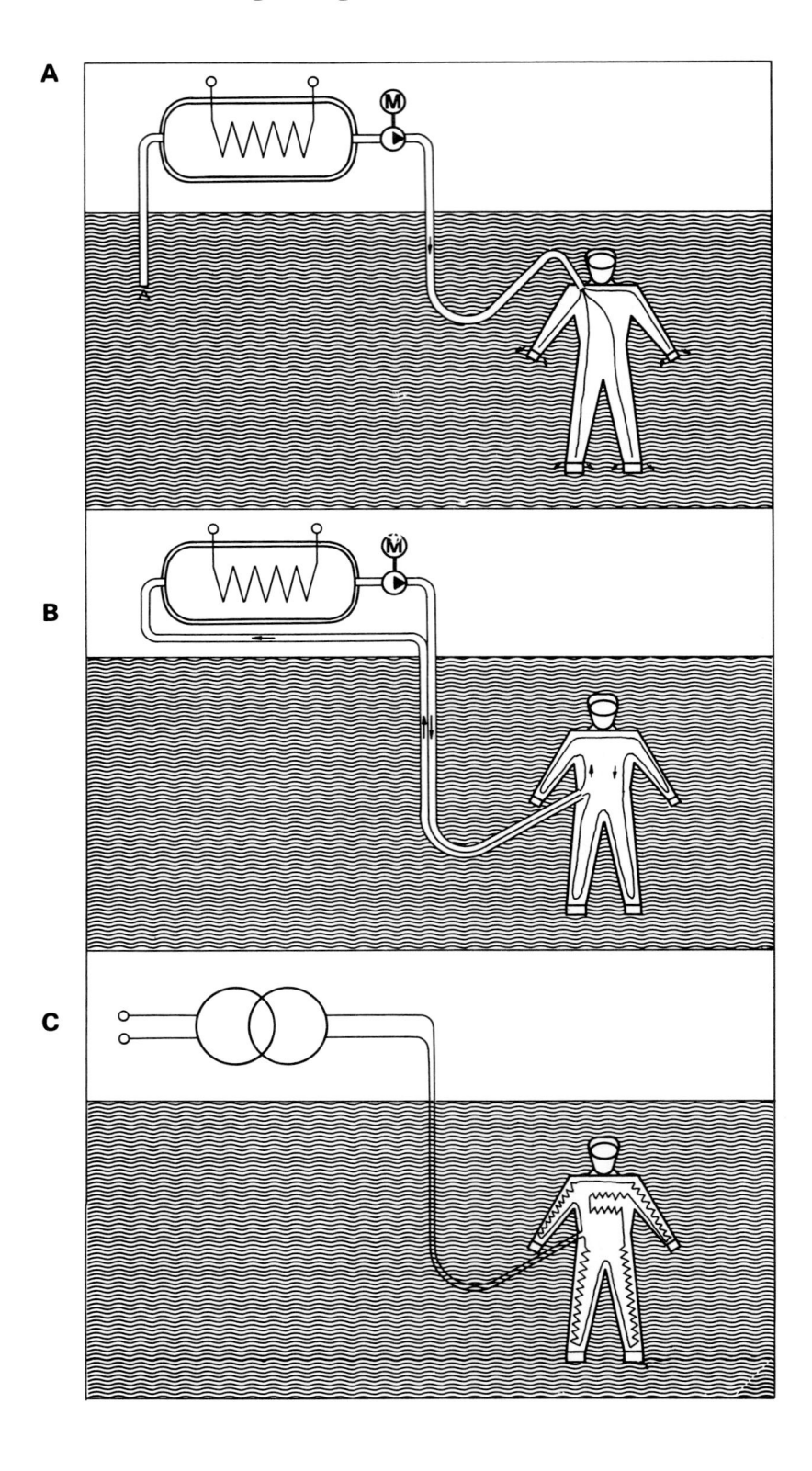

B

C

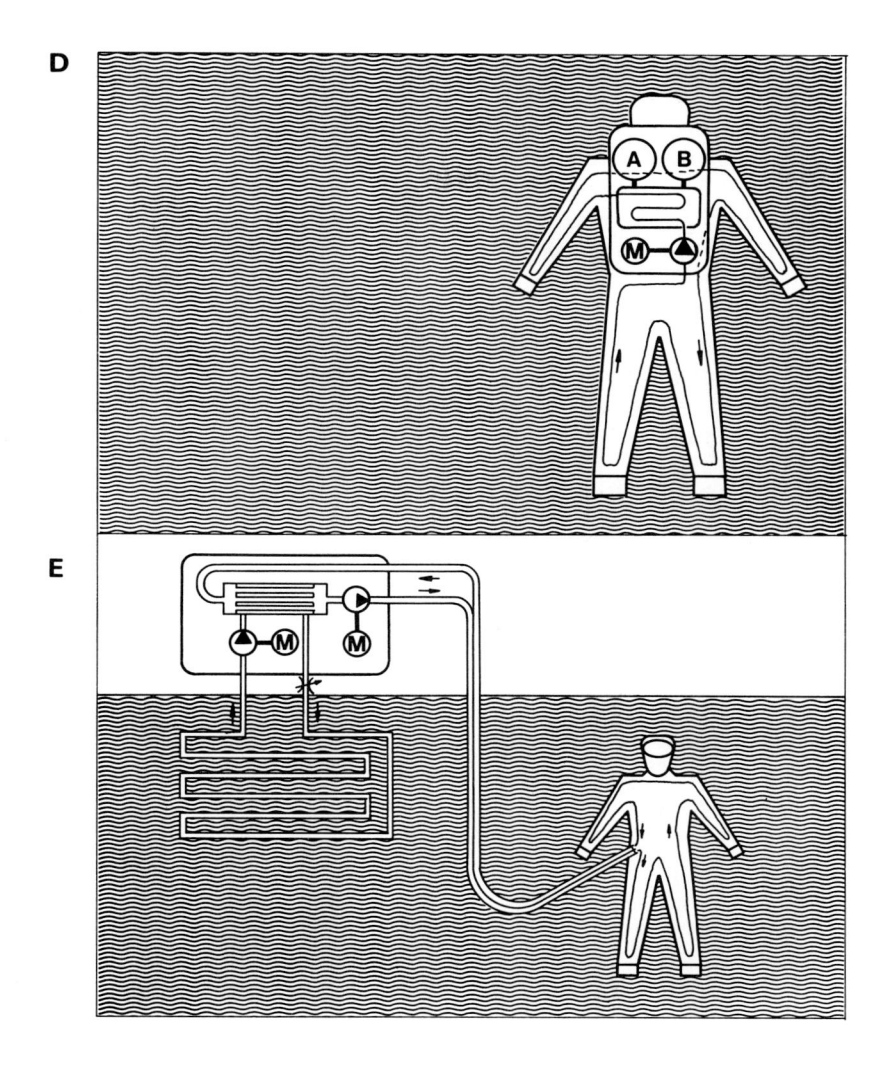

Fig. 7.45. Comparison of different diver heating systems.

- **A** Open warm-water circuit. Electric or other boiler on board vessel support. Warm water is pumped into the diver suit and discharged into the surrounding sea. Simple construction but high energy requirement. Not suitable for submersibles

- **B** Closed warm-water circuit. Boiler heated electrically or by oil. Warm water is pumped into the diver suits and returned to the boiler. Reduced energy consumption. Diver suit more complicated. Conditionally suited for submersibles

- **C** Electrically heated diver suit with woven-in wires supplied with low voltage from transformers. Good efficiency but suit is sensitive to mechanical damage and insulation defects. Principally suited for submersibles

- **D** Suit heated by chemical heat of reaction. Portable system with thermally reactive chemicals and closed warm-water circuit with battery-powered circulation pump. Small power requirement for pumping. System is voluminous and heavy; it is still under development. If refined, would be very suitable for submersibles

- **E** A heat pump is used instead of an electrically heated boiler. Closed warm-water circuit. Energy consumption is only about one-third of a directly converting heater with the same output. Excellent for submersible and already used successfully

solutions require pressure-proof insulation materials. External insulation may be preferred for a number of reasons. Since insulation materials usually have a low specific gravity they contribute to the submersible's buoyancy and thus improve the payload. The chamber is preheated on board the mothership and the steel walls of the chamber act as an efficient heat accumulator. Furthermore the size of the already small pressure chamber is not reduced further.

Suitable insulation materials are syntactic foams in rigid or flexible form and reinforced with glass or other blended resin materials. Syntactic foams are relatively easy to apply but they have the disadvantage of high costs.

Experience and calculations show that the power required to maintain an internal lock-out chamber temperature at 32°C with an ambient water temperature of about 0°C, for an average lock-out chamber, is 7 kW if not insulated and 1 kW if insulated with 2.5 cm of insulating material. The advantage of insulation is therefore considerable.

However, the thermal insulation of divers is more difficult. Wet suits lose their insulating properties at relatively shallow depths because the suit material is compressible and the insulating gas layer enclosed in the material becomes thinner with increasing depth. The same situation is encountered with dry suits but the gas between suit and body and the undergarment is effective as insulation. The manufacture of hard-wearing diver suits of flexible, incompressible materials does not seem to have resolved the problem of retaining the diver's heat without the use of external heating systems.

A submersible carries electrical energy which is stored in its batteries. This electric energy can be converted to heat either directly or transferred to a medium, for example water, which is then supplied to the diver. An electrically heated diving suit is made up of resistance wires which are electrically insulated and woven into the undergarment. Because of the problems caused by the breaking of wires and insufficient insulation an attempt was made to use mercury as a heating element but with little success. Nevertheless improvements are being made in the development of electrically heated systems. At the moment hot water is more dependable as the energy carrier for diver suit heating and is more generally used.

The usual form of heating for diving bells, where hot water is supplied to the bell and then to the diver through an umbilical from the surface as an open circuit system, is obviously out of the question for diver lock-out submersibles. In this case hot water is fed into the diving suit where it is distributed as uniformly as possible and then is discharged. The energy consumption is accordingly high. In submersibles, hot water heating systems on closed circuit operate reasonably well. In one heating system, for example, four separate heating coils are located in a pressure-proof insulated heater. The heating power of the coils is twice 1 kW and twice 0.5 kW, i.e. 3 kW in total. The water is heated and then supplied to the hot water suit of the diver. There it gives off part of its energy and is returned to the heater. This method is considerably more energy-saving than the open circuit described above. The heating suit was originally developed for space missions. It consists of a synthetic material with heating pads that are placed on important areas of the body and in which the warm water circulates through coils. Quick couplings are attached to the suit for the water inlet and outlet connection. It is necessary to vent the suit carefully before use to ensure complete circulation. The water inlet temperature of the suit is about 35°C and the heater outlet temperature about 65°C. The difference is heat lost through the umbilical which is exposed to ambient temperature. The flow rate is between 2 and 3 litres/minute. The maximum differential pressure for the heating garment is 2 bar. About 1.5 kW of heating power is needed.

The power requirement for heating the lock-out chamber, with one diver outside, amounts to about 3 kW. With a battery capacity of roughly 30 kW h (reserves not included), and assuming that about one-half of two-thirds is required for propulsion, lighting, tools etc., operating times of up to five hours can be reached with *Mermaid III/IV*. In practice this means diver lock-out times of up to three hours in one dive.

To conserve energy a heating system on the heat pump principle was specially developed for diver lock-out submersibles by Bruker. This system is, of course, also suitable for under-water habitats and diving bells and has the advantage that for the same output as the heater system less than half as much energy is required. Consequently it is possible to double diver lock-out times. The system consists of a primary circuit, in which the 'refrigerant', e.g. freon R 12, is circulated, and a secondary warm water circuit. The electric motor drives a special compressor in which the freon is compressed and heated. The hot, pressurized gas flows into a condenser in which heat is transferred to a secondary water circuit. The condensated gas passes a reducing valve. With the drop in pressure the temperature is decreased. It is reduced to a level so far below the ambient water temperature that a sufficient temperature difference is achieved and heat can be transferred from the ambient water to the freon in the heat exchanger behind the reducer. The freon is then drawn to the compressor again. An energy saving has been attained in so far as heat was drawn from the sea and merely raised to a higher, useful temperature by the electric motor and compressor. The desired temperature in the secondary circuit can therefore be regulated by the pressure in the primary circuit. To provide an adequate reserve heating power, the temperature is adjusted higher than the average consumption requires and the compressor is switched on and off by a pressure-operated switch. With higher heat consumption the ratio of operation to shutdown time increases. The 'refrigerant' R 12 is a relatively safe gas. It is heavier than air and at more than 4 bar and less than 55°C remains in the liquid stage.

Together with a special umbilical which provides minimal heat loss to the ambient water and the possibility of preheating the breathing gas, this heating system represents an advance. It should not normally be difficult to mount the primary heat exchanger in a

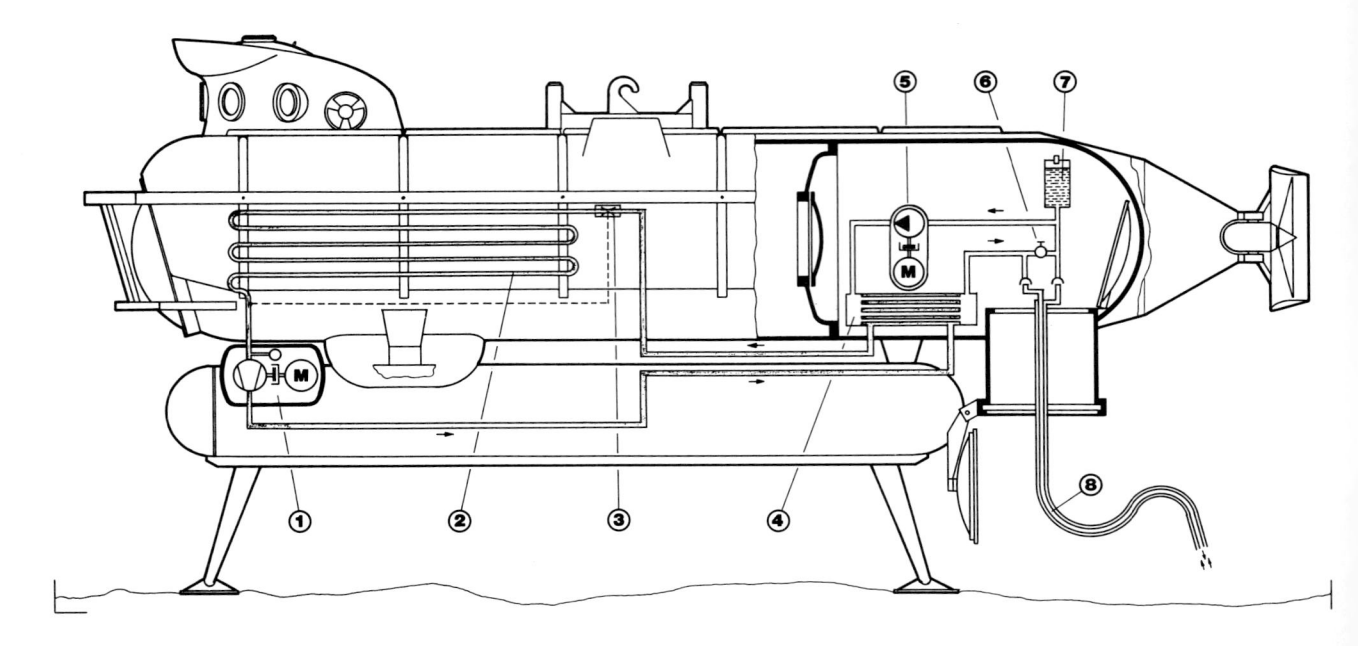

Fig. 7.46. A diver heating system using a closed water circuit and the heat pump principle (patent pending).

1. compressor with electromagnetic clutch and electric motor, here installed in a pressure vessel
2. sea water heat exchanger
3. expansion valve
4. fresh water heat exchanger
5. hermetically encapsulated hot water circulation pump driven by electric motor via permanently magnetic clutch
6. bypass valve
7. compensator tank
8. umbilical connection to heated diver suit

suitable position on the outside of the submersible. At the design stage the compressor and hot-water pump can be planned to be sited in the atmospheric section of the submersible. When electric motors are installed inside the hyperbaric chamber they have to be pressure sealed to reduce fire risk in case of increased oxygen partial pressure. The first heating system built on this principle was installed with compressor, electric motor and pressure switch placed in a separate pressure vessel fitted to the outside of the submersible. The warm water circulation pump was located in the lock-out chamber.

Manipulators

Manipulators have been developed for use on land where remote operations were needed, as in nuclear installations. The development of units for under-water work was relatively simple. The nature of the functions that a manipulator can undertake makes it a most useful tool complementary to the particular skills of a diver. Therefore they are fitted to most lock-out submersibles and are often used for preparatory work prior to the diver locking-out, thus reducing his working time.

Nuclear research facilities need such tools to handle parts in contaminated areas. The movements of the operator's hand are transmitted electrically to the manipulator which is often designed with a force feed-back. Although this principle is also ideally suited for under-water manipulators, the delicate electric sensors and control elements present problems under difficult operating conditions. Therefore manipulators for use under water have to be designed specially for this purpose. Forced feed-back has now been incorporated into modern manipulators.

Robots designed for use in factories will not have a significant impact on under-water operations as the environment is hostile to pre-planned movement.

Typical Tasks for Under-water Manipulators

With simple manipulators it is possible to position acoustic beacons used to mark objects, possibly for later recovery or for dynamic positioning of surface vessels and platforms and for survey work. This type of location work could not be carried out from the surface with the same precision. Placing unarmed explosive charges on wellheads which are no longer needed, attaching lifting lines, clearing debris and cutting cable are further examples of the work that has been done successfully by manipulators. Removal of marine growth, grinding, cutting, drilling and tightening or loosening of bolts are possible, but only with special attachments. For example, manipulators were developed and built for specialized tasks such as the recovery of torpedoes. Basic manipulators have simple claws and clamps with up to three degrees of freedom as distinct from true manipulators with six or more degrees of freedom. The former can only be used to clasp and release objects such as missiles or acoustic beacons. In addition they are sometimes fitted with more functional manipulators in order to overcome reactive forces. For example, the submersible's basic manipulator secures itself by a claw to the object on which it is to do work. Besides mechanical claws, magnetic or suction devices may be considered. A submersible at neutral buoyancy cannot take up any transverse forces (except by its propeller thrust) and moments only within its range of stability and therefore an attachment to a fixed point will help compensate for this reaction. Devices which enable the diver lock-out submersible to attach itself to a structure in mid-water prior to diver lock-out operations are an essential requirement as the use of thrusters and propellors is discouraged.

Hydraulic systems are most suitable for energizing manipulators. A manipulator consists of a structure with several joints and drives. The 'hand' of the manipulator can usually be rotated and swivel about at least one axis. It is usually designed with parallel claws. One design principle is based on drives where joints are pressure-proof, the

Fig. 7.47. A pair of hydraulic manipulators with 6° of freedom. The two parallel claws can be replaced by other claws or tools. In an emergency the manipulators can be discarded.

hollow structures normally being pressure-compensated. This principle offers the best possible protection but it is complicated and maintenance is difficult. Much less costly are manipulators with exposed but corrosion-resistant parts such as hydraulic cylinders and rotary drives.

A manipulator which is designed for the hydraulic system of the *Mermaid* submersibles is the BM-76 shown in Fig. 7.47. At its full extension of 1800 mm it is able to lift weights of 80 kg and its claw can exert a torque 20 m kg. The arm is composed of the basic six functions of upper arm, elbow joint, lower arm, wrist and claw and can be increased by additional elements if necessary. The standard model is able to perform the following motions:

1. Extension and retraction of the upper arm in horizontal direction
2. Swivelling of the lower arm about a vertical axis
3. Lifting and lowering of the lower arm
4. Lifting and lowering of the claw
5. Rotation of the claw
6. Opening and closing of the claw

Hydraulic cylinders and rotary drives are used as moving parts. The parts are made of non-corrosive steel and anodized aluminium. The parallel claw can be replaced by a rotating brush for cleaning and by a cutting wheel, a grinder or a cable cutter. A *Mermaid* submersible is usually equipped with two manipulators which are supported on rollers and mounted on top of the battery pods. One of the arms in the standard version is with a claw whereas the other carries the specific tool for the planned task. For safety reasons each manipulator can be dropped in case it should get entangled and cannot be freed. For this purpose hydraulic bolts are actuated from inside the submersible, after the hydraulic lines have been shut off by means of valves, and separated. The arms are controlled from a joystick.

These claws and manipulators are able to perform numerous tasks and can be manufactured at relatively low cost but two different types of manipulator systems have recently been introduced. The manipulator which was developed by General Electrics (USA) and known as Atmospheric Roving Manipulator System (ARMS) incorporates a more sophisticated forced feed-back. The operator actuates a master arm, the movements of which are followed by the manipulator arm. The operator can 'feel' the forces exerted by the manipulator on the master arm. This system has the advantage that movements can be performed much more positively than with simple on–off or proportional speed control. The Work System Package (WSP) developed by the US Navy is currently the most advanced manipulator, with six functions, a range of tools and a television camera. The tool exchange technique, developed from numerically controlled machine tools, was used for under-water manipulators for the first time in this system. Drills, grinding and cutting wheels, screwdrivers, brushes, chisels, hammers, cutting devices, cable cutters, nail-firing tools and other tools are available. The arm can take a tool from a magazine and return it after use. Quick hydraulic coupling connectors are used for the interchange. The system can be controlled by a television camera on the surface as well as by direct visual contact from inside a submersible or diving bell. In addition the unit can be operated by a diver directly on the site by means of a water-proof control box.

High-pressure air tools, such as drilling machines, cutting wheels, brushes, chain and disc saws etc., are commonly used by divers with the compressed air delivered by compressors from the surface. At greater depths the application of compressed air becomes more and more uneconomic because of the increased back-pressure. Hydraulic tools do not have this disadvantage and are also available for underwater use. Hydraulic, diver-operated tools are in common use in the diver lock-out vehicle which possesses a powerful hydraulic system. On *Mermaid* submersibles, for example, the power which is needed for propulsion whilst under way or manoeuvring is available for hydraulic power tooling after the submersible has 'landed'. The hydraulic pressure and the flow rates are adequate even from very heavy tools. These tools can be stowed and transported on the outside of the submersible. Thus equipped, the diver lock-out submersible is already performing a wide range of light to medium under-water tasks in support of off-shore activity.

The Diver Lock-out: The Future

In common with other methods of under-water intervention, notably the diving bell and, more recently, the unmanned vehicle, the diver lock-out cannot be said to be indispensable when compared to other systems. All systems are being developed to carry out a wider range of operations but some are more efficient in one particular sphere than others. Efficiency also means being cost-effective and therefore diver lock-out operations must also be justified financially. Clearly the significant improvements in the performance of unmanned vehicles, together with their operating cost, have expanded their market in the survey and inspection field, a field which had been dominated in the past by submersibles. In these situations the submersibles find difficulty in competing owing to their high operating costs, which include more personnel and larger motherships than unmanned vehicle operations. The role of the lock-out submersible, however, should not necessarily be evaluated on the same basis as there will always be functions that an unmanned vehicle's manipulator will not be able to carry out and within certain depths the diver's role will exist. The area in which deep diving operations need to be evaluated is notably between bell operations and submersible lock-out operations. The advantages and disadvantages of both are clear. The diving bell operating from a diving vessel, although theoretically supplied with unlimited essential services through an umbilical, is limited to some extent by the physical endurance of the divers and more by the ability of the mothership to keep position dynamically for long periods and in deteriorating weather conditions. The diving bell has very little mobility and cannot be moved whilst lowered.

The lock-out submersible has considerable flexibility and mobility but is constrained by limited supplies of power and gases. Owing to the need to recover the submersible on board a mothership, an operation that can only be carried out in good sea conditions, the weather factor is an important consideration.

The cost-effectiveness of lock-out submersibles is in those operations which require speed and mobility so that they can be completed in a comparatively short time with the minimum of equipment. Heavy construction work requiring diver intervention is better served by diving bells. Some under-water engineering support ships carry both systems which are complementary but use a common hyperbaric complex. If the high cost can be justified, the widest possible range of under-water tasks can be carried out. Ultimately the tasks and operations carried out from diving bells and diver lock-out submersibles will be carried out from a commercial submarine as discussed in Chapter 8. This is the ultimate solution for the future of deep all-round under-water work.

Submarines

8

There is no clear dividing line which separates submersibles from submarines. There are two commonly accepted definitions, Lloyd's Register of Shipping defines a submersible for classification purposes as not exceeding 30 m in length. On the other hand a submarine is often considered as a submersible that can operate without surface support. Purists would say that a true submarine does not need to surface during a mission to renew the internal atmosphere or recharge its power source. At present this requirement is met only by military nuclear-powered submarines and as at present there is no intention of using these large submarines commercially, they are not considered in this chapter. Some craft such as the *Auguste Piccard* are borderline cases, in that they are too large to be operated from a mothership but require a surface escort for a variety of purposes while operating or on passage in open waters. To overcome these borderline problems, it is normal to talk about autonomous submarines. Autonomous in this context refers to the craft's ability to move on the surface or submerged from port to port or from port to operational area unescorted and in all normal weather conditions. At present there are no civilian craft that meet these criteria fully.

History

Submarines are not a new development and the first reported type was made in 1620 by a Dutchman, Cornelius van Drebel, for King James I of England. It was propelled by oars with leather sleeves to provide water-proofing at the oarports and reputedly had some substance to purify the air. It is reported to have navigated in the River Thames at a depth of 12–15 ft (4–5 m) for several hours. The American, Dr David Bushnell, built and operated a small wooden craft in the 1770s in order to attack British warships with mines. From then on all submarine development was for military purposes and only really started at the beginning of this century, although in the early 1800s Robert Fulton did design and build two iron-framed copper-skinned submarines called *Nautilus* and *Mute*. Again in the late 1880s Simon Lake launched the *Argonaut First* but the real advances in submarine design have taken place during this century.

Submarine Design

Submarine design is a specialized field of naval architecture, thorough study of which would require several volumes. Here it is only necessary to touch briefly on the problems of stability, propulsion, buoyancy, hull strength and life-support in order to give the reader a basic understanding of the distinctive requirements of submarine builders and operators.

Stability

When on the surface the submarine acts and behaves in the same way as any other surface ship. It has and requires both a longitudinal and a transverse positive metacentric height which is provided when rolling by the movement of the centre of buoyancy which is below the centre of gravity. As the craft floods her tanks and submerges the centre of buoyancy rises until, when fully submerged, it is above the centre of gravity. This is essential, as the centre of buoyancy remains fixed once the submarine is submerged and the righting moment is provided by the pendulum effect of the movement of the centre of gravity relative to the centre of buoyancy. It should be noted that during submerging and surfacing there will be an instant when the centre of buoyancy and centre of gravity coincide; at this point in time stability is at a minimum. Consequently venting and blowing must be carried out in such a way that chances of a pause at this moment are eliminated.

Propulsion

Although many systems have been tried at different times, the diesel-driven and lead–acid battery combination is the accepted method, except for the military nuclear submarine. Diesel power is used on the surface where air for the engine is readily available and the exhaust can easily be discharged. The power is used to propel the submarine directly or to charge the batteries or a combination. When submerged the batteries provide the motive power as well as power for all other services. In the design of new civilian submarines thought has been given to the use of nuclear power but the cost, size and weight are all prohibitive. Fuel cells and closed-cycle diesel systems are presently under trial, but neither is fully developed and the problems of fuel storage are not yet safely solved.

Buoyancy

It is axiomatic in submarine design that the craft must surface as often as it submerges. To do this it must be able to control its buoyancy. Buoyancy tanks are of two types, hard and soft. The latter are external to the pressure hull, with vent valves at the top and openings at the bottom to allow the water to flow in and out. To flood the tanks and allow the submarine to submerge the vent valves are opened and the waters enter through the bottom, forcing the air out through the top. To surface, the vent valves are closed and the water is expelled through the bottom when compressed air is let into the tanks. The tanks are known as 'soft' as the sides have the same pressure on each side, reducing the strength requirement. Hard tanks have to be strong enough to withstand the full ambient pressure of the maximum diving depth. In addition to controlling buoyancy the tanks control trim by moving weight fore and aft as necessary. While hard tanks are normally inside the pressure hull, it is also possible to have internal soft tanks. In addition to controlling buoyancy by pumping, flooding and blowing, some submarines have drop weights which can be released in an emergency to give a sudden positive buoyancy. Control of buoyancy must be sensitive to ensure neutral buoyancy while cruising submerged to allow for changes of displacement caused by changes of depth, salinity and temperature.

Hull Strength

Inside a submarine the crew are subjected to a pressure similar to that on the surface, i.e. one atmosphere, consequently the hull surrounding them must be able to withstand the full pressure down to the designed working depth of the craft. Submarines and submersibles are made of high-grade steel, except for some submersibles which are built of glass-reinforced plastic and some Russian military submarines which are reputed to be made of titanium. All steel hulls have a design depth at which they are expected to collapse. Different classification societies have different factors of safety. For instance, Germanischer Lloyds vary their factor according to depth while others have a fixed factor independent of maximum diving depth. It is important to ensure that all penetrators and internal pipe systems that may be exposed to the full internal pressure are tested and able to withstand this pressure. Modern design tends to remove the full external pressure from all external systems. Obviously as the maximum designed diving depth increases so also will the hull thickness for any specific grade of steel. Consequently as the hull weight increases so must the displacement to ensure adequate buoyancy. This problem has been met by the use of increasingly high grades of steel which, although producing problems in manufacturing with difficult welding techniques, allow a reduction of thickness and therefore weight against specific strength. The introduction of the commercial submarine in support of the off-shore oil industry will not necessarily be confined to the continental shelf in depths normally covered by diving systems and submersibles but will become cost-effective in deeper depths and more exposed areas. Other points to be considered if great depths are required is the hull shape; the sphere is the best for strength but not ideal for propulsive efficiency or to provide a satisfactory work platform.

Life-support

For men to live in a one-atmosphere submarine submerged for any length of time it is essential that the air be maintained in a reasonable condition, temperature and humidity controlled and food and water provided. All this requires power and this is where a submarine scores over its smaller submersible sisters. Table 8.1 gives typical comparative values, related to discharge time. While the length increases by a factor of seven the battery capacity increases by about a factor of 84.

Table 8.1 Battery capacity of submarines of various lengths

Length (m)	Battery capacity (kW h)
7.28	55.2
24	690
42.5	3260
52	4620

Control of the atmosphere which necessitates removal of CO_2 and replacement of oxygen has been adequately described in other chapters of this book. With the power available it is also possible to make fresh water by reverse osmosis or other advanced processes.

The Justification for a Commercial Submarine

Seven-tenths of the Earth's surface is covered by water and no other planet has as much. In the past the only commercial exploitation was fishing. But even fishing has always been conducted from the surface and man has not been needed to go beneath the surface for commercial success. This situation has changed dramatically since World War II owing to the discovery of oil off-shore in the Gulf of Mexico and later in many other areas world wide. The vast majority of work subsea off-shore is oil-related and the development of oil exploration and production in ever deeper and more inhospitable environments has necessitated the formation of an under-water engineering industry. This industry has continuously been presented with new problems and new challenges. Initially the subsurface work was done entirely by divers and other chapters of this book show how the diver and his equipment have developed to meet this challenge. But in the last few years there has been a change of emphasis with the introduction of the manned submersible and remotely operated vehicle systems. With this plethora of alternative systems what then is the justification for another system, the autonomous submarine? The diver has probably a finite maximum diving depth but more important he has a maximum commercially viable diving depth which is much less than the maximum depth and may be as low as 200-300 m. Also the accidents which inevitably occur, we hope at a reducing rate, make this form of employment socially unpopular and alternatives are sought. The submersible suffers from the disadvantage of working from a mothership and consequently being weather-dependent. The maximum weather conditions for launch and recovery will vary with many factors and in particular the handling system employed, and the size of ship and submersible involved, but a sea state of six is normally accepted as the upper limit. Furthermore due to its size the battery capacity is severely limited, which reduces mission time and the type of work that can be carried out. When compared with the remotely operated vehicle which is also weather-dependent the submarine has the advantage of the 'man on the spot' and can, of course, also operate its own remotely operated vehicle system in any and all weather conditions.

It is not sufficient to produce a good submarine with good underwater and surface performance; it must also be capable of carrying out a variety of tasks as the inevitably high cost of building a submarine would not be justified if used only for a few tasks. Clearly the tasks are in the deeper ranges where divers and other forms of intervention become less cost-effective and the advantages of submarines become

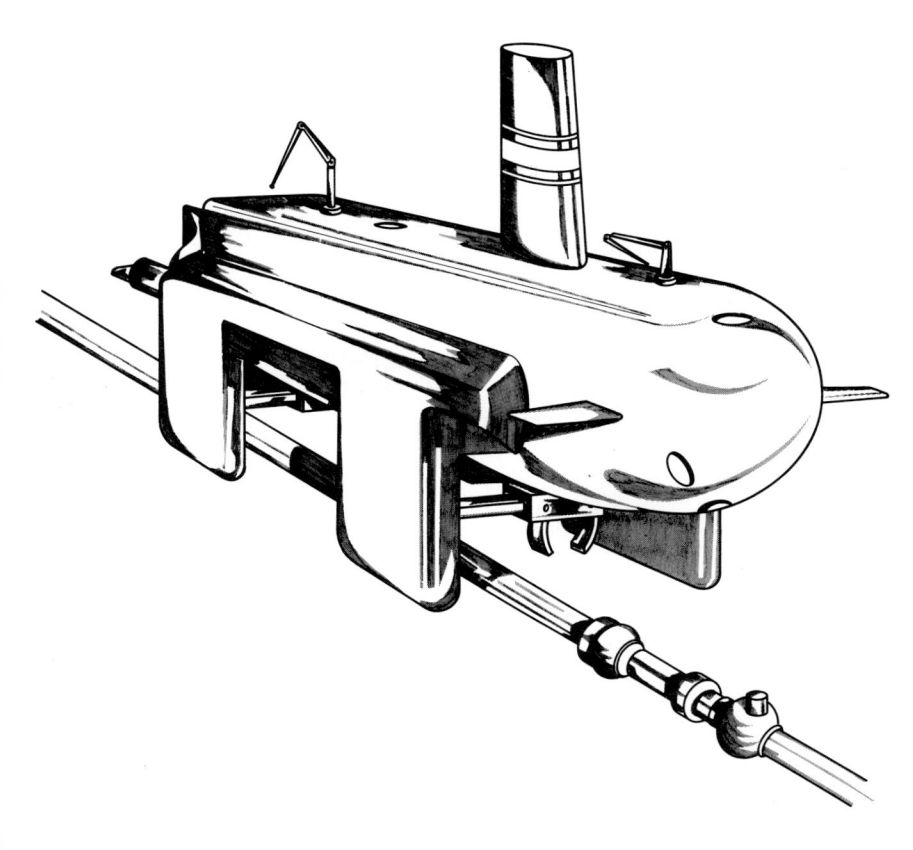

Fig. 8.1. A model of a Kockum General Purpose Submarine fitted with a pipeline alignment frame.

apparent. There have been a number of designs, usually by experienced military submarine designers such as Kockums of Sweden and Ingenieurkontor Lübeck–Gabler of Germany, and these have a number of designed options to cover the requirements of the off-shore oil and gas industry. Both the Kockum and the Gabler designs are very advanced and are ready for building. Submarines that have been built are smaller than those that will be built for commercial use and lack the autonomy to operate independently from surface support, if only in the role of a safety vessel.

The areas of activity to which a submarine must be applied are as follows:

1. Site investigations for installation of platforms requiring core sampling.
2. Route surveys for pipelines requiring side scan profiling and soil sampling.
3. Seismic investigation.
4. Transportation of divers and equipment for tie-ins and subsequent inspection, maintenance and repair of structures and pipelines.
5. Operation of submersibles as part of the total system with entry and exit through the submarine pressure hull to carry out independent surveys and transport personnel and divers to subsea capsules and worksites.

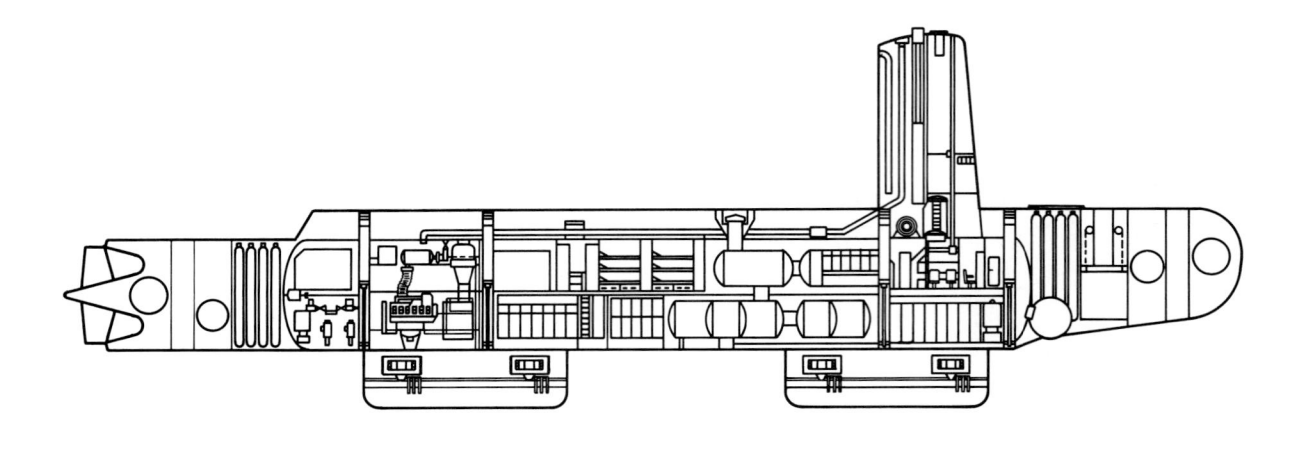

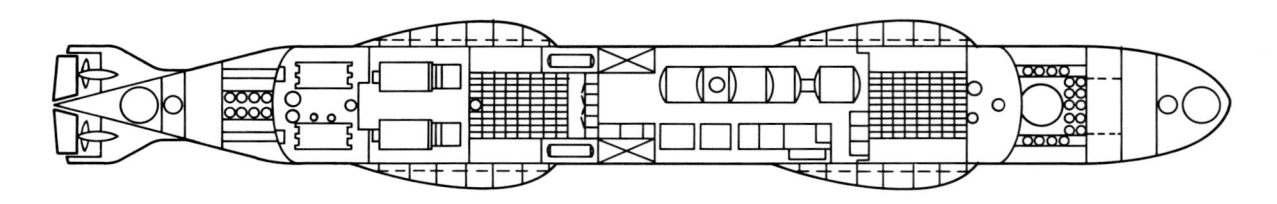

Fig. 8.2. Cross-section of the Kockums General Purpose Submarine.

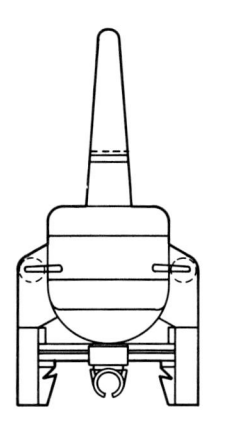

6. Operation of remotely operated vehicles from outside the hull of the submarine, controlled from inside through an umbilical and fitted with television, still cameras, sonar and manipulators, mainly for inspection work inside an adjacent structure at a safe distance from a bottomed submarine.
7. Operation of one-man tethered submersibles through the pressure hull of the submarine, allowing one-atmosphere units as described in Chapter 9 to carry out work needing manual dexterity.
8. Heavy lift capability is a fundamental requirement particularly in regard to pipeline trenching, burial, tie ins and repair. Alignment frames may need to be part of the submarine concept, together with welding chambers.

Specific Submarine Designs

It is estimated that 85% of the work-load for a commercial submarine will be from the off-shore oil and gas industry, with the remaining requirement from research bodies, environmental studies and specifically fishery research. The Hydrospace Survey Vessel HSV-1 is unbuilt but identifies some of the future tasks of the submarine, such as transferring inspection teams at one atmosphere to a seabed production capsule, and at the same time deploying divers to connect an external flowline. This concept is based on an overall length of

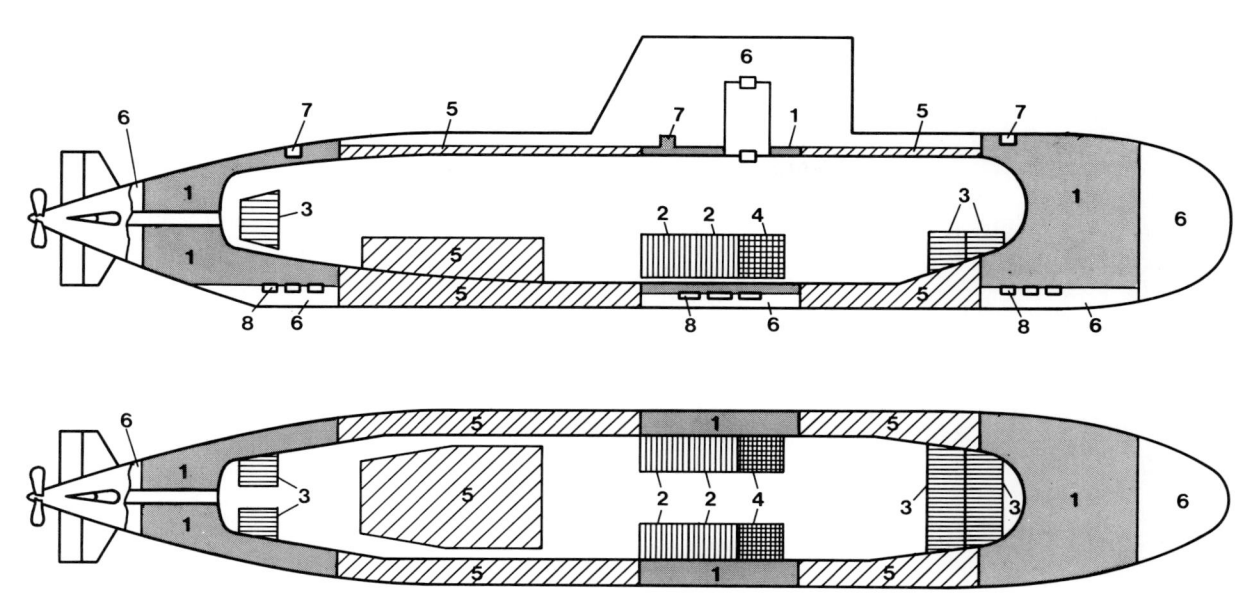

Fig. 8.3. Design for an autonomous commercial submarine.

1. main ballast tanks (MBT)
2. compensating tanks
3. trim tanks
4. compensating fuel tanks
5. fuel oil tanks
6. free flooding spaces
7. MBT venting
8. MBT flood holes

40 m, a diving depth of 305 m, a cargo lift of up to 10 tonnes, a diving team of 11 in addition to the crew and mission cycles of 10–15 days. Up-to-date submarine designs from Kockums, Gabler and Bruker have incorporated these subsystems. Figs 8.1 and 8.2 show the Kockums General Purpose Submarine (GPS).

Alignment Frame

By fitting two power-operated grabs at either end of the submarine and beneath the keel, it is possible to carry out pipeline repair work, re-aligning cutting and welding as required. The divers would be carried in the submarine and locked out to do the work.

Saturation Diving System

A complete saturation diving system is fitted in the submarine which will allow the divers to be both compressed and decompressed as and when required without the need for the submarine to surface. Again the battery power and the large size of the submarine will permit much greater supplies of gas to be carried. Obviously closed-circuit breathing facilities will increase the gas endurance. The saturation system would be similar to those described in Chapter 3. A typical capacity would allow eight divers 24 h diving at 300 m using a semi-closed-circuit system and more if using a closed-circuit breathing system.

Manipulators

Depending on the type of tasks specified for the mission, different manipulators will be fitted from five simple motions to advanced force-feedback systems, with either pincer grips or suction pads according to the requirement.

TV and Photographic Facilities

As with any type of vehicle system the submarine will be fitted with a variety of black and white or colour TV systems as well as ordinary and cine cameras. Depending on the system in use the lighting system will be varied to ensure maximum through-water visual penetration.

Core Driller

It is possible to fit a drilling device capable of taking core samples down to a maximum of 100 m below the seabed. In porous formations a borehole of 152 mm diameter would be possible, while in medium-hard formations a diameter of 119 mm might be possible. The power requirement would be, for the rotary head 40 HP with 100 HP maximum and 15 HP required for both the pressing equipment and the flushing pump. It is estimated that to take cores in a medium-hard formation would take about 60 hours for a 90 m bore hole; this is well within the maximum dive time of the submarine, which would not be less than one week.

Side-scan Sonar

Due to the size and capacity of a submarine it is easy for it to carry, in addition to its normal navigational and communications sonar outfit, such equipment as side-scan or sub-bottom profile equipment when necessary for geophysical studies.

Submersibles

A commercial submarine, unlike a military one, has a very substantial reserve of buoyancy which permits it to carry a large payload. Designs have proved the feasibility of carrying a submersible on the casing. This could be either an observation or a lock-out submersible. It would be both docked to its mother submarine and manned while submerged, thus obviating any weather problems. Divers would be able to return to the submarine saturation system in between sorties.

Remotely Operated Vehicles

In the same way that a submersible is operated from a submerged submarine it is possible to operate a remotely controlled vehicle from a submarine. This was first done successfully in Vancouver when a TREC system was operated from *Auguste Piccard*.

One-man Tethered Submersible

An alternative to the above systems is the *Mantis* one-man system. Feasibility studies have also been done to show how this system could be operated to allow both launching and manning to take place submerged. This is certainly possible, but for safety reasons in a submarine it is considered that an outfit would consist of two completely separate but identical *Mantis* systems.

Heavy Lift Capability

Owing to the very large reserve of buoyancy in these craft it is possible to fit cranes on the casing or to allow even heavier weights to be lifted by attaching them beneath the pressure hull.

Existing Submarines

While little is known about what is being developed in the Soviet bloc, it appears that the Soviets converted a fleet submarine, the *Severyanka*, to a fishery research vehicle in 1957. This remained operational until the early sixties. No other autonomous commercial submarine is known at present.

Borderline Submarines

Several craft have been built or are being built which may be considered borderline cases in that they are too large to operate from a mothership but are not completely autonomous. A short description of some of these is given below:

FNRS 3. This submarine of 28 tonnes was designed from the *FRNS 2* built in 1948 by Auguste Piccard with funds from the Belgian National Fund for Scientific Research (FNRS). The submarine was severely damaged while under tow in heavy weather. It was rebuilt by the French Navy during 1949–53 and achieved a maximum dive of 4125 m. It was de-commissioned in 1960.

Auguste Piccard. This submarine designed by Jacques Piccard and built by Giovanola of Switzerland is 28.5 m long and has a designed maximum operating depth of 700 m. Between July 1964 and October 1965 it carried out 1112 dives taking 32 000 passengers for underwater viewing trips in the Lake of Geneva. Its displacement is 185 tonnes. Since then it has been bought by Horton Maritime of Vancouver and extensively altered in order to fit it for scientific and commercial work which it now carries out.

Aluminaut. This 76-tonne submarine was built entirely of aluminium alloy in 1964 by General Dynamics for Reynolds International. Its designed maximum diving depth was 4572 m but it never went deeper than 1905 m. It was originally intended for deep ocean exploration into minerals and food resources and the salvage of sunken cargo vessels. It has not dived since 1969.

Deep Quest. This submarine of 52 tonnes was designed and built by Lockheed Missile and Space Corporation of California. It is

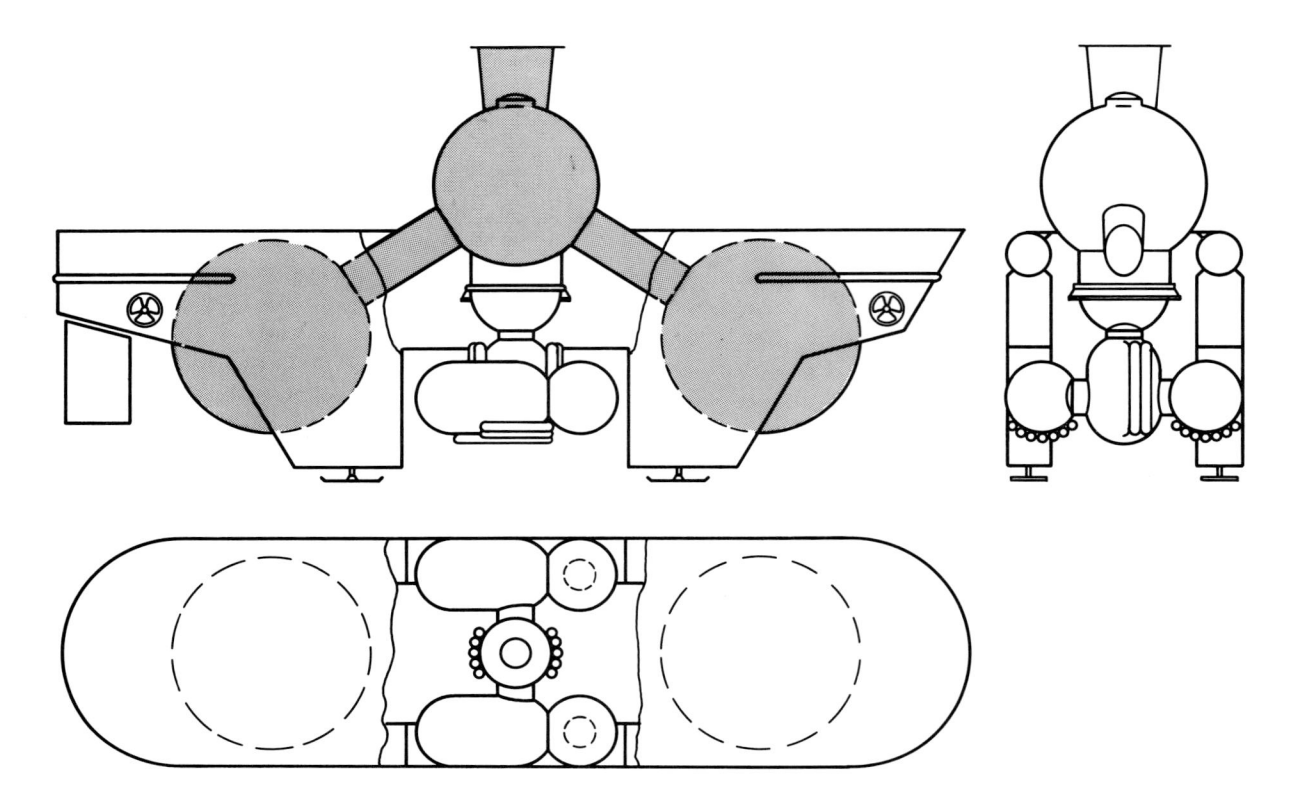

Fig. 8.4. The Deep Subsea Working System (DSWS 600) with a working depth of 600 m.

exceptional in that, in spite of its size, it was designed as part of a system to work from specially constructed surface ship called *Transquest* using a hydraulically powered elevator platform mounted in an open stern well. Its designed operating depth is 2438 m and it is still operational being used for sub-system trials and other purposes.

Argyronete. This was started as a result of an agreement in 1968 between Centre National Pour L'Exploitation des Oceans and Institut Francais du Petrole to build a lock-out submarine with a displacement of just under 300 tonnes and a maximum operating depth of 300 m. Although the hull was complete the vessel has not been completed.

DSRV 1 and 2. These two deep submergence rescue vessels were built in 1970 and 1971 for the US Navy by Lockheed Missile and Space Corporation at Sunnyvale, California. They are designed purely for submarine rescue work down to 1534 m and displace 37 tonnes. They are both air- and submarine-transportable.

Proposed Submarine Designs

Kockums (GPS)

Fig. 8.1 illustrates the design with the following specifications:

Surface displacement	1462 m³
Submerged displacement	1755 m³
Length overall	66 m
Breadth over main ballast tanks	9 m
Diameter of pressure hull	6 m
Nominal diving depth	350 m
Safety factor	NA
Surface speed	8 knots
Submerged speed max.	5 knots
Submerged speed min.	2 knots
Propulsion output	2 × 690 kW
Diesel generator	2 × 800 kW
Battery	lead–acid
Crew max.	26

Gabler Submarines

There are a range of Tours submarine designs from 200/600 to 520/500 class. Fig. 8.3 illustrates the 520/500 design, 52 m in length with a 500 m depth capability and the following specification:

Surface displacement	995 m³
Submerged displacement	1200 m³
Length overall	52 m
Breadth over main ballast tanks	7 m
Diameter of pressure hull	5 m
Nominal diving depth	500 m
Safety factor	1.8
Surface speed	8 knots
Submerged speed max.	10.5 knots
submerged speed min.	0.5 knots
Diesel generator	2 × 490 kW
Battery	lead–acid
Crew max.	17
Life-support (crew days)	15
Cruising ranges	submerged: 3 knots, 210 nautical miles
	surface: 8 knots, 3020 nautical miles
Compression chambers	4 units
Payload	35 tonnes
Negative buoyancy	20 tonnes

In addition to the Gabler range of designs there is the Deep Subsea Working System DSWS/600 illustrated in Fig. 8.4. As an advance of the habitat concept the vehicle is supplied with services from the surface through an umbilical. Designed for 600 m, it is self-propelled at about 5 knots with an overall length of 22 m. It is designed with a number of missions in mind, mainly associated with coring, pipeline inspection and workovers on seabed capsules.

Fig. 8.5. The Bruker *Subcat*, a large submarine catamaran concept for off-shore work, in the alignment and hyperbaric welding mode.

Bruker Subcat

A concept designed by Bruker Meerestechnik of Germany is illustrated in Fig. 8.5. It shows *Subcat* in the pipeline alignment and hyperbaric welding mode. Fig. 8.6 gives an impression of the same catamaran-submarine with its incorporated saturation-diving complex. The submarine rests on the sea bottom, its SCC in the mid-

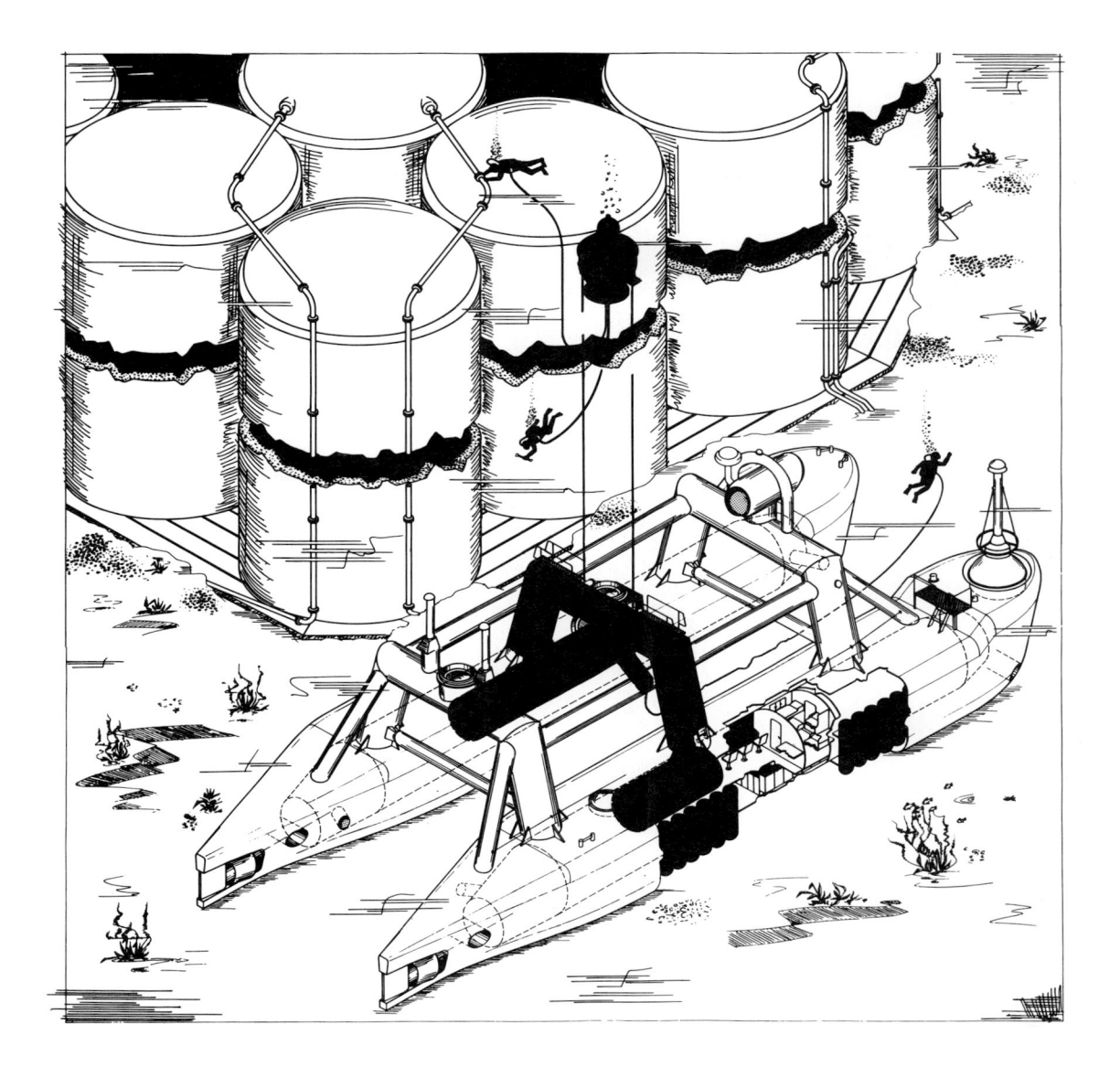

Fig. 8.6. The *Subcat* concept for midwater diving from an SCC.

water diving positon. Semisubmerged in bad weather condition, *Subcat* operates the SCC from the surface in Fig. 8.7.

The Bruker *Subcat* has the following specification:

Displacement above water	ca. 800 m^3
Displacement under water	ca. 900 m^3
Length overall	ca. 36 m
Width overall	ca. 15 m
Draught	ca. 3 m

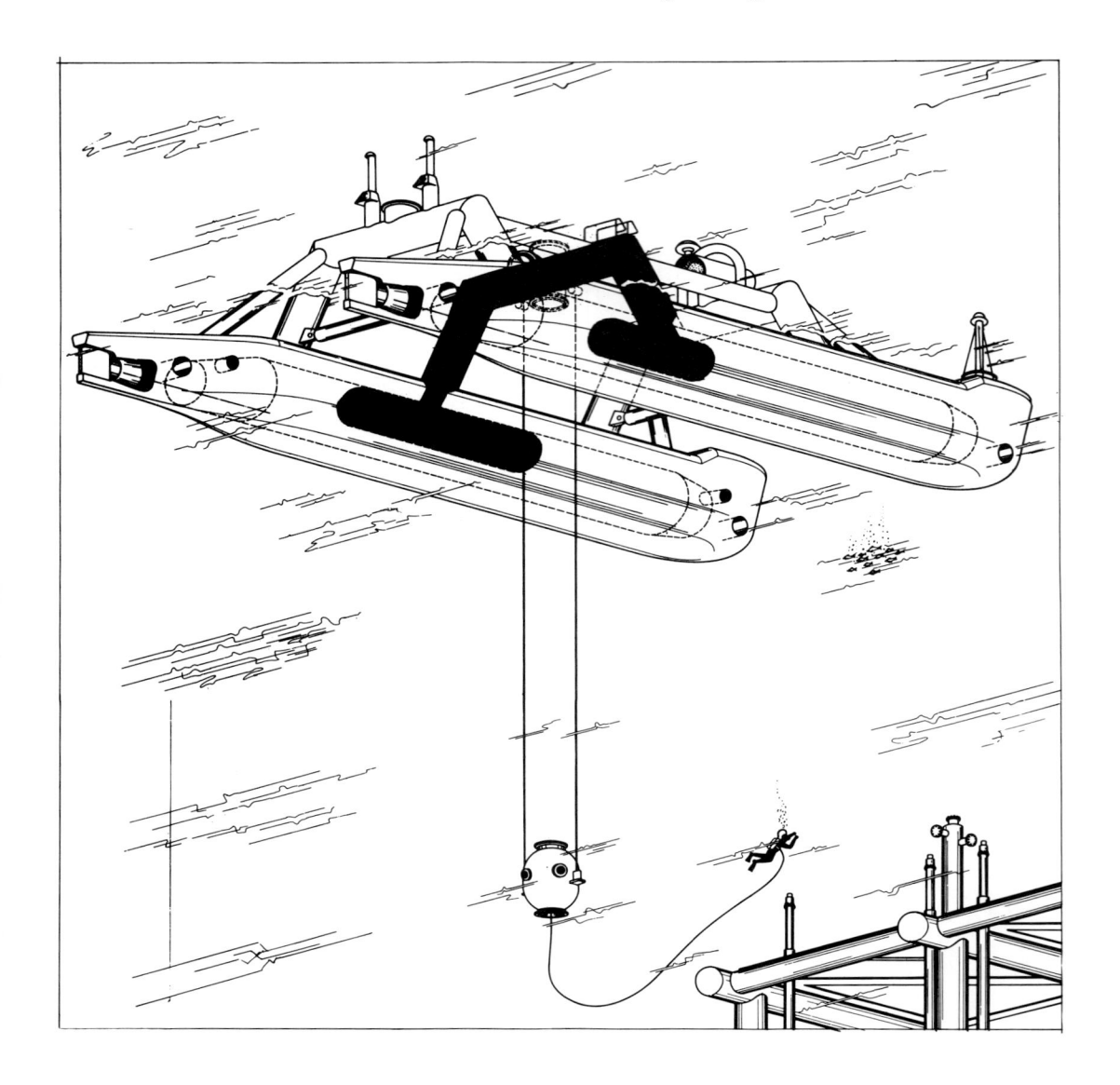

Fig. 8.7. The *Subcat* semi-submerged in the surface diving mode.

Maximum diving depth	300 m
Operating radius	800 nm
Crew (excluding divers)	16 persons
Diving team	12 persons
Surface speed	8 knots
Semi-submerged speed	5 knots
Fully submerged speed	3 knots
Main thrusters	400 kW each

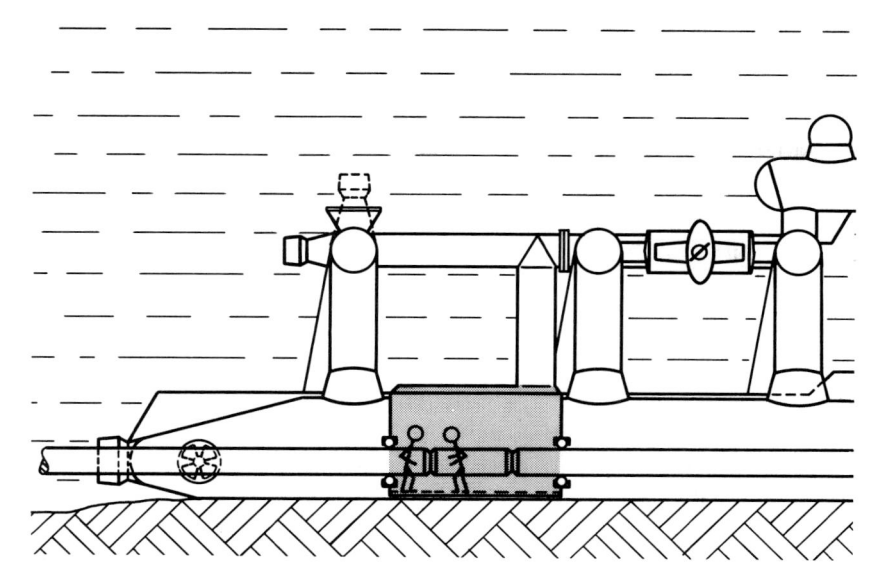

Fig. 8.8. The *Subcat* welding chamber for pipeline construction and repair.

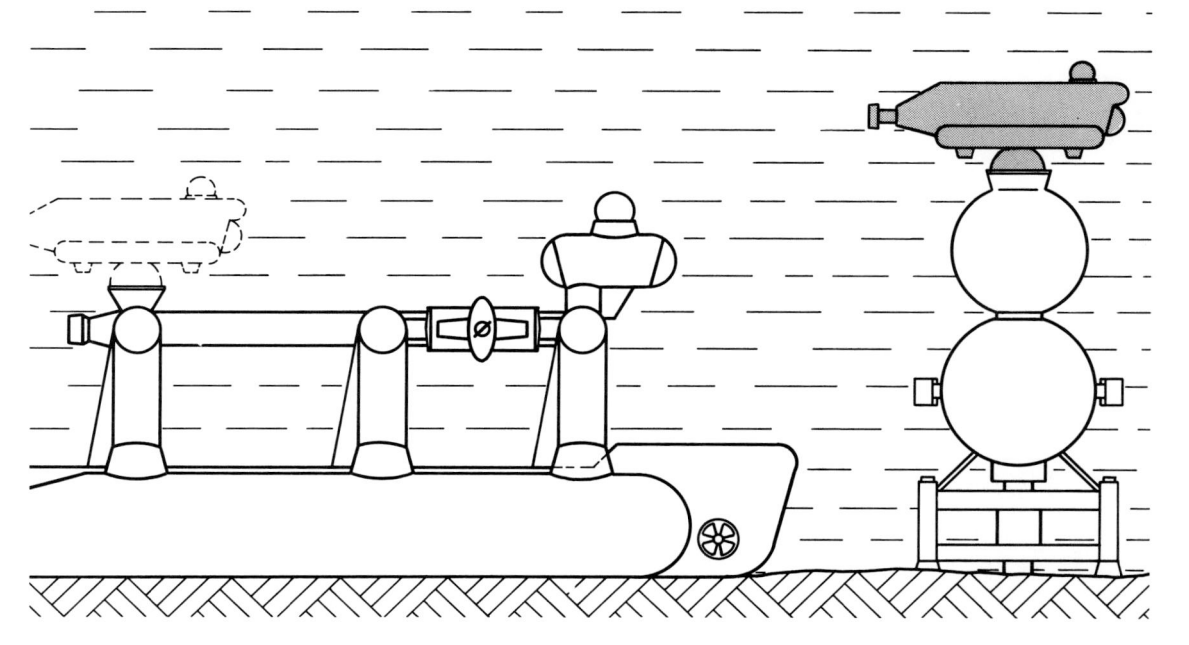

Fig. 8.9. Submersible transfer from *Subcat* to wellhead capsule using the Intertek method.

Lateral thrusters	100 kW each
Battery capacity	4000 kW h
Diesel fuel supply	35 tonnes
Life support (under water)	20 crew days
Payload (under water)	20 tonnes
Gas supply (He, O_2, air)	13440 m^3
Compressed air supply	4600 m^3

CO_2-absorbent material	2.7 m³
Storage room for frozen foods	8 m³
Drinking water supply	16 m³

With its manifold operating abilities, this design certainly represents one of the most advanced concepts among large commercial submarines and its construction will be of great interest to the diving community.

Safety

While it is customary to consider all under-water activities as dangerous, the actual record of submersible safety is good and there is every reason to believe that submarine safety will be even better. One problem of submersibles is their translation through the air–water interface during launch and recovery which does not occur with submarines. At the same time their increased size gives them a better opportunity to fit additional navigational equipment for improved safety. It is also possible to design a resuce sphere which can be fitted into the conning tower. This is large enough to take the entire crew if the submarine should be caught on the bottom for any reason and can be released without external assistance.

Summary

There are real and justifiable reasons why an autonomous submarine should be built for subsurface support and engineering work. That this has not already been done is due to a combination of factors, of which cost is undoubtedly the major one. However, with increasing needs and the possibility of work under ice its day will assuredly come. Gablers have already built two Tours 66 submarines which, although small (8 m in length), have all the characteristics of a submarine, with a diesel engine for surface propulsion and battery charging for submerged operations. It is therefore capable of autonomous operations without having to be re-embarked on board a mothership. The introduction of the commercial autonomous submarine, on the lines of the Gabler Tours 520/500, will be a certain development by the mid 1980s.

One-atmosphere Diving Systems 9

This chapter briefly examines the development of the armoured diving suit, from the early designs of over two hundred years ago to the modern versions which we now call one-atmosphere or atmospheric diving suits (ADS) and some derivatives which have evolved from the basic ADS concept.

The principal feature and main attraction of the one-atmosphere diving suit is for the design to allow a man to operate under water in a normal air atmosphere at a pressure of 1 bar (1 atmosphere absolute) irrespective of depth. Thus in operations where the system is used, it is not necessary to comply with compression, saturation or decompression schedules. This general principle becomes more attractive psychologically, physiologically and, in commercial diving today, financially as the diving depth is increased. The real value of this system then depends on the diver and we continue to refer to him as such even though he is not under pressure and is able to move around the object or structure he is required to work on and carry out the task itself. The arms and legs of the suit are, therefore, of necessity, jointed and must be water-tight and pressure-resistant; the whole suit must be ergonomically designed to allow the diver the greatest possible freedom of movement down to the maximum operational depth.

Development of the One-atmosphere Suit

Probably the first successfully used 'armoured' suit appeared in 1715 and was made of wood by a cooper for John Lethbridge. This device, in which the occupant lay horizontally, incorporated a small window and two leather-sealed armholes. Although his arms were subjected to ambient water pressure, Lethbridge made successful dives to 20 m.

An examination of the many early designs of atmospheric diving suits which followed shows naïvety concerning basic hydrostatics and mechanics. There were only one or two of the 30 or more published designs which might have functioned had they been pursued. The earliest design patents in metal armour suits refer, for example, to Taylor (1838), Phillips (1856), Tasker (1851) and Pekey and Hemengers towards the end of the century, all being patented in America. They show the degree of interest of Americans in this field of innovatory design. The main factors which prevented development and successful application of these early one-atmosphere suits were the limited range of materials and the lack of the necessary metal-working techniques.

In 1913, Neufeldt and Kuhnke patented a design for a universal joint and various models of a complete suit were made during the 1920s using this ball and socket joint, with ball bearings to take the thrust and fabric bellows to keep the water out. The joints of these suits stiffened to the point of being immovable at a depth of about 100 m but, nevertheless, the Neufeldt and Kuhnke suit was used in the most famous of salvage operations, that of recovering the bullion from the wreck of the *Egypt* off Ushant during the early 1930s. Since the wreck lay at 125 m the role was more that of an observation chamber than of a fully working diving suit. The last known new Neufeldt and Kuhnke suit is believed to have been evaluated by the Royal Navy soon after World War II and now stands on display at the RN Experimental Diving Unit at Portsmouth, England.

Some time during or after Neufeldt and Kuhnke's period of manufacture of their suits, it is believed that Roberto Galeazzi Ltd, of La Spezia, Italy, began to make these suits under licence and they began to develop their own design. These suits are available today and their model RM 200/52 is designed for an operational depth of 200 m. The German and Italian designs differed; the former used ball bearings as mentioned above and the latter had gembal rings to support the limb joints. Both designs included a ballast chamber or chambers which could be used by the diver to adjust his overall buoyancy; the material of construction was principally steel.

But back in 1914 Harry Bowdoin filed an application for a patent in the USA for a new design of joint in an atmospheric diving suit. This design showed advanced thinking and an obvious understanding of the problems of joint design. The principle of the Bowdoin joint was that water pressure should be used to counterbalance the hydrostatic thrust between the two components of the joint. In his design, the only factor contributing to the torque loading on the joint was the friction of the three sealing rings, each one sealing against the internal/external pressure differential. There is no known evidence that the Bowdoin joint was ever used in an operational suit.

In 1919, Victor Campos filed a patent for yet another form of joint. This design appears to be the first to use another fluid to support the hydrostatic load on the joint. Like Bowdoin's, it was a rotary type which gave a degree of movement at the shoulders, elbows, wrists, hips, knees and ankles. Campos is reported to have reached a depth of 200 m in this suit, although there is little evidence as to its success.

Whilst Bowdoin and Campos were at work in America, Joseph Peress in England filed a patent for a fluid-supported joint. Whereas the Americans had concentrated on rotary joints, Peress was pursuing the universal joint to achieve angular rather than rotary movement. His 1922 patent allowed for the fluid to be contained in an annular, semi-hemispherical chamber sealed by a rolling fabric disphragm. A suit employing the joint was built from stainless steel but unfortunately, because of its excess weight, no full-scale trials were carried out. In 1933 Peress filed a new patent showing another version of the fluid-supported joint, but excluding the fabric diaphragm. It consisted only of an annular piston moving in an annular semi-hemispherical cylinder. This design proved to be successful and another suit was built using the joint. An interesting innovation was his use of cast magnesium alloy for the body, hatch and joint spacers, the joints themselves being machined in mild steel. This Peress suit was successfully dived to over 150 m during trials and, in the mid-1930s, was used to locate and dive on the wreck of the *Lusitania* off the south coast of Ireland. The suit was evaluated by the Royal Navy at about that time and '... was found to come up to the claims of the inventor, but no use could be made of it as the Navy has no requirements for deep diving.'

The enthusiasm of the earlier designers for exploring the ocean had been particularly directed to the salvage of ships and valuable cargo. The restraints of air diving, which effectively limited operations to much less than the theoretical 100 m, pushed forward the attempts to develop a working one-atmosphere suit. But these earlier developments only marginally extended the depth at which man could operate effectively and below that depth the joints became so stiff that the suit could only be used as an observation chamber, as during the dives on the *Egypt*. Historically, therefore, there has been little problem in designing the pressure-proof one-atmosphere chamber, but until relatively recently the difficulty of achieving acceptably free limb movement had denied the intrepid early designers and divers their aim. Consequently, the one-atmosphere observation chamber was developed by several salvagers and navies; this could be lowered close to wrecks or objects of interest on the seabed and used to control the separate movement of simple tools or grabs. With a view through observation windows and a telephone link to the surface, adequate control of such devices has been achieved in many cases. Although seemingly crude, with experience, the method became very effective and largely met the requirements of salvage and recovery work.

There seems to have been a pause in development of the one-atmosphere suit between the late 1930s and the early 1960s which can be accounted for by the invention and development of the aqua-lung by Cousteau and the operational necessity for fully autonomous free diving during and after World War II. These techniques were then developed and elaborated to take over the so far pre-eminent position of standard diving equipment derived with little real change from Augustus Siebe's original flexible suit of 1837.

Modern One-atmosphere Suits

However, as what is now known as the off-shore oil industry began to develop and as the operational requirements of naval powers extended the range of depth at which effective diving was economically and urgently needed, mixed gas techniques were developed and a vast amount of money was poured into experimental work in diving physiology and engineering. The efforts of the early designers of the one-atmosphere systems might have seemed wasted as experimental and then operational diving moved inexorably towards 600 m. Saturation diving became the logical method of maintaining the cost-effectiveness of ambient pressure diving. However, the very high cost of the necessarily complex equipment, the cost of the divers themselves and the cost of logistic support for saturation diving had opened up the possibility of reintroducing the one-atmosphere suit to carry out at least some of the work tasks of the diver and the now developing manned submersible.

The considerable difference in cost of manufacture, mobilization, transportation, running cost and logistics of the one-atmosphere suit, compared to the deep diving system, was believed to show that the suit would be cost-effective when it could undertake specific work tasks.

Meanwhile, because of the rapid acceleration of interest in, and achievements of, space technology, and the resultant development of the extremely sophisticated space suits eventually used for the moon walks, one American aerospace company, Litton Industries Space Science Laboratory, is known to have applied its space-initiated expertise to the development of a very advanced design of atmospheric diving suit. Inevitably, this complete suit depended on the limb joint design and it seems that, although the performance achieved was excellent, for some reason the concept was not pursued. However, an article on a stage of development was published in the late 1960s. The future need for ambient pressure diving technology in the field of off-shore oil exploration and exploitation operations was becoming more appreciated. The publication of the report and this new awareness of the limitations of conventional diving initiated serious thought at Underwater Marine Equipment Ltd (UMEL). Then a chance remark in October 1968 led to a meeting with Joseph Peress who, although initially reluctant to take an interest in diving matters after a gap of 30 years, was persuaded to tell of his early work. From this meeting a project grew to build a new generation of atmospheric diving suits based on updated Peress joint designs. UMEL and DHB Construction Ltd began work on a prototype joint on which a new patent application was based.

The new limb joint design was, as in Peress' earlier models, fluid-supported, but now without the distortion effects noticeable in the 1933 version. The first of the new suits was called JIM II, after Jim Jarret who had dived the original suit to the *Lusitania* so long ago. The body and dome of the JIM series of suits (Fig. 9.1) are cast in RZ5 magnesium alloy, taking advantage of its high strength-to-weight ratio. The manned all-up weight in air is about 470 kg, including about 70 kg of lead ballast. The suit is lowered from the surface to the seabed on a combined lift cable and telephone umbilical, which in an emergency can be disconnected by the diver. After the ballast has been jettisonned the suit will surface at about 0.5 m/s. Communications with surface control are then transferred to a through-water telephone. The life-support system is in two identical and separate parts, one on either side of the body, consisting of an oxygen supply

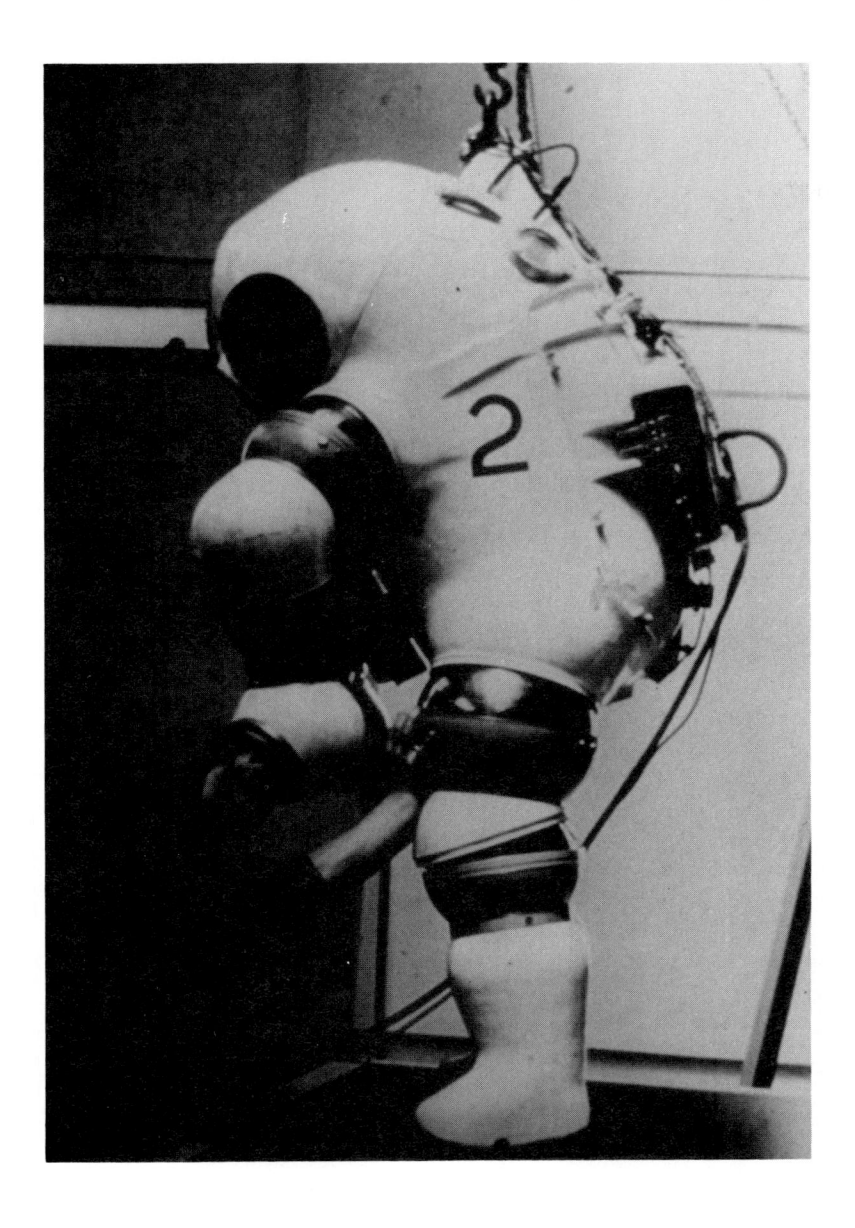

Fig. 9.1. The JIM suit.

cylinder outside the body, leading in via a breakthrough to pressure reducer and automatic pressure sensor and control module. Soda-lime cannisters absorb carbon dioxide from exhaled breath and a change-over valve allows the diver to select either of the two systems at will. The life-support endurance is up to 24 hours. In 1976 an operational dive of 6 hours 50 minutes was carried out at 381 m depth. Life-support could be extended but with rapid recovery, brief between-dive servicing, change of diver and return to the work site, the importance of individual dives lasting over long periods is not significant. Limb joint development has continued at UMEL and the latest types consist of a number of similar fluid-supported shorter elements in place of each of the massive single joints of the 1970 type.

Fig. 9.2. The SAM suit.

Suit body design has also been developed over the period and now includes the SAM version (Fig. 9.2) in both fabricated aluminium alloy and glass-reinforced plastic (GRP). Two complete bodies in each material and fitted with the latest limb designs are being built currently, the latter being rated for a maximum operational depth of 670 m.

All these suits accommodate a range of sizes for a normal range of divers by removal or insertion of spacer sections in the limbs. Payload, particularly in the GRP-bodied SAMs which are exceptional, is generally adequate to allow the diver to take cameras, recorder, refreshments, note books, drawings, etc. with him inside the suit.

The manipulators require tool adaptors for work on some standard fittings and an increasing range of tasks can be carried out particularly where pre-planning of the subsea facilities for future maintenance by ADS has been possible. Intervention diving to great depths is extremely cost-effective when ADS, or one of the derivitives described later, is used. They are helicopter-transportable and require a minimum of space aboard ship or platform, basic launching gear, minimal logistic support and no hyperbaric complex or staff. The one-atmosphere suit is best capable of carrying out certain engineering or inspection tasks when the in situ components, for example of a subsea production system, are modified or adapted to the capabilities of an articulated arm with manipulator—as, indeed, would be required to a similar extent for maintenance by manned or unmanned submersibles. The modifications include either the adoption of tools, valves and fittings to match the vice grips of ADS or the provision of special manipulators to cope with specific items already installed. ADSs may also be used more effectively when cat-walks or special foot-holds are provided to allow access to task areas above the sea-bed level.

The first commercial dives using the JIM suit were in 1974 and by the end of 1977 six ADS units were being successfully used in offshore operations by Oceaneering International Services Ltd, the deepest working dive so far being 438 m.

The need to develop an ADS which can more easily operate above sea-bed level has been recognized. This has led to experiments to provide a thruster package and control system for ADS and the development of other related derivatives, such as WASP in 1977 and OMAS in 1978.

Designed to operate in mid-water areas of structures and above the sea-bed, WASP (Fig. 9.3) is a logical extension of the basic concept. WASP is fitted with articulated arms and manipulators, the body has a full hemispherical window/hatch on a slightly curved upper case aluminium alloy body, the lower part of which is a GRP filament-wound tube and hemispherical lower end cap. Two horizontal and two vertical thrusters on each side provide for horizontal, vertical or rotational movement, controlled by the diver through foot-operated switches. Power, communications, lighting and lift are provided by the slim umbilical and the control, communications and power modules at the surface position are compact.

WASP operates at a fixed state of trim, usually leaning forward at about 30° from vertical but adjustable within a reasonable range by positioning the lead ballast. An electrically operated fan circulates the air within the body through soda-lime cannisters and for emergency use a separate, extra cannister between the diver's legs is available with

Fig. 9.3. The WASP.

an oral–nasal mask providing 36–54 hours endurance beyond the eight hours of the automatic systems. It has a design depth of 620 m.

WASP weighs about 500 kg in air and if required the cable can be released, followed by all the external equipment, which provides about 70 kg positive buoyancy for independent emergency ascent. Emergency batteries allow the vehicle 20 minutes of full thruster power, it is claimed, and it is rated to 610 m depth. With a full hemispherical methyl methacrylate dome and outer protective transparent cover, visibility from the vehicle is excellent and should

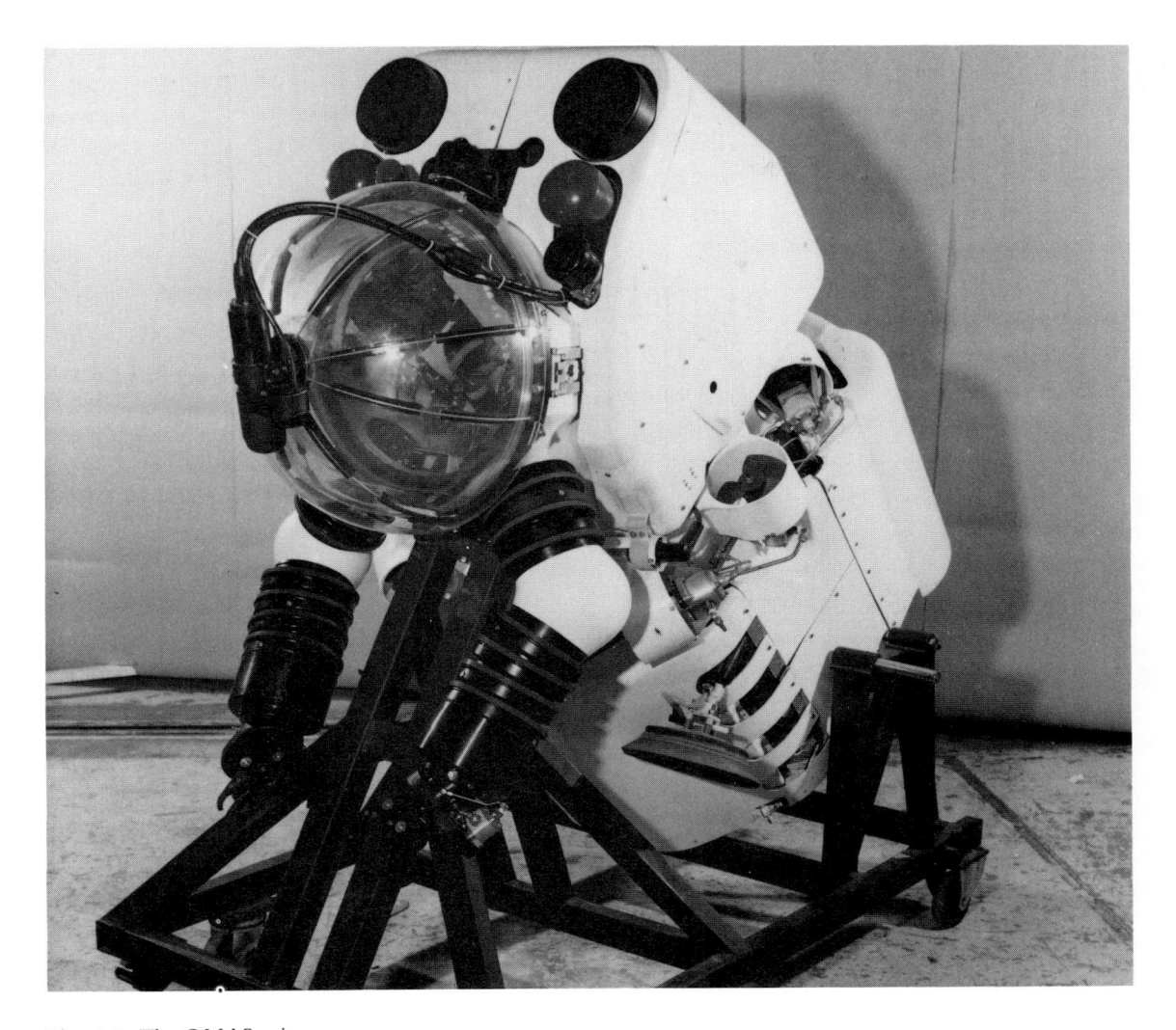

Fig. 9.4. The OMAS suit.

facilitate detailed and comprehensive examination of structures from the sea-bed to surface by skilled inspectors.

In 1978 Vickers Slingsby produced the first OMAS (Fig. 9.4), a mid-water one-man vehicle similar in design to the WASP. Fitted with articulated jointed arms and hydraulic power-assisted manipulators, OMAS weighs about 1000 kg in air. With a hemispherical methyl methacrylate dome, curved upper body and cylindrical lower body, it is designed to adjust the pitch from leaning backwards 45° to leaning forwards 80° from the vertical. It is powered by six thrusters around the body to give movement in all directions. The designed endurance is 72 hours and the operating depth to 620 m. The vehicle is designed to use suction pads to hold onto structures for mid-water inspection.

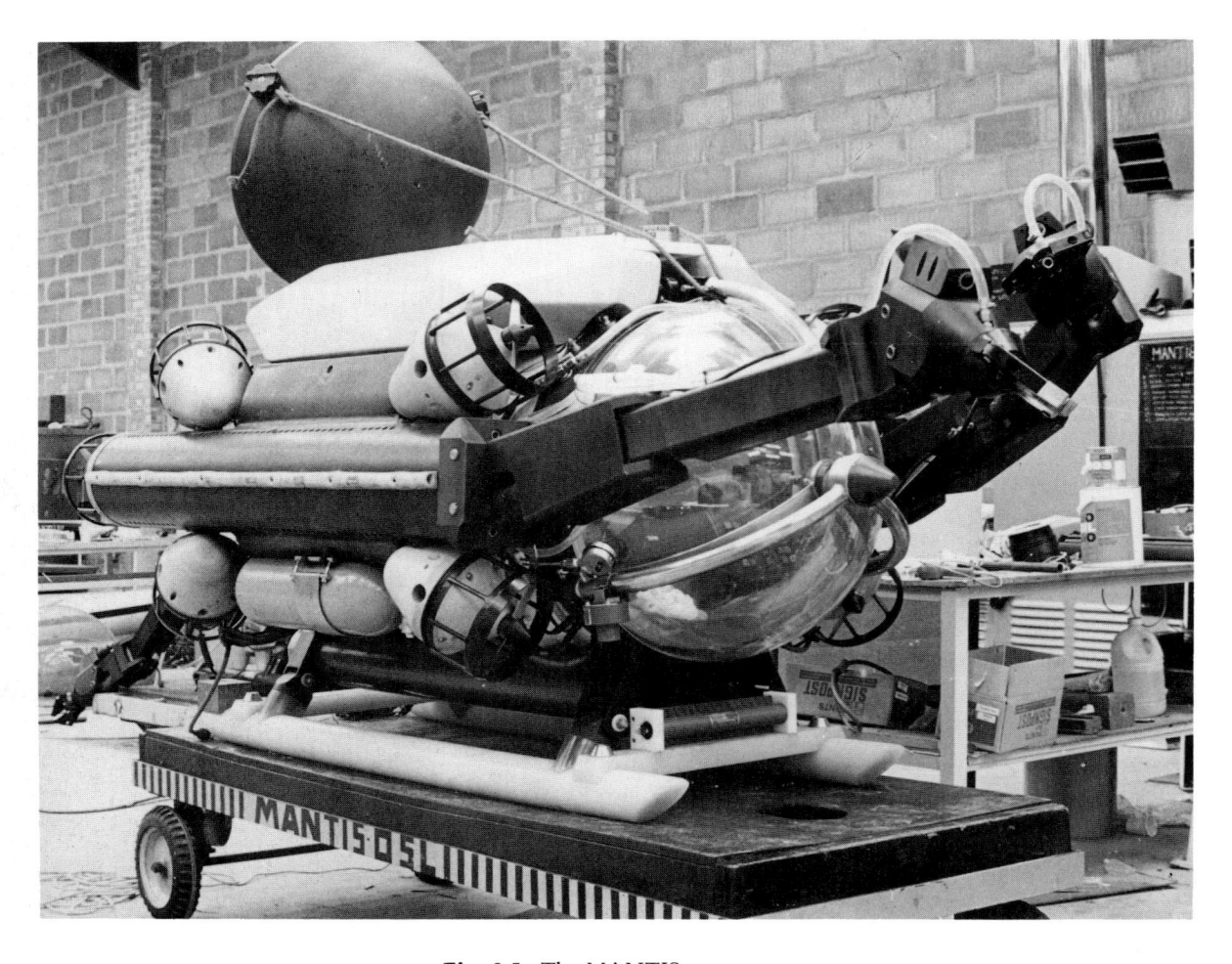

Fig. 9.5. The MANTIS.

A further stage of derivative from the atmospheric diving suit with which this chapter started is the development of MANTIS, a one-man tethered submersible (Fig. 9.5). OSEL, who produced this vehicle in 1978, have really moved out of the area with which we are concerned here. But it belongs within the scope of this chapter because its origins were in ADS. It is a 1 tonne vehicle with its long axis horizontal, a large-diameter acrylic window in the bow and two mechanical manipulator arms in place of arm-operated jointed limbs. Designed for the same types of tasks as we have so far considered, it has unlimited energy endurance via an umbilical, a similar life-support endurance, adequate emergency provisions such as cable release and emergency batteries and, owing to its small size and shape relative to a full submersible, an ability to approach restricted areas of a platform inaccessible to the larger submersibles.

The latest version of the atmospheric suit even in relatively unrefined glass-reinforced plastic is rated to 620 m, and the limbs are capable of far greater depths so there will be a natural progression of ADS diving well beyond the limits of ambient pressure diving. Even now, while it can be said that the diver will never be replaced because he provides a vital close-range, personal and first-hand capability to perform a task, there is a growing body of expert and informed opinion which insists that where possible an alternative to exposing man to ambient pressure should be used. The submersible probably provides the best working conditions for man under water and its safety record is enviably high. But submersibles are expensive to operate and slow to mobilize and require the support of a sophisticated surface vessel. The smaller one-man submersible, autonomous or tethered, will find its place and vehicles like WASP and OMAS will be required to carry out many tasks requiring the power and adaptability of the man on the spot.

The special techniques for carrying out some inspection, repair and maintenance tasks off-shore, as mentioned before, require precision handling and manipulators, particularly for non-destructive testing. For this and other work special tool-kits and procedures will be needed and the criteria by which all manned and unmanned vehicle systems are judged is their capacity to fulfil these tasks.

On most manipulators the mechanical equivalent of the human hand resembles a claw or pipe grip with hinged or parallel action jaws. In the ADS these are a few centimetres beyond the diver's hand but the small displacement and the relatively simple mechanism gives the diver considerable 'feel' in operating the mechanical hand. Some valuable design work is being done on a hydraulically operated design where the diver, by operating a pair of bars connected to hydraulic cylinders, can transmit a quick or slow movement with respective variations in power and a force feedback.

The true one-atmosphere diving suit, however, fits into the whole range of under-water vehicles with very special characteristics. With less logistic requirements, very low running costs and ability to be transported to a distant site and deployed rapidly, it provides man with the physical comfort of a small submersible without the high cost and complexity of ambient pressure diving.

If John Lethbridge could have made articulated arms of wood he would have been able to dive without getting wet in 1715.

10 Life-support Systems and Commercial Diving Equipment

The subject of life support under conditions of pressure involves the widest range of scientific and technical skills with as much emphasis on aspects of human engineering as on space technology. The obligations and social responsibilities that are implied or set out in the *Safety and Health Regulations for Men and Women at Work in Industry* are no less applicable to divers. The primary considerations for a life support system are that it should be capable of the following:

1. Ensuring an oxygen partial pressure (Po_2) within defined limits
2. Restricting carbon dioxide to defined limits
3. Controlling temperature and humidity within a narrow range
4. Removing toxic substances from the breathing gases such as CO, methane, oil, dusts and microbes

Secondary considerations, not necessarily of secondary importance because in combination they can be damaging, are:

1. Supply and removal of domestic water
2. Supply of food and drink
3. Sanitary facilities
4. Illumination and noise levels
5. General living conditions

Table 10.1 Design factors for integrated life-support systems

Individual life support	*Collective life-support*	
	Primary	Secondary
Diving gear	Oxygen	Water supply
Breathing equipment	Carbon dioxide removal	Food supply
Absorbent units (scrubbers)	Temperature and humidity control	Sanitary facilities
Emergency breathing equipment	Removal of toxic substances	Accommodation
		Communication
		Illumination and noise level
		Entertainment
		Firefighting

6. Communications
7. Entertainment
8. Fire hazard

The study of individual primary life support systems where they are applied to breathing systems in diving equipment is dealt with later in this chapter dealing with commercial diving equipment. Here we examine how collective life support systems, as installed in decompression chambers, deep diving research facilities, submersibles fitted for diver lock-out and habitats, need to take account of these primary considerations.

Primary Life-support Factors

Oxygen Partial Pressure (Po_2)

The supply of the oxygen at the correct partial pressure is fundamental to all life-support systems. Most aspects of diving theory related to physiology and decompression depend upon the partial pressure of the various gases and in particular oxygen. Dalton's law of partial pressure states that the total pressure of a gas mixture is the sum of the partial pressures of all the gases in the mixture, assuming that temperatures and volumes remain constant. Therefore at sea level where pressure is 1 bar and the air is assumed to contain only nitrogen and oxygen in a 79:21 ratio, the partial pressure of oxygen is 0.21 bar and that of nitrogen 0.79 bar which corresponds to 21% oxygen and 79% nitrogen in the air. Medical studies have shown that the human body can accept a reduction in oxygen content to 14–15%, corresponding to 0.14–0.15 bar and an absolute minimum of about 11%. This corresponds to a partial pressure of oxygen of 0.11 bar on the surface and will cause oxygen deficiency symptoms known as hypoxia. These symptoms are particularly dangerous because, unlike other manifestations of distress which can be experienced by divers, the symptoms of lack of oxygen are rarely recognized by the affected person himself. He has difficulty in standing upright and walking properly, suffers loss of coordination and his lips go blue resulting in rapid unconsciousness. There are no early symptoms and the onset is swift and dangerous.

An increase in oxygen partial pressure above certain levels under pressure can be equally dangerous, leading to oxygen poisoning. Although pure oxygen can be breathed on the surface and at shallow depths, any further increase of the partial pressure of oxygen above certain levels may cause irreversible changes in the alveoli. A general concensus is that oxygen partial pressures of above 0.6 bar for more than 12 hours will cause irritation of the lungs and therefore there is a reasonable assumption that partial pressure of between 0.2 bar and 0.5 bar can be safely used for within reasonably unlimited periods under pressure. In general, oxygen partial pressures should be kept as low as

Table 10.2 Oxygen consumption related to working performance

Work	Oxygen consumption (litres/min)	Breath volume (litres/min)	Power (W)
Rest			
lying	0.25	6	—
sitting	0.30	7	—
standing	0.40	9	—
Light work			
walking slowly on solid ground*	0.60	13	25
walking at 3.2 km/hour	0.70	16	30
swimming slowly at 0.9 km/hour*	0.80	18	40
Medium work			
walking on soft ground*	1.1	23	70
walking at 6.5 km/hour	1.2	27	80
swimming at 1.6 km/hour*	1.4	30	95
fast walking on solid ground*	1.5	34	105
Hard work			
swimming at 1.85 km/hour*	1.8	40	130
fast walking on soft ground*	1.8	40	130
bicycling at 21 km/hour	1.85	45	140
running at 13 km/hour	2	50	145
Very hard work			
swimming at 2.2 km/hour*	2.5	60	185
running at 15 km/hour	2.6	65	200
running up stairs (100 steps/min)	3.2	80	250
running up hill	4	95	290

*Under water.

possible, even though this may extend the length of the decompression, since it avoids the danger of oxygen poisoning.

Opinion is divided as to what are the reasonable permissible limits of higher oxygen content for shorter exposures in the shallower ranges during decompression. Although 100% oxygen can be breathed to depths of 18 m (equivalent to an oxygen partial pressure of 2.8 bar) this partial pressure should not be exceeded and administered only for short exposures. This is variable as it can be influenced by the following:

1. The duration of exposure
2. The work load
3. The carbon dioxide content of the inhaled gas
4. The physical condition of the diver

Unlike hypoxia, or lack of oxygen, the symptoms of oxygen poisoning usually give adequate warning and the trained diver should immediately recognize them for what they are. Twitching of the

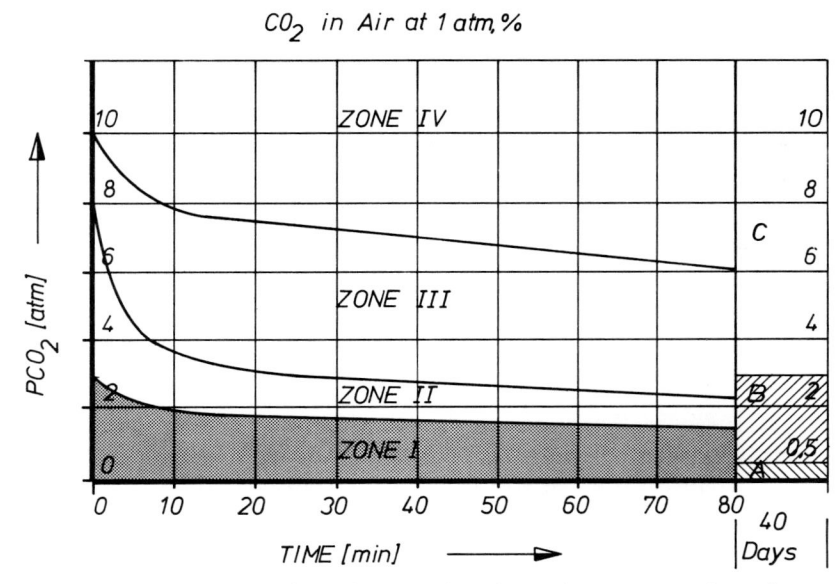

Fig. 10.1. Physiological effects of carbon dioxide in relation to quantity and exposure time.

facial muscles and lips, together with nausea, dizziness and tunnel vision, changes in hearing aptitude, the sensation of ringing in the ears and breathing problems are singly or together the early warning signs of oxygen poisoning. A diver may become confused, distressed and uncoordinated before the final manifestation of severe convulsions with ultimate unconsciousness. The uncontrolled movements of the body during the convulsions can increase the risk to the diver, particularly below water but also in a chamber. The interior design of the chamber should take this into account by providing fittings without sharp cutting edges or projections which might cause injuries to a diver in a convulsive fit.

Carbon Dioxide Partial Pressure (P_{CO_2})

The air that we breathe contains about 0.03% carbon dioxide. This is equivalent to a partial pressure of about 0.0003 bar and it would be desirable if this low value could be maintained throughout in breathing gases under pressure within the life-support systems. Technically this is possible, but the extent of technical effort needed would not be justified, as the human body can fortunately tolerate higher carbon dioxide pressures. Fig. 10.1 shows the permissible carbon dioxide levels by partial pressure. Zones I and II are areas where carbon dioxide partial pressures are permissible, as shown, for short- and long-term exposures up to 40 days. This illustrates that carbon dioxide partial pressure of between 0.005 and 0.03 bar are acceptable in compression chamber atmospheres. This source, published in the NOAA diving manual, represents one viewpoint but others consider the limit of 0.03 bar as being too high and restrict the upper limit to 0.005 bar, but this is perhaps too cautious. For the design of equipment a maximum permissible carbon dioxide partial pressure is 0.015 bar. The effects on the respiratory system of increasing the partial pressure show in an increased breathing rate and at 0.05 bar there is a very pronounced shortness of breath which leads to muscular spasms. If the concentration rises further the body stiffens and the subject becomes unconscious at 0.1 to 0.15 bar partial pressure. Carbon dioxide poisoning is brought on more quickly when combined with too low an oxygen content (hypoxia). Fortunately the recovery from carbon dioxide poisoning is quick after the removal of excess gas and flushing with clean breathing gases.

Temperature and Humidity

In normal ambient conditions we generally accept that a comfortable temperature range is between 18 and 22°C depending to some extent on the degree of physical activity. Similarly a relative humidity of between 50 and 65% is pleasant. These criteria do not change under pressure as long as the composition of air is maintained. In other words the temperature and humidity within their ranges remain the same even at pressures of 5–6 bar.

There is, however, a fundamental change when helium is substituted for nitrogen as the inert gas to overcome nitrogen narcosis and as a lighter gas for easier breathing and quicker decompression. The thermal conductivity of helium is almost seven times as great as that of nitrogen and therefore heat is drawn out of the body much more rapidly. To prevent this dangerous heat loss from the body the oxy-helium breathing gas and chamber gas need to be heated to a higher temperature than for air. Where the helium mixture is high, around 95%, the gases have to be heated to between 30 and 36°C, temperatures that would normally be uncomfortably warm. The same humidity levels of between 50 to 65% are normal.

Under normal atmospheric conditions the body gives off a certain amount of metabolic heat as a normal function. The maintenance of set temperatures will help to achieve thermal equilibrium, making up the metabolic heat loss and keeping the internal body core temperature within safe limits. An excessive rise in core temperature will result in hyperthermia or conversely a reduction in hypothermia. Variations can and are tolerated by the human body but the flexibility of the body, as in most bodily functions, is finite and dependent on the degree of variation from a norm. A reasonable norm for a core temperature is 37°C with the breathing gas in the chamber at 35°C. In diving bells the chamber gas ideally is at 30°C. If these are accepted upper limits it would be impossible to drive the core temperature upwards.

The technical solution, whether using chemical, hot water or electricity systems, should be designed so that the transfer medium does not exceed set limits on the system. On hot water systems as supplied to divers in the water not only temperature but also the flow needs monitoring. Safety systems should be fitted to all systems differing in the type of heating system to which they are applied.

Electrical suits should have a failure mode so that the diver is not exposed to shock or high-temperature hazard.

A system as important as heating, whether supplying heat to a chamber or to a diver in the water, must have a separate back-up, particularly with regard to diver heating systems outside the bell. The back-up systems must be ready to start at an instant's notice.

When designing the dehumidification system for compression chambers the various sources of moisture need to be considered. They are as follows:

1. Body evaporation and respiratory exhalation
2. Precipitation of moisture from CO_2 chemical reaction
3. Evaporation from domestic sanitary and water supplies, particularly from use of showers
4. Increase of humidity from external access to water interface compartments, i.e. divers transfering from bell to compression chambers

The first two causes of humidity, the human body and the chemistry of carbon dioxide absorbents, can be accurately calculated. Only operating experience and the type of diving cycle will provide the extent of additional dehumidification resources needed to control the relative humidity within acceptable limits.

Removal of Toxic Contaminants

Apart from the limits on breathing oxygen, carbon dioxide and the other aspects of temperature and humidity control there are other lesser but important excess substances that need to be considered in some way or other. Table 10.3 lists the contaminants and the exposure limits. Under saturation conditions over long periods the removal of H_2S, hydrogen, hydrocarbons, ammonia, sulphur dioxide, carbon monoxide, methane, oil vapours, small substances, dusts and microbes may become necessary. Carbon monoxide is produced by the body at an average rate of 0.3–1.0 ml/hour. On closed-circuit life-support systems these accumulations, at first negligible, will increase and eventually need to be removed. In addition to CO other contaminants may be produced from internal paint surfaces and instrumentation, such as glue, or may originate in a faulty compressor. For long periods under pressure a limit of 50 mg/m^3 is considered reasonable, this being equal to a volume percentage of 0.0050 (vol%) (DIN 3188). The toxic effect on the human body of carbon monoxide is directly related to the percentage of the gas in the total mixture and not the partial pressure, whilst the toxicity of oxygen and carbon dioxide is related to the partial pressure of the gases in the mixture.

An acceptable carbon monoxide limit, by American standards, is 20 ppm.

The effects of other extraneous toxic substances are known for normal atmospheric conditions and exposure times have been laid down so as not to exceed safe limits. In the absence of generally

Table 10.3. Typical contaminant exposure limits (at atmospheric pressure)

Substance	8-hour weighted average limit	Ceiling concentration	Comments
Ammonia	50 ppm	—	—
Carbon dioxide	5000 ppm	—	—
Carbon monoxide	50 ppm	—	—
Freon-12	1000 ppm	—	—
Hydrogen chloride	—	5 ppm	—
Hydrogen fluoride	3 ppm	5 ppm	10 ppm for max 30 min
Mercury	—	0.1 mg/m^3	—
Nitric oxide	25 ppm	—	—
Nitrogen dioxide	5 ppm	—	—
Oil mist	5 mg/m^3	—	—
Ozone	0.1 ppm	—	—
Phosgene	0.1 ppm	—	Freon decomposition
Stibene	0.1 ppm	—	Lead-acid battery
Sulphur dioxide	5 ppm	—	—

From Bishop, (1973) *The Underwater Handbook*. New York: Plenum Press.

acceptable limits on all these toxic gases whilst under pressure in hyperbaric conditions, the values listed in Table 10.3 represent the medical limits for an eight-hour day and a 40-hour week. They are based on a total working life of 40 years and are considered safe with no harmful consequences in later life.

Secondary Life-support Factors

Water Supply (Fresh Water)

The requirement for fresh water for drinking, washing and for sanitation is dependent on the type of diving and an essential part of the secondary life-support system. For relatively short periods of pressurization associated with bounce or intervention diving there is no need for a permanent supply of water. Small quantities for drinking can be passed through the supply lock which should be a standard part of any compression chamber. For long periods under pressure, where divers are in saturation, a permanent running supply of fresh water is essential for drinking, washing and sanitary purposes. The normal requirement per person is 2–3 litres of pure water for drinking, 20 litres for washing and 15 litres for sanitary systems. The water needs to be supplied internally at 5–6 bar above the internal pressure of the chamber.

Food and Drink

For short duration under pressure the need for food and drink can be met with light refreshments and calorie requirements are met most conveniently by hot soups and drinks, passed through the supply locks normally fitted to surface compression chambers. Diving bells are not normally designed to have supply locks as the divers are transferred under pressure to deck compression chambers. However, detachable supply locks can be fitted to diving bells in the event of a transfer under pressure not being feasible and these small locks can be fitted over a porthole or observation window, enabling the divers to remove the window and pass small amounts of food and water through the opening.

For long exposures and under saturation conditions careful diet control is vital. Because saturation diving demands a large number of personnel under pressure to carry out work continuously under a shift system, the amount of food that needs to be passed into the hyperbaric chambers can be considerable. The diameter and volume of a supply lock is therefore an important design factor in the construction of a chamber. The selection and preparation of food needs to be laid down by dieticians, taking into account the amount of work carried out, the probable energy expended and other factors, not least that helium-enriched gases allow a significantly greater heat loss than breathing air, thus necessitating a compensating increase in daily calories. The calorie requirement is assessed to be 4000 to 6000 calories per day, considerably in excess of the human body requirement at atmospheric pressure. The increased diet needs to contain the correct proportions of proteins, carbohydrates, fat, minerals and vitamins and the selection of the type of food is largely determined by the effect of pressure on the food matter and changes that occur in taste and smell. Although feeding is complicated the needs of the human body for liquids are relatively unchanged at about 2–3 litres per day. The type of liquid is limited to some extent since alcoholic or carbohydrate-based liquids are unsuitable whilst coffee, tea and fruit juices are all acceptable.

A number of points that need to be considered are as follows:

1. Meals should not be prepared inside the chambers because of the dangers of smoke and toxic gases contaminating the atmosphere.
2. Certain food stuffs, raw or cooked, can generate flatulence when eaten and should be excluded from the special diet prescribed.
3. Bread and rolls will deform under pressure, rice congeals, bananas will spoil although oranges will maintain their shape and consistency. These are examples of the effects of pressure on food.
4. Generally a low-fat diet is prescribed to reduce the danger of thrombosis.
5. Cans of food or liquid should not be passed into the chamber as they may implode because of differential air pressures and be difficult to open. Stainless steel cutlery and tableware should be used as plastic is not suitable.

6. The selection of the diet must take account of extraneous gases emitted; these must be within the capability of the life-support system as, if toxic, they must be removed.
7. In under-water habitats, notably in future projects, where food is prepared in the habitat, the usual strictures apply to the thawing of frozen foods, which must not be subsequently refrozen.
8. In hyperbaric rescue chambers food packs not affected by being pressurized need careful selection and the amount must be controlled by the maximum number of occupants for a minimum period of time before recovery and transfer. The knowledge gained from the experience of astronauts in outer space in similar conditions of confinement has helped in the use of hyperbaric feeding and dietary control.

Sanitary Installations

Some classification societies lay down design criteria for the installation of sanitary systems in saturation hyperbaric complexes. In earlier designs the toilet and washing facilities including the shower arrangements were a part of the living accommodation but experience has shown the need for independent pressure chambers to fulfil this function. This allows the chamber to be depressurized, empty, at various times to be cleaned out and disinfected. Whilst some designs allow for a central sanitary chamber which can be used by more than one living chamber, this arrangement has the disadvantage that different pressures and possibly dissimilar mixtures are needed for the competing needs of personnel from different living chambers. Clearly the best arrangement is to connect the separate chambers fulfilling these functions to each living chamber, notwithstanding the additional cost and the need for additional space.

The standard internal fittings of a central or independent chamber will include the following items:

1. Handbasin with hot and cold water
2. Fixed or hand shower with temperature regulation
3. WC fitted with safety exhaust system
4. Drainage system with sewage tanks. The tanks are pressure-proof and a 30–50 litre capacity tank will normally be sufficient for four people under pressure

In hyperbaric rescue chambers a dry toilet can suffice for a limited period.

The design criteria and implementation into systems are discussed in more detail in Chapter 3.

Accommodation

In modern deep diving systems the average volume per diver in the living accommodation is about 5 m^3. National regulations in some countries, for example the UK, legislate a minimum headroom allowing the occupants to stand up if time under pressure exceeds 12

Table 10.4. Space conditions in modern deep diving systems, diving simulators and under-water habitats

System	Total volume (m^3)	Volume per diver (m^3)	No. of separate rooms	Internal diameter of chamber (mm)
Deep diving systems				
Arctic Seal	75	6.25	8	2150
Seaway Falcon	40	4.5	4	2150
Diving simulator				
Cartagena	33	8.25	4*	1750/2900
Zürich	24	8	3*	2000
Under-water station				
Helgoland	40	10	2*	2460
Aegir	48	12	2*	2750

*Excluding wet chamber.

hours. In the earlier days when exposures under pressure were limited to hours rather than days no minimum volumes were ever considered and volumes of less than 2 m^3 per diver were usual and there were no facilities for standing up.

In Table 10.4 are listed the volumes of some systems for different purposes. The operational systems used commercially off-shore, particularly when built into ships, are often constrained by space limitations which do not apply to diving simulators, where no restrictions exist, except for cost. Under-water habitats require greater volumes per person whether they are pressurized or not. Volumes quoted include, and are not in addition to, the fittings such as bunks, tables, cupboards etc. To achieve the best balance of efficiency and comfort, the basis of human ergonomics, careful pre-planning is needed to use the limited space to maximum advantage. Within these structures the main considerations are comfortable sleeping and seating arrangements responding to the individual needs of a diver for privacy and quietness. The bunks should have first claim on space to allow for maximum comfort and size and must be designed to be least affected by the rolling motion of the ship.

Tidiness is a fundamental discipline and the stowage spaces should be designed to hold all small loose equipment and personal possessions. Small design considerations, such as the relative efficiency of sliding doors over hinged ones, need to be settled at the earliest design stage and not during fitting out prior to the first mobilization. At this later stage, however, the choice of colours can be considered to give some warmth to the surroundings. For instance interiors painted in white suggest a cold environment whereas green will be warmer and more pleasing.

Table 10.5. Communication systems for compression chambers diving simulators and deep diving systems

Acoustic	Visual	Audiovisual
Telephones (electric or sound-powered)	Television (vision only)	Television
Press-to-talk systems (sound-powered)	Telewriter	
Talk-back systems	Indicator panel	
Radio systems (wireless)		
Helium voice unscramblers		
Alarms and bells		

Communications

Communications are an essential part of any operation—to the diving bell when the divers are working, to the compression chamber and during the intervening transfer under pressure. A primary and back-up system are minimum requirements for any system, whatever its design and use. The main need to communicate intelligibly, particularly when breathing lighter inert helium gas mixtures, requires helium voice unscramblers. The following systems are used or considered:

1. Sound-powered systems requiring no power
2. Press-button communications systems with loud speakers and amplifiers
3. Talk-back communications systems with loud speakers and amplifiers (not often used due to their higher failure rate)
4. Helium voice unscramblers with amplifiers and loudspeakers (essential for helium-breathing systems)
5. Radio communication for use with hyperbaric rescue chamber when the chamber has been launched into the sea, and communication maintained with a surface vessel

Certain other refinements can be incorporated into diving systems such as television for monitoring inside the chambers, usually restricted to the larger systems both off-shore and simulators on land, and in under-water habitats. The method of transmitting a drawing or hand-written message through telewriters is being considered. Warning devices to indicate communication systems failure, either by indicator lights or by horns, have already been incorporated.

Lighting and Noise Levels

As far as possible the minimum levels of lighting and noise level standards as applied to normal industrial practice should apply to the interiors of hyperbaric chambers. Further design factors apply to maintaining different standards applicable to working areas and rest areas. Although these standards are easier to implement in diving simulators, certainly with regard to noise levels, as the gas supply and compressor facilities can be separated some distance away from the chambers, certain steps can be taken in hyperbaric systems in vessels to reduce noise. This is not always successful as there is also the additional noise from the ship's own machinery. The application of modern techniques using sound-proofing materials can reduce noise levels, especially in the gas circulation, compression and reclamation systems where continuous changes in pressure produce very high noise levels. Noise levels inside the chamber should not exceed 60–70 dB except during short periods of gas changes and pressure changes when levels should not exceed 90 dB (under some circumstances 105 dB).

Similarly lighting levels should vary with area. The diving bell which is the working area should have strong positioned lights to produce the best non-diffused light in the water, directed onto the work and without glare. Lighting inside the chambers should be capable of being controlled so that lights may be reduced for sleeping and increased to give a pleasant light for resting and eating. Table 10.6, based on the German DIN standards, may be used as a guideline.

Table 10.6 Lighting requirements for various areas

Type of area	Power (lux)
Working	150–250
Diving bell	100–110
Living	50–100
Sleeping	20–30

Entertainment

For long periods of saturation, sometimes up to 30 days, there is clearly a need for alternative and optional channels of entertainment. The inherent problems of boredom, possibly interspersed with peaks of stress occurring at different times for individual divers, can to some extent be catered for by having television, film and wireless all available with individual headsets so that low noise levels are maintained. In addition games and literature should be available.

Fire Hazards

The systems for firefighting are covered in Chapter 2, but clearly prevention is fundamental and design and operational considerations should take into account the selection of materials inside the chamber to minimize the risk of toxic gases being released.

Primary Life-Support: Technical Solutions

To produce a safe primary life-support system, removing the toxic gases and maintaining the internal atmosphere in the correct proportion and at the optimum temperature and humidity, allows a number of options. We discuss here the most practical and usual methods as applied to hyperbaric systems. The life-support system applied to transportable recompression chambers for divers has been covered in Chapter 5.

Oxygen Supply

Open air circuit

In compression chambers operating in the air range normally from 0 to 50 m the oxygen supply is guaranteed by the need to ventilate the chamber with clean air to remove the CO_2. Compression chambers filled with air will normally operate on the open-circuit principle where the quantity of fresh air supplied will be proportional to the number of people breathing inside the chamber with an equivalent exhaust of gas to maintain the same correct pressure. For practical purposes the average CO_2 exhaled per person is 0.45 litres/minute and as the maximum permitted CO_2 level should not accumulate above 0.015 bar, the amount of air ventilation needed to disperse this is 30 litres/person/minute. With an oxygen percentage of 21% in the air the oxygen that is supplied in this ventilation to remove CO_2 is already 6.3 litres/minutes, and this will increase proportionally with pressurization, i.e. at 3 bar it will be 18.9 litres. Therefore in chambers where air is the breathing gas and the open-circuit method of ventilating or flushing the system with more air is used, the critical partial pressure relates to CO_2 elimination in which case the oxygen requirement is satisfied.

Closed mixed gas circuit

Outside the normal commercial air diving range between 50 and 60 m where helium is introduced as an inert gas, the closed-circuit system is used for reasons of respiratory control, noise and, not least, cost. The removal of CO_2 by ways other than flushing the system described later requires separate means of re-supplying the chamber atmosphere with oxygen. The supply of oxygen is normally in high-pressure cylinders although theoretically it can be supplied from a liquid oxygen source or solid chlorate candles. The supply of pure oxygen for breathing in the later stages of decompression or for therapeutic treatment is discussed in Chapter 2. The supply of the correct amount of oxygen in the chambers for normal breathing to maintain the correct partial pressure of oxygen is discussed here. Fig. 10.2 shows a standard oxygen supply system as a separate part of the total life-support system for a deep diving system. The system can be subdivided into a number of groups but the overriding design factor must take into account that oxygen, being highly inflammable, requires additional safety factors and the careful selection of materials for handling purposes.

The oxygen supply banks are usually in separate stowages. Individual 50 litre cylinders can be racked together in bottle racks of 10 to 12 cylinders with a charging pressure of 200 bar. In drilling rigs, platforms and vessels these racks are usually stowed on the upper deck. Modern diving support vessels have special stowage facilities below decks for oxygen and often have built-in bulk stowage facilities. Manifold gauges show the storage cylinder pressure and through high-pressure stainless steel or copper alloy piping the oxygen pressure is reduced at source to about 40 bar and distributed to

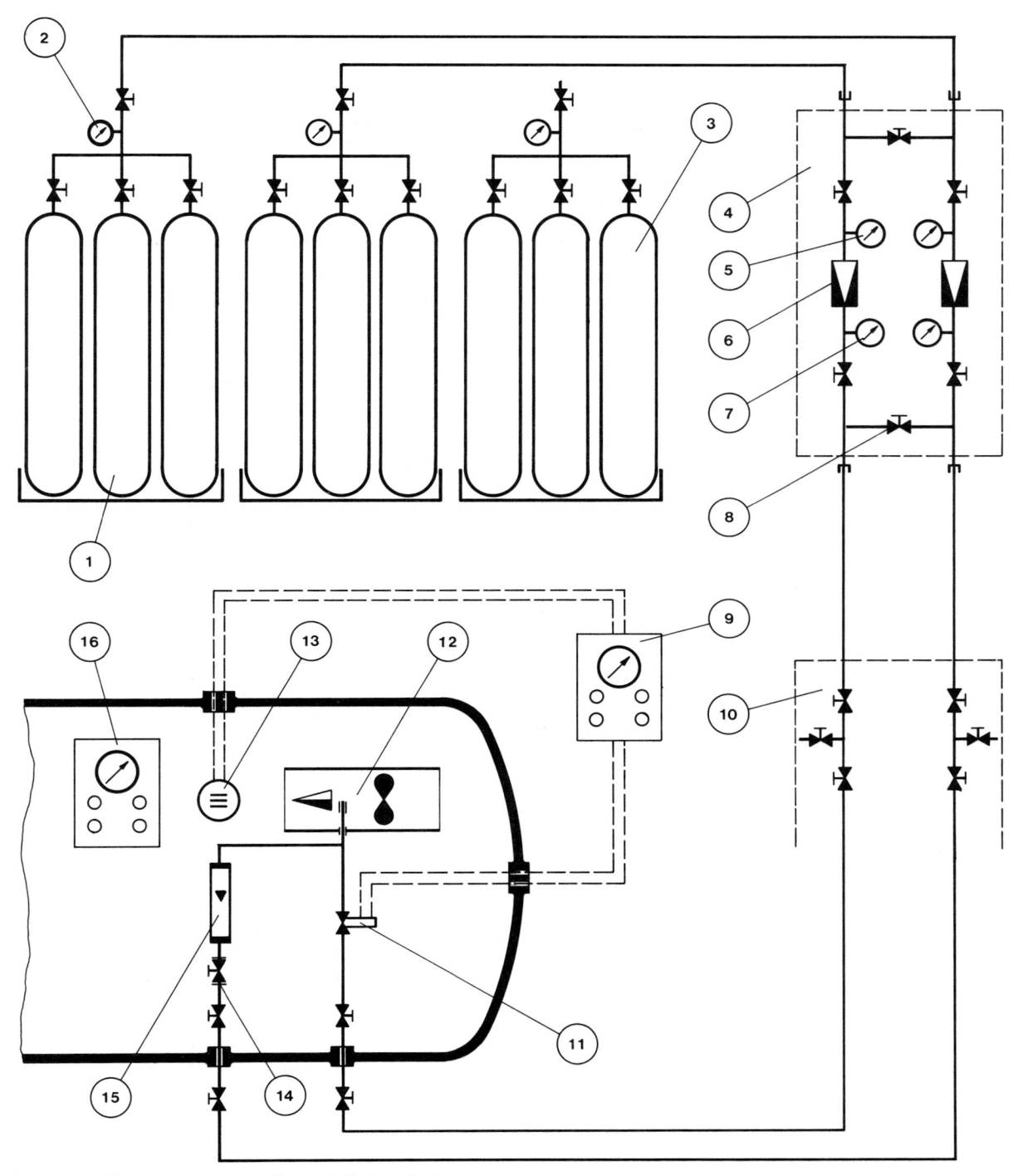

Fig. 10.2. The oxygen system of a typical deep diving system.

1. oxygen storage bank
2. storage pressure gauge
3. oxygen storage bank (reserve)
4. oxygen distribution panel
5. high-pressure gauge
6. pressure regulator
7. operating pressure gauge
8. cross-connect valve
9. oxygen meter
10. control panel (section)
11. solenoid
12. blower
13. oxygen sensor
14. fine adjustment valve
15. flowmeter
16. internal oxygen meter

the various chambers via the control panel where flow is regulated and monitored to maintain the correct partial pressure in the chamber. Automatic partial pressure control systems operate between preset high and low levels controlled by solenoids and by an O_2 partial pressure control meter.

For safety reasons shut-off valves are fitted each side of the hull penetration of the chamber and the best place for the oxygen diffusion into the chamber to give quick and even distribution will be normally behind a blower or adjacent to the circulation flow inlet into the chamber. Alarms are usually fitted on O_2 partial pressure monitoring systems which sound in the event of any malfunction with a manual override. Flow meters to measure the volumes are an integral part of the system. As this is a very sensitive part of the total life-support system it should have a complete back-up system with duplicate instrumentation and cross connections.

Carbon Dioxide Removal

Theoretically there are more than 30 different methods of eliminating CO_2 from a gas mixture and some even produce O_2 in the process. Experiments conducted show that lithium peroxide (Li_2O_2), lithium oxide (Li_2O) and manganese oxide (MgO) can eliminate CO_2. There are procedures which wash out carbon dioxide (monoethanolamine) but require high energy in the process. CO_2 can be frozen out, a method which presented many mechanical problems to Jaques-Yves Cousteau during the *Conshelf III* experiments. The most common process for elimination of CO_2 is using absorbent lime, referred to as soda-lime or baralime, or to a lesser extent lithium hydroxide. Both these chemicals, absorbent lime and lithium hydroxide, are used in granulated form and cannot be re-used. They vary little from different manufacturers. Lithium hydroxide is more efficient than absorbent lime, absorbing nearly twice as much CO_2 for the same amount of absorbent, but is very much more expensive and therefore used in circumstances where weight and space considerations are paramount. These considerations apply to use in submersibles and one-atmosphere vehicles. For design considerations applying to deep diving systems calculations are based on the use of absorbent lime ($Ca(OH)_2$). The efficiency of the absorbent will alter with temperature and humidity and designs must take this into account. Temperatures below 20°C should be avoided if possible and also too dry an absorbent. The absorbent should have the minimum water content stated by the manufacturer. If the circulating gas is too dry the absorbent may need to be humidified artificially.

Deep diving systems may often combine the CO_2 removal and temperature humidity control systems in one unit and it is usual to do so in modern systems. In small compression chambers and in diving bells the CO_2 absorption units are separate, comprising a refillable cannister for the chemical, a blower capable of circulating gas through the unit and into the chamber and an electric drive that is either in a sealed unit using low voltage or air- or water-driven, to reduce fire and explosion hazards.

Fig. 10.3. Lindbergh Hammar carbon dioxide absorption unit.

Fig. 10.3 shows a unit designed by Lindbergh Hammar which is commonly used. The oval casing is stainless steel, as is the refill cannister for the chemicals, with sufficient volume to cater for the maximum number of divers and the operating depth. The blower is driven by a sealed explosion-proof electric motor. Clearly the correct positioning of the unit inside the chamber is very important to achieve the most efficient circulation of gases.

For large deep diving systems with perhaps as many as 24 divers at various stages of saturation for periods of 30 days or more, many large systems are needed, where the small separate units would be insufficient in terms of reliability, endurance and efficiency. Three principle designs are shown in Fig. 10.4. In A, the low-cost system, the blower and refillable cannister are inside. The major disadvantages are the increased noise level, limited maintenance and repairs and the dependence on the divers to refill the cannisters themselves. In B all the obvious disadvantages of the internal systems are overcome by designing the CO_2 unit externally except for the higher costs associated with additional penetrations, pipework and pressure vessels. The higher cost is not nowadays considered to be relevant because of the need for high safety factors in this part of the life-support system. In C a compromise between the external and

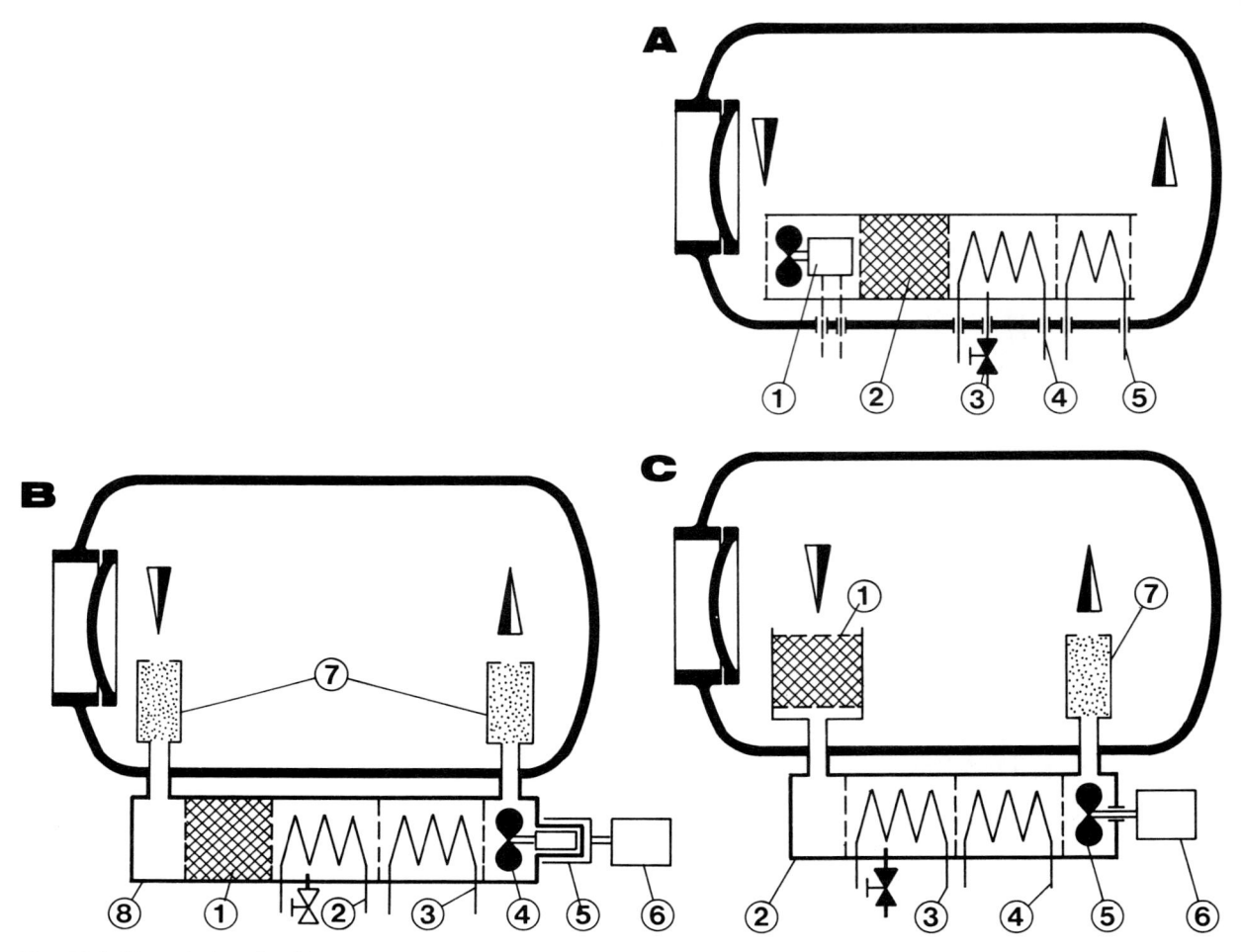

Fig. 10.4. Basic designs for life-support systems.

- **A** Internal life-support system
  1. blower
  2. carbon dioxide absorber
  3. dewatering valve
  4. cooling/dehumidification
  5. heating

- **B** External life-support system
  1. carbon dioxide absorber
  2. cooling/dehumidification
  3. heating
  4. blower
  5. magnetic clutch
  6. driving motor
  7. silencer
  8. pressure vessel

- **C** Semi-external-internal life-support system
  1. carbon dioxide absorber
  2. pressure vessel
  3. cooling/dehumidification
  4. heating
  5. blower
  6. driving motor
  7. silencer

internal systems shows the blower and heat exchanger outside the chamber, enclosed in a pressure vessel, and the CO_2 absorber inside the chamber in a non-pressure-proof container. Clearly combining the advantages and disadvantages of both the other systems, the main technical consideration is the design of a blower drive inside a pressure chamber. Normal electric motors cannot be considered because of the serious fire risk from sparking. Electric drive is possible using metal-clad gas-tight designs with forced helium ventilation to purge the

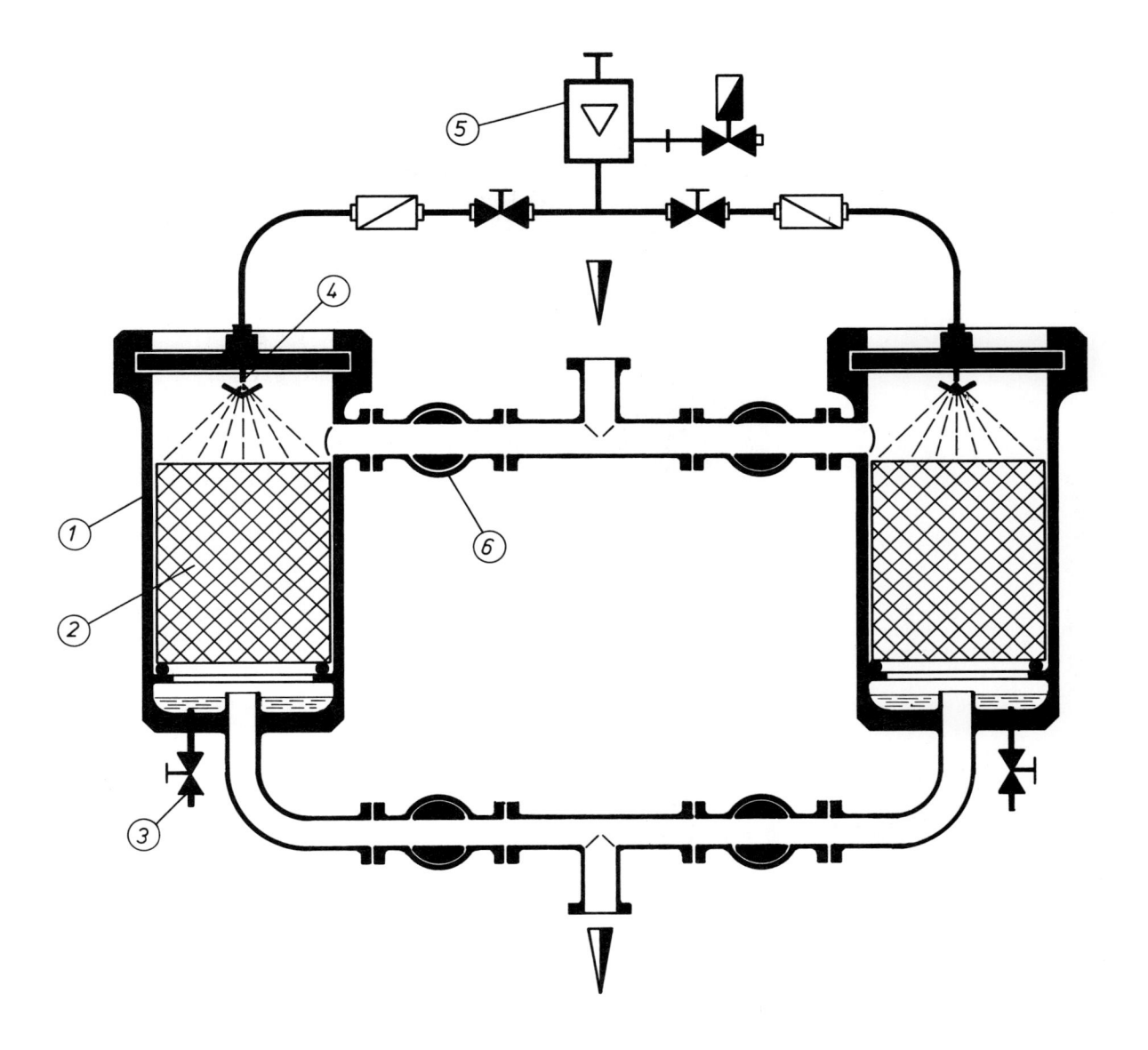

Fig. 10.5. Carbon dioxide absorber with absorbent humidification for an external life support system.

    1 CO_2 absorbent casing
    2 absorbent cartridge (rechargeable)
    3 dewatering valve
    4 atomizer
    5 high-pressure pump
    6 shut-off valve

unit. Other options are hydraulic fluid drives, air-driven motors and magnetic clutches through pressure-proof casings with motors at surface pressure.

Fig. 10.5 illustrates an external life-support system using two filter systems operated either together in parallel or separately isolating one for refill or maintenance purposes. In this Dräger system the filters,

Fig. 10.6. Carbon dioxide absorber, recuperator, blower and drive.

often referred to as scrubbers, are arranged vertically and hold 10-litre absorbent refill cartridges. The pressure-tight lids are constructed with either a bayonet or U-shaped clamp ring. A water atomizer is fitted inside the pressure vessel which, in the event of relatively low humidity conditions and a circulation of dry gases, can increase the humidity to a set degree. Fig. 10.6 illustrates a complete CO_2 unit with blower, recuperator, shut-off valves and heat insulation. Gas flows and the quantity of chemicals have been calculated to provide for CO_2 removal for six divers up to 50 bar.

Complete Integrated Life-support Systems

The integration of the oxygen supply and the CO_2 can now be considered. In Fig. 10.4A the internal CO_2 life-support system has a very limited application nowadays as the more complex deep diving systems use the external and internal/external systems. However, these external systems cannot be used in under-water habitats (the subject of life support in these habitats is discussed separately in Chapter 6). In diving bells the main requirement is to monitor oxygen partial pressure, eliminate carbon dioxide and provide heating if required. Because the purpose of the diving bell is to provide an effective worksite platform for limited periods, only the basic essential needs of the divers need to be considered and as these have to be provided mainly through the umbilical they are

Fig. 10.7. Oxygen meter integrated into control panel (by Saturation Systems).

competing for limited services. In a total closed-circuit system where gases are supplied to the diving bell and subsequently returned to the surface for reprocessing, all the oxygen monitoring and replacement and the CO_2 scrubbing is carried out on the surface. An oxygen meter integrated in the control panel produced by Saturation Systems Inc. is shown in Fig. 10.7. However, in limited operations where the bell divers can control their own gas supply CO_2 scrubbers and oxygen monitoring equipment are provided inside the chamber. For CO_2 removal there are a number of units available. The unit by Lindbergh-Hammar, shown in Fig. 10.3, is compact and very suitable. The same stringent measures against fire and explosion apply to diver bells as well as compression chambers with regard to electric motor safeguards. To avoid problems of corrosion all important components should be made from stainless steel.

Since diving bells, by the nature of their work in the sea, are exposed to cold for long periods, especially in connection with under-water construction work, provision must be made to keep the temperature above 30°C if possible. This can be achieved by using electrically heated radiators but with limited efficiency. A more practical way, if hot water is already being used via the umbilical to the divers, is by heat exchangers and a blower. A water heater unit which works on this principle is shown in Fig. 10.8.

Fig. 10.8. Hot-water-supplied heat-exchanger with electric blower for heating diving bell (by Kinergetics Inc.).

Heating coils can be fitted with some limited success between the bell hull and external insulation which will retain some heat for limited periods of time in the water. Further research into diver heating and bell systems is still necessary and the development of heat pumps deriving energy from the surrounding sea offers some interesting possibilities.

There have not been any agreed standards as to the requirements for diver heating systems in diving bells and for divers in the water. In the colder waters of north-west Europe, a major area of activity, some form of external active body heating should be available at a depth below 50 m. The heating of respiratory gases, normally oxy-helium mixtures, to 30°C is normal practice at diving depths in excess of 150 m. To be less arbitrary, some operational limitations with regard to the type of dive and the length need to be considered. If the temperature of the water is about 10°C active body heating should be provided if the time spent in the water exceeds 1 hour. If the temperature is about 15.5°C then 4 hours is a reasonable diving period without active heating.

Whatever form of active heating is used it must be carefully controlled. There are also dangers in overheating the divers. Hyperthermia can set in after an exhausting dive with heated suits and, after their removal, can lead to unconsciousness. This may be attributable to release of tension, an overheated hot water suit and gas. This creates too high an injection temperature with the inability to eliminate the heat quickly enough. The margin to turn a heat loss into a heat gain is very small. Diver heating systems should be designed on the basis of active diver insulation heating to maintain the thermal equilibrium without the body having to sacrifice its own heat. Unlike the effects of different gases, the parameters of which are well known, much more study is needed in this field.

With regard to the heating of the diver directly through active insulation heating, this can be achieved through three methods:

1. Diesel-fired heater
2. Electrical resistance device
3. Steam generating device

All the systems are designed to take sea water, heat it to a desired temperature, pass it to the diver and dump into the sea again. Each should have safety features to identify the following:

1. Loss of sea water flow
2. Failure of temperature control
3. Loss of heat transfer medium

Diesel-fired heaters are the most common because they require the least outside logistical support. However, they are complicated pieces of machinery and serviceability and maintenance are problems, particularly in fire detection circuits, dirty fuel and temperature oscillations. Some regulations also state that in off-shore operations diesel-fired heaters should be in an explosion-proof housing and protected from the elements.

Electrical resistance heating ranging from 100 to 150 kVA are now becoming commonplace. Adequate precautions against shock should be taken in the design and in this respect the heating elements should heat fresh water which in turn heats the salt water through a separate heat exchanger.

Heating systems using a chemical reaction have been developed. Salt baths of molten salt provide a form of latent heat and can be used for heating water in suits as well as inside chambers. Further developments may give some autonomy to the diver by replacing the hot water umbilical with a closed-circuit hot water suit using a chemical pack as the heat source.

Integrated life-support units in the external mode are shown to have clear advantages and in spite of the cost are generally accepted in deep diving systems. Fig. 10.9, based on a Dräger system, illustrates the most important components of a life-support system and how they function together. The system is based on a maximum operating pressure of 50 bar and designed to eliminate CO_2 and regulate temperature, humidity and the partial pressure of oxygen. The nucleus of the system is the CO_2 scrubber, blower and electrical heater. The cooling system needed for lowering the humidity is electrically operated and the humidity and temperature sensors inside

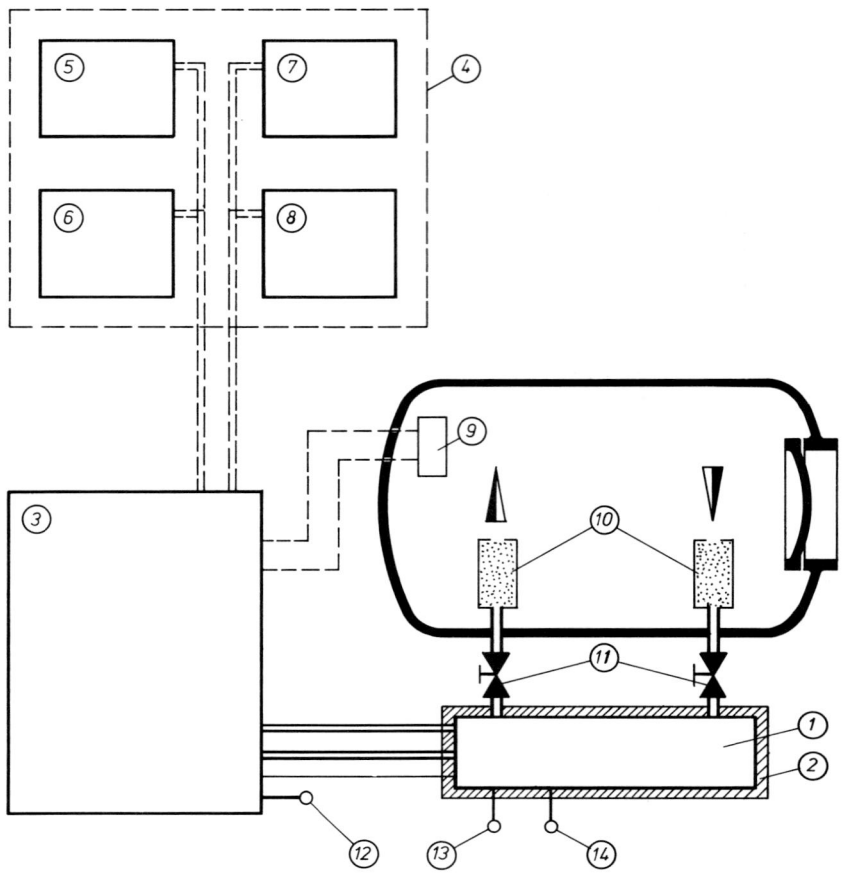

Fig. 10.9. Block diagram of an external life-support system.

1. CO_2 absorber and recuperator
2. insulation
3. cooling aggregate
4. control panel
5. reference input (temperature)
6. actual value read-out and plotter (temperature)
7. reference input (humidity)
8. actual value read-out and plotter (humidity)
9. combined temperature and humidity sensor
10. silencer
11. shut-off valve
12. electric connection
13. water connection for atomizer
14. electric connection for heater

the chamber are monitored from the control panel and with pre-set limits can control the temperature and humidity in the life-support system.

CO_2 scrubbers shown in more detail in Fig. 10.5 have already been described. With a total dual capacity of 20 litres of absorbent lime, sufficient for absorbing 2000 litres of CO_2, the system will maintain this level of efficiency if the circulating gas is not excessively dry. An atomizer is fitted to achieve the correct humidity and the water produced can be drained through a drainage valve which must be fitted to the system. One of the filters can be filled with charcoal or similar material to remove impurities and in this arrangement care should be taken to ensure equal flow characteristics in both scrubbers,

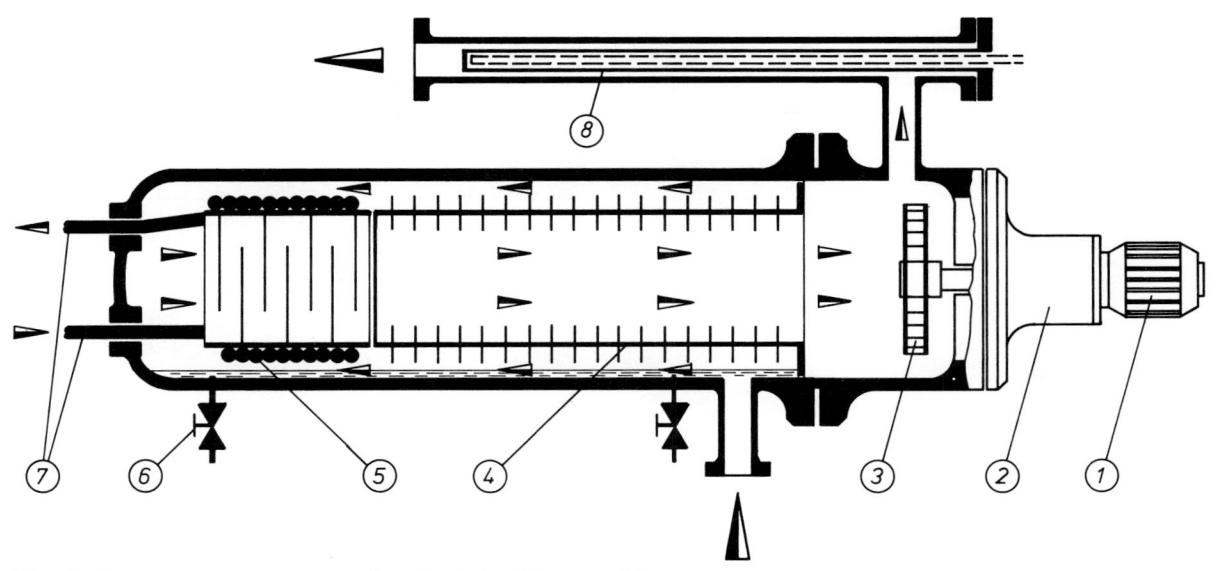

Fig. 10.10. Recuperator, water cooler, circulation blower and heater.

1. electric motor
2. magnetic clutch
3. blower wheel
4. recuperator
5. cooler
6. drainage valve
7. brine inlet and outlet
8. heater

avoiding too great a resistance in one or the other. In the event of the humidity rising above acceptable limits and the cooling system not functioning, the filters can be partially fitted with silica gel in order to absorb some of the water.

Ideally the CO_2 absorption system and the recuperator, water cooler and circulation blower are designed into one unit (Fig. 10.10). Inside the recuperator chamber the gas coming from the CO_2 absorber releases energy to the heat exchanger and is cooled down in the water cooler (to below a certain dew point temperature) until reaching the correct relative humidity. The gas in the recuperator reverses direction after being cooled and passes over a heating coil before re-entering the chamber. As previously mentioned the temperature and humidity are automatically controlled with sensors fitted inside the chamber. The whole assembly should be well insulated to reduce any effect of the temperature outside including pipework and CO_2 scrubbers. Drainage valves should be fitted at the lowest points.

The blower and magnetic clutch system indicated in Fig. 10.10 should be very reliable and fail safe even during long-term operations. Such a system in use generates a flow of gas of 100 m³/hour with a pressure differential in the order of 0.010–0.015 bar and a fan speed of 3000 rpm. The blower or fan wheel is driven without mechanical contact by a magnetic clutch inside a pressure- and gas-tight casing. This design ensures that the electric motor is separated from gas mixtures and conforms with the maximum safety codes to eliminate fire risks associated with oxygen content.

Fig. 10.11. Supply unit and cooling aggregate for an external life support system on the *Arctic Seal*. The system is designed to supply two gas circuits simultaneously.

A sensor can be fitted in the fan to read the flow and this information in respect of gas circulation can be indicated on the control panel.

The recovery of the heat from the heat exchanger is not important and normal heat losses will do this. However, after the gases have passed through the cooling system to achieve the correct humidity they may need to be heated to the correct temperature. In helium-based breathing mixtures the heat losses in the human body are considerable due to the conductivity of the gas and this has to be readjusted in the reheating process. For this purpose an electric heater is placed in a short pipe (Fig. 10.10) directly adjacent to the blower. The gas is separated from the heating elements to again eliminate fire risk and the elements are in the order of 4 kW output. The temperature is regulated by the temperature sensor inside the chamber which will cut out the heating system if temperature rises above a pre-set figure. If this installation is correctly designed and efficiently installed additional separate heaters should not be needed inside the chamber except during pressure changes during decompression. The separate heaters for this purpose, or if the gas heater fails, can be supplied by hot water from the main supply. An additional heating system can be fitted with electrical heating circuits between the external hull of the chambers and the insulation material. This can be effectively used in separate sections to heat parts of the

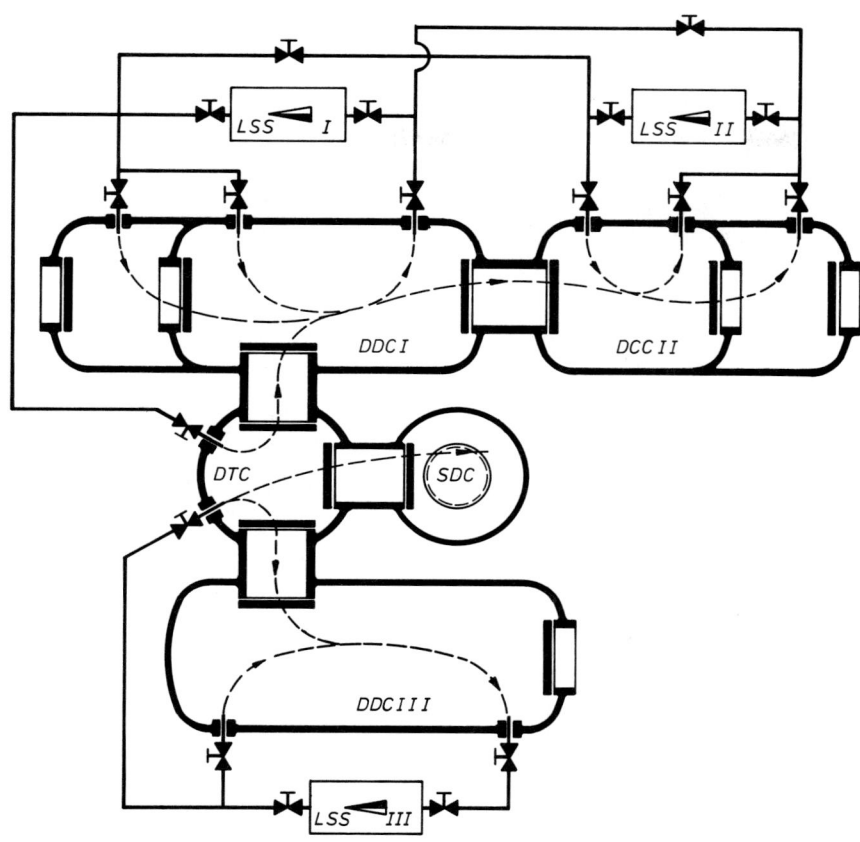

Fig. 10.12. Integration and cross-connection of life-support systems into multiple-chamber complexes.

chamber to compensate for fluctuations and temperature gradients which can occur inside pressurized chambers.

Cooling is carried out by an enclosed unit consisting of the cooling unit itself, the water or brine tank and its pump and a cabinet containing the controls as shown in Fig. 10.11. Standard commercial units are acceptable, designed for either air or water cooling. The cooling liquid is circulated around the system and kept at a set temperature, taking into account the heat absorbed from the heat exchanger in the recuperator. The cooling system is thermostatically controlled between pre-set ranges with the input supplied from the temperature and relative humidity sensors in the chambers.

Ideally a separate life-support system should be designed for separate chambers within a complex and this is necessary where chambers are at different pressures and operating in different circumstances. However economy is good design and where chambers are at the same pressures and same breathing mixtures one system can be designed to undertake the life-support functions of both with cross connections. A stand-by system must be available to be connected into the system as shown in Fig. 10.12. An additional flexible cross-connection can connect the diving bell to the life

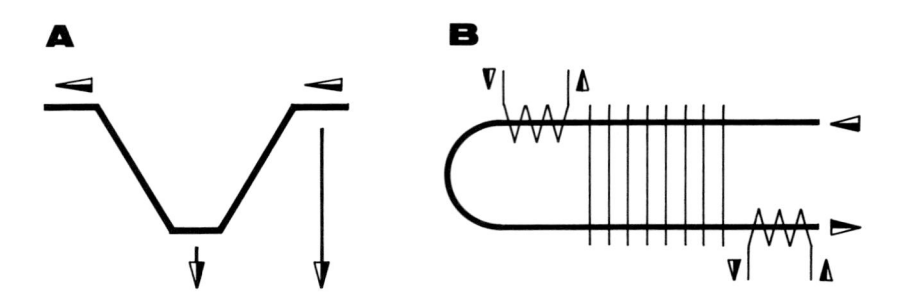

Fig. 10.13. Basic heat balance (A) and counter-current heat exchanger (B).

support system in the event of an emergency requiring the use of the SCC as a deck chamber.

Semi-external/Internal Life-support Systems

The basic features of the systems are shown in Fig. 10.4 and there are various design options open. The CO_2 scrubber can be located inside the chamber, and the blower, dehumidification and heating units can be sited externally within a pressure-proof vessel. If silica gel is used as a drying agent to control humidity this part can also be sited inside the chamber.

An interesting solution on these lines is produced by Kinergetics Inc. The CO_2 scrubber, dehumidification and heating systems, as well as the blower, are installed inside the chamber with the cooling liquid regulator and pumps outside. The cooling liquid is pressurized and also applies pressure to turn the fan in the blower through a magnetic clutch. The basic heat exchange process and recuperator are shown in Figs 10.13 and 10.14. The diagram shows the whole system both inside and outside the chamber, indicating the independent functions of CO_2 removal, dehumidification and temperature control. A rechargeable absorbent container, holding 16 kg and made of stainless steel, is rated for a gas flow of 1400 litres/min. The gas is dehumidified passing through the drying loop after it has passed through the counter-current heat exchanger and been partially cooled down. Further cooling takes place to the required humidity and temperature. The water condensate formed is automatically drained through a valve. This system is claimed to achieve 85% energy saving using the counter-current heat exchanger, compared to a uniflow system described previously. The heating of the gas is carried out in the final phase with hot water, under pressure which drives the fan turbine. Additional heating, if required during peak periods, is provided by an electric heater. The entire system illustrated in Fig. 10.14 and the chamber unit in Fig. 10.15 show the three separate gas phases and the two liquids for heating, power and cooling and the sophistication reached to provide an automatic operation.

Emergency Breathing Systems

Life-support systems can fail and stand-by systems can also be

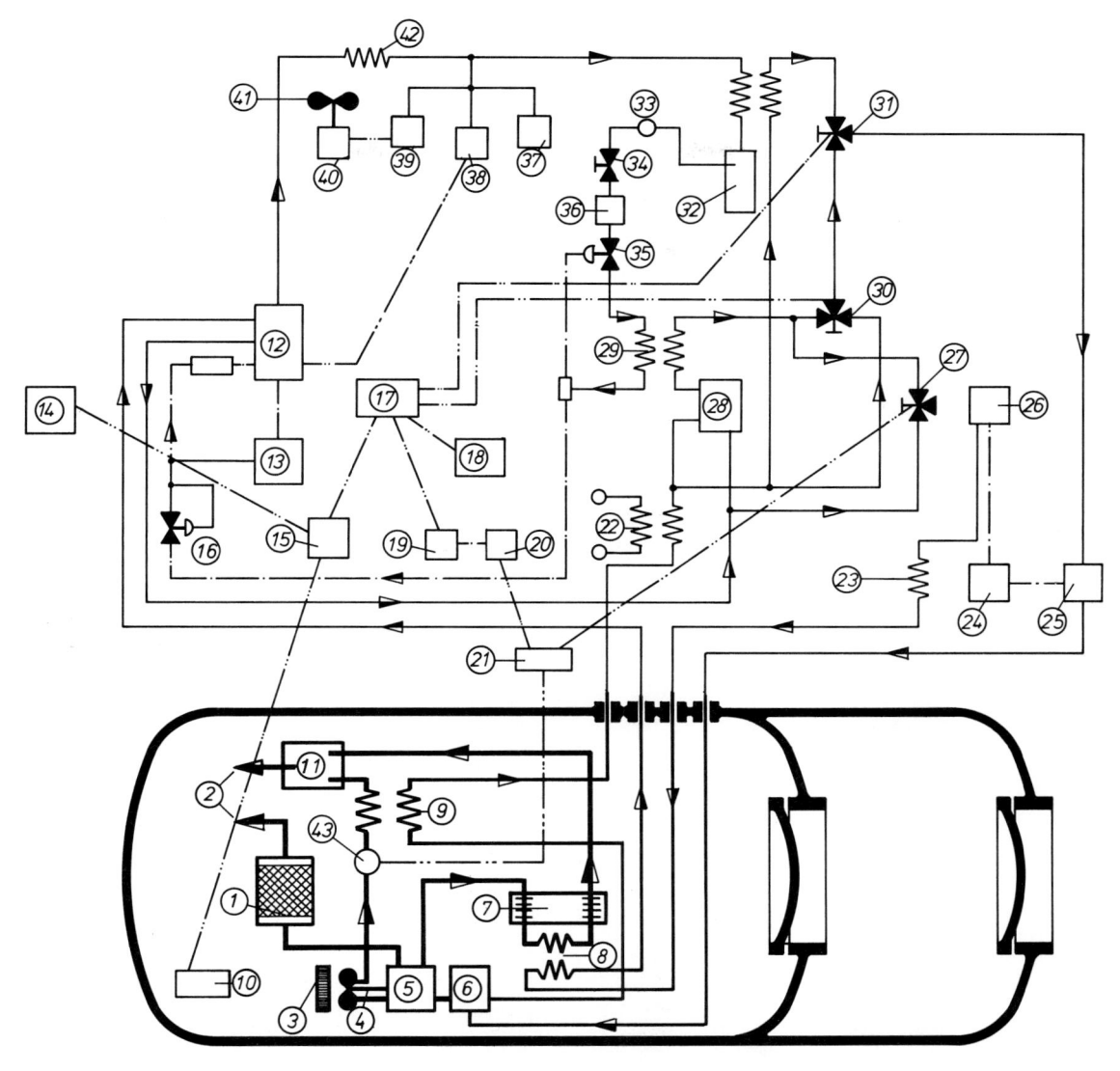

Fig. 10.14. Flow diagram for an external/internal life support system (by Kinergetics Inc.).

1 CO_2 absorber
2 conditioned breathing gas
3 dust filter
4 fan
5 blower magnetic coupling
6 water motor
7 counter-current heat exchanger
8 cold finned tube heat water trap
9 hot finned tube heat-exchanger
10 temperature sensor
11 plenum
12 compressor
13 low-pressure switch
14 temperature read-out
15 temperature read-out
16 back pressure regulator
17 temperature control
18 power supply
19 set point control (temperature)
20 set point control (humidity)
21 humidity control
22 electric heater
23 motor cooler
24 pump motor
25 fluid pump (primary, hot)
26 fluid pump (secondary, cold)
27 control valve (humidity)
28 accumulator
29 evaporator
30 control valve cooling
31 control valve heating
32 receiver
33 sight glass
34 hand valve
35 expansion valve
36 drier filter
37 water cut-in switch
38 high-pressure safety switch
39 motor switch
40 electric motor
41 fan
42 condenser
43 sensor

Fig. 10.15. Chamber aggregate of the Kinergetics Inc. life-support system.

Fig. 10.16. Personal rescue oxygen breathing unit (Comex).

Fig. 10.17. Cylindrical carbon dioxide filter unit by Dräger, installed vertically, with pressure-proof circular bayonet lock for replenishment.

inoperable in situations where there has been a power failure or damage through unforeseen causes. Collision, fire or grounding of the vessel can provide the circumstances that make it necessary to provide an emergency breathing system which does not rely on power. Chamber fire, explosion or breakdown in the supply of oxygen from other causes are real hazards and must be provided for by BIBS (built-in breathing system). These systems provide individual oral–nasal breathing masks already fitted inside the chambers. The breathing mixture, suitable for the occasion, is automatically provided, reduced to the correct pressure, and either closed-circuit or open-circuit depending on the pressures in the chamber. These systems are described in more detail in Chapter 2. BIBS usually have a small connecting hose but with quick connectors they can be moved around to alternative connections inside the chamber. Independent breathing sets can be provided giving maximum mobility but limited endurance.

There are a number of systems available. A Comex breathing system is shown in Fig. 10.16. In the event of the main CO_2

absorption system failing, by inserting a filter cartridge holding several litres of absorbent into the breathing system and exhaling into the surrounding atmosphere, the occupant can survive. At the end of the endurance of the filter it can be replaced as required.

Commercial Breathing Equipment for Divers

The development of breathing equipment has generally been able to keep pace with, and meet the needs of, under-water technology. These developments are naturally becoming constrained by the inevitable barrier imposed in the deeper depths by man's ability to withstand the pressure and at the same time to carry out useful work. The work is directly related to the exploration and production of off-shore oil and gas. Sport diving, using the ubiquitous scuba equipment, was established before the commercial requirement but, within the air range the equipment is still widely used for commercial purposes and is therefore covered in this chapter. The different types of breathing equipment are discussed in detail but a description of any specific manufactured equipment is avoided as it may become outdated. However the basic principle on which it was designed will remain valid. The basic design considerations of any one type of breathing equipment can therefore be directly related to any unit manufactured for commercial use.

The firm basic requirements of any commercial diving set are as follows:

1. It must have an unrestricted supply of oxygen within the defined oxygen partial pressure limits.
2. It must be capable of removing all expired carbon dioxide.
3. It must compensate for the ambient hydrostatic pressure.
4. It must be designed for comfort and for safe operation by the diver.

Compressed Air Breathing Apparatus

Although much greater effort and cost is directed to deep diving, the greatest amount of work is still carried out in the air diving range using open-circuit air breathing sets, either self-contained, i.e. scuba, or surface-supplied. Even with further off-shore development in the deeper depths the greater proportion of work carried out is within about 50 m and this will not significantly change. There is little improvement that can be made in the compressed air set and the advantages and disadvantages of the equipment cannot be affected by any further improvement in design. The fundamental advantage is that the use of air as a breathing medium is simple and inexpensive. The disadvantage of air is the restrictions it imposes on depth: theoretically diving to 90 m is possible but effectively in most commercial operations is limited to about 50 m. Between the two types of equipment the self-contained scuba set has the advantage of mobility but is severely restricted by the limited working times at

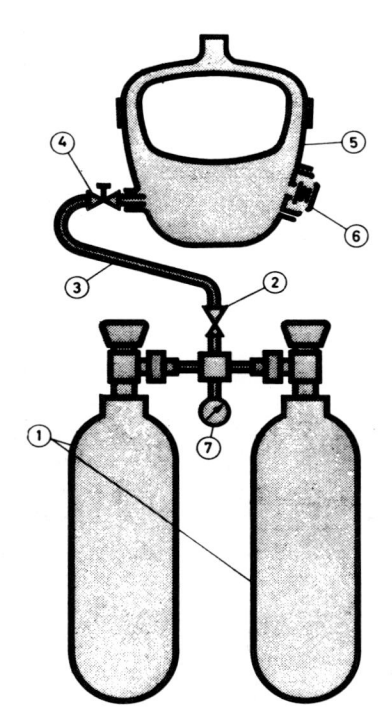

Fig. 10.18. Self-contained open-circuit breathing apparatus with constant air flow.

1 compressed air cylinders with cylinder valves
2 pressure regulator
3 supply hose
4 manually controlled air flow valve
5 full-face diving mask
6 air exhaust valve
7 pressure gauge

depth, directly related to the limited endurance of the air supply carried. This is overcome by the use of surface-supplied air breathing equipment and, because the surface-supplied operation is inherently a much safer method of diving, the scuba method of diving is becoming less used. Both systems are faced with the problem of increased breathing resistance with depth which will affect the working performance of the diver.

Scuba (self-contained air breathing apparatus)

The system works on open-circuit, as does surface supply, where the diver exhales into the surrounding atmosphere. The system cannot be considered really efficient when one considers that in normal breathing only 4% of the total volume is actually consumed by the body. Under pressure, with increased volumes, the rate of efficiency decreases even further. In spite of this it is a very simple, inexpensive and reliable method of diving, in general use more than any other design, but subject to the operational restraints of oxygen tolerance and nitrogen narcosis. There are basically only two types of regulator that deliver the air to the diver at the required pressure and volume, a constant mass regulator and a demand regulator.

Constant Mass Regulator. This regulator produces a constant supply of gas to the diver and is similar in this respect to the constant gas supply to a surface-supplied diver through a breathing hose or umbilical. The diver usually wears a full face mask with an adjustable supply valve allowing the right amount of air into the mask. The additional and surplus air supplied is vented out into the water and this very inefficient method precludes commercial use of this type of regulator. The air is supplied at this constant rate from the air cylinders and the system is illustrated in Fig. 10.18. The constant flow rate must be capable of supplying the diver during maximum exertion so that there is no restriction on breathing. During normal breathing the excess air is exhausted directly into the water. Although not commercially viable, the constant mass regulator does have naval or military advantages because the exhaled air is circulated through a breathing bag or counter lung and rebreathed. In this way the flow through the constant mass regulator can be reduced considerably, increasing the endurance.

Demand Regulator. On demand air supply, controlled by the demand regulator, is activated by the following:

1. The diver creating a slightly negative pressure in the air chamber of the regulator by inhaling.
2. Whilst the diver is descending the ambient water pressure creates an over-pressure in the wet side of the regulator.
3. Manually controlled supply mechanisms are sometimes incorporated in breathing sets to supply additional air.

The basic design and function is illustrated in Fig. 10.19. The design must allow the diver the required volume of air at the correct pressure

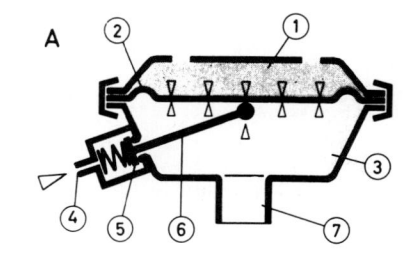

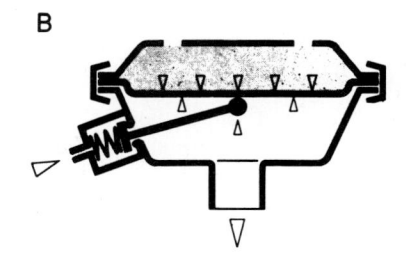

Fig. 10.19. Principle function of a demand regulator.

- **A** Water chamber and air chamber at equal pressure
  1. water chamber
  2. diaphragm
  3. air chamber
  4. air supply
  5. valve
  6. tilt lever
  7. air outlet
- **B** Pressure difference between water and air chamber

with automatic alterations to the volume as pressure varies with depth. In Fig. 10.19 the difference between a single stage and double stage is not considered. In A the water-filled chamber and air-filled chamber are at the same pressure and the diaphragm and lever are therefore in a closed position. No air is being delivered by the action of valve. During the inhalation stage the pressure in the air chamber drops below the pressure in the water chamber and the diaphragm moves downwards, as shown in B in Fig. 10.19, and opens the valve by moving the lever. Air flows out until the pressure on both sides of the diaphragm is equalized. A similar sequence of events takes place during descent when more air is needed as the ambient pressure increases in the chamber open to water. Fig. 10.20 shows the demand valve incorporated into a complete unit.

Whilst the simplest form of scuba diving equipment incorporates a single air cylinder and single-stage regulator to a simple demand valve, the development from this to improved designs has been considerable and varied. Fig. 10.21 illustrates the variations of air diving apparatus and the uses. The total endurance of each system is directly related to the amount of air that is carried in cylinders which can vary, depending on the pressure and capacity in the cylinders.

Single-stage Regulators. The normal pressure in HP air cylinder is between 200 and 300 bar, fully charged, depending on the safe working pressure of the cylinder. This pressure will naturally reduce during a working dive, as the diver consumes his air supply, to a minimum safety level. In any case the pressure needs to be reduced to safe low pressure suitable for inhalation into the lungs. This reduction in pressure takes place in one stage in the single-stage regulator, controlled effectively by the diaphragm/valve combination as illustrated in Fig. 10.23. There are two basic types:

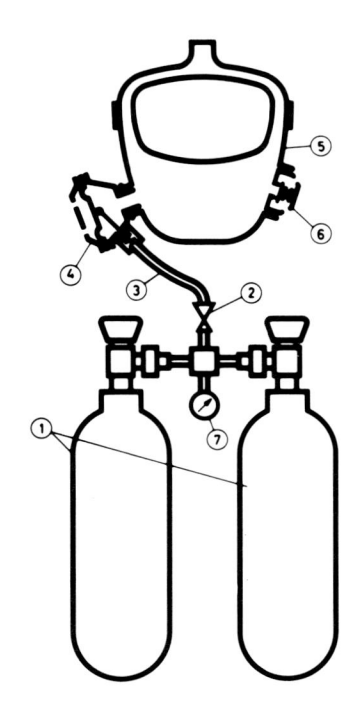

Fig. 10.20. Self-contained open-circuit breathing apparatus with demand regulator.

1. compressed air cylinder with shut-off valves
2. pressure reduction, first stage
3. supply hose
4. demand regulator
5. full-face mask
6. air exhaust valve frequently located in the regulator itself
7. pressure gauge

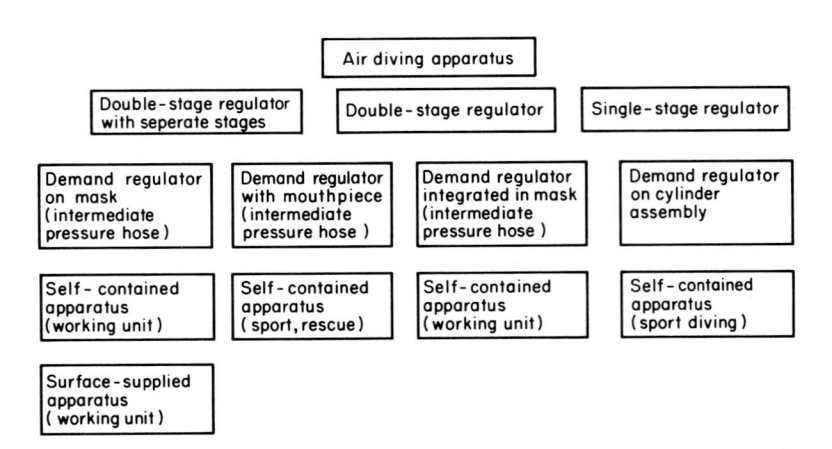

Fig. 10.21. Varieties of air diving apparatus. The first and second stages of the regulator may be designed with a venturi nozzle. Cylinder assemblies may comprise several cylinders.

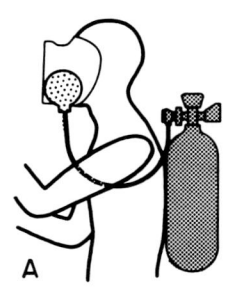

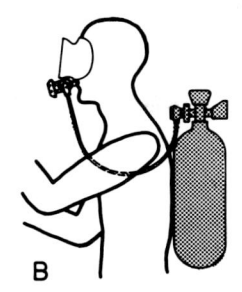

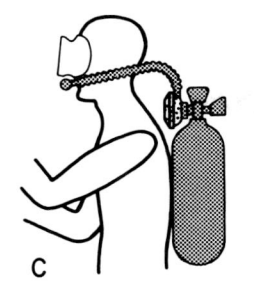

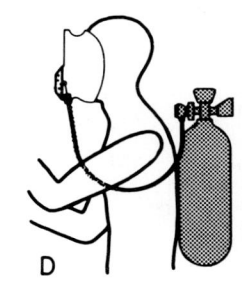

Fig. 10.22. Alternative methods of breathing from supply cylinders.

    A   Regulator mounted on a full-face mask, first and second stages separated
    B   Mouthpiece regulator, first and second stages separated
    C   Regulator mounted on cylinders, single- or double-stage
    D   Regular integrated in full-face mask or helmet, first and second stages separated

1. Upstream valve: single-stage regulator with valve stem opening against pressure and closing with pressure.
2. Downstream valve: single-stage regulator with valve opening in pressure direction and closing against pressure.

The breathing resistances of single-stage regulators are generally greater than those of double-stage regulators. In the upstream valve, a decreasing pressure in the supply cylinders will lead to decreased breathing resistance because the force to open the valve becomes less. The reverse is the case in the downstream valve, where the reduction in supply pressure will increase breathing resistance because a greater force is needed to activate the valve. The single tilt lever mechanism in this type of regulator cannot provide the same degree of efficiency as the double lever mechanisms although the degree of breathing resistance can be improved with the use of injectors.

Double-stage Regulators. By reducing the pressure from the HP supply cylinder to LP for inhalation in two separate stages the breathing resistance is reduced to a more comfortable and constant level. The layout of such a system is shown in Fig. 10.24 where the first and second stage is incorporated in one unit. In the first stage the combined action of the diaphragm and spring reduces the air supply to an intermediate pressure in the range of about 4–9 bar above ambient pressure. This can operate on the downstream principle or the upstream principle. The first stage in the reduction, often referred to as a pressure-reducer, allows the high pressure air from the storage cylinders into the second stage at the correct low pressure which the diver can inhale on demand. This first stage of transfer from high pressure to the diver working pressure is achieved by either of two methods shown in Fig. 10.23. A shows the downstream method

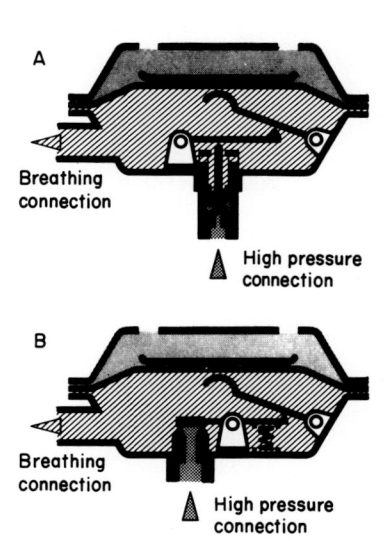

Fig. 10.23. Single-stage regulators.

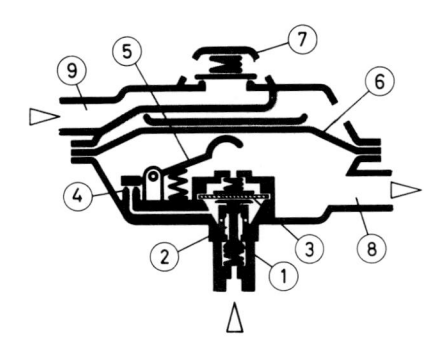

Fig. 10.24. Principles of a double-stage regulator.

1. valve
2. pressure-reducing valve, first stage
3. diaphragm, first stage
4. valve, second stage
5. lever, second stage
6. diaphragm, second stage
7. exhaust valve
8. inhalation connection
9. exhalation connection

where the valve opens against the pressure and B shows the upstream method where the valve opens with the pressure. Whichever system is used a balanced design must allow sufficient flow rate to allow for breathing resistance. In Fig. 10.24 the various parts of a double-stage regulator are shown with their various functions from first stage to second stage and the inhalation and exhalation to and from the diver's respiratory system.

Clearly, when designing a breathing system, the exhalation from the diver's lungs has to be considered as well. The human respiratory system is more comfortable when the exhalation resistance is lower than inhalation resistance. Fig. 10.25 shows the influence that the regulator position has on breathing resistance and the considerable effect hydrostatic water pressure has on this breathing resistance. As it is impossible to mount the regulator at the centre of the breathing cycle because the diver's attitude is constantly changing in the water, the most favourable position needs to be selected. Furthermore the exhaust valve needs to be close to the diaphragm of the second stage.

In Fig. 10.25, when the diver is in a face-down attitude there is a hydrostatic pressure differential of approx. +0.02 bar, due to the difference between the diaphragm and the diver's breathing centre when the regulator is mounted on the cylinder manifold. In addition the inhalation resistance has to be taken into account. In this position the exhalation resistance is less since the exhaust valve is higher than the lungs or breathing centre. If, however, with the second stage the diver is using a single hose regulator in the mouthpiece instead of the double hose, the situation is reversed because in a face-down attitude there is a greater exhalation resistance. Conversely in a face-up attitude the exhalation resistance is less as the second stage regulator is above and therefore at a lower pressure than the lungs. The extent of the exhalation resistance is to a great extent determined by the

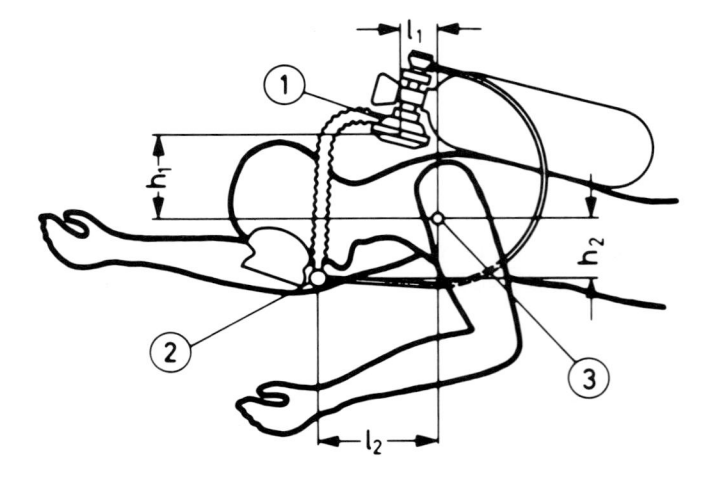

Fig. 10.25. Influence of the position of the regulator on breathing resistance.

1. double hose regulator mounted on cylinder valve
2. single hose regulator (second stage in mouthpiece)
3. respiratory breathing centre

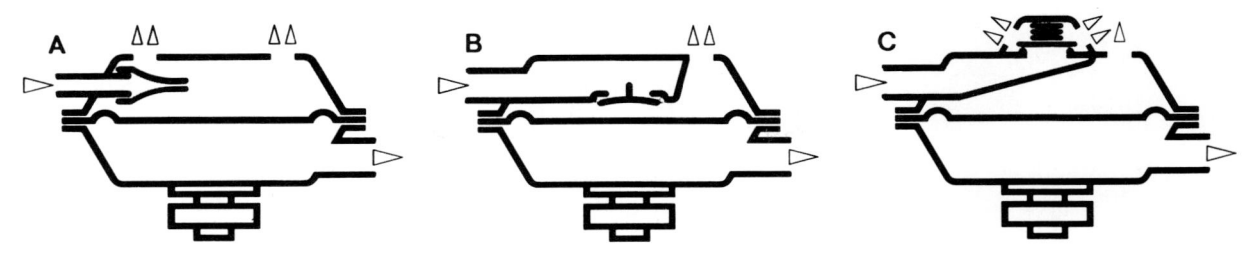

Fig. 10.26. Examples of the arrangement of exhaust valves in regulators.

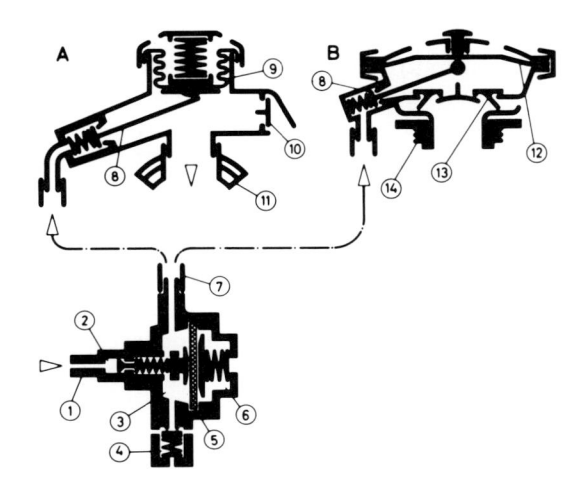

Fig. 10.27. Double-stage regulators with separate first and second stages.

A Mouthpiece regulator
B Regulator for connection to a mask

1 connection to HP storage cylinder
2 high-pressure section
3 intermediate pressure section
4 safety valve
5 diaphragm, first stage
6 regulating spring
7 connecting hose
8 tilt lever
9 bellows, second stage
10 exhaust valve
11 mouthpiece
12 diaphragm, second stage
13 exhaust valve
14 mask connection

position of the exhaust gas in relation to the centre of the body's respiratory system.

The other determining factor in an exhalation system is the design of the exhaust valve. Fig. 10.26 illustrates three principal designs. The most efficient design is one which requires the minimum displacement of water and is shown in C.

The diver breathes either from a mouthpiece or from a breathing mask with a free flow of gas circulating inside. Where the regulators are mounted on the HP storage cylinders the LP gas is passed to the diver through a LP hose, either a single hose in which case the diver exhales into the water from the mouthpiece, or a double hose where the exhaled air is exhausted at the regulator. For convenience, less maintenance and lower cost, the single breathing hose is generally used.

Double-stage Regulator System with Separate First and Second Stage. Rubber bellow hoses for inhalation and exhalation are not generally used in commercial diving as they are not rugged and are prone to damage. The use of the single hose with separate first and second stage, as illustrated in Fig. 10.27, is usual. The regulator can be fitted as a mouthpiece or integrated into an open face mask. In Fig. 10.27 the tilt valve is the basis of the whole operation, reacting to the pressure of sea water and to the respiratory requirements of the diver by opening and shutting the supply from the first stage. From a first stage reducer the gas is supplied to two types of second stage. In Fig. 10.27A a spring bellows is used to act on the tilt valve whilst in Fig. 10.27B a rubber diaphragm is used. The diaphragm is the normal method used to achieve pressure compensation. When the second-stage regulator is fitted to the mask this is the optimum position relative to the centre of breathing as illustrated in Fig. 10.25 and breathing resistance is minimized. There are a number of ways in which the regulator can be fitted to the mask. If fitted at the side near the cheek there is no need to design bubble deflectors which tend to increase the resistance. Single hose regulators will not normally free flow, whatever position the diver adopts in the water, whilst in the double hose regulator there is some likelihood of the air escaping when the mouthpiece is in a higher position than the regulator housing on the inlet to the HP supply.

When comparing the first stage of the combined double-stage regulator incorporating the first and second stage, as illustrated in Fig. 10.24, and the double-stage regulator with the first and second stages separated, as illustrated in Fig. 10.27, there is a need for an additional safety valve to be fitted between the separated first and second stages of the latter. The valve which connects the first and second stage functions on the upstream principle, where the valve closes with the pressure. If the first stage should be defective and a build-up of pressure occurs within the connecting hose between the first and second stage this would be dangerous, hence the need for a safety valve. However in the combined regulator shown in Fig. 10.24 which acts on the upstream principle, illustrated in Fig. 10.23B, there is no chance of a build-up of pressure as the valve seats against the pressure and the air would escape without the need of a safety valve.

The danger of freezing up in the first stage due to external water temperature is prevented by separating the water from the air cavity with a diaphragm whilst still allowing the hydrostatic pressure to be exerted.

Demand Regulator with Injector. Injector systems can produce large air flows with relatively small driving pressure; autonomous hard hat systems are an example of this. In the case of scuba equipment, where the air supply is restricted to the volume in the supply cylinders, a different type of injector can be used in the demand regulator. The principle is based on the fact that air moving through an injector will create a relatively large negative pressure behind the jet. Properly designed and sited, this jet can be applied to the diaphragm, thus increasing the air flow during inhalation but not increasing the inhalation resistance. Fig. 10.28 illustrates the principle of the injector as fitted to a single-stage regulator but it can also be applied to a double-stage regulator. A characteristic of the injector system is that, during the inhalation cycle, after a relatively high initial resistance is overcome, the resistance drops rapidly. If poorly designed or not functioning correctly, there can be a positive pressure which allows more air than the diver can inhale, even resulting in a continuous unchecked air flow. This can be controlled by placing an inhalation valve in the mouthpiece but this increases the initial resistance. Clearly if the injector principle is used the regulator has to be carefully designed and maintained to obtain the advantages.

Fig. 10.28. A single-stage regulator with injector.

High Pressure Connection to First Stage. There are two standard fittings (Fig. 10.29) which connect the demand valve or regulator to the supply cylinders—an international fitting and a 5/8 inch screw connector with an O-ring seal. Both fittings can achieve a pressure seal by hand tightening, without tools, the pressure itself creating a seal. Whichever system is used for the connection, a compatible adaptor is needed to recharge the supply cylinders.

Breathing Connections. Fig. 10.30 illustrates the various types of regulator breathing connections. Five main types can be identified as follows:

1. Hood connection.
2. Full face-mask connection.

Fig. 10.29. High-pressure cylinder valve connections.

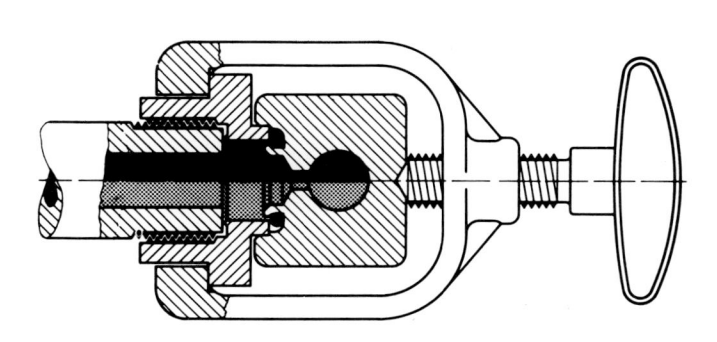

    A 'international' connection
    B 5/8 in screw connection

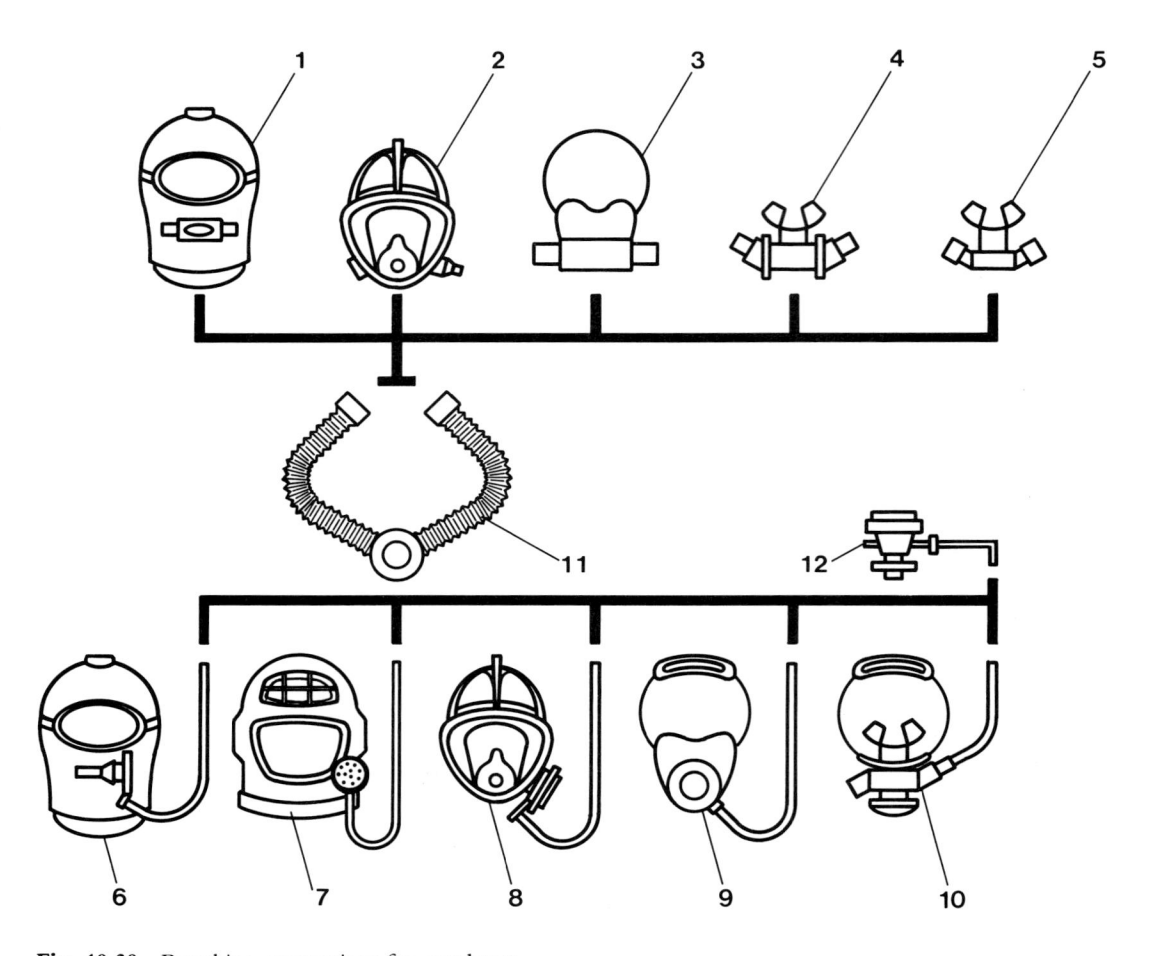

Fig. 10.30. Breathing connections for regulators.

1. hood for constant-volume suit (with mouthpiece or oral mask)
2. diving mask with internal mask
3. oral mask
4. mouthpiece with non-return valves
5. mouthpiece without check valves
6. hood for constant-volume suit with knuckle thread connection
7. helmet with integrated regulator
8. diving mask with knuckle thread connection
9. oral mask with knuckle thread connector
10. mouthpiece regulator
11. double-hose regulator
12. first stage of single-hose regulator

      3. Helmet connection.
      4. Oral–nasal connection.
      5. Mouthpiece connection.

For commercial use only, the hood, face-mask and helmet are in general use. They offer the best protection against the cold and polluted water. With heavy duty constant volume suits an oral–nasal mask is more often used to facilitate communication. If wet suits are worn a full face-mask is considered more practicable.

A full face-mask fitted with an oral–nasal breathing system will have a purge valve to deflect breathing gas over the face plate. Purgers will demist the face plate, expel any water and flush through the dead spaces inside the mask. An oral–nasal mask will also reduce the internal volume of dead space where a build-up of CO_2 may occur. A well designed mask will have a rubber face expansion seal to fit comfortably around the diver's facial contours.

If a double hose regulator is used there is a considerable volume inside the hose which, if filled with water at some stage, will have to be blown out. This volume can be reduced by fitting non-return valves on each side of the mouthpiece and the amount of water can be reduced to a minimum. This is important if, in an emergency, two divers are using the same mouthpiece and supply as the water can be evacuated from the small area in the mouthpiece. The twin breathing hose tubes are made of rubber which is oil-resistant and, as far as is possible, durable in sea water (Neoprene).

To reduce the flow resistance of the internal breathing gas the inside of the tubes should be smooth. The breathing tubes, however, are naturally bulky and exposed to damage under water and, therefore, in commercial diving when breathing on demand from a regulator, the preferred method is to have a single hose which connects the first stage at the supply source on the cylinder to the second stage on a mask, helmet or hood. The connecting low-pressure hose is made as short as possible and is well protected close up to the diver's body.

In sport diving single hoses are more common for the same practical reasons as used for commercial diving. Mouthpieces are usually fitted instead of commercial hoods or full face-masks as there is no requirement for communication, which precludes the use of a mouthpiece, and also for convenience with the smallest possible sealing area around the mouthpiece.

Air storage cylinders

The diving time or endurance of a self-contained open-circuit scuba compressed air diving set is dependent on the volume and pressure of air in the supply cylinders, the depth of the diver and the air consumption of the diver. When the diver is swimming at medium speed near or on the surface the average consumption of air is 20–28 litres/min, increasing to 50–80 litres/min if working hard. These average figures will fluctuate with different divers. The volume of the lungs will remain the same with increase in pressure but the consumption will increase as the depth increases. The consumption will double from the surface to 10 m depth (2 bar) and treble at 20 m depth (3 bar). Assuming an air consumption rate of 22–24 litres/min on the surface, Table 10.7 shows diving time as a function of diving depth and air storage supply. Decompression is required for diving

Table 10.7 Diving time as a function of diving depth and air supply

Diving depth (m)	Diving time (min) with air supply of			
	1400 litres	1600 litres	2800 litres	4200 litres
0	60	70	120	180
5	40	47	80	120
10	30	35	60	90
15	24	28	48	72
20	20	23	40	60
25	17	20	34	51
30	15	17	30	45
35	13	15	27	40
40	12	13	24	36

exposures in the shaded area and furthermore the values do not take into account the time for descent and ascent. The values in Table 10.7 are shown graphically in Fig. 10.31. The no decompression limit is represented by a dotted line. Should this position lie to the left of the dotted curve, for any given depth and time, it will normally be possible to ascend to the surface without decompression. Should the depth time position lie to the right of the curve, decompression is needed and stops will have to be carried out according to the relevant decompression table. For example, from the graph it is possible to surface without stops from 40 m when 1400-litre air storage cylinders are used. It is therefore technically possible to select the optimum air storage cylinders in terms of volume to provide sufficient air for a pre-selected depth and time mission with an adequate reserve. Air storage cylinders carried by divers are normally filled to a pressure of between 200 and 300 bar. Cylinders vary in capacity and are manufactured in alloy steel or aluminium. The common range of capacity is between 7 and 10 litres but some cylinders have a capacity of 15–20 litres. Aluminium cylinders are generally more popular because they are lighter than steel and easier to maintain, but they are expensive. Steel cylinders are more prone to corrosion and need special preventive treatment, especially inside where the onset of corrosion is more difficult to detect. On the outside a zinc spray is applied and then a zinc-enriched paint. Any rusting should be removed. For the inside no entirely reliable method has been devised and generally prevention is the method used by ensuring that the charging air is dry and properly filtered, that the charging process is not too rapid causing excessive heat and that there is some residual pressure inside, when empty, to prevent any moisture entering.

Cylinders should be colour coded at the shoulder to conform to national regulations and are more easily recognizable under water if coloured orange or white. Cylinder valves should be made in brass or stainless steel to avoid seawater corrosion. Often the valves are protected against impact with rubber sleeves. In some designs the

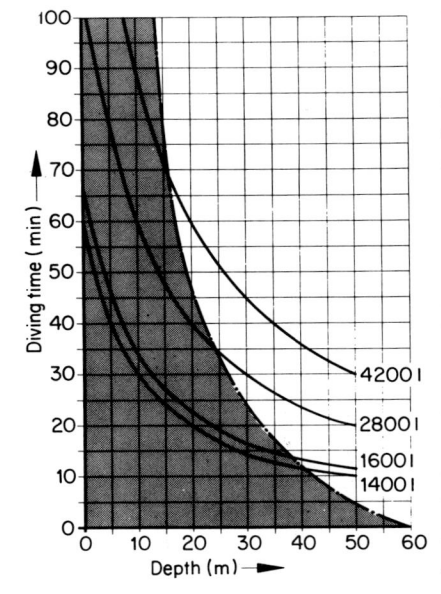

Fig. 10.31. Diving time as a function of diving depth for different air supplies (air consumption rate 22–24 litres/min), showing the no-decompression limit (dotted line).

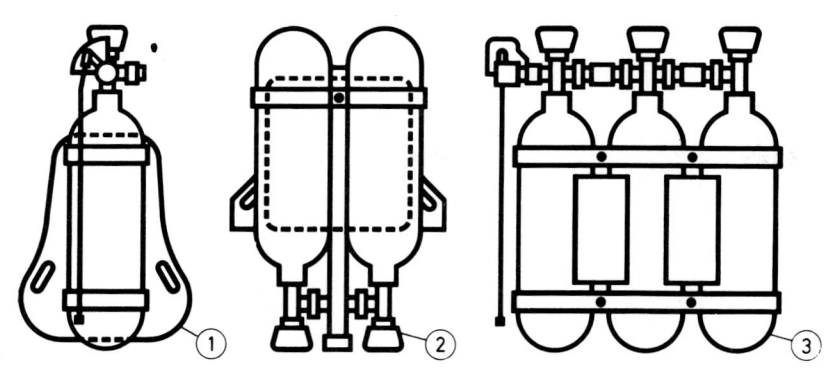

Fig. 10.32. Air cylinder assemblies.

1. Single tank with back pack
2. Double tanks with frame and back pack
3. Three tanks secured in a frame. This assembly is also produced in a triangular form

valves incorporate an air reserve valve if they are not fitted with a pressure contents gauge. To increase endurance two or sometimes three air cylinders are joined together with a cylinder block sometimes designed to allow for variatons in the number of cylinders.

Cylinder Backpack and Harness. The cylinders are secured to the body either directly with a canvas webbed harness or onto a plastic backpack which is moulded to fit the contours of the diver's back. Fig. 10.32 illustrates the backpack and the use of a frame to hold multiple cylinders and act as a shock absorber. The harness, with or without a backpack, must hold the cylinder stationary on the diver's back in the optimum position for breathing. The harness will be fitted with a quick release to discard the breathing equipment in an emergency. Fig. 10.33 illustrates an ideal harness to carry out these functions. The weight of the cylinder assembly is taken by the two shoulder straps, adjusted with D rings, and padded over the shoulders to distribute the weight. A waist belt stops the cylinders from moving and contains the quick release buckle in the centre. Ideally the release should be made with one movement. It should be carefully maintained and tested.

Air Reserve Valves and Pressure Gauges. Although not mandatory, some diving breathing cylinders are fitted with reserve valves which allow a residual volume of high-pressure gas to remain in the cylinder. This air reserve mechanism should serve two purposes: first, to give the diver warning that his air supply is getting low, and second, to provide sufficient air to enable him to surface. On a double cylinder one cylinder can be retained as the reserve, only opened by an air reserve pull rod which equalizes the pressure. The warning that the main supply is running low is given by a resistance in breathing which is caused by a spring-loaded check valve which will begin to close as the air pressure in the main cylinder drops. By pulling on the equalizing rod and equalizing the pressure the diver continues to

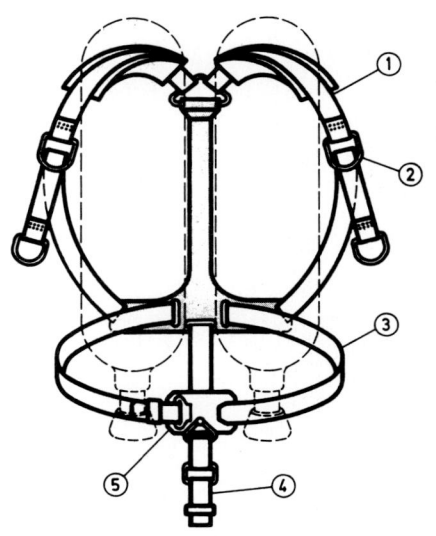

Fig. 10.33. Harness for an air scuba.

1. shoulder strap
2. double-D buckle
3. waist strap
4. battery strap
5. quick-release buckle

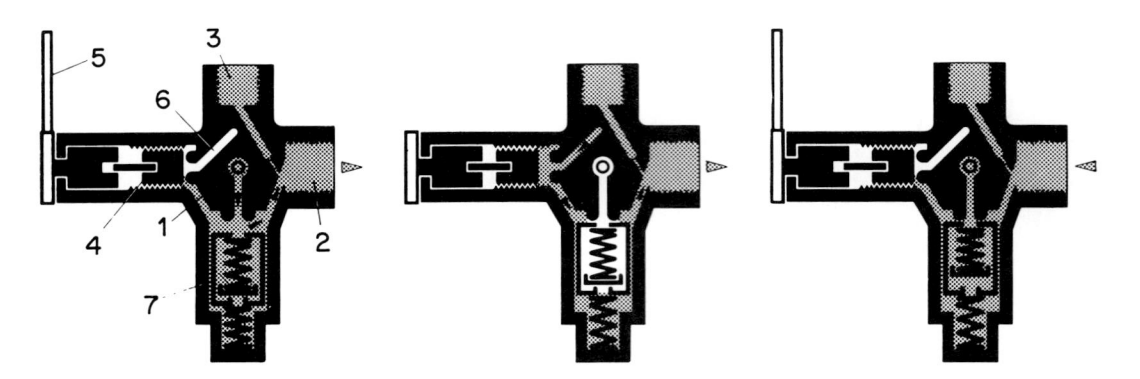

Fig. 10.34. Function of an air reserve system with manual cancelling installed in a cylinder shut-off valve.

A Air flow to regulator with pressure above 40 bar, valve stem lifted
1. cylinder valve seat
2. regulator filling connection
3. connection for pressure gauge
4. air reserve valve
5. lever for air reserve
6. bore directly to cylinder
7. valve stem

B Air flow to regulator with valve opened

C Air flow during recharge (air reserve valve closed), the check valve in the valve stem pushed open

breath normally. This process can, of course, be repeated but there is a danger that the diver may forget the number of times he has equalized, or leave the reserve valve open. Therefore the diver should never assume that the reserve cylinders will automatically provide additional air and should, when breathing resistance is felt, start the ascent to the surface and terminate the dive. Fig. 10.34 illustrates the action of the reserve valve. The design should ensure that the rod actuating the valve cannot be accidentally activated by the diver. An automatic device fitted as part of the regulator is becoming more widely used but it is not entirely acceptable as it may not give a positive warning to the diver.

A simple procedure is to insert a valve into the first stage of the regulator which progressively increases the breathing resistance for the remaining 30 bar of pressure in the supply cylinder. Although it gives a warning this system cannot provide additional reserves of air and for that reason is not entirely adequate.

Another method involves using optical warning signals projected onto the face mask but these are sophisticated electropneumatic systems which are only applicable to advanced closed-circuit, deep diving breathing systems where additional information on the partial pressure of oxygen may also be displayed.

Whatever system is used, a pressure gauge allowing the diver to read the residual pressure in the supply cylinder is essential. The most common arrangement for self-contained air diving equipment, as illustrated in Fig. 10.35, is two supply cylinders with the supply valve manifold facing downwards and a single-hose two-stage regulator with first stage on the air cylinder and second stage on the regulator. To provide reasonable endurance at depths of 30–40 m, extending to 50 m, the air cylinders will contain at least 2800 litres, with two cylinders each with a capacity of above 10 litres, connected to a face mask via the regulator and fitted with a pressure gauge.

Surface Demand Diving Equipment (SDDE)

The development of modern SDDE is an extension of standard diving where air is supplied from the surface, allowing greater endurance with a reduction in flexibility. Since, however, the diving depth will not normally exceed 50 m, with an 80 m umbilical, a wide area of about 1000 m^2 can be covered which is sufficient for most commercial operations. Early surface demand diving equipment comprised a demand regulator worn on the back and connected to a mouthpiece or face mask with a low-pressure hose. The regulator was supplied from the surface with air at 6–7 bar by an umbilical. In the event of a failure of the air supply, the diver made a rapid if not an emergency ascent to the surface. The present-day arrangement is shown in Fig. 10.36 where the air is supplied to the regulator and to the diver from either a bank of high-pressure cylinders or a low-pressure tank with compressor. In addition the diver carries an emergency supply on his back, sometimes referred to as bale-out bottles. The system is compatible for use from a diving bell, habitat or lock-out submersible. The components are identical to a self-contained breathing set except in the function of the reserve bale-out cylinder. The cylinder is fitted with a pressure regulator and an automatic shuttle valve which automatically switches to air reserve in the event of a surface air failure. The main functions of the automatic shuttle valve are as follows:

1. To supply air to the diver in the event of the failure of the main supply.
2. To indicate positively to the diver that he is switched to his reserve supply.
3. To provide an additional safety function by ensuring that the total breathing system cannot be operated unless the reserve cylinder is open ready for emergency use.

Diving suits

The development of diving suits for different situations has been as progressive as the development of the breathing systems to which they have to be compatible. Until 40 years ago the only suit used was the canvas standard diving dress, unaltered in design since its inception. Diving was limited to salvage, harbour works and naval operations, for which it was ideally suited. The introduction of the demand valve, high-pressure and closed and semi-closed breathing systems demanded variations to suit each and every need. The

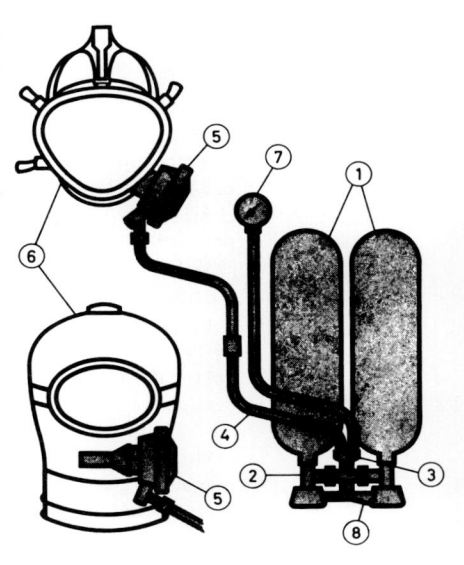

Fig. 10.35. A self-contained air breathing apparatus with cylinders facing downwards.

1 air cylinders
2 cylinder valves
3 pressure regulator
4 pressure hose
5 demand regulator
6 full-face diving mask or hood
7 pressure gauge
8 air reserve lever

Fig. 10.36. A hose-supplied diving apparatus with surface demand.

1. high-pressure storage bank
2. pressure regulator
3. compressor (low pressure) and volume tank
4. air supply hose
5. automatic shuttle valve
6. air reserve tanks
7. pressure regulator with manifold
8. cylinder valve
9. demand regulator
10. diving mask or hood

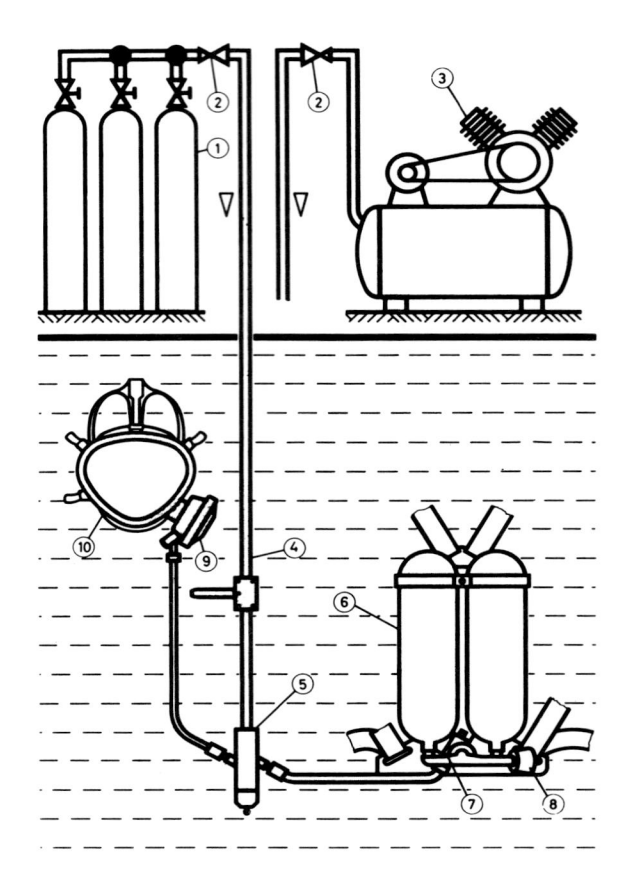

development of the light-weight helmeted diving suit in modern materials was a great improvement on the standard dress, as was the wet and dry suit.

Standard diving dress

The standard diving suit, relatively unchanged since the original Augustus Siebe suit in the 19th century, is based on a helmet and a diving suit joined as one part, allowing control of buoyancy by regulation of the amount of air inside the suit. The air is also the breathing gas. A 'hard hat' helmeted diver is illustrated in Fig. 10.37. The dress is made to fit closely around the body up to the chest but allows adequate clothing and thermal protection to be worn over the surface of the body. The dress therefore covers the body except for the hands and head. Whereas constant pressure corresponding to a water height of B_1 and B_2, shown in Fig. 10.37, acts on the upright diver from the head to the lower extremity of the air bubble, the pressure increases below that to a value which corresponds to H, i.e. the depth of the foot of the diver. The feet of the upright diver, the lowest part of the body, are therefore subject to a greater pressure, which is the difference between H and B. The size of the air pocket is adjusted by opening and closing the spring-loaded inlet valve.

In other attitudes, where the diver is bending, crawling or lying

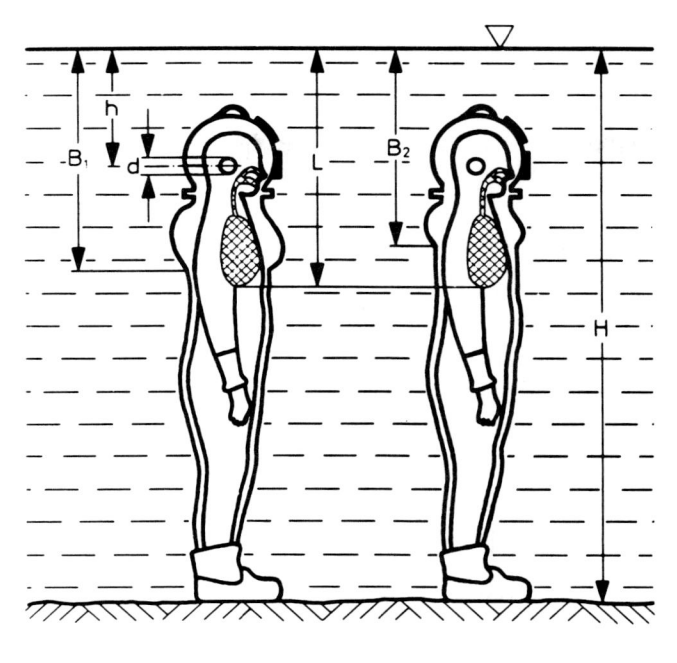

Fig. 10.37. Air cavity inside the diving dress for different settings of the air exhaust valve.

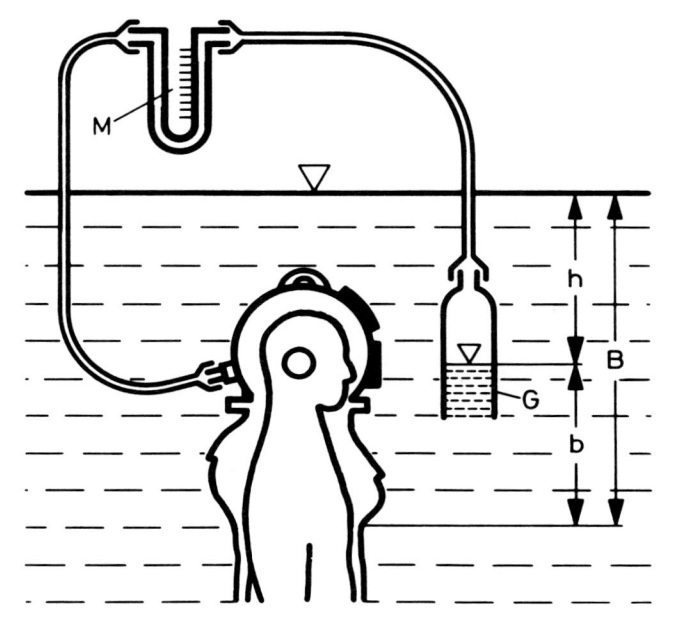

Fig. 10.38. Air pressure measurement in the helmet to determine the water height from the lower edge of the air bubble to the helmet valve.

down, the air may fill the upper parts of the corselet or diving dress before being vented out through the outlet valve. This will, if not checked, blow the diver to the surface and will be dangerous. To counter this the diver should keep the outlet valve open and remove the excess air by raising the helmet from time to time. To calculate the head of water from the bottom of the air bubble to the inlet valve, a mercury pressure gauge can be used as shown in Fig. 10.38. The container should be transparent so as to adjust for the correct height.

Table 10.8 Weight measurements directly beneath the surface of the water using standard diving dress

	Variable air volume (litres)	Absolute weight* (kg)	Maximum inflated volume (litres)
Neutral	41.5	173	217
Normal	15	173	217
Minimum	5	173	217

*Allowing 80 kg for the weight of the diver.

A very real danger whilst using this type of equipment is a fall, particularly in shallow water where the pressure variations are greater. A fall will increase the pressure which may not be balanced by the air pressure. It is possible to calculate the maximum safe increase in depth caused by an inadvertent fall, bearing in mind that the calculations will vary with different diving equipment due to the different internal air volumes. By weighing the diver in water the variable air volume inside the diving suit is calculated, known as V_A. To do this all air initially is vented out of the suit and then weighed. The suit is then inflated until neutral buoyancy is achieved. The difference in weight (kg) determines how many litres of air are required at that depth to maintain neutral buoyancy. For an average diving dress and helmet V_A is about 41.5 litres. Clearly the diver varies the volume of air V_A on the bottom to suit the working conditions. Table 10.8 lists the variable values of V_A when weight measurements are performed immediately below the surface of the water, the smallest value which still allows adequate respiration being 5 litres of air. In addition to V_A, the flexible volume, there is the enclosed volume, V_H, inside the helmet to which the corselet is attached. The volume V_H is the volume of the helmet less the displacement of the diver's head. Fig. 10.39 illustrates the value V_H based on an average standard diving helmet. From these values of V_A and V_H the maximum safe falling depth, h_2, can be calculated from the surface, by the formula:

$$(V_H + V_A)(h_1 + 10) = V_H(h_2 + 10)$$

Furthermore,

$$h_z = h_2 - h_1$$

which is more normally expressed as

$$h_z = \frac{V_A}{V_H}(h_1 + 10) \quad (m)$$

Therefore if $h_1 = 0$, i.e. the fall is from the surface,

$$h_z = \frac{V_A}{V_H} \times 10$$

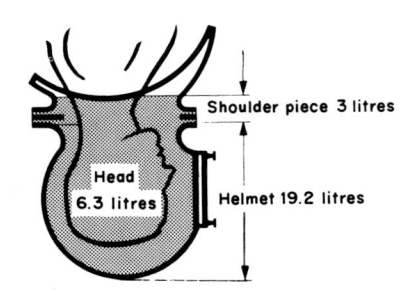

Fig. 10.39. Measuring the helmet volume with water.

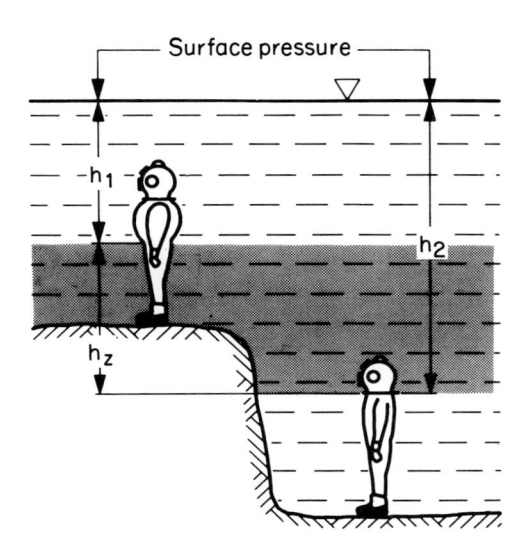

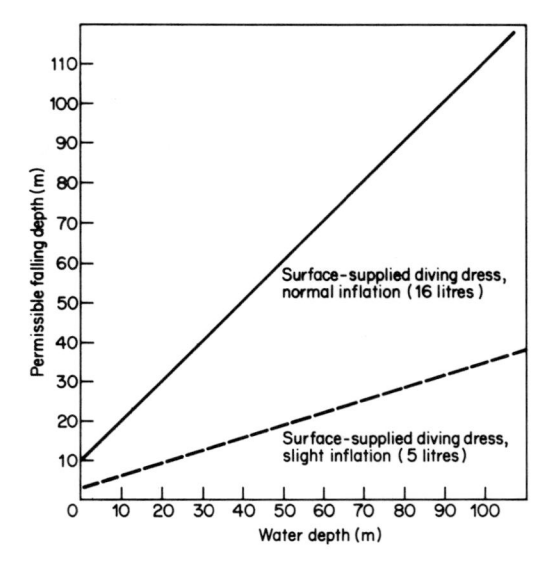

Fig. 10.40. Safe falling depth for a standard hard hat diver.

Fig. 10.41. Safe falling depth for normally and slightly inflated dress.

The figures from Table 10.9 apply in this situation. For falls from other depths, the situation will change, since the air volume in the dress and the enclosed air in the helmet will influence not only the maximum safe falling depth but also the working depth. The value of h_2 increases in direct proportion to that of h_1. Figs 10.40 and 10.41 show the safe falling depths for various types of suit.

An additional danger is that of the standard diver being blown up if he is working in a condition of neutral buoyancy and the outlet valve is restricted. If the diver is blown upwards with a positive buoyancy that cannot be controlled there is a danger of air embolism and rupture of the suit. It is possible to calculate the maximum depth that a diving suit will withstand whilst being blown to the surface. The maximum depth h_1 is calculated on the basis that the pressure inside the suit will not exceed 0.2 bar when surfaced, assuming that the suit is in a well maintained condition.

The formula

$$h_1 = \frac{12 \times V_2}{V_1} - 10 \text{ (m)}$$

where V_1 is the volume of expandable air in a neutrally buoyant suit including helmet and suit and V_2 is the volume of air in the suit after being blown to the surface. Maximum safe depths for blowing up are given in Table 10.10 for two different sizes of suit.

Air Requirement for Standard Equipment. The air flow to the diver is determined by the working depth and the performance of the

Table 10.9 Permissible falling depth from the surface

Degree of inflation	Permissible falling depth = h_z (m)
Neutral	26
Normal	10
Slight	3

Table 10.10. Maximum safe depth in the event of blowing up to the surface

	V_1 (litres)	V_2 (litres)	h_1 (m)
Medium suit	70	113	9.4
Large suit	70	122	10.8

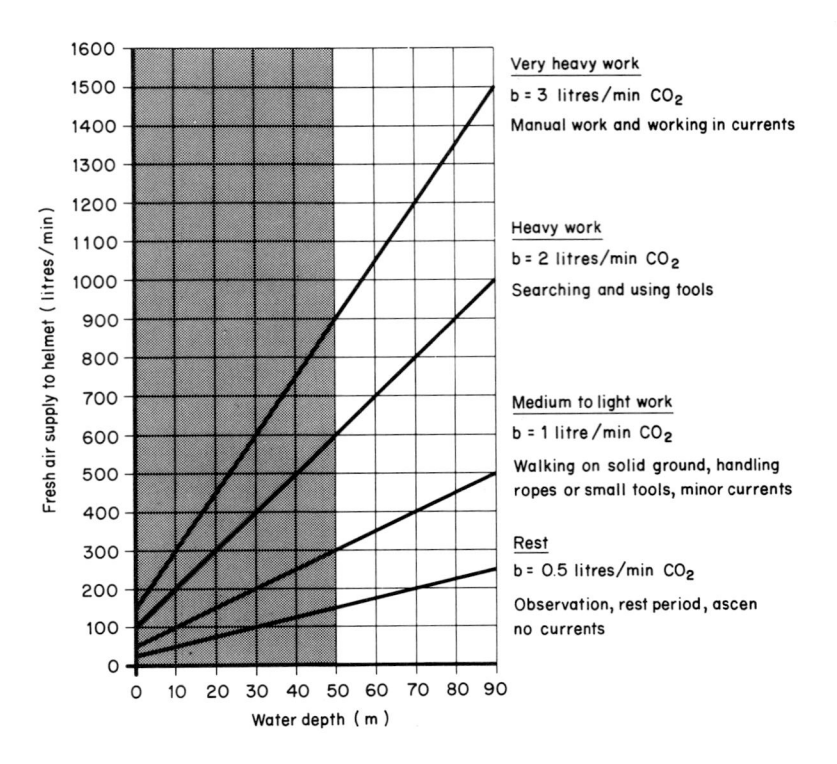

Fig. 10.42. Air requirement for a diver in standard dress for different levels of work effort, with a maximum CO_2 partial pressure of 0.02 bar at various water depths.

diver. The onset of CO_2 poisoning is a more immediate problem than lack of oxygen and although flushing the helmet will reduce the CO_2 it will not eliminate it to the same extent as breathing at atmospheric pressure. It is, however, sufficient if the partial pressure of CO_2 does not exceed 0.02 bar. Since CO_2 partial pressure is directly proportional to the absolute pressure at the respective diving depth, assuming constant CO_2 production, increased air flows are needed to flush the CO_2 out of the system. Fig. 10.42 shows the air requirement for a diver plotted with various degrees of exertion whilst working, on the basis that the CO_2 partial pressure does not exceed 0.02 bar in the helmet. Although the graph is calculated to diving depths of 90 m it is normal nowadays to limit air diving to 50 m.

Air Supply Systems for Standard Diving Equipment. Normally the air is supplied through an air hose or umbilical, sufficient to overcome the bottom pressure and the pressure losses through the hose and to ventilate the diver's helmet to maintain a non-toxic partial pressure of CO_2. An alternative arrangement is to carry the air supply in cylinders on the back, but this is rarely used as the amount of air needed and the very limited capacity of the cylinders will reduce the endurance to the extent that it becomes impractical.

In the past air was supplied by hand pumps but nowadays the air is supplied direct from LP volume or HP storage cylinders on the surface.

Fig. 10.43 shows the arrangement where the main inlet valve is controlled manually by the diver and Fig. 10.44 where the supply is automatically controlled by an air flow regulator. The main advantage of the automatic system is that in the event of a fall and lack of control the increased pressure can be compensated for. A further improvement on this design is shown in Fig. 10.45 where the automatic regulator is positioned on the diver's chest; this allows the diver fine control over his air supply. A further advantage is that the intermediate pressure to the regulator can be higher, allowing a reduction in the size of the air hose giving less drag.

A semi-closed-circuit system is shown in Fig. 10.46 where the air is circulated through a CO_2 absorbent cannister. The air is supplied through a constant mass injector system but, as stated, has little practical application due to severely limited endurance.

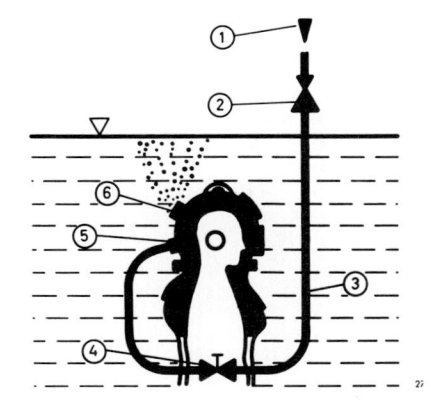

Fig. 10.43. Surface-supplied diving dress with a manually operated air supply.

1 air supply
2 pressure regulator
3 air hose
4 regulating valve
5 helmet connection
6 air exhaust valve

Standard diving dress equipment

The modern standard dress includes the equipment illustrated in Fig. 10.47. The helmet is still manufactured in copper or brass sheet and connected to the breast plate or corselet by an interrupted thread and locked. The diving dress, made of strong vulcanized material, has a heavy rubber collar with bolt holes which is attached to the corselet and secured with corselet brasses. The diving dress is strengthened in those parts which are subject to wear and tear, such as the elbows and knees. The seal around the wrists is achieved by using rubber cuffs. The diver enters the suit by expanding the rubber collar. The helmet will usually have two side windows and one front window and sometimes a top window. The front window with the largest area can be unscrewed and removed. The faceplates may have protective bars fitted on the outside and be made of safety glass. The air hose is connected to the non-return valve at the back of the helmet. The air is conducted around the inside of the helmet and through air ducts to give the best ventilation and prevent any build-up of moisture on the faceplates. The foul air escapes through an outlet valve, usually situated on the right side of the helmet near the diver's ear. A non-return valve is fitted, which works in the opposite way to the inlet valve, allowing the air to escape when at a slightly higher pressure than the surrounding water, and preventing the water from entering. The valve can be temporarily opened by pressing the protruding spindle with the movement of the diver's head inside the helmet or manually from outside. This allows the diver to control his buoyancy. Additionally there is a spitcock which is sometimes fitted in the front of the helmet to act as an outlet valve for further control or to draw water into the helmet to clear the front faceplate. A line telephone is fitted to the helmet. Additional safety features will

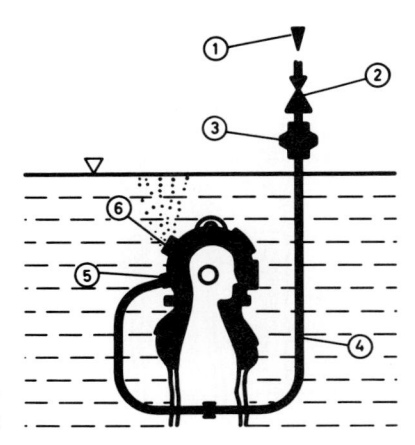

Fig. 10.44. Surface supplied diving dress with gas flow automatically regulated.

1 air supply
2 pressure regulator
3 diver regulator
4 air hose
5 helmet connection
6 air exhaust valve

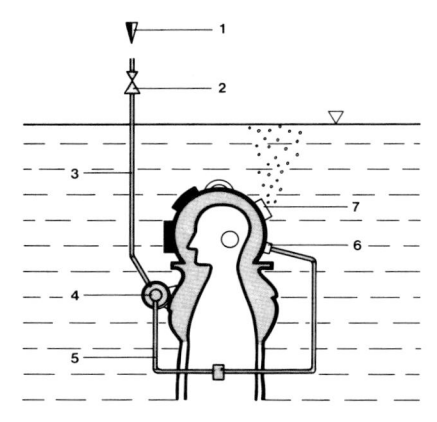

Fig. 10.45. Surface supplied diving dress with gas flow automatically regulated by a regulator on the diver's breast plate.

1. air supply
2. pressure regulator
3. intermediate pressure hose
4. diver regulator
5. air hose
6. helmet connection
7. air exhaust valve

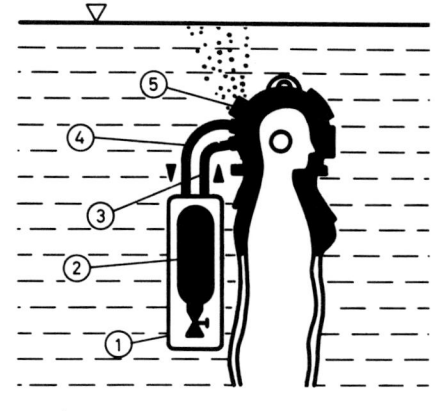

Fig. 10.46. Autonomous semi-closed diving dress with back unit and without air hose.

1. back unit with CO_2 absorbent
2. high-pressure tanks
3. circulating hose, gas input
4. circulating hose, gas output
5. air exhaust valve

include welding visors and the insulation of the helmet during welding.

To counteract the large volume and buoyancy in the upper part of the standard dress, weights need to be distributed around the lower portion of the body to give good stability. In Fig. 10.48A the weights are distributed in such a way that maximum relief and stability is achieved when working in the bent position. By wearing a crotch weight vertically below the air cavity around the chest and helmet the diver's boots can be made lighter. In this arrangement the front weights can also be used as air storage with 400 litres at a pressure of 200 bar, although this is an unusual design. Fig. 10.48B shows the weighted belt favoured by the US Navy and Fig. 10.48C a front and back weight used mainly by British and Russian divers.

The boots are made of stout leather with brass toecaps and wooden soles onto which are attached lead soles. Alternatively they may be of cast iron with leather straps.

The airpipe or umbilical is designed not to kink, buckle or be squeezed. It may be positively or negatively buoyant, although it is usually the latter to withstand currents.

Fig. 10.49 shows a manual air regulator for use where no automatic regulator is fitted. This arrangement, where the valve is on the left side of the chest and easily operated with the diver's right hand, is favoured by British and American divers. A short hose leads from the valve to the helmet and a fine control of the air is achieved by using a needle valve. The pressure is adjusted on the surface to about 6–7 bar above the ambient pressure of the diver. During the ascent it is reduced to 3–4 bar above the ambient pressure.

Standard deep diving dress

Before semi-closed, mixed gas, self-contained breathing apparatus and light-weight deep diving helmet systems were introduced, within the last twenty years, almost all deep diving was carried out using the standard diving suit, with oxy-helium gas. In order to keep the carbon dioxide levels within acceptable limits the flow rates of the breathing gases had to be very high and therefore also the cost. To conserve gas, circulation systems were developed which led to the further development and the introduction of the oxy-helium lightweight helmet (Fig. 10.50). The CO_2 absorbent unit is carried on the back. An injector system supplies a metered quantity of fresh gas which is then circulated around the helmet and passed through the CO_2 absorbent cannister. At depths of more than 60 m the supply would be about 7 bar above ambient pressure, reducing with lesser depths to about 3.5 bar. By introducing a circulation system, only about one-fifth of the fresh gas is needed to ensure a sufficiently low CO_2 content in the helmet. A deflector plate is fitted in the absorber to prevent channelling. Normally the CO_2 absorbent unit is active for about three hours, with an additional reserve. The circulatory system can be by-passed so as to revert to an open demand system.

Although standard equipment is rarely used for deep diving nowadays, particularly in north-west Europe where common

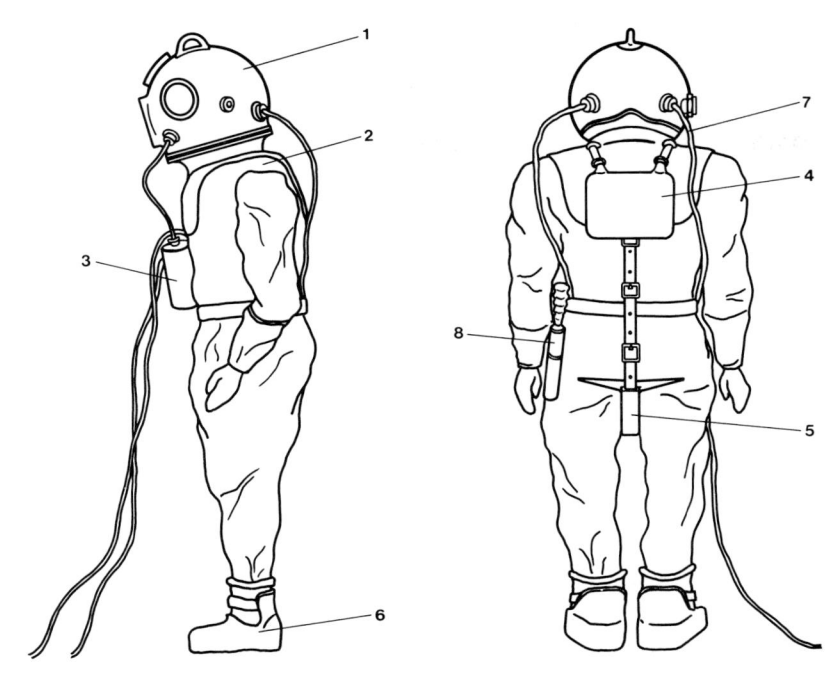

Fig. 10.47. Diver with surface-supplied standard diving dress.

  1 helmet with breastplate
  2 diving dress
  3 front weight with compressed air tanks and connecting hose
  4 back weight
  5 crotch weight
  6 boots
  7 helmet air supply hose
  8 knife and belt

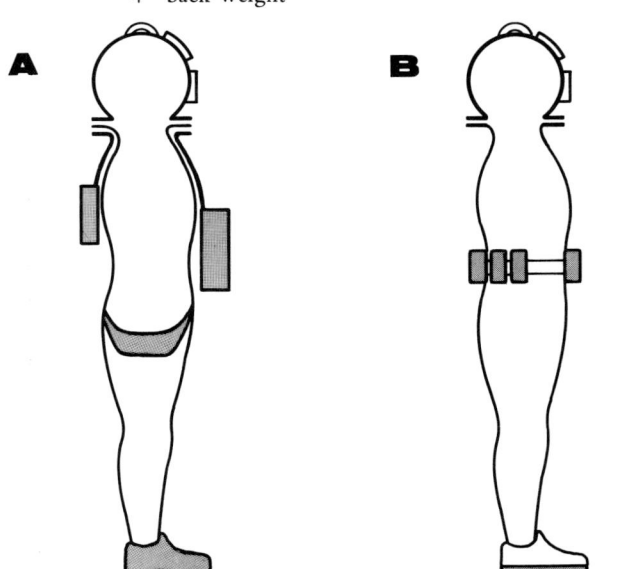

Fig. 10.48. Weight distribution in different standard diving dress.

  A German diving dress
  B American diving dress
  C British diving dress

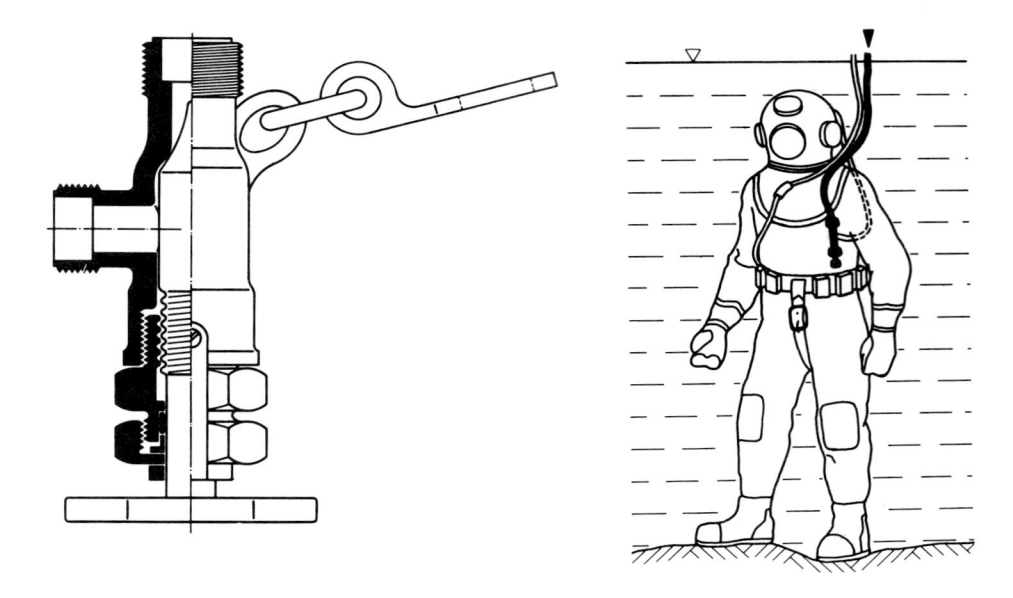

Fig. 10.49. Position and cross-section of an air control valve on a standard diving dress.

practice is to limit surface demand equipment, whether air or mixed gas, to 50 m, it is still used in various parts of the world and is popular with commercial divers in the States and the US Navy where it may be used to depths of 90 m.

Self-contained standard mixed gas breathing set

There are certain, but not many, conditions when a self-contained standard diving set can offer some advantages over a surface-oriented standard gear, in particular where strong currents can produce a high drag effect on the air-breathing air hose or when entering wrecks. Fig. 10.51 shows a back view of the standard self-contained equipment, designed to operate effectively to depths of about 40 m. The CO_2 absorbent cannister is located between the compressed air bottle and the oxygen bottle. The breathing cycle through the helmet is shown in Fig. 10.50, with fresh oxygen replacing the oxygen consumed and an absorbent unit removing the CO_2. Oxygen and compressed air are discharged simultaneously from two cylinders and a desired mixture can be obtained. The mixture may vary from about 60% O_2 and 40% N_2 to 40% O_2 and 60% N_2. The use of these oxygen-enriched breathing mixtures will additionally increase the endurance on the bottom, not only because of the recirculation and reuse of gases but also because bottom times are increased without decompression as the body tissues are absorbing less nitrogen. Open-circuit breathing on air is not practicable as the flow requirements would be in the region of 160 litres/min. In the system illustrated in Fig. 10.51 the pressure of the breathing gases is initially reduced to about 10 bar and, since the diaphragm of the reducer is exposed to the surrounding ambient pressure, the additional pressure is compensated for and the gas flow is

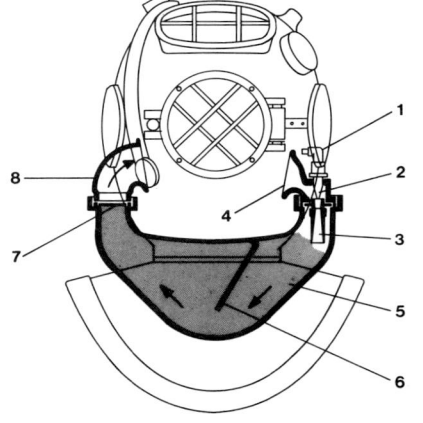

Fig. 10.50. Injector and carbon dioxide absorbent canister for deep diving dress.

1 helium-oxygen supply
2 flow regulator
3 injector
4 intake connection to helmet
5 CO_2 absorbent canister
6 baffle
7 wire mesh strainer
8 exhaust union to helmet

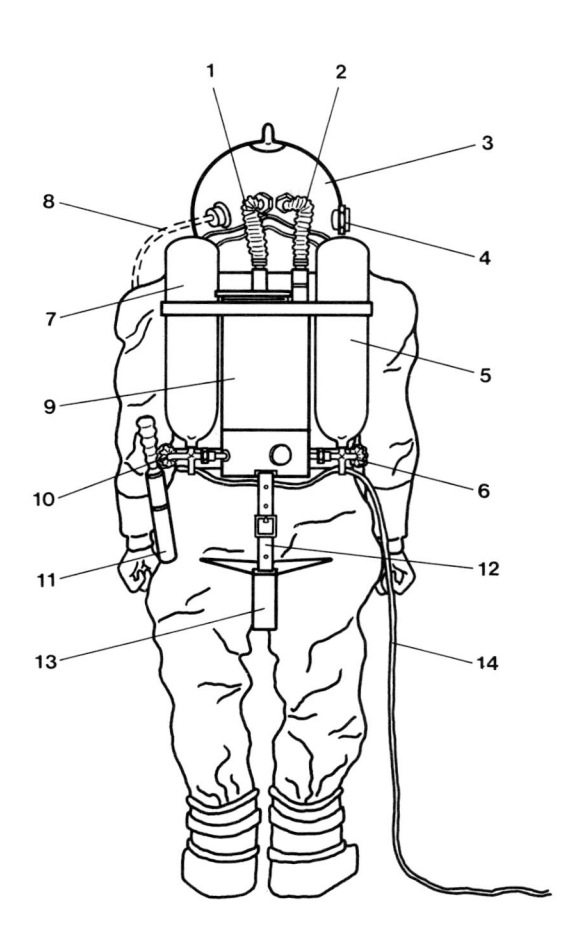

Fig. 10.51. Self-contained mixed gas standard dress.

1. mixed gas intake
2. mixed gas exhaust
3. helmet
4. gas exhaust valve
5. compressed air cylinder
6. compressed air cylinder valve
7. compressed oxygen cylinder
8. telephone cable
9. CO_2 absorbent cannister
10. compressed O_2 cylinder valve
11. diving knife
12. weight harness
13. weight
14. communications and signal line

increased as the depth increases. The gas flow passes from the regulator, through the injector nozzle. With a driving gas flow of 3.6 litres/min the air circulates at about 100 litres/min. The system incorporates a safety valve and a pressure contents gauge. The CO_2 absorbent cannister is interchangeable. The oxygen content of the mixture can be varied within the limits of oxygen partial pressure, at least 0.2 bar with an upper limit dependent on exposure. Although oxygen-enriched mixtures are more economical in terms of endurance, in terms of cost air breathing is more economical as the oxy-nitrogen mixtures have to be prepared and need to be pre-mixed and tested.

The rigid helmet

The improvement in design of the rigid helmet has been very rapid over the last ten years. Now designed to fit onto a light-weight dry suit, the system retains some of the advantages of the heavy standard equipment and some of light-weight self-contained equipment. By using glass-reinforced plastic a very light helmet can be moulded in many designs which would be impossible working with copper or other metals. Rigid helmets can be made smaller and more comfortable. Fig. 10.52 illustrates a modern rigid helmet which

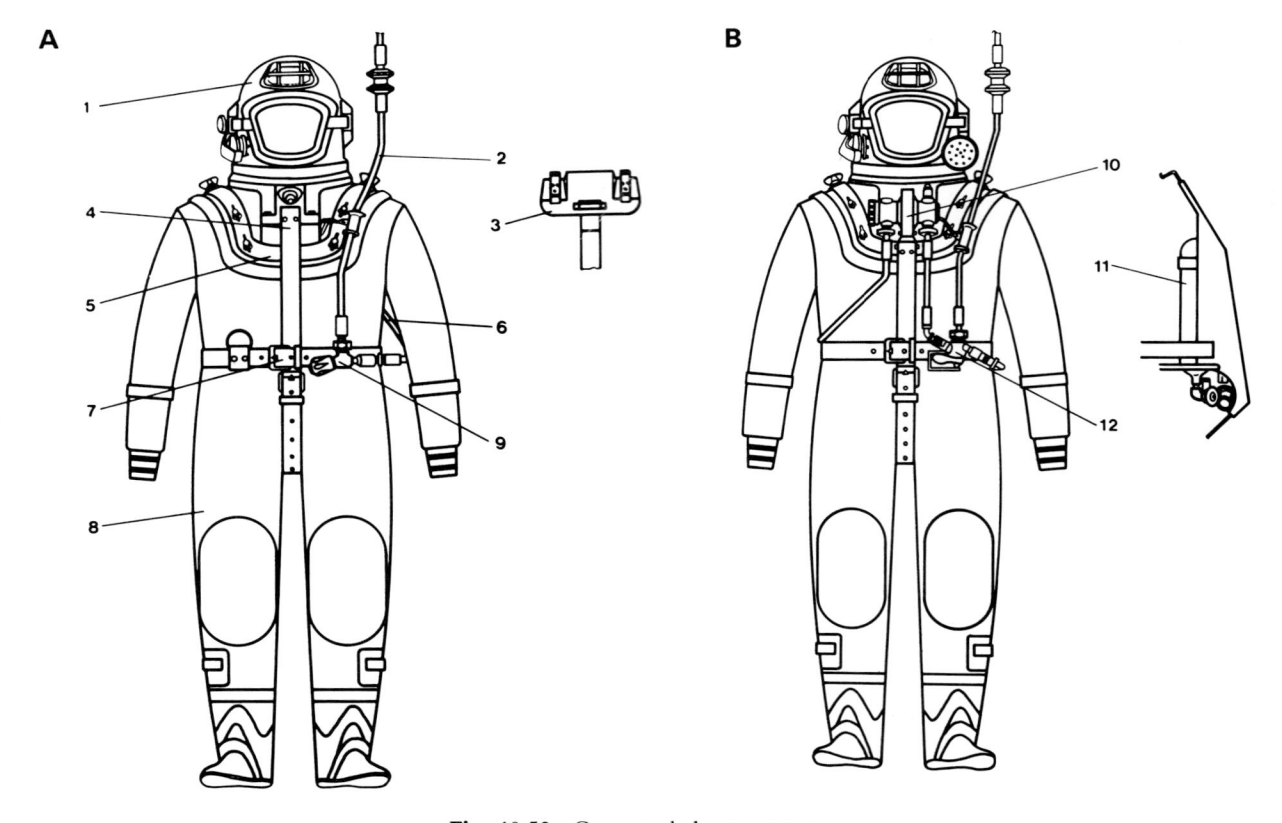

Fig. 10.52. Compact helmet systems

  A Manual air control
  B Diver regulator and air reserve unit

1	diving helmet	7	belt
2	supply hose	8	heavy diving suit
3	back weight	9	manual control valve
4	front weight	10	automatic supply control
5	collar	11	reserve air supply
6	connecting hose	12	emergency switch-over valve

seals onto a light diving suit, giving the diver the flexibility of free swimming with flappers in any attitude or a more rigid upright stance wearing boots. This light-weight equipment is nowadays accepted for diving off-shore.

The helmet, although usually designed with a locking seal which makes a waterproof seal with the collar of a dry suit, can be used with a wet suit. The seal is made around the neck of the diver; although uncomfortable, this is preferable in warm waters where a dry suit would be unbearably hot. The use of these compact, smaller helmets or band masks is now accepted for general use in all but very shallow water, used with a wet suit, a dry suit or a heavy diving suit adapted to fit the helmet. In all but the latter, the equipment can be used for operations from a diving bell.

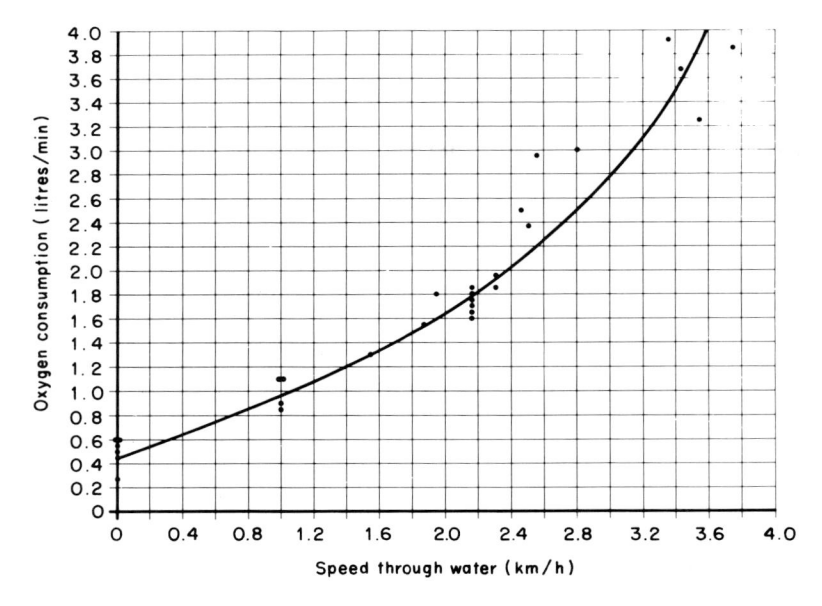

Fig. 10.53. Oxygen consumption during distance swimming.

Fig. 10.69 shows a system of supplying gas on a closed-circuit principle, circulating around the helmet and being returned to the bell. Most modern diving practices use an open-circuit system, supplying gas to the helmet and expelling the air to the surrounding water.

Calculation of Gas Mixtures

Although oxy-nitrogen gas mixtures are not normally used in commercial diving in shallow waters because of the simplicity of compressed air and passing it through the air hose to the working diver, they are used in certain situations in self-contained equipment where endurance is the prime objective. In deeper waters below about 50 m the introduction of helium as an inert gas and the selection of the correct composition of oxygen and the inert gas, nitrogen/helium, and the flow rate required to provide sufficient oxygen to the diver is essential. This is particularly important in semi-closed- or closed-circuit systems where much of the gas is being reused.

Oxygen content of a gas mixture
For the calculation of the total oxygen flow rate in a mixed gas flow the following formula can be applied:

$$O_{2\,tot} = Q \times O_{2\,per} \times 0.01 \text{ (litres/min)}$$

with $O_{2\,tot}$ = oxygen component of total gas flow (litres/min)
  Q = total gas flow rate (litres/min)
  $O_{2\,per}$ = oxygen in mixture (%)

Oxygen partial pressure

The oxygen partial pressure in an apparatus depends on various factors. For an oxygen rebreather with $O_{2per} = 100\%$ only the diving depth has an effect on the oxygen partial pressure. In this case the partial pressure is found by the formula:

$$Po_2 = P_D \text{ (bar)}$$

The situation is different for diving equipment which is supplied with mixed gas.

For open-circuit systems, with gas supplied by a demand regulator, for example, the oxygen percentage in the gas mixture has an effect on the Po_2, in addition to the diving depth.

The consumption of oxygen in the body is not relevant as the system is open-circuit and the gas is not rebreathed. Po_2 is calculated by the formula:

$$Po_2 = O_{2per} \times 0.01 \times P_D \text{ (bar)}$$

In a semi-closed circuit, with a pre-set flow, the consumption of oxygen has to be taken into account, too. For the calculation of Po_2 a formula is obtained as follows:

$$Po_2 = \frac{(Q \times O_{2\,per} \times 0.01 - C)}{Q - C} P_D \text{ (bar)}$$

or

$$Po_2 = \frac{O_{2tot} - C}{Q - C} P_D \text{ (bar)}$$

From this important basic formula and before obtaining the O_2 flow formula in a mixed gas flow an equation can be deduced which is used for calculations of the flow rate when the gas mixture and the diving depth range are known. The formula is:

$$Q = \frac{(O_{2tot} - C)P_D}{Po_2} + C \text{ (litres/min)}$$

where Po_2 = oxygen partial pressure (bar)
C = oxygen consumption rate (litres/min)
P_D = pressure at diving depth (bar)

By rearranging the formulas and computing P_D for a given gas composition and total flow rate, the maximum and minimum permissible diving depth can be determined by assuming a minimum and maximum oxygen consumption rate. For short dives, 1.8 bar and 0.2 bar can be assumed as permissible upper and lower limit of the oxygen partial pressure. For saturation diving, 0.4 bar is a reasonable limit.

Oxygen consumption and mixture calculation

The oxygen consumption of a diver depends in the first place on his working effort. The diving depth does not affect the oxygen consumption if the increased respiratory work due to the higher density of the breathing medium is disregarded.

Table 10.2 shows the oxygen consumption for different kinds of work. The values are average figures and in practice there may be tolerances, as for all physiological data.

Fig. 10.53 shows the consumption of oxygen whilst distance swimming, for periods of 30 min at a depth of 1.5 m in a water temperature of 25°C. Consumption rates of more than 3 litres/min of oxygen were recorded. Table 10.11 shows the maximum possible oxygen consumption related to time. For working purposes it would be reasonable to accept a maximum oxygen consumption of 2.5 litres/min and a minimum consumption of 0.5 litres/min with the average oxygen consumption being 1.3 litres/min. Fig. 10.54 shows the oxygen content required in a gas mixture for a given depth and partial pressure.

By using the following formulae it is possible to calculate the gas mixtures needed for given rates of oxygen consumption and for maximum diving depths using a semi-closed mixed gas rebreathing system with a counterlung or inhalation bag.

Table 10.11 Maximum possible consumption of oxygen related to time

Oxygen consumption (litres/min)	Time
0.25	constantly
1	several hours
2	1–2 hours
4	15–30 minutes
5	1–2 minutes

1. At first the maximum and minimum oxygen percentage in the counterlung is determined for the respective depth range. With the pressure $P_{D\,max}$ at the maximum diving depth and the permissible oxygen partial pressure $Po_{2\,max}$, the maximum oxygen percentage $O_{2\,per\,max}$ in the counterlung is calculated according to the formula

$$O_{2\,per\,max} = \frac{Po_{2\,max} \times 100}{P_{D\,max}}\;(vol\%)$$

and the minimum oxygen percentage $O_{2\,per\,min}$ in the counterlung according to formula

$$O_{2\,per\,min} = \frac{Po_{2\,min} \times 100}{P_{D\,min}}\;(vol\%)$$

2. To calculate the necessary total gas flow Q, the following two equations are arrived at:

$$O_{2\,tot} = C_{min} + \frac{O_{2\,per\,max}}{100}(Q - C_{min})\;(litres/min)$$

$$O_{2\,tot} = C_{max} + \frac{O_{2\,per\,min}}{100}(Q - C_{max})\;(litres/min)$$

from which the following formula is arrived at:

$$Q = \frac{C_{max}(100 - O_{2\,per\,min}) - C_{min}(100 - O_{2\,per\,max})}{O_{2\,per\,max} - O_{2\,per\,min}}\;(litres/min)$$

3. To determine the oxygen component $O_{2\,tot}$ of the mixed gas flow, the total flow rate Q is inserted in the two equations.
4. The oxygen percentage in the mixture is at last calculated from the following formula:

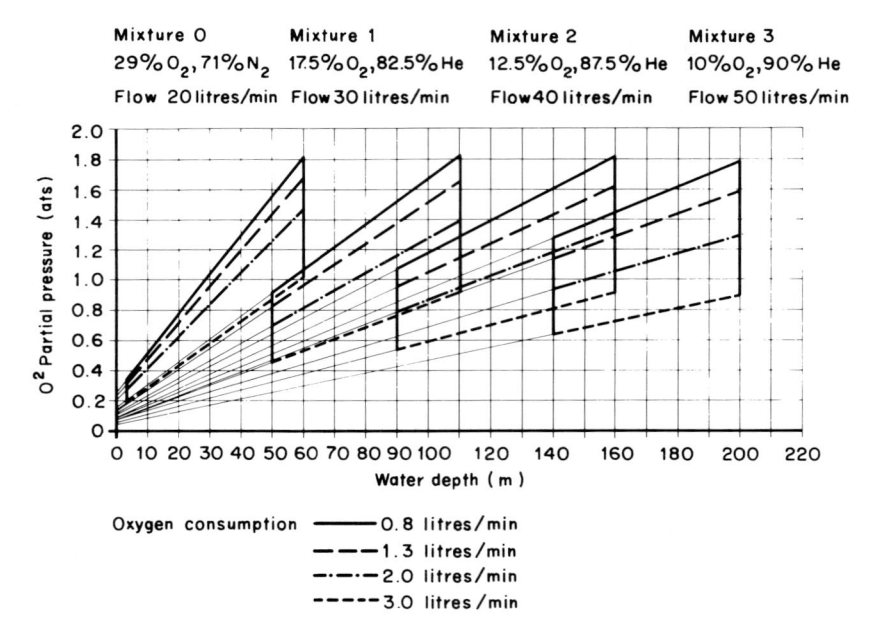

Fig. 10.54. Oxygen partial pressure as a function of oxygen consumption for a deep-diving apparatus with semi-closed circuit and pre-mixed gas supply.

$$O_{2\,per} = \frac{O_{2\,tot} \times 100}{Q} \,(\%)$$

A series of oxygen partial pressure graphs (Fig. 10.54) of a deep diving semi-closed mixed gas set are shown using these formulas.

Deep Diving Techniques (Breathing Equipment)

The methods used to operate divers today have undergone a rapid change within the last decade with experimental dives in the region of 500–700 m. Whilst many of the tasks at the greater depths will need to be carried out by submersibles and remote-controlled vehicles, there will always be a need for divers. Whereas divers can freely descend to about 50 m, beyond this depth the diver is nowadays usually transported either in a diving bell or a submersible or from a habitat. The actual breathing systems will not vary as the same basic life-support principles apply to all, whereas the methods of transportation will vary considerably as discussed in other chapters.

The different types of deep diving equipment are shown in Fig. 10.55. All systems are based on the use of oxygen helium mixtures or trimix, a combination of oxygen, helium and nitrogen. The oxygen content in both mixtures and the nitrogen content in the trimix are relatively low because of the need for a low partial pressure and a high helium content of about 90–95% is normal.

With the very high cost of helium gas it might be assumed that the use of closed circuit, or at least semi-closed breathing systems, would

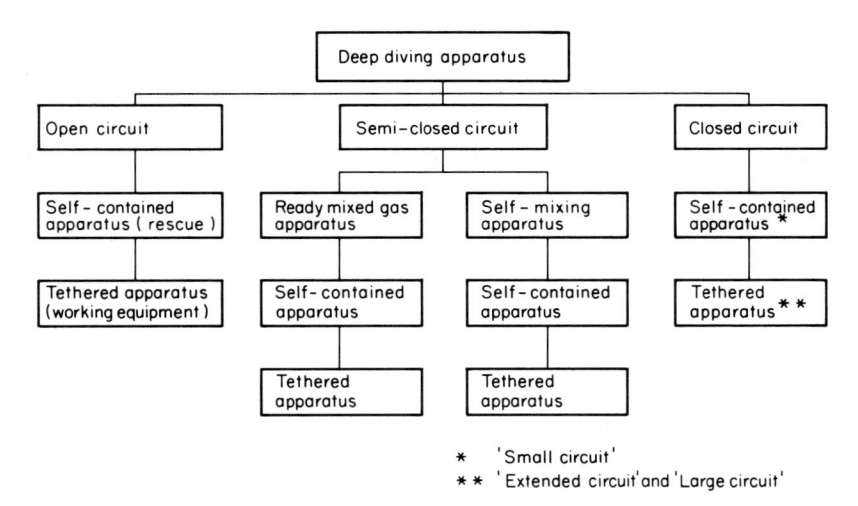

Fig. 10.55. Various options for deep diving equipment.

be preferred so as to economise on gas. So far this has not been the case, largely due to simplicity and reliability of the open-circuit system which overrides the high expenditure on gas. It is not feasable to provide a self-contained open-circuit system at other than shallow air diving depths where, at a depth of 150 m, the gas consumption is about 480 litres/min, in comparison to 30 litres/min on the surface. An external supply is to have a cylinder, or bale-out bottle as it is sometimes called, which can supply sufficient gas, on the same principle as a scuba set, in an emergency if the main supply fails so that the diver can return to the diving bell, submersible or habitat.

Although open-circuit deep diving systems are preferred, systems which work on the semi-closed principle are being introduced and as the reliability and efficiency improves, they will become generally accepted. In this kind of apparatus, a specific helium–oxygen mixture flow is supplied into the circuit with a flow rate and a gas composition which are adjusted in such a way that the permissible oxygen partial pressure limits are safely maintained independent of changing oxygen consumption in the depth range of that mixture. By partial recovery of the gas and simultaneous carbon dioxide elimination, gas consumption is within acceptable limits and hardly exceeds more than 50 litres/minute even at diving depths of 200 m.

The gas supply of a semi-closed circuit apparatus can be either pre-mixed gas or a self-mixing system. Systems with automatic mixing are possible but the design is so complicated that the practical application has to be considered very carefully. When two separate gas components are processed, not only is correct mixing a relatively involved procedure but the necessary monitoring sensors need to function with the minimum of maintenance. The design is much simpler for systems with a ready mixed gas supply. With a constant mass flow of premixed gas only certain depth ranges can be covered but they are great enough to be satisfactory for practical applications.

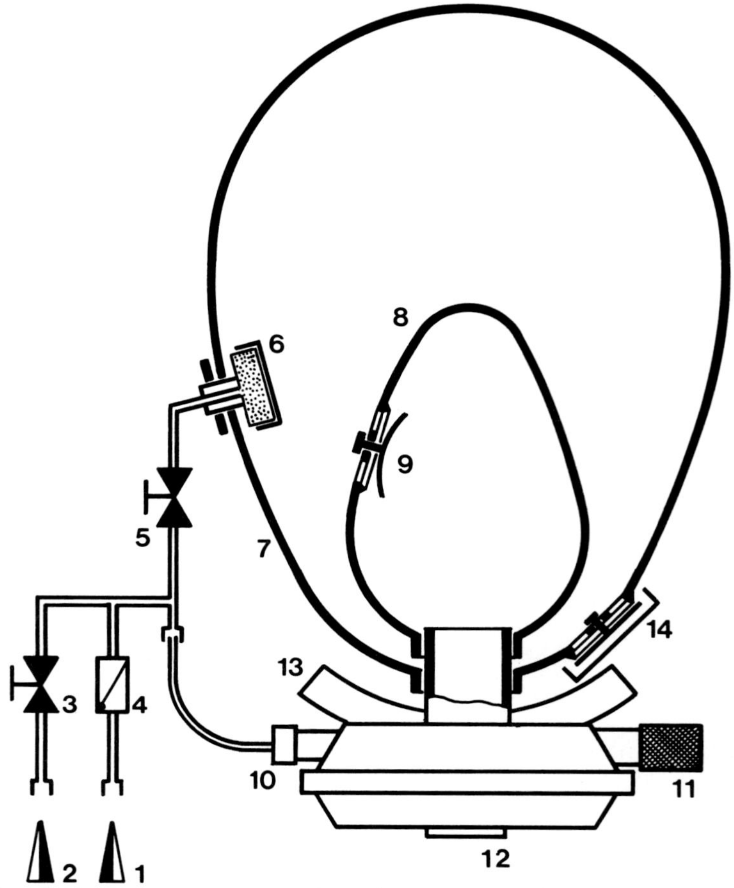

Fig. 10.56. A diving helmet (band mask) for deep diving (open circuit).

1. gas inlet, hose supply
2. gas inlet, emergency supply
3. valve
4. non-return valve
5. valve
6. silencer
7. outer mask (helmet)
8. oral-nasal mask
9. non-return valve
10. gas inlet to regulator
11. adjusting spindle
12. purge valve
13. gas exhaust
14. outlet valve

The diving equipment is relatively simple in design and a further advantage is in the use of different gas mixtures. Depending on the specific application and the desired diving time, gas may be supplied from the mixed-gas cylinders on the apparatus or through a supply hose from a diving bell. The gas umbilical must be small allowing the diver to exit and re-enter through the chamber hatch. The radius of action, given by the length of the umbilical, will rarely inhibit the diver's work. Semi-closed breathing systems can be successfully used to diving depths of at least 200 m with gas consumption a deciding factor. At greater depths the closed circuit is the most desirable diving system if a high percentage of the gas can be recovered. At the same time the desired respiratory balance can be maintained, with the oxygen partial pressure kept constant by an oxygen sensor which measures the partial pressure and controls the oxygen input. The extended closed-circuit system which is designed to be installed in the diving bell or submersible, thereby reducing the surface element, will in future be used more in the deeper depths although the large surface circuit is in current use. For example a DDC on the surface is in the same gas circuit as the SDC and the gas mixture is circulated from the diving bell through a CO_2 absorbent unit into the chamber with additional oxygen to make up the deficiency and

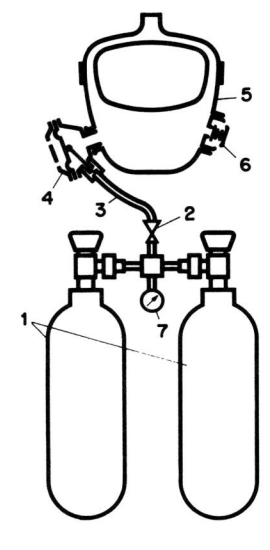

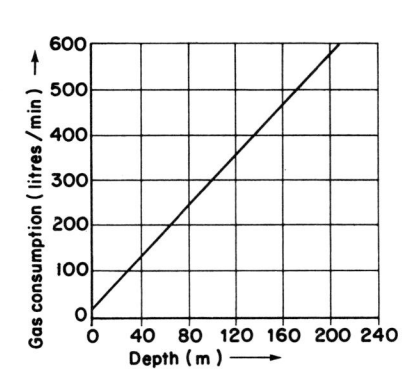

Fig. 10.57. An open-circuit system and its average gas consumption.

1	storage cylinders with shut-off valves	4	demand regulator
2	pressure regulator	5	face mask
3	connection hose	6	air exhaust valve
		7	pressure gauge

recirculated down to the bell. This complete closed-circuit saturation system is illustrated in Fig. 10.00. All monitoring is done on the surface but, although pressure changes are slow, large volumes can be circulated. Another extended circuit is shown in Fig. 10.60 and these systems are described later in the chapter.

Deep diving, open circuit
Fig. 10.56 shows a gas circuit for a helmet working on open circuit. Fig. 10.57 illustrates the proportional increase of gas consumption with diving depth.

Deep diving apparatus with semi-closed circuit, pre-mixed gas
The normal operating range of deep diving with semi-closed circuit is currently between 50 and 200 m where the economy in gas will apply. As stated, the partial pressure of oxygen should not exceed 1.8 bar and be less than 0.2 bar.

Semi-closed diving, self-contained mixed gas
Originally designed for military use, the equipment was adapted for commercial use for deep diving without surface supply or support from a diving bell. Nowadays this type of free diving is limited to about 50 m. At deeper depths the equipment is fitted with a gas umbilical which allows for greater endurance and safety and is suitable for operations from submersibles and habitats where gas supplies are limited.

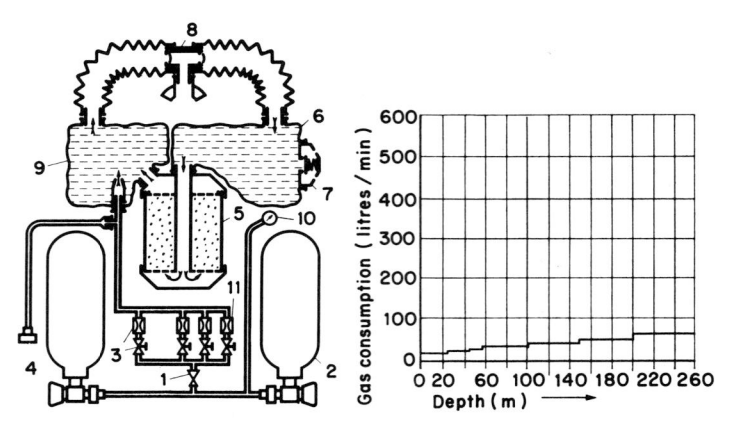

Fig. 10.58. A semi-closed circuit and its average gas consumption.

1 pressure regulator
2 mixed gas storage cylinder
3 bypass valve
4 connecting hose for external gas supply
5 carbon dioxide absorbent canister
6 exhalation bag
7 outlet valve
8 valve with mouthpiece
9 inhalation bag
10 pressure gauge
11 constant mass flow regulator

A self-contained unit is shown in Fig. 10.58 which can be used for deeper dives allowing three separate flow rates to be selected. The mixture in the gas cylinder is selected for the depth and passes to one of the three constant mass flow regulators which can be selected by the diver. The gas passes into the inhalation bag, or counter lung, and is then inhaled by the diver through the inhalation tube and exhaled back into the bag after passing through a CO_2 absorbent unit. Non-return valves are fitted in the mouthpiece.

Semi-closed diving, umbilical-supplied mixed gas

The adaptation of the self-contained semi-closed system to be supplied through an umbilical is shown in Fig. 10.59. The system is designed to allow a diver wearing the apparatus to pass through a hatch with a minimum diameter of 600 mm; the diving time will only be limited by the capacity of the CO_2 absorbent, usually about two or three hours, and by the physical exertion of the diver himself. Fig. 10.59 illustrates a system identical to the self-contained semi-closed system (Fig. 10.58) with the umbilical supply passing directly into the inhalation bag. A flow monitor will register a supply failure and warn the diver either visually or acoustically; in this event the diver opens the supply from the bale-out emergency bottle which, through a reducer, will supply the bag and give sufficient gas for return to the chamber.

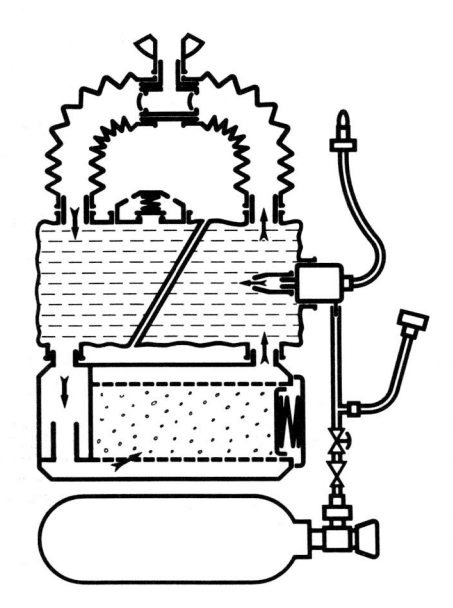

Fig. 10.59. Mixed gas apparatus with a semi-closed circuit and umbilical.

Gas supply to the diver from the surface

A surface-supplied system is illustrated in Fig. 10.60. Although surface-supplied systems are generally not used below about 50 m this

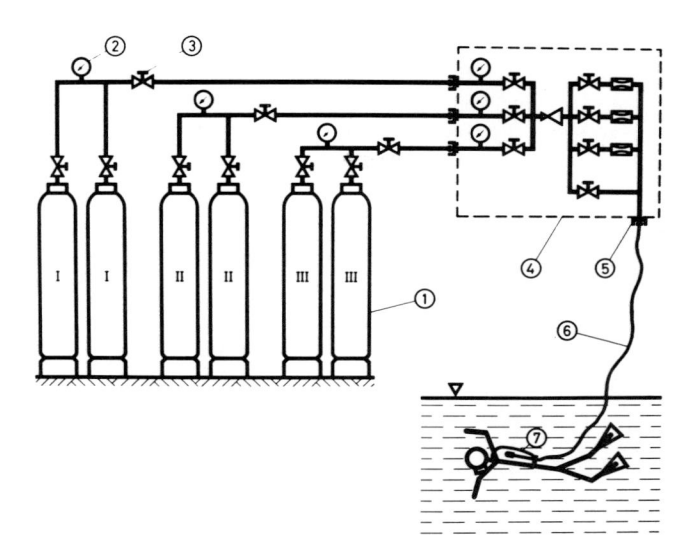

Fig. 10.60. Surface-supplied pre-mix gas supply system.

1. mixed gas cylinders I–III
2. storage bank pressure gauge
3. storage bank supply valve
4. control panel with gauges, valves, pressure regulators
5. umbilical connection
6. umbilical
7. diving apparatus

is a common practice in the Gulf of Mexico and other warmer areas. Also in an emergency, where a diving bell is not available, this may be the only means of providing assistance to a trapped diver or underwater vehicle in distress. A system shown in Fig. 10.60 has ready-mixed gas, possibly subdivided into up to three separate mixtures for different depths. These are separated with shut-off valves and the selected gas mixture passes through a flow regulator, with a predetermined flow rate for the depth and mixture, and then through the umbilical to the diver's breathing bag. The change-over from different mixtures at the correct depth demands accurate depth recording by pneumogauge on the surface control panel.

Gas supplies to the diver from a diving bell (SCC)

The supply of gas through an umbilical is equally relevant from a submersible or a habitat. The correct flow can either be set within the SCC or other under-water chamber or passed at an intermediate pressure and through a flow regulator on the breathing set where it is finally adjusted to the correct working pressure of the diver.

Self-mixing systems

Much of this type of apparatus has not been developed for operational use with the same degree of reliability and ease of maintenance that is generally reflected in other systems. Fig. 10.61 illustrates the self-contained semi-closed self-mixing unit which has been used. Helium and oxygen are stored separately, with a larger helium supply because of the greater quantity needed. With a selected 3 litres/min of oxygen

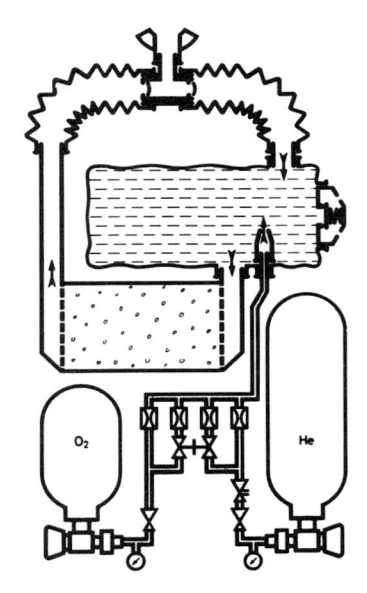

Fig. 10.61. Self-contained self-mixing deep diving apparatus.

which will be adequate for the maximum oxygen consumption, only one regulator is required for the injection of O_2 and supplies it at a constant overpressure to the flow metering device.

On the helium side the output has to be increased as the depth increases and the second stage of a two stage reduction, exposed to ambient pressure, will achieve this. Bypass valves are fitted. The flow control mechanism is designed to produce a correct mixture for any depth within the limits of the apparatus. If the flow rate should fail a signal can be actuated. Similarly if the gas supply is below a preset level this will also be indicated.

When the self-mixing system is not required to be self-contained and can be supplied through an umbilical, the mixing unit will be mounted inside the diving bell or chamber. The pressure regulator, flow control and bypass unit shown in Fig. 10.61 are thus inside this SCC. An oxygen sensor measuring Po_2 can be fitted on the breathing apparatus and so indicate to the diver the correctness of his breathing mixture relative to oxygen content. The actual breathing set can therefore be very small.

Fig. 10.62 shows a completely closed circuit system with an automatic oxygen input control and in Fig. 10.63 a closed circuit system with average gas consumption. In general however operators still prefer to use the less complicated systems using premix gases which are more reliable and easier to handle.

Closed-circuit systems

A perfect closed-circuit breathing system would require only the addition of small quantities of oxygen to replace the metabolic consumption. This ultimate ideal is not likely to be achieved and present systems fall well short of it. These systems are only partially in operational use and they are not favoured because of their complexity and cost. Not until they achieve total reliability, easy maintenance, are rugged and the cost is reasonable will they be generally used.

A small circuit system is illustrated in Fig. 10.62. In this system an oxygen sensor is installed in the breathing circuit to record the partial pressure of oxygen before or inside the inhalation bag, preferably in the bag. The sensor activates the oxygen input through an amplifier depending on the required Po_2 and the consumption of O_2 in the body. The sensor and injection system is very precise. As a safety feature up to three sensors can be fitted so failure of one will bring another into operation. The breathing bag with the carbon dioxide absorbent cartridge is connected to the facemask (or diving helmet) by the exhalation hose and the inhalation hose. In this closed system the circulation of the breathing medium is in the direction of the arrows. The gas storage cylinder supplies inert gas into the circuit through a self-acting pressure controlled valve when the pressure difference between breathing bag and environment is enlarged due to increasing ambient pressure as, for example, during descent. The oxygen cylinder delivers oxygen through the pressure regulator, a regulating valve and line into the breathing bag. Inside this breathing bag a sensor is installed which produces a different electric values

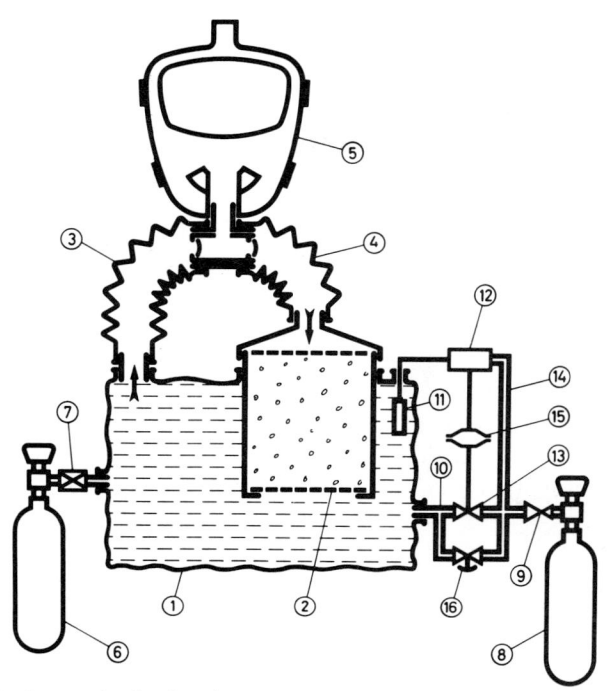

Fig. 10.62. A completely closed circuit with automatic oxygen input control.

1. breathing bag
2. carbon dioxide absorbent
3. inhalation hose
4. exhalation hose
5. face mask
6. inert gas cylinder
7. demand valve
8. oxygen cylinder
9. pressure regulator
10. line
11. sensor (oxygen partial pressure)
12. amplifier
13. oxygen input valve
14. oxygen branch line
15. servomotor
16. oxygen bypass valve

according to changing oxygen partial pressure. The sensor is connected to the amplifier by which the measured electric values are amplified and used to control auxiliary valves which are inserted in an oxygen branch line. This oxygen branch line ends in a solenoid which controls the oxygen input valve. As soon as the oxygen partial pressure drops below a certain value, the oxygen input valve is opened. As soon as the desired partial pressure is reached again, the valve is closed, again by the solenoid. An oxygen bypass valve is connected in parallel to the oxygen input valve which is designed as push-button valve and which can be used by the bearer of the apparatus to fill the circuit with pure oxygen.

Fig. 10.63 illustrates an American system using several O_2 sensors simultaneously to give a mean value of the actual Po_2.

A closed-circuit system as fitted to a diving bell is illustrated in Fig. 10.64. The bell is filled with the required oxy-helium mixture for the depth and the type of dive envisaged. The oxygen partial pressure is regulated by a sensor and the working of the system is shown in Fig. 10.65. The recirculation of the gas applies both to the breathing

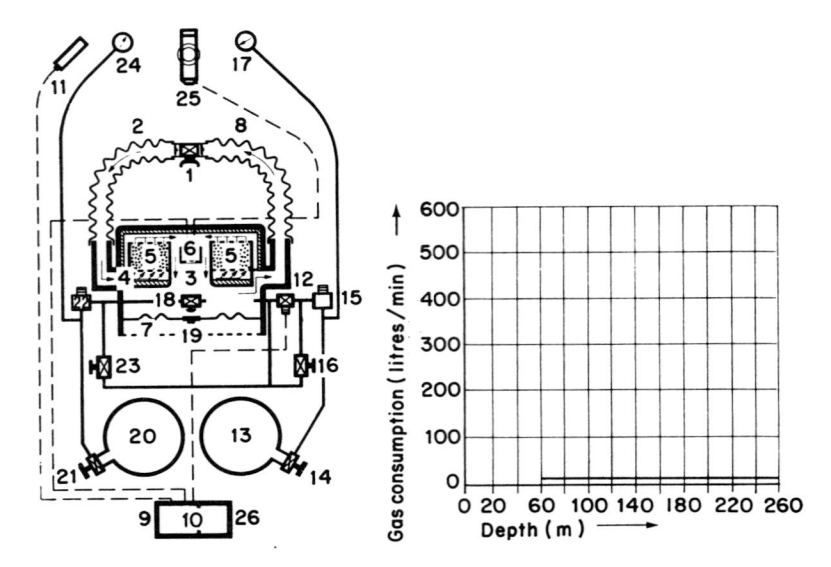

Fig. 10.63. A closed-circuit system and its average gas consumption.

1	mouthpiece non-return valve	13	inert gas container
2	exhalation hose	14	valve
3	breathing bag	15	pressure regulator
4	connection	16	valve
5	carbon dioxide absorbent	17	pressure gauge, inert gas
		18	demand valve
6	oxygen sensor	19	sieve
7	diaphragm	20	oxygen container
8	inhalation hose	21	valve
9	electronic unit	22	pressure regulator
10	electronic unit	23	valve
11	warning signal	24	pressure gauge, oxygen
12	solenoid	25	read-out for P_{O_2}
		26	batteries

apparatus in the water and the chamber environment. The procedure is as follows. The mixed gas is drawn through the compressor and a regulator into a chamber. The regulator can lower the pressure inside the chamber by 2–3 bar below ambient. The suction hose to the diver is connected to this chamber. The CO_2 absorbent unit is connected to the high-pressure side of the compressor and from here gas passes to the overpressure chamber. An overpressure of about 3 bar, with respect to the ambient pressure, is maintained in this tank by a regulator. The gas supply line to the diver is connected to this point, as is the exhaust valve, to supply the bell with regenerated clean gas. The diver has a gas control valve and, since overpressure and suction can be kept very constant, low inhalation resistances can be achieved. There is no danger of the system being subjected to external damage.

Another version is where only oxygen is supplied from the bell, illustrated in Fig. 10.66. The diver carries a helium supply cylinder only and a semi-closed breathing system as previously described. An O_2 sensor in the inhalation hose transmits the partial pressure of oxygen to the bell and through an amplification circuit and solenoid oxygen is injected into the system.

Another example of an extended circuit is for a delivery pump and a suction pump to be sited outside, but attached to, the diving bell and enclosed in a pressure chamber. The push–pull pump pressure vessel supplies gas from the bell to one diver. One such system is illustrated in Fig. 10.69 designed by Normalair Garrett.

Breathing gas for divers is circulated by a push–pull pump contained in a steel pressure vessel attached externally to a bell. One pump/pressure vessel combination supplies gas, from the bell, to one diver. The pressure vessel, designed to withstand external pressure when the bell is used as a one-atmosphere observation chamber, comprises lower and upper housings, divided by a diaphragm to which are attached both the pump and the motor.

A gas control panel, situated within the bell, contains the following: A differential pressure gauge which measures the difference between supply and return gas pressures, which indicates whether the system is functioning correctly; a pressure/vacuum gauge which indicates how far the diver is above or below the bell, i.e. his vertical location; a filter to remove particles in the gas supply line to the diver; an inlet strainer to protect the delivery pump inlet; a non-return valve to prevent emergency gas from passing into the delivery pump; a change-over valve to direct emergency gas (from the emergency bell supply) to the diver; and a water trap to trap slugs of water and prevent them entering the suction pump.

Gas is drawn into the bell penetration through the inlet pipe, containing the inlet strainer; from there it passes to the pressure vessel through a flexible hose. The gas is then routed by pipe to the delivery pump where it is compressed and passed back into the bell. Delivery

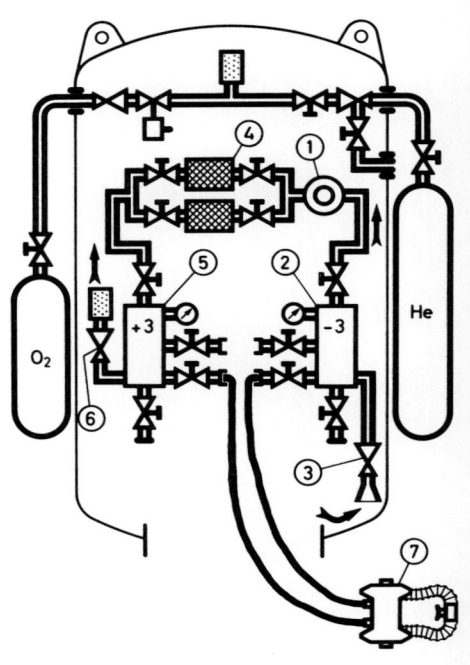

Fig. 10.64. A closed-circuit demand system for diving bell and diving apparatus (extended circuit).

1 pump
2 compensator cylinder
3 supression regulator
4 carbon dioxide regeneration unit
5 overpressure compensation cylinder
6 pressure regulator
7 mixed gas control valve

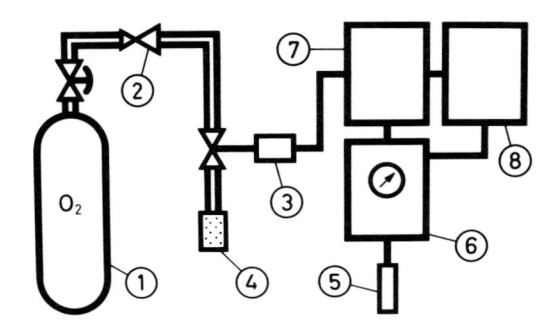

Fig. 10.65. Principles of an oxygen sensor and supply system.

1 oxygen cylinder
2 pressure regulator
3 control valve (solenoid)
4 silencer
5 sensor
6 oxygen meter
7 amplifier
8 energy supply

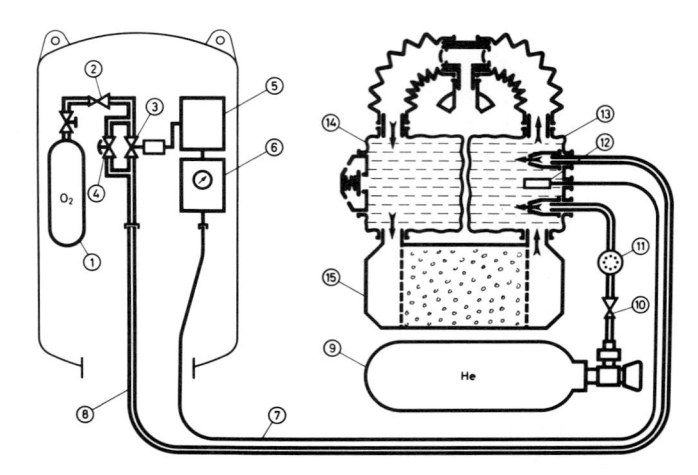

Fig. 10.66. Closed breathing circuit with oxygen supply from the diving bell through a hose.

1. oxygen cylinder
2. pressure regulator
3. solenoid valve
4. oxygen bypass valve
5. amplifier
6. oxygen meter
7. sensor data line
8. oxygen supply hose
9. helium cylinder
10. pressure regulator
11. helium demand valve
12. oxygen sensor
13. inhalation bag
14. exhalation bag
15. carbon dioxide scrubber

gas is supplied to the diver via the non-return valve delivery filter and an excursion umbilical and returns to the inlet connection of the suction pump via the return umbilical hose, a water trap and the pressure vessel. The suction pump delivers the gas back to the bell where it is released into the intake of the bell scrubber.

In an emergency a manual valve on the control panel within the bell connects the bell emergency gas supply to the diver's hose. A non-return valve prevents the emergency gas entering the delivery pump (which could be defective and allow the gas to pass back into the bell). A robust anti-suck valve, having only one element, is connected to the helmet outlet fitted by a flexible hose. Should the element fail, the return pump can suck water but not the diver. Between inlet and outlet an island is positioned which effectively forms a gap in the gas flow system. To bridge this gap, the gas must partially inflate a flexible tube that is subjected to ambient pressure. This tube also controls gas pressure within the helmet. Should there be a breakdown in the supply system or for any other reason the gas return should tend to apply a depression to the helmet, the flexible valve will close. The depression in the gas return line cannot be transmitted to the helmet interior.

An emergency bale-out bottle attached to the diver's back is connected to a distributing tube within the helmet by a diver-operated valve. In the event of complete failure of the gas supply this valve must be opened. The gas will then pass through the helmet to

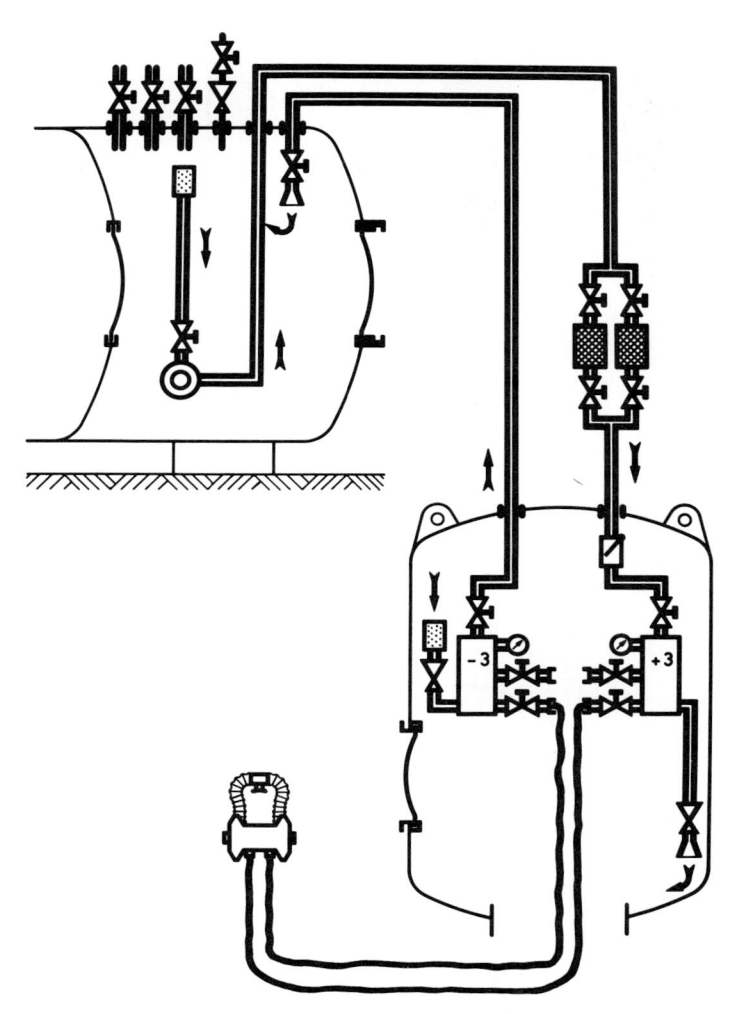

Fig. 10.67. Closed-circuit breathing demand system with surface chamber in the circuit.

the sea via the relief valve. At maximum depth it has a duration of only 2.5 minutes and the diver must return immediately to the bell. During both emergency and bale-out conditions the breathing gas will open the relief valve in the diver's helmet and pass into the sea.

The push–pull system requires a number of self-adjusting valves on or near the diver's helmet to control the gas pressure within the helmet to cover the complete diving spectrum. The diver can then concentrate on his work confident that his gas supply will stay within operational limits. An essential feature of any push–pull system is that the interior of the helmet should never be subjected to a dangerous negative pressure and to ensure that the internal pressure does not become excessive a safety valve must be fitted.

Large closed-circuit systems, where the gases are recirculated from and back to the surface, have also been developed. Figs 10.67 and 10.68 show the different systems. In Fig. 10.67 the recirculating pump

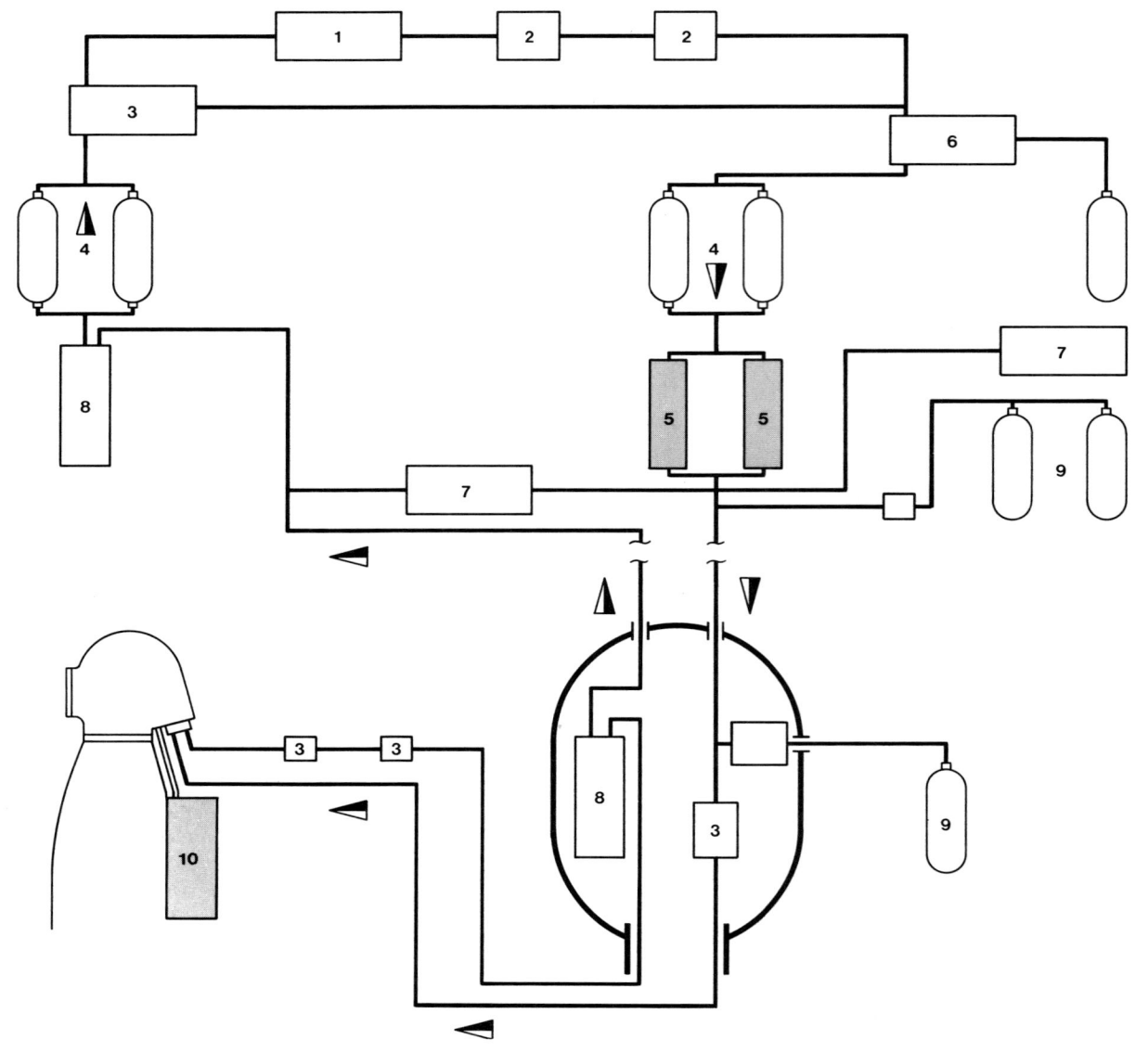

Fig. 10.68. Closed-circuit breathing demand system.

1 compressor	6 O_2 regulating system
2 filter	7 O_2–CO_2 control systems
3 pressure regulating devices	8 water separator
4 buffer	9 emergency supply
5 CO_2 scrubber	10 emergency breathing system

is sited inside a surface chamber. The breathing gas is pumped from the chamber through CO_2 scrubbers to the bell and the divers and returned back to the surface chamber. The surface chamber is at the same pressure as the diving bell and both will vary equally with descent and ascent.

An alternative design is the pressure vessel and pump as illustrated in Fig. 10.69; the bell mounted system can be detached and sited on

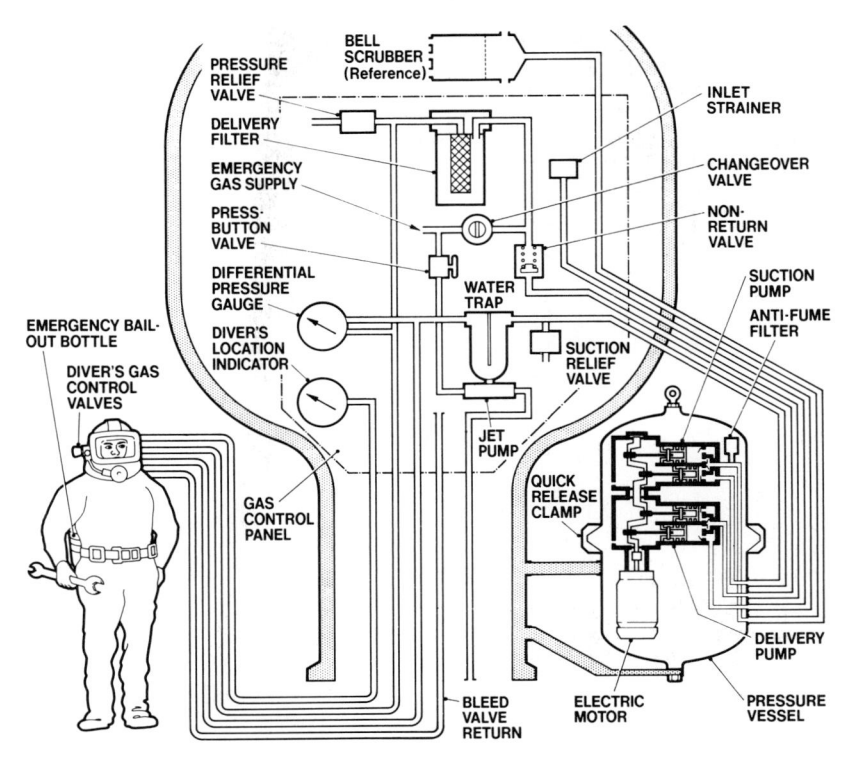

Fig. 10.69. Closed-circuit breathing demand system, bell mounted.

the surface. A circulation compressor which is installed under ambient pressure on the surface, supplies the diver with breathing gas. The gas flows through the diver's helmet on a free-flow principle and by means of a feedback line to the compressor. All devices which are necessary for the preparation of the breathing gas are included in this circuit. A measuring device checks the CO_2 content of the gas inhaled. Simple operating valves and regulators serve to adjust the diver's breathing gas pressure to the water pressure surrounding him. A back pressure control system automatically controls the pressure in the helmet and adjusts it to the surrounding water pressure. A relief valve in the helmet prevents a pressure build-up. The system has an emergency stand-by gas supply which can be used for open-circuit breathing should the primary circuit fail. In all systems the diver continues to carry the emergency bale-out cylinder on his back which allows him to return to the diving bell.

11 Under-water Welding, Repair and Construction Habitats

As early as 1965 the off-shore industry could foresee problems arising from the increasing depths at which pipelines had to be laid for the transport of both gas and oil. Whilst the technique of laying pipelines in these depths became comparatively simple with the rapid introduction of large pipe-laying barges with their ability to operate in bad weather and to continuously weld section upon section on board and then lay the pipe, the final completion was not so easily achieved. At some stage the horizontal pipe laid on the seabed had to be connected to a vertical riser pipe to bring it to the surface and on board the production platform. This required making connections on the seabed. Laid pipe is prone to damage and it is usually impractical to raise the pipe to the surface for joining up. A production field may be interwoven with pipes, one laid on top of another, and there is little opportunity for the pipe to be brought to the surface for repair in the same way that cables are repaired on board cable ships. The pipe may need to be modified at some stage to allow a feeder or branch line to be inserted or a valve fitted. All these major requirements, and others, have led to the development of the under-water welding habitat in which pipes can be cut and welded in a dry chamber environment. The development was begun in the 1960s, mainly by American firms associated with the pipeline construction industry such as Taylor Diving, Ray McDermott, Sub Sea International and Ocean Systems. The initial design, developed originally for pipeline tie-in, or connection, of two horizontal sections of the pipe lying on the sea bed, has since been extended and adapted to undertake riser tie-ins on both steel platform jackets and concrete structures, the repair of damaged off-shore structures and the installation of valve assemblies, bypass assemblies and tie-in assemblies to existing lines. The under-water habitats, or welding chambers as they became known, operating at the ambient pressure at the depth that they were set, initially developed in the USA and were followed by similar developments from European companies associated with the North Sea in Britain, France, Italy and Norway.

Fig. 11.1. Under-water welding habitat by Taylor Diving.

At greater depths the problems associated with obtaining welding performances comparable to those on the surface have led to the more difficult development of chambers operating in a one-atmosphere environment.

Subsea Welding Chambers Under Ambient Pressure

The basic design relies on the ability to place a caisson over the pipe and evacuate the water. To allow the water to be evacuated the interface between the pipe and chamber has to be closed and sealed, usually with inflatable rubber segments, and the gas is introduced into the chamber displacing the water. An under-water welding habitat is shown in Fig. 11.1.

There are a number of variations to suit the particular requirements and Fig. 11.2 illustrates some of these patterns. The basic and most widely used concept is *Type A*, a unit without an alignment frame. An alignment frame can adjust the position of the pipe within certain limits. Therefore in this simple design the pipes are assumed to have been lined up ready for welding. Relatively simple small tasks in shallow water are suitable for this type of chamber which cannot align the pipes. *Type B* is the same concept but with the addition of a

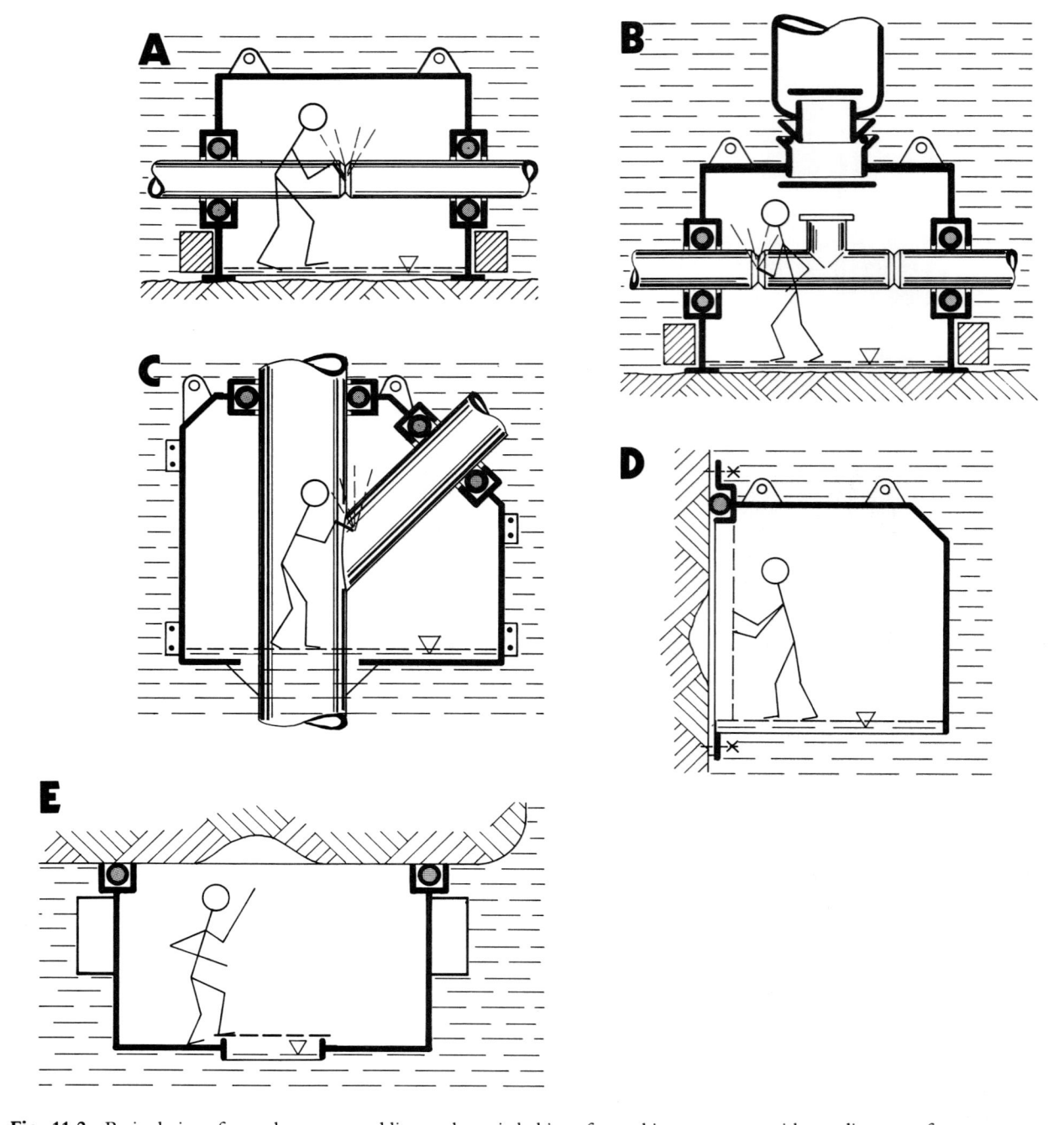

Fig. 11.2. Basic designs for under-water welding and repair habitats for ambient pressure, without alignment frame.

- **A** Basic design with two side entries for the pipeline. Various sizes are available corresponding to the objective
- **B** Welding habitat with dry transfer capsule
- **C** Specially designed habitat fitted to the diagonal of a steel structure
- **D** Repair habitat attached sideways, for example to work on concrete structures
- **E** Repair habitat for work underneath concrete structures or steel floating structures, e.g. ships' bottoms

vertical transfer hatch with a diving bell to transfer the diver welders to and from their task. Apart from the advantages of being able to operate beyond shallow water and outside the scope of surface-orientated diving, in theory at least it may allow non-diving specialists, provided they are familiar with being under pressure, to inspect the work. Nowadays, however, this is not often necessary because of the experience of the divers backed up by qualified inspection divers. The diving bell can also be used for the transfer of equipment including non-destructive test equipment for establishing whether, on completion of the weld, it meets the minimum standards. The classification standards for welds are high and clearly need to be because of the high internal pressures and the conditions in which they operate.

To some extent pipeline welding habitats can be standardized to accept known-diameter pipe lying on the seabed, but other specialized structural repairs are needed on the tubular strength members of steel jackets. In *Type C* an under-water welding habitat is illustrated enclosing a diagonal bracing member at any intermediate depth on a steel structure. In some cases the same welding chamber is standardized so with little or no modification it can be used in similar situations in other areas around a steel structure. In other cases the welding chamber needs to be specially constructed to fit the arrangement of bracing members, particularly when they meet at a nodal point on one of the main members.

For the inspection and repair of vertical flat surfaces, usually associated with concrete structures, the chambers are designed to attach sideways as shown in *Type D*. Although practicable, the problem lies in the secure method of attachment to the flat surface. Work on flat bottom surfaces, such as ships' bottoms or other floating constructions (*Type E*) is relatively simple, using the buoyancy of the chamber and a trimming system as a secure means of attachment.

Subsea One-atmosphere Chambers

The term hyperbaric welding has come to mean fusion welding at hyperbaric pressure carried out in ambient pressure chambers which have just been described. However, welding under pressure in the deeper depths where pipelines need to be connected or repaired presents greater technical and logistical problems, not least that man's ability to carry out useful work below a certain depth becomes doubtful if not impossible. It is certain that production of oil and gas will very soon be undertaken in depths beyond the capacity of divers. Even in relatively shallow waters that are being worked at the moment there is a manpower problem in providing technically qualified welder divers who are graded to produce the very high quality welds required. Research is now being vigorously applied to solving the problem by designing one-atmosphere welding chambers which will need to be pressure-resistant. To achieve this the daunting technical problem of sealing the pipe entry against the pressure of the

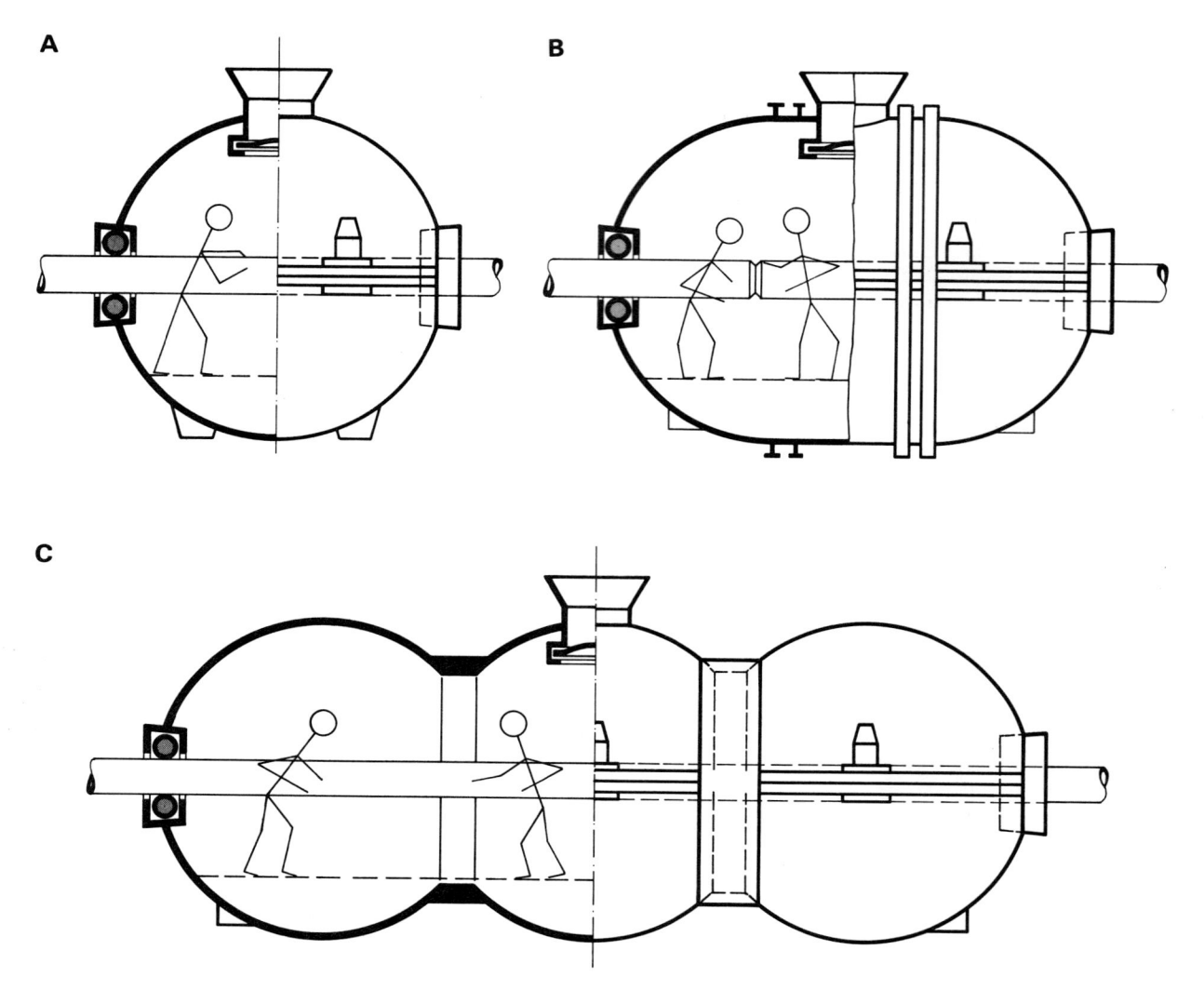

Fig. 11.3. Basic designs of one-atmosphere pressure chambers for welding.

water outside has to be overcome. Fig. 11.3 illustrates some of the designs which are considered and which, because of the constraints of the high pressures envisaged, conform to a spherical or hemispherical configuration. The design always incorporates a lock-on facility which allows a transfer capsule to take the personnel to and from the chamber. They are at one-atmosphere surface pressure, sometimes referred to as a 'shirt sleeves environment'. As stated, the technical problems are daunting. The French company Comex have embarked on a project to repair or join pipelines under one-atmosphere pressure. The necessity of providing additional heavy flange supports at the position of entry into the chamber of the pipe, the pressure sealing arrangements and the need to align the separate pipes are all major problems under development and until they are resolved the diver is still indispensable.

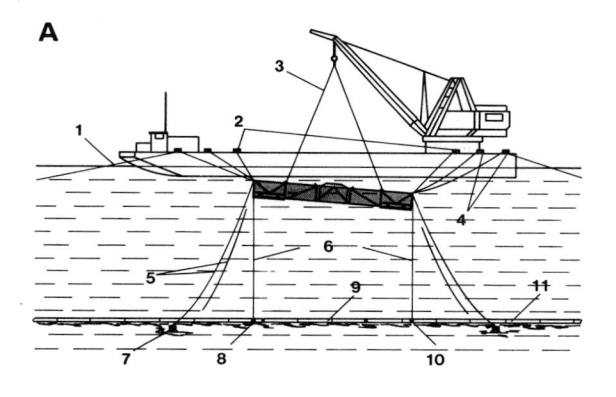

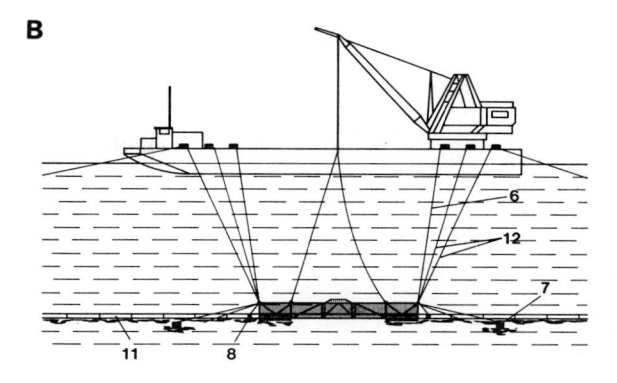

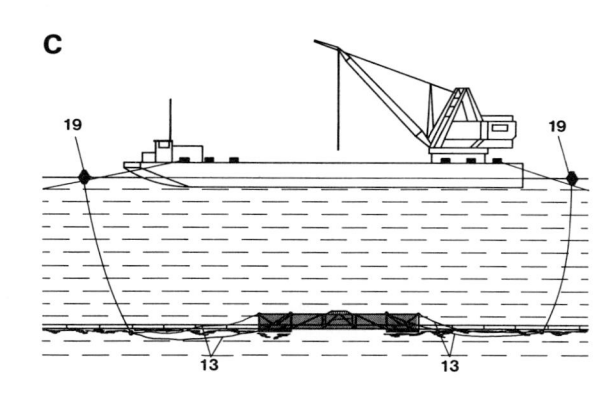

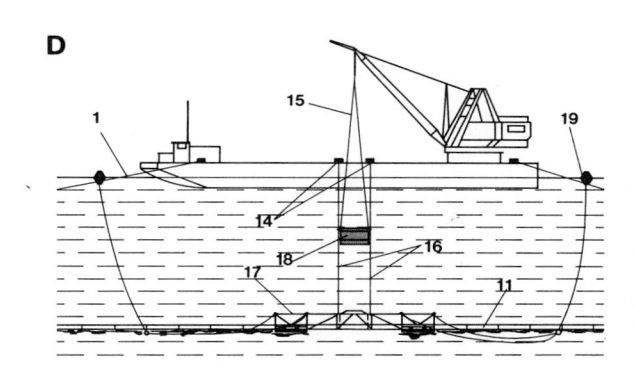

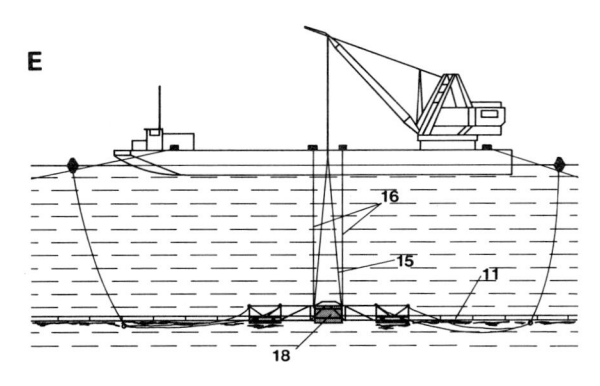

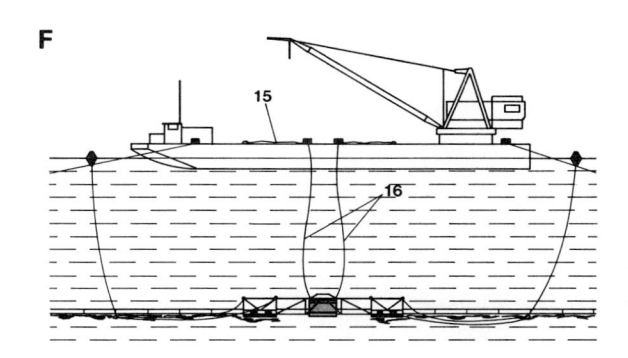

Fig. 11.4. The sequence of events for a mid-point tie-in.

1. mooring line
2. frame guide hoists (constant-tension or hand-held)
3. crane slings
4. frame positioning hoists (constant-tension)
5. wire rope positioning lines (0.25 in wire rope)
6. frame guide lines (0.5 in nylon)
7. 5000 lb anchor
8. guide line clamp
9. break in pipe
10. guide line clamp
11. pipeline
12. positioning lines
13. crane slings
14. habitat guide line hoists (constant-tension)
15. 200 ft sling
16. guide line (in-board side of habitat)
17. alignment frame
18. habitat
19. sling recovery buoys

Fig. 11.5. An alignment frame (end view) (Ray McDermott).

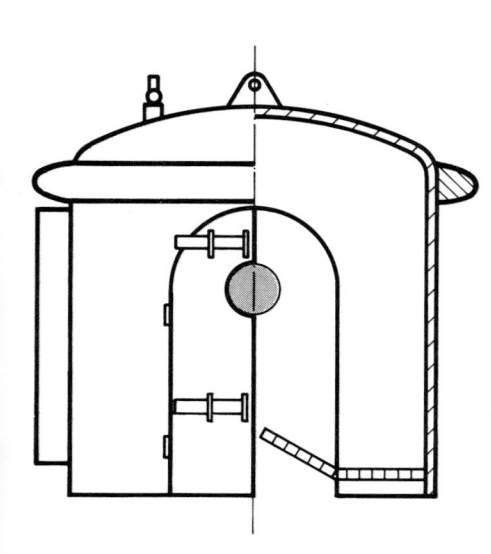

Fig. 11.6. A simple welding habitat.

Welding Chambers with Alignment Frames

The first successful pipeline welds were carried out in 1968 in chambers without any facility for aligning the separate pipes accurately before joining but the need to align the pipes had to be met. By 1975 the first successful submersible pipeline alignment frames were in use. The alignment frames and the welding chambers are separate and Fig. 11.4, taken from a Ray McDermott procedure, illustrates the procedure for lowering the alignment frame over the pipelines and, separately, the welding chamber. Examples of alignment frames on the surface are shown in Figs 11.5 and 11.7. The alignment frames have to handle and position pipeline up to 1200 mm in diameter and the forces needed to do this are considerable. The frame is made of tubular steel. The unit shown in Fig. 11.5 is 55 m in length, 10.5 m wide and 8.9 m high. The weight on the surface will be 400 tonnes and submerged will be 90 tonnes. The tubular structures are capable of being flooded and can be deballasted to provide buoyancy and trim. At each corner, pads, which can be adjusted vertically by hydraulic rams, will level the frame whilst on the seabed. Up to 10 pipe clamps can be incorporated to secure both ends of the pipe. The pipe clamps are modified to match the diameter of the pipe up to 1200 mm. The clamps can be worked separately, hydraulically, to move the pipe either vertically or horizontally and are controlled from the habitat. In addition there are water jet devices to remove the marine growth from the pipe and a closed-circuit television monitoring system to encompass the movements of the separate clamping units.

Fig. 11.7. A pipeline alignment system with a habitat by Sub Sea International.

Fig. 11.8. A large alignment frame with welding habitat before being lowered over a pipe section ready for welding (Taylor Diving and Salvage).

Fig. 11.9. The interior of a welding chamber with a transfer hatch.

Current Welding Chamber Units

There are basic parameters which apply to all welding chambers irrespective of size and depth. A simple unit is illustrated in Fig. 11.6 adapting a vertical pressure cylinder with dished ends. The chamber is designed by Comex Diving in France to accommodate pipe up to 600 mm. Each end of the chamber has a door through which the pipe passes and both doors are secured by locking rams. The ballast is secured in four containers around the bottom of the chamber and the floor of the chamber is made of light retractable grating. The chamber is lowered on a crane and all life-support and industrial gases are supplied from the surface. A medium-sized welding chamber, incorporating an alignment system, is shown in Fig. 11.7 and a large unit in Fig. 11.8. All these units are supplied with life-support from the surface through an umbilical in addition to the power requirement for operating the alignment frame and the welding process.

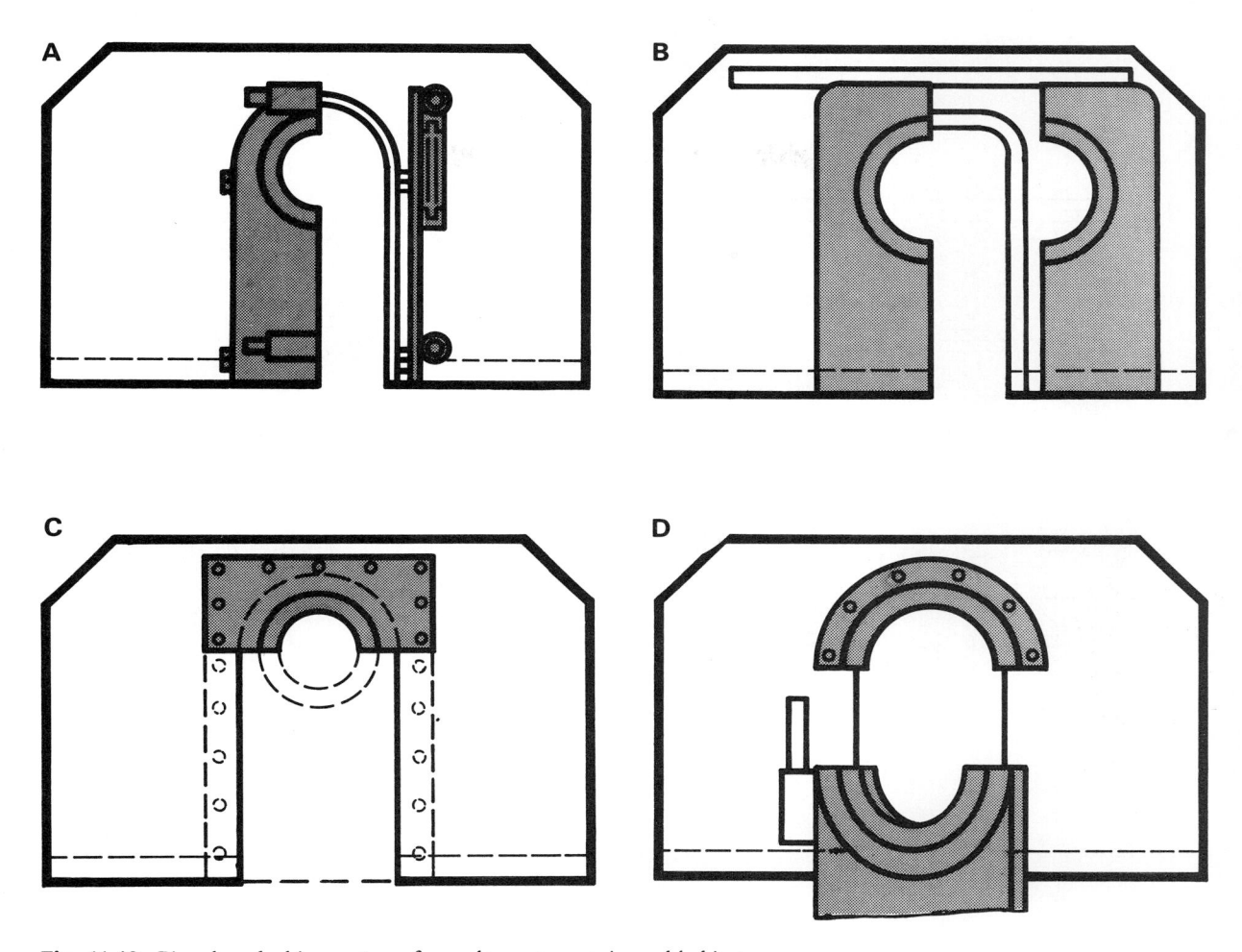

Fig. 11.10. Pipe door locking systems for under-water repairs and habitats.

    A Two-part hinged gate for small habitats and small diameter pipe. Mechanical lock by plugged bolts
    B Two-part sliding gate for large habitats and large diameter pipe. Gate movement and lock by hydraulics
    C Pipeline sealed by double bolted plates. Mainly for small repair chambers
    D Hinged lower segment. For large habitats and largest diameter pipes. Fully hydraulic lock

    The logistics of supplying the various services are similar to those of the diving bell, but on a larger scale. Emergency breathing systems are carried in the unit. The life-support system of the unit comprises the following:

1. Independent CO_2 scrubber system.
2. Oxygen supply.
3. Communication system.
4. Lighting.
5. Temperature and humidity controls.
6. Emergency gas supply.
7. Oral–nasal breathing system.

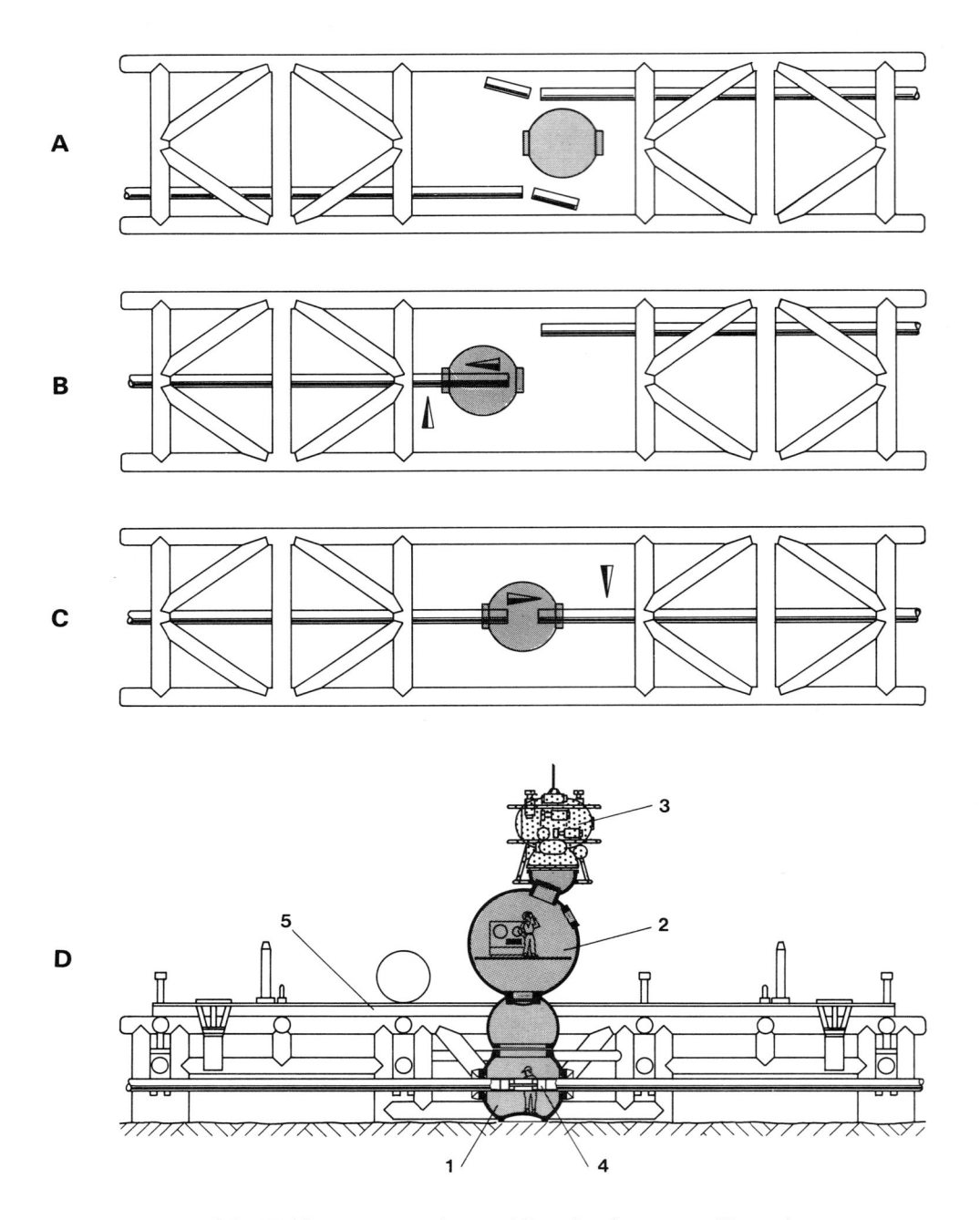

Fig. 11.11. Use of the Weldap one-atmosphere welding chamber system (Comex).

    A The overlapping pipe ends are cut
    B The left-hand pipe is centered and the welding base is moved on to it
    C The right-hand pipe is centered and the welding base is set on both ends
    D The pipes, welding base and plug system are now ready for welding

        1 atmospheric pressure welding base   4 plug system
        2 atmospheric pressure support module   5 alignment frame
        3 atmospheric pressure transfer module

All essential services are sited above the upper level of the pipe entry so that in the event of flooding these main services remain dry and continue to function. Fig. 11.9 shows the interior of the welding chamber with the access hatch above.

Weldap One-atmosphere Chambers

The first one-atmosphere system produced by Comex Diving of France is illustrated in Figs 11.11 and 11.12. Designed ultimately to operate in 1000 m depths, beyond the range of divers, the system has the four distinct parts. Both pipe ends are sealed into a single spherical welding base which is at one-atmosphere pressure, these movements being carried out by the alignment frame. The system is designed to carry out pipeline repairs, pipeline tie-in connections and riser pipeline tie-in.

A lot of preparatory work needs to be carried out before a welding operation takes place. In new constructions the laid pipelines may have to be joined to the vertical riser sections and the production platform but the operation can be preplanned to make the under-water connections as simple as possible. However, when a section of pipe or a tubular structure is damaged and needing repair no two situations are the same. Typical damage to a pipeline may be a single buckle, a double buckle or a hole in the line. The pipe may be exposed, but could be buried, requiring it to be dug out. All pipelines are usually covered with concrete coating reinforced with wire to protect the pipe inside and the damaged area needs to be stripped and cleaned by divers operating either from a diving bell or from a lock-out submersible. This will almost certainly need power tools. If the laid pipeline is damaged a section will have to be cut out. The alignment frame can then be fitted over a new section. Before welding the pipes together, the ends will need precise bevelling. An intermediate section, known as a pup, will be fitted to marry the two sections together.

The various work functions that need to be carried out inside the welding chamber demand the most stringent monitoring of the environment. Noxious and toxic gases will inevitably be produced, particularly during welding, and oral–nasal breathing systems will be needed.

SUPRA (Submersible Under-water Pipeline Repair Apparatus)

The idea of this concept was to develop a new type of under-water work and pipeline repair system which was insensitive to bad weather and heavy sea conditions; needed no heavy surface equipment; was not a submarine; could be operated even from small diver support ships; had versatile equipment; and would offer substantial cost advantages over other systems. The German engineering group consists of Haux-Unterwasser Systemtechnik, Schiffko and Ocean Consult. Fig. 11.13 shows a model of this new rig.

Fig. 11.12. The Weldap one-atmosphere welding chamber sytem.

The SUPRA consists of four pressure cylinders connected to a vehicle of inverted U shape. It carries a habitat for welding operations, to be carried out by divers, and the necessary tools to lift pipe ends, etc. The catamaran-type rig is intended for towing on the surface to the work site by a diving support vessel. The submerging operation, using an integrated ballast and propulsion system, can be remote-controlled or controlled by a diver manning a steering positon in the unit's service capsule. No heavy surface equipment is required for the operation.

Fig. 11.13. SUPRA, a remotely controlled pipeline repair rig.

The rig contains no living quarters, as divers will not remain on the seabed but are carried to the surface by a conventional dive bell system or a transfer submersible. Power is supplied to the rig by umbilical from the mother ship.

Suitable for repair of pipelines with diameters from 12 to 42 inches (305 to 1067 mm), the rig has a pipe alignment system measuring 20 m in length and providing clamp forces of 200–450 kN. The rig is fairly small, measuring 29 × 10 × 7 m, weighs 275 tonnes and carries a 20-tonne payload. Propulsion is by ten 40 kW thrusters. The welding habitat measures 3 × 2.8 × 3.5 m and has a horizontal reach of 20 m. Two cranes are provided, two 100 kN gantry cranes with 20 m longitudinal reach and a swivel crane lifting up to 35 kN with a horizontal reach of up to 18 m. Its maximum diving depth is 500 m.

Development of the rig has the support of the West German Ministry of Research and Technology.

12 Animal Experiment and Equipment Test Chambers

The study of living conditions under high and maximum pressures is increasing and being carried out not only for purely economic reasons. Low pressures are also attracting the interest of both scientists and engineers. The questions to be answered are divided into three areas—human, equipment and materials—and a few examples of each are given below:

1. What is the behaviour of living organisms under the long-term influence of high pressure?
2. What is the limit of pressure endurance?
3. How does high oxygen partial pressure or multi-component gas mixture effect decompression times?
4. Is there an advantage in using linear decompression for certain decompression stages?
5. What is the performance of a measuring probe in 1000 or 10 000 m depth?
6. What is the cause of the narcotic effect of certain inert gases?
7. What is the strength against pressure of a specific material?
8. Is the pressure housing of a new television camera sufficiently strong for all designed depths?
9. Which welding and cutting procedure is best for repair work at varying depths?
10. What is the effect of pressure re-cycling on a new window material?
11. Is a new diving system safe against high pressure, low temperature and high salinity?
12. What is the acoustic behaviour of a diving system in deep water?

Materials change their properties with pressure and temperature and some disease-causing agents die when exposed to high oxygen partial pressures. Gas gangrene might be treated with hyperbaric oxygen; what is the effect of simultaneous treatment of cancer cells with rays and high oxygen partial pressures? These and similar medical, chemical, physiological and physical problems need research which can only be carried out with the use of experimental compression chambers of varying types.

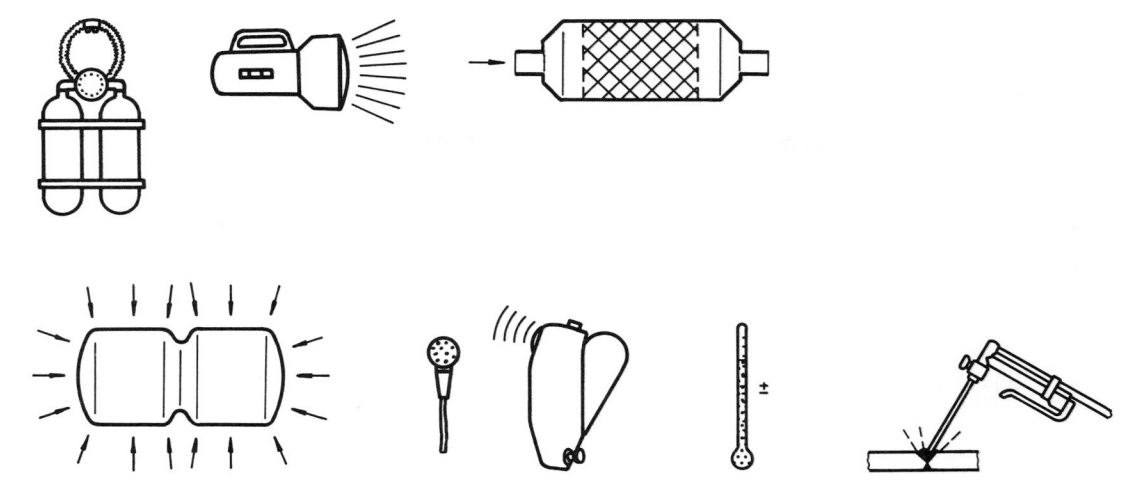

Fig. 12.1. Items of equipment suitable for testing.

Experimental Chamber Applications

To answer the many types of question posed above requires a large variety of chambers. Typical chambers are described for each type of work in the rest of this chapter.

Animal Experimental Chambers

Animal tests are used to solve physiological and respiratory problems from a medical or diving physiological point of view. The chambers must be capable of accommodating any of the following types of animals:

1. Mice.
2. Guinea-pigs.
3. Monkeys.
4. Dogs.
5. Goats.
6. Pigs.
7. Dolphins.

Experiments are mostly to produce decompression profiles, to check oxygen tolerance and bone necrosis and to investigate high-pressure nervous syndrome (HPNS), the effects of high and low temperature, tolerance to various inert gases and problems of liquid breathing etc.

Equipment and Material Testing Chambers

These are similar. All under-water equipment requires extensive trials prior to operational use. This includes both diving and peripheral equipment. Fig. 12.1 explains what may be tested in various types of chambers.

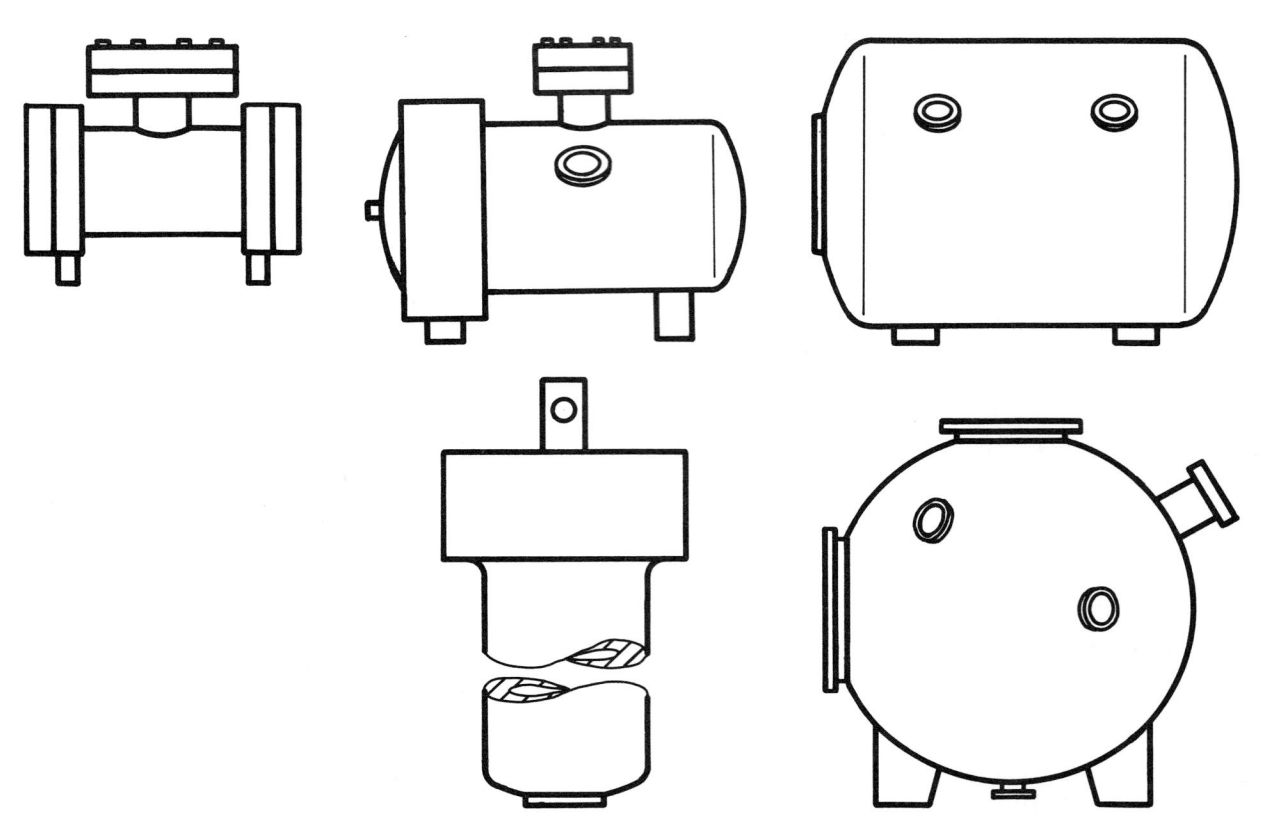

Fig. 12.2. Constructional forms for animal experiment and equipment testing chambers.

Construction of Testing Chambers

The variety of types is relatively small. Cylindrical chambers with dished ends are normal even for pressures up to 1000 bar. Spherical designs are used only when a large volume is required in addition to high pressure. The horizontal cylindrical solution, with a volume of a few litres, is used for small animals such as mice and rats. Occasionally it is used with larger animals such as goats and pigs where a volume of several cubic metres may be necessary. For testing measuring probes, a vertical cylindrical shape is the preferred solution. Two-compartment chambers are rare. The locking system chosen is dictated by the specific application, the size of the chamber, the maximum operating pressure and the money available. Fig. 12.3 shows typical types in common use. The cheapest are those with hinged bolts or studs or a hinged tommy bar, but they are slow to open and close. Bayonet locks are common for pressures up to 100 bar, provided that the door is not too large. For high pressures the sliding cheek or sawtooth thread is a good solution. In the following paragraphs details are given of the peripheral systems in use with these different types of chamber.

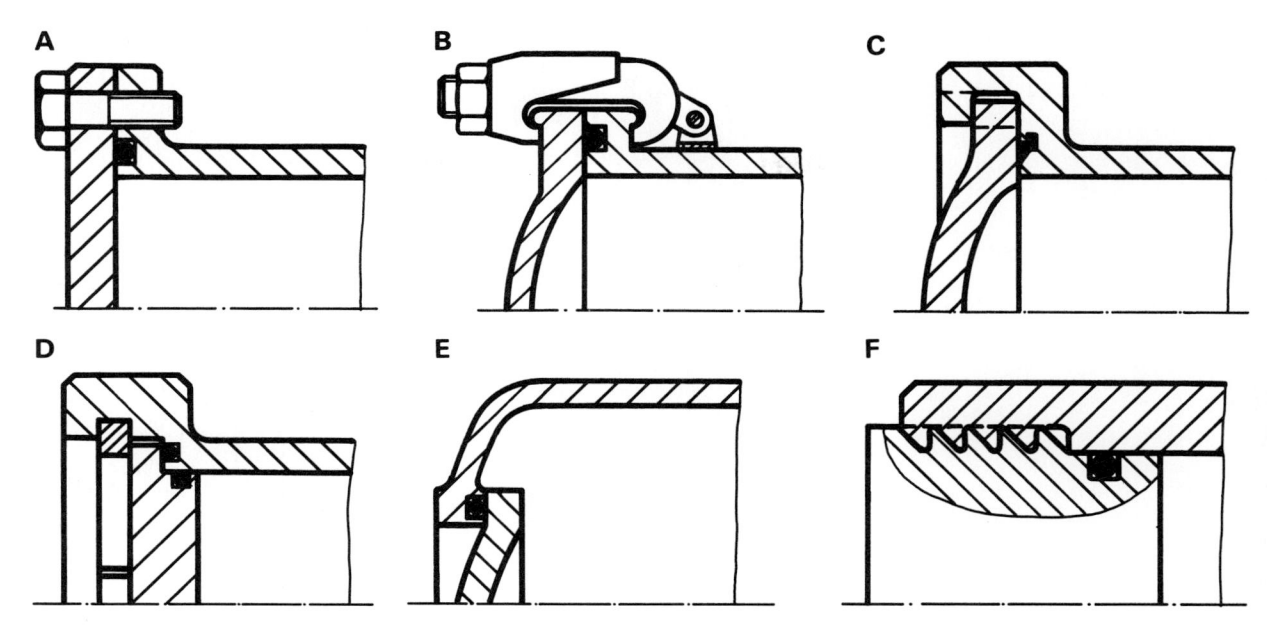

Fig. 12.3. Locking systems for animal experiment and testing chambers.

- **A** Bolted lock with removable screws, bolts or hinged bolts. Simple inexpensive design, but considerable loss of time when locking
- **B** Hinged tommy bars for pressure vessels with relatively low operating pressures. Inexpensive plate lock, but slow when closing
- **C** Bayonet lock or lock with divided U-ring. Normal locking system for high pressures. Quick and safe operation, but expensive
- **D** Sliding-cheek lock for chambers with maximum operating pressures. Quick to lock. Demands high precision in manufacture, therefore expensive
- **E** Inside hatch with seal in direction of pressure for vessels with a large volume. Oval or circular construction. Inexpensive and safe, but space requirement large
- **F** Sawtooth lock for very high operating pressures. Quick closing. Requires high precision in manufacturing, therefore expensive

Design of Animal Experiment Chambers

There are many different designs and the following examples are characteristic.

Simple Compression Chambers for Animal Experiments

Fig. 12.4 shows a typical chamber which needs little technical expertise in design and manufacture and which is therefore cheap and adequate for use with rats and mice. The maximum working pressure is 200 bar and the internal dimensions are 80 mm diameter and 200 mm long. Relatively thick flanges are fitted. The left-hand one is fitted with inlet and outlet valves and a pressure gauge. The right-hand one has a viewport through which the animals can be observed to a limited extent. The top flange has 12 separate screened penetrators through which electrical data from the animals can be

Fig. 12.4. Simple compression chamber for animal experiments (maximum operating pressure 200 bar).

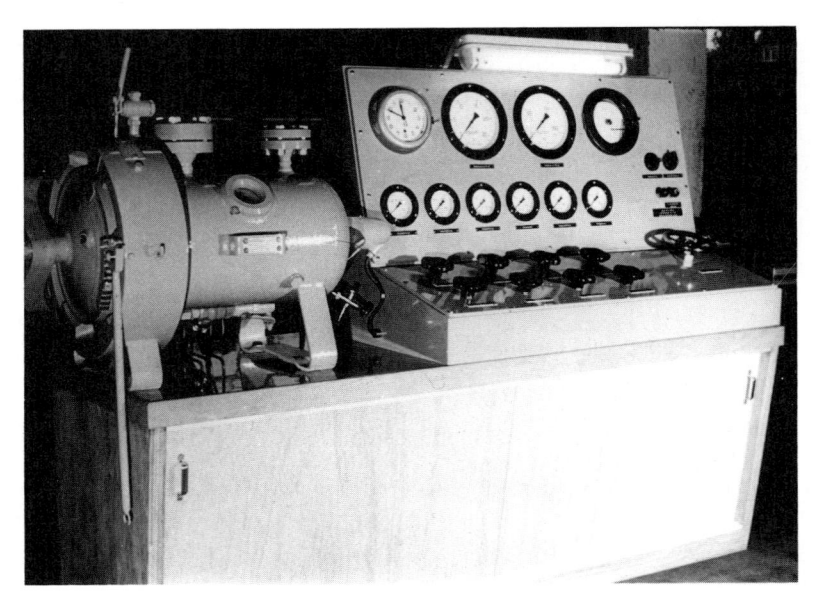

Fig. 12.5. Compression chamber for short-term animal experiments with control panel and desk (maximum operating pressure 100 bar).

extracted. The lock is effected by tightening the 12 counter-sunk screws, which is both slow and laborious.

Standard Test Chamber for Equipment Trials and Short-duration Animal Experiments

The compression chamber shown in Fig. 12.5 is characteristic of the standard test chamber found in many laboratories. The peripherals will vary according to the experimental work carried out; this might be the testing of small items of equipment or components or short-

Experiment and Equipment Test Chambers 499

Fig. 12.6. Compression chamber for animal experiments with installations for continuous production of two-component gas mixtures (operating pressure 3 bar).

duration animal experiments. The chamber is designed for a maximum operating pressure of 100 bar and has a clear internal diameter of 300 mm with a length of 500 mm. The bayonet lock permits quick opening and closing. A safety interlock is part of the door-locking arrangements. Two observation windows are fitted which give a good view when combined with an external floodlight placed at the end of the chamber. Electrical data such as EEG and ECG signals are led through the top flange using separate screened penetrators. Another flange is available for gas connections and gauges. A sample-taking union with a fine adjustment valve and spare connection for future requirements is also fitted. The control panel, which is mounted on the same desk as the chamber, has the normal monitoring facilities: pressure recorder, precision gauges, thermometer and chronometer etc. The valve arrangement is designed to permit the use of various gas mixtures of air, oxygen, nitrogen and helium etc. When small animals are being used an acrylic cage is provided to ensure that they remain in view.

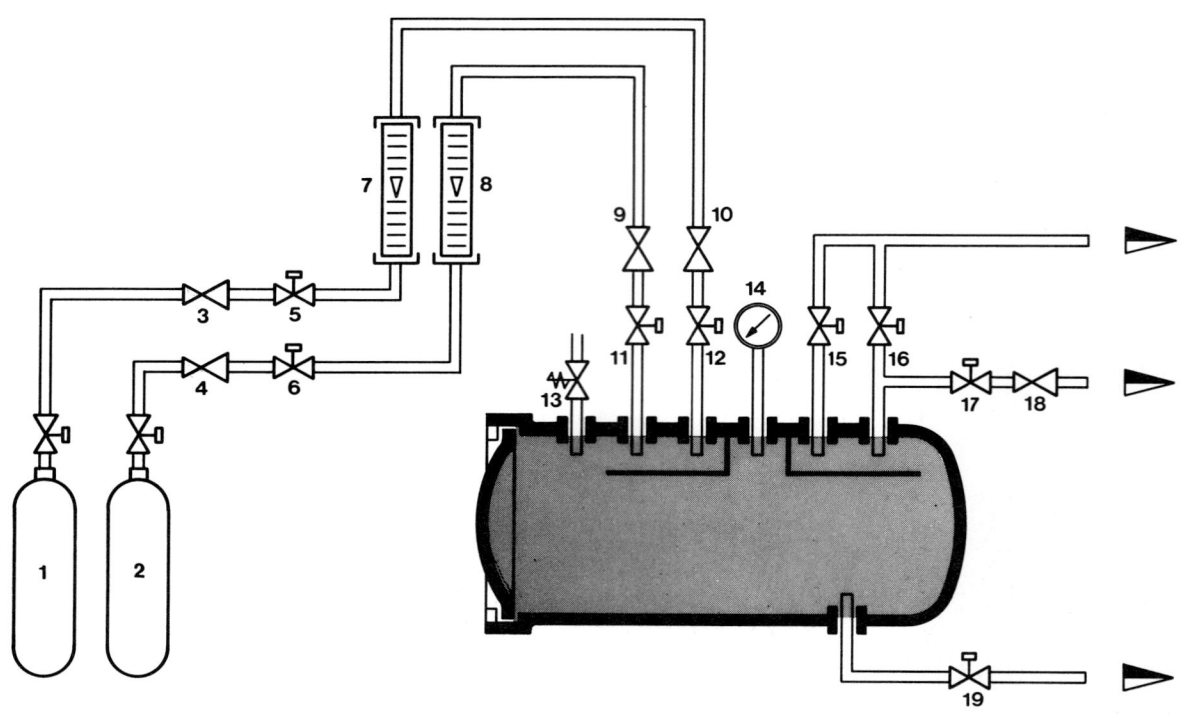

Fig. 12.7. Layout of the installation for the production of two-component gas mixtures and the exhaust system of the animal experiment chamber shown in Fig. 12.6.

1	gas supply, inert component	13	safety blow-off valve
2	gas supply, oxygen	14	external pressure gauge
3, 4	regulators	15	exhaust relief regulator
5, 6	stop valves	16	relief valve
7, 8	gas flowmeters	17	gas sample valve
9, 10	regulators	18	gas sampling regulator
11, 12	inlet valves	19	urine drainage valve

Animal Experiment Chambers for Specific Experiments in the Low-pressure Range

Fig. 12.6 shows an example of a chamber for experiments with rabbits in the low-pressure range (3 bar) but with facilities for continuous variations of any two-component gas mixtures. Fig. 12.7 explains the gas mixing and ventilation arrangements. In this example air and oxygen are taken from two separate storage cylinders through regulators at a differential pressure of 10 bar, then via stop valves to the pressure-proof conical glass flowmeters and thence to the regulators, still at a differential pressure of 10 bar. From there the gases pass through the inlet valves into the chamber. To protect the animals from the high-pressure gas jet, a baffle plate is fitted. To ensure sufficient gas exchange in the chamber, the regulators are capable of gas flows of 20 000 litres/hour while dropping the pressure from 10 bar to 6 bar. This arrangement ensures that, as well as maintaining the chamber at 3 bar, there is sufficient overpressure to permit a

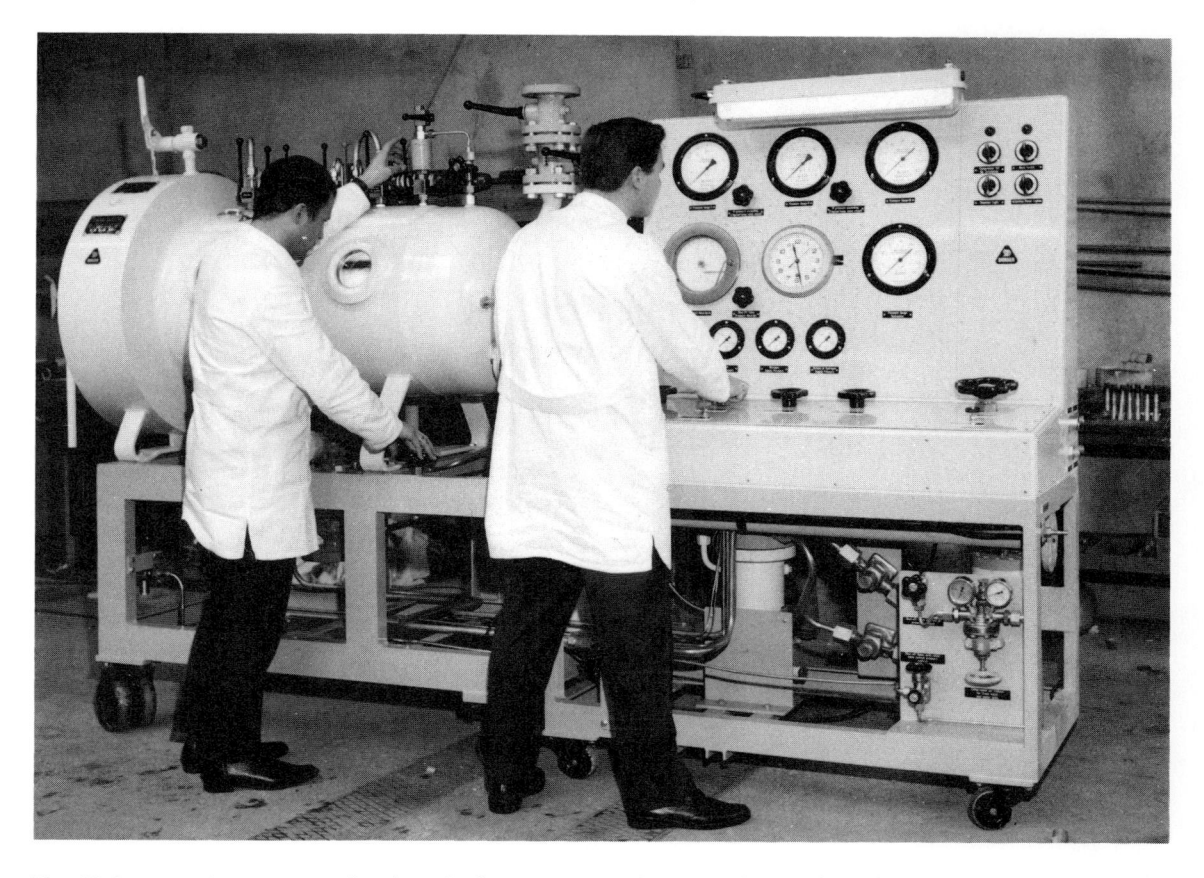

Fig. 12.8. Animal experiment chambers for long-term experiments with complete life-support system (maximum operating pressure 100 bar).

continuous gas flow through the chamber. The relief valve which decides the chamber pressure can be accurately set to any pressure between 0.3 and 3 bar. A valve and regulator allow samples of the chamber gas to be drawn off for continuous sampling. The shut-off valve permits urine drainage at the chamber bottom. The measuring tubes of the conical glass flow meter are easily changed to vary the measurement range.

Animal Experiment Chambers for Long-term Experiments with Small Animals

Many experimental programmes require the long-term exposure of animals to high pressure. This imposes exacting demands on the life-support system of these chambers. Besides monitoring the gas atmosphere, it is sometimes necessary to control the temperature and humidity within narrow limits. Also the animals must be fed and watered and their excrement removed. All this, and at extreme pressures, requires a high level of design expertise. Fig. 12.8 shows a compression chamber system built to these requirements. To

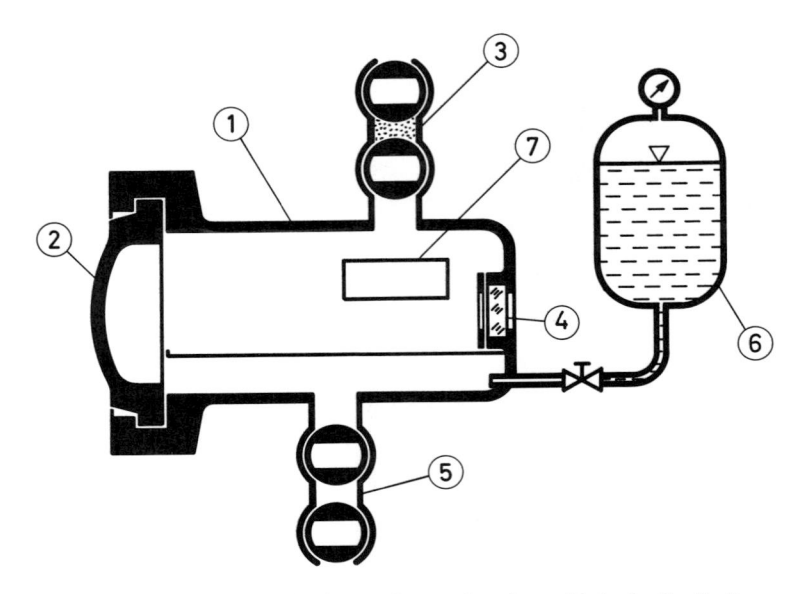

Fig. 12.9. Scheme for an animal experiment chamber with locks for feeding and excrement removal.

1 compression chamber hull
2 door with bayonet lock
3 feeding lock with ball valves
4 viewing window
5 lock for excrement removal
6 tank for high-pressure water flushing
7 food trough

maintain an unobjectionable gas atmosphere a closed-circuit system is employed with a blower driven by a motor. Carbon dioxide is extracted by an absorbent filter. Water vapour is removed either with a water-absorbent filter or by reducing the gas temperature below its dew point. The gas is then reheated in a continuously controlled heat-exchanger. A full set of instruments is provided to monitor these parameters. A lock is fitted at the top of the cylindrical pressure hull through which dry granulated food is fed. Two ball valves in series, with an adequate cross-sectional area, act as a pressure lock. Water is supplied basically in the same manner. In Fig. 12.9 the chamber layout is shown diagrammatically. The animals stand on a perforated grating through which excrement drops; this is washed clean with water under pressure which floods up to the grating level and is then removed through a lock system at the bottom of the chamber. This excrement removal is essential for the health of the animals during long experiments. The chamber is fitted with all normal monitoring facilities and a blood test device can additionally be mounted in the chamber.

Animal Experiment Chamber for Long-term Experiments with Large Animals

Work of this type by French scientists is recorded in many publications. Described here is a chamber in Professor Chouteau's

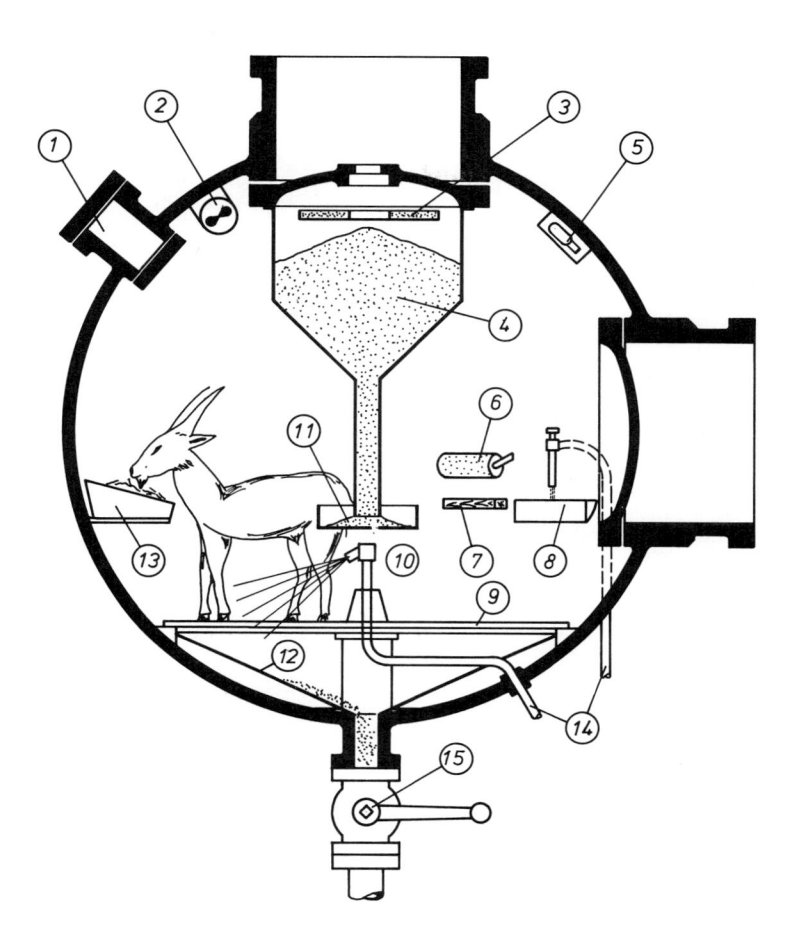

Fig. 12.10. Compression chamber for long-term animal experiments (goats) (maximum operating pressure 150 bar).

1 feeding lock
2 blower
3 silica gel
4 container for granulated food
5 lighting
6 rock salt (for goats)
7 piece of wood
8 water inlet with basin
9 grating floor
10 rotating water jet
11 food trough 1
12 conical chute for excrement catching
13 food trough 2
14 high-pressure water supply
15 shut-off valve

institute at Marseilles which is designed for large animals (goats, pigs, monkeys etc.). Fig. 12.10 shows a cross-sectional drawing of the chamber with the main features and technical layout. The spherical chamber has a diameter of 2400 mm and a volume of 7 m³ with a maximum operating pressure of 150 bar. It is connected to and part of a larger complex and is fitted with doors large enough to let the animals enter. Additional food can be inserted through a supply lock and the animals are under constant observation at the control panel by means of a television camera viewing through a window. The internal feed system has a generous supply of granulated food. The floor is washed with rotating jets and the conical chute leads all excrement to the bottom removal lock in the sphere. The life-support system is typical of first-class design. The closed-circuit system is driven by a centrifugal pump which is inside a pressure-proof housing (Fig. 12.11). Carbon dioxide is removed by a large CO_2 scrubber and H_2O, NH_4 and H_2S are removed in a filter tower by silica gel and a charcoal absorbent which can be by-passed if necessary. The purified gas is re-injected into the chamber through a silencer, oxygen being added directly into the charging line from a storage bank through a flowmeter and precision regulating valve.

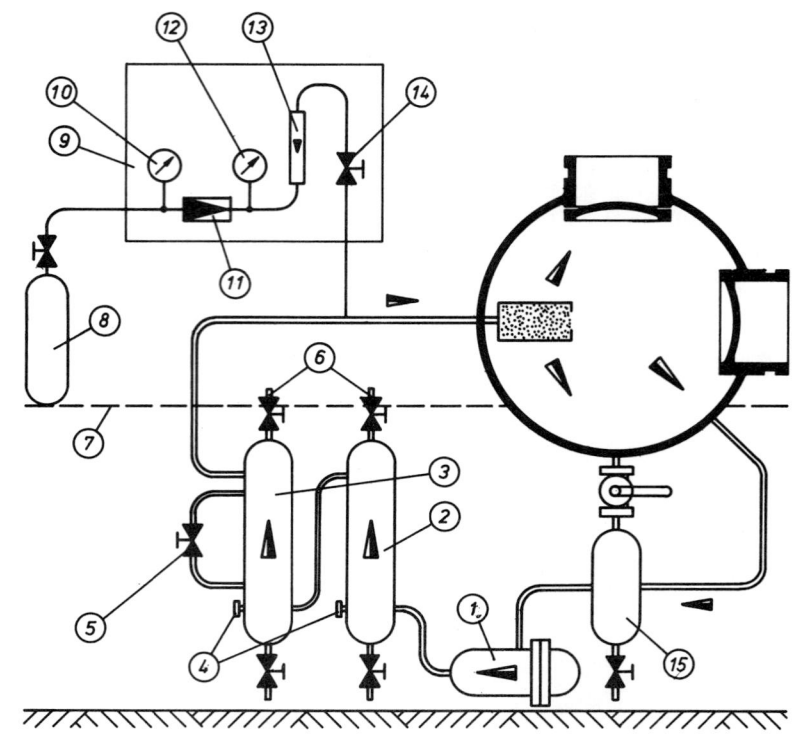

Fig. 12.11. High-pressure life-support system for the animal experiment chamber shown in Fig. 12.10.

1 circulating pump
2 CO$_2$ absorbent cylinder
3 silica gel and charcoal cylinder
4 exhaust valves
5 flow adjustment bypass valve
6 filling valve
7 floor
8 O$_2$ pressure cylinder
9 O$_2$ supply control panel
10 O$_2$ high pressure gauge
11 reducer valve
12 O$_2$ low-pressure gauge
13 O$_2$ flowmeter
14 O$_2$ supply valve
15 excrement disposal tank

Animal Experiment Chambers for Studies of Liquid Breathing

It will certainly be a long time before *Homo sapiens* become *Homo aquaticus,* and even the desirability of this is not definite: suffice it to say that if experimental chambers for this type of work are required a suitable design is shown in Fig. 12.12. The chambers are normally designed for relatively low pressures and need several connections, not only for inlets and outlets but also for measuring such parameters as EEG, ECG etc. As it is necessary to have a full view of the animal under test, care must be taken to position and fix it without interference from recording connections. When larger animals, such as dogs, are used, it is easier to modify walk-in compression chambers. The liquid tank is positioned in the centre of the chamber and a hoist is fitted when heavier animals are involved. To avoid the chance of oxygen poisoning for those monitoring the experiment, a transparent

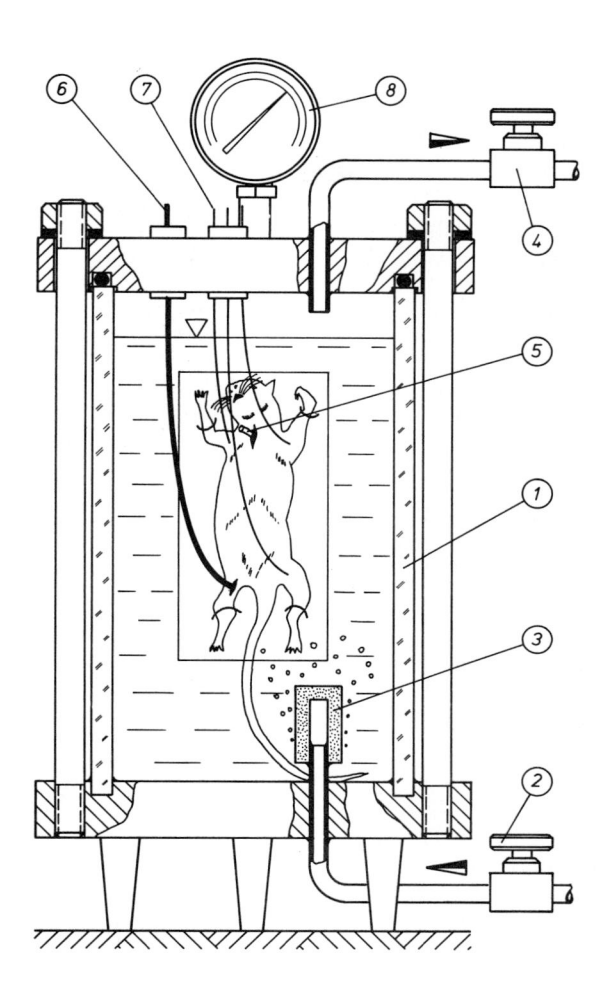

Fig. 12.12. Animal experiment chamber for liquid breathing studies on small animals.

1 Plexiglass cylinder
2 inlet valve
3 oxygen diffuser
4 outlet valve
5 tracheotomy
6 arterial meter
7 ECG leads
8 chamber pressure gauge

flexible plastic cover can be placed over the liquid container to prevent oxygen diffusion.

Design of Equipment and Material Test Chambers

Equipment and material testing chambers do not require life-support systems but the advanced type, as opposed to the pure 'pressure pot', have facilities to vary the temperature and salinity as well as to provide pulsating pressures. From the many types available a few examples are given here.

Small Equipment and Material Test Chambers for Low Operating Pressures

The chamber shown in Fig. 12.13 was developed for testing of equipment such as under-water lights, depth gauges, decompressiometers, under-water photography equipment etc. This unit is built for test pressures of 10, 20 and 30 bars. Its inner diameter is 400 mm and its

Fig. 12.13. Small equipment and material test chamber for low operating pressures (Haux Life Support).

inner height 600 mm. The bayonet closure allows it to be filled easily and a large window in the centre allows good vision into the chamber, which is illuminated by an internal lamp. The pressure is controlled by two check-valves and a precision pressure gauge.

Small Equipment and Material Test Chambers for Medium Operating Pressures

In Fig. 12.14 is shown a chamber for the development testing of diving equipment and other equipment for use under water. The pressure capability must be at least equivalent to the maximum operating depth of the equipment, both to provide the most stringent conditions as well as to produce performance data. This chamber is designed for a working pressure of 100 bar. One of the distinguishing features of this design is the many blind connections, providing plenty of space for manipulator rods, gas penetrators and recording

Fig. 12.14. Compression chamber for equipment and material testing (Submarine Products Ltd).

Fig. 12.15. Compression chamber on a swivel for testing the magnetic properties of materials.

lines of all types. It is important to provide good illumination and viewing facilities for observing the test sample. A door with a U-ring lock is fitted, which allows frequent changes to be quickly undertaken with sequential testing.

Fig. 12.15 shows another example of this type which is designed to test the magnetic behaviour of hollow bodies under pressure. The chamber itself is required to have neutral magnetic properties and

Fig. 12.16. Compression chamber laboratory with super-high-pressure chamber (1200 bar operating pressure) at the University of Kiel.

consequently very careful selection of materials is necessary. Measurements are taken under static conditions but pressure is varied between 0 and 30 bar with a frequency of 0–50 Hz. The chamber can be filled with different liquids and an additional hydraulic system is required for pulsing. Inductive pressure sensors are used, recording on to an oscilloscope or plotter, as mechanical pressure gauges cannot record this information without distortion. The chamber is mounted on a swivel to vary the orientation.

Other specialized chambers have also been designed, such as those with radiographic installations with special windows for filming. Another type was designed to test the acoustic properties of diving equipment. For this work an artificial lung is placed in a small chamber and made to breathe under ambient pressure, the acoustic output being measured by a hydrophone mounted at a distance. All systems are mounted on a solid tubular frame to permit easy handling and prevent damage by rough handling. These are only a few examples of the wide spectrum of types available.

Small Equipment and Material Test Chambers for Maximum Operating Pressures

Oceanographical Instruments for measuring temperature, salinity,

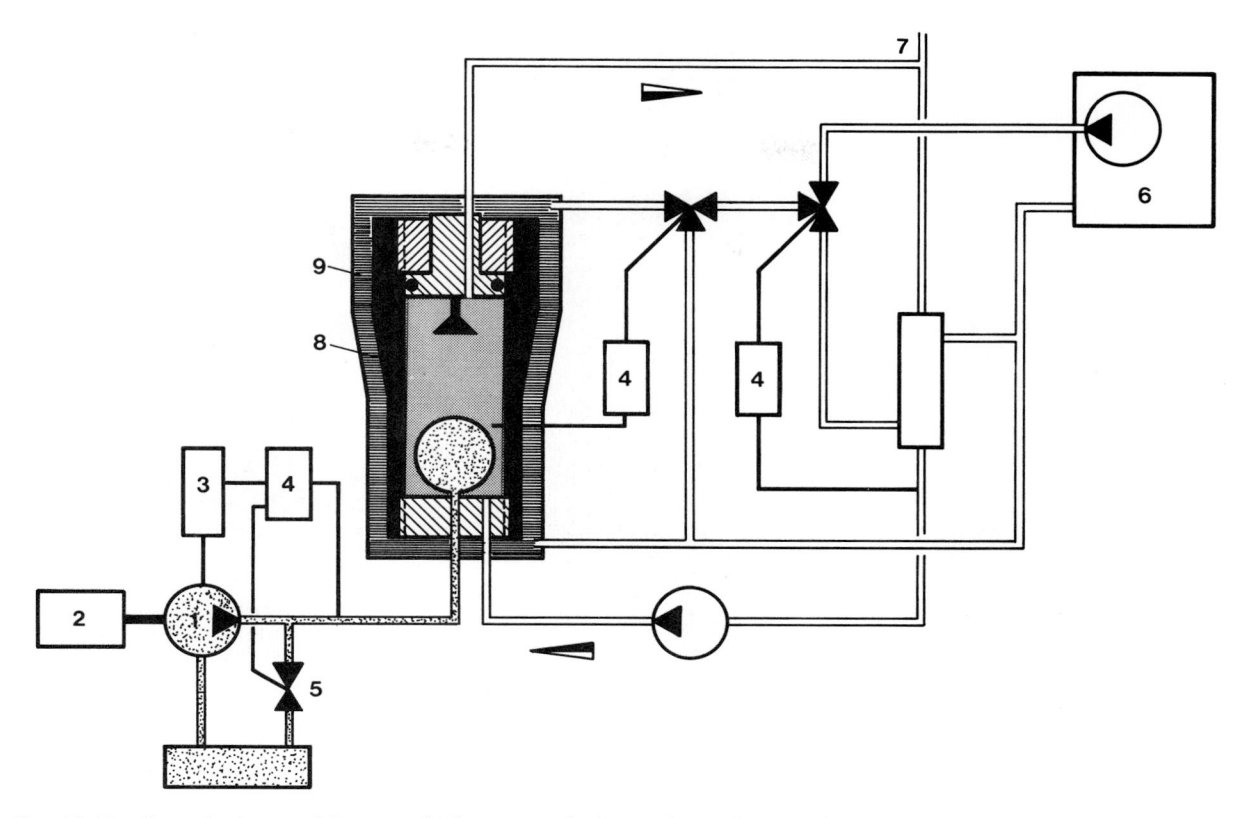

Fig. 12.17. General scheme of the super-high-pressure facility at the Ateliers et Chantiers de Bretagne.

1 compressor
2 electric motor
3 servo-motor
4 regulator
5 relief valve
6 refrigerator
7 filling and gas removal
8 pressure vessel
9 insulation

pH values and currents are often required to work at extreme depth and therefore pressure. Amongst other equipment shown in Fig. 12.16 is an elongated chamber designed to work at 1200 bar. It has an internal diameter of 400 mm and unobstructed internal length of 2000 mm. The chamber, which is filled with sea water for test purposes, is plated with a high-grade titanium alloy as a corrosion protection. It is used for testing deep ocean measuring probes. The chamber is locked with a piston-like piece of stainless steel, water-tight integrity is maintained with a radial O-ring and the longitudinal stress is restrained by ring segments fitting into grooves in the cylinder wall. An hydraulic cylinder, which is hinged to a swivelling eye, guides the hatch into position. The locking mechanism can be swung away to provide unobstructed loading of the chamber. Measurement data are taken from the chamber via electrical penetrators moulded in glass and passing through the lock. A number of hydraulic pumps with extensive controls provide pressurization.

Fig. 12.18. Positioning the locking piston into the super-high-pressure vessel.

Large Equipment Test Chamber for the Simulation of 10 000 m Water Depth

A test facility of outstanding technical interest has been working since January 1976 at the Ateliers and Chantiers de Bretagne. The chamber has an internal diameter of 1000 mm and a clear internal length of 2000 mm and can be pressurized to 1000 bar. According to information received the main purpose of this system is:

1. Analysis of stresses in housing subjected to external pressure.
2. Testing of strengths down to implosion.
3. Functional tests under simulated pressure and temperature conditions of mechanical, hydraulic and electric equipment for use at great depths.
4. Testing of components, connectors and electronic components.
5. Study of the behaviour of materials under hydrostatic pressure (syntactic foam, concrete etc.).
6. Study of sensors and deep-sea nuclear reactor control systems under extreme pressures.

The specific advantages of the facility which should be emphasized are:

1. Large available volume.
2. Automatic control of pressure cycles.
3. System for cooling of water filling.
4. Large number of electric and hydraulic penetrators.
5. Filling of the chamber with fresh or sea water.

Pressure and temperature stability have a tolerance of within 1–2%. Fig. 12.17 gives a schematic layout of the system while the position of the locking piston is shown in Fig. 12.18. Three equidistant pillars are mounted on the vessel's wall and serve as guides. The sawtooth type segments which hold the enormous axial forces are rotated by three hydraulic cylinders mounted on the front end of the vessel. The seal between the vessel and the lock in the lower pressure ranges is made by two O-rings. For high pressure a loose ring is used which expands to make a metal-to-metal contact. Electrical data are extracted through 17 connectors with a total of 91 single connections. Four separate hydraulic connectors permit test samples to receive pressures up to 4000 bar. The control position is impressive, with pre-set electronic controls that permit automatic control of test runs and show the control parameters visually as a comprehensive display.

Appendix I

Research Centres, Institutes, Government Agencies and Training Schools

The following list gives some major centres working in the field of manned under-water engineering.

Admiralty Marine Technology Establishment
Physiological Laboratory, Deep Trials Unit, Fort Road, Alverstoke, Gosport, Hants PO12 2DU, UK

American Bureau of Shipping
45 Broad Street, New York, NY 10004, USA

Association of Diving Contractors
1799 Stumph Boulevard, Gretna, LA 70053, USA

Association of Offshore Diving Contractors
28/30 Little Russell Street, London WC1, UK

Batelle-Columbus Laboratories
Batelle Memorial Institute, 505 King Avenue, Columbus, Ohio 43201, USA

Bergen Diving School
Graydalsveien 255, PO Box 6, YRTE Laksevag, Norway

Bundeslehr- und Forschungsstätte der Deutschen Lebens-, Rettungs-Gesellschaft
Am Pichelsee 20–21, 1 Berlin 20, Germany

Centre d'Etudes et de Recherches Techniques Sous-Marine
DCAN, 8300 Toulon, France

Centre National Pour L'Exploration Des Oceanes
B.P. 337, Brest Cédex, France

Centro de Buceo de la Armada
La Algameca, Cartagena, Spain

Cetravim
Port de la Pointe Rouge, 13008 Marseille, France

Coastal School of Deep Sea Diving
320 29th Avenue, Oakland, Calif. 94601, USA

Comex Services
Traverse de la Soude, 13275 Marseille, Cedex 2, France

Commercial Diving Centre
272 South Fries Avenue, Wilmington, California, USA

Defence and Civil Institute of Environmental Medicine
1133 Sheppard Avenue West, PO Box 2000, Downsview, Ontario, Canada

Department of Energy, Petroleum Engineering Division
Thames House South, Millbank, London SW1, UK

Diving Medical Centre, Royal Netherlands Navy
Bassingracht 106, Den Halder, The Netherlands

Dive Med International
Gruehn Building, 3001 South Hanover Street, Baltimore, MD 21225, USA

Department of Hyperbaric Medicine, St Luke's Hospital,
2900 West Oklahoma Street, Milwaukee, Wis 53215, USA

Department of Naval Medicine
Karolinska Institutet, 104 01 Stockholm 60, Sweden

Department of Physiology, School of Medicine, State University of New York at Buffalo
Sherman Hall Annex, Room 7, State University of New York, Buffalo, New York 14214, USA

Det Norske Veritas
PO Box 300, N-1322 Høvik, Oslo, Norway

Deutsche Forschungs- und Versuchsanstalt für Luft- und Raumfahrt
Institut für Flugmedizin, Godesberger Allee 70, 5300 Bonn 2, Germany

Divers Institute of Technology
PO Box 70312, Seattle, WA 98107, USA

Divers Training Academy
RFD No. 1, Box 193-C, Fort Pierce, FL 33450, USA

Ecole de Plongée de la Marine Nationale
83 Saint Mandrier, France

European Diving Technology Committee, EEC
Commission of the European Economic Community, Brussels

F.G. Hall Laboratories for Environmental Research
Duke University Medical Center, PO Box 2904, Durham, North Carolina 27706, USA

Germanischer Lloyd
2000 Hamburg 36, Neuer Wall 86, West Germany

GKSS-Forschungszentrum Geesthacht GmbH
Postfach 1160, Reaktorstrasse 7–9, 2054 Geesthacht, Germany

Harbor Branch Foundation
Link Port, RR 1 Box 196, Fort Pierce, Florida 33450, USA

Health and Safety Executive
Baynard's House, 1 Chepstow Place, Westbourne Grove, London W2, UK

Institut Za Pomorsku Medicinu
Split, Yugoslavia

Institute of Bio-Medical Research
7205 Wrightsville Avenue, Wilmington, North Carolina 28401, USA

Institute of Environmental Medicine
University of Pennsylvania Medical Center, Philadelphia, Pennsylvania 19174, USA

Institute of Environmental and Offshore Medicine
University Medical Buildings, Forresterhill, Aberdeen, UK

Institute of Naval Medicine
Fort Road, Alverstoke, Gosport, Hants, UK

JAMSTEC Undersea Simulation Facility
Marine Science and Technology Centre, Yokosuka Centre, Japan

Japanese Maritime Self-Defence Forces
Underwater Medical Laboratory, 2-7-1 Nagase, Yokosuka-shi, Kanagawa-ken, Japan

Laboratory of Underwater Biomedicine
Ministry of Public Health, Leningradsky Chausse, 95-a, Moscow 125195, USSR

Lloyd's Register of Shipping
71 Fenchurch Street, London EC3, UK

London Hospital Medical College
Turner Street, London E1 2AD, UK

Makai Hyperbaric Facility
University of Hawaii, Waimanalo, Hawaii 96795, USA

Naval Coastal Systems Laboratory
Panama City, Florida 32401, USA

Naval Submarine Medical Research Laboratory
Building 141, Naval Submarine Base, New London, Groton, Connecticut 06340, USA

Occupational Safety and Health Administration
Department of Labour, Third Street and Constitution Avenue NW, Room N-3716, Washington DC 20210, USA

Övningstanken, Örl Bo
Marinens Dykerikontor, Marinstaben, Stockholm 100, Sweden

Plymouth Ocean Projects Ltd
Fort Bovisand, Plymouth, Devon PL9 0AB, UK

Prodive Ltd
Services Area, Falmouth Docks Oil Exploration Base, Falmouth, Cornwall, UK

Royal Engineers Diving School
Marchwood, Hampshire, UK

Royal Navy Diving School
Holmen, Copenhagen 16, Denmark

Royal Navy Salvage School
Rosyth, Fife, UK

Royal Netherlands Navy Diving Technical Center
Bassingracht, Den Helder, Netherlands

Royal Norwegian Council for Scientific and Industrial Research (NTNF)
Continental Shelf Committee, Sognsveien 72, Oslo 8, Norway

Royal Victoria Infirmary, Department of Surgery
Newcastle-upon-Tyne, UK

Santa Barbara Medical Foundation Clinic
PO Box 1200, Santa Barbara, Calif. 93102, USA

Schiffahrtmedizinisches Institut der Marine
Kopperspahler Allee 120, 2300 Kiel-Kronshagen, West Germany

Science Research Council
3–5 Charing Cross Road, London WC2, UK

Scripps Institute of Oceanography
La Jolla, California, USA

Society of Underwater Technology
1 Birdcage Walk, London SW1, UK

Southwest Research Institute
PO Box 28510, San Antonio, Texas 78284, USA

South African Navy Diving School
West Dockyard, Simonstown, Cape Province, Republic of South Africa

Subsea Oil Services SpA
W & D, Via Venezia 3, Zingonia, Bergamo, Italy

Superintendant of Diving
HMS Vernon, Portsmouth, UK

Taylor Diving and Salvage Co. Inc.
Rt 1, PO Box 795, Engineers Road, Belle Chasse, Louisiana, 77037, USA

Technisches Hochschule, Aachen
Lehrgebiet Grundlagen der Meerestechnik, Eilfschornsteinstrasse 18, 5100 Aachen, West Germany

Undersea Medical Society
9650 Rockville Pike, Bethesda, MD 20014, USA

Underwater Technology Laboratory
1038 G.G. Brown Building, North Campus, University of Michigan, Ann Arbor, Michigan 48104, USA

Underwater Training Centre
Inverlochy, Fort William, Invernesshire, UK

Underwater Engineering Group, CIRIA
6 Storey's Gate, London SW1, UK

University of Alaska Institute of Marine Science
Fairbanks, Alaska, USA

University Hospital, Zürich
Pressure Chamber Laboratory, Rämistrasse, Zürich, Switzerland

University of Miami, Rosenstal School of Marine and Atmospheric Science
Miami, Florida, USA

University of Southern California
Los Angeles, California, USA

University of New York, Department of Physiology
Buffalo, NY 14214, USA

University of Texas Health Sciences Center
PO Box 20708, Houston, Texas 77025, USA

United States Coast Guard
Department of Transport, Nassif Building, 400 Seventh Street West, Washington DC, 20590, USA

United States Department of Commerce, National Oceanic and Atmospheric Administration
11400 Rockville Pike, Rockville, MD 20852, USA

US Navy Coastal Systems Laboratory
Panama City, Florida 32407, USA

US Navy Experimental Diving Unit
Panama City, Florida 32407, USA

US Navy Medical Research Institute
National Naval Medical Centre, Bethesda, MD 20014, USA

US Navy School of Diving and Salvage
Washington Navy Yard, Washington DC 20374, USA

UVBI/DFS
Norwegian Naval Command Vestlandet, Haakonsvern, Bergen, Norway

Westinghouse Ocean Research & Engineering Center
PO Box 1488, Annapolis, Maryland 21404, USA

Wolfson Institute of Occupational Health
University of Dundee Medical School, Dundee, UK

Appendix II Selected Diving Contractors

Aqua Engineers Inc.
PO Box 4025, Christiansted, St. Croix, U.S. Virgin Islands 00820, USA

Aqua Marine B.B. Inc.
110 St. Georges, Cap de la Madeleine, Quebec, Canada G8T 5C9

Atlantic Diving Company, Inc.
Blackburn Industrial Center, Gloucester, MA 01930, USA

British Oceanics Ltd.
East Old Dock, Leith Dock, Leith, Edinburgh, UK

Brundrett Diving and Salvage Co.
1816 Industrial Boulevard, Harvey, LA 70058, USA

Caldwell's Diving Company Inc.
PO Box 401, Toms River, NJ 08753, USA

Can Dive Services Ltd.
250 East Esplanade, North Vancouver, British Columbia, Canada

CCC (Underwater Engineering) Ltd.
62 Brompton Road, London SW3 1BW, UK

C.G. Doris Services UK Ltd.
Unit 4E, Dyce Industrial Estate, Aberdeen, UK

Chinese Salvage Branch
Shanghai, People's Republic of China

Comex Services
Avenue de la Soude, B.P. 143, 13275 Marseille, Cedex 2, France

Comex-Houlder Diving Services Ltd.
Bucksburn House, Howes Road, Bucksburn, Aberdeen, UK

Continental Diving Service
PO Box 2484, Morgan City, LA 70380, USA

Crofton Diving Corporation
284 Huntsman Road, Norfolk, VA 23502, USA

Daspit Bros. Marine Divers Inc.
2013 Todd Drive, Poydras, LA 70085, USA

Deutsche Dampfschiffahrtsgesellschaft 'Hansa'
Schlachte 6, Bremen, Germany

Dive Scan Inc.
5400 Sunnywood Drive, Virginia Beach, VA 23455, USA

Dolphin Services
PO Box 63, 4056 Tanager, Stavangar, Norway

D & W Underwater Welding Services
PO Box 51, Slaughter, LA 70777, USA

EGA Inc.
Route 3, Box EGA, Glen Allen, VA 23060, USA

Energie BV
Sydwende 51, Drachten, Holland

Epic Divers Inc.
PO Box 174, Harvey, LA 70059, USA

Frolich Bros. Marine Divers Inc.
313 West Girod Street, Chalmette, LA 70043, USA

Global Divers & Contractors Inc.
PO Box 68, Maurice, LA 70555, USA

Hydrotech Systems Inc.
PO Box 40901, Houston, TX 77040, USA

Independent Divers Inc.
PO Box 23123, New Orleans, LA 70183, USA

Infabco Diving Services Ltd.
International Base, Greenwell Road, East Tullos, Aberdeen, UK

IUC, International Underwater Contractors
33–25 127th Street, Flushing, New York, USA; and Unit 1b, Woodlands Road, Kirkhill Industrial Estate, Kirkton Avenue, Dyce, Aberdeen, UK

Inter-Coastal Commercial Divers
5791 Tecumseh Road East, Windsor, Ontario, Canada N8T 1E1

International Oilfield Divers Inc.
PO Box 1016, Morgan City, LA 70380, USA

International Underwater Contractors
222 Fordham Street, City Island, NY 10464, USA

J & J Marine Diving Co. Inc.
6618 Overcrest, Pasadena, TX 77505, USA

Johnny Jones Marine Services Inc.
1110 Franklin Lane, Buffalo Grove, IL 60090, USA

K.D. Marine Ltd.
Pitmedden Road Industrial Estate, Kirkton Avenue, Dyce, Aberdeen, UK

Lawrie Diving and Marine Pty. Ltd.
1 Jenkin Street, Port Adelaide, South Australia, Australia

Louisiana South Divers
PO Drawer 490, Belle Chasse, LA 70037, USA

Marine Diving & Salvage
PO Box 800, Pearland, TX 77581, USA

Marine Services Commercial Diving
PO Box 258, Chula Vista, CA 92012, USA

Marine Services Unlimited Inc.
16044 33rd Avenue NE, Seattle, WA 98155, USA

Martech International
PO Box 4324, Houston, TX 77210, USA

McDermott International
Avenue Henri Matisse 16, B-1140 Brussels (Evere), Belgium; and PO Box 40, Kanaaldok B2, Kaai 602606, 203 Antwerp, Belgium

J. Ray McDermott Divers Division
PO Drawer 38, Harvey, LA 70059, USA

Midwest Marine Contracting Inc.
PO Box 335, Shawnee Mission, KS 66202, USA

Nautilus Sermares Ltd.
Merced 116-B, Santiago, Chile

New England Undersea Corporation
PO Box 242, Boothbay Harbor, ME 04538, USA

Oceaneering International Inc.
10575 Katy Freeway, Houston, Texas 77024, USA; 1st Floor, 54 Jermyn Street, London SW1Y 6NQ, UK; and Broadfold Road, Bridge of Don, Aberdeen, UK

Ocean Technical Services Ltd.
43–44 Albermarle Street, London W1X 3FE, UK

Ocean Technology Inc.
PO Drawer NN, Freeport, TX 77541, USA

Odd Berg
PO Box 233, 9001 Tromsø, Norway; and 35 Albert Street, Aberdeen AB1 7DZ, UK

Panoceanic Engineering Corporation
PO Box 61, Alpena, Mich. 49707, USA

Mike Parks Diving Corporation
8027 Liberty Road, Baltimore, MD 21207, USA

Petroleum Divers Inc.
PO Box 885, Harvey, LA 70059, USA

Povodi Vltavy
Závod Dolni Vltava, Rohanský Ostrov, Praha 8 Karlin, Czechoslovakia

Professional Diving Service
206 Hargrove Road East, Tuscaloosa, AL 35401, USA

Saipem
PO Box 4159, 20097 S. Donato Milanese, Milan, Italy

Santa Fe Diving Services Inc.
PO Box 2518, Houma, LA 70361, USA

Santa Fe (UK) Ltd.
Shed 4, Victoria Dock, Leith, Edinburgh EH6 7DZ, UK

Scandive
Lervigsveien 22, N-4000 Stavanger, Norway; and Howe Moss Place, Kirkhill Industrial Estate, Dyce, Aberdeen AB2 0ES, UK

Schaefer Diving Company Inc.
10707 Corporate Dr., Suite 106, Stafford, TX 77477, USA

Sea-Con Services Inc.
PO Box 9308, New Iberia, LA 70560, USA

Seadive Inc.
PO Drawer B, Patterson, LA 70392, USA

Seaway Diving A/S
Øvre Stokkavei 42, PO Box 740, 4001 Stavanger, Norway

S & H Diving Corporation
PO Box 2276, Morgan City, LA 70380, USA

Solus Ocean Systems Inc.
1441 Park 10 Boulevard, Houston, TX 77084, USA; and Abbotswell Road, Aberdeen AB1 4AD, UK

Star Offshore Services Ltd.
Princewall House, 50 Huntly Street, Aberdeen, UK

Submarine Engineering Associates
504 31st Street, Newport Beach, CA 92660, USA

Sub Ocean Services
Hertford Road, Waltham Cross, London E8 7RP, UK

Shiers Diving Contracts Ltd.
21 Millers Lane, Stanstead Abbotts, Ware, Herts SG12 8AF, UK

Sokullu-Sezen Salvage Company
Kuyulubostan Sok. 54/3, Tesvikiye, Istanbul, Turkey

Sub Sea International Inc.
PO Box 61780, New Orleans, LA 70160, USA; and Tyseal Base, Craigshaw Crescent, West Tullos, Aberdeen, UK

Sub Sea Oil Services SpA
Via Venezia 3, Zingonia, Bergamo, Italy

Sylvester Underseas Inspection
900 Hingham Street, Rockland, MA 02370, USA

Taylor Diving & Salvage Co. Inc.
Route 1, Box 795, Belle Chasse, LA 70037, USA

Taylor Diving UK Ltd.
c/o Wharton Williams Ltd, Farburn Industrial Estate, Dyce, Aberdeen, UK

Tecnicas Marinas C.A.
Calle Rendon, No. 156, Cumana, Estado Sucre, Venezuela

Thalassa Offshore (Scotland) Ltd.
Kirkhill Industrial Estate, Mains of Kirkhill, Dyce, Aberdeen, UK

Underwater Completion Team
PO Box 383, New Iberia, LA 70560, USA

V/O Sovsudopodyom
(Salvage, Towage and Dredging Corp.) USSR Ministry of Merchant Marine, 1/4 Zhdanov str., Moscow 103759, USSR

Walker Diving Contractors Inc.
107 Drivers Lane, Laurel Springs, NJ 08021, USA

Wharton Williams Ltd.
Farburn Industrial Estate, Dyce, Aberdeen, UK

Wiswell Inc.
3280 Post Road, Southport, CT 06490, USA

Appendix III Equipment Manufacturers

The following list gives only some of the many equipment manufacturers involved with decompression chambers, deep diving systems, hyperbaric diving simulators, atmospheric diving suits and submersibles.

Alfred Paulsen AS
Stavanger, Norway (decompression chambers and deep diving systems)

Aqua Logistics (International) Ltd.
Neills Road, Bold, St Helens, Merseyside WA9 4TA, UK (decompression chambers, diving simulators and deep diving systems)

Barry Henry Cooke Ltd.
West North Street, Aberdeen, UK (decompression chambers, deep diving systems, diving simulators)

Bruker-Meerestechnik GmbH
am Silberstreifen, 7512 Rheinstetten/Karlsruhe, Germany (submersibles and submarines)

C.G. Doris
83/85 bd Vincent-Auriol, 75640 Paris, Cedex 13, France (decompression chambers and deep diving systems)

Comex Industries
287 Ch. de la Madrague Ville, BP 49, 13314 Marseille, Cedex 2, France (deep diving systems, observation, lockout and rescue submersibles, diving simulators, hyperbaric centers, design and engineering)

Dixie Manufacturing Co.
1501 West Patapsco Avenue, Baltimore, Md 21230, USA (decompression chambers, deep diving systems and hyperbaric centers)

Drass Hyperbaric Technology
Via Venezia 9, 24040 Zingonia (BG), Italy (decompression chambers, diving bells, deep diving systems and diving simulators)

Drägerwerk AG
Werk Druckkammertechnik, Auf dem Baggersand 17, 2400 Lübeck-Travemünde, Germany (decompression chambers, deep diving systems, diving simulators)

Galeazzi, Ditta Roberto
PO Box 378, 19100 La Spezia, Italy (decompression chambers, deep diving systems, diving simulators)

Hannes Keller AG
im Boden 3, 8172 Niederglatt, Switzerland (deep diving systems, decompression chambers, cryogenic helium purifier)

Haux-Life-Support GmbH
Vogesenstrasse 42a, 7517 Waldbronn, Germany (decompression chambers, deep diving systems, diving simulators, work submersibles and handling systems)

Hunting Oilfield Services Ltd.
Main Cross Road, Great Yarmouth, Norfolk, UK (decompression chambers and deep diving systems)

Ingenieurkontor Lübeck
Niels-Bohr-Ring 5, PO Box 1690, 2400 Lübeck, Germany (submarines)

International Submarine Engineering Inc.
2601 Murray Street, Port Moody, British Columbia, Canada (one-atmosphere diving systems)

Marine Dynamics Corporation
320 East D. Street, Wilmington, CA 90744 (decompression chambers, deep diving systems)

Møllerodden A.S.
PO Box 212, 5501 Haugesund, Norway (decompression chambers and deep diving systems)

Normalair Garrett Ltd.
Yeovil, Somerset, UK (powered one-atmosphere diving suit)

OSEL Group
Boundary Road, Harfreys Industrial Estate, Great Yarmouth, Norfolk, UK (one-man submersibles)

Pacific Coast Welding and Machine Inc.
2330 Cleveland Avenue, National City, CA 92050, USA (decompression chambers)

Perry Ocean Engineering
275 West 10th Street, PO Box 10297, Riviera Beach, Florida 33404, USA (decompression chambers, deep diving systems, diving simulators and submersibles)

Renau International Inc.
11505 Todd Road, Houston, Texas 77055, USA (deep diving systems and winches)

Seaforth Maritime Ltd.
West North Street, Aberdeen AB9 2TD, UK (deep diving systems, decompression chambers, diving simulators)

Siebe Gorman & Co. Ltd.
Avondale Way, Cwmbran, Gwent, UK (decompression chambers and deep diving systems)

Slingsby Engineering Ltd.
Kirbymoorside, York YO6 6EZ, UK (submersibles, one-man atmospheric systems)

South West Research Institute
PO Drawer 28510, San Antonio, TX 78284, USA (deep diving systems, diving simulators)

Underwater and Marine Equipment Ltd.
18 Farnborough Road, Farnborough, Hants GU14 6BA, UK (atmospheric diving suits)

Appendix IV
Scientific and Technical Journals, Newsletters and Trade Magazines

Aquanaut
U.H. Dillier-Verlag, Ölbergstrasse 18, CH-9500 Wil SG

Aquatica
Internationale Revue für Unterwassersport und Forschung, Rino Gamba, Lausanne, Switzerland

Der Taucher
Jahr-Verlag KG, Burchardstrasse 14, 2000 Hamburg 1, Germany

Diver
British Subaqua Club, 70 Brompton Road, London SW3, UK

Dräger Informationen aus der Druckkammertechnik
Drägerwerk A.G., Werk Druckkammertechnik, Auf dem Baggersand 17, 2400 Lübeck-Travemünde 1, Germany

International Underwater Systems Design (IUSD)
USD Publishing Ltd, 332 St John Street, London EC1, UK

Journal of Ocean Technology
Marine Technology Society, 1030 15th Street North West, Washington, DC 20005, USA

Journal of the Society for Underwater Technology (SUT)
1 Birdcage Walk, London SW1H 9JJ, UK

Meerestechnik (MT)
Organ des Deutschen Komitees für Meeresforschung und Meerestechnik (DKMM) Verein Deutscher Ingenieure, c/o VDI-Verlag GmbH, Düsseldorf, Germany

Mondo Sommerso
Etas Compass, Milan, Italy

MTS Memo
Marine Technology Society, 1730 M Street NW, Washington DC 20036, USA

North Sea Letter and European Offshore News
The Financial Times Business Information Service Ltd, Braeken House, 10 Cannon Street, London EC4S 4BY, UK

North Sea Observer (Journal for North Sea Activities)
J.P. Petersen, PO Box 235, Skoyen, Oslo 2, Norway

Noroil
Noroil Publishing House Ltd, PO Box 480, Hillevågsvn 17, 4001 Stavanger, Norway

Norwegian Oil Review
S.E. Haugan, Norwegian Information Publisher A/S, Kongensgt 6, Oslo 1, Norway

Océans
Société Océans, 4 rue Luce, La Pointe Rouge, 13008 Marseille, France

Ocean Industry (Engineering, Construction, Operations)
Gulf Publishing Company, 3301 Allen Parkway, Houston, Texas 77019, USA

Oceanology: The Weekly of Ocean Technology
1001 Vermont Avenue North-West, Washington DC 20005, USA

Offshore Engineer
Thomas Telford Ltd, Telford House, PO Box 101, 26/34 Old Street, London EC1P 1JH, UK

Offshore
The Penn Well Publishing Company, 1421 South Sheridan Road, Tulsa, Oklahoma 74101, USA

Offshore Research Focus
CIRIA, 6 Storey's Gate, London SW1P 3AU, UK

Offshore Services and Technology
Kingston Publications Ltd, Rowe House, 55/59 Fife Road, Kingston-upon-Thames, Surrey, UK

Ozean + Technik (Informationsdienst für Meerestechnik und Meereswirtschaft)
Handelsblatt GmbH, Kreuzstrasse 21, 4000 Düsseldorf 1, Germany

Petroleum Review
Institute of Petroleum, 61 Cavendish Street, London W1M 8AR, UK

Plongées
Société Francaise d'Edition et de Presse, Paris, France

Poseidon
Militärverlag der Deutschen Demokratischen Republik (VEB), Berlin, East Germany

Pressure
Undersea Medical Society Inc., 9650 Rockville Pike, Bethesda, Maryland 20014, USA

Scanshore
Aas & Wahl Forlag A/S, Sørkedasvein 10A, Oslo 2, Norway

Sea Technology
Compass Publications Inc., Suite 1000, 1117 North 19th Street, Arlington, Va. 22209, USA

Skin Diver Magazine
Petersen Publishing Company, 8490 Sunset Boulevard, Los Angeles, California 90069, USA

Sous Marine
Jean Albert Foëx, Paris, France

Sporttaucher
Verband Deutscher Sporttaucher, Verlag Schmidt-Römhild, Mengstrasse 16, 2400 Lübeck 1, Germany

Submarin
Heering Verlag GmbH, Ortlerstrasse 8, 8 München 70, Germany

The Oilman
Maclean-Hunter Ltd., 30 Old Burlington Street, London W1X 2AE, UK

Undersea Technology
Compass Publications Inc., 617 Lynn Building, 1111 North 19th Street, Arlington, Va. 22209, USA

Appendix V Bibliography

Aerospace Technologie Division (1968) *Soviet Naval Medicine and Underwater Physiology* ATD Report 67–7. Washington, D.C.: Aerospace Technical Division, Library of Congress.
Alnor, P.C., Herget, A. & Seusing, J. (1964) *Drucklufterkrankungen*. Munich: J. Ambr. Barth.
Bennett, P.B. & Elliot, D.H. (1975) *The Physiology and Medicine of Diving and Compressed Air Work,* 2nd ed. London: Baillière Tindall.
Berrill, N.J. (1966) *The Life of the Ocean*. New York: McGraw-Hill.
Boerema, I. (1964) *Clinical Application of Hyperbaric Oxygen*. Amsterdam: Elsevier.
Bond, G.F. (1964) *Sealab I Chronicle*. US Navy Medical Corps.
Bond, G.F. (1965) *Sealab II Chronicle*. US Navy Medical Corps.
Brady, E.M. (1960) *Marine Salvage Operation*. Cambridge, Md.: Cornell Maritime Press.
Brohult, S., Oldenburg, I. (1970) *Havsforskning i Dag*. Stockholm: Sveriges Radios.
Bühlmann, A. (1961) *Der Weg in die Tiefe*. Documenta Geigy, Bulletin 1–5. Basel: Geigy.
Bulenkow, S.Y. (1968) *Manual of Scuba Diving*. Moscow: Spravochnik Ploutsa Podvodnika.
Busby, R.F. (1976) *Manned Submersibles*. Office of the Oceanographer of the US Navy.
Cassel, B. (1967) *Havet Dykaren Fynden*. Stockholm: P.A. Norstedt u. Söners.
Cayford, I.E. (1966) *Underwater Work*. Cambridge, Md.: Cornell Maritime Press.
Coker, R.E. (1966) *Das Meer—Der Grösste Lebensraum*. Hamburg and Berlin: Paul Parey.
Committee on Hyperbaric Oxygenation (1966) *Fundamentals of Hyperbaric Medicine*, Publication No. 1298. Washington, DC: National Academy of Sciences.
Cousteau, J.-Y. & Dugan, J. (1963) *The Living Sea*. New York: Harper and Row.
Cousteau, J.-Y. (1953) *The Silent World*. New York: Harper and Row.
Davis, R.H. (1962) *Deep Diving and Submarine Operations*. London: Saint Catherine Press.
Dietrich, G. (1970) *Erforschung des Meeres*. Frankfurt: Umschau.
Dugan, J. (1956) *Man Under the Sea*. New York: Harper and Row.
Ebner, H. (1969) *Konstruktive Probleme der Ozeanographischen Forschung*. Cologne: Westdeutscher.
Ehm, O.F. & Seemann, K. (1965) *Sicher Tauchen*. Rüschlikon: Albert-Müller.
ETA Offshore Seminars (1976) *The Technology of Offshore Drilling, Completion and Production*. Tulsa: Petroleum Publishing.
Fock, H. (1968) *Marinekleinkampfmittel*. Munich: I.F. Lehmanns.
Foëx, J.A. (1964) *Histoire Sous-Marine Des Hommes*. Paris: Robert Lafont.
Fontanesi, S. & Moretti, G. (1969) *Techniche, Sistemi e Mezzi di Immersione Profonda Rassegna Panoramica Della Loro Evoluzione*. Luglio: Annali di Medicina Navale.
Freihen, W. (1970) *Tauchen*. Wiesbaden: Falken-Verlag Erich Sicker.
Gabler, U. (1964) *Unterseebootsbau*. Darmstadt: Wehr und Wissen.
Gabler, U. (1978) *U-Bootbau*. Koblenz and Bonn: Wehr und Wissen.
Geyer, S. & de Haas, W. (1965) *Tauchschulung-Tauchtraining*. Rüschlikon: Albert-Müller.
Geyer, R.A. (1977) *Submersibles and Their Use in Oceanography and Ocean Engineering*. Amsterdam: Elsevier.
Gierschner, N. (1980) *Tauchboote*. Transpress VEB Verlag für Verkehrswesen.
Goodfellow, R. (1977) *Underwater Engineering*. Tulsa: Petroleum Publishing.
Gosović (1971) *Ronjenje u Sigurnosti*. Split: Institut za Pomorsku Medicinu.
Halstead, B.W. (1965) *Dangerous Marine Animals*. Cambridge, Md.: Cornell Maritime Press.
Hass, H. (1973) *Welt unter Wasser*. Vienna: Fritz Molden.
Haux, G. (1969) *Tauchtechnik I*. Berlin: Springer.
Haux, G. (1970) *Tauchtechnik II*. Berlin: Springer.
Haux, G. (1979) *Tauchtechnik*. Izdatelstvo Sudostroenie.
Myers, J.J., Holm, C.H. & McAllister, R.F. (1969) *Handbook of Ocean and Underwater Engineering*. New York: McGraw-Hill.

Idyll, C.P. (1969) *Exploring the Ocean World*. New York: Thomas Y. Crowell.
Kenny, J.E. (1972) *The Business of Diving*. Houston: Gulf Publishing.
Kenyou, L. & de Haas, W. (1966) *Tauch mit!* Rüschlikon: Albert-Müller.
Kurowski, F. (1970) *Unsere Zukunft das Meer*. Karl Ueberreuter.
Kurowski, F. (1974) *In die Tiefen der Meere*. Würzburg: Arena-Verlag Georg Popp.
Kurze, G. (1973) *Zukunft Weltmeer*. Leipzig: VEB Fachbuch.
Lambertsen, C.J. (1967) *Underwater Physiology, Proceedings of the Third Symposium on Underwater Physiology, Washington*. Baltimore: Williams and Wilkins.
Landois-Rosemann (1960) *Lehrbuch der Physiologie des Menschen*. Munich and Berlin: Urban & Schwarzenberg.
Larson, H.E. (1959) *A History of Self-Contained Diving and Underwater Swimming*. Washington, D.C.: National Academy of Sciences.
Lerris, O. (1969) *Teori for Sportsdykkere*. Nordborg: C. Lerris.
Lippens, P. (1973) *Station Helgoland*. Rüschlikon: Albert-Müller.
Loftas, T. (1970) *Letztes Neuland—die Ozeane*. Frankfurt: Suhrkamp.
Marfeld, A.F. (1972) *Zukunft im Meer*. Berlin: Safari.
Marine Technology Society (1970) *Progress into the Sea*. Washington, D.C.
Marine-Nationale-GERS (1961) *La Plongée*. Paris: Arthaud.
Masubuchi, K. (1970) *Materials for Ocean Engineering*. Cambridge, Mass.: M.I.T. Press.
Mattes, W. (1964) *ABC des Tauchsports*. Stuttgart: Frank'sche Verlagsbuchhandlung.
McCallum, R.I. (1967) *Decompression of Compressed Air Workers in Civil Engineering*. Newcastle-upon-Tyne: Oriel.
Miles, S. (1976) *Underwater Medicine*. London: Staples Press.
Miscevic, D. (1971) *Osnovi Ronjenja*. Zagreb: Narodna Tehnika SR Hrvatske.
Moslener, C.D. (1962) *Tauchen mit Verstand*. Lübeck: Antäus.
Pauli, D.C. & Clapper, G.P. (1967) *An Experimental 45-Day Undersea Saturation Dive at 205 Feet*. Washington, D.C.: Naval Research Department of the Navy.
Penzias, W. & Goodman, M.W. (1973) *Man Beneath the Sea*. New York: Wiley Interscience.
Piccard, J. (1961) *Seven Miles Down*. New York: G.P. Putnam & Sons.
Piccard, J. (1972) *Tauchfahrt im Golfstrom*. F.A. Brockhaus.
Rebikoff, D. (1955) *Licht im Meer*. Hamburg: Barakudagesellschaft.
Rensch, H. (1969) *Tauchen*. East Berlin: Deutscher Militärverlag.
Rensch, H. (1970) *Tauchen, Handbuch für Sporttaucher*. East Berlin: Deutscher Militärverlag.
Rössler, E. (1975) *Geschichte des Deutschen Ubootbaus*. Munich: J.F. Lehmann.
Ross, F. (1970) *Undersea Vehicles and Habitats*. New York: Thomas Y. Crowell.
Schiffahrtmedizinisches Institut der Marine (1968) *Neue Wege des Tieftauchens und der Tiefseeforschung*.
Shilling, C.W., Werts, M.F., Schandelmeier, N.R. (1976) *The Underwater Handbook*. New York and London: Plenum.
Soule, G. (1968) *Undersea Frontiers*. New York: Rand McNally.
Stelzner, H. (1943) *Tauchertechnik*. Lübeck: Charles-Coleman.
Stelzner, H. (1962) *Physiologie des Tauchens*. Lübeck: Charles-Coleman.
Stenuit, R. (1966) *The Deepest Days*. New York: Coward-McCann.
Strauss, R.H. (1976) *Diving Medicine*. New York: Grune and Stratton.
Sweeney, J.B. (1970) *Oceanographic Submersibles*. New York: Crown.
Tailliez, P. (1954) *To Hidden Depths*. New York: E.P. Dutton.
Technical University (1969) *Meerestechnik, 1. Aufbauseminar Vorlesungsmanuskripte*. Berlin: Technical University.
The British Sub-Aqua Club (1976) *The British Sub-Aqua Club Diving Manual*. Eaton Publications.
Titcombe, R. (1973) *Handbook for Professional Divers*. London: Adlard Coles.
US Navy (1974) *Directory of World-wide, Shore-based Hyperbaric Chambers*. Supervisor of Diving, US Navy.
US Navy Bureau of Medicine and Surgery (1956) *Submarine Medicine Practice*. Washington, D.C.: US Navy.
US Navy Department (1974) *US Navy Diving Manual*. Washington, D.C.: US Navy.
Various (1970) *La Plongée Profonde*. Paris: Editions Technip.
Various (1971) *Prace Podwodne*. Gdansk: Wydawnictwo Morskie.
Various (1975) *Pomorska Medicina*. Beograd: Izdanje Mornorickog Glasnika.
Various (1975) *The NOAA Diving Manual*. National Oceanic and Atmospheric Administration.
Victor, H. (1972) *Meerestechnologie*. Munich: Carl Thiemig.
Witthöft, H.J. (1979) *Energie aus der Nordsee*. Herford: Koehler.
Woods, J.D. & Lythgoe, J.N. (1971) *Underwater Science*. Oxford: Oxford University Press.
Woudstra, F.G.A. (1967) *Tussen Zeesterren en Amphoras*. Amsterdam: A.J.G. Strengholt.
Zinkowski, N.B. (1971) *Commercial Oil-Field Diving*. Cambridge, Md.: Cornell Maritime Press.

Picture Sources

We are grateful to the following people or organizations for supplying illustrations which appear on the pages indicated.

Ateliers et Chantiers de Bretagne: 510

Berg, Odd: 135, 142, 157, 161

Bruker Meerestechnik: 311, 330, 334, 335, 348, 378

Comex Industries: 42, 46, 124, 125, 177, 436, 490, 492

DDG Hansa: 147

DFVLR: 74

Drass: 51, 134, 202

Drägerwerk: 3, 14, 26, 66, 67, 69, 73, 75, 78, 84, 87, 88, 92, 93, 95, 98, 99, 101, 102, 104, 121, 128, 129, 131, 138, 139, 143, 144, 170, 171, 174, 176, 180, 183, 184, 185, 186, 193, 197, 206, 208, 211, 214, 216, 219, 225, 226, 241, 247, 256, 260, 265, 266, 277, 278, 279, 281, 282, 283, 285, 289, 290, 291, 303, 423, 426, 428, 436, 437, 501, 508

Galeazzi: 44, 77, 127

Haux: 149, 154, 155, 162, 163, 175, 183, 191, 204, 215, 216, 220, 245, 251, 276, 432, 506

International Underwater Contractors: 231

Kinergetics: 428, 436

Makai Undersea Test Range: 246, 286, 301

NOAA Diving Manual: 242

Ocean Consult: 493

Oceaneering International: 401, 402

OSEL: 404, 406

Ray McDermott: 486, 488

Royal Navy: 55

Schenk, B.: 24, 53, 99

Saturation Systems Inc.: 427

Spanish Navy: 13

Submarine Products: 507

Sub Sea International: 149, 487

Sub Sea Oil Services: 12

Taylor Diving and Salvage: 48, 165, 481, 487

Umel: 401, 402

Vickers Slingsby: 405

Wagner, J.: 20, 21

Wharton Williams: 405

Index

Aachen, Technical University, 8, 16, 17, 34
Abandon ship procedure, 132, 231
Acrylic glass, 86, 187, 237, 243, 310
Acrylic screen, 8
Adaptors, 216
Adelaide, 299
Aegir under-water habitat, 245, 246, 253, 286, 302
   arrangement of rescue chambers, 268
   operation, 245
   plan of, 301
A-frame, 148, 149, 150
Air circulating system, 285
Air compressor, 90
Air diving with diving bell, 111
Air exhaust valve in hard hat, 453
Air filters, 90
Air injection into moonpool, 141
Air injector, 90
Air purification, 90
Air reserve valves, 449, 450
Alignment frame, 481, 486
Aluminaut, 389
Aluminium alloy, 69, 226, 402
Aluminium plates, 20
Ammonia, 413
Anchor
   bottom, 159, 190, 201
   guide-wire, 157, 160
   submersible, 345–9
   systems, 345
   weight, 345, 348
   winch, 201
Animal experiment chambers, 494–511
Anti-fouling paint, 253
Anti-suck valve, 476
Aquanauts, 240, 264
Arctic Seal, 122, 135, 157, 194, 432
Arctic Surveyor, 121, 154
Argentinian Navy, 41–2
Argonaut I, 381
Argyronete, 240, 248, 390
Armoured diving suits, 397
Arms, 379
Ateliers et Chantiers de Bretagne, 25, 509, 510
Atmospheric diving suit, 397
   launching gear, 403
   life-support, 401, 403, 404
   modern designs, 339, 400

Atmospheric diving suit (*continued*)
   tasks, 397, 407
   tools, 403
Auguste Piccard, 52, 381
Autonomous submarine, 381

Babcock design, 150, 151
Back pack, 449
Baffle tubes, 153
BAH1, 300
Bale-out bottle, 112, 476
Ballast and trim systems, 189, 243, 260, 338, 340
   atmospheric diving suit, 403
   solid, 341
   tanks, 338, 339, 382, 383
   submersible, 338–45
   submersible compression chamber, 189–91
   under-water habitat, 269
   weights, 342
Balloons, inflatable, 200
Band mask, 462
   open-circuit, 468
Baralime, 422
Bathyscope, 52
Batteries, 196
   submersible, 326
   under-water habitats, 253, 254, 259
Bayonet fittings, 184, 189, 213, 216, 225
Beaver Mk IV, 310, 331
Belos, 175
Ben Franklin, 52
Bennett, P., 40
BIBS, 166, 287
Bleed-off valve, 74
Blower, 284, 423, 424, 431
Blowing down mating dome, 359
Body metabolism, 316
Boiler steel, 276
Bolted lock, 219
Bond, G., 22, 292
Borovikov, P.A., 253
Bottom anchor, 159, 190, 201
Bottom fix, 239
Bottom lock-out, 279
Bounce diving, 109, 120
   on air, 111

Bounce diving (*continued*)
   on mixed gas, 112
Bowdoin joint, 398
Breathing apparatus for divers, 438–79
Breathing connections, 445, 446
Breathing resistance, 441
Bruker Meerestechnik, 375, 392
   Mermaid, 310, 311, 312, 330, 339, 344, 375, 378
   Subcat, 392, 393
Buffalo system, 5, 8, 9, 18, 36–7, 50
   barriers, 18
   principle for lock-out procedure, 279
Bunks, 417
   retractable, 67
Buoys, supply, 250, 251, 253
Buoyancy control, *see* Ballast and trim systems
Bushnell, D., 381
Bühlmann, A., 23, 24, 33, 52

Cachalot deep diving system, 35
Cages, protective, 5, 155, 280
Caisson, 481
Camell Laird, 222, 248
Canadian National Diving Research Facility, 49–50
Canadian Navy, 310
Cannon, B., 302
Capshell, 168, 169, 170
Capsule systems, 169, 355
Carbon dioxide,
   absorbents, 22, 228, 293, 422–6, 435
   in deck compression chambers, 94, 102
   for deep diving dress, 460
   for transportable recompression chambers, 229, 230
   in under-water habitat, 263
   with injector, 222
   exposure limits, 411
   partial pressure (P_{CO_2}), 226, 411
   physiological effects of, 411
   scrubbers in submersible, 367
   in under-water habitat, 283, 284
   see also Gas supply systems
Carbon monoxide, 413
Caribe, 298
Carpenter, S., 293

Carrier gas, 141
Catamaran designs, 241, 271
Caterpillar, 16
Centre of gravity, 343
Challenger, 56
Chariots, 45
Chemical test tubes, 286
Chernomor, 275, 299, 305
Chlorate candles, 420
Chouteau, Professor J., 502
Circling compressor, 478
Closed-circuit systems, 229, 472, 473
  breathing demand, 477
  diesel, 382
  gas consumption, 420
  mixed gas, 420
  for submersible, 363
Cold lights, 99
Comex Industries, Marseilles, 2, 17, 41, 45, 47, 57–58, 177, 312, 358, 437, 484, 490, 491
Commercial diving equipment, 408–79
Communication systems, 103, 114, 137, 418
  in deck compression chamber, 103–4
  in submersible, 324, 369, 370
  in submersible compression chamber, 196, 197
  in transportable compression chamber, 212
  in under-water habitat, 253, 287
Compensator bellows, 354
Compressed air, 326
  breathing apparatus, 438–51
  deck compression chamber, 69, 90
  deep diving systems, 141
  standard diving equipment, 456, 457, 458
  storage cylinders, 447
  systems in submersibles, 366, 367
  see also Gas supply systems
Compressor, 252
Connecting systems, *see* Mating systems
Constant mass regulator, 439
Constant tension device, 125, 163, 201
Construction habitats, 480
Contaminants, 413, 414
Continental Oil Company, 231
Continental plateau, 234
Control centre, layout of, 134, 135, 160
Control panel, 67
  deep diving system, 134–8
  deck decompression chamber, 67, 134, 171, 174
  deck transfer chamber, 137
  internal piping, 138

Control panel (*continued*)
  submersible compression chamber, 137
Core temperature, 412
Cork, 277
Cousteau, J.-Y., 239, 240, 243, 292, 293, 399
Crane transfer, 147–8, 232
Crown frame, 151
Cryogenic purification, 145

Dalton's law, 409
Dead man's handle, 338
Deck compression chambers, 65–104, 127–8
  air supply, 66, 71, 72, 89, 90
  carbon dioxide absorption, 102
  charging systems, 91
  combination, 76
  communication systems, 103–4
  components, 79
  compressed air system, 72, 89–92
  configurations, 118
  cooling, 100–2, 127
  dehumidification, 102
  design, 116, 127
  doors, 67, 79–86
  heating, 100–2
  life-support equipment, 71
  lighting, 98–100
  living accommodation, 104
  main compartment, 68, 71
  main dimensions, 126
  materials, 69–71
  medical lock, 87–9
  mobile, 65, 77–8, 93
  modular design, 75, 76, 130
  one-lock, 66–76
  operation with submersible, 319
  oxygen supply, 71, 72
  for saturation diving, 78–9
  silencers, 103
  stationary, 66
  and submersible, 319–22
  supply lock, 88
  transfer compartment, 71
  transfer of personnel, 70
  truck-mounted, 78
  two-lock, 76
  ventilation, 92–8
  window design, 86–7
Deck transfer chamber, 128–31
Decompression procedure, 20
Deep Diver, 308, 337
Deep diving dress, 452, 458
Deep diving systems, 106–71
  for bounce diving, 109, 120
  breathing equipment, 466, 467
  capsule systems, 169–71

Deep diving systems (*continued*)
  components, 108, 117, 123
  configurations, 118–23
  control room, 134–8
  deck compression chamber, 127–8
  deck transfer chamber, 128–30
  diving equipment, 167–9
  general layout, 109
  modular design, 109, 130
  observation dive, 109–11
  procedures, 109–16
  rescue chamber, 132–4
  sanitary installations, 129, 165–7
  for saturation diving, 109, 114–15, 120
  short-duration dives, 111–14
  submersible compression chamber, 124–7, 145–65
  work systems, 170, 390
Deep Ocean Pressure Facility, 27, 34
Deep Quest, 255, 389
Deep Subsea Working System, 390
Dehumidification, 102, 412–13
Delta Southern County Inc., 47
Denise, 292
Derrick crane, 147, 148
Det Norske Veritas, 37, 38, 87, 188
Deutsche Forschungs- und Versuchsanstalt für Luft- und Raumfahrt, 62–4, 74, 251
DHB Construction Ltd., 400
Diaphragm rings, 353, 354
Dick Evans Inc., 123
Diesel generator, 252
Dished head, 83
Diver(s)
  diet, 263, 415, 416
  entertainment, 419
  evacuation, 230
  falling distance, 454, 455
  heating systems, 372, 373, 428, 429
    in submersibles, 371, 376
  helmets, 457, 461
  living space, 24, 104, 286, 416–17
  lock-out submersibles, 380
  lock-out trunking, 341
  monitoring in submersibles, 369
  training, 12
Diving
  apparatus, 408
    for deep diving, 167
  bounce, 109, 111, 112, 120
  excursion, from under-water habitat, 265
  in pipelines, 205
  methods, 106, 107
  saturation, 78, 106, 107, 114, 115, 172
  simulator complexes, 9
  from submersible, 313, 316

Diving (*continued*)
   tower, 19, 20
Diving bells, *see* Submersible compression chambers
Diving suit, 375, 451, 475
   see also Atmospheric diving suit
Diving vessels, 120
Dixie manufacturing Co., 38
DLRG, Berlin, 18–21
Dome for dry transfer, 203, 356, 357
Doors
   circular, 84
   closures, 82
   cross-sections, 83
   for deck compression chamber, 67, 79–86
   design, 80, 81, 184
   dogs, 81
   double bottom hatch, 184
   double, 179, 186
   flat, 83
   frames, 84
   hinges, 81
   hydraulic drive, 13, 182, 186
   locking systems, 41, 57
   oval, 84
   one-way pressurization, 79, 80
   rectangular, 84
   sandwich designs, 83
   seals, 27, 85
   single, 179
   slide lock, 186
   space requirements, 179
   submersible, 353
   for two-way pressurization, 81, 82
   titanium alloy, 177
   for under-water habitats, 280
   for welding habitats, 489
Drainage of mating domes, 358, 359
Drass Spa, 33, 50–51, 133, 134
Drebel, Cornelius van, 381
Drillship, 153
Drum winches, 163
Dräger systems, 34, 41, 58, 59, 62, 120, 174, 212, 425, 429, 436, 498, 500
   flexible transportable recompression chamber, 208
   hyperbaric diving chamber, 2, 3, 16, 31–2
   Igloo, 241
   piggy-back transportable recompression chamber, 222
   Subcom, 119, 170, 171
   telescopic chamber, 222
   transportable recompression chamber modules, 225
DSRV 1 and *2*, 390
Duke University, USA, 39–41
DVLR, 74

Dynamic hydraulic tests, 26
Dynamic positioning, 153

Ebner, 34
Ecofloat, 200, 201, 278
Edelhab I, 304
Egypt, 398, 399
Electrical supply, *see* Power supply
Elk River, 275, 276
Emergency provisions
   air supply, 451
   breathing systems, 434, 437
   food and drink, 263
   gas supply, 261
   life-boat, 268
   life-support, 134
   resupply of stores, 263
   satellites, 269
   of under-water habitat, 258
EMS, Comex, Marseilles, 58
Energy, *see* Power supply
Entertainment for divers, 419
Epoxy resin, 200
Equipment test chambers, 494–501
Ergometer, 5
   frame, 36
Evacuation of divers, 133, 230
Evacuation of water in dry transfer systems, 358
Excrement removal lock in animal chambers, 502
Excursion diving from under-water habitat, 265
Exhaust valves in regulators, 443
Experiment chambers, 494–511
Extended circuit, 475

F.G. Hall Laboratory for Environmental Research, 39, 40
Fabric, 222
Falco, A., 292
Ferraro, I., 300
Fibreoptic lights, 99
Fire hazard, 96, 419
   control in under-water habitat, 269
   detection systems, 167
   fighting systems, 98, 166
   of oxygen, 141
   precautions, 67, 96
   suppressants, 166, 167
Flowmeter, 137, 212
Fluid joint, 398
FNRS 2 and *3*, 389
Food and drink, 415–16
   emergency supply, 263
   lock, 67, 87
   in animal chambers, 502
Force feed-back, 377

Frame rigging, 151
Free escape, 203
Freon, 375
Friedrich Heinke, 174
Fuel cells, 254, 382
Fulton, R., 381
Fust, 64

Gabler, 385, 387, 391
Galathee, 305
Galeazzi, 398
   hyperbaric diving simulator, 43, 45, 50
   transportable recompression chamber, 222
Gas bag, 145
Gas chromatograph, 138
Gas cylinders, 141
Gas mixtures, calculation of, 139, 463
Gas supply systems, 9, 140, 143, 420–38
   deck compression chamber, 137
   deep diving systems, 138–45
   to diver from submersible compression chamber, 471
   purification, 142
   self-mixing, 471, 472
   storage, 140, 145, 364
   for submersible, 324–6, 360–9
   see also Compressed air, Carbon dioxide *and* Oxygen
Gauges, precision, 137
Gebruder Sulzer, 52
General Corporation, 379
General Electric Co., 301
German Navy, 204
Germanischer Lloyd, 383
GKSS Research Centre, 59
Glass foam, 200
Glass-reinforced polyester resin, 200, 242, 277, 312, 402
Grab, 399
Grating, 9
Guidance systems, 159, 160
Guide cable, 152
Guide-wires, 151, 157, 160, 201
GUSI, 37, 59–62
Gusto winch, 159

Hahn and Clay, 56
Hammock, 222
Hand pump, 457
Handling systems
   diving bells, 145–64
   submersibles, 320, 321
Hangar for submersibles, 326, 327
Hansa, 147
Hard hat divers, 452

Harness for air scuba, 449
Hartmann, H., 300
Hatches, see Doors
Haux systems, 491, 492, 506
  Ecotransfer, 222
  Transcom 3, 220
Heat exchangers, 9, 101, 424, 434
Heat loss, 432
  of divers, 371
Heat pump, 375, 376
  in submersible, 372
Heating coil, 32
Heating systems, 100–2, 114, 284, 318, 428, 429, 431, 432
Heave compensator, 159, 160
Helgoland, 62, 64, 235, 243, 245, 251, 258, 259, 260, 261, 266, 267, 279, 281, 282, 289, 290, 291, 303
  emergency gas supply, 262
  supply buoy, 253
  transport, 247
  trim and ballast system, 272, 273
  umbilical, 247
Helicopter transport, 209, 218, 232
Heliox, 113
Helium, 325
  reclaim, 145
  storage, 142
  see also Gas supply systems
Helium unscrambler, 103, 198
Hemengers, 397
High-pressure connection, 445
High-pressure drain pump, 360
High-pressure water pump, 98
Hinged bolts, 189
Hoist wire, 151
Holokai, 246
Horton Maritime, 389
Hoses, 451
Hot-water systems, 138, 166
Humidification, 425
Hunuc, 304
Hyco, 310
Hydraulic cylinders, 131, 184
Hydraulic legs, 310
Hydraulic manipulator, 378
Hydraulic pulsing, 508
Hydraulic pumps, 26, 509
Hydraulic thruster, 172
Hydrocarbons, 413
Hydrogen, 413
Hydrolab, 253, 278, 308
Hydrospace Survey Vessel HSV-1, 306, 386
Hydrosphere, Comex, 57
Hydrostatic water pressure, effect of, 442
Hyperbaric diving simulators and pressure testing facilities, 1–64
  applications, 2, 28–31

Hyperbaric diving simulators and pressure testing facilities (*continued*)
  Argentine Navy, 41–3
  Buffalo system, 5, 8, 9, 18, 36–7, 50
  Canadian National Diving Research Facility, 49–50
  classification, 27–8
  Comex, 18, 57–8
  design configurations, 4–24
  DFLVR, 62–4
  DLRG, 18–21
  Dräger, 2, 3, 16, 31–2
  Drass, 33, 50–1
  Duke University, 39–41
  GUSI, 37, 59–62
  for high operating pressures, 15
  Iraqi Armed Forces, 41
  Italian Navy, 43–5
  Kantonhospital, Zürich, 23
  living chambers, 24
  locations, 28, 29
  large-volume, 17
  for maximum operating pressure, 16
  modular designs, 13
  Norwegian Under-water Institute, 37–8
  Ocean Simulation Facility, 56–7
  Royal Navy, UK, 2, 7, 54–6
  Spanish Navy, 13, 58–9
  spheres, 15
  standard designs, 10
  Sub Sea Oil Services, 32–3, 50
  Technical University, Aachen, 8, 16, 17, 34
  University Hospital, Zürich, 52–4
  US Navy, Panama City, 23
  Westinghouse Ocean Research, 34–6
Hyperbaric dry transfer with submersible, 361
  for maximum operating pressures, 16
Hyperbaric life boat, see Rescue chamber
Hyperbaric medical treatment centre, 209, 231
Hyperbaric welding, 483
Hyperthermia, 412, 428
Hypoxia, 409, 412

Igloo, 241
Igloo designs, 235, 241, 242
Ikhtiandr 66, 67 and *68*, 293, 298, 300
Infra-red heaters, 284
Infra-red scan equipment, 167
Ingenieurkontor Lübeck, 385
Injectors, 90, 222, 228, 441

Institute of Oceanology, Moscow, 4
Insulation, 371, 374, 412
Internal combustion engine for under-water habitat supply, 255
International Under-water Contractors, 231
Intervention capsules, 163
Iraqi Armed Forces, 41
Italian Navy, 43–5

Jarret, J., 400
JIM suits, 400, 401
Joint frame, 148

Kantonhospital, Zürich, 23–4
Karnola, 299
Kattenturm, 147, 158, 159
Keller, H., 23, 52
Keel-hauling, 125
Kitchen in under-water habitat, 289
Kitjesch, 293
Kockelbockel, 299
Kockums, Malmö, 45, 47
  General Purpose Submarine, 385, 386, 390, 391
Kokkinowrachos, Prof., 34
Kuhnke, 398
Kvaerner Brug, 37

L2, L3, L4 and L5, 312
La Chalupa, 240, 245, 246, 280, 304
Lake Lab, 304
Lake, S., 381
Leg designs for submersibles, 310, 348, 349, 350, 351
Lethbridge, J., 397
L-frame, 148, 150, 151
Life-support systems, 9, 15, 17, 47, 54, 65, 110, 191, 207, 225, 236, 408–79
  animal test chambers, 502, 503
  atmospheric diving suit, 401
  basic designs, 424
  calculation of gas mixtures, 463–6
  cooling, 433
  design factors, 408, 409, 419
  emergency breathing systems, 434
  external, 423, 432
  external-internal, 435
  integrated, 426
  layouts, 430, 433
  semi-external-internal, 434
  submarine, 383
  submersibles, 316, 361
  transportable recompression chambers, 226, 229
  under-water habitats, 249, 281–6

Life-support systems (*continued*)
    under-water igloo, 242
Lifting cable, 193
Lighting, 99–100, 418–9
Limb joint, 400, 401
Lindbergh Hammar, 423
Linear decompression, 137
Link, E.A., 292
Liquid breathing, 504
Liquid oxygen, 420
Lithium hydroxide, 422
Litton Industries Space Science Laboratory, 400
Live boating, 314
Living accommodation, 416–17
    hyperbaric diving simulators, 24
    under-water habitat, 286
    deck compression chamber, 104
Loudspeaker systems, 196, 198
LR 1, 336
Lusitania, 399

MacInnes, 243
Macrospheres, 200
Magnesium alloy, 399
Magnetic clutch, 425, 431
Magneto inductor, 197
Makai Undersea Test Range, 239, 245, 268
Malter 1 and *2*, 300
Man in Sea 1 and *2*, 292
Manipulators, 202, 307, 377, 378, 379, 388
Manometer outlay, 137
MANTIS, 389, 406
Mariana Trench, 52
Marine growths, 253
Material test chambers, 495, 505, 511
Mating systems, 73, 131, 179, 188–9, 209, 352, 479
Medical supply lock, 87, 88
Medusa 1 and *2*, 298, 299
Mercury, 344
Mermaid submersibles, 310, 311, 312, 330, 339, 344, 375, 378
Microballoons, 200
Mid-water inspection, 405
Moonpool systems, 153
    aeration, 141, 153
    angle, 153
    cursor, 153, 158, 159
    for submersible compression chamber, 146–60
    for submersible, 327
Motherships for submersibles, 327
Motion compensators, 158
Multi-layer construction, 27
Multiple joint, 150
Mute, 381

NASA, 301
National Oceanographic Atmosphere Administration, 240, 248, 305
    diving manual, 411
NATO, 216
Nautilus, 381
Neufeldt, 398
Neumann Eschweilter, 34
Nitrogen purging of battery pods, 259
No-decompression limit, 448
Noise level in chambers, 418, 419
Non-destructive testing, 483
Non-magnetic properties, 69, 73
Normalair Garrett, 475
North American Rockwell, 310
Northrop Corporation, 56
Norwegian Trench, 38
Norwegian Underwater Institute (NUI), 37–8
Novoindustria Acciaio, 50
Nozzle injector, 71
Nuclear energy for under-water habitat, 255

Observation chambers, 172, 203, 207
Observation dive, 109, 110
Observation slot, 32
Ocean Consult, 491, 492
Ocean Simulation Facility, Panama City, 18, 21, 56–7
Ocean Systems, 480
Oceaneering International Services Ltd., 403
Oceanlab, 240, 248, 305
Odd Berg, 157
Oktopus, 298
OMAS suit, 403, 405, 407
One-atmosphere diving suit, *see* Atmospheric diving suit
One-atmosphere pressure chambers for welding, 483, 484
Open-circuit systems, 229, 439
    air, 420
    for deep diving, 467
    gas consumption, 469
    in submersible, 362
    warm-water, 372
Open diving bell, 172, 202, 203, 204
Optical warning signals, 450
Oral–nasal masks, 67, 447
OSEL, 406
Overboard dumping systems, 166
Overboard handling of submersible compression chamber, 147–53
Oxyhelium storage, 142
Oxygen, 166, 325, 409, 463
    breathing systems, 95, 96, 436
    consumption, 410, 448, 455, 463, 464, 465, 466

Oxygen (*continued*)
    dumping systems, 96, 97
    exposure limits, 410
    meter, 427
    monitoring, 229
    partial pressure (P_{O_2}), 226, 404, 464
    poisoning, 409, 410
    storage, 141–2, 420
    supply systems, 420–2, 364–5, 475
    see also Gas supply systems

Parallelogram arm, 156
Parallelogram frame, 161
PC1202, *15* and *16*, 310, 311, 336, 338
Pekey, 397
Permon 2, *3* and *4*, 293, 298
Perress, J., 398, 399
Phillips, 397
Physalie, 58
Piccard, A., 23
Piccard, J., 52, 389
Pinger for submersible navigation, 322, 324
Pipe door-locking systems, 489
Pipeline operations, 48, 480–96
Piping for gas systems, 90, 142
Platform leg guide trolley, 161
Pneumofathometer, 137
Polyurethane foam, 200, 277
Power supply, 101
    distribution panel, 138
    submersible, 326, 327–30
    submersible compression chamber, 195–7
    under-water habitat, 253–6, 258–9
Powered drum, 163
Precontinent 1, *2* and *3*, 245, 292, 293
Pressure
    equal, 179
    external, 179
    gauges, 449, 450
    internal, 179
    sensors, 508
    testing facilities, large-scale, *see* Hyperbaric diving simulators and pressure testing facilities
Prinul, 253
Propellors, 328
Propulsion units, 111, 328
PRV-2, 311
Push-pull systems, 363, 364, 477, 478, 479
PX-15, 24, 52

Radial crane, 147
Radial davit, 148, 149
Radiotelephone buoy, 288
Radiographic unit, 20

Ray McDermott, 120, 480, 486
Reclaim, 56
Recuperator, 426, 431
Regulator, 439–44
Repair habitat, 480
Rescue bell, 204, 205
Rescue chamber, 38, 132–4, 232
   one-man, 266, 269
Riser tie-in, 480
Risk analysis, 258
Robin, 302
Robinsub 1, 300
Rocker arm, 157
Rotary unit, 184
Rotating hatch, 219
Roumania LS 1, 299
Royal Dutch Navy, 9, 11
Royal Navy, UK, 2, 7, 54–6, 398, 399
   hyperbaric diving simulator, 54, 55
Royal Norwegian Council for Scientific and Industrial Research, 38
Royal Swedish Navy, 45, 176
Rubber, 237
   -coated fabric, 276
   plating, 200
   strips, 278

Sadko 1 and *2*, 245, 293, 299
Sagittaire, 58
Sanitary installation, 129, 165, 288, 414, 416
   deep diving system, 127, 129, 165–7
   under-water habitat, 289
Saturation diving, 78, 106, 107, 114, 115, 172
Saturation Systems Inc., 37, 427
Sawtooth-type closure, 511
Schafstall, G., 62
Schenk, B., 52
Schiffko, 491, 492
Scrubber, 426
Scuba, 438–9
SDDE, 451, 452
SDL-1, 332
Seabed chamber, 314
Seabed vehicle, 248
Sealab 1, *2* and *3*, 243, 244, 245, 262, 267, 275, 280, 288, 292, 293, 301
Seashore 2, 151
Seatopia, 304
Seaway Falcon, 131, 155, 183
Self-mixing gas system, 471, 472
Semi-closed circuits, 229
   deep diving set, 467, 468, 469
   gas consumption, 470
   in submersible, 362
   umbilical-supplied mixed gas, 470

Semi-submersible, 152
Severyanka, 389
Sewage systems, 166, 289
   see also Sanitary systems
Shelf 1, 303
Shelf Diver, 308
Shell, 169
Shirt-sleeves environment, 484
Shock absorber, 153
Shower, 416
Shuttle valve, automatic, 451
Siebe, A., 399, 452
Signal system, 196, 198
Silencer, 90, 92, 103
Silica gel, 431
Silica glass, 187
Skadok, 152, 246
Skid for deck compression chamber, 68
Skirt for dry transfer, 356, 357
Slip rings, 163
SM 351 (URF), 312
Smith Mountain Dam, 35
Sodalime, 422
Sodasorb, 367
Sol 1, 310
Solus Ocean Systems Inc., 120
Sonar, 196, 385, 388
Sound-powered telephone, 32, 103, 197, 370
Space conditions, 417
Spacer sections, 403
Spanish Navy, Cartagena, 13, 58–9, 403
Spindle gear, 189
Spindle locking, 131
Sprinkler systems, 98
Sprut, 300
Stabilizing fins and tanks, 153
Stachiw, I., 187
Starfish House, 239, 293
Steel, 27, 237, 383
   stainless, 73
Stolt Nielsen, 183
Stretchers, 212, 216
Struthers Nuclear and Process Co., 36
Sub-Igloo, 242, 243, 304
Sub Sea International, 149, 189, 480, 487
Sub Sea Oil Services, 12, 32–3, 50
Subcat, 392, 393
Subcom, 119, 170, 171
Submarine, 240, 306, 381–96
   alignment frame, 387
   battery capacity, 383
   Bruker *Subcat*, 392–6
   buoyancy, 382
   core drilling, 388
   diesel-powered, 382
   escape gear, 2, 31, 32

Submarine (*continued*)
   Gabler, 385, 387, 391
   heavy lift capability, 389
   hull strength, 383
   Kockums, 385, 386, 390, 391
   life-support, 383–4
   manipulators, 388
   nuclear-powered, 381
   propulsion systems, 382
   remote operated vehicles, 388
   safety, 396
   saturation diving from, 387
   submersible carrier, 388
   sonar, 388
   tasks for, 385
   television facilities, 388
Submersible, 306–80
   anchoring system, 345–9
   ballast and trim systems, 338–45
   catamaran design, 241
   communication systems, 324
   deck compression chamber installations, 319–22
   diver heating, 371–6
   diver monitoring equipment, 369–71
   doors, 353
   effect of weather, 318
   gas systems, 324–6, 360–9
   hull configurations, 332–8
   hydraulic systems, 316, 331
   launching, 320, 321
   legs, 310, 348, 349
   life-support, 316–19
   manipulators, 307, 376–9
   mating systems, 353–60
   motherships, 326–7
   navigation, 322–4
   oxygen systems, 364, 366
   power supply, 326, 327–30
   pressure testing facilities, 25–6
   propulsion, 327–30
   ship maintenance, 326
   support requirements, 324
   testing, 27, 41
   transfer, 314, 315, 349–60, 395
   water supply, 326
Submersible compression chamber, 105, 110, 112, 124–7, 172–202
   ballast systems, 189–91
   buoyancy, 189, 200–1
   communication systems, 197–8
   component parts, 182–202
   control panel, 137
   doors, 182–6
   fendering systems, 193
   gas systems, 192–3, 198–200
   guide systems, 125, 160, 201
   handling, 145–64
   insulation, 200–1

Submersible compression chamber (*continued*)
  launching, 154
  manipulators, 202
  mating systems, 124, 145, 179–82, 188–9
  moonpool systems, 153–64
  observation, 202, 206–7
  one-compartment, 174–7
  open, 203–6
  oval, 177
  overboard handling systems, 147–53
  power supply, 195–7
  pressure strength, 179, 180
  roll-over, 124
  spherical, 176, 180
  tasks for, 202, 203
  transfer, 181, 183, 202
  two-compartment, 177–9
  umbilical cables, 193–4
  vertical cylinder, 174
  winch systems, 161–4
  windows, 187–8
Supply bank, 140
Supply buoy, 250, 251, 252, 253
Supply containers, 257, 258
Supply locks, 16, 87, 88, 371, 414, 415
SUPRA, 491–3
Surface-demand diving equipment, 451, 452
Surge zone, 153
Swedish Navy Diving Centre, 5, 45–6, 312
Syntactic foam, 374

Talisman, 124
Talk-back systems, 198
Tappet drive, 183
Tasker, 397
Taurus, 311, 334, 336
Taylor Diving and Salvage, 165, 397, 480, 481, 487
  hyperbaric diving simulator of, 47–9
Tektite 1 and *2*, 239, 245, 267, 279, 280, 301, 303
Telephone systems, 32, 103, 197, 235, 196, 370
Telescopic chambers, 210, 211
Telescopic frame, 160, 161
Television systems, 103, 130, 137, 167, 198, 207, 288, 369, 388
Temperature, 15, 412–13
Tension rod, 355
Tents for under-water use, 237, 243
Testing chambers, 24, 27, 494, 495, 508, 509
Therapeutic decompression, 141, 212
Thrusters, 172, 202, 403

Tie-rods, 189
Titan, 63, 64
Titanium, 83, 182, 286, 177, 209, 225, 231, 383, 509
Tools, under-water, 169, 379
Tours class submarine, 391
Toxic contaminants, 413
Trailer, 220
Training tower, 203
Transfer systems, 12, 32, 69, 70, 116, 121, 216
  flanges, 188
  lock, 16
  to submersible compression chambers, 124
  from transportable recompression chamber to deck compression chambers, 217
  of transportable recompression chamber, 212
  to under-water chamber, 355, 356, 357
  to under-water habitats, 274, 275
  under pressure, 124, 349, 353, 354, 355
Transponder, 322, 324
Transportable box for telescopic chamber, 211
Transportable recompression chambers, 208–33
  CO_2 absorption unit, 228, 230
  communication systems,
  component parts, 214
  connection to deck compression chamber, 219
  hatch systems, 219
  inflatable, 221, 222
  instrumentation, 212, 216
  life-support systems, 226–30
  mating systems, 209, 215
  medical lock, 225
  one-man, 209–222
  rigid, 213–19
  safety devices, 213
  semi-rigid, 210, 220, 225
  two-man, 223–6
  storage, 221
  telescopic, 210–13
  transfer, 212, 216, 226
  transportation, 209, 216, 231
  ventilation, 212, 213
Transquest, 390
Trec, 388
Trim systems, *see* Ballast and trim systems
Trimix, 113, 141
Trolleys, 152, 154, 160, 161
Trunk designs, 353, 355
  for under-water habitats, 280
Two-way pressure door, 81

U-ring clamp, 219
U-ring segment, 189
US Navy, 56, 148, 222, 243, 262, 310, 379, 390
Ultrasonics, 198
Umbilical cables, 112, 163, 193–4, 248, 252, 451
  coated, 194
  cutter, 194
  handling systems, 164
  sheathed, 164, 194
  taped, 164, 194
  for under-water habitat, 254
  winches, 163
UMEL, 400
Under-water habitats, 234–305, 480–93
  air conditioning, 285
  ballast and trim systems, 243, 269–75
  breathing systems, 287
  communication systems, 253, 287–8
  connection dome, 280, 281
  control panel, 265
  cylinder storage, 260
  cylindrical, 237
  doors, 280
  electrical systems, 290, 291
  ellipsoid, 238
  emergency supply, 258, 260, 261
  flooding tanks, 272
  food supply, 263, 290
  gas systems, 250, 261, 281–
  heating, 284
  humidity control, 285
  insulation, 277, 284
  kitchen, 289, 290
  life-support systems, 249, 281–92
  lock-out and trunking, 278, 279, 280
  logistic support, 249–58
  lowering procedures, 269, 271, 273
  mobile, 240–1, 247, 248
  modular hull, 238
  monitoring systems, 282
  observation facilities, 278
  personnel transfer, 274, 275, 276
  power supply, 253–6, 258–9
  rescue facilities, 263–9
  sanitary systems, 288–9
  satellites, 235
  sleeping space, 286
  sphere, 237, 243
  stock pot, 257
  supply systems, 250, 252, 256–7, 263
  water supply, 256, 260
  welding, repair and construction, 480–96
Under-water rescue vehicle, 47, 312
University Hospital, Zürich, 52–4

University of Kiel, 508
Upstream valve, 441

Vecto Offshore Inc., 160
Ventilation, 92, 93, 95
Vickers Slingsby, 405
Videotape recorder, 104
Visual communication in submersibles, 369
Voice communication in submersibles, 370
VOL 1, 310

Wasp suit, 403, 404, 407
Water atomizer, 426
Water bag, 260, 288
Water heater, 428
Water supply systems, 164, 326, 414
  level gauges, 340
  removal, 102
  tanks, 165
  for ballast, 340
Weldap system, 490, 491, 492
Welding chambers and habitats, 48, 315, 480–93
Westinghouse Ocean Research, 34–6

Westy, C., 292
Winch systems, 145, 149, 151, 161, 162
Windows, 87–8, 161, 187, 369
Wireless communication, 288
Work System Package (WSP), 379

Zip fastener, 222